Contents

Welcome to Myanmar (Burma)

Now is the moment to visit this extraordinary land, scattered with gilded pagodas, where the traditional ways of Asia endure and areas that were previously off-limits are opening up.

A World Apart

'This is Burma,' wrote Rudyard Kipling. 'It is quite unlike any place you know about.' Amazingly, more than a century later, Myanmar retains the power to surprise and delight even the most jaded of travellers. Be dazzled by the 'winking wonder' of Shwedagon Paya. Contemplate the 4000 sacred stupas scattered across the plains of Bagan. Stare in disbelief at the Golden Rock at Mt Kyaiktiyo, teetering impossibly on the edge of a chasm. These are all important Buddhist sights in a country where pious monks are more revered than rock stars.

Traditional Life

In a nation with more than 100 ethnic groups, exploring Myanmar can often feel like you've stumbled into a living edition of *National Geographic*, circa 1910! The country, for instance, has yet to be completely overwhelmed by Western fashion – everywhere you'll encounter men wearing skirt-like *longyi*, women smothered in *thanakha* (traditional make-up) and betel-chewing grannies with mouths full of blood-red juice. People still get around in trishaws and, in rural areas, horse and cart. Drinking tea, a British colonial affectation, is enthusiastically embraced in thousands of traditional teahouses.

International Interest

In 2013 Myanmar remained a Starbucks-free nation – but that could soon change. As the country makes tentative steps towards democracy, sanctions have been dropped and the world is rushing to do business here. In recent years conveniences such as mobile phone coverage, internet access and internationally linked ATMs have all improved or made their debut. Relaxing of censorship has led to an explosion of new media and an astonishing openness in public discussions of once-taboo topics, including politics. Swaths of the county, off-limits for years, can now be freely visited.

Simple Pleasures

The pace of change is not overwhelming, leaving the simple pleasures of travel in Myanmar intact. You can still drift down the Ayeyarwady river in an old river steamer, stake out a slice of beach on the blissful Bay of Bengal, or trek through forests to minority villages scattered across the Shan Hills without jostling with scores of fellow travellers. Best of all you'll encounter locals who are gentle, humorous, engaging, considerate, inquisitive and passionate – they want to play a part in the world, and to know what you make of their world. Now is the time to make that connection.

Why I Love Myanmar

By Simon Richmond, Author

On a recent afternoon in Yangon I was invited into the shack-like home of Patrick, the great-grandson of Burma's last king. With his daughter, he runs a humble English-language school in the shadow of Shwedagon Paya. As I chatted with this courteous, religious, eccentric man about his life, it underlined what I've always loved about Myanmar – meeting and sharing time with its charming people. Slow down, sit, listen and connect – it's the best way to appreciate what's truly golden about this land.

For more about our authors, see page 424

Myanmar (Burma)

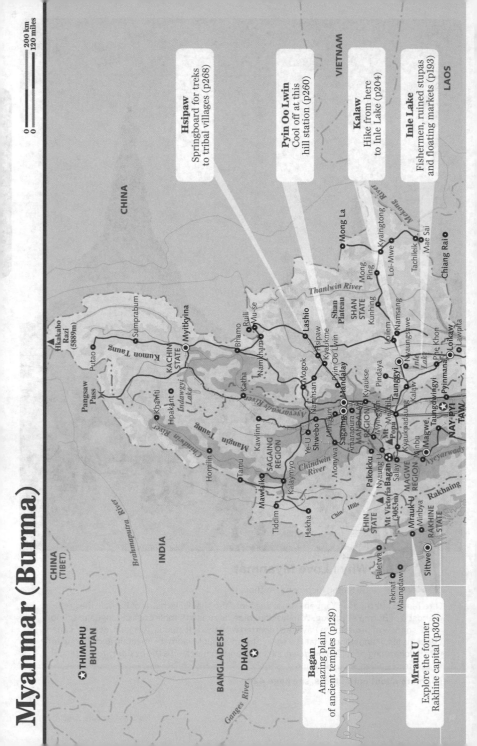

0 ——— 200 km
0 ——— 120 miles

Hsipaw
Springboard for treks to tribal villages (p268)

Pyin Oo Lwin
Cool off at this hill station (p260)

Kalaw
Hike from here to Inle Lake (p204)

Inle Lake
Fishermen, ruined stupas and floating markets (p193)

Bagan
Amazing plain of ancient temples (p129)

Mrauk U
Explore the former Rakhine capital (p302)

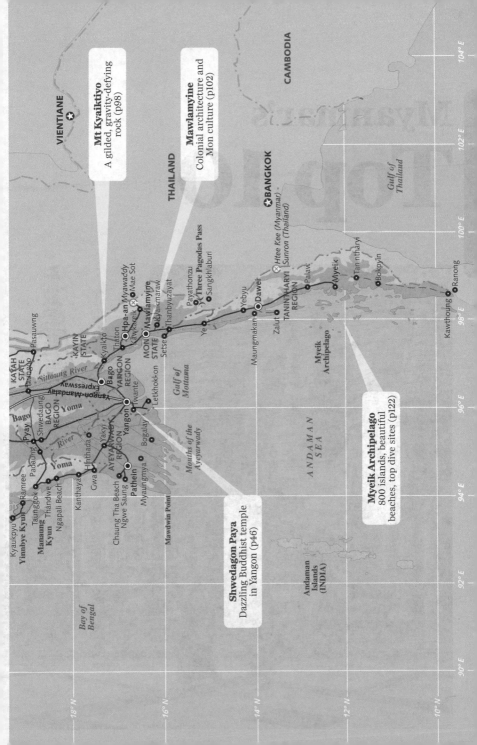

Myanmar's
Top...

Mt Kyaiktiyo
A gilded, gravity-defying
rock (p98)

Mawlamyine
Colonial architecture and
Mon culture (p102)

Shwedagon Paya
Dazzling Buddhist temple
in Yangon (p46)

Myeik Archipelago
800 islands, beautiful
beaches, top dive sites (p122)

Myanmar's
Top 10

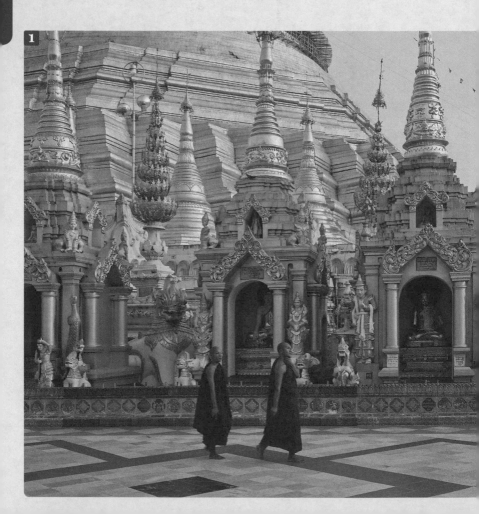

Shwedagon Paya

1 Is there a more stunning monument to religion in Southeast Asia? We don't think so. In fact, the sheer size and mystical aura of Yangon's gilded masterpiece may even cause you to question your inner atheist. But it's not all about quiet contemplation: Shwedagon Paya (p46) is equal parts religious pilgrimage and amusement park, and your visit may coincide with a noisy ordination ceremony or fantastic fortune-telling session. If you're looking for one reason to linger in Yangon before heading upcountry, this is it.

Inle Lake

2 Virtually every visitor to Myanmar makes it here at some point, but Inle Lake (p186) is so awe-inspiring and large that everybody comes away with a different experience. If you're counting days, you'll most likely be hitting the hotspots: water-bound temples, shore-bound markets and floating gardens. If you have more time, consider day hikes or exploring the more remote corners of the lake. Either way, the cool weather, friendly folk and that placid pool of ink-like water are bound to find a permanent place in your memory.

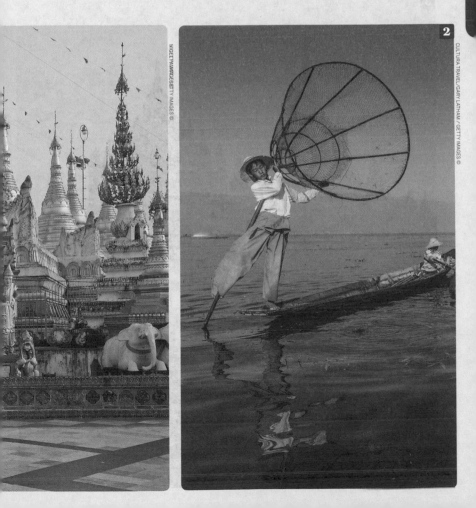

NIGEL PAVITT/GETTY IMAGES ©

CULTURA TRAVEL/GARY LATHAM / GETTY IMAGES ©

Bagan

3 More than 3000 Buddhist temples are scattered across the plains of Bagan (p165), site of the first Burmese kingdom. Dating back to between the 11th and 13th centuries, the vast majority of the temples have been renovated, as Bagan remains an active religious site and place of pilgrimage. Yes, there are tour buses and crowds at the most popular sunset-viewing spots, but they can be avoided. Pedal off on a bike and have your own adventure amid the not-so-ruined temples, or float over the temple tops in a hot-air balloon.

Mrauk U

4 The temples, monasteries, former palace and ruined city walls of the former Rakhine capital of Mrauk U (p302) continue to paint a picture of what an amazing place this town must have been at its zenith in the 16th century. And best of all, with giant structures such as the Dukkanthein Paya and Kothaung Paya sharing real estate with rural villages and emerald-green rice fields, Mrauk U emerges as much more than a museum piece.

Right: Buddha statue

JEREMY WOODHOUSE / GETTY IMAGES ©

Kalaw

5 Boasting an almost Himalayan atmosphere, Kalaw (p204) is one of Myanmar's best bases for upcountry exploration. Hiking with Danu, Pa-O and Taung Yo villagers through the forests, fields, roads and trails that link the town and Inle Lake, you may even forget which country you're in. Trekking in the area is also one of the few travel experiences in Myanmar in which the authorities don't seem to mind if you stray off the beaten track.

Pyin Oo Lwin

6 A one-off curiosity, Pyin Oo Lwin (once known as Maymyo; p260) makes a great escape from hectic and humid Mandalay. It was once the British summer capital and still has many colonial-era buildings scattered across the city, while there's a lovely, manicured botanical garden to stroll. The local taxis are colourful horse-drawn wagons, and an increasing number of sophisticated restaurants make it one of the best provincial cities in Myanmar to eat in.

Above: National Kandawgyi Gardens (p262)

AUSTIN BUSH / GETTY IMAGES ©

DAVID LAZAR / GETTY IMAGES ©

Mt Kyaiktiyo (Golden Rock)

7 A crowded, windy, potentially vomit-inducing ride up a remote hill simply to look at a big gilded rock is, admittedly, a tough recommendation. But if you ask us, you can't say you've been to Myanmar if you haven't ascended Mt Kyaiktiyo (p98), home to the country's most important religious pilgrimage site after the Shwedagon Paya. The journey may be difficult, but at the top you'll be rewarded by a scene replete with stunning vistas and a uniquely Myanmar-style spiritualism.

Mawlamyine

8 A virtual time capsule, the former capital of British Burma Mawlamyine (p102) has changed little since the colonial era, and its busy harbour, antique buildings, hill-top temples and imposing churches fool visitors into believing that Kipling and Orwell never left town. Even if you're not interested in history, the attractions surrounding Mawlamyine, with destinations ranging from tropical islands to deep caves, not to mention the area's unique Mon culture, are strong draws, yet like the city itself they see few visitors.

Hsipaw

9 Attractive, laid-back Hsipaw (p268) is ideally placed for quick, easy hikes into fascinating Shan and Palaung villages, as well as more strenuous treks to barely visited hamlets. The surrounding area feels far less discovered than the hiking available around Kalaw, or much of Southeast Asia. Hsipaw itself is a historic town with a royal past – it has its very own Shan palace and an area known as 'Little Bagan', which is also full of ancient stupas.

Top right: Produce Market

EITAN SIMANOR / GETTY IMAGES ©

Myeik Archipelago

10 It's hard to believe that a place such as the Myeik Archipelago (p122) still exists in mainland Southeast Asia. Although accessing the area remains time-consuming and expensive, those who can afford the investment will be among the handful of people who can claim witness to one of the final frontiers in Asia, not to mention a beach junkie's fantasy destination, with more than 800 islands of white-sand beaches, some of the region's best dive sites and only two islands claiming any sort of accommodation.

MARK WEBSTER / GETTY IMAGES ©

10

Need to Know

For more information, see Survival Guide (p379)

Currency
Burmese kyat (K)

Language
Burmese

Visas
Needed by everyone. Single-entry tourist/ business visas last 28 days/10 weeks and are extendable.

Money
Cash mainly. ATMs accepting international cards available in major cities and tourist areas. Bring only pristine US bills for exchange.

Mobile Phones
Prepaid SIM cards available.

Time
GMT/UTC plus 6½ hours.

When to Go

Mandalay
GO Nov-Feb

Pyin Oo Lwin
GO Nov-Feb

Mrauk U
GO Oct-Mar

Bagan
GO Nov-Feb

Yangon
GO Nov-Jan

Warm to hot summers, mild winters
Tropical climate, wet & dry seasons

High Season
(Dec–Feb)

➡ Rains least (if at all, in some places) and is not so hot.

➡ Book accommodation and transport well ahead for this busy travel season.

Shoulder
(Oct–Nov, Mar–Apr)

➡ March to May Yangon often reaches 104°F (40°C). Areas around Bagan and Mandalay are hotter.

➡ Cooler in the hill towns of Shan State.

➡ All forms of transport booked solid during Thingyan in April.

Low Season
(May–Sep)

➡ The southwest monsoon starts mid-May and peaks from July to September.

➡ The dry zone between Mandalay and Pyay gets the least rain. Rain can make roads impassable anywhere (especially in the delta region).

Useful Websites

Go-Myanmar.com (www.go-myanmar.com) Plenty of up-to-date travel-related information and advice.

7 Days in Myanmar (http://7daysinmyanmar.com) Multimedia showcase for the country, crafted by 30 internationally renowned photographers in April 2013.

Myanmar Image Gallery (www.myanmar-image.com) Pictures and text on myriad Myanmar-related subjects.

Online Burma/Myanmar Library (www.burmalibrary.org) Database of books and past articles on Myanmar.

Ministry of Hotels & Tourism (www.myanmartourism.org) Government department with some useful information.

Irrawaddy (www.irrawaddy.org) News and features site.

Lonely Planet (www.lonelyplanet.com) Good for pre-planning.

Important Numbers

Country code	☑95
International access code	☑00
Emergency (Yangon)	☑500 005
Fire (Yangon)	☑191
Police (Yangon)	☑199

Exchange Rates

The US dollar is the only foreign currency that's readily exchanged and/or accepted as payment for goods and services. **For current exchange rates see www.xe.com.**

Australia	A$1	K897
Europe	€1	K1350
Japan	¥100	K953
UK	UK£1	K1614
US	US$1	K981

Daily Costs

Budget less than $50

➡ Guesthouse: $10–30

➡ Local restaurant or street-stall meal: $2–5

➡ Travel on buses: $1–5

Midrange $50–150

➡ Double room in a midrange hotel: $50–100

➡ Two-course meal in midrange restaurant: $5–10

➡ Hiring a guide: $10 per person per day

➡ Pathein parasol: $1–20

Top end more than $150

➡ Double room in top-end hotel: $150–600

➡ Two-course restaurant meal plus bottle of wine: $40–70

➡ Driver and guide: $100 per day

➡ Fine lacquerware bowl: $200

Opening Hours

Government offices, post offices, telephone centres 9.30am to 4.30pm Monday to Friday

Shops 9.30am to 6pm Monday to Saturday

Restaurants 8am to 9pm

Cafes, teashops 6am to 6pm

Internet cafes noon to 10pm

Banks 9.30am to 3pm Monday to Friday

Arriving in Myanmar

Yangon International Airport If you haven't arranged a transfer with your hotel or travel agent, a taxi from the airport to the city centre will be $8 to $12 (K8000 to K12,000; 45 minutes to one hour).

Mandalay International Airport A whole/shared taxi into Mandalay costs K12,000/4000 (one hour); free shuttle buses for Air Asia and Golden Myanmar customers.

Overland Arrival Walk across borders with Thailand at Tachileik–Mae Sai, Myawaddi–Mae Sot, Kawthoung–Ranong and Htee Khee–Sunron.

Getting Around

A few remote destinations are accessible only by flight or boat, but many others, including key tourist sites, can be reached by road or rail. Poor and over-stretched infrastructure means patience and a tolerance for discomfort are part and parcel of the journey.

Flights Fast; reasonably reliable schedules, but government or crony-owned businesses.

Bus Frequent; reliable services and generally privately owned; overnight trips save on accommodation.

Car Total flexibility but can be expensive; for some destinations you need a government-approved guide and driver.

Boat Chance to interact with locals and pleasant sightseeing, but slow and only covers certain destinations.

Train More interaction with locals and countryside views but also uncomfortable, slow and frequently delayed.

For much more on **getting around**, see p390

What's New

Opening Up the Country

Four cross-border checkpoints with Thailand can now be used to enter or exit Myanmar; there's a chance in 2014 that the crossing into China at Mu-se will also be freely open in both directions without the need for permits. This, in conjunction with an easing of restrictions on some of the places you can travel in Myanmar, is expanding the range of itineraries and adventures to be had. See p393 for more information.

Social Enterprise Restaurants

Dine well, without feeling guilty about how much you're spending, at Yangon's trio of social enterprise restaurants, the best of which is sophisticated Shwe Sa Bwe. (p67)

Cooking in Thanlyin

A shopping trip to the market in a horse-drawn buggy is the fun introduction to the Flavours of Myanmar cooking class in Thanlyin, an easy day trip from Yangon. (p81)

Exploring the Deep South

Colonial architecture in Dawei and Myeik, the beautiful Myeik Archipelago and the untouched coastline of Tanintharyi Region – all excellent reasons for setting your travel compass to Myanmar's south. (p97)

Bagan's Boutique Stays

There is a fresh crop of boutique resorts in New Bagan, which is changing accommodation options for the better, including Blue Bird Hotel, Areindmar Hotel and Bagan Lodge. (p141)

Taung Kwe Paya

The relaxation of some travel restrictions to Kayah State allows you now to more easily visit the dazzling Taung Kwe Paya in the state capital of Loikaw. (p217)

Yoma Cherry Lodge

A lovely new place to stay at the prime beach resort of Ngapali, that's affordable, attractive and has a secluded bay virtually to itself. (p294)

Mrauk U Regional Guides Society

If you're one of the few foreign visitors fortunate enough to make it to Mrauk U, hire the services of these knowledgeable local guides dedicated to the principles of community-based tourism. (p303)

Hsipaw's Shan Palace

Newly opened again to the public is this melancholic, suburban-English-style 'palace' where Mr Donald, nephew of the last *sao pha* (sky lord) of Hsipaw, and his wife are your charming hosts. (p269)

Meinmahla Kyun Wildlife Sanctuary

Spot estuarine crocodiles, rare Irrawaddy dolphins and masses of birds cruising through the mangroves around this island sanctuary a day's travel south of Yangon. (p92)

For more recommendations and reviews, see lonelyplanet.com/myanmar-burma

If You Like...

Buddhas & Temples

Yangon's Shwedagon Paya (p46), Mandalay's Mahamuni Paya (p228) and Bagan's plain of temples (p165) shouldn't be missed, but there are also many other lesser-known Buddhist religious sites that will impress you with their beauty and spiritual power.

Shwesandaw Paya A 10-storey tall, seated buddha watches over Pyay, its hilltop location providing sweeping views of the town. (p160)

Win Sein Taw Ya Gawp at the 560ft-long buddha reclining on the lush hillsides of Yadana Taung, accessible from Mawlamyine. (p108)

Mrauk U Fall under the spell of the old Rakhaing capital, dotted with ruined and restored temples and monasteries. (p302)

Sagaing Leafy paths shade the routes to 500 hilltop and riverside stupas, and a community of some 6000 monks and nuns. (p252)

Culinary Delights

Street eats There are street vendors serving great, cheap snacks and meals everywhere in Myanmar, but the best selection is in Yangon. (p64)

Tea time Breakfast or an afternoon snack at a Myanmar teahouse is a unique experience that provides more than a caffeinated kick. (p360)

Alcoholic beverages Raise a glass of toddy made from the sap of the palm, or wine produced from Shan Hills grapes. (p357)

Ethnic variations Hunt out **Jing Hpaw Thu** (p278) in Myitkyina for authentic Kachin food, or Shan specialties at **Shan Yoe Yar** (p65)in Yangon.

Artisan Crafts

Markets Drop by Yangon's **Bogyoke Aung San Market** (p73) for handicrafts from around the country, and the central markets in Pyay (p160) or **Shwe** (p298) for colourful, lively shopping scenes.

Lacquerware Watch artisans craft, paint and engrave lovely bowls, cups and other ornaments at workshops in **Myinkaba** (p140), **New Bagan** (p144) and **Kyaingtong** (p213).

Parasols Keep the sun off with the graceful, painted paper umbrellas that are a speciality of **Pathein**. (p88)

Puppets If you enjoyed the classic marionette shows in Mandalay, why not adopt a puppet character of your own. (p242)

Activities & Adventures

Overnight treks Head to Kalaw (p204), Pindaya (p202) or Hsipaw (p268) for short, easily arranged hilltribe village treks.

Balloon rides Marvel at Bagan's temples, bathed in the beautiful light of dawn, from the basket of a hot-air balloon. (p129)

Boat journeys Ride sections of the Ayeyarwady (Irrawaddy) River; explore the Chindwin from Monywa or sail from Yangon to Pathein. (p25)

Bicycling Pedal your way around Bagan, or arrange a more challenging cross-country bike ride. (p130)

Eco-exploration Head to **Melnmahla Kyun Wildlife Sanctuary**, Indawgyi Lake or Moeyungyi Wetlands for bird- and wildlife-spotting. (p92)

Mountain climbing Take on **Mt Victoria** (p309) in Chin State or head for the foothills of the Himalayas in **Hkakabo Razi National Park** (p289).

Diving Swim among the myriad dive sites around the beautiful islands of the Myeik Archipelago. (p122)

Surreal Sights

Nay Pyi Taw In a country of intermittent power supply and pot-holed roads, the 24-hour street lights and empty, pristine highways of Nay Pyi Taw are remarkable. (p156)

Jumping cats Applaud the kitties that have been trained to leap through hoops by the monks at Inle Lake's **Nga Hpe Kyaung**. (p194)

Giant spectacles Sometimes even Buddha needs spectacles; the faithful believe the buddha wearing a massive pair of glasses at Shwedaung can cure eyesight afflictions. (p163)

Holy snakes Whether draped around their favourite buddha statue or being tenderly washed at 11am, **Paleik**'s star residents are its pythons. Other holy snakes reside in **Bago** and a village on the way to Twante. (p84)

Ethnic Diversity

Kyaingtong Mingle with Shan and tribal people from the surrounding hills at the central market and twice-weekly water-buffalo market. (p210)

Hsipaw Trek out of this low-key country town to encounter Shan and Palaung tribal villagers. (p268)

Mawlamyine Soak up the laid-back atmosphere of this tropical town that's the heart of Mon culture. (p102)

Myitkyina Proud of its Kachin culture and host to two huge, colourful tribal festivals, including a new one that reunites Lisu villagers from both sides of the Myanmar–China border. (p276)

Loikaw Arrange visits to Kayan villages from the newly-opened-to-travellers capital of Kayah State. (p216)

BARTOSZ HADYNIAK / GETTY IMAGES ©

LEE FROST / GETTY IMAGES ©

(Top) Myanmar woman, Kalaw (p204)
(Bottom) Lacquerware, Kyaingtong (p213)

Month by Month

January

Peak season and if Chinese New Year falls within the month even busier, with local and regional tourists. Plan ahead to secure transport tickets and hotels of choice. Note New Year's Day is not a public holiday in Myanmar.

🎉 Yangon Photo Festival

With Aung San Suu Kyi as its patron, this celebration of photography, held at Yangon's Institute Francais, includes exhibitions, conference and workshops (www.yangonphoto.com).

🎉 Independence Day

Celebrating the end of colonial rule in Burma, this major public holiday on 4 January is marked by nationwide fairs, including a week-long one at Kandawgyi Lake, Yangon.

🎉 Manao Festival

Costumed dancing, copious rice beer and 29 cows or buffalo sacrificed to propitiate *nat* (traditional spirits) are part of this Kachin State Day event, held in Myitkyina on 10 January.

🎉 Ananda Pahto Festival

Stretching over a couple of weeks in January (but sometimes in December depending on the Myanmar lunar calendar), this is one of the biggest religious festivals in Bagan.

February

Still a busy travel season, with the weather getting warmer. If Chinese New Year happens to fall in this month, watch out for a boost in travel activity.

🎉 Irriwaddy Literature Festival

First held in Yangon in 2013, the 2014 festival saw a change of location to Mandalay. Local writers are joined by celebrated international literary and media figures including the likes of Jung Chang, Fergal Keane and Tan Twan Eng (http://irrawaddylitfest.com).

🎉 Shwedagon Festival

The lunar month of Tabaung (which can also fall in

PAYA PWE

Nearly every active paya (Buddhist temple) or *kyaung* (Buddhist monastery) community hosts occasional celebrations of their own, often called *paya pwe* or 'pagoda festivals'. Many occur on full-moon days and nights from January to March, but the build-up can last for a while. All such festivals follow the 12-month lunar calendar and so their celebration can shift between two months from year to year. To check dates of these and other festivals go to the festival calendar of the **Britain-Myanmar Society** (www.shwepla.net/Calendar/ThinkCal.mv).

March) signals the start of the Shwedagon Festival, the largest *paya pwe* in Myanmar.

April

While joining in the water frolics of Thingyan can be fun, it's steaming hot in Myanmar during this month. Also, with many locals off work and on the move during the New Year celebrations, securing transport, booking hotels and even finding a restaurant open for a meal can be tricky.

✯✯ Buddha's Birthday

The full-moon day of Kason (April or May) is celebrated as Buddha's birthday, the day of his enlightenment and the day he entered *nibbana* (nirvana). Watering ceremonies are conducted at banyan trees within temple and monastery grounds.

✯✯ Water Festival (Thingyan)

Lasting from three days to a week, depending on whether the holiday falls on a weekend, this celebration welcomes in Myanmar's New Year.

✯✯ Dawei Thingyan

Male residents of the seaside town of Dawei (Tavoy) don huge, 13ft-bamboo-frame effigies and dance in the streets to the beat of the *kalakodaun*, an Indian drum.

June

Pack your raincoat and a sturdy umbrella as this month Myanmar is doused by monsoon rains. Roads can be flooded and flights to coastal destinations are sharply reduced.

✯✯ Start of the Buddhist Rains Retreat

The full moon of Waso is the beginning of the three-month Buddhist Rains Retreat (aka 'Buddhist Lent'), when young men enter monasteries and no marriages take place. Prior to the full-moon day, a robe-offering ceremony to monks is performed.

August

The monsoon is still in full swing so be prepared for damp days and transport hitches.

✯✯ Taungbyone Nat Pwe

Myanmar's most famous animist celebration is held at Taungbyone, 13 miles north of Mandalay, and attracts thousands of revellers, many of them homosexual or transgender.

September

The rainy season starts to wind down. Watch out for boat races in places such as Inle Lake.

✯✯ Thadingyut

Marking the end of Buddhist Lent, this festival of lights celebrates the descent of Buddha from heaven. People place candles in their windows and it's a popular time for weddings and monk pilgrimages.

October

Rain is still a possibility but that means everything is very green – making this a great time to visit Bagan, for example.

✯✯ Tazaungdaing

The full-moon night of Tazaungmon (which can also fall in November), known as Tazaungdaing, is a second 'festival of lights', particularly famous for the fire-balloon competitions in Taunggyi.

November

The start of the main tourist season sees cooler weather and still-lush landscapes.

✯✯ National Day

Held on the waning of Tazaungmon (usually in late November), this public holiday celebrates student protests back in 1920, seen as a crucial step on the road to independence.

December

Peak travel season with many visitors heading to the country over the Christmas–New Year break. Christmas is celebrated by many Christian Kayin, Kachin and Chin people.

✯✯ Kayin New Year

On the first waxing moon of Pyatho (which can also happen in January), the Kayin New Year is considered a national holiday, with Kayin communities (clustered in Insein near Yangon and Hpa-An) wearing traditional dress.

Itineraries

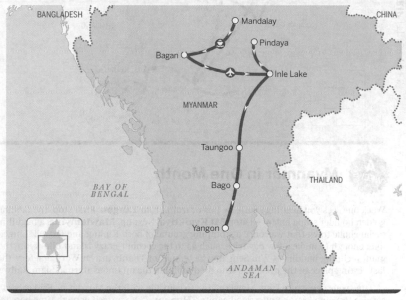

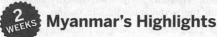 **Myanmar's Highlights**

Fly into **Mandalay**. Apart from its sights such as Mandalay Hill, Mahamuni Paya and its craft shops and markets, the old capital can be used as a base for day trips to places such as Mingun, home to a giant earthquake-cracked stupa; U Bein's Bridge at Amarapura; Monywa, where you can climb halfway up inside the world's tallest standing buddha; and quiet riverside villages such as A Myint.

Consider catching the fast boat from Mandalay to **Bagan**; set aside two or three days to explore the thousands of ancient temples scattered across the countryside. For amazing views take off at dawn for a balloon ride or climb up sacred Mt Popa.

Fly to beautiful **Inle Lake**, where motor-powered dugout canoes take you to floating markets under the flight path of egrets. Make a day trip to the Shwe Oo Min Cave near **Pindaya** to see 8000 buddha images. If you're not flying directly back to **Yangon**, consider breaking your road journey at the pilgrimage town of **Taungoo** or at **Bago**, another past royal capital stacked with impressive temples.

Before leaving Yangon, visit the Shwedagon Paya and go souvenir shopping at Bogyoke Aung San Market.

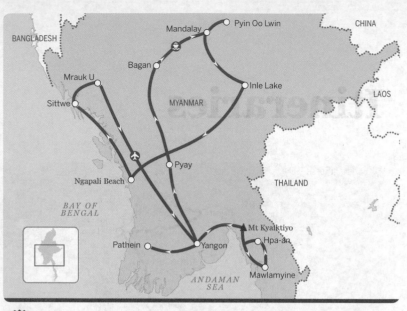

Myanmar in One Month

Week one sees you heading south, by bus or train, from **Yangon**. First stop: the fabulous, golden boulder stupa balanced atop **Mt Kyaiktiyo**. Next up, **Mawlamyine**, a beguiling, melancholic town that was once a stomping ground of both Kipling and Orwell. Linger long enough to make a few day trips, such as to the coconut-crazy island Bilu Kyun, the giant reclining buddha at Win Sein Taw Ya temple, or Thanbyuzayat War Cemetery, the last resting place of the prisoners who died building the infamous Burma–Siam Railway.

Time your departure from Mawlamyine to coincide with the Monday or Friday boat service to Kayin State's underrated capital, **Hpa-an**. Give yourself enough time here to climb nearby Mt Zwegabin, before taking the overnight bus back to Yangon.

Week two starts with a journey north along the Yangon–Bagan Highway, pausing at historic **Pyay**, famed for its pilgrimage site, Shwesandaw Paya, and the ancient city ruins of Thayekhittaya. Continuing north, switch buses in Magwe, to reach the remarkable temple-strewn plains of **Bagan**. A boat ride away is **Mandalay**, bigger and less exciting than many visitors imagine, but a great base for visiting several ancient-city sites.

If the heat is getting you down, drive two hours and breathe fresh cool air in the colonial-era getaway of **Pyin Oo Lwin**. Chill out even more around the shores of magical **Inle Lake**, perhaps getting there via an overnight trek from Kalaw. Fly from Heho direct to Thandwe for some R&R on beautiful **Ngapali Beach**. Tan topped up, head north by plane or boat to Rakhaing State's capital of **Sittwe**. Linger a day to catch its atmospheric market and breezy seaside promenade, then take a river trip to **Mrauk U**. Once a powerful, cosmopolitan city, it's now one of Myanmar's most atmospheric backwaters, an idyllic location dotted with hundreds of ancient stupas and monasteries. Reserve a day for another river trip to visit nearby Chin villages.

Fly back to Yangon where you can do some last-minute sightseeing and shopping, perhaps making a day trip to the Delta town of Twante, or learning how to cooking Burmese food in Thanlyin. Alternatively, squeeze in an overnight break in **Pathein** to pick up some traditional paper parasols.

Plan Your Trip
Before You Go

For all its recent changes, Myanmar is still far from a spontaneous, hassle-free destination to visit. Careful pre-trip planning, from getting your visa and travel money sorted, to booking hotels and weighing up transport options, will make travelling here all the smoother.

Getting Your Visa

These days, getting a visa is relatively straightforward (see p388 for more information). The key things to know immediately are:

➡ Everyone requires a visa to visit Myanmar.

➡ Start the process no later than three weeks before your trip, a month before to be safe.

➡ If there is no Myanmar embassy or consulate near where you live, it's possible to apply for a visa online and pick up the stamp at the airport on arrival.

➡ If you're crossing the land border to enter the country, you will need to have your visa already in your passport.

➡ Short-notice visas are available at Bangkok's **Myanmar Embassy** (☏66-2233 7250; www.myanmarembassybkk.com; 132 Sathorn Nua Rd; ⊙application 9am-noon, collection 3.30-4.30pm); the cost is 1260B for same-day processing, 1035B for the next day.

Arranging Permits

There are large areas of Myanmar (mainly in Chin, Kachin, Kayah and Kayin States and Mandalay and Tanintharyi Regions) that are off limits, or accessible only with permission. Securing such permission:

➡ takes time – a minimum of at least two weeks, but more commonly around a month

Predeparture Checklist

➡ Apply for a **visa**

➡ **Book** hotels, flights and river cruises

➡ Sort out any necessary **permits** for travel to restricted areas

➡ Stock up on **brand-new US dollar bills**

➡ Arrange any necessary **vaccinations**

Don't Forget

➡ All-purpose electrical-plug adapter

➡ Torch (flashlight) for power blackouts

➡ Warm jacket for chilly overnight bus rides

➡ Colour passport photos for permits

➡ Flip flops or sandals

➡ Bug spray

➡ Prescription medicines

Check Travel Advisories

Australia (www.smarttraveller.gov.au)

Canada (www.voyage.gc.ca)

New Zealand (www.safetravel.govt.nz)

UK (www.gov.uk/foreign-travel-advice)

USA (http://travel.state.gov/travel)

➡ requires the help of an experienced travel agency

➡ involves paying fees to the government-owned travel agency, MTT, even if you're dealing with another agency

➡ usually means dancing to the MTT's tune when it comes to how you visit the area in question and who you go with.

Sometimes areas that are possible to visit, with or without a permit, suddenly become off-limits; that's how it can be in Myanmar.

Accommodation Choices

Some things to keep in mind:

➡ A tax of at least 10% goes to the government no matter where you stay.

➡ Stick with budget family-run guesthouses and minihotels, if you prefer the bulk of your money to go local enterprises and people.

➡ Top-end hotels can employ staff of 100 or more and often fund community projects.

➡ Advance bookings are strongly advised for the busiest holiday season from December through to February.

➡ Staying at hotels that use local products can keep more of your money in the country.

➡ Staying in a monastery is usually only possible at ones that run meditation courses for foreign students (see p383).

➡ Online accommodation rental operations, such as Airbnb (www.airbnb.com), do have some listings for Yangon.

Family-Run Guesthouses

Often with just five or so rooms and a lounge, which are shared with three or four generations of a family living in-house, these budget-level guesthouses can be a highlight of your trip, offering connections with local life and inexpensive deals (under $20 for a double).

Most rooms come with a fan or some sort of air-conditioning unit, though electricity frequently cuts out after midnight. Some guesthouses are better than others, however, and like budget hotels, you'll find some with squashed mosquitoes left on the walls.

Budget Hotels

In many towns your only options will be a couple of four-storey, modern, 'Chinese-style' hotels. In some there are dark cell-like rooms with a shared bathroom on the ground floor (usually for locals only), and two types of nicer rooms on upper floors. Some have lifts. Some keep their generators on 24 hours; others just for a few hours at night and in the morning. Most cost $20 to $50 for a double.

Have a look before taking the higher-priced 'deluxe' rooms; they often cost an extra $10 for a refrigerator and writing desk you may not use. Other deluxe rooms offer more space, nicer flooring and maybe satellite TV.

Midrange & Top-End Hotels

Upper-midrange and top-end hotels may be owned and run by various local entrepreneurs and/or foreign companies. Some are former government hotels now leased to local owners. Some owners are part of Myanmar's growing middle class and aren't linked with the former government. Conversely, other owners are members of the generals' families or cronies of the military – for example, the owners of the Aureum Palace and Myanmar Treasure chains.

If you're concerned about a hotel's ownership make pre-trip enquiries. Also ask about things such as employment practices and whether funds are provided for community projects and local charities.

Transport Options

Online booking of flights is possible, and a good idea if you want to secure seats during the busy high season. Bear in mind, though, that Myanmar's domestic airline industry can become over-stretched at peak times and that delays and changes to flight times need to be taken in one's stride.

For more details see p390.

Train

Train travel in Myanmar is an experience (not always a good one!) but does have its fans. Take note of the following:

Monks, Bagan (p129)

➡ Myanmar Railways (MR) does not currently offer online bookings.

➡ Travel agencies can sort out tickets for you (recommended particularly outside of Yangon and other major cities) but may only be able do so a few days in advance of travel.

➡ Payment by non-Myanmar citizens for tickets at stations must be in US dollars.

➡ Do not take a train if you are on a tight travel schedule – they are notorious for long delays.

➡ Be prepared for some discomfort on the journey as carriages rock and roll on the narrow gauge tracks.

➡ For more details see p397 and the Myanmar page of **The Man in Seat 61** (www.seat61. com/Burma).

Boat

A cruise along Myanmar's major rivers is the stuff of many travellers' dreams, a chance to soak up Myanmar's largely unsullied landscape and lifestyle in all its lush glory. The main drawback of this mode of travel is speed – or lack thereof. Boat trips for many routes are loosely scheduled in terms of days, not hours. Make sure you bring plenty of diversions and/or a willingness to make conversation with fellow passengers.

The level of comfort on the boats depends on your budget. IWT ferries and private boats may be relatively inexpensive but you get what you pay for – they are very low frills and highly uncomfortable for lengthy journeys. You certainly won't go hungry, though, as all long-distance ferries have an on-board cook and are visited at most stops by a variety of locals selling food and drink.

For more about travelling by boat in Myanmar see p393.

Routes

There are 5000 miles of navigable river in Myanmar, with the most important river being the Ayeyarwady (Irrawaddy). Even in the dry season, boats can travel from the delta region (dodging exposed sandbars) all the way north to Bhamo, and in the wet they can reach Myitkyina.

The ability of you being able to make such a journey though is another matter, as foreigners are barred from certain routes – at the time of research, for example, it was not possible for foreign visitors to buy tickets on IWT ferries between Yangon and Pyay or on any boats heading into or out of Myitkyina. This situation may change in the future.

The key riverboat routes that *can* be built into a travel itinerary include the following:

Yangon–Pathein On the IWT ferry.

Yangon–Mandalay Rarely offered route on luxury cruises.

Mandalay–Bagan On the IWT ferry or private boats.

Mandalay–Bhamo–Katha A few private fast-boat services, but mostly done on the IWT.

Mawlamyine–Hpa-an By private boat.

Sittwe–Mrauk U By private boats or IWT ferry.

Khamti–Monywa Newly opening up Chindwin River route on IWT ferries and private boats. A few luxury boats also sail along the Chindwin.

One other key thing to keep in mind is the direction in which to travel. Journeys which head north (ie against the flow of the river) take days longer than those going south with the river – this is especially the case on the lumbering IWT ferries.

Luxury Cruises

For creature comforts, such as a bed with a mattress and fully plumbed bathroom, your only option will be a berth on a luxury cruise boat. Rates will usually include all meals and excursions from the boat. The starting point for most trips is either Bagan or Mandalay, but occasionally itineraries will originate in Yangon.

Amara Cruise (www.amaragroup.net) Owned by a German and his Myanmar wife, this company runs cruises from Mandalay to Bagan (four days, three nights single/double from €1230/1520) and Bhamo (seven days, six nights single/double from €2390/2980). Its two medium-sized teak boats each have seven comfy cabins and are traditionally styled but recently built. The company also runs a local charity, the Amara Foundation (www.amara-foundation. com), which supports projects in the Ayeyarwady Delta region.

Pandaw Cruises (www.pandaw.com) Offers various high-end cruises aboard a replica of the

Ballooning in Bagan (p129)

teak-and-brass IFC fleet, such as a 14-night trip between Yangon and Mandalay (single/double from $3463/6920) and a 20-day itinerary that charts the Chindwin and upper reaches of the Ayeyarwady (single/double $6837/11,403).

Paukan Cruises (www.ayravatacruises.com) Beautifully restored river steamers are used for this company's trips, which range from one or two days between Mandalay and Bagan (single/twin from $680/1560) to 10-day itineraries including sights along the Chindwin River (single/twin $6280/9560).

Road to Mandalay (www.orient-express.com) Part of the Orient Express group, this luxe operation offers cruises of between three and 11 nights on two boats. The *Road to Mandalay*, a 43-berth liner that is huge by Ayeyarwady standards, includes an on-board swimming pool and wellness centre. In high season it does mostly Bagan–Mandalay, but there are occasional trips to Bhamo, too. The newly constructed four-deck *Orcaella* has 25 cabins and also has a small top-deck pool, a fitness and wellness centre, and boutique. Short cruises start at £1640 per person.

Sanctuary Ananda (☎44-20-7190 7728; www.sanctuaryretreats.com) Launching in December 2014 is this brand-new Myanmar-built craft with 20 suites spread over three decks. There's a small plunge pool on the top deck and a spa/gym inside. Itineraries range from the three-day Bagan–Mandalay route (from $1221 per person) to the 11-day sailing between Mandalay and Yangon ($5214).

Viking River Cruises (☑44-80 8159 9358; www.vikingrivercruises.co.uk) This British operator runs two 30-room boats, the *Viking Mandalay* (refurbished in 2013) and the *Viking Sagaing*. Both are used on its two-week Memories of Mandalay itinerary originating in Bangkok with flights to Mandalay where you board the boat for a trip downriver to Yangon. Rates start around £4450 per person including flights from the UK.

Putting Together Your Own Trip

If you're used to having a car at the airport waiting for you, and guides showing you where to go, that can be done *and* arranged privately. Just because many roads are rough doesn't mean you have to sacrifice all comforts. Either contact a Yangon-based agent before a trip, or give yourself a couple of days to do so once you arrive. The agent can help set up private guides,

transport and hotels. Ask to pay as you go to ensure that your money is spread out and to use different guides at each destination rather than one guide for the whole trip. Talk with more than one agent, telling them what you want, to gauge offers.

Some agents are keen to ensure you have adequate travel insurance covering medical emergencies for your trip. Their concerns are well founded, as quality medical care in Myanmar isn't readily available. An insurance policy that covers medi-vac is wise.

Travel Agencies

Most visitors to Myanmar use private domestic travel agencies to book a tour, hire a car or book a domestic flight.

There are hundreds of businesses across the country calling themselves travel agencies, but only a handful can be considered full-service, experienced tour agencies, who have a track record of arranging visits to more remote places in Myanmar.

Among the best ones we've encountered or have had recommended are the following, all with offices in Yangon.

HOW TO SKIP OVERNIGHT BUSES

There's not one obvious way to travel by bus between Myanmar's four big destinations: Yangon, Inle Lake, Mandalay and Bagan. Most travellers start in Yangon and bus to Mandalay one night, then pick between Inle Lake or Bagan next; this requires at least a couple of overnight buses.

If you like being able to see scenery out the window, or sleeping in beds, you can travel to these places without taking an overnight bus. It does take pre-planning and a bit more time – around a week of travel time and a total cost of at least K43,400 if you take the following buses and/or pick-up trucks:

ROUTE	DURATION (HR)	COST (K)
Yangon–Taungoo	9	4300–5000
Taungoo–Meiktila	6½	4000
Meiktila–Taunggyi (for Inle Lake)	6	5000
Taunggyi–Kalaw	3	2500
Kalaw–Mandalay	9	7000–10,000
Mandalay–Nyaung U (for Bagan)	7–8	7500–9000
Bagan–Magwe	8	4500
Magwe–Pyay	7	4100
Pyay–Yangon	7	4500

Asian Trails (Map p44; ☑01-211 212; www. asiantrails.travel; 73 Pyay Rd, Dagon) In business since 1999, this experienced outfit can arrange specific-interest tours of Myanmar, including cycling and mountaineering; we also like the sound of its Irrawaddy Dolphin tour where you shadow fishermen who practice cooperative fishing with this rare species. It can facilitate visits to far northern Myanmar and other remote areas.

Ayarwaddy Legend Travels & Tours (Map p40; ☑01-252 007; www.ayarwaddy legend.com; 104 37th St, Kyauttada) Can provide advice on visiting off-the-beaten-track areas such as mountain climbing in Chin State.

Columbus Travels & Tours (Map p44; ☑01-229 245; www.travelmyanmar.com; 586 Strand Rd, Lanmadaw) Established in 1993, Columbus also has branches in Mandalay, Bagan and Inle.

Diethelm Travel (Map p40; ☑01-203 751; www.diethelmtravel.com/myanmar; 412 Merchant St, Botahtaung) Among the many things this reputable, five-decades-old Swiss-owned operation can do is arrange walking tours of Yangon, visits to an elephant camp near Kalaw, or a beach safari from Ngapali. Its offices in Yangon occupy a beautifully restored heritage building.

Exotissimo Travel (Map p50; ☑01-558 215; http://myanmar.exotissimo.com/travel/tours; 147 Shwegonedine Rd, Bahan) Operating in Myanmar since 1995, this Southeast Asian specialist tour company also has a Mandalay office.

Good News Travels (Map p40; ☑095-9511 6256, 01-357 070; www.myanmargood newstravel.com; Room 1101, 11th floor, Olympic Tower, cnr Bo Aung Kyaw St & Mahabandoola Rd, Kyauktada) The owner, William Myatwunna, is extremely personable and knowledgeable, and can help arrange visits to remote parts of Myanmar. Highly recommended. Also has an office in Bagan.

Journeys Myanmar (☑01-664 275; www. journeysmyanmar.com; 53 Nagayone Pagoda Rd, (Off Pyay Road), Mayangone) Can arrange river trips on a wide range of luxury craft and other options. Also biking tours and sailing holidays in the Myeik Archipelago.

Khiri Travel (Map p40; ☑09 7313 4924, 01-375 577; http://khiri.com; 1st floor, 5/9 Bo Galay Zay St, Botataung) The friendly team

here is run by multilingual Dutchman Ed Briels, who has over a decade's experience in tourism in Myanmar. Biking and kayak trips, walking tours of markets and meetings with fortune-tellers are some of their offerings.

Myanmar Himalaya Trekking (Map p50; ☑01-227 978; www.myanmar-explore. com; Room 201, Summit Parkview Hotel, 350 Ahlone Rd, Dagon) Worth consulting if you're interested in off-the-beaten-track trekking adventures.

Oway (Map p50; ☑01-230 4201; www.oway. com.mm; 2nd floor, Bldg 6 Junction Square, Pyay Rd, Kamayut) New and technically savvy company offering online bookings for a wide range of hotels and all domestic flights. It also arranges visas online which can be picked up at international airports.

SST Tours (Map p40; ☑01-255 536; www. sstmyanmar.com; Rm S-6, 2nd floor, Aung San Stadium, Mingalar Taung Nyunt) Standing for 'Supreme Service Team', SST lives up to its name as well as being a specialist for eco-tours. The managers have excellent contacts in the country's national parks and reserves and can arrange trips that will delight nature lovers.

Budgeting

Having decided on all the transport and accommodation options, you'll be in a position to budget more accurately for your trip.

In Myanmar, in the vast majority of cases, you'll be paying for everything in cash – either US$ or the local currency, kyat. If you're dealing with a travel agent you can usually pay in advance for some of your expenses (hotels, transport), on top of which a processing fee of around 5% may be charged.

Only brand new greenbacks – bills from 2006 or later that are in absolutely perfect condition, ie with no folds, stamps, stains, writing or tears – will be accepted for payment or exchanged for kyat. Keep them in a flat wallet as you travel.

ATMs accepting international cards are becoming more common, and a few places such as hotels, major tourist restaurants and shops now take credit cards. But with dodgy power supplies and telecommunications, such electronic means of payment cannot be guaranteed – so come prepared with plenty of cash.

Plan Your Trip

Responsible Travel

Since 2010, the question of whether it is right or wrong to travel to Myanmar has been superseded by that of how to travel responsibly and sustainably. Read on to discover how best to tread lightly in the country, engage respectfully with locals and make a positive impact.

Avoid Package Tours

Travelling independently rather than on a package tour will give you more control over where your money goes. If you pay for tours with overseas agents before arriving in Myanmar, often less of your money finds its way into the pockets of local citizens. Tours also tend to provide less interaction with locals.

If you prefer working with tour agents in your own country, or in Mynamar, ask them the following questions:

➡ Who are your owners and do they have any links to the government?

➡ What are your policies with regard to using the services of government or government-linked businesses?

➡ Do you have any charitable programs in place to assist local communities and/or individuals?

➡ Can I contribute directly to a clinic, school or orphanage as part of a trip? (Always do this in person.)

➡ Can I hire different guides at each destination rather than travel with one guide for the whole trip?

Top Tips

➡ Travel independently or in small groups rather than in a big tour group.

➡ Support small independent businesses and those that have charitable and sustainable tourism programs in place.

➡ Spread your money around: buy souvenirs across the country, not just in Yangon, and hire different guides at each destination.

➡ Talk to locals but take their lead on the substance of the conversation – don't force people into awkward and potentially dangerous talk about politics and human rights.

➡ Contribute to local charitable causes.

➡ Be environmentally conscious in your travel choices: opt for buses, trains and river cruises over flights; avoid using air-conditioning.

➡ Be sensitive to, and respectful of, local customs and behaviour: dress and act appropriately when visiting religious sites and rural villages.

➡ Read up about Myanmar's history, culture and current situation.

➡ Check out Dos & Don'ts For Tourists (www.dosanddontsfortourists.com).

BURMA OR MYANMAR?

What to call the Republic of the Union of Myanmar (to use its official name as of 2011) has been a political flashpoint since 1989. That was the year in which the military junta decided to consign Burma, the name commonly used since the mid-19th century, to the rubbish bin, along with a slew of other British colonial-era place names, such as Rangoon, Pagan, Bassein and Arakan.

The UN recognises Myanmar as the nation's official name; Myanmar is more inclusive than Burma, given that its population isn't by any means 100% Burman. However, nearly all opposition groups (including the NLD), many ethnic groups and several key nations including the US continue to refer to the country as Burma. As Aung San Suu Kyi told us in 2010, 'I prefer Burma because the name was changed without any reference to the will of the people.'

We use Myanmar as the default name for the country, with Burma used for periods before 1989 and where it's the name of an organisation, eg Burma Campaign UK. 'Burmese' is used for the Bamar people (not to all the country's population, which we term 'the people of Myanmar'), the food and the language.

Choose Goods & Services Carefully

For all its recent positive changes Myanmar continues to be plagued by human rights abuses and distressing extremes of poverty and wealth. Much of the blame for this situation rests with its government – past and present.

For this reason, groups including **Tourism Concern** (www.tourismconcern.org.uk/burma.html), **Tourism Transparency** (www.tourismtransparency.org) and **EcoBurma** (www.ecoburma.com) encourage visitors to minimise the amount of money they spend on government-owned or government-friendly businesses and services.

However, disentangling the complex web of financial connections in Myanmar's economy is like unpicking the Gordian knot. The government has divested itself of certain nationalised businesses – the supply of petrol being a key example – but it still controls chunks of the economy, either directly or via companies owned and run by the military.

Some cronies, such as Tay Za, owner of the Htoo group of companies, are easily identifiable; other 'private' companies are run by government members or supporters on the sly, or by their family members. Such links may not be obvious, partly because there is no equivalent of surnames in Myanmar, so each member of a family has his or her own name.

Taxes (both the official kind and the bribes that are a necessary part of getting things done) are a fact of life in Myanmar, with no business being able to avoid financial dealings with those in power. Also, when it comes to buying souvenirs and products, keep in mind who may be supplying them. Bottom line: the only way ensure that none of your money will benefit the government is to not visit Myanmar.

Spread your Money Around

Critics of independent travel argue that travellers' spending usually bottlenecks at select places, even if those spots are privately run. Familiarity can be reassuring – your trishaw-driver buddy or the plate of noodles that didn't make you sick. But the more places at which you spend money, the greater the number of locals likely to benefit. A few things to consider:

➡ Don't buy all of your needs (bed, taxi, guide, meals) from one source.

➡ Be conscious that behind-the-scenes commissions are being paid on most things you pay for when in the company of a driver or guide. If all travellers follow the same lead, benefits go to only a select few.

➡ Plan en-route stops, or take in at least one off-the-beaten-track destination, where locals are less used to seeing foreigners.

➡ Mix up the locations from where you catch taxis and trishaws – and try to take trips with drivers who aren't lingering outside tourist areas.

➡ Try to eat at different family restaurants, and if you're staying at a hotel, eat out often. In Ngapali Beach, for example, local restaurants are just across the road from the beach and hotels.

➡ Buy handicrafts directly from the artisans as you travel around the country, or if you're spending most of your time in the same location, don't get all your souvenirs from one private shop.

➡ Don't raise political questions and issues in inappropriate situations; allow the local to direct the conversation.

➡ Show equal caution regarding what you ask or say on the phone or via email.

➡ Be wary of places that treat minority groups as 'attractions'.

➡ Think very carefully before accusing anyone of cheating you or of theft. Innocent people can suffer greatly by implication. For example, a bus driver can end up in very hot water if you report your camera stolen during a bus ride.

Interact, But Don't Endanger

One way you can positively help people is to talk and talk and talk, and make new friends. Many locals cherish outside contact because they have so little. The two-way exchange that comes from it is reassurance for them that Myanmar is part of the world and not forgotten.

This said, bear in mind that people who campaign against the authorities are still being arrested and imprisoned in Myanmar. Ensure you don't behave in a way that will get locals into trouble. Some things to keep in mind:

Charity & Direct-Aid Volunteerism

Tourism isn't going to fix all of Myanmar's problems, of course, but there are some small things you can do to help during your visit.

➡ Ask guesthouse owners, agents, teachers and monks about where you can donate money for medical or school supplies.

➡ Stop at a village school and ask what materials they lack. Often less than $100 can get a book, notepad and pen for every student needing them.

➡ Patronise socially responsible businesses that support charitable causes.

THE PERILS OF MASS TOURISM

Since 2010 the National League for Democracy (NLD) and other groups campaigning for democracy and civil rights in Myanmar have dropped their boycott to tourism. The NLD now 'welcome visitors who are keen to promote the welfare of the common people and the conservation of the environment and to acquire an insight into the cultural, political and social life of the country'. At the same time it recognises the perils of mass tourism, and urges the government and businesses to avoid further damaging the environment in the process of developing tourism infrastructure.

Author, historian and chairman of Yangon Heritage Trust, Thant Myint-U told us 'Now that tourism is beginning to take off and seems set to grow significantly over the coming years, I think we need to also have a serious public discussion about both the potential dangers as well as the benefits of mass tourism, learning lessons from the experience of nearby countries, and looking at concrete options for how tourism might best be managed.'

Such a discussion is beginning to happen. An international conference on responsible tourism was held in Nay Pyi Taw in Febuary 2012, sponsored by Germany's Hanns Seidel Foundation and the UK-registered NGO, International Centre for Responsible Tourism. In August 2013 the *Irrawaddy* also reported that the Ministry of Hotels and Tourism is working to educate citizens about tourism's darker side, but needs cooperation from civil society and local communities to get the message out.

Outside of small donations, some NGOs prefer tourists to stick with their trips and leave bigger projects for them. But we've also encountered travellers who have acted as 'direct-aid volunteers'. They felt there wasn't time to wait for aid to reach locals, so they come twice yearly to fund projects on their own. One, who has built and overseen many new school projects, told us: 'When I finish one, I only have to drive 10 minutes to the next village to find another in need.'

In Tony Wheeler's *Bad Lands* the founder of Lonely Planet writes about how he and his wife financed the construction of a 300m wooden bridge connecting the floating village of Maing Thauk to land at Inle Lake.

Giving Gifts & Donations

Travellers handing out sweets, pens or money to kids on hiking trails or outside attractions have had a negative impact (as you'll certainly see when begging kids follow you around a pagoda). It's not the best way to contribute to those in need, and many locals will advise you not to give to children anyway. If you want to hand out useful items keep this in mind:

➡ Try to give directly to schools, clinics and village leaders, not kids. A rewarding way to spend a day is going to a village school, asking a teacher what supplies are lacking, buying them and handing them out to each of the students.

➡ Foreign-made gifts (eg pens) are generally cherished items, and more likely to find a place in a bookcase than actually get used. If you want to give useful items, buy locally. This puts money into the local economy, and locals are more likely to use the gift!

➡ Give only to those with whom you have made some sort of personal bond, not to random supplicants who happen to ask. Otherwise you'll encourage a culture of begging.

➡ If you do decide to help a begging family, ask what they need. Often you can accompany them to the market and pick up food (a bag of rice, some vegetables, some fish).

➡ Some items from outside the country are greatly appreciated, though. It's a good idea to carry books and magazines.

Back at Home

Your trip to Myanmar doesn't have to end once you're back home.

➡ Alert Lonely Planet and fellow travellers via the Thorn Tree discussion board (www.lonelyplanet.com/thorntree) if you have advice on how to travel in Myanmar.

➡ Consider posting photos and perceptions of your trip on a blog – but take care to ensure your words don't have repercussions for locals you may have met while travelling.

➡ Write to your local Myanmar embassy and elected politicians to express your views about the human rights situation.

➡ Contact the various pro-democracy activist groups in your country.

➡ Email the people in Myanmar you became friendly with – let them know they are not forgotten.

A HISTORY OF SANCTIONS

From the late 1980s and for over 20 years, economic sanctions by mainly the US, EU, Canada and Australia were applied in an attempt to force political and social change in Myanmar. It was a controversial policy: while the NLD, the leading democracy group of the time, insisted they were necessary as a way of keeping up pressure on the military junta, others pointed out the harm that sanctions did to Myanmar's citizens, who in the main were struggling to make a living.

In 1995 the NLD also called for a tourism boycott, which led to criticism of Lonely Planet's continued coverage of the country. In 2010 the travel boycott was officially dropped by the NLD, who now welcome independent tourists who are mindful of the political and social landscape; however, those on large group-package tours are discouraged.

During 2012, as the pace of reform in Myanmar continued, the EU, Australia and the US all largely suspended their economic sanctions against the country. Sanctions on some specified individuals still remain, as do ones on the import of gems into the US.

Regions at a Glance

Yangon & Around

Temples
Food
Beaches

Temples
Yangon's unmissable Shwedagon Paya, Bago's plethora of temples, the water-bound Yele Paya at Kyauktan and Pathein's Shwemokhtaw Paya make the entire region perfect for those with a passion for *paya*.

Food
Home to some of the country's best Burmese food, Yangon also has a plethora of restaurants serving tasty takes on more familiar international cuisines. The city also offers a vibrant street-food scene that ranges from Indian nibbles to Shan noodles.

Beaches
They may not rank among Southeast Asia's prime sand strips, but Chaung Tha Beach and Ngwe Saung Beach are clean, relaxed and the easiest seaside resorts to reach from Yangon.

p36

Southern Myanmar

Beaches
Temples
Culture

Beaches
The Myeik Archipelago covsers more than 800 largely uninhabited islands, making it the country's, if not mainland Southeast Asia's, ultimate beach destination.

Temples
There are enough temples in and around Mawlamyine alone to keep you busy for a lifetime, but the indisputable highlight of the region is Mt Kyaiktiyo (Golden Rock) – a must-do religious pilgrimage for everyone in Myanmar.

Culture
You will probably never have heard of the Mon people before, so let one of the excellent Mawlamyine-based guides introduce you to the culture via the area's tidy sugar-palm-lined towns, seaside temples and island-bound villages.

p97

Bagan & Central Myanmar

Temples
Shopping
Elephants

Temples
You'll find thousands of them in Bagan, but also worth seeking out are the Nat shrine at Mt Popa and the pilgrimage temples of Shwesandaw Paya in Taungoo, Shwesandaw Paya in Pyay, and Shwenyetman Paya in Shwedaung.

Shopping
Bagan is also famous for its exquisitely decorated lacquerware; watch artisans create it in workshops in Myinkaba and New Bagan. Across the Ayeyarwady River, Pakokku is famous for its patterned blankets.

Elephants
Nay Pyi Taw has a herd of elephants at its zoo and you can watch elephants working at jungle logging camps on trips to teak plantations outside Taungoo.

p128

Eastern Myanmar

Outdoors
Culture
Food

Outdoors

Tramping between tea plantations in Pindaya; buzzing around in a boat on Inle Lake; scaling mountains outside Kalaw; visiting a Loi longhouse outside Kyaingtong...just a few of the outdoor pursuits possible.

Culture

The country's far east boasts exceptional cultural diversity, even by Myanmar standards. Learn about Pa-O culture around Inle Lake, or Shan culture and language and their similarities with those of neighbouring Thailand in Kyaingtong.

Food

From *shàn k'auq·s'wèh* (Shan-style noodle soup) to *ngà t'ămìn jin* (a turmeric-tinged rice dish), a stay in eastern Myanmar is your chance to try authentic Shan food.

p183

Mandalay & Around

Temples
Culture
Shopping

Temples

Arguably more interesting than Mandalay's fine monastic buildings are the older stupas and temples on the sites of several former capitals, including what would have been the world's biggest stupa (Mingun) had it been finished.

Culture

Myanmar's cultural capital offers intimate traditional dance performances, marionette shows, and the famed Moustache Brothers' vaudevillian rants.

Shopping

Even if you're only window-shopping there's an impressive range of antiques (not all real!) and craft work, notably stuffed embroidery, silk, stone carving and the manufacture of gold leaf.

p221

Northern Myanmar

Outdoors
Culture
Boats

Outdoors

Hike to unspoilt hill-tribe villages, accessible on short hikes from Hsipaw and Kyaukme. With permits and serious money, intrepid travellers can trek deep into Myanmar's Himalayan foothills from Putao.

Culture

Immerse yourself in the region's cultural mix, including Chinese-influenced Lashio, Shan and Palaung villages around Hsipaw and the Kachin capital Myitkyina, home to two of Myanmar's biggest and most colourful 'minority' festivals.

Boats

You'll hardly see another foreigner on the no-frills public boats chugging down the Ayeyarwady River. Alternatively, join a tour that takes you on the remote and dramatic Malikha River near Putao.

p258

Western Myanmar

Temples
Beaches
Boats

Temples

Temples and a ruined palace are scattered across the lush hillsides of the old Rakhine capital of Mrauk U. Sittwe's giant Lokananda Paya and the teak buildings of the Shwezedi Kyaung monastic complex are also worth searching out.

Beaches

Idyllic stretches of palm-fringed sand hardly come more perfectly formed than those of Ngapali Beach.

Boats

The only way to reach Mrauk U or the Chin villages further up the Lemro River is by a leisurely boat ride. For the really adventurous there's also the day-long coastal hop from Sittwe to Taunggok via the island port of Kyaukpyu.

p291

On the Road

Northern Myanmar p258

Mandalay & Around p221

Western Myanmar p291

Eastern Myanmar p183

Bagan & Central Myanmar p128

Yangon & Around p36

Southern Myanmar p97

Yangon & Around

🔖 01 / POPULATION C4,447,000

Includes ➡

Best Places to Eat

➡ Shwe Sa Bwe (p67)

➡ Taing Yin Thar (p69)

➡ Shan Yoe Yar (p65)

➡ Feel Myanmar Food (p65)

➡ Union Bar & Grill (p66)

➡ Nilar Biryani & Cold Drink (p63)

Best Places to Stay

➡ Strand Hotel (p61)

➡ Mother Land Inn 2 (p59)

➡ Alamanda Inn (p62)

➡ Garden Home Bed & Breakfast (p62)

➡ Governor's Residence (p61)

➡ Loft Hotel (p60)

Why Go?

'A city of blood, dreams and gold' is how Pablo Neruda described Yangon. Nearly a century after the Chilean poet lived in what was then known as Rangoon, the former capital is emerging from bloody and neglectful military rule into an era of glittering possibilities. Exiles are returning and foreign investors and adventurers flooding in, triggering a blossoming of new restaurants, bars, shops, building sites and traffic jams.

Yangon's awe-inspiring Buddhist monument Shwedagon Paya is the one sight in Myanmar you cannot miss. Vibrant streets lined with food vendors, colourful open-air markets, evocative colonial architecture – some of the most impressive you'll find in Southeast Asia – are reasons for lingering. It's also easy to make day trips or go further afield to the charming city of Pathein (Bassein) or the relaxed beach resorts of Chaung Tha and Ngwe Saung.

When to Go
Yangon

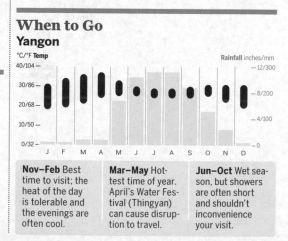

Nov–Feb Best time to visit; the heat of the day is tolerable and the evenings are often cool.

Mar–May Hottest time of year. April's Water Festival (Thingyan) can cause disruption to travel.

Jun–Oct Wet season, but showers are often short and shouldn't inconvenience your visit.

YANGON

ELEVATION 46FT

Even though it is no longer the nation's official capital, Yangon remains Myanmar's largest and most commercially important city. Its downtown skyline is dominated by the 'winking wonder' of Shwedagon Paya, a dazzling Buddhist temple that attracts pilgrims from all over the world.

Since the 2010 elections, Yangon's fortunes have skyrocketed along with its land prices, as both local and foreign investors scrambled to grab a foothold here. At the same time, decades of economic stagnation are only too apparent in the city's slums, shanty housing and creaking, frequently overwhelmed infrastructure – something you'll quickly realise as you crawl into town in a taxi from the airport.

In December 2013 a masterplan for Yangon was unveiled. Funded by the Japanese government's aid and development agency JICA, it proposed 103 priority projects costing over $5 billion – around 100 times the current budget of the Yangon City Development Committee.

History

In 1755 King Alaungpaya conquered central Myanmar and built a new city at Dagon, a village that had existed for centuries around the Shwedagon Paya. He renamed the place Yangon, meaning 'end of strife',

and, a year later, following the destruction of Thanlyin (Syriam) across the river, built it up into an important seaport.

In 1841 the city was virtually destroyed by fire; the rebuilt town again suffered extensive damage during the Second Anglo-Burmese War in 1852. The British, the new masters, renamed the city Rangoon (a corruption of Yangon) and mapped out a grand building plan for what would become the capital of their imperial colony.

It's easy to get a sense of how prosperous colonial Rangoon was from the monumental architecture that still graces the city's downtown. By the 1920s Rangoon was a key stopover point for steamships in the region; notable international visitors included Rudyard Kipling, W Somerset Maugham, Aldous Huxley and HG Wells. In 1937 Amelia Earhart dropped in during the second of her attempts to fly around the world.

Early-20th-century Rangoon was also the spawning ground for Burmese independence. When that independence came in 1948, Rangoon continued as the nation's capital. However, the city's fortunes took a turn for the worse when military rule was imposed in 1962. The Burmese road to socialism as promulgated by General Ne Win and his cohorts drove Rangoon, like the rest of the country, to the brink of ruin.

In 1989 the junta decreed the city would once again be known as Yangon. After decades of neglect, streets were cleaned and

---

YANGON & AROUND IN...

Two Days

Follow our **walking tour** of downtown Yangon. Drop by the gorgeous **Musmeah Yeshua Synagogue**, then browse the traditional market **Theingyi Zei** and the more tourist-oriented **Bogyoke Aung San Market**. Stroll through **People's Park** before ascending to **Shwedagon Paya** in time for sunset.

Start day two at the riverside **Botataung Paya**. Take a taxi to the **National Museum** to view the magnificent Lion Throne and other treasures. Spend the afternoon admiring the giant reclining Buddha at the **Chaukhtatgyi Paya** and the gorgeous sitting Buddha at nearby **Ngahtatgyi Paya**. An amble around **Kandawgyi Lake** can be followed by sunset drinks at **Vista Bar**.

Four Days

Hop on the ferry to **Dalah** to view the city from the Yangon River. Once in Dalah negotiate with a taxi or motorbike taxi for a tour to **Twante** to view pottery makers, Shwesandaw Paya and the snake-infested Mwe Paya. Back in Yangon, visit the incense-clouded temple **Kheng Hock Keong** and head to **19th St** for a grilled-food feast.

On day four board the **Yangon Circle Line** and get off at Tadakalay station to visit kitsch, fun **Melamu Paya**. Eat at **Taing Yin Thar** or **Minn Lane Rakhaing Monte & Fresh Seafood**, both at the north end of Inya Lake. Live it up back downtown at the **Strand Bar** or the **Union Bar & Grill**.

many public buildings painted. However in November 2005, quite unexpectedly, the government announced that the newly constructed city of Nay Pyi Taw in central Myanmar was to be the nation's capital. Yangon again suffered as government ministries departed from the downtown area, leaving behind empty and uncared-for state-owned buildings.

In late 2007 Yangon was the centre of huge nationwide fuel protests, which were led by Buddhist monks. The protests quickly escalated into antigovernment demonstrations, which culminated in the deaths of many protestors and worldwide condemnation.

In May 2008 the worst natural disaster in Myanmar's recent history hit the south of the country. Yangon was declared a disaster area by Myanmar's government. Many of the city's pagodas, temples, shops and hotels had minor to serious damage from falling trees, lampposts and fences. However, when reconstruction work began, it was found that most of the city had escaped major structural damage. By mid-June 2008 electricity and telecommunications were back to normal, and shops and restaurants had reopened with brand-new corrugated-tin roofs.

◉ Sights

Yangon is divided into 33 townships and addresses are usually suffixed with these (eg 3 Win Gabar Lane, Bahan).

Back in the mists of time, Yangon was a village centred on Shwedagon Paya, but the British shifted its centre south towards the Yangon River. This is Downtown Yangon. Shwedagon and nearby Kandawgyi Lake are covered mainly by Dagon and Bahan townships; in the latter is the area referred to as Golden Valley, a choice address for the city's monied elite.

Further north are more leafy areas surrounding Inya Lake and stretching up to Yangon International Airport. The city's townships also spill south across the Yangon River to Dalah.

◉ Downtown Yangon

★ **Botataung Paya**   BUDDHIST TEMPLE
(ဗိုလ်တထောင်ဘုရား; Map p40; Strand Rd, Botataung; admission $3/K3000, camera $1/K1000; ◷6am-9.30pm) Botataung's spacious riverfront location and lack of crowds give it a more down-to-earth spiritual feeling than Shwedagon or Sule Paya. Its most original feature is the dazzling zig-zag corridor, gilded from floor to ceiling, that snakes its way around the hollow interior of the 131ft golden *zedi* (stupa).

Also look out for a bronze Buddha that once resided in the royal palace in Mandalay, and a large pond full of hundreds of terrapin turtles.

The temple is named after the 1000 military leaders who escorted hair relics of the Buddha from India to Myanmar over 2000 years ago. For one six-month period this paya (religious monument) is said to have harboured eight strands of the Buddha's hair before they were distributed elsewhere.

A bomb from an Allied air raid in November 1943 scored a direct hit on the unfortunate paya. After the war the Botataung was rebuilt in a very similar style to its predecessor, but with one important and unusual difference: unlike most *zedi*, which are solid, the Botataung is hollow, and you can walk through it.

There's a gold leaf-coated maze inside the *zedi*, with glass showcases containing many of the ancient relics and artefacts, including small silver-and-gold Buddha images, which were sealed inside the earlier stupa. Reconstruction also revealed a small gold cylinder holding two small body relics and a strand of hair, said to belong to the Buddha, which is reputedly still in the stupa.

On the northern side of the stupa is a hall containing a large **gilded bronze Buddha**, cast during the reign of King Mindon. At the time of the British annexation, it was kept in King Thibaw Min's glass palace, but after King Thibaw was exiled to India, the British shipped the image to London. In 1951 the

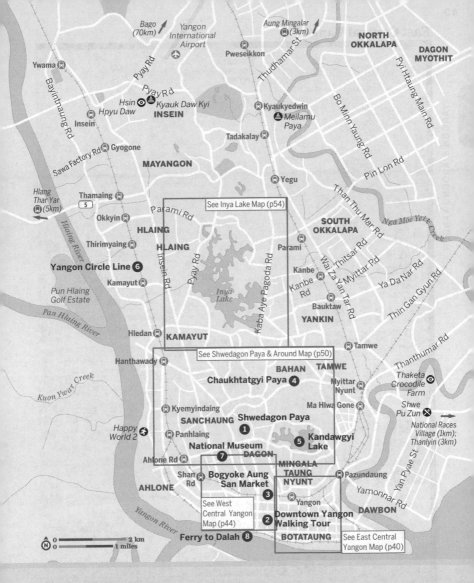

Yangon Highlights

1 Offer a slack-jawed prayer of wonder at the **Shwedagon Paya** (p46), the pyramid of gold that is the Burma of old

2 View grand colonial architecture on a **walking tour** (p56) of downtown Yangon

3 Pick up some Burmese-style slippers or a *longyi* (sarong-style lower garment)

at **Bogyoke Aung San Market** (p73)

4 Be dazzled by the giant reclining Buddha at the **Chaukhtatgyi Paya** (p53)

5 Take an early-morning or evening stroll on the boardwalk around **Kandawgyi Lake** (p51)

6 See Yangon's 'burbs from

the rockin' and rollin' train on the **Yangon Circle Line** (p75)

7 Witness the treasures of Myanmar's past at the poorly maintained but worthwhile **National Museum** (p41)

8 Shuttle across the Yangon River on the **Dalah ferry** (p78) for a glimpse of the workings of the city's port

East Central Yangon

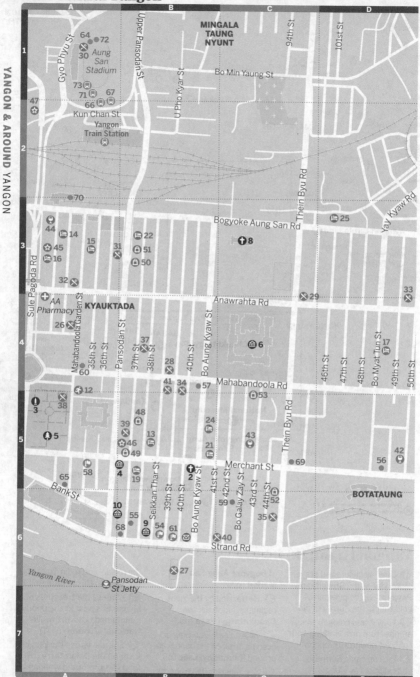

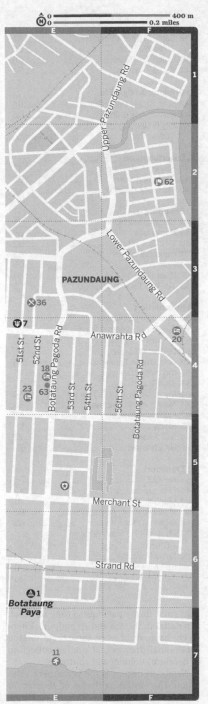

image was returned to Myanmar and placed in the Botataung Paya.

In the southwest corner of the temple is a *nat* (spirit being) **pavilion** containing images of Thurathadi (the Hindu deity Saraswati, goddess of learning and music) and Thagyamin (Indra, king of the *nat*) flanking the thoroughly Myanmar *nat* Bobogyi.

The terrapin turtle pool is in the southeast corner. Most of the turtles are fairly small but every now and again a truly monstrous one sticks its head out of the water.

The nearby **Botataung Jetty** provides a good view of activity on the Yangon River.

Sule Paya
BUDDHIST STUPA

(ဆူးလေဘုရား; Map p44; cnr Sule Paya Rd & Mahabandoola Rd, Pabedan; admission $2/K2000; ⊙ 5am-9pm) It's not every city where the primary traffic circle is occupied by a 2000-year-old golden temple. This 46m *zedi*, said to be older than Shwedagon Paya, is an example of modern Asian business life melding with ancient Burmese tradition.

Just after the sun has gone down is the most atmospheric time to visit the temple.

The central stupa's name, Kyaik Athok, translates in the Mon language as 'the stupa where a Sacred Hair Relic is enshrined'. As with many other ancient Myanmar shrines, it has been rebuilt and repaired many times over the centuries.

The gilded *zedi* is unusual in that its octagonal shape continues right up to the bell and inverted bowl. Near the north entrance look for the small golden *karaweik* (royal barge designed in the shape of a mythical bird), which you can load with a prayer card, then winch up a chain to deposit the card in a shrine higher up the stupa (K1000).

The exterior base of the temple is surrounded by small shops (including an internet cafe and a guitar shop) and all the familiar nonreligious activities that seem to be a part of every *zedi* in Myanmar.

Besides its significance as a landmark and meeting place, maybe its most mundane function is as a milestone from which all addresses to the north are measured.

National Museum
MUSEUM

(အမျိုးသားပြတိုက်; Map p44; 66/74 Pyay Rd, Dagon; admission $5/K5000; ⊙ 9.30am-4.30pm Tue-Sun) Even though the museum's collection is appallingly labelled and lit, the treasures that lie within this cavernous building deserve a viewing.

The highlight is the spectacular 26ft-high, jewel-encrusted Sihasana (Lion

East Central Yangon

Throne), which belonged to King Thibaw Min, the last king of Myanmar. It's actually more of an entrance doorway than a throne but let's not quibble – it's a damn sight more impressive than your front door! Further signs that the kings of old didn't understand the meaning of the word 'subtlety' are the ornate beds, silver and gold rugs, flashy palanquins (one of which is palatial in its size and splendour), kitchen chairs made of ivory, some breathtaking ceremonial dresses and a large collection of betel-nut holders and spittoons.

Newly on display is the permanent exhibition *The Vanishing Tribes of Burma*, 70 photographic images by Richard K. Diran, who spent 17 years documenting around 40 ethnic groups, some of whose way of life had been practically unchanged for centuries.

The upper floors are less impressive and take you on an amble through natural history, prehistory and a very poorly lit art gallery. Look for the model of the colonial-era State House demolished in 1978; the chandeliers that hang on each floor of the museum are all that remain of it.

Mahabandoola Garden

PARK

(မဟာဗန္ဓုလပန်းခြံ; Map p40; Mahabandoola Garden St, Kyauktada; ⊙6am-6pm) **FREE** This recently revamped park offers pleasant strolling in the heart of the downtown area and views of surrounding heritage buildings including **City Hall**, the **High Court** and the old **Rowe & Co** department store.

The park's most notable feature is the **Independence Monument** (Map p40), a 165ft white obelisk surrounded by two concentric circles of *chinthe* (a half-lion, half-dragon deity). There's also a good children's playground.

When laid out by the British in 1868, the park was called Fytche Sq after Sir Albert Fytche, chief commissioner at the time. Later it was renamed Victoria Park to commemorate the queen whose statue used to stand where the Independence Monument is today.

After Independence, the park was renamed to honour General Thado Mahabandoola, a Burmese hero who conquered Assam and died in action in the First Anglo-Burmese War in 1824.

For a year or two following the 1988–90 prodemocracy uprisings, the park was occupied by soldiers; many of the more violent events of the time took place nearby.

Ministers Office

HISTORIC BUILDING

(ဝန်ကြီးများရုံး; Secretariat; Map p40; 300 Thein Byu Rd, Kyauktada) This spectacular red-brick complex takes up a 6.5-hectare block but has been off limits to the public since 1962. Built in stages between 1889 and 1905, the Secretariat was the British seat of government for Burma. General Aung San and six of his colleagues were assassinated here in 1947. The complex also housed independent Burma's first National Assembly.

When the capital moved to Nay Pyi Taw in 2005 the building, renamed the Ministers Office, was mostly abandoned and its roof suffered damage during Cyclone Nargis.

A reprieve came in 2011 when the Ministry of Construction selected it as one of five key Yangon heritage buildings to undergo basic renovations. The plans include a cultural centre and historical museum which will include Aung San's old office and the room where he was gunned down.

It's likely to be years before the barbed wire comes down and the public can once again re-enter the grounds and view the building from the flame tree–shaded lawns surrounding it. A technical study has put the cost of full restoration of the 400,000-sq-ft building at at least $100 million; the Anawmar Group has so far committed $30 million to the project.

Musmeah Yeshua Synagogue

SYNAGOGUE

(မယ်ရှီမီးရာရေရှုဘာဂျူးဘုရားကျောင်း; Map p44; 85 26th St, Pabedan; ⊙10am-noon & 4-6pm) Watched over by trustee Moses Samuels, a member of Yangon's now tiny community of Jews, the lovingly maintained interior of this 1896 building contains a *bimah* (platform holding the reading table for the Torah) in the centre of the main sanctuary and a women's balcony upstairs. The wooden ceiling features the original blue-and-white Star of David motif.

The synagogue was once the focal point of an influential community of Sephardic Jews from India and Baghdad that at its height in the early 20th century numbered 2500. Very occasionally services are held in the synagogue.

Mr Samuels' son Sammy runs the tour agency Myanmar Shalom (info@myanmar shalom.com); it's best to contact him directly to be sure of gaining access to the synagogue or if you have specific questions about the Jews of Yangon.

Strand Hotel

HISTORIC BUILDING

(Map p40; www.ghmhotels.com; 92 Strand Rd, Kyauktada; ⊛) Opened in 1901, and run by the famed Sarkies brothers (they also owned Raffles in Singapore and the Eastern and Oriental in Penang), this historic hotel hosted the likes of Rudyard Kipling, George Orwell and W Somerset Maugham in its early years.

The hotel was built by Turkish-Armenian contractor Tigran Nierces Joseph Catchatoor, who is buried around the corner in the cemetery next to the **Armenian Church of St John the Baptist** (Map p40; 66 Bo Aung Kyaw St, Kyauktada).

West Central Yangon

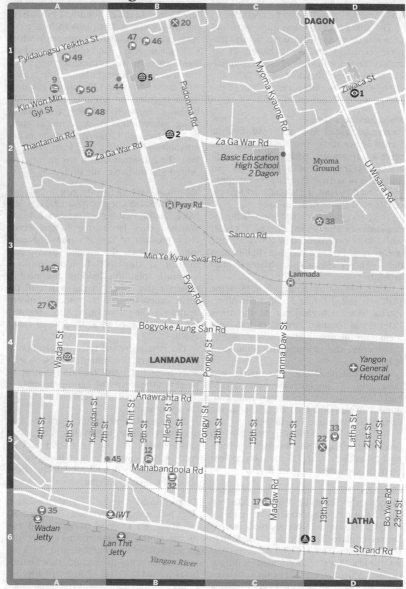

In 1913 an annex was built next door; this now houses the Australian Embassy. During WWII, the Japanese took over the running of the Strand, which they renamed the Yamato Hotel.

Burmese nationals were allegedly not allowed to stay in the hotel until 1945.

From 1962 to 1989, in what was quite possibly its darkest period, the Strand was owned and managed by the Burmese government. In 1979 when Tony Wheeler reviewed the Strand for the first edition of this guidebook he found a 'tatty and dilapidated' colonial relic where you were

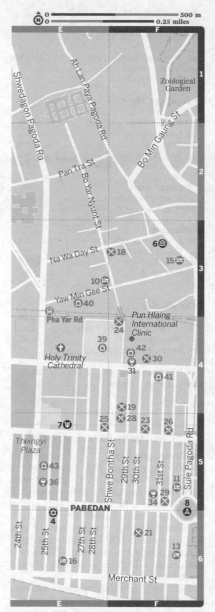

Yangon Heritage Trust HISTORIC BUILDING
(Map p40; ☏ 01-240 544; http://yangon heritagetrust.org; 22/4 Pansodan St, Kyauktada; ⊙ 9am-5pm Mon-Fri) FREE The small gallery of historic photographs here gives an idea of how downtown Yangon used to look. There's a great view of lower Pansodan St's grand facades from the open balcony, particularly of the bomb-damaged Yangon Region Court and the art-deco Myanmar Economic Bank 2 opposite.

Kheng Hock Keong BUDDHIST TEMPLE
(ခိန်ဟုက်ဗုဒ္ဓဘာသာဘုရားကျောင်း; Map p44; 426-432 Strand Rd, Latha; ⊙ 5am-9pm) FREE Supported by a Hokkien association, Yangon's largest Chinese temple is most lively from around 6am to 9am when it's thronged with worshippers offering candles, flowers and incense to the Buddhist and Taoist altars within.

The temple is dedicated to the sea goddess Mazu, who occupies the central altar and is flanked by to the right by Guan Gong, the embodiment of loyalty and bravery, and on the left by Bao Sheng Da Di, the god of medicine.

The current building dates to 1903 and replaced a wooden temple that was erected here in 1861.

St Mary's Cathedral CHURCH
(စိန်မေရီကာသီဒရယ်ဘုရားရှိုးကျောင်း; Map p40; ☏ 01-245 647; 372 Bo Aung Kyaw St, Botataung; ⊙ mass 6am & 5pm, plus 8am & 10am Sun) Myanmar's largest Catholic cathedral is an impressive red-brick building dating to 1909. The neo-gothic design is mainly down to Dutch architect Jos Cuypers, who modified a more Byzantine structure created by Henry Hoyne-Fox.

The floridly decorated interior with its red, white and green brick patterns and painted statues is quite an eye-opener.

Sri Varatha Raja Perumal HINDU TEMPLE
(စရိဝါရသရာဂျာပေရူမာလ်ဘုရားကျောင်း; Map p40; cnr Anawrahta Rd & 51st St; ⊙ 6.30-11.30am & 4.30-8.30pm) Dedicated to Vishnu, this lavishly decorated Hindu temple dates to 1927 and has the classic South Indian *gopuram* style of of entrance tower. It can easily be combined with a visit to the nearby teahouse Lucky Seven and is a location for catching the Murugan Festival (commonly known as Thaipusam) in January or February.

Sri Kali HINDU TEMPLE
(သျှီရီကာလီဘုရားကျောင်း; Map p44; Anawrahta Rd; ⊙ 5-11am & 3-9pm) Another of several colourful Hindu temples that can be found in

more likely to encounter rats than a soft bed and a hot shower. Having closed for three years of renovations the Strand reopened to its present luxurious incarnation in 1993 (p61).

West Central Yangon

the city centre. This is one of the locations for the Murugan Festival, famous for colourful street processions featuring acts of ritual self-mutilation.

Former Pegu Club   HISTORIC BUILDING
(ပဲခူးကလပ်(ဟောင်း); Map p44; Za Ga War Rd, Dagon) Despite being in a very sorry state, this teak building exudes a magnetic attraction. It was once the most exclusive British club in Burma, and it's believed that Rudyard Kipling was inspired to write his poem *Mandalay* after spending a night here.

Ghosts of the Raj haunt the rotting but still regal interior, which is so dilapidated you shouldn't think of entering without the guidance of the caretaker, whom you should tip for the tour.

In a fairy tale, a heritage-loving investor would cast a repairing wand across the complex; in reality, the chances of the Pegu Club being restored to its former glory are slim.

⊙ Shwedagon Paya & Around

★ **Shwedagon Paya**   BUDDHIST STUPA
(ရွှေတိဂုံဘုရား; Map p50; www.shwedagon pagoda.com; Singuttara Hill, Dagon; admission $8/K8000; ☉4am-10pm) Visible from almost anywhere in Yangon, this is one of Buddhism's most sacred sites. The 325ft *zedi*, adorned with 27 metric tons of gold leaf and thousands of diamonds and other gems, is believed to enshrine eight hairs of the Gautama Buddha as well as relics of three former buddhas.

Four long, graceful entrance stairways lead to the main terrace which, depending on the time of day you visit, can be quiet and contemplative or bustling and raucous. If you prefer the quiet and reflective, then visit in the cool of dawn. Otherwise pay your respects when the golden stupa flames crimson and burnt orange in the setting sun.

The following covers the history and layout of Shwedagon Paya. Freelance guides (they'll locate you before you can find them) can provide more details. Tour agencies can also arrange guides; a good tour, including the surrounding area, is offered by Khiri Travel (p27).

➤ History

Legend has it that there's been a stupa on Singuttara Hill for 2600 years, ever since two merchant brothers, Tapussa and Ballika, met the Buddha. He gave them eight of his hairs to take back to Myanmar, a land ruled over by King Okkalapa. Okkalapa enshrined the hairs in a temple of gold, together with relics of three former buddhas, which was then enclosed in a temple of silver, then one of tin, then copper, then lead, then marble and, finally, one of plain iron-brick.

Archaeologists suggest that the original stupa was built by the Mon people some time between the 6th and 10th centuries. In common with many other ancient *zedi* in earthquake-prone Myanmar, it has been rebuilt many times. During the Bagan (Pagan) period of Myanmar's history (10th to 14th centuries), the story of the stupa emerged from the mists of legend to become hard fact. Near the top of the eastern stairway is a brick inscribed with the date 1485.

In the 15th century, the tradition of gilding the stupa began. Queen Shinsawbu, who was responsible for many improvements to the stupa, provided her own weight (88lb or nearly 40kg) in gold, which was beaten into gold leaf and used to cover the structure. Her son-in-law, Dhammazedi, went several better, offering four times his own weight and that of his wife in gold.

In 1612 Portuguese renegade adventurer Filipe de Brito e Nicote raided the stupa from his base in Thanlyin and carried away Dhammazedi's 30-ton bell, with the intention of melting it for cannons. As the British were to do later with another bell, he accidentally dropped it into the river, where it remains.

During the 17th century, the monument suffered earthquake damage on eight occasions. Worse was to follow in 1768, when a quake brought down the whole top of the *zedi*. King Hsinbyushin had it rebuilt to virtually its present height, and its current configuration dates from that renovation.

British troops occupied the compound for two years immediately after the First Anglo-Burmese War in 1824. In 1852, during the Second Anglo-Burmese War, the British again took the paya, the soldiers pillaged it

once more and it remained under military control for 77 years, until 1929. Prior to the British takeover of southern Myanmar there had been defensive earthworks around the paya, but these were considerably extended by the British. The emplacements for their cannons can still be seen outside the outer wall.

In 1871 a new *hti* (the umbrella-like decorative top of a stupa), provided by King Mindon from Mandalay, caused considerable head-scratching for the British, who were not at all keen for such an association to be made with the still-independent part of Myanmar.

The huge earthquake of 1930, which totally destroyed the Shwemawdaw in Bago, caused only minor damage to Shwedagon. The following year when the paya suffered from a serious fire, it wasn't so lucky.

After another minor earthquake in 1970, the *zedi* was clad in bamboo scaffolding, which extended beyond King Mindon's 100-year-old *hti*, and was refurbished. The stupa also had to be repaired following 2008's Cyclone Nargis.

During recent centuries, the Shwedagon Paya was the scene for much political activity during the Myanmar independence movement – Aung San Suu Kyi spoke to massive crowds here in 1988 and the temple was also at the centre of the monks' protests in 2007.

➤ Temple Layout

The hill on which the stupa stands is 167ft above sea level, with the entire complex covering 46 hectares. As is common with all temples in Myanmar, the main terrace is approached by four **zaungdan** (covered walkways) each of which is flanked at its entrance by a pair of 9m-tall *chinthe*. If you don't want to climb the steps, there are elevators at the southern, eastern and northern entrances, while the western *zaungdan* has sets of escalators.

All but the western *zaungdan* are lined with stalls selling flowers – both real and beautifully made paper ones – for offerings, buddha images, ceremonial umbrellas, books, antiques, incense sticks and much more. There are also fortune tellers and money exchange booths.

You emerge from the shade of the *zaungdan* into a visual cacophony of technicoloured glitter at the marble-floored **main terrace**, littered with pavilions and worship halls containing buddha images and two giant cast-iron bells.

(Continued on page 50)

Shwedagon Paya

WHAT TO LOOK FOR

A pair of giant **Chinthe** ❶ guard the southern covered entrance, from Shwedagon Pagoda Rd; of the four covered arcades leading up Singuttara Hill this is considered the main entrance.

Halfway up, branch off in either direction for a peaceful stroll along the lower terrace of Shwedagon. Flanking this concrete footpath that encircles the hill are monasteries and resting houses for pilgrims.

Continue around to the northern covered entrance, climb the final flights of steps and emerge onto the main terrace to a dazzling explosion of decoration. Ahead rises the golden **central stupa** ❷ surrounded by **planetary posts** ❸, as well as many other shrines, *tazaung* (small pavilions) and religious statuary.

In the terrace's northeast corner an open-sided pavilion covering the **Shwedagon inscription** ❹ stones stands in the shadow of the **Naungdawgyi Paya** ❺.

For a close-up detail of the jewel-encrusted **hti** ❻ at the top of the central stupa view the gorgeous photos in the **photo gallery** ❼ or use one of several telescopes doted around the main terrace – there's one outside Shwedagon's small museum.

TIPS

» **When to go** Early morning or late afternoon towards sunset Monday to Friday.

» **Temple etiquette** Dress respectfully and remove your shoes before entering the temple precincts. Walk clockwise around the stupa.

» **Viewpoints** The north gate and northwest corner between the Friday and *Rahu* planetary posts are prime photo spots.

Hti
The stupa's uppermost section is encrusted with 5448 diamonds, 2317 rubies, sapphires, and other gems, as well as 1065 golden bells. At the very top sparkles a single 76-carat diamond.

Stupa
Rising 325ft, the stupa sits on an octagonal base with a bell-shaped dome and conical-shaped spire. Around the base four smaller stupa mark the cardinal directions, in between which are 64 smaller pagodas.

Southern covered entrance

Lower terrace of Shwedagon

Chinthe
30ft-tall pairs of these legendary half-lion, half-dragon beasts guard each of the four covered walkways up Singuttara Hill to the paya's central platform.

SIMON RICHMOND ©

Photo gallery
Displays snaps of Shwedagon dating back to the late 19th century. Close-ups of the jewel-encrusted *hti* taken during one of the regular renovations of the pagoda reveal all of its glittering detail.

SIMON RICHMOND ©

Naungdawgyi Paya
The 'Elder Brother Pagoda' stands on the site where Buddha's eight hair relics were said to have first been enshrined by the two merchant brothers who brought them for King Okkalapa.

Museum

Northern covered entrance

⑥

⑦

②

⑤

④

③

Shwedagon inscription
Dating to 1485, three sandstone slabs faintly inscribed in Pali, Mon and Burmese relate how the brothers Tapussa and Ballika brought the eight sacred hairs from the Buddha to Myanmar.

Planetary posts
Twelve of these represent the days of the week and the ascending node of the moon; follow locals by pouring water over the Buddha statue at the post that corresponds with the day of your birth.

SIMON RICHMOND ©

SIMON RICHMOND ©

Shwedagon Paya & Around

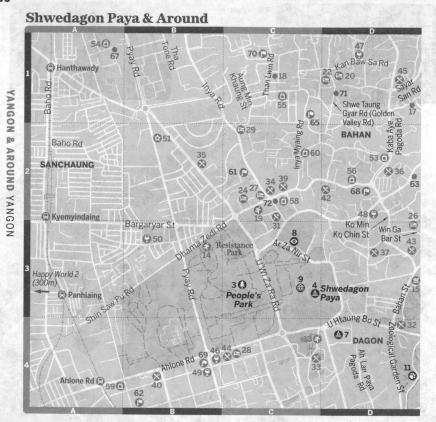

(Continued from page 47)

At the centre of the terrace **Shwedagon Paya** sits on a square plinth, which stands 21ft above the clutter of the main platform and immediately sets the stupa above the lesser structures. Smaller stupas sit on this raised platform level – four large ones mark the four cardinal directions, four medium-sized ones mark the four corners of the plinth and 60 small ones run around the perimeter.

From this base, the *zedi* rises first in three terraces, then in 'octagonal' terraces and then in five circular bands. The shoulder of the bell is decorated with 16 'flowers'. The bell is topped by the 'inverted bowl', another traditional element of stupa architecture, and above this stand the mouldings, then the 'lotus petals'. These consist of a band of down-turned petals, followed by a band of up-turned petals. The banana bud is the final element of the *zedi* before the jewel-encrusted *hti* tops it.

Around the stupa's base **12 planetary posts** conform to the days of the week; locals pray at the station that represents the day they were born. If you want to join them, and don't know the day of your birth, the fortune tellers at the temple have almanacs that will provide the answer. Note that Wednesday is divided into births in the morning and births in afternoon – for the latter you worship at the Rahu post at the northwest corner of the stupa base.

Before leaving the main terrace pop into the small **museum** (Map p50; Shwedagon Paya, Dagon; ☉9am-4pm Tue-Sun) FREE which is chock full of buddha statues and religious ornaments. Look for the scale model of the stupa and the beautiful painting of the temple by MT Hla. The **photo gallery** is also well worth a look, particularly for the close-up snaps it displays of the top of the stupa.

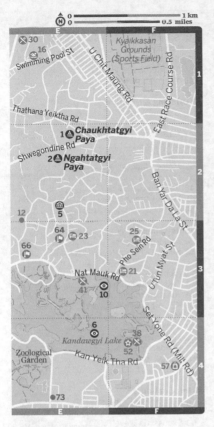

Kandawgyi Lake

LAKE

(ကန်တော်ကြီး; Map p50; Kan Yeik Thar Rd, Dagon; admission K2000) Also known as Royal Lake, this artificial lake, built by the British as a reservoir, is most attractive at sunset, when the glittering Shwedagon is reflected in its calm waters. The boardwalk, which runs mainly along the southern and western sides of the lake, is also an ideal place for an early-morning jog or stroll.

Just east of the Kandawgyi Palace Hotel, on the southern side of the lake, floats a **Shin Upagot** shrine. Upagot is a Bodhisattva (Buddhist saint) who is said to protect human beings in moments of mortal danger.

The eastern side of the lake is dominated by a small park, a kids' playground, a **paintball attraction** (K8000 for 50 balls, open 9am to 9pm) and the fanciful or monstrous (depending on your taste) Karaweik Palace (p72), a reinforced concrete reproduction of a royal barge. There are plenty of lakeside cafes here, good spots for a drink at sunset.

On the north side of the lake **Utopia Tower** (Map p50; admission K500; ⊙9am-9pm) is another quirky feature. This giant pile of artificial rocks houses restaurants, bars, karaoke and snooker and, on the 5th floor, a viewing deck. On the ground floor the **Summit Art** (Map p50; ☎09-500 5849; ⊙9am-5.30pm Tue-Sun) showcases the impasto canvases of owner-painter Myint Soe and other local artists.

Maha Wizaya Zedi

BUDDHIST TEMPLE

(မဟာဝိဇယဇေတီ; Map p50; U Htaung Bo St, Dagon; admission K200; ⊙5am-9pm) This well-proportioned *zedi*, built in 1980 to commemorate the unification of Theravada Buddhism in Myanmar, is connected by a pedestrian bridge to the southern gateway to Shwedagon Paya. The *zedi* is hollow, its inside decorated with a forest of fake trees and a beautiful blue dome showing star constellations.

The king of Nepal contributed sacred relics for the *zedi* relic chamber and General Ne Win had it topped with an 11-level *hti* – two more levels than the *hti* at Shwedagon.

Dargah of Bahadur Shah Zafar

MAUSOLEUM

(ဗဟိုရ်ရှား၁ဒါရ်ဂါတော်; Map p44; Ziwaca St, Dagon; ⊙8am-8pm) **FREE** A place of pilgrimage for Indians, Muslims and others interested in the history of the Raj, this functioning mosque houses the mausoleum of India's last Mughal emperor. Bahadur Shah Zafar II was exiled to Rangoon along with his wife

★ People's Park

PARK

(ပြည်သူ့ရင်ပြင်; Map p50; U Wisara Rd, Dagon; admission $5/K5000; ⊙7am-7pm) This recently renovated park is notable for its splendid views of the west side of Shwedagon Paya. There are lots of pleasant features such as flower gardens and ponds; fountains, including one made up of concentric rings of white elephants; and tree-top observation platforms linked by fun swinging bridges.

More quirky aspects include a decommissioned Myanmar Airways Fokker you can climb inside, a fighter jet and an old steam train.

At the park's northwest corner is the **Natural World Amusement Park** with things like bumper cars and a log flume rollercoaster (K1000 a ride). Facing onto Damazedi Rd is the kid's amusement park **Happy Zone** (Map p50; Dhamma Zedi Rd; ⊙9am-9pm).

Shwedagon Paya & Around

(who is also buried here) and family in 1858 following the failed Sepoy Rebellion in Delhi. The ex-emperor, who had a reputation as a talented Urdu poet, died four years later in November 1862.

William Dalrymple, who chronicles Bahadur Shah Zafar's life in *The Last Mughal*, writes of how his shrouded corpse was hastily buried in an anonymous grave in his prison enclosure, so that, as the British Commissioner in charge insisted, 'No vestige should remain to distinguish where the last of the Great Mughals rests.'

A mausoleum was later built on the location of the prison, but the grave itself remained a mystery until 1991 when workmen discovered it 3½ft underground during excavations for a new structure at the site. Today it is covered in silks and strewn with sweet-smelling petals.

★ **Chaukhtatgyi Paya** BUDDHIST TEMPLE
(ခြောက်ထပ်ကြီးဘုရား; Map p50; Shwegondine Rd, Tamwe; ☺6am-8pm) Housed in a large metal-roofed shed, this beautiful 65m-long reclining Buddha is hardly publicised at all, even though it's larger than a similar well-known image in Bago. The statue's placid face is topped by a crown encrusted with diamonds and other precious stones.

Close to the Buddha's feet is the small shrine to Ma Thay, a holy man who has the power to stop rain and grant sailors a safe journey.

Attached to the temple complex is the **Shweminwon Sasana Yeiktha Meditation Centre** (ရွှေမင်းဝံသာသနာ့ရိပ်သာ) where large numbers of locals gather to meditate. It's not hard to find someone to show you around the adjoining monasteries.

★ **Ngahtatgyi Paya** BUDDHIST TEMPLE
(ငါးထပ်ကြီးဘုရား; Map p50; Shwegondine Rd, Tamwe; admission $2/K2000; ☺6am-8pm) Virtually across the street from Chaukhtatgyi Paya is a gorgeous 46ft-tall seated Buddha image at the Ngahtatgyi Paya. Sitting in calm gold-and-white repose with a healthy splash of precious stones to boot, it's one of the most impressive sitting buddhas in southern Myanmar. In fact, it's worth going to see for its carved wooden backdrop alone.

Yangon Zoological Gardens ZOO
(ရန်ကုန်တိရစ္ဆာန်ဥယျာဉ်; Map p50; Kan Yeik Tha Rd, Mingalar Taung Nyunt; adult/child K2000/1000; ☺8am-6pm, last entry 4.30pm) Yangon's 1901-vintage zoo is a chance to view up close 45 species of mammals and 68 species of birds who, on the whole, appear to be well fed and cared for. However, enclosures are often too small and the chained elephants and circus-like weekend animal shows are upsetting spectacles for animal lovers.

The leafy grounds are nicely landscaped, with handsome architectural features such as the King Edward VII 1915 Carnivore House.

Bogyoke Aung San Museum MUSEUM
(ဗိုလ်ချုပ်အောင်ဆန်းပြတိုက်; Map p50; 15 Bogyoke Aung San Museum St, Bahan; ☺9.30am-4.40pm Tue-Sun) FREE A melancholy air hangs over the home in which General Aung San lived with his family for just over two years before he was assassinated in July 1947.

Daw Kin Kyi, his widow, and three children, including Aung San Suu Kyi, stayed on until 1953, when their second son Lin drowned in the pond in the colonial mansion's grounds.

You'll have to work hard to imagine what life was like inside the house, which is sparsely furnished and has old family photos and a few personal possessions.

YANGON & AROUND YANGON

MAUSOLEUMS AROUND SHWEDAGON PAYA

Several prominent Myanmar citizens are buried nearby Shwedagon Paya. Near the north entrance to the stupa is the **Martyrs' Mausoleum** (အာဇာနည်ဗိမာန် ; Map p50; Arzani St, Bahan; admission $3/K3000; ☺9am-4pm Tue-Sun), housing the remains of General Aung San and the six comrades who were assassinated on 19 July 1947. The complex has recently reopened after being closed to the public after a North Korean terrorist strike here in 1983 killed 20 people (but not the target, visiting South Korean general Chun Doo-Hwan). The old timber mausoleum in Myanmar-style that was destroyed in the bomb blast was replaced with a stark Soviet-style concrete complex.

South of the stupa along Shwedagon Paya Rd are four mausoleums. The one closest to the stupa is for Burma's last queen, **Suphayalat**. Having been exiled to India with her husband and daughters in 1885, she was allowed to returned to Rangoon in 1919, three years after King Thibaw's death, but was kept under house arrest by the British colonial authorities until her death in 1925.

Next in line are the tombs of Aung San's widow, **Daw Khin Kyi**, the famous writer **Thakin Kodaw Hmaing** and former UN secretary-general **U Thant**. A chapter in *The River of Lost Footsteps* by his grandson Thant Myint-U recounts the horrific details of U Thant's burial in 1969 when students fought with the military and there were riots leading to hundreds of dead, many more imprisoned and martial law being imposed.

◉ Inya Lake & Northern Yangon

Inya Lake   LAKE

(အင်းယားကန်) Inya Lake, created by the British as a reservoir in 1883, is roughly five times larger than Kandawgyi. This is one of the most exclusive areas of the city to live; University Ave Rd, on the lake's southern side, was the address of Aung San Suu Kyi's home where she spent her years of house arrest, as well as the US Embassy.

The best spots to view the lake from are the parks running along part of Pyay Rd and Kaba Aye Pagoda Rd. The paths are open to the sun so bring an umbrella for shade.

If you're into sailing, drop by the **Yangon Sailing Club** (Map p54; ☑ 01-535 298; http://moewai.net; 132 Inya Rd, Kamaryut; ☺ 9am-8pm), which is open to nonmembers on Friday nights for drinks and has a lovely lakeside setting.

★ Meilamu Paya   BUDDHIST TEMPLE

(မယ်လမှုဘုရား; Thudhamar Rd, North Okkalapa; ☺ 6am-8pm) **FREE** Situated next to the Nga Moe Yeik creek, this Disneyland-ish pagoda is a hoot. Large-than-life 3D stucco depictions of the Bud-

Inya Lake

dha's life and practice litter the compound. Search out the giant crocodile housing a gallery depicting the legend of Mei La Mu, the girl born from a mangrove fruit, after whom the temple is named. There are teahouses in the complex overlooking the creek and you can take a boat across the water to another cluster of stupas.

The temple is a short walk from Tadakalay Station on the Yangon Circle Line.

Kaba Aye Paya
BUDDHIST TEMPLE

(ကမ္ဘာအေးဘုရား; Map p54; 68 Kaba Aye Pagoda Rd, Mayagone) FREE This overly glitzy 'world peace' *zedi*, about 5 miles north of the city centre, was built for the 1954–56 Sixth Buddhist Synod. The centrepiece is a 118ft-high hollow paya with five gateways, each guarded by an image of Buddha. In the centre is a statue that has claimed to be the largest Buddha cast from silver in Myanmar.

Mahapasana
CAVE

(မဟာပါသာနလိုဏ်ဂူ; Map p54; Kaba Aye Pagoda Rd, Mayagone; ⊙24hr) FREE Totally artificial, this 'great cave' is where the Sixth Buddhist Synod was held in 1954–56 to coincide with the 2500th anniversary of the Buddha's enlightenment. Measuring 456ft by 371ft, the cave, which can accommodate up to 10,000 people, took only 14 months to build. It helped that there were 63,000 labourers. Grand religious ceremonies are still held here.

State Fine Arts School
HISTORIC BUILDING

(အနုပညာအထက်တန်းကျောင်း; Map p54; 131 Kaba Aya Pagoda Rd, Bahan; ⊙9am-4.30pm) FREE Built in the early 20th century as the grand home of shipping and rubber magnate Lim Chin Tsong, this is another crumbling but highly evocative slice of Yangon's architectural heritage. On the ground floor, beneath the pagoda-like tower, is a gallery of student art.

Explore upstairs to find murals painted by Ernest and Dod Proctor, who later in their careers had their works hung in London's Tate Gallery and National Portrait Gallery.

Kyauk Daw Kyi
BUDDHIST TEMPLE

(ကျောက်တော်ကြီး; Mindhama Hill, Mingalardon; ⊙6am-6pm) FREE Not far from the airport, this immense seated Buddha was carved from a single piece of marble found outside Mandalay in 1999. The partially finished statue was painstakingly transported to Yangon by boat and train (on a specially built track) a year later, events that are depicted in the complex's modern murals.

After the detailing was finished, the Buddha was positioned in its current home at the top of a hill and encased in glass.

Hsin Hpyu Daw
ELEPHANT ENCLOSURE

(ဆင်ဖြူတော်; Mindama Rd, Insein; ⊙8am-5pm) FREE A small, unmarked park close by the Kyauk Daw Kyi is home to four white elephants – actually light pink in colour. Found upcountry and brought to Yangon in 2002, their discovery was regarded, by the military at least, as a good omen for the country. The elephants, who spend much of the day chained, might think otherwise.

Myanmar Gems Museum & Gems Market
MUSEUM, MARKET

(မြန်မာ့ကျောက်မျက်ရတနာပြတိုက်   နှင့် ကျောက်မျက်အရောင်းပြခန်း; Map p54; ☑ 01-665 365; 66 Kaba Aye Pagoda Rd, Mayagone; admission $5; ⊘ 9.30am-4pm Tue-Sun) The glitter has dimmed at this small museum, on the 4th floor of a building that mainly operates as a shopping plaza for jewelry stalls, since the government carted off the biggest gems to another repository in Nay Pyi Twa. Still, there's a few eye-catching pieces of bling and precious stones, including a small bust of General Aung San carved from jade.

Activities

Apart from the swimming pools listed here, nonguests can use the pools at the following hotels: Savoy and Chatrium ($10); Parkroyal ($20 including the gym); and Governor's Residence (free as long as you eat at the restaurant).

Kokine Swimming Club
SWIMMING

(Map p50; 23 Sayar San Rd, Bahan; admission K2000; ⊘ 6am-8pm, closed 10am-3pm Mon) Offering two well-maintained 30m outdoor pools, this club for serious swimmers has been going since 1904.

Kandawgyi Swimming Pool
SWIMMING

(Map p50; Bahan St, Bahan; admission K4000; ⊘ 7am-noon, 3-8pm) Near Kandawgyi Lake, this pool is well patronised but not as nice as Kokine; there's also a paddling pool for toddlers.

Keinnayi Souvenir Shop
BICYCLE RENTAL

(Map p40; 118 Mahabandoola Garden St, Kyauktada; per day K5000; ⊘ 9am-6pm) Should you be brave enough to take to downtown Yangon's traffic-clogged streets by bicycle, this upstairs shop, next to Myanmar Travels & Tours, can rent you a set of wheels.

Bike World Explores Myanmar
BICYCLE TOUR

(Map p54; ☑ 01-527 636; www.cyclingmyanmar. com; 10F Khapaung Rd, Hlaing; bike rental & guide $13) Contact Aussie expat Jeff Parry about the downtown Yangon guided bike rides he leads on Friday nights from 10pm to midnight and the Sunday all-day rides into the countryside around the city.

City Walk
Yangon's Colonial Treasures

START THONE PAN HLA TEASHOP
FINISH GOLDEN TEA TEASHOP
LENGTH APPROX 1.4 MILES; TWO TO THREE HOURS

We recommend starting this tour in the cool hours of the morning, with a coffee and Burmese-style breakfast at ❶ **Thone Pan Hla**, a typical Myanmar teahouse. It's also advisable to do the walk on Sunday when downtown Yangon's traffic is at its lightest.

Near the teahouse is the 2200-year-old ❷ **Sule Paya**, the geographic and commercial heart of the city, and where the British-designed grid street pattern was centred. Make a circle around the temple to get the right angle for your photograph; good views can also be had from the pedestrian bridge that rises from the west side of Mahabandoola St to the terrace level of the pagoda.

To the east of Sule Paya is ❸ **City Hall**, a colossal lilac- and purple-painted colonial building adorned with traditional Myanmar decorations such as peacocks, *nagas* (serpents) and three-tiered *pyatthat* turrets. Nip around the back to see the Municipal Corporation of Rangoon insignia on the iron gates.

On the next corner further east on Mahabandoola Rd is the ❹ **former Immigration Department**, once Rowe & Co department store, dubbed the 'Harrods of the East'. At the time of research the building was being restored to become a bank. Across the street is the ❺ **Immanuel Baptist Church**, originally built in 1830, though the present structure dates from 1885.

Continuing south you'll pass the Queen Anne–style ❻ **High Court** with its bell clock tower and rooftop lion statues. Pop into the recently renovated ❼ **Mahabandoola Garden** to enjoy the greenery and take a closer look at the Independence Monument. Exit on Sule Pagoda Rd, heading towards Yangon River past the monumental 1939, neo-classical ❽ **Myawaddy Bank**, built to house the Reserve Bank of India.

Turning left a colonnade of Ionic columns stretches along the Strand facade of the ❾ **former Yangon Region Office Complex**. There are plans to turn the building into a five-star hotel. Next door is the red-brick

10 Customs House, built in 1915, and still functioning for its original purpose, as is the nearly century-old two-faced bracketed clock hanging from the building's white tower.

On the corner with Pansodan St stands the pastel-coloured **11 Yangon Region Court**, one of the oldest masonry structures in Yangon dating from around 1900. Bomb damage from WWII is still visible on the Bank St side of the complex. The opposite corner is taken up with the grand **12 Port Authority** building with its striking square corner tower and bas-relief sculptures of ships on the facade.

Two blocks further along Strand Rd is the **13 Strand Hotel**. The air-conditioned lobby, cafe and bar make a good rest stop. Consider writing a postcard and then posting it at the **14 Central Post Office**, dating from 1908; note the lovely beaux-arts portico as you enter.

Return to turn right on lower Pansodan St. Monumental buildings line what was considered Yangon's prime business address a century ago. Several, such as the **15 Myanmar Agricultural Development Bank** (former Grindlays Bank) and the graceful **16 Inland Waterways Department** (once the the headquarters of the Irrawaddy Flotilla Company),

have weathered the passage of time well, while others, including the **17 Lokanat Gallery Building**, are in desperate need of love and attention. This crumbling Italianate-style building, constructed by the Jewish-Baghdadi trader Isaac A Sofaer, still has original features such as the floor tiles imported from Manchester.

At the corner with Merchant St and north along 37th St are many streetside **18 bookstalls**; the area is known as Yangon's open-air library for obvious reasons. Turn right at the junction of Mahabandoola Rd and head west until you reach the corner occupied by the **19 Ministers Office**, a giant red-brick pile also known as the Secretariat from when it was the nucleus of British power in the country.

Return to Sule Paya along Mahabandoola Rd, noting the **20 Central Telegraph Office**; during the 1950s close on 200,000 international cables a year passed through this building.

West of Sule Paya continue down Mahabandoola Rd through the chaotic Indian and Chinese quarters. Several mosques are found here, including the 1918 **21 Mogul Shiah Mosque** and the **22 Surti Sunni Jamah Mosque**, Yangon's oldest Muslim place of worship dating to the 1860s. End the walking tour with a well-earned cuppa at **23 Golden Tea**.

Nemita by Lilawadee Spa   SPA

(Map p50; 01-544 500; http://chatrium.com; Chatrium Hotel, Pho Sein Rd, Tamwe; 1hr massage $25; 10am-midnight;) International-standard spa that offers a full range of treatments, including reasonably priced massage and foot reflexology.

Seri Beauty and Health   MASSAGE

(Map p50; 534 205; www.seribeautynhealth.com; 118 Dhama Zedi Rd, Bahan; massage per hr K5000; 9am-6pm) Not Yangon's most upscale beauty parlour but conveniently located and offering reasonably priced massages and a full range of beautification services. There's another branch two door down (114 Dhama Zedi Rd, Bahan).

Thu Ti Leithwei
Boxing School   BOXING

(Map p54; www.myanmar-boxing-school.com; 893 Wun Tharet Khitta Lan, Kabaye; 1hr session K5000) Lone Chaw, three-time winner of Myanmar's National Championship, runs this school where you can get fit learning the moves of luthwei (Burmese boxing). Be warned – it's a high-intensity workout.

Dora   CRUISE

(Map p40; 01-531 313; www.cruiseinmyanmar. com; Botataung Jetty, Botataung; morning or sunset cruise $60) Enjoy the scenery along Yangon's river and harbour on this pricey one-hour cruise (minimum five people needed). Drinks and snacks are included and the 63ft teak-decked boat is handsomely appointed. Day trips to Twante can also be arranged. For a fraction of the cost you could do a return trip on the Dalah ferry.

🎓 Courses

Several monasteries and meditation centres in Yangon welcome foreigners, although stays of 10 days are generally preferred. For more information on meditation courses, see p383.

Mahasi Meditation Centre   MEDITATION

(Map p50; 01-541 971; www.mahasi.org.mm; 16 Thathana Yeiktha Rd, Bahan) Yangon's most famous meditation centre was founded in 1947 by the late Mahasi Sayadaw, perhaps Myanmar's greatest meditation teacher. The Mahasi Sayadaw technique strives for intensive, moment-to-moment awareness of every physical movement, every mental and physical sensation and, ultimately, every thought. The centre only accepts foreigners who can stay for at least one week. A dhamma (Bud-

dhist teachings) talk in English (3pm; two hours) is open to anyone to attend.

Dhamma Joti Vipassana Centre   MEDITATION

(Map p50; 01-549 290; www.vridhamma.org; Ngahtatgyi Paya Rd, Bahan) Following the Vipassana teachings of SN Goenka, this simple, peaceful retreat is a short walk from Shwedagon Paya and Kandawgyi Lake. Meditators must sign up for the introductory 10-day course and share accommodation.

Panditarama
Meditation Centre   MEDITATION

(Map p50; 01-535 448; www.panditarama.net; 80A Than Lwin Rd, Bahan) Established in 1990 by Sayadaw U Pandita, formerly a chief mediation teacher at the Mahasi centre, this respected facility also runs the Panditarama Forest Meditation Centre at Hse Main Gon, 40 miles northeast of Yangon off the highway to Bago. Courses in English are run for visitors prepared to commit to stays of one week or more.

Chanmyay Yeiktha
Meditation Centre   MEDITATION

(Map p54; 01-661 479; www.facebook.com/chanmyaymeditation.centreyangon; 55A Kaba Aye Pagoda Rd, Mayangone) Meaning 'peaceful retreat' Chanmyay Yeiktha was founded by another Mahasi desciple, Sawadaw U Janaka. There is also a countryside branch at Hmawbi, around a one-hour drive north of Yangon; one-month stays are preferred.

🎊 Festivals & Events

Crowds of pilgrims descend on the Shwedagon for a *paya pwe* (pagoda festival), one of the more important Myanmar holidays. This takes place over the March full moon day, the last full moon before the Myanmar New Year. In the Western calendar it normally falls in late February/early March.

Other major festivals in Yangon:

Independence Day   CULTURAL

(4 Jan) Includes a seven-day fair at Kandawgyi.

Thaipusam   HINDU

(Jan or Feb) Held at Yangon's Hindu temples, it involves colourful processions and ritual piercings of the flesh. The date depends on the lunar calendar.

Water Festival/Thingyan   CULTURAL

(Apr) The Myanmar New Year is celebrated in wet pandemonium.

Buddha's Birthday　　　BUDDHIST
(☉Apr/May) Celebrate the Buddha's enlightenment.

Martyrs' Day　　　CULTURAL
(☉19 Jul) Commemorates the assassination of General Bogyoke Aung San and his comrades.

🛏 Sleeping

The sharp increase in the number of visitors to Yangon, coupled with a dearth of decent hotels and guesthouses, has caused a spike in prices. In the wet season rates are what you'll find quoted here, but expect many places, particularly the larger hotels, to hike their rates substantially over busy periods in December through February, when booking ahead is essential.

Several new hotels are in the works, but at the time of research few were anywhere near completion. Much of Yangon's budget accommodation is dank and dreary, and many midrange places are poor value for money.

Downtown Yangon is a convenient, if noisy place to be based. Hotels in Dagon and Bahan are convenient for walking to Shwedagon Paya and Kandawgyi Lake, while those further north will speed up access to and from the airport.

Budget accommodation ($) are places that offer a double room or dorm bed for under $50; midrange places ($$) are those where rates are between $51 and $200; top end ($$$) is over $200.

🛏 Downtown Yangon

★**Mother Land Inn 2**　　BUDGET HOTEL $
(Map p40; ☎01-291 343; www.myanmarmotherlandinn.com; 433 Lower Pazundaung Rd, Pazundaung; s/d $25/30, dm/s/d with shared bathroom $10/24/28; ▣❀@☎) It's often fully booked and is a long walk or a short taxi ride from the core of downtown, but the Motherland remains a backpacker favourite for its professional service, cleanliness, well-proportioned rooms, travel advice

---

RESTORING OLD YANGON

'It is one of the best-preserved colonial cityscapes in the world,' says Thant Myint-U, chairman of the Yangon Heritage Trust (YHT) of Yangon's downtown area, 'but whether it survives the transition to democracy and renewed prosperity remains to be seen.'

Set up in April 2012, the YHT has a seemingly impossible task: to protect the city's architectural legacy, under threat from a double whammy of decades of neglect combined with landowners eager to take advantage of the booming property market and sell to developers who have little to no interest in heritage preservation. Currently 189 properties are listed as historically significant by the Yangon City Development Committee (YCDC). All are either government-owned or religious buildings. Hundreds more privately owned buildings are not listed as well as some buildings, such as the Pegu Club, which remain government properties.

The YHT is pushing for laws and public policy to protect key buildings and sensitively develop Yangon. It's working with the YCDC on what to do with vacant government buildings so that best-practice conservation methods are put in place, and reaching out to the public, 'to give people, especially the young, a sense of the historical importance of the downtown landscape'.

A 'blue plaque' scheme for 200 notable buildings, sponsored by the Dutch conglomerate Phillips, was launched at the end of 2013. LED-illuminated plaques with details in Bamar and English on a building's history and significance are being affixed across the downtown area; the first two are on the British Myanmar–style City Hall and Basic Education High School 2 Dagon (formerly Myoma School, Burma's first 'nationalist' place of education).

The YHT is also working with the leaseholders and owners of buildings, such as the Ministers Office and the former Burma Railways Company complex on the corner of Sule Paya Rd and Bogyoke Aung San Rd, to ensure their heritage value is protected during ongoing restoration work. It's a process fraught with difficulties, as the row over the development of the former Yangon Region Office Complex on the Strand shows. At the time of research this handsome building, once used for law courts, was at the centre of a dispute between lawyers' groups and the government over plans to turn it into a five-star hotel called the State House.

and services. The free airport transfer and a solid included breakfast are other pluses.

Three Seasons Hotel
GUESTHOUSE $

(Map p40; ☑01-297 946; phyuaung@mptmail. net.mm; 83-85 52nd St, Pazundaung; s/d/tr $30/35/45; ❋@🛜) The nine rooms in this homey guesthouse are large, spotless and well endowed with everything that would make your granny smile. The outdoor terrace, with tree shade, is a nice place to sit and watch the world cruise by.

Staff are very friendly and helpful and it is located on a block that is especially quiet at night, so you should be able to sleep undisturbed.

Ocean Pearl Inn
HOTEL $

(Map p40; ☑01-297 007; www.oceanpearlinn. com; 215 Botataung Pagoda Rd, Pazundaung; s/d/tr $25/30/38; ❋🛜) A paint job and rooms washed and polished by a team of cleaning addicts make the Ocean Pearl one of the tidiest choices in the budget range. Another perk is free airport pickup.

New Yangon Hotel
HOTEL $

(Map p44; ☑01-210 157; www.newyangonhotel. com; 830 Mahabandoola Rd, Lanmadaw; r $30-60; ❋🛜) Not many of the rooms in this newly renovated hotel, steps from Lan Thit Jetty, offer views of the river. Never mind; the rooftop bar does, and that's the main plus of staying here.

Yoma Hotel
HOTEL $

(Map p40; ☑01-299 243; www.yomahotelone.com; 146 Bogyoke Aung San Rd, Pazundaung; s/d from $27/32; ❋🛜) Although it's a bit of a hike from the city centre, this is one of the tidier and better-run budget places in town. The rooms are a bit frumpy and vary in size and facilities, and clearly date from another era, but it's clean and has friendly staff.

There are five floors and no lift, so if you're on the top floor you can eat that extra cake without guilt.

Beautyland Hotel II
HOTEL $

(Map p40; ☑01-240 054; www.goldenlandpages. com/beauty; 188-192 33rd St, Kyauktada; s/d $20/25, with air-con from $28/38; ❋🛜) Exceedingly tidy rooms with friendly and confident service make this one of the better budget choices in central Yangon. The cheapest rooms don't have windows, while the more expensive front-side rooms boast heaps of natural light.

May Fair Inn
GUESTHOUSE $

(Map p40; ☑01-253 454; maytinmg@gmail.com; 57 38th St, Kyauktada; s/d/tr $15/24/30; ❋🛜) Family-run, and ever reliable, this old-fashioned place is best for the traveller looking for tranquility rather than a party.

Hninn Si Budget Inn
GUESTHOUSE $

(Map p40; ☑01-299 941; www.hninnsibudgetinn. com; 213-215 Botataung Pagoda St, Pazundaung; s/d with shared bathroom $23/30; ❋🛜) Sparkling-clean new backpacker guesthouse with 15 mostly windowless rooms with sparse decoration.

Okinawa Guest House
GUESTHOUSE $

(Map p44; ☑01-374 318; 64 32nd St, Pabedan; d $28, d/m/s/d with shared bathroom $8/16/22; ❋) The interior of this bougainvillea-fronted guesthouse is a bizarre hotchpotch of decorations and building styles that blend wood, bamboo and red brick. The handful of rooms are small and dark but very clean, although noise can be an issue.

White House Hotel
HOTEL $

(Map p44; ☑01-240 780; whitehouse.mm@gmail. com; 69/71 Kon Zay Dan St, Pabedan; s/d air-con $25/30, with fan & shared bathroom $17/22; ❋🛜) Pluses are the generous breakfasts, rooftop terrace, cold beer, expansive views and useful travel desk. The negatives are a thigh-burning number of stairs, small and sometimes windowless rooms, and basic bathrooms.

There's also a curfew from midnight to 5am, so not for late-night revellers.

Tokyo Guest House
HOTEL $

(Map p40; ☑01-386 828; tokyoguesthouse.yangon@gmail.com; 200 Bo Aung Kyaw St, Botataung; s $11-17, d $22-26; ❋🛜) Highlights at this friendly budget hotel are the sunny terrace with views and the room cleanliness. Lowlights are the fact that said rooms are windowless and very cramped.

Cherry Guest House
HOTEL $

(Map p40; ☑01-255 946; 278/300 Mahabandoola Garden St, Kyauktada; s/d $20/25; ❋🛜) Located on the 4th floor of this (relatively) quiet street, the 20 rooms here are a useful fallback if other budget options are full.

★ Loft Hotel
HOTEL $$

(Map p44; ☑01-393 112; www.theloftyangon.com; 33 Yaw Min Gee St, Dagon; r $150-240; ❋@🛜) Designer fairydust has been cast over a 1960s warehouse to transform it into this new and very appealing boutique hotel in a very handy location. New York City-style loft rooms and split level suites sport exposed-brick walls, floor-to-ceiling windows, arty black-and-white prints and contemporary furnishings.

May Shan Hotel
HOTEL $$

(Map p44; ☑ 01-252 986; www.mayshan.com; 115 Sule Paya Rd, Kyauktada; s/d/tr $45/55/79; ✵@⑦) The single rooms are pretty tight and lack windows, but the combination of convenient location, gracious service and ample amenities make the May Shan a top option in this area. The triple rooms (ask for room 601) are spacious and overlook Sule Paya.

Panorama Hotel
HOTEL $$

(Map p40; ☑ 01-253 077; www.panoramaygn.com; 294-300 Pansodan St, Kyauktada; s/d $80/100; ✵@⑦) Centrally located and boasting distant views over the Shwedagon Paya, the aptly named 10-storey Panorama is not the most modern place but rooms are vast and generally well appointed.

Aung Tha Pyay Hotel
HOTEL $$

(Map p40; ☑ 01-378 663; www.aungthapyayhotel.com; 74-80 38th St, Kyauktada; r/ste $75/85; ✵@⑦) A good addition to Yangon's stock of midrange hotels, this new place is simply decorated. Spruce rooms are functional and spacious, with attached bathrooms with shower only. It's not worth paying extra for the suites, which offer little more than the standard rooms.

Yangon Home Stay
HOMESTAY $$

(Map p44; ☑ 09 4202 80430; http://yangonhomestay.com; 2nd fl, 32-34 16th St, Lanmadaw; d from $40; ✵⑦) Friendly Burmese-French couple Aldrich and Gladyis manage this pleasantly renovated apartment in Chinatown that's worth hunting down. The five cosy rooms (a couple without windows) share a bathroom. There's a big, well-equipped kitchen, and lounge with library and gym equipment.

Excellent Burmese-style massages can also be arranged (K15,000 for one hour).

East Hotel
HOTEL $$

(Map p40; ☑ 01-7313 5311; www.east.com.mm; 234-240 Sule Pagoda Rd, Kyauktada; r $90; ✵@⑦) A dash of contemporary style helps this newish hotel stand out from the downtown midrange crowd. Take note, though, if you prefer your ablutions to be private from your

room buddy: the bathrooms are not sealed off from the rest of the bedroom.

Panda Hotel
HOTEL $$

(Map p44; ☑ 01-212 850; www.myanmarpandahotel.com; 205 Wadan St, Lanmadaw; r $90-120; ✵@⑦) This 13-storey high-rise west of the city centre offers bright and enticing rooms with excellent bathrooms. It's in a peaceful residential area and is popular with tour groups.

New Aye Yar Hotel
HOTEL $$

(Map p40; ☑ 01-256 938; www.newayeyarhotel.com; 170-176 Bo Aung Kyaw St, Botataung; s/d from $75/80; ✵@⑦) A high-rise midranger that has avoided the tropical rot that has struck down so many of its cousins.

Eastern Hotel
HOTEL $$

(Map p40; ☑ 01-293 815; www.myanmareasternhotel.com; 194-196 Bo Myat Tun St, Botataung; s/d $45/55; ✵@⑦) The 40 rooms here are utterly unremarkable, but are clean and reasonably priced for amenities such as satellite TV, hot water and fridge.

★ Strand Hotel
HOTEL $$$

(Map p40; ☑ 01-243 377; www.hotelthestrand.com; 92 Strand Rd, Kyauktada; r from $633; ✵@⑦) Yangon's most storied hotel is a luxury affair, with heaps of charm and history and a high level of service. If you can't afford to stay, visit for a drink in the bar, high tea in the lobby lounge or a splurge lunch at the cafe.

★ Governor's Residence
LUXURY HOTEL $$$

(Map p44; ☑ 01-229 860; www.governorsresidence.com; 35 Taw Win St, Dagon; r/ste from $300/432; ✵@⑦) In the 1920s the Governor's Residence was a guesthouse for important nationals of the Kayah ethnic group, but now, after a masterful restoration, it's the epitome of colonial luxury. The glorious rooms have ever-so-lightly-perfumed air, teak floors, cloudy soft beds and stone baths with rose-petal water.

The pool merges gently into the lawns and sparkles in reflected beauty. A major plus is the excellent range of free daily activities including bike rides and cooking classes.

Parkroyal Yangon
CASINO HOTEL $$$

(Map p44; ☑ 01-250 388; parkroyalhotels.com; 33 Ah Lan Pya Pagoda Rd, Dagon; r from $220; ✵@⑦) This well-run, centrally located business hotel offers rooms featuring all the

There are good kids' playgrounds at Mahabandoola Gardens, People's Park, Yangon Zoological Gardens and **Happy World Kandaw Mingala Garden** (Map p50; Shwedagon Pagoda Rd, Kandaw Mingala Garden, Dagon; ⊙ 9am-9pm). **Thirimingala Zei** (3rd fl, Thirimingala Zei, Lower Kyee Myin Dyaing Rd, Kyeemyindaing; ⊙ 9am-9pm) is an amusement park chain with a branch near the south entrance to Shwedagon Paya.

For more suggestions check out the *Yangon Golden Guide,* sold at bookshops and at the gift shop Pomelo (p73).

amenities you'd expect at this price. It also has a good pool, tennis courts and gym including aerobics and yoga classes ($20 for outside guests).

🛏 Shwedagon Paya & Around

★ Garden Home Bed & Breakfast   GUESTHOUSE **$$**
(Map p50; 01-541 917; www.gardenhomebnb. asia; 10 Bogykoke Museum Rd, Bahan; s/d/tr $80/105/125; ❄@🛜) Opposite the German Embassy and within walking distance of Kandawgyi Lake and Shwedagon Paya; you'd be wise to book well ahead to secure one of the 10 simply and tastefully decorated rooms at this best new addition to Yangon's accommodation scene. The garden bar is lovely and the attached art gallery is also a plus.

★ Alamanda Inn   BOUTIQUE HOTEL **$$**
(Map p50; 01-534 513; www.hotel-alamanda. com; 60B Shwe Taung Gyar Rd/Golden Valley Rd, Bahan; s/d from $110/120; ❄@🛜) Set in a blissfully quiet compound, the French-run Alamanda combines 10 spacious and attractively decorated rooms, the most expensive of which is the suite in the old servants' quarters with its own private garden. There's an excellent attached French restaurant and bar.

Classique Inn   HOTEL **$$**
(Map p50; 01-525 557; www.classique-inn.com; 53B Shwe Taung Gyar Rd/Golden Valley Rd, Bahan; s/d from $50/70; ❄@🛜) Located in a secluded villa in the posh Golden Valley neighbour-

hood, this leafy, family-run place offers eight cosy, attractive rooms which vary greatly in size. Deluxe rooms have teak and bamboo furnishings. Warm service (including travel arrangements), good breakfast and a homey atmosphere are all pluses.

Rainbow Hotel   HOTEL **$$**
(Map p50; 01-543 681; www.myrainbowhotel.com; 3 Win Gabar Lane, Bahan; s/d $40/55; ❄@🛜) The main selling point of the aged Rainbow is its quiet location, a short walk north of Kandawgi Lake. Rooms and furnishings have seen better days but the comfy lobby with an art gallery has a winning charm.

Guest Care Hotel   HOTEL **$$**
(Map p50; 01-511 118; www.guestcarehotel. com; 107 Dhama Zedi Rd, Bahan; s/d from $60/70; ❄@🛜) There are several classes of room here (with little noticeable difference between them), and it's worth taking a look at a few before committing, as some are in much better nick than others. For character you'll find a few bits of beautifully carved wooden furniture tossed about the place.

Winner Inn   HOTEL **$$**
(Map p50; 01-535 205; www.winnerinnmyanmar. com; 42 Than Lwin Rd, Bahan; s/d from $50/55, ste $75; ❄@🛜) This low-slung building is in a quiet, leafy suburb and has spotless rooms with old-fashioned desks, and pictures on the walls. The communal areas have plenty of well-positioned chairs waiting for you to collapse into them with a book.

Holiday Hotel   HOTEL **$$**
(Map p50; 01-860 4076; www.myanmarholidayhotel.com; 51A Pho Sein Rd, Bahan; r $60-80; ❄@🛜) Attached to a long-standing halal Chinese restaurant, the Holiday is a new hotel that will win no awards for its design, but nonetheless makes for a friendly, reasonably good value base.

Savoy Hotel   BOUTIQUE HOTEL **$$$**
(Map p50; 01-526 289; www.savoy-myanmar. com; 129 Dhama Zedi Rd, Bahan; s/d $295/315, ste s/d $379/418; ❄@🛜🍽) Everything inside the Savoy is done so well it's easy to forgive the fact that it's situated on a busy street corner. Hallways, rooms and even the lavish bathrooms are stocked with photographs, antiques, handicrafts and sculptures, and it takes little imagination to feel as if you are some Raj-era royal.

Chatrium Hotel   HOTEL $$$

(Map p50; ☑01-544 500; www.chatrium.com; 40 Natmauk Rd, Tamwe; r/st $299/500; ❋@☞☒) Since Hilary Clinton stayed here there's been a steady stream of VIPs checking in. It's easy to see why. It might not be Yangon's most historic or charming hotel but it's very professionally run and offers more style than most at this price point. The large pool, gym and excellent spa are other pluses.

Nonguests can use the pool for $10.

Summit Parkview   HOTEL $$$

(Map p50; ☑01-211 888; www.summityangon. com; 350 Ahlone Rd, Dagon; s/d from $184/207; ❋@☞☒) If one of the Summit's room overlooking the jewel-encrusted Shwedagon Paya isn't for you, feel free to take the same type of room overlooking the pool; they're a little cheaper. A necessary refurbishment of some rooms was underway during our most recent visit.

🛏 Inya Lake & Northern Yangon

Bike World Explores
Myanmar Inn   GUESTHOUSE $$

(Map p54; ☑01-525 820; bwemtravel.com; 10F Martin Ave, Hlaing; r $50-70; ❋@☞) In an out-of-the-way location, near the Israeli Embassy, and run by an Australian-Burmese couple as an extension of their bicycle tour company, the Inn offers cramped but fully equipped rooms. New and more spacious rooms were under construction during our visit.

Inya Lake Hotel   HOTEL $$

(Map p54; ☑01-966 2866; www.inyalakehotel. com; 37 Kaba Aye Pagoda Rd, Yankin; r from $160; ❋@☞☒) If you'd prefer chilling out in a serene lakeside location, this mammoth property, designed by a Russian in the 1950s, offers big, light-filled rooms with wooden floors and balconies. There's a good-sized pool and tennis courts.

Sedona Hotel   HOTEL $$$

(Map p54; ☑01-666 900; www.sedonasmyanmar. com; 1 Kaba Aye Pagoda Rd; r $100-160, ste $350-900; ❋@☞☒) You know exactly what you'll be getting at the Singapore-owned Sedona: peace, quiet and very professional service. What you won't be getting is any indication you're in Myanmar, but as you sink into one of the comfortable beds, you probably won't be that bothered.

🍴 Eating

Yangon is where you may first experience Burmese cuisine. As such, be sure to arm yourself with a bit of culinary knowledge (see p355) before hitting the city's rapidly expanding range of restaurants, as well as its excellent street stalls and buzzing teahouses.

It's not all about Burmese eats. Yangon has always been Myanmar's most cosmopolitan city and its culinary diversity reflects that. On top of all the regional styles of Myanmar cooking, such as Shan and Rakhine, there's a decent selection of international restaurants, including Thai, Japanese, Korean, French, Italian and Indian ones. You're likely to encounter more than your fair share of Chinese (Burmese Chinese, actually) while upcountry, so unless you're a huge fan of the genre, it's worth investigating the other options.

Eat early – by 10pm all but a couple of places and a few large hotel restaurants will be closed. In terms of value for money few of the top-end restaurants can really justifiy their high prices.

🍴 Downtown Yangon

Street eats are plentiful and available pretty much any time of the day. Downtown's teahouses are also good places for a light meal or bite.

Along Anawrahta Rd, west of Sule Paya Rd towards the Sri Kali temple, are a number of shops serving Indian food, much of it southern Indian in origin and Muslim-influenced. Further west is the Chinatown district where you'll find plenty of Chinese-Burmese eateries.

Nilar Biryani &
Cold Drink   MUSLIM INDIAN $

(Map p44; 216 Anawrahta Rd, Pabedan; meals from K800; ☺4am-10pm; 📵) Giant cauldrons full of spices, broths and rice bubble away at the front of this bright and brash Indian joint. It's never less than packed, and with good reason: the biryanis are probably among the best your lips will meet.

The chicken has been cooked so slowly and for so long that the meat just drips off, the rice is out of this world and the banana lassi is divine. Nothing on the menu costs more than K1800, and most is a fraction of that. It's far and away the best of several similar nearby places.

YANGON'S STREET EATS

It doesn't take long to see that much of life in Yangon takes place on the streets. Likewise, for the average person in Myanmar, eating at a proper restaurant is an infrequent extravagance and most eating is done at home or on the street.

Yangon's street-food options can be both overwhelming and challenging (pork offal on a skewer, anyone?), so as a guide in this jungle of meals, here are some of our favourite street eats and the best places to eat them.

Samusa thoke During the day a line of **vendors** (Map p40; Mahabandoola Garden St, Kyauktada; samosas K500) near Mahabandoola Park sell this 'salad' of sliced samosas served with a thin lentil gravy.

Fruit juice Several **vendors** (Bogyoke Aung San Rd, Pabedan; juice from K1000; ⊙10am-5pm) at Bogyoke Aung San Market sell refreshing fresh-squeezed juice – don't miss the creamy avocado, sweetened with condensed milk.

Bein moun & moun pyar thalet These delicious 'Burmese pancakes' (K200), served sweet (*bein moun*) or savoury (*moun pyar thalet*), can be found at most Yangon corners at all times of the day and night.

Dosai At night along Anawratha St, several streetside vendors sell this thin southern Indian crepe (from K500), known in Burmese as *to-shay*.

Mohinga This soup of thin rice noodles and fish broth is available just about everywhere, but our favourite bowl is at **Myaung Mya Daw Cho** (Map p40; 149 51st St, Pazuntaung; noodles from K500; ⊙4.30-9am). There's no English sign here; simply look for the green sign near some trees. They also have a more formal branch near Shwedagon Paya (p66).

Grilled food Every night, the strip of 19th St between Mahabandoola and Anawrahta Rds hosts dozens of **stalls and open-air restaurants** (Map p44; 19th St, Latha; meals from K5000; ⊙5-11pm) serving delicious grilled snacks and draught beer.

Lassi Shwe Bali (Map p44; Bo Sun Pat Rd, Pabedan; lassi per glass from 600K; ⊙10am-10.30pm), on the corner with Mahabandoola Rd, serves deliciously curdy glasses of this Indian yogurt drink.

Buthi kyaw Every evening a lone **vendor** (Map p40; cnr Anawratha & Thein Byu Rds, Pazuntaung; K500; ⊙4-9pm) sells this tasty snack of battered and deep-fried chunks of gourd served with a spicy/sour dipping sauce.

Burmese sweets Every afternoon in front of FMI Centre a handful of **streetside vendors** (Map p44; Bogyoke Aung San Rd, Pabedan; from K50) sell delicious Burmese sweets ranging from *shwe-t'aumi'n* ('golden' sticky rice) to *mou'n-se'in-ba'un* (a type of steamed cake topped with shredded coconut).

---

999 Shan Noodle Shop SHAN $
(Map p40; 130/B 34th St, Kyauktada; noodle dishes from K500; ⊙6am-7pm) A handful of tables are crammed into this tiny, brightly coloured eatery behind City Hall. The menu includes noodles such as *shàn k'auq swèh* (thin rice noodles in a slightly spicy chicken broth) and *myi shay* (Mandalay-style noodle soup) and tasty non-noodle dishes such as Shan tofu (actually made from chickpea flour) and the delicious Shan yellow rice with tomato.

**Nam Kham Family
Shan Restaurant** SHAN $
(Map p40; 134 37th St, Kyauktada; noodles from K800; ⊙6am-7pm Mon-Sat) This tiny restaurant split across two neighbouring units serves the usual Shan noodle dishes plus a variety of point-and-choose curries, soups, stir-fries and other dishes served over rice.

New Delhi INDIAN $
(Map p44; 274 Anawrahta Rd, Pabedan; mains from K500; ⊙5.30am-9.30pm; ▣) This grubby place serves tasty Muslim-influenced South Indian dishes such as a rich mutton curry, as well as meat-free options including *puris* (puffy breads), *idli* (rice ball), various *dosai* (savoury pancakes) and banana-leaf *thalis* (meals; K1000).

Ingyin New South India Food Centre SOUTHERN INDIAN $

(Map p44; 232 Anawrahta Rd, Pabedan; mains from K600; ☯5am-10pm; ⌨) The cheery staff here do the crispiest and tastiest *dosai* in central Yangon. It's a good place for a *thali* as well, and it has tea and Indian sweets if you require dessert.

★ Shan Yoe Yar SHAN $$

(Map p44; ☑01-221 524; www.facebook.com/ShanYoeYar; 169 Wadan St, Lanmadaw; mains K2000-7000; ☯7am-10.30pm; ☎⌨) A century-old wooden mansion has been expertly renovated into Yangon's most upmarket Shan restaurant. Among the delicious dishes on the menu are a luscious Mine Tauk aubergine curry and Inlay-style pork curry. Set menus (from K10,000) include one vegetarian dish.

★ Feel Myanmar Food BURMESE $$

(Map p44; ☑01-511 6872; www.feelrestaurant. com; 124 Pyidaungsu Yeiktha St, Dagon; meals from K3000; ☯6am-8.30pm) This long-running operation is a superb place to get your fingers dirty experimenting with the huge range of tasty Burmese dishes, which are laid out in little trays that you can just point to. It's very popular at lunchtime with local business-people and foreign embassy staff.

Danuphyu Daw Saw Yee Myanma Restaurant BURMESE $$

(Map p44; 175/177 29th St, Pabedan; meals from K2000; ☯9am-9pm; ⌨) Ask locals where to eat Burmese food in central Yangon and they'll most likely point you in the direction of this longstanding shophouse restaurant. All dishes are served with sides of soup du jour (the sour vegetable soup is particularly good) and *ngapi ye,* a pungent dip served with par-boiled vegies and fresh herbs.

There's a brief English-language menu, but your best bet is to have a look at the selection of curries behind the counter.

★ Ichiban-Kan JAPANESE $$

(Map p40; ☑01-394 824; 17-18 Aung San Stadium, Gyo Phyu St, Mingalar Taung Nyuit; noodle dishes $5-7; ☯11.30am-2pm, 5.30-10pm; ☎⌨) Our favourite Japanese restaurant is intimate and tasteful and seems to have been lifted straight from the Tokyo backstreets of yesteryear. The food, which covers a wide range of Japanese dishes, is as well presented and highly authentic.

Be Le CHINESE $$

(Junior Duck; map p40; ☑01-249 421; Pansodan St Jetty, Kyauktada; dishes from K1200; ☯10am-10.30pm; ⌨) Occupying the old ferry terminal, this pleasant Chinese restaurant is one the best places in town to soak up a river view (not that it has much competition!) and some breezes. The food is decent; most go for the roast duck (K7100 for a small portion).

It's part of the Golden Duck chain of restaurants which also has a branch (Map p50; ☑01-240 216; Kan Taw Mingalar Garden, Shwedagon Pagoda Rd, Dagon; ☯10am-10pm; ☎) with a great view of the south of Shwedagon Paya.

Shwe Mei Tha Su MUSLIM BURMESE $$

(Map p44; 173 29th St, Pabedan; meals from K2000; ☯9am-9pm) Located next door to Danuphyu Daw Saw Yee, and lacking a roman-script sign, this is the Muslim version of the traditional Myanmar curry house. The sour soup is replaced with a hearty dhal, the meat-based curries are rich and spicy, and sides include a smoky *balachaung.*

Aung Mingalar Shan Noodle Restaurant SHAN $$

(Map p44; Bo Yar Nyunt St, Dagon; mains from K1500; ☯7am-9pm; ⌨) Aung Mingalar is an excellent place to indulge simultaneously in people-watching and noodle sipping. It's a simple and fun restaurant with trendy city-cafe overtones.

Bharat Restaurant SOUTHERN INDIAN $$

(Map p40; ☑01-281 519; 356 Mahabandoola Rd, Kyauktada; mains from K1000; ☯6am-8.30pm; ⌨) Specialising in southern Indian dishes, Bharat's tidy interior and marble-topped tables make a nice change from the long cafeteria-style tables at the Indian places on Anawrahta Rd.

Lotaya SHAN $

(Map p44; Bogyoke Aung San Market, Pabedan; mains K1000-3800; ☯9am-5pm Tue-Sun; ⌨) Located at the back of market next to the footbridge over the train lines, this simple place serves Shan noodles and Thai- and Chinese-style dishes, in addition to iced coffees and fruit drinks. They're not the best Shan noodles in town, but it's a good place to refuel while shopping.

365 Café
INTERNATIONAL, JAPANESE $$

(Map p40; 5 Ah Lan Paya Pagoda Rd, Dagon; mains K3300-7800; ☺24hr; 🖥📶) Open around the clock, this stylish cafe serves a largely Japanese-influenced menu, with a few Western and Chinese dishes thrown in for good measure.

Zawgyi House
BURMESE, INTERNATIONAL $$

(Map p44; 372 Bogyoke Aung San Rd, Pabedan; mains K2300-7800; ☺9am-9pm; 🖥📶) This cafe and gift shop is very much a hang-out for expats and passing businesspeople, all of whom appreciate the expensive shakes, juices, ice creams and sandwiches.

Japan Japan
JAPANESE $$

(Map p40; 239 Pansodan St, Kyauktada; mains K2500-4000; ☺11am-10pm; 🖥📶) A kitschily decorated Japanese restaurant with Japanese staff who like to make a fuss over you. The food is reasonably cheap and filling with some superb sushi.

★ Union Bar & Grill
INTERNATIONAL $$$

(Map p40; ☑09 42010 1854; www.unionyangon.com; 42 Strand Rd, Botataung; mains $8-14; ☺restaurant 10am-11pm, bar to 2am; 🖥📶) Occupying a corner of the Red Cross Building, this new restaurant and bar oozes urban sophistication with nods to its dock-side location in the artwork. The brasserie-style menu of appealing pizzas, burgers, sandwiches and salads is high-quality comfort food.

It's a monied Yangonite and expat scene, particularly on Friday and Saturday nights when the central bar buzzes, but can also be a pleasantly relaxed spot for a quiet Sunday brunch.

Monsoon
SOUTHEAST ASIAN $$$

(Map p40; ☑01-295 224; www.monsoonmyanmar.com; 85-87 Thein Byu Rd, Botataung; mains from K2200; ☺10am-11pm; 🖥📶) Located in an airy colonial town house, Monsoon is a good option for those intimidated by Yangon's more authentic options. The menu also spans the rest of mainland Southeast Asia, with dishes from Thailand, Vietnam, Cambodia and Laos.

✖ Shwedagon Paya & Around

Myaung Mya Daw Cho
BURMESE $

(Map p50; ☑01-559 663; 118A Yay Tar Shay Old St, Bahan; noodles K500; ☺5-11am) A great breakfast stop before or after visiting Shwedagon Paya is this famous place specialising in *mohinga*. You can eat the fish-soup noodles inside or get them as a takeaway outside for K300.

★ Aung Thukha
BURMESE $

(Map p50; ☑01-525 194; 17A 1st St, Bahan; meals from K2000; ☺9am-9pm) This longstanding institution is a great place to sample a wide range of Myanmar food – everything from rich, meaty curries to light, freshly made salads. The flavours are more subtle here than elsewhere, emphasising herbs rather than oil and spice. It's almost constantly busy, but manages to maintain gentle, friendly service and a palpable old-school atmosphere, making the experience akin to eating at someone's home.

Sharky's
PIZZA/DELI $$

(Map p50; ☑01-524 677; 117 Dhama Zedi Rd, Bahan; pizza from K7500; ☺9am-10pm; 🖥📶) Ye Htut Win (aka Sharky) worked in catering for 20 years in Switzerland before returning to Yangon with the dream of making cheese and other quality eats. The result is this gourmet heaven – part deli, part restaurant serving excellent thin-crust pizza and other dishes with Sharkey's own fine ingredients. The tempting selection of gelato is reason enough to make a beeline here.

SK Hot Pot
HOT POT $$

(Golden Happy Hot Pot; map p50; ☑01-559 339; 18 Ko Min Ko Chin St, Dagon; meals from K5000; ☺10.30am-11pm; 📶) This vast hall is Yangon's most famous and most popular hotpot joint. Join hundreds of other diners in choosing the raw ingredients (starting at K800 for vegtables) from the bank of freezers then cooking them in vats of a spicy Sichuan-style broth (K2800).

Although it's open during the day it's most fun to come at night when the main dining hall is packed.

House of Memories
BURMESE, INTERNATIONAL $$

(Map p50; ☑01-525 195; www.houseofmemoriesmyanmar.com; 290 U Wi Za Ra Rd, Bahan; mains K4000-5000; ☺11am-11pm; 🖥📶) Located off U Wi Za Ra Rd, and housed in a mock-Tudor colonial villa stuffed with antiques and old photos (and including an office where General Aung San once worked), this an interesting place to dine on dishes such as hearty beef curry and an authentically smoky-tasting grilled eggplant salad.

There's live music in the piano bar downstairs on weekend evenings.

Onyx Restaurant
STEAKHOUSE $$

(Map p50; www.facebook.com/onyxmyanmar; 135 Dhama Zedi Rd, Bahan; mains K4500-6000;

⏱11am-11pm Mon-Sat, 5-11pm Sun; 🛜📶) Go up a side road, past the wood carving shop, to find this lauded steakhouse hiding in a worse-for-wear black-and-white house. It's a lot nicer inside – even vaguely romantic. Locals swear by the quality and value for money of the meat dishes.

Sabai@DMZ
THAI $$

(Map p50; 📞01-525 078; 162 Dhama Zedi Rd, Bahan; mains from K2500; 📶) This semi-formal Thai-owned place boasts a Thai chef and an extensive and appetising menu. The range of salads is particularly impressive for someone craving a light lunch in the heat of the day.

Acacia Tea Salon
PATISSERIE $$

(Map p50; www.acaciateasalon.com; 52 Sayasan St, Bahan; mains K7000; ⏱10am-10pm; 🛜📶) This colonial-style tea salon, patisserie and restaurant occupies a chic whitewashed mansion. There's a takeaway section stocking all the lovely cakes, biscuits and savouries made here. For an indulgent time, treat yourself to one of their afternoon teas (K15,000 to K25,000).

The Corriander Leaf
INDIAN $$

(Map p50; 📞09 4318 5008; Bldg 12, Yangon International Hotel Compound, Ahlone Rd, Dagon; mains K6000-8000; 🛜📶) If you're wanting a decent Indian meal at a white-tablecloth restaurant, the Corriander Leaf fits the bill. It has a good selection of vegetarian dishes.

Garden Bistro
INTERNATIONAL $$

(Map p50; 📞01-546 488; cnr Bahan St & Kan Yeik Thar St, Bahan; mains K3800-5000; ⏱7am-10.30pm; 🛜📶) Popular for breakfast meetings with the embassy and business crowd, the Garden Bistro is also a pleasant spot for

---

DON'T MISS

EATING FOR A GOOD CAUSE

In a city where poverty is rife and social problems abound there's a strong chance you may end up feeling guilty about dining out in a restaurant where the bill may be the equivalent of what a waiter earns in a month. But at three Yangon restaurants and cafes, set up as social enterprises or self-sustaining charitable businesses to help those in need, you can dine with a clear conscience.

LinkAge (Map p40; 📞09 4958 3618; 1st fl, 221 Mahabandoola Garden St, Kyauktadar; meals K1000-3000; ⏱10am-10pm; 🛜📶) This Burmese restaurant and art gallery is run by Forever, a humanitarian and development project which helps provide street kids and those from poor families with cooking and catering skills. The colourful art on the bright yellow walls and the balcony (with seating in good weather) overlooking the street make for a great atmosphere and the food is very tasty and well presented. Try the delicious red snapper fish fillet or, if you're really hungry, the multi-course set meal (K6000 to K8000).

Yangon Bakehouse (Map p50; www.yangonbakehouse.com; Pearl Condon, Kaba Aye Pagoda Rd, Bahan; sandwiches & salads K2500-5000; ⏱7am-5pm Mon-Fri, 8am-5pm Sat; 🛜📶) Works with disadvantaged women who have fallen on hard times because of debt or family problems, some of them having resorted to sex work. A model enterprise of its kind, the bakehouse pays its trainees twice the going monthly wage as well as providing counselling and valuable work skills. It's not surprising that it has built up a loyal clientele for its delicious bakes, hearty sandwiches, fresh salads and good coffee. It's mainly takeaway but there's a few shared tables if you want to eat in.

⭐ **Shwe Sa Bwe** (Map p54; 📞01-661 983; www.facebook.com/ShweSaBwe; 20 Malikha St, Mayangone; lunch/dinner from K11,000/23,000; 🛜📶) Based in a beautifully decorated mansion close to the north shore of Inya Lake, this fine-dining restaurant and catering training school was started by French expat François Stoupan and has an intake of 22 students per year. They are chosen from across Mynamar and come from disadvantaged (but not destitute) backgrounds. Training is provided in both front-of-house and kitchen skills under the supervision of chefs from France. As a prelude to a meal here François will give you a tour of the premises and explain the aims of the venture. The results are amazing – quite simply the best fine-dining in Yangon for the price. No wonder the graduates go on to work at the city's best hotels and restaurants.

a light meal or afternoon tea overlooking Kandawgyi Lake. Tip: there's direct access to the lakeside boardwalk here without you having to pay the K2000 entry fee.

Royal Garden
CHINESE **$$**

(Map p50; ☑01-546 923; Nat Mauk Rd, Bahan; mains K4000-7000; ⊙6.30am-10.15pm; 🗑🞵) Kicking off with dim sum for breakfast and rolling through to roasted duck for dinner, this big lakeside restaurant offers up a tasty and keenly priced selection of Chinese goodies.

Sai's Tacos
TEX-MEX **$$**

(Map p54; ☑01-514 950; 32A Inya Myaing Rd, Bahan; mains K2200-6000; ⊙11am-9pm Mon-Fri, 8am-9pm Sat & Sun; 🗑🞵) Safe to say this is the world's only Tex-Mex restaurant with a Shan twist. Set up to help train young Shan in restaurant skills, this cute home-style place serves up reasonably authentic dishes including the, fajitas, burritos and tacos, both soft and crispy shell. Also available: Shan noodles!

Nervin Cafe & Bistro
INTERNATIONAL **$$**

(Map p50; www.nervincafe.com; Karaweik Oo-Yin Kabar, Kandawgyi Nature Park, Mingalar Taung Nyunt; mains K5000; ⊙10am-10pm; 🗑🞵) The most modern of the cluster of cafes at the east end of Kandawgyi Lake, Nervin offers up light meals such as club sandwiches with fries and fresh salads, along with caffeinated drinks and smoothies.

Padonmar
BURMESE **$$**

(Map p50; ☑01-122 0616; www.myanmar-restaurantpadonmar.com; 105-107 Kha Yae Bin Rd, Dagon; ⊙11am-11pm; 🗑🞵) Padonmar (meaning 'lotus flower') may be geared to the coach tour crowd, but still serves high-quality, value-for-money food. In good weather you can dine in the garden, but the interior, painted with traditional scenic and figurative murals, is also lovely.

Le Planteur
FRENCH **$$$**

(Map p50; ☑01-541 997; www.leplanteur.net; 22 Kaba Aye Pagoda Rd, Bahan; mains $19-32, set lunch $25, set dinner $45-78; ⊙11.30am-1.45pm, 6-10pm; 🗑🞵) A meal at this fine-dining restaurant set in a mansion with a lovely garden (used in the dry season for outdoor dining) is a pricey affair. Dishes are expertly prepared, if overly fussy, and run the gamut from foie gras to prime rib.

There's an excellent wine cellar and a stylish cocktail lounge. For dinner guests, free transfers in one of its vintage motors can be arranged.

Alamanda Inn
FRENCH **$$$**

(Map p50; ☑01-534 513; 60B Shwe Taung Gyar Rd/Golden Valley Rd, Bahan; meals K9000-16,000; ⊙7am-11pm; 🗑🞵) In a quiet residential neighbourhood, this breezy open-air restaurant and bar under a covered patio is a relaxing place to put the cares of Yangon behind you. The house specialities are tagines and couscous, but it also does good steaks and sandwiches as well as killer cocktails.

Golden Kitchen by IndoChine
SOUTHEAST ASIAN **$$$**

(Map p50; ☑09 3120 5450; 135 Dhama Zedi Rd, Bahan; mains $10-15; ⊙11am-11pm; 🗑🞵) The Singapore-based IndoChine group has brought its signature mix of Lao and Vietnamese dishes to Yangon. It's classy, with splashes of colourful contemporary art to admire while you eat.

Next door, it also runs **Mojo by Indo-Chine** (Map p50; ☑01-511 418; 135 Dhama Zedi Rd, Bahan; ⊙11.30am-2am), a tapas and wine bar that hosts a range of weekly events including dance parties.

🍴 Inya Lake & Northern Yangon

Minn Lane Rakhaing
Monte & Fresh Seafood
RAKHINE BURMESE **$$**

(Map p54; 16 Parami Rd, Mayangone; mains from K2000; ⊙11am-10pm) If you want spicy, skip Thai and head directly to this boisterous Rakhine-themed grilled-seafood hall, popular with local families on a night out. The eponymous *monte* (actually *moún-di*) is a noodle soup (K600) featuring rice noodles and an intensely peppery broth.

If you prefer your pepper on the side, order Rakhine salad, a spicy noodle salad. And of course there's all manner of grilled crab, oyster, shrimp, squid and shellfish, all for low prices.

Café Dibar
INTERNATIONAL, ITALIAN **$$**

(Map p54; ☑09 500 6143; 104 University Ave Rd, Kamaryut; mains K3500-7000; ⊙10am-10pm; 🗑🞵) Like your corner Italian place back home: not outstanding, but always reliable. Specialising in pizza and pasta, but with a few other dishes (sandwiches, salads, burgers) thrown in.

Isola Garden Cafe & Restaurant   INTERNATIONAL $$

(Map p54; ☑01-532 124; 80 University Ave Rd, Bahan; mains K5000-10,000; ⏰10am-10pm; 🛜📶) The best thing about Isola is its serene location beside Inya Lake. Peacocks and swans strut on the lawn, where you can enjoy light meals such as pizza, pasta and sandwiches. It's ideal for afternoon tea (for one/two K5000/9000). You'll also find here a florist and interior-decor shop with some interesting local crafts.

Green Elephant   BURMESE $$

(Map p54; www.greenelephant-restaurants.com; University Ave Rd, Bahan; mains K5000-8000; ⏰11am-10pm; 🛜📶) Popular with tour groups, the Green Elephant is a safe but tasty enough introduction to Myanmar cuisine. It has a new, easier-to-find location opposite Aung San Suu Kyi's home near Inya Lake. You'll also find an upmarket crafts shop here.

★ Taing Yin Thar   MYANMAR $$$

(Map p54; ☑01-966 0792; cnr May Kha Rd & Parami Rd, Mayangone; mains K3000; ⏰10am-midnight; 🛜📶) An airy wood-beamed dining hall with verandas for outdoor dining is the setting for this pan-Myanmar restaurant. On the menu are a wide range of ethnic dishes that you're unlikely to find elsewhere, including plenty of vegetarian options.

L'Opera Restaurant   ITALIAN $$$

(Map p54; ☑01-665 516; www.operayangon.com; 62D U Tun Nyein St, Mayangone; mains $10-30; ⏰restaurant 11am-2pm & 6-10pm, cafe 8am-5pm; 📶) One of the better and more elegant restaurants in Yangon, L'Opera boasts well-trained and smartly dressed waiters, but more important is the Italian owner and chef's meticulous preparation. The outdoor garden seating is a bonus in good weather. Next to the bakery at the front of the property is the small cafe Il Fornaio.

> **DON'T MISS**
>
> ## YANGON'S TOP TEAHOUSES
>
> The following is our shortlist of Yangon's traditional teahouses. All are great places to grab a snack as well as a reviving brew, with a cup of tea costing K250. See p360 for more about ordering drinks and food in teahouses.
>
> **Lucky Seven** (Map p40; 49th St, Pazundaung; snacks from K300; ⏰6am-5.30pm Mon-Sat, to noon Sun; 📶) The most central of this small chain of high-class traditional teashops, Lucky Seven is much more than a pitstop for a cuppa. Its streetside tables are fringed by greenery and an ornamental pond. The *mohinga* is outstanding – order it with a side of crispy gourd or flakey-pastry savoury buns.
>
> **Thone Pan Hla** (Map p44; 454 Mahabandoola Rd, Pabedan; snacks K400-600; ⏰6am-7.30pm) Close to Sule Paya Thone, so a good pitstop as you wander the downtown area. There's an English-language menu of teahouse staples including fried rice for breakfast.
>
> **Shwe Khaung Laung** (cnr Bogyoke Aung San Rd & 31st St, Pabedan; snacks K450) In addition to good tea, this Chinese-style teahouse serves decent steamed buns and noodles and baked cakes and pastries.
>
> **Shwe We Htun** (Map p40; 81 37th St, Kyauktada; snacks from K300; ⏰6am-6pm, to noon Sun) A buzzing old-school teahouse on the bookstall street, serving better-quality food than most. There's no roman-script sign but you'll know it by the crowds.
>
> **Man Myo Taw Café** (Map p40; cnr Mahabandoola Rd & 39th St, Kyauktada; snacks K450; ⏰5am-8pm) Representing the Chinese end of the spectrum, this tidy place offers good steamed buns and coffee.
>
> **Golden Tea** (Map p44; 99 Bo Sun Pat Rd, Pabedan; snacks from K300; ⏰6am-9pm) This centrally located Muslim-run place is a good choice for breakfast; later in the day they serve tasty *s'uanwi'n-mauk'in* (semolina cakes)
>
> **Yatha Teashop** (Map p40; 353 Mahabandoola Rd, Kyauktada; snacks from K200; ⏰5.30am-8.30pm Mon-Sat, to 12.30pm Sun) A classic Muslim-style teahouse, providing fresh samosas and *palata* (fried flatbread).

🍷 Drinking & Nightlife

Places that fit the Western concept of a bar or a club are becoming slightly more common. However, most places close by 10pm and locals prefer hanging out in a teahouse or air-conditionded cafe as much as one of the ubiquitous beer stations and beer gardens – the last two being favourite places to catch satellite TV broadcasts of soccer matches.

There are several social events that, should you be in town at the right time, provide an opportunity to mingle with the local and expat population. At the time of research, the best was the free drinks party every Tuesday night from 7pm at Pansodan Gallery (p72). It's an immensely friendly scene with gallery owner Aung Soe Min and his expat wife helping the crowd connect with local culture and art. The couple also run **Pansodan Scene** (Map p40; www. pansodan.com; 144 Pansodan St, Kyauktada), a community art space with a cafe further down Pansodan St – it's possible the party will have moved here by the time you read this.

For more information on Yangon's nightlife and entertainment scene check out **Myanmore** (www.myanmore.com), which publish a free weekly pamphlet guide available in several bars, cafes and restaurants around town.

🍸 Downtown Yangon

★ Bar Boon   CAFE-BAR
(Map p44; FMI Centre, 380 Bogyoke Aung San Rd, Pabedan; ☺8.30am-9pm; 🗐) Recharge and relax at this contemporary-styled cafe serving excellent coffee, iced tea and Dutch beer along with tasty snacks and pastries. The outdoor terrace offers brilliant people-watching near Bogyoke Aung San Market.

Kosan   BAR
(Map p44; 108 19th St, Latha; ☺6pm-2am; 🗐) A reasonably decent mojito for K800? No wonder this Japanese-owned bar with seats spilling onto buzzing 19th St is popular with partying locals and expats. The next-door grilled-food joint **Kaung Myat** is where Anthony Bourdain ate when he was in town.

Strand Bar   HOTEL BAR
(Map p40; Strand Hotel, 92 Strand Rd, Kyauktada; ☺to 11pm; 🗐) Primarily an expat scene, this classic bar inside the Strand Hotel has any foreign liquors you may be craving behind its polished wooden bar. Friday nights (5pm to 11pm) it gets packed as all drinks are half price.

50th Street Bar & Grill   BAR
(Map p40; ☑01-397 060; www.50thstreetyangon; 9-13 50th St, Botataung; ☺11am-midnight; 🗐) One of Yangon's longest established Western-style bars, in a handsomely restored colonial building, 50th Street continues to draw in the crowds with its mix of event nights ($6 pizzas and jazz on Wednesday, salsa every second Tuesday, live music on Friday), free pool table and all-day happy hour on Sunday.

Coffee Club   CAFE
(Map p44; http://coffeeclub.com.mm; cnr 11th St & Mahabandoola Rd, Latha; ☺9am-7pm; 🗐) Above a mobile-phone shop is this hip cafe hangout where you can get a soy latte or extra-strong espresso fix with a side order of gourmet sandwich, pie or cake (courtesy of Yangon Bakehouse). Slip back in time by leafing through the stock of vintage news magazines.

Zero Zone Rock Restaurant   BAR
(Map p44; 4th fl, 2 Theingyi Zei Market, Latha) This rooftop bar is more fun than the unintentionally self-deprecating name suggests. Live music starts at 7pm, there's a 'fashion show' of parading girls, the draught beer is cheap and the cool breezes are free.

Sky Bistro   BAR
(Map p40; 20th fl, Sakura Tower, cnr Sule Paya Rd & Bogyoke Aung San Rd, Kyauktada; ☺9am-10pm; 🗐) Certainly not the sexiest place in Yangon for a night out, but the views from the 20th floor are pretty impressive and happy hour runs from 4pm to 10pm. Bar snacks and other dishes are also available.

Wadan Jetty Beer Station   BEER STATION
(Map p44; Wadan Jetty, Lanmadaw; ☺6am-9pm) Entering the docks from the main road, turn right at the waterfront to find this small beer station with a cluster of outdoor seating. It's a great spot for sunset drinks when you can also watch (or join in) with locals playing football or the local sport of *chinlon*.

Hola Dance Club   COCKTAIL BAR
(Map p40; ☑01-392 625; 94 Bo Galay Zay St, Botataung; ☺6pm-midnight; 🗐) The main reason for heading to this classy, art deco–decorated restaurant and bar is to at-

tend salsa nights, which run from 8pm on Tuesday and Thursday. Contact them to find out about taking Latin dance lessons with the resident instructors.

Shwedagon Paya & Around

⭐**Vista Bar**   COCKTAIL BAR
(Map p50; www.vistabaryangon.com; 168 Shwegondine Rd, Bahan; ⊙5pm-1.30am; 📞) The knockout view of Shwedagon Paya is the big draw of this rooftop bar above an Yves Rocher beauty shop. The cocktails, which start at K3500, are pretty decent, too.

Winstar   BEER STATION
(Map p50; Sanchaung St, Sanchaung; ⊙11am-2am) Very much a local party scene, this street of beer stations and small restaurants is a short walk north of People's Park. Winstar is the biggest beer station along the strip, and has an English menu and a relaxed vibe popular with all ages. It's a great place to come watch a soccer match.

Ginki Kids   BAR
(Map p50; 📠 01-527 256; 18 Kan Baw Sa Rd, Bahan; ⊙10am-midnight) Handy if you're staying around Golden Valley, this long-running drinking hole is decorated with posters of Kurt Cobain, Elvis, the Beatles and Native Americans. The partially open upstairs level is the place for a cooling beer.

Water Library   COCKTAIL BAR
(Map p50; www.mywaterlibrary.com; 83/95 Pyay Rd, cnr Manawharri Rd, Dagon; ⊙bar 5pm-2am, restaurant 11.30am-2pm & 6-10pm; 📞) Attached to the fine-dining restaurant of the same name, this chic cocktail bar specialises in homemade spirits such as tamarind-infused bourbon, gummy bear–infused gin and M&M-infused vodka. The mixologists know their trade and there's a patch of lawn outside to sit on.

Coffee Circles   CAFE-BAR
(Map p50; 107 Dhama Zedi Rd, Bahan; mains from K3000; ⊙7am-midnight; 📞) Located in front of the Guest Care Hotel, this chic cafe-bar serves real coffee and offers a menu that ranges from Thai to burgers. There's an outdoor section on the roof from which you might just glimpse the tip of Shwedagon Paya.

Fuji Coffee House   CAFE
(Map p54; 📠01-535 371; www.fujicoffeehouse.com; 116 University Ave Rd, Kamaryut; ⊙7.30am-

10.30pm; 📞) Next to the US Embassy, this classy lounge cafe has the atmosphere of an upmarket hotel lobby.

Flamingo Bar   BAR
(Map p50; Yangon International Hotel compound, 330 Ahlone Rd, Dagon; entrance K2000 incl 1 drink) At press time, this was the venue being used by YG Events (www.facebook.com/EventsYG) to host its fab gay-friendly parties on the last Saturday of the month from 10pm to 2am. Check the Facebook page to see whether the party has moved on.

JJ City   CLUB
(Map p50; Mingala Zei, Set Yone Rd, Mingalar Taung Nyunt; entrance K3000; ⊙8pm-2am) Just your typical, bog-standard wet market by day, multistorey entertainment complex by night... Enter lifts stained with betel spit to emerge at JJ, ostensibly a disco. Most appear to come for the bizarre 10pm fashion show and the working girls. The entrance fee includes one free drink.

Pioneer   CLUB
(Map p50; 330 Ahlone Rd, Yangon International Hotel Complex, Dagon; admission K6000; ⊙7pm-3am) This disco sees a relative mix of people, from upper-class locals to profit-seeking 'dancing girls'. Like other clubs in Yangon, it's similar to your first school dance: a handful of girls actually hit the floor while the guys fidget nervously.

At the same location there are also dance parties held at the smaller venue **MBox** (Map p50; 330 Ahlone Rd, Yangon International Hotel Compound, Dagon).

Inya Lake & Northern Yangon

GTR Club   CLUB
(Map p54; 37 Kaba Aye Pagoda Rd, Mayangone) If you fancy mingling and dancing around with Yangon's elite youth this is the place to do it. There's a good sound system, drink prices are reasonable and there's usually no cover charge.

☆ Entertainment

Thamada Cinema   CINEMA
(Map p40; 5 Ah Lan Paya Pagoda Rd, Dagon; tickets from K600) Easily the best cinema for foreigners, Thamada is comfortable and shows fairly recent international (including Hollywood) films.

Nay Pyi Daw Cinema CINEMA
(Map p40; Sule Paya Rd, Kyauktada; tickets from K600) One of the busiest cinemas in the city, this place hosts the European Film Festival in September each year.

Karaweik Palace TRADITIONAL DANCE
(Map p50; ☑01-290 546; www.karaweikpalace.com; Kandawgyi Park Compound, Mingalar Taung Nyunt; dinner & show K20,000; ⊙6-9pm) Although the buffet meal served here is universally slated, the stage inside this concrete replica of a Burmese royal barge is one of the few places in Yangon where you can watch a cultural show of traditional dance and puppetry.

National Theatre THEATRE
(Map p44; Myoma Kyaung Rd, Dagon) Opened in 1991, the National Theatre is a boxy modern structure, which little reflects traditional Burmese architecture. That said, the venue is increasingly being put to good use for a variety of shows.

Alliance Française CULTURAL CENTRE
(Map p50; ☑01-536 900; http://afrangoun.org; 340 Pyay Rd, Sanchaung; ⊙library 2-5pm Mon, 10.30am-12.30pm & 2-6pm Tue-Fri, 9am-12.30pm & 2-6pm Sat; ☎) French and local culture is promoted not only by a library and various French-language evening courses, but also by various events including film screenings and art shows.

American Center CULTURAL CENTRE
(Map p44; ☑01-223 140; http://burma.usembassy. gov/american-center.html; 14 Taw Win St, Dagon; ⊙8am-4.30pm Mon-Fri; ☎) American films are sometimes shown here for free as well as public talks on various topics. The centre's library has a collection of 18,000 volumes, including a good Myanmar section.

DON'T MISS

CONTEMPORARY ART GALLERIES

The relaxing of censorship has resulted in a blossoming of Yangon's art scene, as evidenced by a flurry of new galleries joining longstanding exhibition spaces.

Lokanat Gallery (Map p40; 58-62 Pansodan St, Kyauktada; ⊙9am-5pm Mon-Fri) FREE The grand dame of the art scene has been hosting shows, which change on a weekly basis, since 1971. It's worth visiting for a chance to peek inside the crumbling but evocative early-20th-century building.

Pansodan Gallery (Map p40; 1st fl, 286 Pansodan St; ⊙10am-6pm) Owner-artist Aung Soe Min stocks a huge variety of Myanmar contemporary and antique art, the latter including some truly unique antique prints, advertisements and photos that make wonderful souvenirs. The gallery's Tuesday-evening soirees are not to be missed.

River Gallery (Map p40; www.rivergallerymyanmar.com; Strand Hotel Annex, 92 Strand Rd, Kyauktada; ⊙10am-6pm) Started by New Zealander Gill Pattison in 2005, this classy gallery features the works of some 30 leading and emerging artists. Exhibitions have included the National Portrait Awards in 2011.

New Zero Art Space (Map p44; www.newzeroartspace.net; 202 United Condo, Ah Lan Pya Pagoda Rd, Dagon) FREE Aiming to empower a new generation of artists, New Zero promotes edgier works in a variety of forms including sculptures, video, performance art and photography.

Gallery Sixty Five (Map p44; http://gallerysixtyfive.webstarts.com; 65 Yaw Min Gee St, Dagon; ⊙10am-6pm) On the ground floor of a colonial-era mansion, this private gallery is dedicated to revolving exhibits of contemporary creations.

KZL Art Studio & Gallery (Map p50; www.kzlartgallery.com; 184/84A Shwe Tuang Gone/ Golden Hill Rd, Bahan) The three-story Golden Valley home of artist Khin Zaw Latt, who has an international reputation, includes a gallery of his and other artists' works, plus his studio space.

Myanmar Deitta (Map p54; www.deitta.org; 3rd fl, Pyan Hlwar Bldg, 4A Parami Rd, Mayangone; ⊙11am-5pm Mon-Fri) From the Pali word for 'in front of one's eyes', Deitta is a new nonprofit working with documentary photographers, film-makers and multimedia artists. The planned Witness Yangon documentary art space should be up and running now.

🛍 Shopping

There is quite a lot in the way of interesting art, furniture and antiques to be bought in Yangon. Unfortunately much of it is too large to fit in most people's luggage and there are few bargains to be had. Prices for tailormade clothes, however, are among the lowest in Southeast Asia.

It's worth checking out the many **bookstalls** (Map p40; cnr Merchant St & Pansodan St, Kyauktada) around Bogyoke Aung San Market or along 37th St, which is also regarded as something of a university library for the people. Several stalls have small selections of novels and nonfiction books in English, French and German.

Every Yangon township has its own *zei* (market, often spelt *zay*) – exploring them can be fun, educational and a chance to interact with the locals. Fans of fresh markets should make a point of visiting the hectic **morning market** along 26th St, adjacent to Theingyi Zei. Another photogenic **morning market** unfolds along the southernmost end of 42nd St, and a tiny but lively **night market** is held every evening near the Methodist Telugu Church.

🏠 Downtown Yangon

⭐ **Bogyoke Aung San Market**   MARKET

(Map p44; Bogyoke Aung San Rd, Dagon; ⊙10am-5pm Tue-Sun) Half a day could easily be spent wandering around this sprawling covered market, sometimes called by its old British name, Scott Market. It has more than 2000 shops and the largest selection of Myanmar handicrafts and souvenirs you'll find under several roofs, from lacquerware and Shan shoulder bags to puppets and jewellery.

Pick up some nice slippers here, convenient for all the on-and-off demanded by paya protocol, and a *longyi*; U Maung Maung in the main hall has a good selection ranging from cotton ones for K5500 to silk-mix ones for K9500.

Other shops worth seeking out include **Yo Ya May** (1st floor), specialising in hill tribe textiles, particularly those from Chin State, and **Heritage Gallery**, next door, which has a good selection of reproduction and authentic antiques with an emphasis on lacquerware.

⭐ **Pomelo**   HANDICRAFTS

(Map p40; www.pomeloyangon.com; 89 Thein Byu Rd, Botataung; ⊙10am-9pm) The best selection of contemporary handicrafts in Yangon – and all produced by projects supporting disadvantaged groups in Myanmar. Fall in love with the colourful papier mache dogs and bags featuring bold graphic images as well as the exquisite Chin weavings and jewellery made from recycled materials.

Bagan Book House   BOOKSHOP

(Map p40; ☑01-377 227; 100 37th St, Kyauktada; ⊙9am-6.30pm) This Yangon institution has the most complete selection of English-language books on Myanmar and Southeast Asia, and owner U Htay Aung really knows his stock, which includes tomes dating back to the 19th century.

Theingyi Zei   MARKET

(Map p44; Shwedagon Pagoda Rd, Pabedan) Most of the merchandise at downtown Yangon's largest market is ordinary housewares and textiles, but it's also renowned for its large selection of traditional herbs and medicines, which can be found on the ground floor of the easternmost building.

Traditional herbal shampoo, made by boiling the bark of the Tayaw shrub with big black *kin pun* (acacia pods), is sold in small plastic bags; this is the secret of Myanmar women's smooth, glossy hair.

Inwa Bookshop   BOOKSHOP

(Map p40; 301 Pansodan St, Kyauktada; ⊙9am-6pm) This bookshop sells a small selection of English-language books as well as foreign magazines such as *Time* and *The Economist*.

Tip-Top Tailors   TAILOR

(Map p40; 287 Mahabandoola Rd, Botataung; ⊙9.30am-6pm Mon-Sat) Three generations of the same family have run this reliable tailor shop. Bring them your own fabric and they can craft a shirt from as little as K4000. Trousers cost K10,000.

Globe Tailoring   TAILOR

(Map p44; ☑01-253 924; 367 Bogyoke Aung San Rd, Pabedan; ⊙9.30am-5.30pm) Well regarded by local expats for women's and men's tailoring, this tailors is run by U Aung Soe, who also has a Japanese language school. A shirt without/with fabric costs K8000/10,000, trousers K20,000 with fabric.

Parkson Mall   DEPARTMENT STORE

(Map p44; 380 Bogyoke Aung San Rd, Dagon) The old FMI Building has undergone a makeover to become a branch of this Malaysian department store, packed with luxury international-brand items over four floors. In the basement there's a small branch of the fancy supermarket **Marketplace by City Mart**.

Shwedagon Paya & Around

FXB Product Outlet HANDICRAFTS
(Map p50; Hnin Si Myaing Residence, 21 Kabar Aye Pagoda Rd, Bahan; ⊗9am-5pm Mon-Sat) The showroom of this international NGO, dedicated to fighting poverty and AIDS, has fabric-based products, including adorable soft toys, cushions, rugs and other crafts.

Nandawun SOUVENIRS
(Map p50; www.myanmarhandicrafts.com; 55 Baho Rd, Ahlone; ⊗9am-6pm) This housebound shop spans two storeys and just about every Myanmar souvenir, from lacquer vessels to replicas of antique scale weights. The upstairs bookshop has a good selection of titles on obscure Myanmar topics. There's also a branch in the National Museum.

Monument Books BOOKS, TOYS
(Map p50; 150 Dhama Zedi Rd, Bahan; ⊗8.30am-8.30pm; ⊛) Yangon's most modern and well-stocked bookshop. In addition to a good selection of books on topics local and international, there's an attached cafe with internet access and a reasonably selection of Western toys.

Mingala Zei MARKET
(Map p50; cnr Ban Yar Da La St & Set Yone Rd, Mingalar Taung Nyunt; ⊗6am-6pm) A little southeast of Kandawgyi, this market offers textiles, clothes, electrical appliances, plasticware, preserved and tinned foodstuffs, modern medicines, and even cosmetics from China, Thailand and Singapore.

Marketplace by City Mart SUPERMARKET
(Map p50; Dhama Zedi Rd, Bahan; ⊗9am-9pm) One of the best-stocked outlets of Yangon's top supermarket chain offers a complex which also sports the **Popular** bookstore, with its reasonable selection of English-language titles and **Ananda Coffee and Cocoa**, selling locally produced coffee and chocolate.

Patrick Robert HOMEWARES
(Map p50; ☑01-513 709; Mangosteen Mansion, 24 Inya Myaing Rd, Bahan; ⊗10am-5pm Mon-Sat) The French designer who restored the Governor's Residence in the 1990s has an interior-design shop inside his home in Golden Valley. You'll find many attractive gifts and decorative home items here, most locally made and using materials such as mother of pearl, lacquer and teak.

Inya Lake & Northern Yangon

Augustine's Souvenir Shop ANTIQUES
(Map p54; www.augustinesouvenir.com; 25 Thirimingalar St, Kamayut; ⊗11.30am-7pm Mon-Fri, 2-7.30pm Sat & Sun) This handsome house doubles as one of Yangon's most captivating shopping destinations. A virtual museum of Myanmar antiques, there's a particular emphasis on wooden items, including carved figures, chests and wall hangings.

Elephant House HANDICRAFTS
(Map p54; University Ave Rd, Bahan; ⊗10am-9pm) Attached to Green Elephant restaurant, this shop sells a decent selection of Burmese housewares, primarily high-quality and attractive lacquerware.

Junction Square MALL
(Map p50; Kyun Taw Rd, Hliang; ⊗9am-10.30pm; ⊛) Currently Yangon's fanciest shopping mall but likely to be out-classed by in-the-works projects, Junction Square is worth a mooch for fashions and other items. There's a multiplex cinema here, too.

ℹ Information

DANGERS & ANNOYANCES
You are far less likely to be robbed here than in almost any other big city in Southeast Asia. Having said that, rich foreigners and badly lit side streets at night don't mix, and you should show some caution at such times.

A far bigger danger is getting hit by a belligerent motorist, stumbling on the uneven paving slabs or even disappearing completely into a sewage-filled pothole. Keep your eyes peeled for such obstacles and carry a torch at night.

EMERGENCIES
Your home embassy may be able to assist with advice during emergencies or serious problems. It's a good idea to register with your embassy upon arrival or, if possible, register online before you arrive, so that embassy staff will know where to reach you in case of an emergency at home.

There isn't always an English-speaking operator on the following numbers; you may have to enlist the aid of a Burmese speaker.
Fire Department (☑191)
Police (Map p40; ☑199)
Red Cross (☑01-383 680)

DON'T MISS

YANGON CIRCLE LINE

The nearly 32 mile Yangon Circle Line ($1/K1000) is a slow-moving, three-hour train trip around Yangon and the neighbouring countryside. The ancient carriages shake at times like washing machines on full spin cycle – not great if you suffer from travel sickness. However, hopping on the line is a great way to experience commuter life, interact with passengers and vendors on the trains, and see off-the-beaten-track areas of the city.

Disembark at any station and take a taxi back to the city centre once you've had enough or use the train to avoid traffic-clogged roads to get part of the way to northern attractions such as Kyauk Daw Kyi (Insein station) and Meilamu Paya (Tadakalay station).

Trains leave at 6.10am, 8.20am, 8.35am, 10.10am, 10.45am, 11.30am, 11.50am, 1.05pm, 1.40pm, 2.25pm, 4.40pm and 5.10pm from platform 6/7 at the Yangon train station, accessed off Pansodan St; tickets are bought on the platform. Trains go in either direction and some don't always do the full circuit. The train is least crowded after 10am and before 4pm, and at weekends.

At the time of research there were plans to run trains with air-conditioned carriages on this line ($2/K2000) – they would be more comfortable in the heat of the day but the trade-off will be a partial sensory shut-off from all that's happening on regular trains.

INTERNET ACCESS

Nearly all hotels and many restaurants, cafes and bars offer free wi-fi access; there's even free wi-fi at Shwedagon Paya! There's also plenty of internet shops around town. Server speeds have improved, but still tend to be frustratingly slow in comparison to almost any other country.

LAUNDRY

Almost all of Yangon's budget and midrange guesthouses and hotels offer laundry services. Rates at the midrange and top-end hotels are not cheap.

Shine (Map p40; ☑ 01-703 229; 23 Botataung Pagoda Rd, Pazundaung; ☺ 8am-5.30pm) The per piece rate at this laundry starts from K600 for underwear. A normal wash takes three days. There are other branches around the city.

MEDICAL SERVICES

There are several private and public hospitals in Yangon, but the fees, service and quality varies. There are also some useful pharmacies in town.

AA Pharmacy (Map p40; 142-146 Sule Paya Rd, Kyauktada; ☺ 9am-10pm) Just north of Sule Paya.

International SOS Clinic (Map p54; ☑ 01-667 871; www.internationalsos.com; Inya Lake Hotel, 37 Kaba Aye Pagoda Rd, Mayangone) Your best bet in Yangon for emergencies, this clinic claims to be able to work with just about any international health insurance and has a 24-hour emergency centre with an expat doctor.

Pun Hlaing International Clinic (Map p44; ☑ 243 010; 4th fl, FMI Centre, Bogyoke Aung San Rd, Dagon; ☺ 9am-7pm Mon-Sat, 10am-

7pm Sun) This is your best bet for centrally located healthcare.

MONEY

You'll get the best rates for changing money at the airport and at official bank exchange counters in places such as Bogyoke Aung San Market and Shwedagon Paya. There are also many ATMs dotted around Yangon that accept international Visa and Mastercards; there's a K5000 charge for using these ATMs.

POST

Central Post Office (Map p40; cnr Strand Rd & Bo Aung Kyaw St, Kyauktada; ☺ 7.30am-6pm Mon-Fri) A short stroll east of the Strand Hotel. Stamps are for sale on the ground floor but go to the 1st floor to send mail.

DHL (Map p44; ☑ 01-215 516; www.dhl.com; 58 Wadan St, Lanmadaw; ☺ 8am-6pm Mon-Fri, 8am-2pm Sat)

TOURIST INFORMATION

Myanmar Travels & Tours (MTT; Map p40; ☑ 01-374 281; www.myanmartravelsandtours. com; 118 Mahabandoola Garden St; ☺ 8.30am-5pm) The people at this government-run information centre are quite friendly and helpful, although their resources are very limited. This is the place to go to arrange the necessary paperwork and guides for areas of the country that still require travel permits. They also can arrange local sightseeing tours to a variety of locations.

USEFUL WEBSITES

Yangon Life (www.yangonlife.com.mm) Expat-run site packed with plenty of useful info.

TRANSPORT TO/FROM YANGON

The following box shows travel times and costs between Yangon and Myanmar's main destinations. The range in train fares is that between ordinary and sleeper class. For more detailed information see the Getting There & Away sections of each of the specific destinations.

DESTINATION	BUS	TRAIN	AIR/FERRY
Bago	2½hr; K1500	3hr; $2-4	N/A
Chaung Tha Beach	7hr; K10,000	N/A	N/A
Dawei	16hr; K13,000	N/A	flight 70min; $126
Heho (for Inle Lake & Kalaw)	N/A	N/A	flight 1-3hr; $102-112
Hpa-an	7-8hr; K5000-8600	N/A	N/A
Hsipaw	15hr; K14,500-16,500	N/A	N/A
Kalaw	10-12hr; K10,000-16,500	N/A	N/A
Kyaikto	5hr; K8000	4-5hr; $3-10	N/A
Lashio	15hr; K14,500	N/A	flight 1hr, 45min; $157
Loikaw	19hr; K12,500-16,000	N/A	flight 1hr; $63
Mandalay	9hr; K10,500	15 ½hr; $11-33	flight 1hr; $75-135
Mawlamyine	7hr; K5000-10,000	9-11hr; $5-14	N/A
Myitkyina	N/A	N/A	flight 2hr; $180
Nay Pyi Taw	5hr; K6000	9-10hr; $7-18	flight 45min; $65-75
Ngwe Saung Beach	6-7hr; K9000	N/A	N/A
Nyaung U (for Bagan)	10hr; K13,000-18,000	16hr; $20-40	flight 70min; $100-110
Pathein	4hr; K3600	N/A	ferry 17hr; $8 deck, $40 cabin
Pyay	6hr; K5500	7-8hr; $5-13	N/A
Sittwe	N/A	N/A	flight 1hr, 15min; $120-146
Taunggyi (for Inle Lake)	12hr; K15,000	N/A	N/A
Taungoo	6hr; K4300-5000	7hr; $5-13	N/A
Thandwe (for Ngapali)	14hr; K14,000	N/A	Flight 55min; $100-120

Yangonite (www.yangonite.com) Another excellent expat-authored site with plenty of listings and other features.

ⓘ Getting There & Away

AIR

Yangon International Airport (☑ 01-533 031; www.ygnia.com; Mingalardon; ☎) is Myanmar's main international gateway as well as the hub for domestic flights.

BOAT

There are several jetties along the Yangon River, but those interested in travelling by boat only need to be familiar with two – all other departure points are for cargo or routes that don't allow foreign passengers.

Pansodan St Jetty (Map p40) is the jumping-off base for daytime river-crossing boats to Dalah (round trip K4000, 10 minutes) which leave roughly every 20 minutes between 5.30am and 9pm.

Lan Thit Jetty (Map p44) is where **IWT** (Inland Water Transport; Map p44; ☑ 380 764, 01-381 912) runs ferries to Pathein Monday and Friday at 5pm (deck class/private cabin $8/40, 17 hours). Foreigners must buy tickets from the deputy division manager's office next to Building 63 on Lan Thit Jetty.

A few privately owned companies operate **luxury cruises** between Yangon, Bagan and Mandalay; see p25.

BUS

The two major bus terminals that service Yangon – Aung Mingalar Bus Terminal and Hlaing Thar Yar Bus Terminal – are located several miles outside of central Yangon.

Most signs at the bus terminals are in Burmese; however, English-speaking touts anxious to steer you in the right direction are in abundance.

To avoid the hassle and attention make sure your taxi driver (both of the major terminals are around 45 minutes to one hour from the city centre) knows where you want to go and, even better, the name of the specific bus company. Showing the driver your ticket will do; if you don't have a ticket, ask a Burmese speaker to write the information on a slip of paper.

Keep in mind that journey times can differ immensely from the estimates we've given, and depend on road conditions and the health of your bus.

Many hotels can book tickets for you and several agents and bus companies have offices alongside **Aung San Stadium**; expect to pay a couple thousand kyat more here than for tickets bought at the stations – a few bus companies offer transfers from Aung San Stadium to the bus stations, which can be handy.

Bus companies with offices at the Aung San Stadium:

Elite Express (Map p40; ☏01-656 831) Runs high-quality air-con buses to Mandalay, Monywa, Nay Pyi Taw, Pyin Oo Lwin (Maymyo) and Taunggyi.

Mandalar Minn (Map p40; ☏09 7323 1000) Departures for Bagan, Mandalay and Pyin Oo Lwin.

Shwe Mandalar (Map p40; ☏01-249 672) Departures for Bagan, Mandalay and Pyin Oo Lwin.

Teht Lann Express (Map p40; ☏01-255 557) Departures for Lashio, Mandalay and Pyin Oo Lwin.

Aung Mingalar Bus Terminal

Located about 3 miles northeast of the airport as the crow flies, Aung Mingalar is the official bus terminal for all 150 bus lines leaving for the northern part of Myanmar, as well as for Kyaiktiyo (Golden Rock), Mawlamyine (Moulmein) and destinations to the south.

A taxi here from downtown Yangon costs K7000 and takes around 45 minutes to one hour.

Hlaing Thar Yar Bus Terminal

This is the bus terminal for travel to Ayeyarwady Division and destinations west of Yangon including Chaung Tha Beach, Ngwe Saung Beach and Pathein.

TAUKKYAN WAR CEMETERY

On the road to Bago, a few miles beyond Yangon's airport at Mingaladon, you reach **Taukkyan** (ေတာ်ကြီ) location of the huge **Taukkyan War Cemetery**, maintained by the Commonwealth War Graves Commission.

It contains the graves of 6374 Allied soldiers who died in the Burma and Assam campaigns of WWII. There is also a memorial bearing the names of the almost 27,000 soldiers who died with no known grave. As you walk around reading the names of those who died and the epitaphs commemorating them, the heat of the sun seems to fade and the noise of the road recedes, leaving you alone in the silence of your own thoughts in this immensely sad place.

You can get to Taukkyan on bus 9 (၉) from Yangon or aboard any Bago-bound bus from the Aung Mingalar Bus Terminal.

By taxi (K7000) the terminal is 45 minutes to one hour west of the city centre on the other side of the Yangon River on Hwy 5 (Yangon-Pathein Rd). More than 20 bus lines operate out of here.

CAR

Rates for hiring a car and driver run approximately $80 to $100 per day depending on your ultimate destination and the state of the vehicle you hire. Drivers can be arranged through a travel agent or hotel front desk.

TRAIN

Yangon train station (☏01-202 178; ⊗6am-4pm) is located a short walk north of Sule Paya; advance tickets should be purchased at the adjacent **Myanmar Railways Booking Office** (Map p40; Bogyoke Aung San Rd; ⊗7am-3pm), where you can also check the latest timetables.

Major destinations that can be reached by daily departures from Yangon include Bagan, Bago. Kyaikto, Mandalay, Mawlamyine, Nay Pyi Taw, Pyay, Taungoo and Thazi. There's a chance that in 2014 a new service to Pathein will commence.

Though inexpensive, trains are slow, uncomfortable and tend to be plagued by delays; see p397 for more details. The one destination you might consider using a train to get to is Kyaiktiyo. Every Saturday a service using

DALAH & TWANTE တွံတေး

One of the easiest and most enjoyable short trips out of Yangon is to board a double-decker ferry (round trip K4000; every 15 minutes) that shuttles between Pansodan Jetty and **Dalah** (ဒလ) across the Yangon River. As well as the breezy views provided on the 15-minute journey, there's a lively scene on board as hawkers jostle to sell everything from sun hats and *paan* (areca nut and/or tobacco wrapped in a betel leaf and chewed as a mild stimulant) to bags of speckled eggs. Tip: take the ferry around 5.30pm for a cheap sunset cruise back and forth across the river.

Dalah, which is one of Yangon's townships, is no great shakes; the main aim is to continue on to **Twante**, a pleasant town 30 to 45 minutes' drive west into the delta. Chances are you'll be approached on the ferry by someone offering their services as a motorbike taxi; the going rate is around K10,000 round trip including stops at the various sights. Regular taxis charge around K30,000, while a squashed seat in a pick-up van to Twante is K1000.

Twante's main sight is **Shwesandaw Paya** (ရွှေဆံတော်ဘုရား; camera fee K200; ⊙6am-9pm). Standing 250ft tall, this *zedi* was first built by the Mon 2500 years ago and is said to contain two hair relics of the Buddha. One corner of the compound commemorates King Bayinnaung's (also spelt Bayint Nyaung) defeat of a local rebellion. Near the southern entrance is a 100-year-old sitting bronze buddha in Mandalay style. Instead of focusing on the floor, the buddha's eyes stare straight ahead. Along the western side of the *zedi* stand some old bronze buddhas.

Twante's **Oh-Bo Pottery Sheds** (အိုးဘို အိုးလုပ်ငန်း) supply much of the delta region with well-designed, utilitarian containers of varying shapes and sizes. You'll be able to view the process from making the clay, casting the pots on human-powered wheels and firing in kilns, which can take three to four days. Pots the size of a small child that are used to store rice and water go for K25,000 but there are plenty of smaller ones for sale in the shops that are close to the Twante Canal.

On the way to or from Twante make a detour off the main road to visit the **Mwe Paya** (မြွေဘုရား) a beautifully situated temple amid a fish pond which is reached by four bridges. The temple is home to scores of sleepy snakes who are tended to by Buddhist nuns. Nearby is a copy of the **Mahabodi Pagoda** in Bodhgaya, India, where the Buddha gained enlightenment.

Twante has plenty of street-food stalls; should you prefer a sit-down meal there's a couple of beer gardens on the way into the town, including **Relax Garden** (84 Myoe Shaung Rd, Twante; mains K1500-3000; ⊙9am-9pm).

---

air-conditioned carriages departs for the Golden Rock at 6.25am ($10; 4½ hours); it returns on Sunday at noon arriving in Yangon (in theory) at 4.25pm. The air-conditioned carriages are eventually destined to be used on the Yangon Circle Line, once station platforms on that route have been upgraded.

ⓘ Getting Around

TO/FROM THE AIRPORT

Taxi drivers will approach you before you exit the airport terminal. The fare for a ride from the airport to downtown Yangon is around K8000 and will take an hour (more if traffic is heavy). **JTB Polestar** (☎ 01-382 528; www.jtb-pst.com; airport transfer $10) offers coach transfers to major hotels for $10, as well as a chauffeur service.

BUS

With taxis in Yangon being such a fantastic deal, you'd really have to be pinching pennies to rely on buses. They're impossibly crowded, the conductors rarely have change, the routes are confusing and there's virtually no English spoken or written.

If you're determined, the typical fare within central Yangon is K100 (use small bills – bus conductors don't tend to have change). Prices often double at night, but they're still cheap and still crowded.

TAXI

Yangon taxis are one of the best deals in Asia, despite not using a meter. Most drivers speak at least some English (although it's advisable to have someone write out your destination in

Burmese) and are almost universally honest and courteous.

All licensed taxis have a visible taxi sign on the roof, but many other drivers will give you ride for a negotiated fare. If you'd prefer to book a taxi, a service we've had recommendations for is **Golden Harp** (📞 09 4500 19186, 09 4281 17348), run by ex political prisoners.

The following should give you idea of what to pay: a short hop (say from the Strand to Bogyoke Market) will be K1000; double this distance will be K2000; from downtown to Shwedagon Paya and the southern half of Bahan township will be K3000 depending on the state of traffic; from downtown to the Inya Lake area K4000.

From downtown to either bus terminal, drivers ask for K7000 and the trip takes from 45 minutes to an hour. You can also hire a taxi for about K5000 an hour. For the entire day, you should expect to pay $60-80, depending on the quality of the vehicle and your negotiating skills. Be sure to work out all details before you agree to a price and itinerary.

For all types of taxi the asking fares usually leap by 30% or so after sunset and on weekends. Late-night taxis – after 11pm or so – often cost double the day rate, mainly because the supply of taxis is considerably lower than in the day, so the drivers are able to charge more.

TRAIN

Yangon Circle Line ($1; see p75) loops out north from Yangon to Insein, Mingaladon and North Okkalapa townships and then back into the city.

TRISHAW

In Myanmar, trishaw passengers ride with the driver, but back-to-back (one facing forward, one backward). These contraptions are called *saiq-ka* (as in side-car) and to ride one costs about K1000 for short journeys. Given the heaviness of downtown Yangon's traffic during the day, you may find trishaw pedlars reluctant to make long journeys across town at this time.

AROUND YANGON

As well as the excursion to Twante there are several other destinations within Yangon Region that can easily be done in a day, the most easily organised being to the varied sights around Thanlyin and Kyauktan. A visit to the Taukkyan War Cemetry can also be combined with a journey out to the historic town of Bago in neighbouring Bago Region.

If you have more time, a journey southwest into the delta region, properly known as Ayeyarwady Region, is highly recommended. The landscape – a vast wobbly mat of greenery floating on a thousand rivers, lakes and tributaries – is stunning. This is one of the rice bowls of Myanmar, where the farming of the grain continues in the age-old manner. The laid-back and very easily negotiated city of Pathein is the natural base for exploring.

Should you be looking for nothing more than sand, sea and swaying palms then the resorts of Chaung Tha Beach and Ngwe Saung Beach, lapped by the waves of the Bay of Bengal, are your answer.

Yangon Region

Thanlyin & Kyauktan
သံလျင်/ကျောက်တန်း

One of the easiest escapes from Yangon is to the rural towns of Thanlyin and Kyauktan, east of the city across the Bago River. There are interesting sights and activities in both towns and along the way.

During the late 16th and early 17th centuries, Thanlyin was the base for the notorious Portuguese adventurer Filipe de Brito e Nicote. Officially a trade representative for the Rakhine (Arakan), he actually ran his own little kingdom from Thanlyin, siding with the Mon (when it suited him) in their struggle against the Bamar.

In 1599 his private army sacked Bago, but in 1613 the Bamar besieged Thanlyin and de Brito received the punishment reserved for those who defiled Buddhist shrines: death by impalement. It took him two days to die, due, it is said, to his failure to take the recommended posture for the stake to penetrate vital organs.

Thanlyin continued to be a major port and trading centre and for a while was the base of the French East India Company. It was the first place in Myanmar to receive Christian missionaries and have its own church.

The ruins of a **Portuguese-built church**, dating to 1750, can be found not far from the Thanlyin Bridge.

After the town was destroyed by Bamar king Alaungpaya in 1756, its role as a port was eclipsed by Yangon. Under British colonial rule the town became

Around Yangon

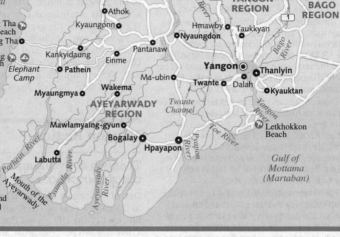

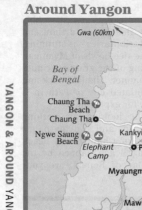

DON'T MISS

AROUND YANGON HIGHLIGHTS

➡ Admire the artistry and skill needed to make silk and cotton parasols in **Pathein** (p86), the ideal base for exploring the delta.

➡ Cycle around the historic temples of former capital **Bago** (p81), where you can view a partial reconstruction of a royal palace.

➡ Combine a cooking course in **Thanlyin** (p79) with a trip to the crocodile farm and the National Races Village.

➡ Ride a motorbike taxi along jungle tracks between the beach resorts of **Chaung Tha** (p91) and **Ngwe Saung** (p94), crossing three rivers by ferry en route.

known as Syriam and flourished again as an important oil refinery; the plant is still operating today.

⊙ Sights

Thanlyin is a relaxing place, with shaded streets and a busy market to stroll through. There is little of the ancient city to be seen.

In the third week of January Thanlyin's Hindu community celebrates (or endures depending on your opinion) **Thaipusam**, the ritual of penitence in which devotees repent bad deeds by impaling themselves with hooks and nails and walking over hot coals.

Kyaik-khauk Paya   BUDDHIST STUPA
(ကျိုက်ခေါက်ဘုရား; Kyaik-khauk Pagoda Rd, Thanlyin; admission K1000; ⊙6am-8pm) A couple of miles south of Thanlyin's centre is this gilded Mon-style stupa, similar in design to Shwedagon and said to contain two Buddha hairs delivered to the site by the great sage himself. There are stupendous views from its hilltop location.

Yele Paya   BUDDHIST TEMPLE
(ရေလယ်ဘုရား; Kyauktan; admission $2; ⊙first/last boat 7am/4.30pm) At Kyauktan, 7.5 miles southeast of Thanlyin, is a sparkling floating temple adrift on a chocolate river. You can feed the massive catfish splashing about at the temple complex's edge. To reach the islet,

catch one of the launch ferries (K5000 return) reserved for foreigners from the riverbank.

Also in the town is a small pagoda perched on the top of a hill beside the river and a hectic, flyblown and rather fishy market, which reaches its climax in the morning.

Thaketa Crocodile Farm FARM
(သာကေတမိကျောင်းမွေးမြူရေးဝန်း; Thaketa Industrial Estate, Tharkyta; admission K1400; ⊗ 6am-6pm) Off the main road from Yangon to Thanlyin, at the end of a bumpy road leading into the Thaketa Industrial Estate, is this farm that breeds crocodiles for their leather. Some of the saltwater crocs are monsters and watching their fanged mouths snap around tossed pieces of fish will send a chill down your spine.

Boardwalks keep you at a safe distance and lead over concrete pools and the mangroves next to Pazundaung Creek.

National Races Village PARK
(တိုင်းရင်းသားများ ကျေးရွာ; Yandar Rd, Thaketa; admission K3000; ⊗ 9am-6pm) You'll quickly understand why locals call this quirky park the people's zoo. The lush, landscaped compound presents an idealistic view of Myanmar's many different ethnicities. Traditional houses of the Kachin, Kayah, Kayin, Chin, Bamar, Mon, Rakhine and Shan are staffed by people in native costume who sell local products and crafts.

The park, just north of the Yangon side of the Thanlyin Bridge, is large so you'd be well advised to rent a bike (K1000) to get around it.

🔁 Courses

Flavours of Myanmar
Cooking School COOKING COURSE
(☑ 09 863 5066, 01-375 050; www.myanmargood newstravel.com; 103 Bogyoke Ne Win Rd, Thanlyin; course plus transfer from Yangon $50) Top Yangon travel agency Good News Travels is behind this cooking school/restaurant operation.

The setting with giant Pathein parasols providing shade in a garden planted with mango trees is delightful; lessons are given at the outdoor cooking stations following a horse-and-cart trip to the local market to shop for ingredients.

The half-day course also includes a visit to a monastery to present gifts of food to the monks.

🍴 Eating

For eats, **Pwint** (Kyaik-khauk Pagoda Rd, Thanlyin; mains K1700-3000; ⊗ 9am-9pm) is a reliable Burmese restaurant on the main road less than mile after the Thanlyin Bridge. There's no roman-script signage.

If you've hired a driver, ask to refresh at **Shwe Pu Zun** (14A Minnandar Rd, Dawbon; ice cream & drinks from K650; 📷), a huge modern bakery and cafe, located between Yangon and Thanlyin, specialising in sweets; the *faluda* ('fa-lu-da' on the menu, a mixture of custard, ice cream and jelly; K1200) is famous.

Near the ferry landing in Kyauktan are several **food vendors**.

ℹ️ Getting There & Away

The most convenient way to visit both Thanlyin and Kyauktan is to hire a taxi in Yangon (K40,000 for a half-day). By taxi, it takes about 30 minutes to get to Thanlyin.

If you're passionate about Myanmar's uncomfortable local transport or are counting kyat, buses to Thanlyin (K200, one hour, 16 miles) leave frequently throughout the day from Sule Pagoda; look for lines 213, 217 and 258.

In Thanlyin, motorcycle taxis can take you to Kyaik-khauk Paya (K1500) and Yele Paya (K5000).

Bago Region

Bago (Pegu) ပဲခူး

If it wasn't for its abundance of religious sites and the remains of its former palace it would be hard to tell that this scrappy town – 50 miles northeast of Yangon on the old highway to Mandalay – was once capital of southern Myanmar. The awarding of a contract to a South Korean consortium to build the country's new Hanthawady International Airport (due for completion in 2018) is set to revive Bago's fortunes.

In the meantime, the great density of blissed-out buddhas and treasure-filled temples makes Bago an appealing and simple day trip from Yangon, or the ideal first stop when you leave the city behind.

Many of Bago's monuments are actually centuries old, but don't look it, due to extensive restorations. This is an excellent place to explore by bicycle, as most attractions are near each other. Bikes can be rented at Bago Star Hotel.

Bago

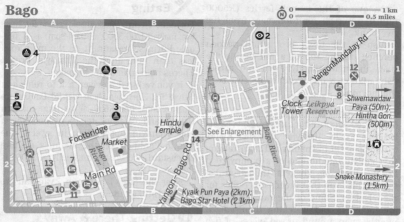

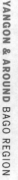

Bago

Sights
1	Kanbawzathadi Palace	D2
2	Kya Kha Wain Kyaung	C1
3	Maha Kalyani Sima (Maha Kalyani Thein)	B1
4	Mahazedi Paya	A1
5	Shwegugale Paya	A1
6	Shwethalyaung Buddha	B1

Sleeping
7	Emperor Motel	A2
8	Hotel Mariner	D1
9	Mya Nanda Hotel	A2
10	San Francisco Guest House	A2

Eating
11	Hadaya Café	A2
12	Hanthawaddy	D1
13	Three Five Restaurant	A2

Transport
14	Bus Station	B2
15	Bus Station	D1
	Taxi Stand	(see 15)

History

Bago was reputedly founded in AD 573 by two Mon princes from Thaton, who saw a female *hamsa* (mythological bird) standing on the back of a male *hamsa* on an island in a huge lake. Taking this to be an auspicious omen, they founded a royal capital called Hanthawady (from the Pali-Sanskrit 'Hamsavati', meaning the 'kingdom of the *hamsa*') at the edge of the lake.

During the later Mon dynastic periods (1287–1539), Hanthawady developed into a walled city of one square mile with 20 gates and became the centre of the Mon kingdom of Ramanadesa, which consisted of all southern Myanmar.

The Bamar took over in 1539 when King Tabinshwehti annexed Bago to his Taungoo kingdom. The city was frequently mentioned by early European visitors – who knew it as Pegu – as an important seaport. In 1740 the Mon, after a period of submission to Taungoo, re-established Bago as their capital, but in 1757 King Alaungpaya sacked and utterly destroyed the city. King Bodawpaya, who ruled from 1782 to 1819, rebuilt it to some extent, but when the river changed its course the city was cut off from the sea and lost its importance as a seaport. It never again reclaimed its previous grandeur.

Sights & Activities

Shwethalyaung Buddha
BUDDHIST TEMPLE
(ရွှေသာလျောင်းဘုရား; ⊙5am-8pm) FREE
Legend has it that this gorgeous reclining Buddha was built by the Mon king Mgadeikpa in the 10th century. Measuring 180ft long and 53ft high, the monument's little finger alone extends 10ft.

Following the destruction of Bago in 1757, the huge buddha was overgrown by jungle and not rediscovered until 1881 when a contractor unearthed it while building the Yangon–Bago railway line.

In 1906 an open-sided pavilion was erected over the statue and in the 1930s a mosaic was added to the great pillow on which the Buddha's head rests.

On the rear side of the plinth, in a series of 10 murals, the legend of how the buddha came to be built by Mgadeikpa is depicted. His reign was marked by corruption and violence, but one day his son was out hunting in the forests when his eye fell upon a Mon girl who caused his heart to flutter. Even though she was a Buddhist and he, like everyone in his father's kingdom, worshipped pagan idols, the two became lovers and married after he promised her that she could continue to practise Buddhism.

Back at the court the king was furious when he discovered this and ordered the execution of both the girl and his son. Yet when the new bride prayed in front of the pagan idol it cracked and broke. The king was seized with fear and, realising the error of his ways, ordered the building of a statue of the Buddha and the conversion of the population to Buddhism.

Near the huge head of the image stands a statue of **Lokanat** (Lokanatha or Avalokitesvara), a Mahayana Buddhist deity borrowed by Burmese Buddhism.

A Japanese war cemetery, **Kyinigan Kyaung**, can be seen on the grounds of a monastery just north of Shwethalyaung.

Shwemawdaw Paya BUDDHIST STUPA

(ရွှေမောတောဘုရား; Shwemawdaw Paya Rd; 5am-8pm; admission with a Bago Archaelogical Zone ticket, $10) A pyramid of washed-out gold in the midday haze and glittering perfection in the evening, the 376ft-high Shwemawdaw Paya stands tall and proud over the town. The stupa reaches 46ft higher than the Shwedagon in Yangon. At the northeastern corner of the stupa is a huge section of the *hti* toppled by an earthquake in 1917.

According to murky legend the original stupa was a small, ramshackle object, built by two brothers, Kullasala and Mahasala, to enshrine two hairs given to them by Gautama Buddha. In AD 982 a sacred tooth was added to the collection; in 1385 another tooth was added and the stupa was rebuilt to a towering 277ft. In 1492 strong winds blew over the *hti* and a new one was raised.

The stupa has collapsed and been rebuilt many times over the past 600 years; each time it has grown a little taller and the treasures mounted in it have grown a little more abundant. The last time it was destroyed was in 1930 when a huge earthquake completely levelled it, and for the next 20 years only the huge earth mound of the base remained.

The Shwemawdaw Paya is a particularly good destination during Bago's annual pagoda festival, in March/April.

Hintha Gon Paya BUDDHIST STUPA

(ဟင်္သာကုန်း) FREE Located a short walk behind the Shwemawdaw, this shrine was once the one point in this whole vast area that rose above sea level and so was the natural place for the *hamsa* to land. Images of this mythical bird decorate the stupa built by U Khanti, the hermit monk who was the architect of Mandalay Hill.

Walk to it by taking the steps down from side of the Shwemawdaw from the main entrance. This paya is also a big spot for *nat* worship and festivals and with a bit of luck you'll catch the swirling, veiled forms of masculine-looking *nat* dancers accompanied by the clanging and crashing of a traditional orchestra.

Kyaik Pun Paya MONUMENT

(ကျိုက်ပွန်ဘုရား; admission with a Bago Archaelogical Zone ticket, $10.) Built in 1476 by King Dhammazedi, the Kyaik Pun Paya consists of four 100ft-high sitting buddhas (Gautama Buddha and his three predecessors) placed back to back around a huge, square pillar, about a mile south of Bago just off the Yangon road.

According to legend, four Mon sisters were linked with the construction of the buddhas; it was said that if any of them should marry, one of the buddhas would collapse. One of the four buddhas disintegrated in the 1930 earthquake, leaving only a brick outline (since restored) and a very old bride.

Maha Kalyani Sima
(Maha Kalyani Thein) BUDDHIST TEMPLE

(မဟာကလျာဏီသိမ်တော်ကြီး) This 'Sacred Hall of Ordination' was originally constructed in 1476 by Dhammazedi, the famous alchemist king and son of Queen Shinsawpu. Like almost everything in Bago it has suffered a tumbledown history and has been destroyed and rebuilt many a time.

Next to the hall are 10 large tablets with inscriptions in Pali and Mon describing the history of Buddhism in Myanmar.

🛈 BAGO ARCHAEOLOGICAL ZONE TICKET

To gain access to Bago's main sites including Shwemawdaw Paya, Kyaik Pun Paya and Kanbawzathadi Palace, foreigners must buy the Bago Archaeological Zone ticket ($10/K10,000). Nearly all of the sights charge an additional K300 for camera and K500 for videocameras.

If you can't get enough of buddha statues then across the road from the Maha Kalyani Sima is the **Four Figures Paya**, with four buddha figures standing back to back. An adjacent open hallway has a small reclining buddha image, thronged by followers, and some macabre paintings of wrongdoers being tortured in the afterlife.

Relaxing in the sun next to these two monuments is the serene **Naung Daw Gyi Mya Tha Lyaung**, a reclining buddha sprawled out over 250ft and built in 2002 with public donations.

Mahazedi Paya
BUDDHIST STUPA

(မဟာစေတီဘုရား) The design of the Mahazedi Paya (Great Stupa), with its whitewashed stairways leading almost to the stupa's summit, is unusual for southern Myanmar and certainly one of the more attractive religious buildings in Bago.

Originally constructed in 1560 by King Bayinnaung, it was destroyed during the 1757 sacking of Bago. An attempt to rebuild it in 1860 was unsuccessful and the great earthquake of 1930 comprehensively levelled it, after which it remained a ruin. This current reconstruction was only completed in 1982.

The Mahazedi originally contained a Buddha tooth, at one time thought to be the most sacred of all Buddha relics; the tooth of Kandy, Sri Lanka. After Bago was conquered in 1539, the tooth was moved to Taungoo and then to Sagaing near Mandalay. Together with a begging bowl supposed to have been used by the Buddha, it remains in the Kaunghmudaw Paya, near Sagaing, to this day.

THE HAMSA

In deference to legend, the symbol for Bago is a female *hamsa* (*hintha* or *hantha* in Burmese; a mythological bird) standing on the back of a male *hamsa*. At a deeper level, the symbol honours the compassion of the male *hamsa* in providing a place for the female to stand in the middle of a lake with only one island. Hence, the men of Bago are said to be more chivalrous than men from other areas of Myanmar. In popular culture, however, men joke that they dare not marry a woman from Bago for fear of being henpecked!

Shwegugale Paya
BUDDHIST STUPA

(ရွှေဂူကလေးဘုရား) A little beyond the Mahazedi Paya, this *zedi* has a dark *gu* (tunnel) around the circumference of the cylindrical superstructure. The monument dates to 1494 and the reign of King Byinnya Yan. Inside are 64 seated buddha figures. In the evening many locals venture out here.

From the *zedi*, cross a rickety wooden footbridge and you'll arrive at a **nat shrine** with life-sized statues of Ko Thein and Ko Thant, the *nat* of the temple compound.

Kya Kha Wain Kyaung
MONASTERY

(ကြာခတ်ဝိုင်းကျောင်း) The sight of some 500 monks and novices, filing out in the early morning from one of largest monasteries in Myanmar to collect alms, is worth getting up early for. Otherwise, join the tour groups visiting here at 10.30am to see the monks gathered to eat lunch in a giant hall.

You're free to wander around; most of the monks think it's hilarious that tourists come and watch them eat, but the atmosphere is a bit like a zoo. Prior to the protests of 2007 there were supposedly 1500 monks in residence here; now it's more like 500.

On the way to or from the monastery it's worth having a look around Bago's lively **market**.

Kanbawzathadi Palace
PALACE

(ကမ္ဘောဇသာဒီနန်းတော်; admission with Bago Archaeological Zone ticket $10; ⊘ 9am-6pm) At the heart of ancient Hanthawady was the Kanbawzathadi Palace, the remains of which have been excavated just south of Shwemawdaw Paya. The stumps of the huge teak posts that held up part of the palace have been left in situ, while the posts themselves occupy a museum that's a slipshod reconstruction of the Great Audience Hall, originally dating from 1599.

Another reconstructed building in the compound is the Bee Throne Hall.

Snake Monastery
MONASTERY

(မြွေကျောင်း) A story goes that a revered monk had a dream that the python you can see snoozing in this monastery was the reincarnation of a *nat*; another is that it is the reincarnation of the monk himself.

Either way, over 125 years later, the self-same python has grown to be at least 17ft long and a foot wide, making it probably one of the largest snakes in the world. No wonder locals flock here to pay their respects.

The **Shwe Taung Yoe Paya** *zedi*, nearby on a small hilltop, is great for watching sunsets; however you have to cross a festering rubbish dump to reach it.

The monastery and *zedi* are about mile south of Hintha Gon Paya; locals should be able to direct you there.

✴️ Festivals & Events

Shwemawdaw Paya Festival RELIGIOUS
On the full moon of Myanmar's lunar month of Tagu (March/April) this festival attracts huge crowds of worshippers and merrymakers.

🛏 Sleeping

The cheapest places to stay are located on the busy road and – make no mistake about this – noisy main road, so rooms towards the back of these hotels are the choice pickings. Electricity is generally available only from the evening to early morning.

Emperor Motel HOTEL $
(✍052-21349; 8 Main Rd; r $5-10; ❄️🛜) The pick of the downtown budget selection – which is not saying much. Musty rooms are painted pink; the more expensive ones have a bit of light and space. The rooftop offers great views of the surroundings.

San Francisco Guest House HOTEL $
(✍052-22265; 14 Main Rd; d/d $10/15; ❄️) The rooms are rough and ready and there's a curfew from 10pm to 5am. The guys who run it offer motorbike tours of Bago's sights (K8000).

Mya Nanda Hotel HOTEL $
(✍052-19799; 10 Main Rd; s/d from $8/18; ❄️) An acceptable, if grubby, budget choice, and the staff here can arrange motorbike taxis and guides.

Bago Star Hotel HOTEL $$
(✍052-30066; http://bagostarhotel.googlepages.com; 11-21 Kyaikpon Pagoda Rd; s/d $35/40; ❄️🛏) This self-styled 'Country style, Bangalow type Hotel' has a summer-camp feel. Located just off the highway and only a short walk to the ever-watching eyes of the Kyaik Pun Paya, it offers A-frame cabin-like rooms, a murky small pool and – a big plus – bikes can be rented (K3000 a day). Generators keep the air-conditioning humming.

Hotel Mariner HOTEL $$
(✍052-201 034; hotelmariner.hm@gmail.com; 330 Shwemawdaw Paya Rd; r $35-45; ❄️🛜) New six-floor property that significantly ups the standard of Bago's midrange accommodation offerings. Some rooms offer grandstand views of Shwemawdaw Paya.

★ Han Thar Gardens HOTEL $$$
(✍09 4281 77217; hanthargardens@gmail.com; 34 Bullein Tar Zone Village, Yangon-Mandalay Rd; r from $150; ❄️@🛜) Overlooking fields and a golf course, this beautifully designed property has environmentally friendly features such as no air-conditioning in the airy 50ft ceiling rooms of the main building. Run by an overseas-educated Myanmar woman, it also features an excellent restaurant – worth visiting in its own right – serving delicious Burmese food, including local specialities such as *pazun chin* (pickled prawn salad).

🍴 Eating

Hanthawaddy CHINESE, BURMESE $$
(192 Hintha St; mains K2000-8000; ⊙ lunch & dinner; 🍴) The food here isn't amazing, but it's the only restaurant in central Bago with a bit of atmosphere. The open-air upper level is breezy and offers great views of Shwemawdaw Paya.

Kyaw Swa CHINESE $$
(445-446 Yangon-Bago Rd; mains K5000-9000; ⊙8am-9pm; 🛜🍴) A couple of miles south of Bago's centre, this barn-like Chinese restaurant serves decent meals, including roast duck and grilled lobster.

Three Five Restaurant INTERNATIONAL, BURMESE $
(10 Main Rd; mains K1200-4000; ⊙7am-10pm; 🍴) This friendly but shabby place offers a menu spanning Bamar, Chinese, Indian and European dishes; the food is cheap and good. If you're feeling adventurous, try 'goat fighting balls' (goat testicles), prepared in a number of ways.

Hadaya Café TEAHOUSE $
(14 Main Rd; ⊙2am-midnight) This popular, central teahouse, keeping very long hours, has a good selection of pastries and good-quality tea and coffee.

ℹ️ Getting There & Away

TRANSPORT TO/FROM BAGO
The following table shows travel times and costs between Bago and several main destinations. The range in train fares is between ordinary and upper class. For more detailed information refer

to the Getting There & Away sections of each of the specific destinations.

DESTINATION	BUS	TRAIN
Kyaikto	1½hr; K3500	3hr; $2-4
Mandalay	9hr; K14,000	14hr; $10-27
Mawlamyine	6hr; K7000	7hr; $4-8
Taungoo	6hr; K6000	5hr; $3-6
Yangon	2hr; K2000	2hr; $2-4

BUS

Bago's **bus station** (Yangon-Mandalay Rd) is about halfway between the town centre and the Bago Star Hotel, located across from the Hindu temple. Many buses passing through Bago can also be waved down from outside your hotel, though unless you have booked a ticket in advance there is less likelihood of getting a seat.

Buses to Yangon depart approximately every 30 minutes from 6.30am to 5.30pm.

Going south, buses to Kinpun, the starting point for Mt Kyaiktiyo (Golden Rock), leave every hour or so during the day. During the rainy season (May to October), buses go only as far as Kyaikto, 10 miles from Kinpun.

Heading north, for Mandalay, Taungoo and Inle Lake, apart from a handful of direct services from Bago, it's also possible to hop on services coming from Yangon – book ahead with a local agent, such as **Sea Sar** (☑ 09 530 0987; seasar. tickets918@gmail.com), or ask your hotel to help.

TAXI

A more expensive but more convenient alternative is to hire a taxi for a day trip from Yangon.

With bargaining this should cost about $80/ K80,000, but it does give you the additional advantage of having transport between sites once you get to Bago and saves traipsing all the way out to the bus station in Yangon.

One-way taxis back from Bago straight to your hotel in Yangon cost $40/K40,000.

A guide and driver for a day trip to Mt Kyaiktiyo (Golden Rock) can be hired for around K55,000 return.

For any of the above, you can inquire at the town's **taxi stand** (Yangon-Mandalay Rd) or through any of the central Bago hotels.

TRAIN

Bago is connected by train with Yangon and Mawlamyine and stops north towards Mandalay.

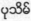 Getting Around

Trishaw is the main form of local transport in Bago. A one-way trip in the central area should cost no more than K500. If you're going further afield – say from Shwethalyaung Buddha, at one end of town, to Shwemawdaw Paya, at the other – you might as well hire a trishaw or motorcycle for the day, either of which should cost around K7000.

Ayeyarwady Region

Pathein   ပုသိမ်

Myanmar's fourth city and the most important delta port outside Yangon lies at the heart of an area that produces the finest rice

---

OFF THE BEATEN TRACK

MOEYUNGYI WETLANDS

About an hour northeast of Bago and close to the village of Pyinbongyi is the **Moeyungyi Wetlands** (မိုးညွန့်ကြီးရေနတ်ကွင်း), a 15-sq-mile lake and marsh that is one of Myanmar's handful of national parks. Sitting on a migration route of birds fleeing the icy Siberian winter and attracting thousands of local waders, the wetlands, which started life as an artificial water-storage reservoir in 1878, will bring a big grin to any birder's face. The last census revealed some 125 different species including great flocks of egrets, cormorants, white storks and large numbers of the beautiful swamp hen (purple gallinule) as well as sarus cranes with their brilliant red heads.

Your best chance of seeing exotic birds is from December to February and during this time a small 'resort' offers excellent boat tours (up to six people) on the lake including a guide for $15 per person for about two hours. The boat will take you whizzing over the lake to the marshy reed beds in the centre where the birds congregate in vast numbers.

Should you want to stay nearby, the resort offers accommodation in floating **houseboats** (☑ 052-70113; s/d $55/65; ☉ Nov-Mar) from November to March. The price includes three meals and a boat ride, and it's essential that you book in advance. The rooms, though novel, are somewhat overpriced and even serious birders may prefer to make a half-day tour from Bago.

Pathein

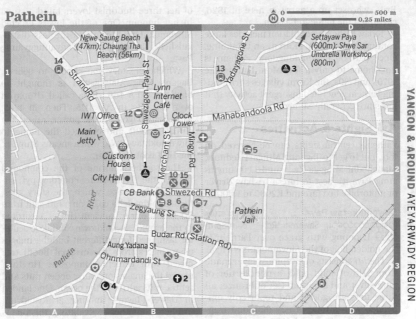

in Myanmar, including *pawsanmwe t'àmìn* (fragrant rice). There's a general air of prosperity in the city, which has a busy, buzzy atmosphere, particularly along the river and in the markets near the Shwemokhtaw Paya, Pathein's principal religious site.

Most travellers only stop off briefly on their way to the beaches, but the workshops that produce colourful, hand-painted parasols, along with the shady, tree-lined village lanes to the northeast of the town centre, are worth a little more than a token glance. If you care to look for it, there are also architectural remnants of colonial days in Pathein, including the central jail dating from 1879.

Adding to the allure is the fact that Pathein can be reached by boat from Yangon. The discomfort of the overnight trip on aged IWT ferries, laden to the gills with cargo, is compensated for by the insight provided on the pattern and pace of everyday life in the delta region.

History

The town was the scene of major clashes during the struggle for supremacy between the Mon and the Bamar. Later it became an important trade relay point for goods moving between India and Southeast Asia. The city's name may derive from the Burmese word for Muslim (*Pathi*) – due to the heavy presence of Arab and Indian Muslim traders here centuries ago; there's still a large Muslim population in the city. The colonial

Pathein

◎ Sights

▣ Sleeping

✕ Eating

◔ Drinking & Nightlife

ⓘ Transport

Brits, who set up a garrison here in 1826, corrupted the name to Bassein.

Today, Pathein's population includes large contingents of Kayin (Karen) and Rakhine. Once part of a Mon kingdom, Pathein is now home to only a few Mon. During the 1970s and '80s, the Kayin villages surrounding Pathein generated insurgent activity that has since generally calmed.

◉ Sights & Activities

Pathein's central sights can be covered on foot, but to get to Tagaung Mingala Zeditaw, Mahabodhi Mingala Zedi amd Leikyunyinaung Paya it's best to hire a trishaw driver or motorbike taxi (around K2000 to K3000).

Shwemokhtaw Paya
BUDDHIST STUPA

(ရွှေမုဋ္ဌောဘုရား; Shwezedi Rd; ⊘6am-8pm) **FREE** Looming with grace over Pathein is the golden bell of the Shwemokhtaw Paya.

The *hti* consists of a topmost layer made from 14lb of solid gold, a middle tier of pure silver and a bottom tier of bronze; all three tiers are gilded and reportedly embedded with a total of 829 diamond fragments, 843 rubies and 1588 semiprecious stones.

This large complex is unusually well layered in legend. One states that it was originally built by India's Buddhist King Ashoka in 305 BC. Standing just 7.5ft tall, this original stupa supposedly enshrined Buddha relics and a 6-inch gold bar.

Another legend says a Muslim princess named Onmadandi requested each of her three Buddhist lovers build a stupa in her honour. One of the lovers erected Shwemokhtaw, the others the less distinguished Tazaung and Thayaunggyaung Paya.

Whichever story you choose to believe, Bagan's King Alaungsithu is thought to have erected a 46ft stupa over this site in AD 1115. Then, in 1263, King Samodagossa took power, raised the stupa to 132ft and changed the name to Shwemokhtaw Paya, which means Stupa of the Half-Foot Gold Bar.

The southern shrine of the compound houses the Thiho-shin Phondaw-pyi sitting buddha image, which, the story goes, floated to the delta coast on a raft sent from Sri Lanka during ancient times. According to the legend, an unknown Sinhalese sculptor fashioned four different buddha images using pieces from the original Bodhi tree mixed with cement composite. He then placed the images on four wooden rafts and set the rafts adrift on the ocean. One landed in Dawei (Tavoy), another at Kyaikkami (Amherst), another at Kyaiktiyo (this one is now at Kyaikpawlaw); and the fourth landed near Phondawpyi, a fishing village about 60 miles south of Pathein, from where it was transferred to Pathein.

A marble standing buddha positioned in a niche in the fence running along the western side of the stupa marks a spot where Mon warriors once prayed before going off to battle. In the northwestern corner of the compound is a shrine dedicated to

---

PATHEIN PARASOLS

Pathein is famous throughout Myanmar for the quality of its handmade parasols, used to shade the carrier from the searing sun. Covered in silk or waterproofed cotton, the parasols come in a variety of bright and organic colours.

One type that can be used in the rain is the saffron-coloured monks' umbrella, which is waterproofed by applying various coats of tree resin; a single umbrella may take five days to complete, including the drying process. Parasols and umbrellas can be ordered in any size directly from the workshops, and are a bargain given the amount of work that goes into making them.

Workshops welcome visitors who want to observe this craft, which is a lot more interesting than it might sound. The most centrally located shops are at the southern end of Merchant St, but here you'll only see the finishing decorative steps of the typical 40-stage process needed to make the best parasols.

To see the whole process head to **Shwe Sar Umbrella Workshop** (☎042-25127; 653 Tawya Kyaung Rd; ⊘8am-5pm), the best of several workshops scattered in the vicinity of Twenty-Eight Paya, off Mahabandoola Rd. This workshop has been run by the same family for three generations, and is just around the corner from the Settayaw Paya.

Shin Upagot, the bodhisattva who floats on the ocean and appears to those in trouble. Turtles swim in the water surrounding the small pavilion.

Also in this northwest corner is an unusual golden Ganesh shrine, dedicated to the elephant-headed god worshipped by Hindus as the god of wisdom and wealth.

Settayaw Paya BUDDHIST TEMPLE

(စက်တော်ရာဘုရား) FREE This charming paya, spread across a green hilly setting, is dedicated to a mythical Buddha footprint left by the Enlightened One during his legendary perambulations through Southeast Asia. The footprint symbol itself is an oblong, 3ft-long impression.

Tagaung Mingala Zeditaw BUDDHIST STUPA

(ဟာကောင်းမင်္ဂလာစေတီတော် (တကောင်းဘုရား)) FREE Interesting from an artistic perspective, this pagoda is centred on a graceful stupa that sweeps inward from a wide, whitewashed base to a gleaming silver superstructure. It's about 2 miles south of the city centre.

Look for the small squirrel sculpture extending from the western side of the upper stupa, representing a previous life of the Buddha as a squirrel. One of the pavilions at the base of the stupa contains a very large sitting buddha image.

Twenty-Eight Paya BUDDHIST TEMPLE

(နှစ်ကျိပ်ရှစ်ဆူဘုရား; ⊙9am-5pm) This rectangular shrine contains 28 sitting and 28 standing buddha images. None of them are particularly distinguished except that the latter appear in the open-robe style rather than the closed-robe pose that is typical of Mandalay standing images. You may have to ask the caretaker to unlock the building.

At one end of the hall stands a group of crude sculptures depicting a scene from the Buddha's life in which he teaches a disciple the relativity of physical beauty by comparing a monkey, the disciple's wife and a *deva* (celestial being).

St Peter's Cathedral CHURCH

(Mingyi Rd) FREE The focal point of a Catholic educational compound is this 1872-vintage cathedral distinctively plastered emerald green. If you're not here for daily mass at 6am (also 4pm on Sunday), friendly Father William, the Chinese-Kayin priest, will happily let you peek inside.

A short walk further south, just off Merchant St, is another colonial-age religious building: the **Zerbadi Sunni Jamae Mosque**. The dilapidated building has a ruinous charm.

Mahabodhi Mingala Zedi BUDDHIST TEMPLE

(မဟာဗောဓိမင်္ဂလာစေတီ) FREE West of Tagaung Mingala Zeditaw, a little way towards the river, stands this temple patterned after the Mahabodhi stupa in Bodhgaya, India.

Leikyunyinaung Paya BUDDHIST TEMPLE

(လိပ်ကျွန်းညီနောင်ဘုရား) FREE This temple, about a mile directly south of Mahabodhi, was renovated by the miltary regime in the early 1990s to create a facsimile of Ananda Paya in Bagan. Forced labour was used in the renovation, so many locals avoid praying here.

🎊 Festivals & Events

Vesakha RELIGIOUS

The people of Pathein celebrate the Buddha's birth, enlightenment and passing away with a huge *paya pwe* (pagoda festival) during the full moon of Myanmar's month of Kason (April/May). The festival is held at the Shwemokhtaw Paya.

🛏 Sleeping

Day to Day Motel HOTEL $

(☑042-23368; Jail St; r from $10; 🕸🤶) This new guesthouse has high-standard rooms in a quieter part of town, opposite the Sikh Temple dating from 1938. A big roof terrace provides a pleasant place to sit and take in the surrounding leafy view.

Taan Taan Ta Guest House HOTEL $

(☑042-22290; 7 Merchant St; s/d from $10/15; 🕸) This popular budget guesthouse is often full, even though it's very much no-frills. If you're not on a shoestring, check out the more expensive double rooms on the top floor, which feature air-conditioning, TV and fridge.

★ La Pyae Wun Hotel HOTEL $$

(☑042-24669; 30 Mingyi Rd; s/d $20/33; 🕸🤶) Offers white-tiled rooms that are as polished as the staff. The huge bathrooms, rather bizarrely, only have cold showers. Breakfast isn't included and loving couples will be delighted to hear that it's twin rooms only – so we'll have none of that hanky-panky, please!

Pammawaddy Hotel HOTEL $$

(☑042-21165; newpammawaddy@gmail.com; 14A Mingyi Rd; r $15-35; 🕸🤶) An acceptable backup, if the better La Pyae Wun Hotel across

OFF THE BEATEN TRACK

MAWDIN POINT

If you follow the Pathein River until it empties into the Andaman Sea you'll reach **Mawdin Point** (မော်တင်စွန်း) a place of great religious significance to Myanmar's Buddhists. This is where the religion is first believed to have to have been introduced to the country, no doubt by sailors from the Indian subcontinent; **Mawdin Paya** has graced the point for centuries.

The best time to visit is during the 15-day Mawdin Paya festival in February or March. Throughout the year, the point can be reached by either bus (K4000; six hours) departing Pathein at noon and returning at 5am the next day; or by boat (K3000; 10 hours) leaving Pathein at 5am and returning at 6pm.

As the point is near a naval base you should arrange a permit before setting off here – Pathein guide Soe Moe Aung (p90) can arrange this and provide guiding services to the area ($30 a day) which also includes Thamee Hla (Diamond Island), an important sea-turtle hatchery.

the road is full. Rooms improve as you go higher up in the building.

✗ Eating & Drinking

★ Shwe Ayar   BURMESE MUSLIM $
(32-35 Mingalar Rd; mains K1500) It doesn't look like much but this place offers high-quality biryani which you can supplement with chicken or mutton. The lentil and bean soup is so delicious you'll want a second helping. Find it opposite Zaw Optical.

Zone Pan   BURMESE $
(Budar Rd/Station Rd; meals from K1500; ⊙ 8am-9pm) This typical Myanmar curry house features a good range of tasty curries, soups and salads. To cut the grease of a Myanmar meal, try the mouth-puckeringly tart *shauk-thi dhouq* (lemon salad). There's no English sign here; look for the light-blue shopfront opposite Lucky One Tea Shop.

New City Tea Centre   TEAHOUSE $
(Mingyi Rd; snacks from K200; ⊙ 5.30am-8.30pm) Next to La Pyae Wun Hotel and perfect for the breakfasts that your hotel doesn't provide. This shady teahouse provides plates of freshly baked naan and chickpeas (only until 9.30am) and other snacks and a morning caffeine kick.

Man San Thu   TEAHOUSE $
(3 Shwezigon Paya St; snacks from K200; ⊙ 6am-11pm; 🕸) You can't miss this place, spread over two floors and with a bright orange facade. Inside there's a real buzz as patrons dig into all the teashop snacks (including dim sum) and surf the net on the free wi-fi.

Myo Restaurant   BURMESE $
(5 Aung Yadana St; mains from K2000; ⊙ 7am-10pm) A bustling bar and restaurant that extends a loving welcome to all comers. The meals, which focus on all your favourite Bamar staples, are done with more style than most places. And, to keep you entertained while you wait for your supper, there is a TV playing all the premiership matches, and draught beer to boot.

Shwe Zin Yaw Restaurant   BURMESE $
(24/25 Shwezedi Rd; mains from K1500; ⊙ 8am-9pm; 🕸) Oh you lucky, lucky taste buds, finally you're going to get something different, including goat curry and sardine salad!

🔒 Shopping

Apart from the parasol workshops, there's the **night market** that is set up each evening in front of Customs House, where teenagers cruise, flirt and hang out while vendors purvey food, clothing and tools and just about every other requisite for daily life at low prices. Just south of Shwemokhtaw Paya is the **Central Market**, and just south of that the **New Market**, with all manner of goods.

ℹ Information

If he doesn't find you first, young guide **Soe Moe Aung** (🖉 09 2503 22368; http://travel-topathein.wordpress.com) is worth tracking down. A mine of local information, he can help arrange all kinds of trips and adventures in the area, including boating along the Pathein River; motorbike taxis in the countryside to visit Kayin villages and out to the beaches; and the necessary permits for Mawdin Point.

Money can be changed at **CB Bank** (cnr Merchant St & Shwezedi Rd) where you'll find an ATM accepting international cards.

Internet is available at **Lynn Internet Café** (Shwezigon Paya St; per hr K400; ☺9am-11pm).

❶ Getting There & Around

BOAT

To Yangon (deck/cabin $8/40) boats leave Wednesday and Sunday at 2pm, arriving in Yangon the next day at 11am. Tickets must be bought with dollars only at the **Inland Water Transport Office** (Mahabandoola Rd; ☺10am-noon), located in a wooden colonial-era building near the jetty.

BUS

If you're bound for Yangon (four hours), head to the informal **bus company offices** (Shwezedi Rd) located directly east of Shwe Zin Yaw Restaurant. The cheapest air-con service is offered six times a day by **Ayer Shwe Zin** (☏ 09 4974 5191) for K3600; other operators charge K6000.

Insanely uncomfortable minibuses ply the route from Pathein to Chaung Tha Beach (K3000, 2½ hours, 36 miles) every two hours between 8am and 4pm, departing from an informal **bus station** (Yadayagone St) a couple of blocks northeast of the clock tower.

To Ngwe Saung Beach (K4000, two hours, 29 miles), buses leave from yet another **bus station** (Strand Rd) at 9am, 11am and 3pm.

TRAIN

Pathein's train station is the terminus of a branch line from Kyankin, 61 miles south of Pyay on the west bank of the Ayeyarwady (Irrawaddy) River. During 2014 a new direct line to Yangon is scheduled to open.

TAXI

Share taxis for up to four people can be arranged from your hotel in Pathein for Chaung Tha (K50,000), Ngwe Saung (K40,000) and Yangon (K100,000).

Chaung Tha Beach
ေခ်ာင္းသာကမ္းေျခ

Travel 25 miles west of Pathein to discover the closest thing Myanmar has to a partying beach resort. Chaung Tha is where locals head when they want to relax. There's paddling in the water, floating about on rubber rings, plodding up and down on ponies, wasting money on tacky souvenirs, boisterous beach football games, happy family picnics and setting off Chinese fireworks in the evening.

It's not the most awe-inspiring piece of coastline, but if you need to squeeze some sand and sun into your visit to Myanmar, it is a relatively convenient and affordable option. Unlike Ngwe Saung Beach further south, a few places here are open year-round.

◉ Sights & Activities

The beach itself is the main focus, with the pretty **Kyauk Pahto pagoda** on a rock about two thirds of the way down. Walk to the far southern end and you can take a boat to nearby **Aung Mingalar Island** (K1000 return) where there's a small fishing village and the **Aung Mingalar Mya Kyunnyo pagoda** up on a hill.

Get up early if you want to browse the village **market** (open 5.30am to 9.30am) located behind Chaung Tha's bus station. The rest of the village lies around here and along the main road as it veers left after Hotel Max. Continue to the wooden jetty at the end of the road, where you should be able to persuade a fisher to take you up the river and around the **mangroves** (from K10,000 per hour). This is also the route to Ngwe Saung.

A modest coral reef lies a short way offshore with decent **snorkelling** possible both here and around the headland at the beach's northern end. During the rainy season the water clarity is terrible.

The best snorkelling, though, is about a two-hour boat ride away. Boats, which can be arranged through your hotel or the couple of tourist information providers, cost K50,000 per hour for six people. If you haven't got your own gear it's possible to rent a tatty snorkel and mask from hotels and the tourist info spots. You can also rent canoes for about K10,000 a day, or bicycles for about K2000 a day.

Day Trips

Whitesand Island (The Pyu Kyun), visible a short way offshore, is a popular snorkelling and swimming sport. Boats (K3000 return, 30 minutes) leave from the jetty at the south end of the village every hour or so from 8am (last one back leaves at 5pm). There's very little shade on the low-lying island; bring plenty of water. Don't attempt to swim over – it's a very long way.

About 9 miles north from Chaung Tha is **Chauk Maung Na Ma**, with a similar white sand beach to Ngwe Saung: it's quiet, and you can snorkel, fish and meet local people. It's also a good place for a picnic. You can walk here in around two hours in the dry season.

Whether or not you're not planning to overnight at **Ngwe Saung Beach**, the trip here on a motorbike taxi (K18,000 return) is highly recommended. The route, which takes about two hours, is through wild and glorious country and involves three river crossings on small wooden country boats that have just enough room for the motorbike and a couple of passengers. You will pass serene beaches and several rustic villages amid the forests as you whiz over tracks and trails between shocking-green rice paddies.

Sleeping

Of all Myanmar's beach destinations, Chaung Tha offers the most affordable accommodation. All but a few hotels close down for at least part of the rainy season from mid-May to mid-September; those that remain open discount room rates, sometimes by up to 50% off the high-season rates quoted here.

Most places, including even the most expensive resorts, have electricity only from 1pm to 3pm and 6pm to 6am. Wi-fi is now promised by most places, but seldom actually delivered (if it does work, it will usually only be available when the power is on at night).

If none of the budget places recommended here are available, there are several similarly priced off-beach guesthouses south of the bus station, along the way to the pier.

OFF THE BEATEN TRACK

MEINMAHLA KYUN WILDLIFE SANCTUARY

Since 2012, Fauna and Flora International (www.fauna-flora.org), the world's oldest conservation organisation, has been working with the Ministry of Environmental Conservation and Forestry to help promote eco-tourism in Myanamar. One of the locations they are focusing on is **Meinmahla Kyun Wildlife Sanctuary** (☎045-45578; office in Bogalay), a swampy, mangrove-covered island in the south of the Ayeyarwady Delta that can make for an adventurous three- or four-day return trip from Yangon.

The 137-sq-km sanctuary is the premier place to see wild estuarine crocodiles in Myanmar and, if you're lucky, you may also spot rare Irrawaddy dolphins. Between November and February it's also the pitstop for vast numbers of migratory waterbirds on the East Asian–Australasian Flyway. On the aptly named Turtle Island, 7 miles south of Meinmahla Kyun, turtles nest and hatch between October and March. It's possible to take a day trip to this island and camp there overnight.

Aside from the wildlife, the great attraction of this trip is experiencing life in the delta, where the main livelihood activities are rice farming, fishing and crabbing. This also makes it a great destination for fresh seafood.

The sanctuary headquarters is in **Bogalay**, 92 miles southwest of Yangon. Express boats run by **Shwe Pyi Tan Express** (☎01-230 3003; www.shwepyitan.com) leave daily at 6am from Phone Gyi Jetty (K12,000; six hours); the IWT ferry leaves daily at 6pm from Lan Thit Jetty (deck class/private cabin $5/25; 12 hours). Bogalay can also be reached by bus (K3000; five hours) with departures roughly every two hours during the day from Hlaing Thar Yar Bus Terminal.

You must first register with the park headquarters in Bogalay – this process will be much smoother and quicker if you let them know you're coming in advance. From Bogalay, the park staff will organise return boat transport to Meinmahla Kyun (K70,000 per boat for up to eight people). You can also book canoe tours along the mangrove-lined creeks on the island (K30,000 per day, up to three passengers), and basic accommodation at the ranger stations (K15,000 per person) with mattresses, sheets and mosquito nets provided.

Specialist tour operators in Yangon, including **SST Myanmar** (Map p40; ☎01-255 536; www.sstmyanmar.com; Rm S-5-6, 2nd fl, North Wing, Aung San Stadium, Mingalar Taung Nyunt), can arrange round trips to the sanctuary.

★ **Hill Garden Hotel** HOTEL **$**

(🖉 09 4957 6072; www.hillgardenhotel.com; r $25; 🛜) Even though it's a 20-minute walk north along the coast from the centre of Chaung Tha, the Hill Garden's elevated, lush location, friendliness and rustic-design bamboo-and-rattan chalets make this an excellent choice for getting away from it all. The bathrooms are top grade and there are mosquito nets over the comfy beds.

Shwe Ya Min Guesthouse & Restaurant GUESTHOUSE **$**

(🖉 042-42127; Main Rd; s/d $15/20; ❇🛜) Although it's located on the opposite side of the road from the beach, the bright rooms here are scrubbed clean, neatly tiled and come with desk, soft bed and decent bathrooms. The attached restaurant serves a justifiably well-regarded pancake breakfast, and gracious, friendly service rounds out the package.

Dream Light HOTEL **$**

(🖉 042-42201; s/d $15/20; ❇🛜) If you don't need a room right on the beach, this pastel-hued castle-like complex near the market intersection is an adequate, although slightly musty budget choice.

Grand Hotel HOTEL **$$**

(🖉 042-42329; www.grandhotel-chaungtha.com; Main Rd; r K50,000-109,000; ❇🛜) There were some renovations going on at this beachside property when we dropped by, the three-storey deluxe sea-view rooms were finished and sleep up to three in good comfort with plenty of facilities. A major plus is the hotel's Grand Bistro restaurant and attached bakery, offering not only fresh bakes but also the promise of authentic cappuccino (electricity supply permitting!).

Shwe Hin Tha Hotel HOTEL **$$**

(🖉 042-42118; Main Rd; r incl breakfast & dinner $40-60; ❇🛜) Located near the bus drop-off point, this is Chaung Tha's most popular backpacker choice, possibly because of its breezy seaside bar. The rooms and bungalows are unremarkable, but it's located at the quiet northern end of the beach and has intermittent wi-fi.

Diamond Hotel HOTEL **$$**

(🖉 042-42380; Main Rd; r $40-90; ❇🛜🏊) The bungalow-based rooms here are large enough, but leave you rather close to your neighbour. Rooms come with amenities such as TV and fridge and rainbow-coloured balustrade on the balconies. There's a small pool and hot showers at night when the power is on.

Golden Beach Hotel RESORT **$$**

(🖉 042-42128; Main Rd; r K55,000-88,000; ❇🛜🏊) This 56-room resort doesn't have the park-like manicured grounds that others do, but the hotel room–style duplex bungalows are in good shape and there's a very nice swimming pool. The cheapest rooms don't face the sea.

Hotel Ayeyarwady HOTEL **$$**

(🖉 042-42332; Main Rd; r K40,000; ❇🛜) Located across the road from the beach just south of the market intersection, this turquoise-painted 1960s-style 'motel' complex offers simple but tidy rooms. Cold water showers only, we're afraid.

Belle Resort RESORT **$$$**

(🖉 042-42112; www.belleresorts.com; Main Rd; r $76-115; ❇🛜🏊) The rooms are understated sophistication with sprawling beds, massive windows with equally massive ocean views and satellite TV. Enter the stylish bathrooms and things get even better with hot water throughout the day. Downsides are that wi-fi is best in the lobby, service can be a bit patchy and food is not brilliant.

Hotel Max RESORT **$$$**

(🖉 042-42346; www.maxhotelsgroup.com; Main Rd; r $70-250; ❇@🛜🏊) Offering a smidge more electricity than other properties, this crony-built place is as fancy as it gets for Chaung Tha. It's well run and maintained but the rooms lack feel dowdy and old-fashioned compared to Belle Resort.

🍴 Eating

Unlike at nearby Ngwe Saung, there aren't many independent restaurants here, so plan on eating most of your meals at your resort.

A standout during our visit was **Shwe Ya Min Restaurant** (mains K1500-2000; ⊙ all day), where the service is charming and more than a bit of care goes into the food. The menu at this attractive guesthouse-based restaurant is largely seafood-based and includes all the Myanmar and Chinese-Burmese staples. And even if you're not staying here, you'd be well advised to consider the restaurant's famous breakfast, which features thick, sweet Myanmar-style pancakes.

Also of note is the **Grand Bistro** and **Bakery** at the Grand Hotel; the bakery supplies baked goods to all the other hotels in the

BUSES FROM CHAUNG THA BEACH

DESTINATION	FARE (K)	DURATION (HR)	DEPARTURE	TYPE
Yangon	8000	7½	6am	bus
Yangon	10,000	7½	9.30am	air-con bus
Pathein	4000	2½	7am, 9am, 11am, 1pm	minibus

area and in high season churns out muffins, doughnuts, cakes and other sweet treats.

ℹ Information

A long-established guide on the Chaung Tha scene is Mr George, who along with his family members operates out of **Tourist Information Chaung Tha Beach** (🕿 09 4973 4562; www. myanmartravelbeach.weebly.com; Main Rd) opposite Shwe Hin Tha Hotel.

Also reliable, friendly and less pricey is **Ko Chit Kaung**, who runs the parasol showroom and souvenir shop near Shwe Yan Min – contact him via the Shwe Yan Min guesthouse. Both can arrange snorkelling trips, day trips and various modes of transport around the area.

ℹ Getting There & Around

The twisting 25-mile road between Chaung Tha and Pathein can be traversed in two hours by private car; buses and minibuses usually take about 2½ hours. The route passes through rubber plantations spread across the hills – it's a depressing example of the effects of deforestation. Over half the villages passed along the way are Kayin.

BUS

For buses to Yangon, the 9.30am departure by Asia Dragon is the most comfortable and terminates more conveniently at Aung San Stadium in the downtown area rather than Hlaing Thar Yar Bus Terminal in the west of the city.

To continue up the coast to Gwa, and from there to Ngapali, you'll first have to return to Pathein. From there take a bus to Nga Thein Chaung (one hour) where you'll have to change buses for Gwa (four hours). From Gwa it's around eight hours to Ngapali, so reckon on the trip taking around two days and having to overnight in Gwa.

MOTORBIKE

Motorbike taxis can be hired to take you to Pathein (K12,000) or directly to Ngwe Saung Beach (K18,000).

BOAT

If it's calm, consider taking a boat (seats six; K65,000, two hours) to and from Ngwe Saung. This is handy if you're in a group but be prepared to wade ashore with your bags and ask to be dropped as close to your hotel as possible. Bring plenty of water and sunblock.

TAXI

Share taxis for up to four people to Pathein (K50,000), Ngwe Saung (K50,000) and Yangon (K150,000) can be arranged with your hotel's assistance.

Ngwe Saung Beach ငွေဆောင်ကမ်းခြေ

Forgive us for thinking that Ngwe Saung Beach has a split personality. These days the northern end of the beach has the air of a weekend getaway destination for nouveau-riche Yangonites, and is home to an uninterrupted chain of walled, upscale resorts. At the southern end a palpable abandoned aura pervades, and this is where you'll find foreign backpackers and budget bungalows. The factor linking these two disparate places is an attractive 13-mile string of sand and palms that, although it won't rate as one of the region's best beaches, has finer sand and clearer and deeper water than nearby Chaung Tha Beach.

⊙ Sights & Activities

Above all else Ngwe Saung is an indulgent, lie-back-and-do-absolutely-nothing sort of beach, and most visitors are happy to comply; the kind of beachside activities that are common at Chaung Tha, such as food sellers and pony rides, are noticeably absent here. However, if sitting around doing nothing more strenuous than wiggling your toes in the sand sounds boring then there are a few calorie-burning activities you can take part in.

A boat trip out to **Bird Island**, just visible way out on the horizon, for a day of snorkelling and, dare we say it, birdwatching, is the most popular water-based excursion. Boats can be arranged through many hotels for between $65 and $85, depending on the size of your group and the boat it will require.

If you don't have the stomach or budget for a boat trip, at low tide you can simply walk over to **Lovers' Island** at the southern end of the beach. The water surrounding this island is also a good place to **snorkel** among dancing clouds of tropical fish. Masks and snorkels can be hired from some hotels (Shwe Hin Tha Hotel and Treasure Resort are the most reliable) for K2500 per day. Diving trips can be arranged via the dive shop **Zawgyi** in the village.

Further south of Lovers' Island is the new Ngwe Saung Yacht Club & Hotel constructed for the Southeast Asian (SEA) Games in 2013; a marina is planned and it's possible you may be able to arrange sailing trips from here.

Halfway between Ngwe Saung and Pathein is an **elephant camp** (admission $5, elephant rides $10; ⏱8am-noon). Around five working elephants live here and it's possible to go for a 30-minute elephant ride through the forest – the romance of which wears off in about 30 seconds. If you thought horses attracted a lot of large biting insects, just wait until you get on the back of an elephant! To get there, hop on any outbound bus, or Tom Tom at Sandalwood (p96) can arrange a motorcycle taxi for about $10.

🛏 Sleeping

Ngwe Saung was one of the venues for the SEA Games in December 2013, which meant that there was a fair amount of construction and upgrading of properties going on when we visited. **Ngwe Saung Yacht Club & Hotel**, which includes a camping ground with two- and four-person tents, should be worth checking out.

There are few budget places here and those that do exist are of a pretty poor quality. The midrange is reasonably well served but at these places you'll only be granted electicity between 6pm and 6am. For anything close to 24-hour power you'll need to check into one of the top end resorts.

Silver Coast Beach Hotel　　HOTEL **$$**
(☎042-40324; htoo.maw@mptmail.net.mm; r $25-60; ❄) At the southern end of the beach, steps from Lovers' Island, this secluded resort is a bargain-hunter's fantasy, featuring reasonably well-maintained beachside bungalows. The cheaper ones have no air-conditioning or hot water, but you'll rarely need that in high season.

There's plenty of space and hardly a soul around to disturb the peace of your own slab of palm-bedecked perfection.

Shwe Hin Tha Hotel　　HOTEL **$$**
(☎042-40340; bungalows $25-50; ❄) Set at the blissful southern end of the beach, this place has a magnetic pull for backpackers who agonise over whether to opt for cheap-and-simple bamboo huts or one of the more solid, no-frills bungalows. Either way they can be sure that it will be clean and well maintained and that hot water will appear on request.

There's a book exchange, various travel services and plenty of like-minded clientele to waste away the days with.

EFR Seconda Casa　　HOTEL **$$**
(www.efrsecondacasa.com; Myoma St; r $55 & $70; ❄@🛜) Slap in the middle of the village strip, with beach access, is this newish and appealing place offering two grades of room: the cheaper (and nicer) rattan and wood huts with mattress on the floor, or the concrete rooms with rooftop viewing decks.

Silver View Resort　　HOTEL **$$**
(☎042-40317; silverviewresort@gmail.com; r $45 & 55; ❄🛜) Also located south of the village and popular with vacationing locals, this attractive, compact compound offers mint-green painted bungalows, most offering sea views, and all well maintained. The restaurant promises wi-fi.

⭐ **Bay of Bengal Resort**　　RESORT **$$$**
(☎042-40304; www.bayofbengalresort.com; r/ste from $150/180; ❄@🛜⛱) Quite possibly the poshest beach resort in Myanmar, this immense compound dominates the far northern end of Ngwe Saung. The ground-floor Bengal Suites have a spacious sitting area and huge balcony, and bathrooms with a stone tub and an open-air shower. Reasons to leave your room include tennis courts, a huge pool and a spa.

Nonguests can dip into to the pool for K5000 and the Pier Restaurant is a lovely place to dine with an extensive international menu and prices that are not too steep, considering.

Emerald Sea Resort　　RESORT **$$$**
(☎042-40247; www.emeraldseahotel.com; r $110, bungalows $120-140; ❄🛜⛱) Located south of the village, this cosy resort may not be as flashy as the newer places along the beach, but it makes up for it with attractive design

and excellent service. The rooms themselves are beautifully created with minimal decor, making the virgin-white and very comfortable interiors all the more classy.

There's a decent restaurant (advance notice is often required), a spa and a beautiful stretch of beach out front. Electricity is only 24 hours in high season.

Sunny Paradise Resort
RESORT $$$

(☏042-40227; www.sunnyparadiseresort.com; r $65-260; ❈@♠❀) Yet another imposing compound north of the village, Sunny Paradise also includes two adjacent properties: Dream Paradise and Ocean Paradise (offering the cheapest rooms with no direct beach access). The attractive wooden bungalows in the Sunny Paradise section are the pick of the rooms, with pricetags from $200 upward.

Aureum Palace
RESORT $$$

(☏042-40218; www.aureumpalacehotel.com; r/ villa from $160/240; ❈@♠❀) Designed in glitzy royal Myanmar style with plenty of gilded traditional carvings and soaring teak pillars, the Aureum is exactly the kind of place you'd expect a crony such as Tay Za to own. Nonetheless the standards are high and it's professionally run with the promise of round-the-clock power.

The cheapest rooms are on the small side.

✖ Eating

Break out of your hotel restaurant at least once in order to eat in the village, where there is a good range of cheap restaurants. There is little to distinguish one from another – most places share a facsimile menu that focuses on seafood-based dishes prepared in the Chinese style.

★ Royal Flower
ASIAN, SEAFOOD $$

(Myoma St; mains K4000; ⊙6-10pm; 🖻) Offering by far the classiest ambiance of Ngwe Saung's same-same restaurants, Royal Flower distinguishes itself with the nightly concerts by a mellow guitar-playing duo – and you're welcome to join in if you can play or sing. The grilled fish is excellent.

West Point
ASIAN, SEAFOOD $$

(www.facebook.com/westpointseafoodrestaurant; Myoma St; mains K4000; ⊙8am-10pm; 🖻) The closest thing you'll get to seaside dining in the village (the view is distant!), West Point is nonetheless a breezy and pleasant joint to pick from a menu offering all the usual seafood, Chinese and Thai offerings as well as Rakhine dishes.

Golden Myanmar Restaurant
CHINESE, BURMESE $$

(mains K2000-4000; ⊙7am-10pm; 🖻) When asked for a good place to eat, most locals will point you in the direction of this place, located in the middle of the village and larger than most of its brethren. The prawn curry we sampled was tasty and fresh.

❶ Information

Located towards the northern end of the village, **Sandalwood** (☏09 856 8130), a cafe-information centre, is the place to go for local info. Ask for local expert and guide Tom Tom, who can arrange a day trip or snorkelling excursion, and rents motorcycles. If he's not here, Tom Tom can also be found at the Shwe Hin Tha Hotel or another Sandalwood tea shop in the market behind the main village strip (accessed off the road on the left, heading out of town towards the pagoda).

❶ Getting There & Around

Air-con buses to Yangon (K9000, six hours) leave at 6.30am and 8am. For Pathein (K3000, two hours), minibuses go at 7am, 8am, 9am, 11am and 3pm. The buses leave and arrive at the junction between the village and the beach resorts.

Taxis can be arranged for Pathein (K40,000) and Yangon (K110,000).

There are a few trishaws available to carry you between the resorts and the village (K1000), and motorbikes (with or without a driver) can be hired via Sandalwood or from some hotels for about K12,000 per day including fuel.

Southern Myanmar

Best Places to Eat

➡ San Ma Tau Myanmar Restaurant (p112)

➡ Daw Yee (p105)

➡ Hla Hla Hnan (p118)

Best Places to Stay

➡ Cinderella Hotel (p105)

➡ Golden Sunrise Hotel (p101)

➡ Hotel Zwegabin (p112)

➡ Garden Hotel (p117)

➡ Soe Brothers Guesthouse (p111)

➡ Sandalwood Hotel (p105)

➡ Mountain Top Hotel (p101)

Why Go?

In addition to being largely unexplored, far off the beaten track and tragically neglected (do you get the picture?), the pleasures of southern Myanmar exist on a variety of other levels.

The caves around sleepy Hpa-an will escort visitors to unparalleled depths and darkness, while the ascent to the sacred golden boulder at Mt Kyaiktiyo (Golden Rock) might have you believing that you've gone to heaven. And somewhere in-between are the history-soaked coastal cities of Mawlamyine and Myeik. Yet perhaps the region's, if not the country's, most dramatic intersection of water, land and sky is the Myeik Archipelago, home to some of the most gorgeous – and untouched – coastline in Southeast Asia.

And did we mention that you'll probably be the only one there?

When to Go

Southeastern Myanmar

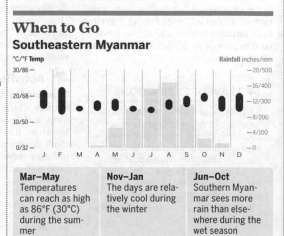

Mar–May	Nov–Jan	Jun–Oct
Temperatures can reach as high as 86°F (30°C) during the summer	The days are relatively cool during the winter	Southern Myanmar sees more rain than elsewhere during the wet season

MON STATE

Mon State (မွန်ပြည်နယ်) seems to have a bit of everything that's wonderful about Myanmar: golden temples, a palpable colonial past, charming villages and even some scenic coastline. Travelling in this region is generally easy (at least, for Myanmar), relatively free from bureaucracy, and the distances short; yet, strangely, few visitors seem to make it down here.

History

Once native to a broad region stretching from southern Myanmar to Cambodia, the Mon have been absorbed – sometimes willingly, sometimes unwillingly – by the more powerful Burmese and Thai cultures in Myanmar and Thailand respectively over the last thousand years.

Though no one knows for sure, the Mon may be descended from a group of Indian immigrants from Kalinga, an ancient kingdom overlapping the boundaries of the modern Indian states of Orissa and Andhra Pradesh. They are responsible for much of the early transmission of Theravada Buddhism in mainland Southeast Asia.

Since 1949 the eastern hills of the state (as well as mountains further south in Tanintharyi Region) have been a refuge for the New Mon State Party (NMSP) and its tactical arm, the Mon National Liberation Front (MNLF), whose objective has been self-rule for Mon State. In 1995, after years of bickering and fighting, the NMSP signed a ceasefire with the Myanmar government. Since then, peace has largely been maintained, and as of 2013, foreign travellers have tentatively been allowed to travel by land to previously off-limits areas south of Mawlamyine.

ℹ TRAVEL RESTRICTIONS

It's possible to travel as south as Mawlamyine by train, or to Dawei by bus, but beyond this point foreign tourists who wish to continue southward are generally required to take a boat or fly. Likewise, foreign travellers wishing to travel between Myanmar's southernmost cities, Dawei, Myeik and Kawthoung, can generally only do so by plane or boat.

Mt Kyaiktiyo (Golden Rock)
ကျိုက်ထီးရိုးတောင်

🎵 057

We'll admit it: a giant gilded rock on the top of a mountain seems like an odd, perhaps even gaudy, destination. But there really is something special about the boulder stupa of Kyaiktiyo.

The monument, an enormous, precariously balanced boulder coated in gold and topped with a stupa, is a major pilgrimage site for Myanmar Buddhists. Its image adorns many a local's car windscreen or family hearth, and every good Buddhist dreams of the day he finally set eyes on this holiest of shrines.

Not surprisingly, the atmosphere surrounding Kyaiktiyo during the height of the pilgrimage season (from November to March) is charged with magic and devotion: pilgrims chant, light candles and meditate all through the night; men (only) are permitted to walk along a short causeway and over a bridge spanning a chasm to the boulder to affix gold leaf squares on the rock's surface. And the boulder itself is stunning, especially when bathed in the purple, sometimes misty, light of dawn and dusk.

During the rainy season (June to October) the mountain is covered in a downright chilly and nearly permanent coat of mist, fog and rain. Although the area's hotels are open during this period, most restaurants and food stalls aren't, and the majority of pilgrims are foreigners.

There are several other stupas and shrines scattered on the ridge at the top of Mt Kyaiktiyo, though none is as impressive as Kyaiktiyo itself. Even so, the interconnecting trails sometimes lead to unexpected views of the valleys below.

🏃 Activities

Climbing the Mountain

Kinpun, a busy hub of restaurants, souvenir shops and hotels, is the base camp for Mt Kyaiktiyo. It's from here that large trucks climb the seven winding, uphill miles to the rock (per person K2500). The truck beds are lined with padded wooden slats for benches and seat about 40 people. Five passengers are allowed in the much more comfortable front seats (per person K3000) but these are usually reserved in advance by groups or families. As an individual traveller it's difficult to secure a

1 Sail, cruise, snorkel, dive or simply beach bum among the 800+ islands of the **Myeik Archipelago** (p122).

2 Reach for enlightenment at the golden, gravity-defying **Mt Kyaiktiyo (Golden Rock)** (p98).

3 Discover seemingly hidden lakes, hanging Buddhist art and a sparkling spring in the **caves** around Hpa-an (p113).

4 Compose prose to rival Kipling's *'By the old Moulmein Pagoda, lookin' lazy at the sea'* in go-slow **Mawlamyine** (p102).

5 Travel back in time at the historic, atmospheric and allegedly haunted port city of **Myeik** (p119).

6 Exploring the remote ruins, sacred temples, unknown beaches and one ogre-infested island **around Mawlamyine** (p106).

7 Be among the scant handful of foreign tourists to have visited the sleepy southern capital of **Dawei** (p117).

LEGEND OF THE BALANCING BOULDER

Legend states that the boulder at Mt Kyaiktiyo maintains its precarious balance due to a precisely placed Buddha hair in the stupa. Apparently King Tissa received the Buddha hair in the 11th century from a hermit who had secreted the hair in his own topknot. The hermit instructed the king to search for a boulder that had a shape resembling the hermit's head, and then enshrine the hair in a stupa on top. The king, who inherited supernatural powers as a result of his birth to a *zawgyi* (an accomplished alchemist) father and *naga* (dragon serpent) princess, found the rock at the bottom of the sea. Upon its miraculous arrival on the mountain top, the boat used to transport the rock then turned to stone. This stone can be seen approximately 270yd from the main boulder – it's known as the Kyaukthanban (Stone Boat Stupa).

front seat, while a group of five has a better chance. Regardless, you could be in for a wait of an hour or more, as trucks don't leave until they are completely packed to the brim.

The ride takes about 45 minutes and usually includes a stop around halfway up to allow trucks coming from the opposite direction to pass. The first truck in the morning leaves at 6am and the last truck down departs at 6pm, though you should try to be at the terminal earlier to avoid the risk of being stranded for the night.

In the old days trucks only went as high as Yatetaung terminal, leaving pilgrims with a 45-minute, unforgiving uphill, sweaty schlep to the top. Nowadays the trucks proceed virtually to the peak of Mt Kyaiktiyo, terminating steps from Mountain Top Hotel and the ticket checkpoint, leaving us to ask, Where's the sacrifice?

Perhaps it's the requisite K6000 entrance fee for foreigners, payable a short walk from the truck terminal, just after the Mountain Top Hotel. Tickets are valid for two days. Women wearing shorts or skimpy tops risk being denied entry.

Hiking & Other Activities

If you have the time to extend your stay in the vicinity there are several other rewarding hikes that take in eye-popping views and quiet religious meditation. You can start your journey from Kinpun, the Yatetaung bus terminal, or even the shrine itself.

From Kinpun the most obvious short hike is to Maha Myaing Pagoda (မဟာမြိုင်ဘုရား), a miniature Kyaiktiyo, an hour's climb from Kinpun. Any of the Kinpun hotels can point you in the right direction.

From Yatetaung bus station it's a 45-minute climb to the top of Mt Ya-The (ရသေ့တောင်), a 30-minute walk down to Mo-Baw Waterfall (မိုးဘောရေတံခွန်) and a 1½-hour walk to

the Sa-ma-taung Paya and Kyaung (monastery; ဆမတောင်ဘုရား၊ဆမတောင်ကျောင်း).

From Kyaiktiyo itself a trail continues along the crests of the surrounding peaks for another couple of hours to the Kyauk-si-yo Zedi (ကျောက်ဆည်ရိုးစေတီ) and Kyaik-tiyo Galay Paya (ကျိုက်ထီးရိုးကလေးစေတီ).

If you'd like to spend more time in the area or want to give something back to the community, the Seik Phu Taung Youth Development Centre (☎ 057-60353; www.facebook.com/SeikPhuTaungYouthDevelopmentCentre), located between Kyaikto and Kinpun, is an established, temple-based orphanage that accepts volunteer English teachers. Basic food and lodging is provided and a minimum stay of two weeks is the norm.

Sleeping & Eating

Although Kyaiktiyo can be visited as a day trip from Bago and, in theory, Yangon, this isn't recommended; the advantage of staying near the shrine is that you can catch sunset and sunrise – the most magical times.

Because Kinpun is the starting point for Mt Kyaiktiyo, there are numerous restaurants along the town's main street, capitalising on the mountain's popularity. Similarly, there is a veritable food court of restaurants at the summit, past the shrines and plaza area and down the steps. It's worth noting that foreigners aren't permitted to stay in one of the many *zayat* (rest shelters) for pilgrims at the top.

On the Mountain

If you want to catch the best light and most enchanting atmosphere at the shrine (and yes, you do) then you simply have no choice but to stay at one of the four overpriced hotels near the top.

Mountain Top Hotel
HOTEL **$$**

(☎09 871 8392, in Yangon 01-502 479; grtt@golden
rock.com.mm; r incl breakfast $100-120; ❄️🛜)
Yes, the rooms in the Mountain Top Inn are
grossly overpriced, but they're clean and well
maintained, with good service. It is also situ-
ated right on the summit of the mountain
only a couple of moments' stroll to the shrine
complex – an unbeatable position. The more
expensive 'deluxe' rooms have air-con, a TV, a
mini bar and great views.

Yoe Yoe Lay Hotel
HOTEL **$$**

(no roman-script sign; ☎09 872 3082; www.yoe
yoelayhotel.com; r incl breakfast $80-100; ❄️)
Towering over the pilgrims' village north of
the boulder, the Yoe Yoe Lay packs a spread
of clean but generally bland and overpriced
rooms, some new and claiming great views,
others needing an update. The place is worth
seeking out at night when it's lit up like a
gaudy Christmas tree.

Kyaik Hto Hotel
HOTEL **$$**

(☎094 981 9196, in Yangon 01-392 801; www.
kyaikhto.com; r incl breakfast $75-140; ❄️🛜) This
former government-owned hotel is where
most package tourists stay. It's unremarkable
and rather institutional-feeling, but has the
benefit of being located a short walk from the
Golden Rock. We've come across reports of
things missing from rooms here, so take care
to look after your valuables if you choose to
stay here.

Golden Rock Hotel
HOTEL **$$**

(☎09 871 8391; grtt@goldenrock.com.mm; r incl
breakfast $80-100; ❄️) The Golden Rock Hotel,
just a few minutes up from the Yatetaung bus
terminal, has recently renovated, comfortable
rooms in a secluded-feeling location. The only
problem is that its positioning – halfway between everywhere but not really anywhere –
makes it inconvenient both for accessing the
boulder and food and drink.

🛏️ Kinpun

Bawga Theiddhi Hotel
HOTEL **$**

(no roman-script sign; ☎094 92 99899; r incl breakfast $20-80; ❄️🛜) Kinpun's newest – and
flashiest – hotel has rooms that are clean,
spacious and equipped with TV, fridge and
free wi-fi, making them good value.

Sea Sar Hotel
HOTEL **$**

(☎09 872 3288; r incl breakfast $10-35; ❄️🛜) The
rooms here cover a lot of ground, some good,
some not so good. The best are the various air-

con bungalows out back, some of which are
relatively new and attractive.

Pann Myo Thu Inn
GUESTHOUSE **$**

(☎057-60285, 094 981 8038; r incl breakfast $6-35;
❄️) Sprawling around the home of a local
family, the somewhat aged-feeling cheapest
rooms here are fan-cooled and share bathrooms. The newer 'bungalow' rooms offer a
lot more space and air-con.

★ Golden Sunrise Hotel
HOTEL **$$**

(☎09 872 3301, in Yangon 01-701 027; www.golden
sunrisehotel.com; s/d incl breakfast $45/58; ❄️) A
few minutes' walk outside the centre of Kin-
pun village in the direction of the highway, the
Golden Sunrise is one of the best-value hotels
in southern Myanmar. The low-slung, semi-
detached rooms are undisturbed by noise,
decked out with attractive wood furniture,
and are immaculately clean. The private ve-
randas overlooking the secluded gardens are
the perfect place to relax at the end of the day
with a drink.

ℹ️ Getting There & Away

The major transport hub for Mt Kyaiktiyo is the
similar-sounding town of Kyaikto. This is where
the train station is, and the town's main street is
where you'll board (or disembark from) buses.
Frequent pick-ups cruise the road between
Kyaikto's train station and Kinpun from 7am to
4pm (K500, 20 minutes).

The one destination you might consider using
a train to get to is Kyaiktiyo. Every Saturday a
service using air-conditioned carriages departs
for the Golden Rock at 6.25am ($10; 4½ hours);
it returns on Sunday at noon arriving in Yangon,
in theory, at 4.25pm. The air-conditioned car-
riages are eventually destined to be used on the
Yangon Circle Line, once station platforms on
that route have been upgraded.

Tickets for relatively comfortable Win Express
buses can be purchased in Kinpun across from
Sea Sar Hotel. The ticket price includes truck
fare to Kyaikto.

DESTINATION	BUS	TRAIN
Bago	K5000; 3hr; frequent 8am-4pm	N/A
Hpa-an	K5000; 3hr; frequent 11am-4pm	N/A
Mawlamyine	K7000; 4hr; frequent 11am-4pm	$3-6; 4hr; daily noon & 11.30pm
Yangon	K5000; 5hr; frequent 8am-4pm	$3-8; 5hr; daily noon & midnight

Mawlamyine မော်လမြိုင်

📍 057 / POPULATION C300,000

With a ridge of stupa-capped hills on one side, the sea on the other and a centre filled with mosques and crumbling colonial-era buildings, Mawlamyine is a unique combination of landscape, beauty and melancholy. Indeed, the setting inspired two of history's finest writers of the English language – George Orwell and Rudyard Kipling. Orwell lived here for some years (his famous 1936 essay 'Shooting an Elephant' is about an experience he had as a police officer in Mawlamyine), and generations of his fam-

ily were born and bred here. Relatively little has changed since those days, and if you've wondered what life was like during the Raj, Mawlamyine is about as close as it comes to a living time capsule. But it's not all about history; the area around Mawlamyine has enough attractions, from beaches to caves, to keep a visitor happy for several days.

Formerly known as Moulmein, the city served as the capital of British Burma from 1826 to 1852, during which time it developed as a major teak port. A great deal of coastal shipping still goes on, although Pathein and Yangon have superseded it as Myanmar's most important ports. The

Mawlamyine

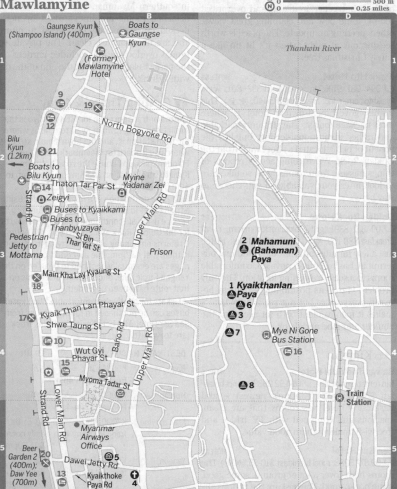

city is composed roughly of 75% Mon, plus Kayin (Karen), Bamar, Indian, Chinese and other ethnic groups.

⊙ Sights & Activities

★**Kyaikthanlan Paya** BUDDHIST TEMPLE
(ကျိုက်သံလန်ဘုရား; Kyaik Than Lan Phayar St; ⊙daylight hours) FREE Rudyard Kipling's visit to Myanmar allegedly only spanned three days, but this stint resulted in a few lines of prose that turned Burma into an oriental fantasy: 'By the old Moulmein Pagoda, lookin' lazy at the sea…' The 'Moulmein Pagoda' cited in the poem 'Mandalay' was most likely **Kyaikthanlan Paya**, the city's tallest and most visible stupa.

A favoured spot for watching the sunset, the best way to approach the temple complex is via the long covered walkway that extends from Kyaik Than Lan Phayar St. This walkway also had an impact on Kipling, who was later to comment of it: 'I should better remember what the pagoda was like had I not fallen deeply and irrevocably in love with a Burmese girl at the foot of the first flight of steps. Only the fact of the steamer starting next noon prevented me from staying at Moulmein forever.'

Directly north and linked by a covered walkway is **Mahamuni (Bahaman) Paya** (မဟာမုနိ(ဗြဟ္မာ)ဘုရား; ⊙daylight hours) FREE, the largest temple complex and easily the most beautiful in Mawlamyine. It's built in the typical Mon style with covered brick walkways linking various shrines. The highlight is the Bahaman Paya itself, a jewel-box chamber shimmering with mirrors, rubies and diamonds and containing a century-old replica of its namesake in Mandalay.

Below Kyaikthanlan is the 100-year-old **Selndon Mibaya Kyaung** (စိန်တုံးမိဖုရားကျောင်း; ⊙daylight hours) FREE, a monastery where King Mindon Min's queen, Seindon, sought refuge after King Thibaw Min, took power. On the next rise south stands the isolated silver-and-gold-plated **Aung Theikdi Zedi** (အောင်သိဒ္ဓိစေတီ; ⊙daylight hours) FREE.

U Khanti Paya (ဦးခန္တီဘုရား; ⊙daylight hours) FREE was built to commemorate the hermit architect of Mandalay Hill fame; supposedly U Khanti spent some time on this hill as well. It's a rustic, airy sort of place centred around a large buddha image.

U Zina Paya (ဦးဇိနဘုရား; ⊙daylight hours) FREE, on the southern spur of the ridge, was named after a former monk who dreamt of finding gems at this very spot, then dug them up and used the proceeds to build a temple on the same site. One of the shrine buildings contains a very curvy, sensual-looking reclining buddha; there are also statues depicting Gautama Buddha's meeting with a sick man, an old man, a dead man and an ascetic – encounters that encouraged him to seek a meaning behind human suffering.

Mon Cultural Museum MUSEUM
(မွန်ယဉ်ကျေးမှုပြတိုက်; cnr Baho & Dawei Jetty Rds; admission K2000; ⊙10am-4.30pm Tue-Sun) Recently renovated, and unlike most of Myanmar's regional museums, actually worth a visit, Mawlamyine's museum is dedicated to the Mon history of the region. The collection includes stelae with Mon inscriptions, 100-year-old wooden sculptures depicting old age and sickness (used as *dhamma*-teaching devices in monasteries), ceramics,

SOUTHERN MYANMAR MAWLAMYINE

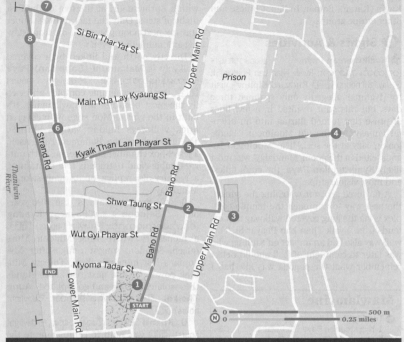

City Walk
Colonial Mawlamyine

START BAHO RD
FINISH STRAND RD
LENGTH 2.5 MILES; TWO TO THREE HOURS

Between 1826 and 1852 Mawlamyine was the capital of British Burma. An abundance of British residents, from officials to Anglo-Burmese, led to the city being known as 'Little England', a legacy still palpable in the architecture.

Start near the **1** **park** on Baho Rd, formerly known as Dalhousie St. Head north, turning east on **2** **Shwe Taung St** (look for the corner with the motorcycle taxi drivers), an atmospheric strip of brightly coloured, low-slung houses, home to the descendants of Indian civil servants. Cross Upper Main Rd to **3** **St Patrick's Cathedral** founded by the De La Salle brothers in 1829. At the back of the church compound is an overgrown graveyard with headstones, many with English names, some dating back to the mid-19th century.

Head north on Upper Main Rd. If you haven't already been, turn east on Kyaik Than Lan Phayar St and ascend the covered stair-

way to **4** **Kyaikthanlan Paya** (p103) – most likely the inspiration for Kipling's 'Mandalay'. From here you'll also have a great view of Mawlamyine's prison, built in 1908 and possibly the setting for George Orwell's lesser-known 1931 short story *A Hanging*.

Head west on Kyaik Than Lan Phayar St, veering south into any of the atmospheric side streets and taking in the tiny mosques and colonial-era homes in this, the predominately Muslim neighbourhood of **5** **Shwe Taung Quarter**. Emerge on **6** **Lower Main Rd**, Mawlamyine's main commercial strip, home to many old multistorey shophouses. Continue north until you reach **7** **Surtee Sunni Jamae Masjid**, a mosque built in 1846 to serve the Muslim officers and civil servants of British Burma.

Continue north, turning west on Phat Tan St. You're now on the riverside **8** **Strand Rd**, where, heading south, you'll pass the former grand mansions, shipping company offices and theatres that indicate Mawlamyine's former role as a wealthy trading port.

silver betel boxes, royal funerary urns and Mon musical instruments, most of which are accompanied by English-language descriptions.

Gaungse Kyun (Shampoo Island)
ISLAND

(ခေါင်းဆေးကျွန်း ; ⊙daylight hours) **FREE** This picturesque little isle just off Mawlamyine's northern end is so named because, during the Ava period, the yearly royal hair-washing ceremony customarily used water taken from a spring on the island.

You can hire a boat out here from the pier at the north end of town, not far from the former Mawlamyine Hotel, for around K2000 return.

Peace rather than sights is the reason for venturing out here, but you can visit Sandawshin Paya, a whitewash-and-silver *zedi* (stupa) said to contain hair relics, and a nearby Buddhist meditation centre. Many nuns, with a menagerie of pet dogs, live on the island.

First Baptist Church
CHURCH

(cnr Upper Main & Dawei Jetty Rds; ⊙daylight hours) **FREE** Founded by American Adoniram Judson in 1827, this was the country's first Baptist church. In addition to this place of worship, Judson's legacy also includes having been the first person to translate the Bible into Burmese. As a result of his work, today Myanmar has the third-highest population of Baptists in the world after the United States and India.

🛏 Sleeping

Most of Mawlamyine's accommodation is a K2000 motorcycle taxi ride from the train station or Mye Ni Gone bus station.

★ Cinderella Hotel
HOTEL $

(☏057-24411; www.cinderellahotel.com; 21 Baho Rd; r incl breakfast $25-65; ✲@🛜) Where else could you afford to stay in the nicest place in town? This shockingly purple structure has numerous and capable staff who look after huge rooms with heaps of amenities: 24-hour electricity, TV, air-con, wi-fi and huge fridges positively stuffed with junk food.

Sandalwood Hotel
HOTEL $

(☏057-27253; 278 Myoma Tadar St; r incl breakfast $15-50; ✲🛜) A modern multistorey hotel, conveniently located in 'downtown' Mawlamyine. The tile-walled rooms are spacious and spotless, if a tad institutional. Communicating in English can be problematic.

Breeze Guest House
BACKPACKER HOTEL $

(☏057-21450; breeze.guesthouse@gmail.com; 6 Strand Rd; r incl breakfast $7-25; ✲🛜) The rooms aren't much but the staff at this colonial-style villa on Strand Rd are an endless source of information, pleasant conversation and superb guiding skills.

OK Hotel
HOTEL $

(☏057-25097; okhotel.mlm@gmail.com; cnr Strand Rd & Thaton Tar Par St; s/d incl breakfast $20/30; ✲) Street noise and tiny size aside, these capable budget rooms near the market area represent good value.

Shwe Myint Mo Tun Hotel
HOTEL $

(☏057-27347; r incl breakfast $25-40; ✲🛜✲) The pool here – Mawlamyine's only one – is the highlight of this new hotel. Otherwise the rooms, located in four-room bungalows or a two-storey poolside structure, are pretty standard and rather gaudily decorated.

Ngwe Moe Hotel
HOTEL $

(☏057-24703; cnr Kyaikthoke Paya & Strand Rds; s/d incl breakfast $35/45; ✲🛜) Located in a large building overlooking the river on Strand Rd, the rooms here are clean and comfortable and come with air-con, TV and fridge, but not a lot of character.

Mawlamyaing Strand Hotel
HOTEL $$

(☏057-25624; www.mawlamyaingstrandhotel.com; Strand Rd; r incl breakfast $60-110; ✲@🛜) Mawlamyine's biggest and flashiest hotel has four storeys of spacious and modern rooms that are on par with business-class rooms just about anywhere else – with the added benefit of great views over the town and river.

Attran Hotel
HOTEL $$

(☏057-25764; www.attranhotel.com; Strand Rd; r incl breakfast $50-80; ✲🛜) Overlooking the river is this orderly plot of comfortable, if dull, cement bungalows. 'River View' rooms are larger and in addition to the space and views, include wide-screen TV and fridge.

🍴 Eating & Drinking

★ Daw Yee
BURMESE $

(no roman-script sign; off Strand Rd; meals from K2000; ⊙9am-10pm) Simply put, humble Daw Yee does some of the best Burmese food we've come across in the country. Highlights of our meal included an insanely fatty prawn curry and a deliciously tart soup of young tamarind leaves and tiny shrimp. The only downside is locating it; continue south along Strand Rd until you see Beer Garden 2, then start asking the locals for Daw Yee – everybody knows it.

Mi Cho Restaurant MUSLIM-BURMESE $
(no roman-script sign; North Bogyoke Rd; meals from K1500; ⊘10am-9pm) This busy hole-in-the-wall serves excellent Muslim-style Burmese cuisine, in particular a rich biryani and a delicious dhal soup. There's no English-language sign here; look for the green awning.

Beer Garden 2 BURMESE $
(58 Strand Rd; meals from K3000; ⊘9am-10.30pm; 📶) Simply select your vegies and proteins from the refrigerators and staff will slather them with a delicious, spicy sauce and grill them for you.

May South Indian Chetty Food INDIAN-BURMESE $
(cnr Strand Rd & Main Kha Lay Kyaung St; meals from K1500; ⊘9am-9pm) This place specialises in comically cheap South Indian-influenced 'chetty' set meals: choose your curry and rice and a seemingly endless succession of soups, dips and other spicy sides will follow.

Grandfather and Grandmother Restaurant CHINESE-BURMESE $
(Strand Rd; mains K1000-2500; ⊘6.30am-10pm; 📶) Does what it says on the label; the money raised at this teashop-cum-restaurant goes to a charity helping the town's elderly. The sign is written in Burmese only; look for silhouettes of old people walking with canes.

Mya Thanlwin Restaurant CHINESE-BURMESE $
(Strand Rd; mains K1000-3000; ⊘11am-11pm; 📶) The riverside setting and draught beer here are better draws than the mediocre dishes from the expansive English-language menu.

ⓘ Information

A **police station** (Strand Rd) is located over the road from the government jetties. The **post office** (Myoma Tadar St) is a couple of blocks further inland.

Mawlamyine's only international ATM is at **CB Bank** (Strand Rd; ⊘9.30am-3pm Mon-Fri); foreign exchange is available here, as well as at **AGD Bank** (Strand Rd; ⊘9.30am-2.30pm Mon-Fri) and **Myanmar Oriental Bank** ((MOB.); cnr Strand Rd & Main Kha Lay Kyaung St; ⊘10.30am-3pm Mon-Fri).

Internet is available at the **cafe** (21 Baho Rd; per hr K500; ⊘9am-9pm) at the Cinderella Hotel.

ⓘ Getting There & Away

At press time, **Myanma Airways** (📞09-871 8220, 21500; ⊘9am-3pm) was the only domestic airline flying out of Mawlamyine, while Thai airline **Nok Air** (📞in Yangon 01-533 030, international call centre +662 900 9955; www.nokair.com) operates a route between Mawlamyine and Mae Sot, in Thailand.

Public ferries used to run between Mawlamyine and Hpa-an, but this service was recently cancelled. Instead, contact Breeze Guest House to charter a boat (up to 14 people) for the two-hour trip to Hpa-an (K60,000).

Buses for destinations north of Mawlamyine use the **Mye Ni Gone bus station**, located near the train station; a motorcycle taxi to/from here should run about K2000. For routes south of Mawlamyine (including Myawaddy), head to **Zay Gyo bus station**, a couple miles south of the city; a motorcycle taxi to/from this station should run about K3000. Note that vans (actually share taxis) to Myawaddy depart only on odd-numbered days. When we were in town, foreigners were tentatively allowed to take the bus only as far south as Dawei, although this could very well change by the time you read this.

A press time, foreigners were not yet allowed to take trains to destinations south of Mawlamyine.

ⓘ Getting Around

Motorcycle taxis are found on just about every corner in Mawlamyine (short trips K500; longer journeys from K1000).

For destinations outside of town you'll want a driver. This can be arranged at Breeze Guest House, or you can call **Ko Min Naing** (📞09 730 75120, 057-22247), who has a new car and speaks a bit of English.

Around Mawlamyine

If you're finding Mawlamyine a bit too sleepy, you'll be delighted to find that the town functions as a great base for a variety of easy and worthwhile day trips.

Many people save themselves time and hassle by hiring a car (per day K60,000) and guide (per day $15) in order to explore fully. The best place to organise this is through the Breeze Guest House, where Mr Antony and Mr Khaing are both highly informed and entertaining guides.

TRANSPORT TO/FROM MAWLAMYINE

DESTINATION	BUS	TRAIN	VAN (SHARE TAXI)
Bago	K5100-10,000; 5hr; daily 8am, 9am, 1pm, 2pm, 7pm, 9pm, 8.30pm & midnight	$4-12; 7hr; daily 8am, 7.30pm & 9pm	N/A
Dawei	K8000-10,000; 10hr; 7pm	$6-15; 16hr; daily 4.30am & 7.20am	N/A
Hpa-an	K1050; 2hr; hourly 6am-4pm	N/A	N/A
Kawthoung	K38,000-40,000; 35hr; daily 7pm	N/A	N/A
Kyaikto (for Mt Kyaiktiyo; Golden Rock	K5100-10,000; 4hr; daily 8am, 9am, 1pm, 2pm, 7pm, 9pm, 8.30pm & midnight	$3-7; 4hr; daily 8am, 7.30pm & 9pm	N/A
Mandalay	K15,000; 13hr; daily 5pm & 6pm	N/A	N/A
Mae Sot (Thailand)	N/A	N/A	N/A
Myawaddy	N/A	N/A	K8000-10,000; 4-6hr; frequent 5-10am
Myeik	N/A	K15,000-17,000; 20hr; daily 7pm	N/A
Nay Pyi Taw	N/A	$8-22; 15hr; daily 6.15am	N/A
Pyin Oo Lwin	K16,500; 17hr; daily 5pm & 6pm	N/A	N/A
Yangon	K5100-10,000; 7hr; daily 8am, 9am, 1pm, 2pm, 7pm, 9pm, 8.30pm & midnight	$5-16; 10hr; daily 8am, 7.30pm & 9pm	N/A
Ye	N/A	$3-7; 6hr; daily 4.30am & 7.20am	K6000; 4hr; frequent 6am-1.30pm

North of Mawlamyine

👁 Sights

Nwa-la-bo Pagoda   BUDDHIST TEMPLE
(နွားလသိုဘုရား; ⊙ daylight hours) `FREE` A local pilgrimage site, Nwa-la-bo is still relatively unknown outside Mon State and, currently, very few foreigners make it out here. This is surprising because the pagoda is a smaller but, geologically at least, far more astonishing version of Kyaiktiyo. Unlike at that shrine, where just one huge boulder perches on the cliff ledge, Nwa-la-bo consists of three sausage-shaped **gold boulders** piled precariously atop one another and surmounted by a stupa.

ℹ Getting There & Away

Nwa-la-bo can't be reached during the rainy season (from approximately June to October) and is at its best on a weekend when pilgrims will add more flair to the scene and transport is a little more regular. From Mawlamyine you'll have to wait at the roundabout before the bridge for a northbound bus or pick-up to Kyonka village (K1000), located around 12 miles north of town. From here clamber into the back of one of the pick-up trucks that crawl slowly up to the summit of the mountain (K2000 return) in 45 minutes. Allow plenty of time as the trucks don't leave until beyond full, and don't leave your descent too late in the day as transport becomes scarcer after 3pm. Alternatively, motorcycle taxis will do the trip to Kyonka for K7000.

DON'T MISS

BILU KYUN

Bilu Kyun (ဘီလူးကျွန်း; Ogre Island) isn't quite as scary as it sounds. Rather than a hide-away for nasty monsters, it's a beautiful and fascinating self-contained Mon island directly west of Mawlamyine. Roughly the size of Singapore, Bilu Kyun comprises 78 villages that are home to more than 200,000 people. It's a green, fecund place, home to palm-studded rice fields and fruit plantations, and has the jungly vibe of a tropical island – without the beaches. Many of Bilu Kyun's villages are associated with the production of various handicrafts and household items, from coconut fibre-mats to slate tablets.

There's public transportation to Bilu Kyun, but the boats run a confusing schedule from a variety of piers. The local authorities also require notice to visit Bilu Kyun, so the best way to approach the island is via a day tour with Mr Antony or Mr Khaing at Breeze Guest House. They charge $30 per person for the tour, which typically runs from 9am to 5pm, circling the island, stopping in at various craft workshops and even tacking on a swim stop. The fee covers transportation and lunch.

At research time, foreigners were not allowed to stay overnight on Bilu Kyun.

South of Mawlamyine

◉ Sights & Activities

Pa-Auk-Taw-Ya Monastery BUDDHIST MONASTERY

(ဖားအောက်တောရဘုန်းကြီးကျောင်း; 22853; www.paaukforestmonastery.org) **FREE** Only 9 miles south of Mawlamyine, the monastery teaches *satipatthana vipassana* (insight-awareness meditation) and, at 500 acres, is one of the largest meditation centres in Myanmar. Foreigners can visit for the night or several days; sleeping and eating is gratis.

Win Sein Taw Ya BUDDHIST TEMPLE

(ဝင်းစိန်တောရ; ☉daylight hours) **FREE** If you thought you'd seen some big old buddhas, just wait till you get a load of this one. Draped across a couple of green hillsides at Yadana Taung, and surrounded by a forest of other pagodas and shrines, is this recently constructed, 560ft-long reclining buddha. It's easily one of the largest such images in the world.

Many other stupas and standing buddhas dot the area, including 500 statues lining the road to the Win Sein Taw Ya. Aside from inflated buddhas, the area affords some gentle walks with wonderful panoramas.

Every year around the first couple of days of February a crazy coloured festival takes place here to celebrate the birthday of the monk who constructed the buddha. As well as a host of itinerant traders, monks and nuns, magic men and the odd hermit or two, the festival often hosts a major kickboxing tournament, which leads to the slightly surreal sight of hundreds of cheering monks baying for blood in the ring!

Kyauktalon Taung BUDDHIST TEMPLE

(ကျောက်တစ်လုံးတောင်; ☉daylight hours) **FREE** Kyauktalon Taung is a strangely shaped, sheer-sided crag rising out of the surrounding agricultural land and crowned with stupas. It's a sticky 20-minute climb to the summit. On the opposite side of the road is a similar but smaller outcropping surmounted by a Hindu temple.

Kandawgyi LAKE

(ကန်တော်ကြီး; ☉daylight hours) **FREE** This lake formed by Azin Dam (a water storage and flood-control facility that's also used to irrigate local rubber plantations) also boasts a tidy recreation area and is a favourite picnic spot with locals. Don't miss the tasty *buthi kyaw,* deep-fried gourd, sold here. At the northern end of the lake stands the gilded stupa of Kandawgyi Paya.

❶ Getting There & Away

Hop on a Mudon-bound bus or pick-up from Mawlamyine's Zay Gyo bus station and ask to be dropped at the junctions for any of the sights (K800 to K2000, 45 minutes, hourly from 6am to 4pm). Alternatively, a round-trip motorcycle taxi from Mawlamyine to any of the sights will run between K4000 and K7000.

Thanbyuzayat & Around

◉ Sights & Activities

Thanbyuzayat
HISTORICAL SITE

(သံဖြူဇရပ်; ⊘ daylight hours) FREE Thanbyuzayat (Tin Shelter), 40 miles south of Mawlamyine, was the western terminus of the infamous Burma–Siam Railway, dubbed the 'Death Railway' by the thousands of Allied prisoners of war (POWs) and Asian coolies who were forced by the Japanese military to build it. Half a mile west of town lies the **Thanbyuzayat War Cemetery**, containing 3771 graves of Allied POWs who died building the railway.

Most of those buried were British but there are also markers for American, Dutch and Australian soldiers. As you walk around this simple memorial, maintained by the Commonwealth War Graves Commission, reading the heart-rending words inscribed on the gravestones it's impossible not to be moved to the brink of tears.

Daw Pu (no roman-script sign; meals from K1500; ⊘ 6am-3pm), a Burmese restaurant located across from the pick-up-truck stand, west of the clock tower, is a good place to eat.

Kyaikkami
VILLAGE

(ကျိုက္ခမီ) Located 5.5 miles northwest of Thanbyuzayat, Kyaikkami was a small coastal resort and missionary centre known as Amherst during the British era. The town is an atmospheric seaside destination, although you'll probably not do any swimming at the rocky and rather muddy beach. Instead, the main focus is **Yele Paya** (ရေလယ်ဘုရား), a metal-roofed Buddhist shrine complex perched over the sea.

Along with 11 Buddha hair relics, the shrine chamber beneath Yele Paya reportedly contains a buddha image that was supposed to have floated here on a raft from Sri Lanka in ancient times. A display of 21 Mandalay-style buddha statues sits over the spot where the Sinhalese image is allegedly buried. Pilgrims standing at the water's edge place clay pots of flowers and milk into the sea in order to 'feed' the spirits.

Adoniram Judson (1788–1850), an American missionary and linguist who has practically attained sainthood among Myanmar Baptists, was sailing to India with his wife when their ship was blown off course, forcing them to land at Kyaikkami. Judson stayed on and established his first mission here; the original site is now a Catholic school on a small lane off the main road.

The only accommodation in town is **Kaday Kywe Guest Villa** (☏ 75019; Bogyoke Rd; r K6000-50,000; ❀). A short walk from Yele Paya, this hotel has tidy but overpriced air-con rooms with attached bathrooms, while the cheaper rooms are little more than fan-cooled closets. There's a basic restaurant directly across the street.

Setse Beach
BEACH

(စက်စဲကမ်းခြေ) Not a picture postcard beach by any stretch of the imagination, but as the grime of travel washes away you probably won't care. This low-key Gulf of Mottama (Martaban) beach is a very wide, brown-sand strip. The beach is lined with waving casuarina trees and has been a popular spot for outings since colonial times.

Though a few locals stop by for a swim, almost no foreigners visit this area and facilities are minimal. At low tide you can walk along the beach to the small temple on the rocks at the northern end.

You can stay at the privately owned **Shwe Moe Guesthouse** (☏ 09 870 3283; r $20), which has spacious but run-down beach bungalows. A few modest restaurants offer fresh seafood, including the **Pyay Son Oo Restaurant**, which is very close to the hotel.

❶ Getting There & Away

To Thanbyuzayat, there are frequent departures from a **stall** (Lower Main Rd) near Zeigyi (K1500, two hours, from 6am to 5pm). Kyaikkami-bound buses leave from a nearby **stop** (Lower Main Rd) (K1000, 2½ hours, hourly from 6am to 4pm).

During the first half of the day there are regular pick-up trucks from Thanbyuzayat to Kyaikkami (K500) and Setse (K500). The last return departure for both is about 4pm.

East of Mawlamyine

◉ Sights & Activities

Kyaikmaraw
VILLAGE

(ကျိုက်မရော) This small, charming town, 15 miles southeast of Mawlamyine, is the site of **Kyaikmaraw Paya** (ကျိုက်မရောဘုရား; ⊘ daylight hours) FREE, a temple of serene, white-faced buddhas built by Queen Shin Saw Pu in 1455. Among the temple's many outstanding features are multicoloured glass windows set in the outside walls, an inner colonnade decorated in mirrored tiles, and beautiful ceramic tile floors.

THE DEATH RAILWAY

The strategic objective of the 'Burma–Siam Railway' was to secure an alternative supply route for the Japanese conquest of Myanmar and other Asian countries to the west.

Construction on the railway began on 16 September 1942 at existing terminals in Thanbyuzayat and Nong Pladuk, Thailand. At the time, Japanese engineers estimated that it would take five years to link Thailand and Burma by rail, but the Japanese army forced the POWs to complete the 260-mile, 3.3ft-gauge railway in 13 months. Much of the railway was built in difficult terrain that required high bridges and deep mountain cuttings. The rails were finally joined 23 miles south of the town of Payathonzu (Three Pagodas Pass); a Japanese brothel train inaugurated the line. The railway was in use for 21 months before the Allies bombed it in 1945.

An estimated 16,000 POWs died as a result of brutal treatment by their captors, a story chronicled by Pierre Boulle's book *Bridge on the River Kwai* and popularised by a movie based on the book. Only one POW is known to have escaped, a Briton who took refuge among pro-British Kayin guerrillas.

Although the statistics of the number of POWs who died during the Japanese occupation are horrifying, the figures for the labourers, many from Myanmar, Thailand, Malaysia and Indonesia, are even worse. It is thought that 80,000 Asians, 6540 British, 2830 Dutch, 2710 Australians and 356 Americans died in the area.

Covered brick walkways lead up to and around the main square sanctuary in typical 15th-century Mon style. The huge main buddha image sits in a 'European pose', with the legs hanging down as if sitting on a chair, rather than in the much more common cross-legged manner. A number of smaller cross-legged buddhas surround the main image, and behind it are two reclining buddhas. Another impressive feature is the carved and painted wooden ceiling. Perhaps as impressive as the temple is the route there, which passes through bright green rice fields studded with sugar palms and picturesque villages.

Kha-Yon Caves

CAVES

(ခရံု့; ⊙ daylight hours) **FREE** Spirited away in the back of the little-known, dark and dank Kha-Yon Caves are rows of ghostly buddha statues and wall paintings that come lurching out of the dark as the light from a torch catches them. Close by is another, smaller, cave system with an open cavern and a small cave-dwelling stupa. Bring a torch or buy candles from the stall near the entrance.

ⓘ Getting There & Away

Pick-ups nip between Mawlamyine's Zay Gyo bus station and Kyaikmaraw (K800, one hour, hourly from 6am to 4pm).

For Kha-Yon Caves, head to Mawlamyine's Mye Ni Gone bus station, take any bus towards Hpa-an and ask to be dropped at the junction for the caves (K1050, 30 minutes, hourly from 6am to 4pm).

KAYIN STATE

The limestone escarpments and luminous paddy fields, coupled with a fascinating ethnic mix, would make Kayin State (ကရင်ပြည်နယ်) a Myanmar highlight but sadly, like so many of the nation's border regions, significant parts of the state remain off limits to foreign visitors.

Ever since Myanmar attained independence from the British in 1948, the Karen have been embroiled in a fight for autonomy – a war that is by some accounts the world's longest-running internal conflict. In 2012, after more than 60 years of fighting, the main insurgent body, the Karen National Union (KNU), and the Burmese government signed a ceasefire agreement. The KNU's military component, the Karen National Liberation Army (KNLA), continue to control parts of the northern and eastern parts of the state, but the newfound peace has meant the opening up of parts of Kayin State to the outside world, most notably in the 2013 general opening of the border at Myawaddy.

Hpa-an ဘားအံ

☑ 058 / POP C50,000

Hpa-an, Kayin State's scruffy, riverside capital, isn't going to inspire many postcards home. But the city is the logical base from which to explore the Buddhist caves, sacred mountains and cloud-scraping islands of the surrounding countryside.

Hpa-an

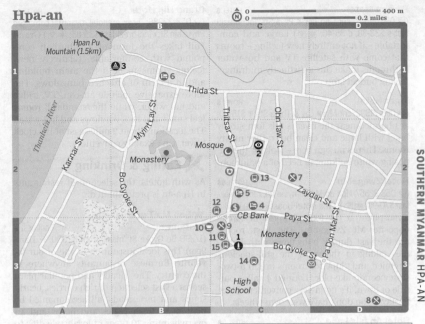

☉ Sights & Activities

Hpa-an's vibrant **Morning Market** (off Thitsar St; ☉5am-11am) is fun to explore and **Shwey-inhmyaw Paya** (ရွှေရင်မှော်ဘုရား; off Thida St; admission free; ☉daylight hours), down by the waterfront, is a good place from which to watch the world sail on by. Some might also describe the central **clock tower** as a 'sight' at night when it's lit up like a gaudy lollipop.

🛏 Sleeping

Accommodation options are fairly limited in Hpa-an and, unless you have your own transport, you're relegated to the cheaper places in town that inspire little to write home about.

★ Soe Brothers
Guesthouse   BACKPACKER HOTEL $
(☎058-21372, 09 497 71823; soebrothers 05821372@gmail.com; 2/146 Thitsar St; r $6-25; ❄) A classic backpackers' crash pad, the rooms here are correspondingly basic, but the family that runs the place is lovely and highly tuned in to travellers' needs. The vast majority of rooms are small, fan-cooled and share basic but clean communal bathrooms; the three 'luxury' rooms have a bit more space, air-con and no queues for the toilet. There are lots of welcoming communal

areas to relax or chat, and hassle-free excursions, boat hire and bus tickets can be arranged here.

Parami Motel HOTEL $

(☎058-21647; cnr Ohn Taw & Paya Sts; incl breakfast s $33-38, d 35-40; ❄📶) Large and comfortable – if not entirely new-feeling – rooms that come with satellite TV and hot-water bathrooms make this a distinctly midrange-feeling budget stop.

Tiger Hotel HOTEL $

(☎058-21392; cnr Myint Lay & Thida Sts; r $15-30; ❄) Located near the river is this four-storey hotel with large and clean but rather musty rooms. There's no sign here – look for the imposing white building in need of a paint job.

Hotel Zwegabin HOTEL $$

(☎058-22557; Hpa-an-Mawlamyine Rd; r incl breakfast $70-90; ❄📶) This hotel boasts a park-like atmosphere at the foot of limestone karsts opposite Mt Zwegabin. The best rooms are the vast duplex bungalows with balconies taking in the view; the still-spacious 'Premier' and 'Superior' rooms are in a two-storey condo-like bloc. Located 4 miles outside of town, it's not a very convenient place to stay if you don't have your own wheels.

Hotel Angels Land HOTEL $$

(☎058-21256; angel.landhotel@gmail.com; Padauk Rd; r incl breakfast $50-80; ❄) This new hotel, run by an enthusiastic team of Burmese women, boasts 22 sumptuous-feeling, well-equipped (TV, air-con, fridge, hot water), although somewhat overpriced rooms. Inconveniently located about 1 mile south of town, near Hpa-an's City Hall.

WORTH A TRIP

HPAN PU MOUNTAIN

Across the Thanlwin River from Hpa-an, Hpan Pu Mountain (ဖားပုတောင်) is a craggy, pagoda-topped peak that can be scaled in one sweaty morning. Getting there involves hopping on one of the river crossing boats (K500, every 30 minutes from 7am to 5pm) from the informal **jetty** near Shweyinhmyaw Paya. Upon reaching the other side, you'll walk through a quiet village then begin the steep but relatively short ascent to the top. The views of the river, the surrounding rice fields and limestone cliffs (including Mt Zwegabin) are astounding.

Grand Hill Hotel HOTEL $$

(☎058-22286; www.grandhillmyanmar.com; Sin Phyushin St; r incl breakfast $35-85; ❄📶) Grand Hill takes the form of a suburban compound with comfortable, relatively new-feeling rooms in both the main building and in a strip of attached bungalows. The more expensive include air-con, TV, fridge and hot water, while the 'standard' rooms feel small and lack windows and hot water. The location, about 2 miles east of the clock tower, isn't exactly convenient.

Eating & Drinking

As with hotels, the selection of restaurants in Hpa-an is pretty limited.

★San Ma Tau Myanmar Restaurant BURMESE $

(1/290 Bo Gyoke St; meals from K2000; ⏰11am-9pm) This local institution is one of our favourite Burmese restaurants anywhere in the country. The friendly and popular place serves a vast selection of rich curries, hearty soups and tart salads, all accompanied by platters of fresh vegies and herbs and an overwhelming 10 types of local-style dips to eat them with.

White TEAHOUSE $

(cnr Thitsar & Bo Gyoke Sts; snacks from K200; ⏰6am-4pm) This teahouse, located near the clock tower, serves decent tea and freshly baked naan – great for breakfast.

New Day CAFE $

(3/624 Bo Gyoke St; drinks from K600; ⏰8am-7pm) This modern cafe features real coffee, tasty fruit shakes and a variety of baked goods.

Lucky 1 CHINESE-BURMESE $

(Zaydan St; mains from K800; ⏰10am-9pm; 📋) This grubby place is the closest thing Hpa-an has to a bar and, in addition to draught beer, also serves decent Chinese-style dishes.

Information

The **post office** (off Bo Gyoke St) is on a side road off Bo Gyoke St on the way to the bus station.

Hpa-an doesn't yet have an ATM that accepts international cards, but money can be exchanged at **CB Bank** (cnr Thitsar & Paya Sts; ⏰10am-2pm Mon-Fri).

Slow internet is available at the **cafe** (1/290 Bo Gyoke St; per hr K500; ⏰11am-9pm) attached to San Ma Tau Myanmar Restaurant.

❶ Getting There & Away

BOAT

With the advent of improved roads and new bridges, the government ferry that previously ran between Hpa-an and Mawlamyine has been cancelled. In its place, it's possible to charter a private boat, which seats about 10 people, taking approximately two hours to reach Mawlamyine (K60,000). This can be arranged at Soe Brothers Guesthouse.

BUS & VAN (SHARE TAXI)

Hpa-an's bus station is located about 4 miles east of town, but tickets can be bought and buses boarded at the **ticket stalls** (Bo Gyoke St) near the clock tower; every second bus to Mawlamyine makes a brief stop to pick up passengers at an unmarked **stand** (Bo Gyoke St) nearby. Staff at Soe Brothers can also arrange tickets.

Vans (share taxis) to Myawaddy depart, on odd-numbered days only, from a **stall** (Bo Gyoke St) near the clock tower intersection.

DESTINA-TION	BUS	VAN (SHARE TAXI)
Bago	K5000; 6hr; 4 departures 7am-7pm	N/A
Kyaikto	K5000; 4hr; 4 departures 7am-7pm	N/A
Mawlamyine	K1000; 2hr; hourly 6am-4pm	N/A
Myawaddy	N/A	K8000-10,000; 4-6hr; daily 6am & 7am
Yangon	K5000; 7-8hr; 4 departures 7am-7pm	N/A

Around Hpa-an

The real highlights of Hpa-an are all scattered about the divine rural countryside out of town. While many of these sights are potentially accessible by public transport, you'd need to be prepared to give your leg muscles a workout. Therefore, almost everyone takes a motorbike (or *thoun bein,* motorised trishaw) tour organised by the Soe Brothers Guesthouse, which circumnavigates Mt Zwegabin, stopping at all of the sights mentioned here. A full-day tour costs K30,000 per vehicle (up to six passengers), while a half-day tour, hitting destinations of your choice, runs from K15,000 to K20,000.

Some of the closer attractions can also be reached by bicycle. Bikes (per day K2000) and motorcycles (per day K8000) can be rented at Soe Brothers, who have also put together a good map of the surrounding area and its attractions. At press time, Khiri Travel (p28) were planning to offer kayaking excursions in the wetlands around Hpa-an; check the website to see if their Hpa-an branch has opened by the time you're in town.

◉ Sights & Activities

Kaw Ka Thawng Cave
CAVE
(ကောကသောင်ဂူ; ⊙daylight hours) FREE

More popular among locals than travellers, this area actually consists of three caves, only two of which are generally open to the public.

Kaw Ka Thawng Cave is about 7 miles from Hpa-an along the road to Eindu. From the **stall** on Zaydan St in Hpa-an, hop on a pick-up truck to Eindu (K1000) and ask to be dropped off at Kaw Ka Thawng Cave. A round-trip in a *thoun bein* or motorcycle taxi will run K4000 or K5000.

The first cave you'll come to, Kaw Ka Thawng, has been quite gentrified and has slippery tile floors and numerous buddha statues. Continuing along a path, you'll pass the stairway to another somewhat concealed cave that's not normally open (allegedly a monk found a used condom here and decided to lock it). Near the end of the path, you'll reach an inviting spring-fed swimming hole, popular with local kids, and another water-filled cave that also serves as a swimming hole. There are a few simple restaurants here.

Splitting from the path before the first cave, a long bridge leads to Lakkana Village, a picturesque Kayin village, the backdrop to which includes Mt Zwegabin, and which has been featured in numerous Myanmar films and videos.

The countryside here is drop-dead gorgeous and you could easily spend a day walking and swimming.

Kawgun Cave & Yathaypyan Cave
CAVE
(ကောဂွန်းဂူရသောပြန်ဂူ; ⊙daylight hours) The 7th-century artwork of the Kawgun Cave (admission K3000, camera K500) consists of thousands of tiny clay buddhas and carvings plastered all over the walls and roof of this open cavern.

Just over a mile away, and built by the same exiled king, is the Yathaypyan Cave

DON'T MISS

MT ZWEGABIN

Hpa-an is hemmed in by a wrinkled chain of limestone mountains. The tallest of these is Mt Zwegabin, about 7 miles south of town, which as well as being a respectable 2372ft is also a home of spirits and saintly souls.

It's a demanding two-hour hike to the summit – up more steps than you'd care to count, and with aggressive monkeys as constant adversaries – but once at the top the rewards are staggering views, a small monastery and a stupa containing, yes, you guessed it, another hair from the buddha. If you arrive at the top before noon you can take advantage of a complimentary lunch (rice, orange and tea) and the 11am **monkey feeding** – different primates, different menus. The descent down the east side of the mountain takes around 1½ hours, and from the bottom it's another 2 miles to the main road from where you can catch a pick-up truck back to town. The whole trek takes roughly six hours or about half a day.

To get to the mountain, there's a pick-up every weekday at 8am, from a **stall** on Ohn Taw St in Hpa-an, in front of the high school (K500, 30 minutes). You'll be dropped off at the Zwegabin junction, where it's a 15-minute walk through a village to the base of the mountain on the west side past hundreds (1150 to be precise – don't believe us? Get counting!) of identical buddha statues lined up row after row. Alternatively, a *thoun bein* or motorcycle taxi from Hpa-an to the base of the mountain should run about K2000. At research time foreigners were not allowed to stay overnight on Mt Zwegabin.

(admission free), which contains several pagodas as well as a few more clay wall carvings. Both caves are inaccessible during the rainy season (June to October). A round-trip on a *thoun bein* or motorcycle taxi should run about K5000.

Kawgun was constructed by King Manuaha after he was defeated in battle and had to take sanctuary in these caves. Impressive as it is today, you can only imagine what it was like a few years back, before a cement factory, in its quest for limestone, started dynamiting the nearby peaks – the vibrations caused great chunks of the art to crash to the floor and shatter.

If you have a torch you can traverse Yathaypyan Cave, which takes about 10 minutes, after which you'll emerge at a viewpoint.

Kyauk Kalap
BUDDHIST MONASTERY

(ကျောက်ကလပ်; ⊙ daylight hours) **FREE** Standing proud in the middle of a small, artificial lake is Kyauk Kalap, a tall finger of sheer rock mounted by one of the most unlikely pagodas in Myanmar. The rock offers great views of the surrounding countryside and nearby Mt Zwegabin, and is allegedly the best place to see the sunset over this mountain.

A round-trip *thoun bein* or motorcycle taxi from Hpa-an to Kyauk Kalap will run about K5000.

The compound is a working monastery and is closed every day from 12pm to 1pm to allow the monks to meditate. The 30 or so

monks here are vegetarian and free vegetarian food is served from the temple from 9am to 5pm.

The monastery is also where the highly respected monk U Winaya, whose solid support of democracy leader Aung San Suu Kyi is well known in Myanmar, first resided. U Winaya passed away several years ago and his body was entombed in a glass case at Thamanyat Kyaung, another monastery about 25 miles southeast of Hpa-an. On one night in April 2007, the monk's body was stolen (allegedly by soldiers) and has never been recovered.

Saddan Cave
CAVE

(ဆဒ္ဒန်ဂူ; ⊙ daylight hours) **FREE** This huge cave is simply breathtaking. As you enter the football stadium–sized cavern you'll be greeted by (what else?) dozens of buddha statues, a couple of pagodas and some newer clay wall carvings.

Saddan Cave can be traversed only during the dry season (around November to April) and is 17 miles from Hpa-an along the road to Eindu. To get there, take a pick-up to Eindu (K1000). From the village take a motorbike taxi (K2000) for the remaining 2 miles to the cave.

In absolute darkness (bring a torch; otherwise for a donation of K3000, they'll turn on the lights for you) you can scramble for 15 minutes through black chambers as high as a cathedral, truck-sized stalactites and, in places, walls of crystal. To add to the general atmosphere, thousands, possibly hundreds of thousands, of bats cling to the cave roof. In places the squealing from them is deafening and the ground underfoot becomes slippery with bat excrement!

Emerging at the cave's far side, the wonders only increase and the burst of sunlight reveals an idyllic secret lake full of ducks and flowering lilies hidden in a bowl of craggy peaks. There is another cave on the far side of the lake that is actually half flooded, but local fishers occasionally paddle through the cave for 10 minutes to yet another lake. You may be able to persuade one to take you along.

Myawaddy မြ၀တီ

☑ 058 / POPULATION C50,000

For decades, Myawaddy, located on the Moei River opposite the Thai city of Mae Sot, alternated between dodgy border town (that is, when the border was actually open) and intermittent battleground. But with the fighting between the Myanmar army and various Karen insurgent groups now largely over, and with the 2013 opening of the

border ostensibly paving the way for Asian Highway 1 (AH1) to be Southeast Asia's first real transnational conduit, things are set to change for Myawaddy. This said, as of now, there's still little of interest for most tourists and the town is really only a transit point.

⊙ Sights

There's little in terms of visit-worthy sights in Myawaddy. The town's most important temple is **Shwe Muay Wan Paya** (ရွှေမှော်ဝန်းဘုရား; Dar Tu Kalair St; ⊙ daylight hours) , a traditional bell-shaped stupa gilded with many kilos of gold and topped by more than 1600 precious and semiprecious gems. Another noted Buddhist temple is **Myikyaungon Paya** (မြေကျောင်းကုန်ဘုရား; Nat Shin Naung St; ⊙ daylight hours) **FREE**, called Wat Don Jarakhe in Thai and named for its gaudy, crocodile-shaped sanctuary. Both are within walking distance of the Friendship Bridge.

🛌 Sleeping & Eating

All accommodation and food is located along AH1, Myawaddy's main strip.

WORTH A TRIP

MAUNGMAGAN BEACH မောင်းမကန်

Dawei's most accessible beach is Maungmagan, a wide, sandy strip spanning approximately 7 miles along a pretty bay. The sand veers toward the coarse, gray end of the spectrum, but on weekdays at least you're likely to have it all to yourself, save for the occasional fisherman.

Opposite the beach is a collection of three pretty island groups: Maungmagan, Hienze and Launglon, known collectively in English as the Middle Miscos. Due to a natural profusion of wild boar, barking deer, sambar and swiftlets (sea swallows), these islands belong to Myanmar's only marine sanctuary – established by the British in 1927 and still officially protected.

Places to stay at Maungmagan include the delightful Burmese/French-run **Coconut Guesthouse & Restaurant** (☑ 09 737 00052; Phaw Taw Oo St, Maungmagan; s/d $20/25; @), located near the village and a brief walk from the beach, and the waterfront yet bland and overpriced **Maungmagan Hotel** (☑ 09 422 201819; Maungmagan; r incl breakfast K40,000-80,0000, bungalows incl breakfast K80,0000; ❄), located at the rocky southern end of the beach. It has no roman-script sign. Burmese and European food is available at the former's **restaurant** (Phaw Taw Oo St, Maungmagan; mains from K2500; ⊙ 7.30am-11pm), and there is also a string of beachside seafood shacks at the road head – on weekends and holidays this end of the beach draws a crowd – not to mention some basic restaurants in Maungmagan village.

Maungmagan is around 11 miles west of Dawei via a narrow, patched blacktop road that winds through villages, rubber plantations and over a high ridge. There's a daily, very crowded **truck** (Arzarni Rd) that departs from near Dawei's Si Pin Tharyar Zei at around 7am (per person K1000), otherwise motorcycles go to Maungmagan for around K5000, *thoun bein* for around K12,000, and a car can be arranged at Dawei Regional Tourism Services for a hefty K40,000. From Maungmagan village, trucks depart from the market area when bursting from 7am to 8am (1000K).

Myawaddy Hotel HOTEL $$
([☎]058-50519; cnr AH1 & Nat Shin Naung St; r incl breakfast K25,000-40,000; [❄][🛜]) Conveniently located 0.3 miles from the border, the Myawaddy Hotel has small but clean and well-equipped (air-con, TV, fridge) rooms with 24/7 electricity.

ⓘ Getting There & Away

DESTINATION	BUS	VAN (SHARE TAXI)
Hpa-an	N/A	K10,000-15,000; 6hr; frequent 6am-5pm
Mawlamyine	N/A	K10,000-15,000; 4-6hr; frequent 6am-5pm
Yangon	K12,000; 16hr; 5am	K40,000; 14hr; frequent 6am-5pm

The daily bus to Yangon departs from a small office on Pattamyar St.

White vans (share taxis) wait on the corner of AH1 and Pattamyar St, a short walk from the border. Note that vans to Hpa-an and Mawlamyine depart only on even-numbered days.

TANINTHARYI REGION

Simply put, the deep south of Myanmar, known today as Tanintharyi Region (တနင်္သာရီတိုင်း), is a beach bum's dream. The coastline consists of bridal-white beaches fronting a vast archipelago of more than 800 largely uninhabited islands, nearly all of which have only recently opened to general tourism. We certainly weren't the first foreigners to be drawn to the area. A 1545 Portuguese expeditionary chronicle refers to Tanancarim, somewhere along the northwest

ⓘ GETTING TO THAILAND: MYAWADDY TO MAE SOT

In 2013, the Friendship Bridge linking Myawaddy and Mae Sot, in northern Thailand's Tak Province, became one of three newly opened land borders between the two countries. Regardless of where or how you entered Myanmar, you can exit the country here. Likewise, if you've already procured a Myanmar visa in Bangkok or elsewhere, you're free to cross here and proceed to other destinations in Myanmar.

However it's important to understand that, if you're crossing here from Thailand, a Myanmar visa is *not* available at the border; this must be obtained in advance. It's also worth noting that in the recent past fighting between the Myanmar Armed Forces and splinter groups of the Democratic Karen Buddhist Army (DKBA) has occasionally led to this border being closed. Be sure to check the situation before you cross here.

Getting to the border Vans (share taxis) and buses linking Myawaddy with Hpa-an, Mawlamyine and Yangon terminate a short walk from the Friendship Bridge.

At the border The Myanmar immigration office ([☎]058-50100; AH1, Myawaddy; [🕑]6am-6pm) is at the foot of the Friendship Bridge. After walking across the 420m bridge, if you don't already have a visa, the Thai Immigration office ([☎]055 56 3004; AH1, Mae Sot; [🕑]6.30am-6.30pm) will grant you permission to stay in Thailand up to 15 days.

If you're crossing from Thailand and don't already have a Myanmar visa, it's possible to cross for the day, paying a fee of US$10 or 500B for a one-day visit and leaving your passport at the border. Then you're free to wander around Myawaddy as long as you're back at the bridge by 5.30pm Myanmar time (which is half an hour behind Thai time) to pick up your passport and check out with immigration.

Moving on Mae Sot's bus station is located 2 miles east of the border and has good connections to destinations in northern Thailand and Bangkok. Mae Sot's airport is 2 miles east of the border, from where Nok Air ([☎]in Mae Sot 0 5556 3883, nationwide call centre 1318; www.nokair.com; Mae Sot Airport, Th Intharakhiri (AH1), Mae Sot; [🕑]8am-5pm) operates four daily flights to Bangkok and a daily flight to Chiang Mai (and a daily flight to Yangon, if you're so inclined). Both the bus station and airport can be reached by frequent *sŏrng·tăa·ou* (pick-ups) that run between the Friendship Bridge and Mae Sot from 6am to 6pm (20B).

For further information, head to shop.lonelyplanet.com to purchase a downloadable PDF of the Northern Thailand chapter from Lonely Planet's *Thailand* guide.

coast of the Thai-Malay Peninsula, and this Portuguese rendering became Tenasserim in later European records. The region subsequently became a Thai protectorate known as Tanaosi, and ultimately Tenasserim once again under British colonial rule following the First Anglo-Burmese War in 1826.

Dawei ထားဝယ်

☎059 / POPULATION C140,000

The area near the mouth of the Dawei River has been inhabited for five centuries or more, mostly by Mon and Thai mariners. English trader Ralph Fitch mentions a stop at 'Tavi' during his 1586 sea journey between Bago and Melaka in a written account stating that tin from the area 'serves all India'. The present town dates to 1751 when it was a minor 'back door' port for the Ayuthaya empire in Thailand (then Siam). From this point it bounced back and forth between Burmese and Siamese rule until the British took over in 1826.

Despite being the administrative capital of Tanintharyi Region, the Dawei of today remains a sleepy, tropical seaside town, only relatively recently connected to the rest of Myanmar by air, road and rail. Yet Dawei's laid-back demeanour is threatened by the so-called Dawei Project, consisting of a proposed deep-sea port and vast industrial zone. The port would allow ships to avoid the Strait of Malacca altogether, turning the beach at Maungmagan into what developers call the 'new global gateway of Indo-China', and the industrial zone is touted as the largest in Southeast Asia, although at press time efforts to fund the project had fallen flat.

Sights

For a relatively small town, Dawei has a disproportionate amount of interesting architecture, with many old wooden houses in the two-storey vernacular, with hipped rooflines and plenty of temple-like carved wood ornamentation. Mixed in are more modest thatch-roofed bungalows, colonial-style brick-and-stucco mansions, shophouses and offices, including the bright green, almost church-like 1941 **Division Development Committee** (Arzarni Rd) and the imposing 1928 **Office of Tanintharyi Division** (Arzarni Rd).

Payagyi BUDDHIST TEMPLE

(ဘုရားကြီး; ⊙daylight hours) FREE The main Buddhist monastery in town, colloquially referred to as Payagyi (Big Pagoda), is an expansive glittering, Disneyland-like compound centred around **Shwe Taung Za Paya**, an immense gilded stupa.

A sculpture of Dharani, the earth goddess, standing in the corner of one of the compound's main *thein* is a much-venerated object of worship among the people of Dawei, who rub her breasts, thighs and shoulders for good luck.

Shwethalyaung Daw Mu & Shinmokhti Paya BUDDHIST TEMPLE

(ရွှေသာလျောင်းတော်မူဘုရားကြီးနှင့် ရှင်မုဋ္ဌိုးဘုရား; ⊙daylight hours) FREE Completed in 1931 and measuring 74m long and 21m high, Shwethalyaung Daw Mu is the largest reclining buddha in the country. A couple of miles up the road is Shinmokhti Paya, dating back to 1438 and one of four shrines in the country housing a Sinhalese Buddha image supposedly made with a composite of cement and pieces of the original bodhi tree. Shinmokhti Paya is located about 6 miles from Dawei; a round trip *thoun bein* stopping off at both temples should run around K7000.

Festivals & Events

During the annual **Thingyan** festival in April, Dawei's male residents don huge, 13-foot (4m) bamboo-frame effigies and dance down the streets to the beat of the kalakodaun, an Indian long drum. The origin of this custom, peculiar to Dawei, seems to be a mystery but it's most likely linked to a similar custom brought by Indian immigrants many decades ago.

Sleeping

Dawei has a good selection of recommendable budget/midrange accommodation, and by the time you read this, the multi-storey **Golden Hotel** (Ye Yeik Thar St) should be finished.

Garden Hotel HOTEL $

(☎059-22116; 88 Ye Rd; r $10-40; ❄📶) An attractive, spacious 1940s-era building encompassing both fan-cooled cheapies and several larger, well-equipped air-con rooms. All are spotless and looked over by a team of competent, helpful staff.

Dawei

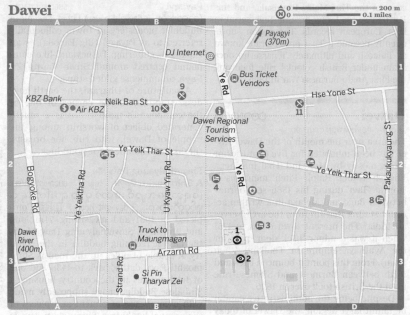

Dawei

⊙ Sights
1 Division Development
  Committee..C3
2 Office of Tanintharyi Division.............C3

🛏 Sleeping
3 Diamond Crown Hotel.........................C3
4 Garden Hotel.......................................C2
5 Golden Hotel.......................................A2
6 Hotel Zayar Htet San..........................C2
7 Pearl Princess Hotel...........................D2
8 Shwe Moung Than Hotel.....................D2

✗ Eating
9 Hla Hla Hnan....................................... B1
10 Meik Hswe... B1
11 Tha Hto (Daw Zan) C1

Diamond Crown Hotel HOTEL $
(☑ 059-22517; 651 Ye Rd; r incl breakfast $30-40;
❄️ 🛜) This place combines rather tight and
somewhat worn rooms in the original wing
and larger more modern rooms in a brand-
new, multistorey addition.

Shwe Moung Than Hotel HOTEL $
(☑ 059-23763; 665 Pakaukukyang St; r K15,000-
50,000; ❄️ 🛜) Packing a chintzy, almost
nouveau riche feel, the rooms here are
nonetheless spacious and bright. If you can

function without TV, the 4th-floor cheapies
are a good deal.

Pearl Princess Hotel HOTEL $
(☑ 059-21780; pearlprincess.dawei@gmail.com;
572 Ye Yeik Thar St; r/bungalows incl breakfast
$40/45) An attractive antique wooden
villa holding nonetheless musty and skel-
etal rooms. A better bet are the 'bungalows',
which include a separate sitting room.

Hotel Zayar Htet San HOTEL $$
(☑ 059-23902; 566 Ye Yeik Thar St; r incl breakfast
$40-60; ❄️ 🛜) This new hotel is easily the
most stylish and contemporary accommo-
dation in Dawei, if not in the entire region.
It's not a steal, but isn't necessarily bad
value, as the rooms come standard with
flat-screen TV, air-con, fridge, tub and free
wi-fi. The most expensive rooms are huge,
with similarly large TVs.

✗ Eating

Come evening, a few basic stalls unfold
around the intersection of Hse Yone and
Neik Ban Sts.

★ Hla Hla Hnan BURMESE $
(Neik Ban St; dishes from K300; ⊙noon-9pm) In
addition to selling the requisite ingredients
for *leq·p'eq thouq*, Burmese tea leaf salad,

TRANSPORT TO/FROM DAWEI

DESTINATION	AIR	BOAT	BUS
Kawthoung	$111; 80min; 2 daily	$80; 12hr; 4.30am	N/A
Mawlamyine	N/A	N/A	K9000-11,000; 9-12hr; 5am
Myeik	$71; 35min; 2 daily	$35; 4hr; 4.30am	N/A
Yangon	$126; 70min; 2 daily	N/A	K13,000; around 16hr; 4pm

this vendor also serves a selection of other equally delicious Burmese-style salads including ginger, tomato, pennywort (a type of herb) and *shauq-thi* (a type of citrus fruit). There's no roman-script sign, or English-language menu, but orders can be made by pointing to the raw ingredients.

Tha Hto (Daw Zan) BURMESE $
(Hse Yone St; meals from K2000; ⊙11am-9pm) For 40 years Daw Zan has been serving a generous spread of tasty Burmese curries to the people of Dawei. There's no roman-script sign so look for the glut of parked motorcycles a couple doors away from Wonder Luck Guesthouse.

Meik Hswe MUSLIM-BURMESE $
(Neik Ban St; snacks from K200; ⊙6am-9pm) Seemingly connected to a mosque (although there is no roman-script sign) it has good snacks and frothy tea. Come Sunday this Muslim teashop also does hearty dishes of biryani.

❶ Information

Currency exchange and an international ATM are available at **KBZ Bank** (Neik Ban St; ⊙9.30am-3pm Mon-Sat).

Internet can be accessed at **DJ Internet** (Ye Rd; per hr K400; ⊙9am-9pm).

The English-speaking staff at **Dawei Regional Tourism Services** (☑09 410 04311, 09 450 990747; 301 Ye Rd; ⊙8am-9pm) can sell plane tickets, help arrange boat tickets and provide car, motorcycle and bicycle hire.

❶ Getting There & Away

When we were in town, only **Air KBZ** (☑in Dawei 059-23833, in Yangon 01-372 977; www.airkbz.com; Neik Ban St; ⊙9am-5.30pm) and **Myanma Airways** (☑in Yangon 01-374 874; www.myanmaairways.aero) were operating out of Dawei's tiny airport.

Three companies operate speedboats from Dawei, with boats bound for Myeik and Kawthoung. Boats depart daily at 4.30am, but the ocean pier is 20 miles downstream from Dawei, so you'll need to meet at midnight for the ferry transfer. Tickets are sold at various locations near Si Pin Tharyar Zei and near the bus ticket vendors on Ye St; that

said, it's probably a lot easier to let Dawei Regional Tourism Services or your hotel suss it out for you.

Dawei's bus station is inconveniently located a couple miles northeast of the city centre, but tickets can be purchased in advance from the various **vendors** (Ye Rd) near the canal on Ye Rd (although you'll still have to board your bus at the station). At press time, foreigners were generally not allowed to travel by bus south of Dawei, although this could very well change.

Dawei does have a train station, but when we inquired, foreigners were not allowed to travel by train north to Ye.

Getting Around

The centre of Dawei is accessible on foot.

Dawei's **airport** is about 2 miles northeast of town; a motorcycle taxi should run about K2000. Dawei's **bus station** is located northeast of the airport; a *thoun bein* to/from here will run about K5000.

Myeik

☑059 / POPULATION C200,000
Myeik – known to the colonials as Mergui and locally as Beik (Myeik is the written rather than the spoken form) – sits on a peninsula that juts out into the Andaman Sea. Because of its location roughly halfway between the Middle East and China, not to mention the safe harbour offered by the peninsula and facing islands, Myeik became an important international port over 500 years ago.

The Portuguese were allegedly the first Europeans to visit Myeik, while the Siamese, who ruled the area during the 17th century, installed Englishman Samuel White as harbourmaster. White proceeded to plunder visiting ships at will and to tax the local population for every shilling he could squeeze out of them, exploits described in Maurice Collis's 1936 biography of the man, *Siamese White*. The British eventually re-occupied the city following the First Anglo-Burmese War in 1826, so that along with Sittwe, Myeik became one of the first

Myeik

Andaman Sea

Pataw Padet
Kyun (700m)

3

Jetty

Air
KBZ

Speedboat
Ticket Vendors

Sake Nge
Jetty **6**

Sun Far

12

Yae Twin St
Gadae Ya
Ta Nar St

Assumption
Church

2

5

Strand Rd

Nar Yi Shin St

Zay Taung
Bat St

Bo Gyoke Rd

4

Clock
Tower

Thmata
Yone St

1 **Theindawgyi
Paya**

AGD Bank

Independence
Monument

S.H.S. (2) St

Mosque

10

S.H.S. (1) St

Kanphyar Rd

9

Sa Ga War St

8 **11**

7

General
Aung San
Monument

Internet Cafe (100m);
Zan Pya (150m);
Dolphin Guest
House (1.6km);
Palé Mon Hotel (2.75km);
Airport (3.7km)

0   200 m
0   0.1 miles

---

cities in Myanmar to become part of British India. The city continued to retain its international roots into the 20th century, as this 1901 British census of Myeik indicates:

A considerable proportion of the population in the town and mines is Baba or half-Chinese, the men retaining the pigtail but talking Burmese or Siamese [...] Of the Musalmans [Muslims], between 2000 and 3000 are Malays and the rest nearly all Zarbadis. Living in boats among the island in a very low stage of civilisation is a wild people of obscure origin, called by the Burmese Salon, by the Malays Orang Basin, by the Siamese Chaunam (waterfolk), and by themselves Maw Ken (drowned in the sea).

The Japanese invaded in 1941, but by 1945 Myeik was back in British hands, until independence was achieved in 1948.

Sights

With a temple-capped hill at its back, a wide harbour at its breast, and a hilly island opposite, Myeik is one of Myanmar's more handsome towns. The town's history has also led to a palpable multicultural feel, and even today, there are still distinct Muslim, Chinese and Catholic quarters.

Despite a 1989 fire that destroyed as many as 3900 buildings, Myeik remains home to some beautiful classic architecture, much of it allegedly haunted. Crumbling Chinese-style godowns line parts of Strand Rd, several grand shophouses can be found in the blocks that surround Sake Nyein Zei, and some beautiful old Sino-Portuguese mansions can be found along S.H.S. (2) St, east of Assumption Church.

★**Theindawgyi Paya**   BUDDHIST TEMPLE
(သိမ်တော်ကြီးဘုရား; off Bo Gyoke Rd; ⊙daylight hours) **FREE** The city's most

Myeik

venerated Buddhist temple, Theindaw-gyi Paya sits on a ridge overlooking the city and harbour. A beautiful, Mon-style ordination hall of wood, brick and stucco contains an impressive painted and carved ceiling, a 'European pose' buddha towards the front entry, 28 smaller buddhas along its two sides, a large meditation buddha in the centre and a sizable reclining buddha at the back. A tall gilded stupa stands on a broad platform with excellent views of the city below and islands in the distance.

Myeik Harbour   LANDMARK
(Strand Rd) Myeik's vast harbourfront is worth a stroll to watch stevedores load-ing and offloading cargo from ships big and small. Until it was destroyed in 2001, the southern end of the harbour was also home to the tomb of Mary Povey White, the wife of the notorious Siamese-employed harbourmaster Samuel White, who died of cholera in 1682.

Pataw Padet Kyun   ISLAND
(ပတောပဒတ်ကျန်း) This island, located di-rectly opposite Myeik's harbour, is named for its two prominent hills. A large, hollow reclining buddha, **Atula Shwethalyaung**, lies at the foot of rocky, jungle-covered Padet Hill to the south. At 66m it's the third-long-est reclining buddha in Myanmar – but with a twist: it's a hollow cement form with an interior walkway lined with comic-strip-like stories of the buddha's past lives.

Boats can be chartered from the small jetty at the west end of Pyi Taw Thar St (round trip K3000).

Bu Paya Zedi   BUDDHIST TEMPLE
(ဗုးဘုရားစေတီ; off Bo Gyoke Rd; ☉ daylight hours) **FREE** Yet another hilltop temple; in addition to views over town, Bu Paya Zedi has an appealingly abandoned feel and abundance of mouldy, crumbing statues.

Sake Nyein Zei   MARKET
(စိတ်ငြိမ်းဈေး; Bo Gyoke Rd; ☉ 6am-6pm) Near the harbour, Myeik's municipal market is a colourful collection of enclosed stalls cover-ing an entire city block.

🛌 Sleeping

Sun Guest House   GUESTHOUSE $
(☏ 059-41745; 1 S.H.S. (1) St; r incl breakfast $30-50; ❋ 🛜) Ascend a modern shophouse to eight cosy rooms looked after by two charmingly overbearing yet almost entire-ly non-English-speaking women. Rooms come equipped with air-con and TV, and good local-style breakfast is served.

Myeik Guest House   HOTEL $
(cnr Strand Rd & Sake Nge Jetty Rd; r $25; ❋) Lo-cated directly opposite Myeik's main pier, most of the rather bare rooms here don't have windows, but compensate with air-con, TV and fridge.

Dolphin Guest House   GUESTHOUSE $
(☏ 059-42868; 139 Kanphyar Rd; s/d incl break-fast $35/40; ❋ 🛜) A vast villa housing equally spacious rooms – the double rooms nearly echo (they're also the only rooms with TV) – inconveniently located 1 mile northeast of the town centre.

Myaseesein Hotel   HOTEL $
(☏ 059-41272; Strand Rd; s/d incl breakfast $30/50; ❋) A grand exterior and an address on Strand Rd are masks for bare, small, overpriced rooms.

Palé Mon Hotel   HOTEL $
(☏ 059-41841; palemon.myeik@gmail.com; Kanph-yar Rd; r $35-45; ❋ 🛜) A cavernous place with worn, bare rooms, inconveniently located near the airport. A last resort only.

🍴 Eating

A local speciality in Myeik is *kaq kyi kaiq* (scissor-cut noodles): rice noodles that have been cut into short strips and stir-fried with egg and seafood – a lot like *phat Thai*. Try them at the friendly **vendor** (no roman-script sign; K800) near the mosque in the Muslim quarter.

Shwe Mon
BURMESE $

(Sake Nge Jetty Rd; meals from K2000; ⊙11am-9pm) Burmese curry restaurant serving what is one of the richest, tastiest chicken curries we've come across yet.

Zan Pya
MUSLIM-BURMESE $

(Kanphyar Rd; mains K1500; ⊙7.30am-6.30pm) Hole-in-the-wall, with no english sign, serving heaped plates of delicious chicken biryani that often sell out early. Look for the large aluminum pots a couple doors down from OK Mobile.

Karaweik
BURMESE $

(Kanphyar Rd; mains from K1500; ⊙11am-10pm; 🗐) The best bang for your kyat; a popular place with inviting, open air-seating that serves immense bowls of *kyè òu* (see p358) and other noodle and rice dishes. There is no roman-script sign; look for the white villa.

G Apparao Restaurant
MUSLIM-BURMESE $

(Kanphyar Rd; snacks from K200; ⊙6am-9pm) Muslim teashop serving good tea and a variety of freshly made snacks.

G-Naidu
INDIAN-BURMESE $

(Kanphyar Rd; mains from K500) Teashop-restaurant selling southern Indian–style dishes such as dosai. Look for the blue interior.

ⓘ Information

When we were in town there was not yet an international ATM, but **AGD Bank** (Bo Gyoke Rd; ⊙9am-2pm) has a currency exchange counter.

Air tickets can be bought at **Sun Far** (✆41160; Pyi Taw Thar St; ⊙7am-5pm).

Internet is available at a **cafe** (Kanphyar Rd; per hr K400; ⊙9am-10pm) just east of the town centre.

ⓘ Getting There & Away

At press time, foreigners were not yet allowed to travel by bus to/from Myeik; this may have changed by the time you read this.

AIR

Air KBZ (✆ in Myeik 059-42224, in Yangon 01-372 977; www.airkbz.com; 53 (B) St; ⊙9am-6pm) and Myanma Airways (p119) link Myeik with Kawthoung ($80 to $88, 45 minutes, twice daily) and Yangon ($130 to $147, two hours, twice daily), the latter via a stop in Dawei ($75 to $78, 30 minutes, twice daily).

BOAT

Three companies operate speedboats from Myeik, departing from **Sake Nge Jetty** and bound north to Dawei ($25, five hours, 11am) and south

to Kawthoung ($40, seven hours, 8am). Tickets are sold from various **vendors** (Sake Nge Jetty Rd; ⊙6am-7pm) opposite Sake Nge Jetty.

ⓘ Getting Around

Most destinations in central Myeik are walkable; a motorcycle taxi to/from Dolphin Guest House will run K1000, to Myeik's airport, just east of town, about K2000.

Myeik Archipelago

In the extreme south of the Tanintharyi coast where Myanmar and Thailand share a narrow peninsula, are the beautiful islands of the Myeik Archipelago (also known as the Mergui Archipelago). Far beyond the value of any local product (rubber, marine products or swiftlets' nests) the region has huge, almost completely untapped potential in the beachgoing and ecotourist market. For a run down of some of the archipelago's noteworthy islands and dive sites, see p125. Most of the islands are uninhabited, though a few are home to tiny villages with mixed populations of Burmese and 'sea gypsies', also known as the Moken, a nomadic seafaring people who sail from island to island, stopping off to repair their boats or fishing nets (for more on the Moken, see p333).

✖ Activities

The vast expanse of the Myeik Archipelago coupled with the area's lack of infrastructure mean that to explore the area, you'll have to sign on to a multiday live-aboard diving tour or a boat excursion, neither of which come particularly cheap.

Diving

Most visitors approach Myeik Archipelago via multiday, live-aboard diving tours, all of which are based out of Thailand. The various outfits run pre-scheduled three- to eight-day excursions generally to sites south of Black Rock. Fees for a five-day trip can range from about $800 to $1500, which includes accommodation and meals, but generally not the Myeik Archipelago entrance fee (excursions south of Black Rock $100 per person for the first five days, excursions north of Black Rock $150 per person for the first five days plus $20 per every additional day).

Recommended outfits operating out of Ranong include **A One Diving Team** (✆ in Thailand +66 81891 5510; www.a-one-diving.com; Ranong, Thailand), with capable Western divemasters; the more budget-oriented **Andaman International Dive Center** (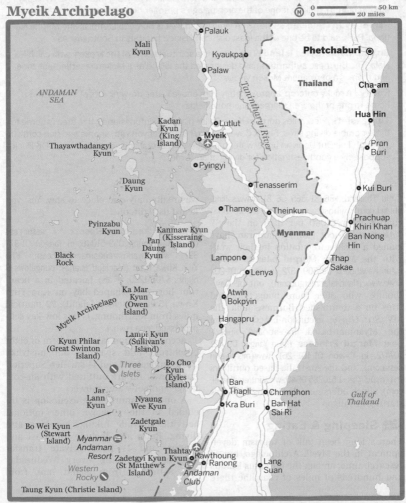 in Thailand +66 89814 1092, in Thailand +66 77 834 824; www.aidcdive.com; 97/21 Th Phetkasem, Ranong); and the French-run **Smiling Seahorse** (✆ in Thailand +66 84452 4413, in Thailand +66 86011 0614; www.thesmilingseahorse.com; 170 Th Ruangrat, Ranong; ⊙ 9am-6pm), which offers long excursions to more remote destinations such as Black Rock. Elsewhere in Thailand, **Thailand Dive & Sail** (✆ in Thailand +66 87469 7801; www.thailanddiveandsail. com; Khao Lak, Thailand), based out of Khao Lak, has experienced divemasters.

Boating

If you'd rather stay above water, various outfits, including some of the diving outfits listed earlier, conduct multiday island-hopping excursions, which offer visits to Moken villages, snorkelling, kayaking and visiting beaches, among other activities. Fees for all-inclusive five-day excursions range from $1300 to $2000, and outfits include **Burma Boating** (✆ in Thailand +66 21070 445; www.burmaboating.com), which runs the Austrian-captained SY *Meta IV*, a beautiful vintage Thai teak sailboat; the Thailand-based **Sailing Charter Phuket**

Myeik Archipelago

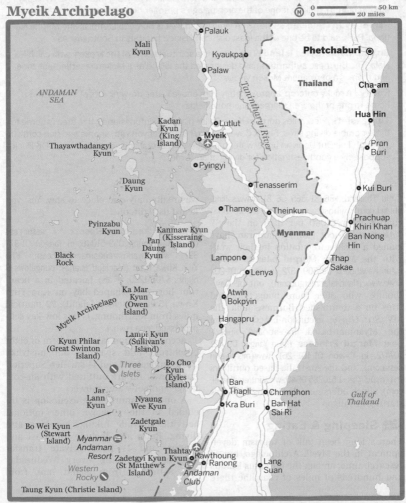

ISLANDS OF THE MYEIK ARCHIPELAGO

The Burmese used to say there were more than 4000 islands in the Myeik Archipelago, though British surveyors recognised only 804. The British took the liberty of naming many of the islands, although some are also interchangeably known by their Burmese and sometimes Moken names (some islands are even known by old Thai or Arabic names). Most are uninhabited – some little more than rocky outcrops – some have Navy and Army stations and are off limits, while others are home to Burmese and occasionally small Moken communities.

The more noteworthy islands and diving spots in the Myeik Archipelago include the following (from north to south):

Kanmaw Kyun (Kisseraing Island) A large island (409-sq-km) home to Burmese, Karen and Moken villages and expansive rubber plantations.

Black Rock A remote, rocky outpost that is the northernmost extent of most diving excursions. The site is home to clear water and rich sea life, including manta rays (typically around March), making it one of the archipelago's premier diving sites.

Lampi Kyun (Sullivan's Island) A large island that is home to Lampi Island Marine National Park, said to be one of the least disturbed island habitats in Southeast Asia.

Bo Cho Kyun (Eyles Island) This island is a spiritual home of the Moken, who call it Pu Nala. The Burmese authorities have designated the island as a Moken resettlement zone, and there is a permanent Moken village.

Rocky I A rocky outcrop, approximately 10m above water, drawing lots of sea life and home to one of the area's largest anemone fields.

Three Islets A few miles north of Kyun Philar (Great Swinton Island), this area is home to three notable diving sites: Shark Cave, an underwater canyon with sharks and rich coral; In Through The Out Door, an underwater passage with several species of coral; and OK Rock, supposedly a good destination for diving at any time.

(✉ in Thailand +66 81 365 56 81; www.sailing-phuket.com), whose excursions (whole boat charter from €1080 per day) on the SY *Nakamal*, 42-foot (13m) catamaran, have gained a positive reputation in their work with the Moken; **Mergui Islands Safari** (✉ in Kawthoung 09 509 1672, in Yangon 01-202 064; www.islandsafarimergui.com), out of Kawthoung, who offer more budget-oriented trips on a refurbished Burmese junk, the MV *Sea Gipsy*; excursion-based trips on the Myanmar-based live-aboard speedboat **Mergui Princess** (✉ in Yangon 09 421 107472, in Yangon 01-401 261; www.merguiprincess.com); and the Australia-based outfitters **Intrepid** (✉ +1 510285 0640; www.intrepidtravel.com), which offers nine-day sailing packages starting in Yangon.

🛏 Sleeping & Eating

There's long been talk of tourism development in the Myeik Archipelago, but at research time, among the 800-plus islands and hundreds of miles of coastline there was really only one place to stay. Yes, you heard us right, one.

Myanmar Andaman Resort RESORT $$$
(✉ in Kawthoung 059-51046, in Yangon 01-377 891; www.myanmarandamanresort.com; Kho Yinn Khwa Kyun (Macleod Island); bungalows 3 nights $700-1220; ❄ 🛜) Located in a beautiful horseshoe-shaped bay on Kho Yinn Khwa Kyun (Macleod Island), 72 nautical miles from Kawthoung, is this low-key self-professed 'eco resort'.

Accommodation takes the form of eight beachfront and spacious but unstylish 'Suite' bungalows and 14 smaller 'Superior' bungalows. All are outfitted with air-con, fridge and hot-water showers.

A one-day snorkelling excursion is included in the package; other optional activities include hiking, kayaking and diving. Rates also include breakfast and dinner, and 1½-hour private transfer to/from Kawthoung every Wednesday and Saturday (from island 7am, from

Kyun Philar (Great Swinton Island) Home to a freshwater spring where passing boats fill up and a small Burmese/Moken village, there's decent snorkelling here and the surrounding islands offer good diving.

Nyaung Wee Kyun A seasonal home for the Moken, this island also has beaches, clear water and wildlife, making it a popular stopover for boat tours. A resort has long been under construction on nearby 115 Island.

High Rock From the surface it's little more than a tree-topped limestone outcropping, but High Rock is home to an abundance of marine life, including at least five types of nudibranch, making it a lauded dive site.

Taung Taw Win Kyun (South Twin Island)/Myauk Taw Win Kyun (North Twin Island) Home to at least three good dive sites including Pinnacle, north of Myauk Taw Win Kyun (North Twin Island), a known manta ray gathering site during February/March. Taung Taw Win Kyun (South Twin Island) has clear blue water and fan coral.

Bo Wei Kyun (Stewart Island) South of this island is a rocky outcrop with above- and underwater caves. Nearby Maccarthy Rock has a beautiful limestone cliff more than 30m high and good diving. Cavern Rock, nearby, is another good dive site.

Kho Yinn Khwa Kyun (Macleod Island) This horseshoe-shaped island 40 nautical miles from Kawthoung is home to Myanmar Andaman Resort, the only real beach accommodation in the entire Myeik Archipelago. There are at least 20 known dive sites around the island, including North Rock, where sea snakes and sea turtles are often sighted.

Western Rocky An underwater cave that has been known to draw sharks makes this arguably the Myeik Archipelago's finest dive site.

Thahtay Kyun Opposite Kawthoung, this beach-free island, known in Moken as Pulau Ru, is home to Andaman Club. The resort offers trips to beaches on Zadelgale Kyun and Zadetgyi Kyun (St Matthew's Island), each about 45 minutes away by speedboat.

Kawthoung noon). The resort is open from October to April.

Kawthoung ကော့သောင်း

🎵 059 / POPULATION C20,000

This small port at the southernmost tip of Tanintharyi Region – the most southern point of mainland Myanmar (500 miles/800km from Yangon and 1200 miles or 2000km from the country's northern tip) – is separated from Thailand by a broad estuary in the Pagyan River. To the British it was known as Victoria Point and to the Thais it's known as Ko Song (Second Island). The Burmese name, Kawthoung (also spelt Kawthaung), is a mispronunciation of the latter.

It's one of the earliest British possessions in Myanmar, obtained after the first Anglo-Burmese War in 1826. Today, the town is a scrappy border post and jumping-off point for boating and diving excursions into the Myeik Archipelago.

◉ Sights

Cape Bayint Naung   PARK
(ဘုရင့်နောင်အငူ; Strand Rd; ⊙24hour) FREE At the southern end of the harbour lies this park, named for King Bayinnaung, a Burmese monarch who invaded Thailand several times between 1548 and 1569. A bronze statue of Bayinnaung, outfitted in full battle gear and brandishing a sword pointed at Thailand – not exactly a welcoming sight for visiting Thais – stands at the crest of a hill on the cape.

Anandar Paya   BUDDHIST TEMPLE
(အာနန္ဒာဘုရား; ⊙daylight hours) FREE Towering over Kawthoung is this hilltop temple with great views of the city.

🛏 Sleeping & Eating

A knot of stalls, teashops, beer gardens and restaurants can be found at the southern end of Strand Rd, opposite the park at Cape Bayint Nuang.

Garden Hotel
HOTEL $

(☑ 059-51731; www.gardenhotelmm.com; Shwe Minwon Rd; s/d $25/40; ❄ ☎) Probably the best place in town, the Garden combines tidy, tiny single rooms on the ground floor and larger double rooms upstairs. A downside is that the hotel is located an uphill hike about 1 mile north of the jetty.

Kawthaung Motel
HOTEL $

(☑ 059-51474; www.mountpleasanthotelmyanmar.com; Bosonpat St; r incl breakfast $20-45; ❄ ☎) A former government hotel, the Kawthaung has recently renovated, mostly spacious and very mint-green rooms, some with great views over the ocean. Located about half a mile west of the jetty.

Honey Bear Hotel
HOTEL $

(☑ 059-51352; Strand Rd; r 800B; ❄ ☎) Overlooking the jetty, the Honey Bear consists of 39 relatively modern but simple rooms equipped with TV, air-con, hard beds and cold-water showers.

Penguin Hotel
HOTEL $

(☑ 059-51145; 339 Sabel St; r incl breakfast $20-70; ❄ ☎) The rooms at the Penguin are new-feeling, but a tight fit, particularly the fan-cooled singles. Located a couple of blocks west of the jetty, behind the market.

Andaman Club
RESORT $$$

(☑ in Thailand +66 2287 3031, in Yangon 01-572 535; www.andamanclub.com; Thahtay Kyun; r incl breakfast $107-155, ste incl breakfast $224-382) Located on Thahtay Kyun, a large private island directly south of Kawthoung, is this 205-room luxury resort. It's worth pointing out that there's no beach on the island, but golf, gambling, spas and excursions to other islands can be arranged. Andaman Club can be reached by boat from Ranong's Saphan Pla Pier or by an hourly shuttle boat from Kawthoung.

Daw Moe
BURMESE $

(Neikban St; meals from K2000; ⊙ 9am-9pm) This tin-roofed restaurant, with no roman-script sign, serves a disproportionately vast spread of Burmese dishes. Located on the uphill portion of Neikban St, about a half mile from the pier – locals will point you in the direction.

LOCAL KNOWLEDGE

CLIVE WHITE: DIVE GUIDE

How long have you been diving in the Myeik Archipelago?

I'm a professional underwater photographer and dive guide with 14 years of experience in the Myeik Archipelago.

What's unique about the area?

The archipelago consists of more than 800 islands, including many unexplored areas. The islands and pinnacles are formed from limestone and are of varying sizes, some islands covering many acres, some just breaking the surface. These intricate structures are the perfect substrate for soft corals, which grow in abundance. These limestone formations also have large underwater caves and interesting swim-throughs.

Is the archipelago home to any notable animals or coral?

The amazing diversity of marine life in the region ranges from large fauna, such as sharks, rays and other pelagic animals, to many smaller species such as nudibranches, harlequin shrimp and cuttlefish. There are some very special finds here such as frogfish, ornate ghost pipefish and seahorses. There have even been sightings of the extremely rare lacey scorpionfish; this species is the Holy Grail for underwater photographers.

What are some particularly recommendable dive spots in the Myeik Archipelago?

Any trip to the region is incomplete without visiting the premier dive site, Black Rock. Interesting fauna can be found here, and it is also a famous giant manta ray aggregation site. The Three Islets group of islands have a well-known swim-through called In Through The Out Door. This is a must-visit dive site for those looking for diverse macro life and an exhilarating dive full of surprises. The islands and pinnacles at Western Rocky are another highlight of the archipelago due to a huge, cavern-like swim-through approximately 100-ft (30m) long.

❶ GETTING TO THAILAND: KAWTHOUNG TO RANONG

Kawthoung (also known as Victoria Point), at the far southern end of Tanintharyi Region, is, as of 2013, one of Myanmar's new 'open' borders for foreign tourists. But there are a few caveats, and the following information is liable to change, so be sure to check the situation locally before you travel.

Getting to the border The bright green **Myanmar border post** (Strand Rd; ⊕ 7am-4pm) is located a few steps from Kawthoung's jetty.

If crossing from Thailand, the **Thai border post** (Saphan Pla Pier, Ranong; ⊕ 7.30pm-4.30pm) is at Saphan Pla Pier, located about 6 miles, a 60B motorcycle taxi ride or 20B *sŏrng·tăa·ou* (pick-up), from Ranong.

At the border If you've arrived in Kawthoung from elsewhere in Myanmar, you're free to exit the country here. After clearing Myanmar immigration, you'll be herded to a boat (per person from 50B) for the 20-minute ride to Ranong. On the Thai side, the authorities will issue you permission to stay in Thailand up to 15 days, or you can enter with a Thai visa obtained overseas.

If approaching from Thailand, after passing Thai immigration, board a waiting boat (per person from 50B) for the 20-minute ride to Kawthoung. Upon arriving at the Myanmar immigration office, you'll most likely be greeted by an English-speaking tout who insists on 'helping' by translating and making photocopies in return for an exorbitant fee; you can ignore this, but it might complicate things. If you haven't already obtained a Myanmar visa, you'll need to pay $10 for a border pass, which will allow you to stay in a 24-mile radius of Kawthoung for up to 14 days; your passport will be kept at the border. If you already possess a Myanmar visa obtained from abroad, you'll be allowed to enter, but will most likely be regarded with some suspicion, and will probably be required to show or purchase tickets for onward travel.

Moving on Ranong is a 60B motorcycle taxi ride or 20B *sŏrng·tăa·ou* (pick-up) from Saphan Pla Pier. **Happy Air** (❷ in Ranong 081 891 5800; www.happyair.co.th) and **Nok Air** (❷ in Thailand 1318; www.nokair.com) offer daily flights between Ranong and Bangkok (from 2000B, 1½ hours to 1¾, four to six departures daily), while major bus destinations include Bangkok (240B to 680B, 10 hours), Hat Yai (410B, five hours) and Phuket (240B, five to six hours).

❶ Information

Exchange (but no international ATM) is available at the huge branch of **KBZ Bank** (Bosonpat Rd; ⊕ 9am-3pm Mon-Sat), located a brief walk from the pier.

Internet is available at **Myanmar Info-Tech** (Strand Rd; per her K900; ⊕ 8am-10pm) in the temple-like Shwe Nan Taw Plaza, at the southern end of Strand Rd.

❶ Getting There & Away

At press time, foreigners were not allowed to travel by bus to/from Kawthoung.

AIR

Air KBZ (❷ in Kawthoung 09 4306 9018, in Yangon 01-372 977; www.airkbz.com; Bosonpat St; ⊕ 7.30am-5pm) and Myanma Airways (p119) link Kawthoung with Yangon ($192, three hours, twice daily) via stops in Myeik ($54, 45 minutes, twice daily) and Dawei ($112, 80 minutes, twice daily).

BOAT

Three companies run speedboats, departing daily at 3am for Myeik ($40, seven hours) and Dawei ($80, 12 hours).

❶ Getting Around

Everything listed here is located no more than a brief walk from the jetty; Garden Hotel is a K1000 ride in a *thoun bein*.

Kawthoung's airport is approximately 8 miles from the jetty; a *thoun bein* will run about K4000.

Bagan & Central Myanmar

Why Go?

This heartland of the Bamar people has been the location of three former Burmese capitals – Bagan, Pyay and Taungoo – as well as the latest surreal one, Nay Pyi Taw. Of this quartet, it's Bagan with its wondrous vista of pagodas and stupas, many dating back to the 12th century, that's the star attraction. The tallest and most majestic of Bagan's temples, built of brick, decorated inside with beautiful frescos and topped with gilded *hti* pinnacles, mix Hindu and buddhist images with locally brewed *nat* (spirits) in nooks and crannies.

Most visitors fly directly to Bagan, but central Myanmar also provides scenic rewards for adventurous travellers. It may be known as the 'dry zone', but the region is far from a desert. Beside highways and rickety train tracks amble ox carts through rice fields and rolling plains, all rimmed by the Shan Mountains to the east and the snaking Ayeyarwady (Irrawaddy) River to the west, creating scenes that hark back centuries.

Best Places to Eat

➡ Black Bamboo (p135)

➡ Grandma Café (p161)

➡ Maw Khan Nong (p158)

➡ Mona Liza 2 (p164)

➡ Starbeam Bistro (p139)

Best Places to Stay

➡ Blue Bird Hotel (p143)

➡ Hotel Chindwin (p148)

➡ Hotel@Tharabar Gate (p139)

➡ Myanmar Beauty Guest House II, III & IV (p154)

When to Go

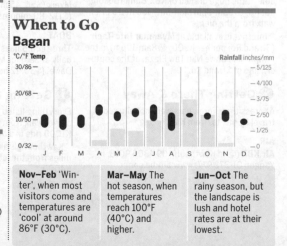

Bagan

Nov–Feb 'Winter', when most visitors come and temperatures are 'cool' at around 86°F (30°C).

Mar–May The hot season, when temperatures reach 100°F (40°C) and higher.

Jun–Oct The rainy season, but the landscape is lush and hotel rates are at their lowest.

History

Conquering armies led by various peoples, including the Pyu, the Mon and the Burmese, have marauded across this central plain, the 'heart of Myanmar', over the centuries. The area around Pyay served as the Pyu capital from the 5th to 9th centuries AD and some historians consider the Pyu to be founders of Myanmar's 'first empire', although little is known of this vanished group.

Bagan's burst of spiritual creativity lasted two-and-a-half centuries, beginning in 1047 and ending as the pounding footfall of Kublai Khan's raiders approached in 1287. The latest empire to lodge in the area is the military junta, which founded the new capital of Nay Pyi Taw in 2005.

ℹ Getting There & Away

Bagan is the main entry point to the region for visitors arriving by air, although Mandalay is also convenient for northern destinations such as Monywa. Yangon is a convenient international entry point for more southerly destinations such as Pyay or Taungoo. Nyaung U is the principal gateway to Bagan, with a train station, a jetty and the airport. Most visitors by boat come downriver from Mandalay on a fast boat or a slower, luxury cruise. The majority of long-haul bus routes (eg Yangon–Mandalay) miss Bagan, but there are a few direct bus links between Bagan and Yangon, Mandalay and Inle Lake, including some luxurious sleeper options. Trains to the Bagan area are slow and impractical, with the exception of the Yangon–Bagan sleeper trains. The more interesting road route from Yangon to Bagan is via Pyay and Magwe.

BAGAN

☑ 061

One of Myanmar's main attractions, this is a temple town. The area known as Bagan (ပုဂံ) or, bureaucratically, as the 'Bagan Archaeological Zone', occupies an impressive 26-sq-mile area, 118 miles south of Mandalay and 429 miles north of Yangon. The Ayeyarwady River drifts past its northern and western sides. See p165 for more on the temples.

The area's most active town and main transport hub is Nyaung U, in the northeast corner. About 2.5 miles west, Old Bagan is the former site of the village that was relocated two miles south to New Bagan in 1990. Between the two is Myinkaba, a village boasting a long-running lacquerware tradition. One thing to keep in mind, particularly for travellers exploring the region, is that

Bagan is most definitely not Siem Reap or even Luang Prabang. It's more of an overgrown village and lacks anything resembling a night scene, although it does have basic traveller amenities. Plan your partying somewhere else.

Connecting the towns are paved roads making a 12-mile oval. In between and around these towns is the bulk of the Bagan action: the plain, featuring most of the temples, all connected with a vast network of bumpy dirt roads and trails.

🏃 Activities

Boat Trips

Sunset chasing in Bagan isn't restricted to the tops of temples. An interesting alternative is a dusk **boat trip** (per boat $10-15) on the Ayeyarwady. The hour-long tours offered by the boat folk at the Old Bagan jetty tend to cater to package tourists, but drop by to arrange your own cruise.

You can also arrange an interesting boat and taxi side-trip to the mountaintop **Tan Kyi Paya**, one of four stupas that marked the original edges of the city. Another possible boat trip is to three temples north of Nyaung U.

Ballooning

The best way to truly appreciate Bagan's size and sprawl is from the basket of a hot-air balloon belonging to **Balloons over Bagan** (☑ 061-60058; www.balloonsoverbagan.com; office in Bagan Thiripyitsaya Sanctuary Resort; per person stand-by rate $320). These magical 45-minute rides over one of the world's most highly acclaimed ballooning spots only run from October to March. Sometimes sunrise flights are booked up to a month or more in advance, but *if* there's space, any hotel or guesthouse should be able to arrange a ticket.

The slickly run company, owned by an Australian-Burmese couple and employing about 100 locals, has 10 balloons that usually fit up to 10 passengers and a pilot. The experience begins with a pick up from your hotel in one of their fleet of lovingly restored, pre-WWII Chevrolet CMP buses partly made of teak. You can have coffee and snacks while watching the UK-made balloons fill with hot air, and sparkling wine and snacks after you land and watch them get packed up again.

Although sunset flights are offered (depending on weather conditions), the sunrise ones are preferable as the cooler dawn air allows pilots to fly the balloons at lower altitude for a closer view of the temples.

❧ Courses

**Bagan Thiripyitsaya
Sanctuary Resort** COOKING CLASS
(☎ 061-60048; www.thiripyitsaya-resort.com) This resort offers a variety of courses, including a three-hour cooking course covering four or five traditional dishes for a maximum of four participants ($100 per person). Other classes include meditation training with a monk (one/two hours $70/100).

ℹ Information

For travel information, try Nyaung U's Ever Sky Information Service or the government-run MTT office in New Bagan.

Nyaung U and New Bagan have post offices. It's possible to get an online fix at internet cafes in Nyaung U and New Bagan. Free wi-fi is now widely available at most guesthouses and hotels around Bagan, plus some restaurants and cafes.

The Map of Bagan (www.dpsmap.com/bagan; K1000) is sold at most hotels and at the airport. It shows many of the area's paths, but isn't always 100% accurate.

ℹ Getting There & Around

To orient themselves, many visitors opt for a 'greatest hits' tour of the temples on horse cart or by car, then follow it up by checking more remote or lesser-known temples by bike.

FROM THE AIRPORT

Taxis between Nyaung U airport and hotels in Nyaung U, Old Bagan and New Bagan cost K5000, K6000 and K7000 respectively. Horse carts and taxis are cheaper from the Old Bagan or Nyaung U jetties, if you arrive by boat.

BICYCLE

Bikes are widely available and can be an ideal way of getting around, despite the direct exposure to sun and some dirt roads that slow you up. Essentially all accommodation places rent bicycles: in Nyaung U it costs about K2000 per day to K5000 per day, depending on the condition and model of bike.

Traffic is pretty light on all roads. Early-morning or late-afternoon rides along the sealed Bagan–Nyaung U Rd are particularly rewarding. It's worth planning ahead a little, as the bulk of the temples in the Central Plain have little shade and nowhere to get lunch. The most convenient temple dining options are in and around Old Bagan.

HORSE CART

A popular but uncomfortable and slow way of seeing the ruins is from the shaded, padded bed of a horse cart. Drivers speak some English (at least), know where to find the 'keyholders'

to locked sites and can point out temples with few or no tourists around. Some might stop by a shop in the hope of securing a commission; it's OK to say 'no thanks'. A cart works best for two passengers, but it's possible to go with three or (for a family with younger children) four.

From Nyaung U or Old Bagan, a day with a horse cart and driver costs about K15,000 to K20,000; a half-day is about K10,000. Prices are sometimes a little higher out of Old Bagan due to the proliferation of high-end hotels.

PICK-UP TRUCKS

A pick-up (K500; hourly 7am to 3pm) runs from outside the Nyaung U market, ending near the junction in New Bagan and passing Wetkyi-in, Old Bagan and Myinbaga on the way. This could be used to jump from one place to the next, then walk around the temples, particularly on the North Plain or around Old Bagan.

TAXI

Hiring a shared taxi for the day in Nyaung U costs about $35 and drivers are usually quite knowledgeable about which temples to visit. Old Bagan hotels will charge anything up to $75 to hire an unshared taxi. Chartered taxis are also convenient ways of making day trips to Mt Popa and Salay. Taxis between Nyaung U and New Bagan cost about K7000, or K15,000 return.

TRISHAW

There's little trishaw activity outside Nyaung U, where you can get one at the jetty or bus station; the pedal into town is around K2000.

Nyaung U ညောင်ဦး
☎ 061

A bustling river town with more action than is on offer elsewhere in Bagan, Nyaung U is where most independent travellers hang their hat (or backpack). Roaming the back roads towards the jetty or stopping at scrappy teashops will attract friendly wide-eyed looks. There are a handful of temples to see, including the Shwezigon Paya, and a lively market. Visitors staying in New or Old Bagan tend to make it here at some stage, either to experience the restaurant scene (the closest the Bagan area gets to nightlife) or for transport links to other destinations around Myanmar.

Guesthouses and roadside restaurants now push a couple of miles west, along the road to Old Bagan, reaching the small village of **Wetkyi-in** (Giant Pig). The town was named for a mythical pig that, according to local legend, inhabited the lake there and was responsible for the deaths of many

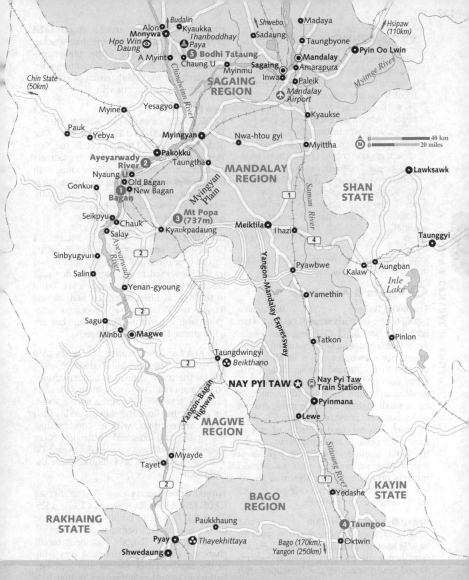

Bagan & Central Myanmar Highlights

1 Watch from a **hot-air balloon** (p129) as the sun rises or sets over the temple-studded plain of Bagan

2 Hit the **Ayeyarwady River** on a Bagan–Mandalay boat, or on a half-day trip to nearby temples (p129)

3 Pay respects to Myanmar's 37 **nat** at their spiritual home, the monkey-tastic volcanic mountaintop temple at **Mt Popa** (p144)

4 Hang with elephants at a working camp (p154) east of **Taungoo**

5 Ponder what the Buddha would have felt to see his likeness fashioned as a 30-storey concrete statue at **Bodhi Tataung** (p151)

local people before eventually being killed by a future king of Bagan.

◉ Sights & Activities

Thanakha Gallery MUSEUM, SHOP
(☑061-60179; cnr Yarkinnthar Hotel Rd & Main Rd; ⏱9am-9pm) FREE Claiming that it's the 'Only One Thanakha Gallery In the World', this sizeable complex has a small gallery devoted to the myriad medicinal and cos-metic uses of the thanakha tree (*Limonia acidissima*), from its roots to its bark. It has a small plantation of the trees, around which bounce a posse of cute bunny rabbits, to which you can feed bunches of greens. Really, the place is a glorified shop for the thanakha cosmetics of **Shwe Pyi Nann** (www.shwepyinann.com), as well as a good range of other Bagan and Myanmar souve-nirs. A restaurant, internet cafe and beauty salon round out the complex.

Bagan Nyaung U Golf Club GOLF
(☑061-60035; www.amazing-hotel.com; green fee for 9/18 holes incl clubs & caddy $40/70; ⏱6am-6pm) Just south of town, this government-owned facility is run by the Amazing Bagan Resort and has about half a dozen pagodas scattered around its 18-hole, par-72 course, making for some memorable match play. Buggy rental is available for US$15/30 per nine/18 holes.

🛏 Sleeping

★**New Wave Guesthouse** GUESTHOUSE $
(☑061-60731; Bagan–Nyaung U (Main) Rd, Wetkyi-in; r $25-50; ❉🛜) Opened in 2013, it is to be hoped this place sparks a new wave of smarter guesthouses around Bagan. The attractive rooms include hotel-like touches such as hairdryer and kettle, plus hand-crafted wooden beds. Highly recommended but watch out for rapidly rising prices, as it was very new during our visit.

New Park Hotel HOTEL $
(☑061-60322; www.newparkmyanmar.com; 4 Thiripyitsaya; s $20-40, d $25-45; ❉@🛜) One of the best all-round budget hotels, the New Park is tucked away in the leafy backstreets off Restaurant Row. The older rooms, with bungalow-style front decks, are comfortable, wood-floor set-ups, with spic-and-span bath-rooms. The newer wing brings more space, a fridge, TV and even a rain shower.

Eden Motel GUESTHOUSE $
(☑061-60812; Anawrahta Rd; r $15-25; ❉🛜) Spread over three buildings and split in two by the busy road to the airport, Eden isn't exactly paradise. The best rooms are found in the newest Eden Motel III and include flatscreen TV and a well-appointed bath-room with a bathtub. The young staff are quite attuned to backpacker needs.

May Kha Lar Guest House GUESTHOUSE $
(☑061-60907; Main Rd; s $13-20, d $18-28; ❉🛜) One of the more appealing budget options on the main road, the reception includes lots of handy traveller info and a shrine room. On the ground floor the cheap, gaudily tiled rooms are compact, with air-conditioning, ceiling fan and attached bathroom. Nicer upstairs options have wooden floors and TV. The cheapest singles and doubles share the bathroom.

Winner Guest House GUESTHOUSE $
(☑061-61069; Main Rd, Wetkyi-in; s $9-20, d $15-23; ❉🛜) This little family-run guesthouse on the road to Old Bagan is one of the old school cheapies. Bargain basement rooms share the common bathroom. A new wing at the rear includes air-con and a private bathroom. Another advantage is that it is somewhat nearer the temples than the aver-age Nyaung U address.

Grand Empire Hotel HOTEL $
(☑061-60206; grandempirehotel.nyu@gmail.com; Main Rd; s $25, d $30-50; ❉🛜) An interest-ing fusion concept, we are not convinced it entirely works. Hidden behind a garish new Chinese-like exterior is essentially an old hotel with minimal upgrades. It's only worth investing in higher-priced rooms if

accommodation is at a premium. Cheaper rooms involve outside access from strange portacabin style doors.

★ Oasis Hotel
BOUTIQUE HOTEL $$

(✆061-60923; www.oasishotelbagan.com; Anawrahta Rd; superior $50-80, deluxe $70-100; ✳🛜❄) A welcoming little boutique hotel, the thoughtfully decorated rooms include a parquet wooden floor and Burmese handicrafts, as well as the basics such as a flatscreen TV and in-room safe. The deluxe rooms are a worthwhile investment thanks to additional space and a location next to the brand new swimming pool.

Thante Hotel
HOTEL $$

(✆061-60315; www.thanteyu.com; Anawrahta Rd; s/d/tr $50/60/85; ✳🛜❄) Just off the main road, this 37-room hotel offers roomy bungalows on shady grounds and has an inviting swimming pool. The decor is dated, but the rooms are spacious and come with new air-con systems, satellite TV, refrigerator, bathtub, wooden floor and deckchairs on the small porch. There is a good bakery and restaurant on site.

Yar Kinn Tha Hotel
HOTEL $$

(✆061-60051; Anawrahta Rd; r $30-60; ✳🛜) This long-running hotel provides fair value for money thanks to stable prices, particularly now that most nearby guesthouses have hiked their rates up. The $35 rooms with balcony include a garden view, but the $60 bungalow rooms are the best investment with oodles of space.

Bagan Princess Hotel
HOTEL $$

(✆061-60661; www.baganprincesshotel.com; Bagan-Nyaung U Rd; r $50-60; ✳@🛜❄) Built around a small pool, this curiously designed hotel in Wetkyi-in offers amply proportioned rooms, all with separate Jacuzzi bathtubs as well as showers in the large bathrooms. Spend a little extra for one of the upper-level deluxe rooms, which have more light and direct pool access.

Bagan Umbra Hotel
HOTEL $$

(✆061-60034; baganumbra@gmail.com; Bagan-Nyaung U Rd; s $40-60, d $45-70; ✳@🛜❄) Formerly the Golden Express Hotel, this kitsch complex features a chapel-like reception and four bright motel-style units. The best value of the four classes are the superior single/double rooms, with wood floors, a bit more space and tubs. A planned new wing will bring a bit of boutique to Bagan Umbra.

Amazing Bagan Resort
RESORT $$$

(✆061-60035; www.amazing-hotel.com; deluxe $140, ste $210; ✳@🛜❄) The smartest resort in the Nyaung U area, Amazing Bagan does indeed boast an amazing lobby complete with a hanging display of supersized Pathein umbrellas. The bungalow suites in brick buildings mimicking old Bagan architecture are best. Personal touches include sun hats in the rooms, free internet and bicycles. Located next to the golf club.

✗ Eating & Drinking

Nyaung U's Yar Kinn Thar Hotel Rd (aka Restaurant Row) is a strip of atmospheric open-air eateries geared towards foreign visitors. It's touristy, but easily the epicentre of Bagan action as far as such a thing exists. Many of the restaurants are copycats, with similar 'everything goes' menus (Chinese, Burmese, Thai, Indian, pizza and 'Western' options).

★ Myo Myo Myanmar Rice Food
BURMESE $

(Bagan–Nyaung U (Main) Rd; meals K2000-4000; ⊙7am-6pm) One of the most popular

---

WHERE TO STAY?

There are three distinct accommodation bases around Bagan, each catering to a different style of visitor.

Old Bagan Closest to the big-time temples, most of Bagan's high-end hotels cluster in and around the riverside and the old palace walls. It's a central location (particularly good for quick visits to Bagan), with plenty of day-time eating options, but less nightlife than Nyaung U. Doubles from $85.

New Bagan Only founded in 1990, New Bagan has by far the best midrange choices, with rooms from around US$25 to US$125. There's also a couple of appealing riverside restaurants.

Nyaung U The budget heart of Bagan, with the liveliest restaurant scene and the bulk of the transport connections, Nyaung U is a real town, with guesthouses from $15. On the downside it's a 2-mile bicycle ride to the temple zone.

Nyaung U

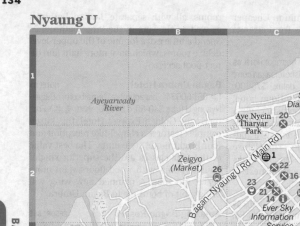

Nyaung U

◉ Sights
1 Thanakha Gallery	C2

🛏 Sleeping
2 Amazing Bagan Resort	D4
3 Bagan Princess Hotel	A3
4 Bagan Umbra Hotel	A4
5 Eden Motel	D1
6 Grand Empire Hotel	D1
7 May Kha Lar Guest House	D1
8 New Park Hotel	C2
9 New Wave Guesthouse	A3
10 Oasis Hotel	D2
11 Thante Hotel	D2
12 Winner Guest House	A3
13 Yar Kinn Tha Hotel	C2

✗ Eating
14 Aroma 2	C2
15 Beach Bagan Restaurant & Bar	D1
16 Black Bamboo	C2
17 Fuji Restaurant	D1
18 Myo Myo Myanmar Rice Food	B3
Pyi Wa	(see 16)
19 Red Pepper	C2
20 San Kabar Restaurant & Pub	C1
21 Shwe Ya Su	C2
22 Weather Spoon's Bagan	C2

🍸 Drinking & Nightlife
23 Hti	C2

🛍 Shopping
24 Mani-Sithu Market	D1

ℹ Transport
25 Buses to Old Bagan	D1
26 Nyaung U Bus Station	B2
27 Pick-ups to Mt Popa	D1

Burmese restaurants in the Bagan area, the owners specialise in the personalised table-top buffets that characterise the national cuisine. However, here they really go to town, with 25 dishes or more appearing at the table, including seasonal specials such as asparagus. Bring a crowd to share.

Aroma 2 INDIAN $

(Yarkinnthar Hotel Rd; dishes K2000-8000; ☉11am-10pm; 🔊) 'No good, no pay' is the mantra of this justifiably confident operation serving delicious veggie and meat curries on banana leaves (or plates) with an endless stream of hot chapattis and five dollops of condiments (including tamarind and mint sauces). With some advance notice, the chef can also whip up various biryani rice dishes.

Weather Spoon's Bagan RESTAURANT $

(Yarkinnthar Hotel Rd; mains K2000-5000; ☉7am-10pm; 🔊) Brits abroad may be familiar with the name, borrowed from one of the UK's discount pub chains. Owner Winton studied balloon piloting in Bristol and clearly spent some time in the local boozers. But Bagan benefits from his experience and he offers the best burger in town, as well as some Asian and international favourites. Lively drinking spot by night.

San Kabar Restaurant & Pub ITALIAN $

(Main Rd; pizza K4000-6000; mains K2500-5500; ☉7am-10pm; 🔊) Famous as the birthplace of Bagan pizza, the San Kabar's streetside candlelit courtyard is all about its thin-crust pies and well-prepared salads. There is so much variety on offer here that staff present diners with not one, but three menus.

Fuji Restaurant JAPANESE $

(Main Rd; mains K2000-4000; ☉8am-9.30pm) An unexpected find in downtown Nyaung U, this Japanese restaurant is one of the cheapest you are likely to find in Myanmar. There is no sushi and sashimi, maybe a blessing given the distance to the coast, but plenty of classics such as ramen, udon, kyoza and tofu. Affordable international and Burmese dishes also make a cameo appearance.

Pyi Wa BAMAR, INTERNATIONAL $

(Yarkinnthar Hotel Rd; noodles & dishes K1500-4000; ☉7am-10pm) Slightly less stylish than some, but Pyi Wa is the only restaurant on the row with a Bagan-era *zedi* (stupa) as a neighbour and staff light up its base at night. The best dishes are Chinese, but do

try the 'potato cracken', fried potato wedges that go particularly well with a bottle of Myanmar Beer.

Shwe Ya Su BEER STATION $

(Yarkinnthar Hotel Rd; dishes K1500-4000; ☉7am-10.30pm) Thanks to the barrels of draught Myanmar Beer, this place has become quite the local hangout. It's a lively spot to revive with twinkling fairy lights hanging from the trees and tasty barbecued snacks.

★ Black Bamboo EUROPEAN $$

(☏061-60782; off Yarkinnthar Hotel Rd; dishes K3500-7000; ☉9am-10pm; 🔊) Run by a French woman and her Burmese husband, this garden cafe and restaurant is something of an oasis. It's a lovely place to relax over a decent steak-frites, a well-made espresso or a delicious homemade ice cream. Service is friendly but leisurely.

Red Pepper THAI, EUROPEAN $$

(☏09-4926 0229; cnr Anawrahta Rd & Thirpyitsaya 3 St; meal K4000-12,000; ☉11am-3pm & 6-10pm) Serving a broad range of Thai dishes, freshly made with an authentic spicy kick, this relaxed venue takes a stab at sophistication with silky pillows on concrete benches in a courtyard facing the main road. It had just reopened following a renovation during our visit.

Beach Bagan Restaurant & Bar PAN-ASIAN $$

(☏061-60126; www.thebeachbaganrestaurant.com; 12 Youne Tan Yat; dishes K5000-10,000; ☉8am-9pm) Signs lead past backstreets from the Nyaung U market to this slick, breezy spot with plenty of parking space for tour buses. The restaurant overlooking the river has wicker chairs and offers Thai, Chinese and Myanmar dishes. Try the roof-top bar for a sunset cocktail, with a happy hour from 4pm to 6pm.

Hti BAR

(5 Thiripyitsaya; ☉5-10pm) One of Nyaung U's only real bars, Hti is the Burmese name for parasol, and this certainly puts most other would-be bars in the shade. The cocktail list is impressive and food is available including Asian and international dishes, plus a barbecue grill. Shishas on demand.

🛍 Shopping

There is a good selection of souvenirs at the Thanakha Gallery (p132) and at shops along Restaurant Row.

BAGAN & CENTRAL MYANMAR NYAUNG U

Mani-Sithu Market
MARKET

(☉6am-5pm Mon-Sat) Near the roundabout at the east end of the main road, this market offers a colourful display of fruit, vegetables, flowers, fish and textiles and is best visited early in the day to see it at its liveliest. There are plenty of traveller-oriented goods (woodcarvings, T-shirts, lacquerware) at its northern end.

❶ Information

For phone calls, try to use internet based comms such as Skype, as government sanctioned calls are overpriced.

Ever Sky Information Service (✆061-60895; Yarkinnthar Hotel Rd; ☉7.30am-9.30pm) On the restaurant strip, this friendly place has travel and transport information and a used bookshop. Staff can get share taxis (to Mt Popa, Kalaw, Salay, around Bagan) for the best available rates.

KBZ Bank (13C Anawrahta Rd) Centrally located bank with an ATM that accepts most international bank cards.

Internet (Thanakar Complex, Yarkinnthar Hotel Rd; ☉9am-9pm)

Post Office (Anawrahta Rd; ☉9.30am-7pm)

❶ Getting There & Away

AIR

The Nyaung U Airport is about 2 miles southeast of the market. Airlines connect Bagan daily with Mandalay ($50 to $55, 30 minutes), Heho ($70 to $75, 40 minutes) and Yangon ($100 to $110, 70 minutes).

Travel agencies sometimes have cheaper tickets than the airline offices. Try **Seven Diamond** (✆061-60883; Main Rd) on Main Rd.

BOAT

Boats to Mandalay go from either Nyaung U or Old Bagan, depending on water levels. The Nyaung U jetty is about half a mile northeast of the Nyaung U market.

The government-run IWT ferry (aka 'slow boat') heads to Mandalay on Monday and Thursday at 5am ($15, two days) and overnights beyond Pakokku. At the time of writing there were no southbound passenger ferries operating to Magwe or Pyay, possibly a blessing in disguise given the slow journey times.

If open (unlikely!) the IWT office, about 300yd (275m) inland from the jetty, sells tickets; alternatively book a ticket through your hotel or an agency, who can also secure tickets for the faster **Malikha 2** ($35, 11 hours) or **N Mai Hka** (Shwe Keinerry; $35, 12 hours) boats to Mandalay.

BUS

The main bus station serving Bagan is on the main road in Nyaung U.

During peak season, it's wise to book bus tickets for Mandalay, Taunggyi (for Inle Lake) and Yangon a couple of days in advance.

Note, some Mandalay-bound buses go via Myingyan, others via Kyaukpadaung and

❶ TRANSPORT OPTIONS TO BAGAN

The following table provides a quick comparison of the various ways of getting to Nyaung U from Yangon and Mandalay

To/from Yangon	Duration	Cost	Frequency
Air	70min	$100-110	frequent
Bus	10hr	K13,000-18,000	frequent
Car	9hr	K150,000	charter
Train	16hr	$30-50	daily
To/from Mandalay	**Duration**	**Cost**	**Frequency**
Air	30min	$50-55	frequent
Boat (slow)	2 days	$15	2 weekly
Boat (fast)	11hr	$35	daily in high season
Bus	7hr	K7500-9000	frequent
Car	6hr	K130,000	charter
Train	8hr	US$4-10	daily

Meiktila. It is worth paying a little more for the minibuses as they can save two or three hours compared with the slower buses. The Yangon-bound service goes via Meiktila and Nay Pyi Taw. There are lots of different operators serving Yangon, but JJ Express leads the way in comfort with only three seats per row in a sort of business class airline configuration.

PICK-UP TRUCKS

The lone daily pick-up service to Mt Popa (K3000 each way, one hour) leaves at 8.30am from in front of the south entrance to the market, and returns at 1pm. From the bus station, half-hourly pick-ups go to Chauk (two hours), where there are onward connections to Salay (one hour). Pick-ups between Nyaung U, Old Bagan and New Bagan run along the main street, starting from the roundabout outside the Nyaung U market.

TAXI

As Bagan has limited bus connections to other major destinations, many travellers share taxis to destinations around the country, but some vehicles are in better condition than others so check out the car before embarking on an epic journey. Ask at Ever Sky or at your hotel. Some sample taxi fares: Inle Lake (K150,000, 12 hours), Kalaw (K130,000, 10 hours), Magwe (K70,000, five hours), Mt Popa (K40,000, 1½ hours), Salay (K50,000, two hours), Mt Popa and Salay (K60,000).

TRAIN

The elaborate and over-the-top Bagan train station is located in splendid isolation about 2.5 miles southeast of Nyaung U. The shop **Blue Sea** (☑ 061-60949; Main Rd) in Nyaung U sells tickets and charges a K20,000 commission. The train to Mandalay takes eight hours and departs at 7am (ordinary/upper class $4/10), while the train to Yangon takes 16 hours and departs at 5pm (ordinary/upper class/sleeper $30/40/50). There is an English language timetable and prices on display at the station.

Old Bagan ပုဂံမြို့ဟောင်း

☑ 061

The core of the Bagan Archaeological Zone contains several of the main temple sites, city walls, a museum, a reconstructed palace, restaurants, a few shops and a cluster of mid-range to top-end hotels. It's right on a bend of the Ayeyarwady River and it's well worth wandering down to the waterfront to watch the comings and goings of the river trade.

In 1990 the government forcibly relocated a village that had grown up in the 1970s in the middle of the walled area of 'Old

Bagan'. We're told one of the reasons for this was the increased incidence of treasure hunting and gold prospecting around the ruins in the wake of the 1988 street protests, when the authorities' attentions were diverted elsewhere.

Some claim the villagers had a week's notice of the move; others say it was longer and they put off the inevitable to the last minute. Either way, there was certainly resistance to the uprooting of homes and belongings for a new home in a peanut field, now developed as the thriving village of New Bagan.

BAGAN'S BEST

Bart D'hooge, Chief Pilot for Balloons over Bagan (p129), has been flying hot-air balloons at Bagan since 2007.

Best temple

Sulamani Temple is a beautiful impressive temple with some well preserved wall paintings. It is great to stroll around and take in the atmosphere. Just to the south of the temple there is a little lake, a nice place to sit around and spot some Bagan birdlife. Just be aware that you are in snake territory.

Best non-temple thing to do

A sunset cruise on the river can be a great way to end the day. The boat heads upstream, they cut the engine and drift back down with sunset as a backdrop. Bring a few drinks along for the ride.

Best shopping

Tun Handicrafts/Moe Moe's (p144) is run by a lovely lady who produces good-quality laquerware. The range on display is just the tip of the iceberg: ask to see the special room, with the really nice bits. The staff can show the entire lacquerware process in the workshop, which is a fascinating insight into this Bagan tradition.

Best restaurant

The Black Bamboo (p135) has delicious food and they prepare homemade ice cream and desserts.

Best nightlife

Check out Hti bar (p135) in Nyaung U which serves a wide variety of cocktails.

Best place to hang out with locals

Sarahba III (p140; also known as Gyi Gyi's after the owner) is where the locals come to eat, which is always a good sign. The ingredients are all market fresh and the beef curry is amazing.

Secret spot

If I told you this, it wouldn't be a secret any more... Try and find a small temple for sunrise or sunset, one that is peaceful and serene, away from the crowds. There are certainly enough temples to choose from. Avoid the most popular spots unless you like queuing to climb the stairs.

Sights

Archaeological Museum MUSEUM
(ကျောက်စာသမိုင်းပြတိုက်; Bagan-Nyaung U Rd; admission K5000, child under 10yr free; 9am-4.30pm Tue-Sun) Housed in an out-of-character, 19th-century-style temple, this government-run museum features many fine pieces from Bagan (reclining buddhas, original images, inscribed stones and mural re-creations) and an unexpected room of modern-art renderings of the temples. No photography allowed inside.

Bagan Golden Palace PALACE
(ပုဂံရွှေနန်းတော်; Bagan-Nyaung U Rd; admission K5000; 6.30am-10pm) Following similar government-mandated palace reconstruc-

tion jobs in Bago, Mandalay and Shwebo, this towering concrete-and-steel-reinforced edifice was opened to much fanfare in 2008. Built opposite the excavated site of the actual palace just in from the Tharabar Gate, it's unlikely to bear much resemblance to the original. Either way, it's a sign of the ongoing Disneyfication of Bagan.

Sleeping

Old Bagan's hotels provide views of the river, proximity to the temples and nice pool areas, but don't necessarily offer much more comfort than you get at New Bagan's best – and less expensive – accommodation. Definitely book ahead, as they fill up months in advance of peak season.

All places listed have restaurants, bars and pools, plus satellite TV and extras such as a minibar in the room. Prices listed are walk-in rates during low season, and don't include the 10% service charge and 10% government tax, so expect some hefty surcharges at peak times. Yangon agents or online hotel booking websites often have discounted rates available.

Aye Yar River View Resort RESORT **$$$**
(✆ 061-60352; www.ayeyarriverviewresort.com; r $115 360; ✿@✿✿) Following a major facelift, this former government hotel offers the best all-round value in Old Bagan. The most expensive rooms are set in spacious bungalows with expansive river views, while those closer to the pool are pretty impressive as well, including little details such as rain showers and private balconies.

Hotel@Tharabar Gate HOTEL **$$$**
(✆ 061-60037; www.tharabargate.com; r $160-200, ste $300; ✿@✿✿) Recently renovated in 2013, this hotel is a fine option for those that are willing to forgo a river view. Lush gardens of tropical plants and bougainvillea line walkways to the inviting wooden-floor bungalows with decks. The two-room suites at the far end go traditional, with gold-coloured ogres and *naga* spirits on the walls.

Bagan Thiripyitsaya Sanctuary Resort RESORT **$$$**
(✆ 061-60048; www.thiripyitsaya-resort.com; r $120-180, ste $380; ✿@✿) This Japanese joint-venture hotel is located on the river, about 500m south of the Old Bagan walls. It boasts the largest swimming pool in the Bagan area, but the rooms are mostly set in ageing four-room bungalow-style duplexes with covered decks and limited river views. The restaurant is good with panoramic river views and there's a wide range of activities on offer.

Bagan Thande Hotel HOTEL **$$$**
(✆ 061-60025; www.hotelbaganthande.com; economy $85, superior $110, deluxe $150-200, ste $350; ✿@✿) Opened for King Edward VIII in 1922, this riverside hotel carries a bit of dated formality and is arguably overdue a makeover. The simple 'superior' bungalows have decks looking over the pool and nearby Gawdawpalin Pahto. Best for views, though, are the riverfront deluxe rooms at the river's edge. Breakfast is served under the shade of tropical trees, with a river view.

Bagan Hotel River View HOTEL **$$$**
(✆ 061-60032; www.kmahotels.com; r from $100-250; ✿@✿✿) This 107-room hotel has bungalows with teak floors in a nice setting. The owner runs the luxurious KMA Hotels group, with hotels in locations from Nay Pyi Taw to Taungoo, and has a history of cosy relations with the generals.

✕ Eating

Old Bagan's restaurants (between the Ananda Pahto and Tharabar Gate) make for a convenient stop for lunch. The nearby hotel restaurants add a little style (and kyat) to a meal. Alcohol is not served at restaurants within the Old Bagan area as they are in close proximity to the temples. However, this rule does not apply to the luxury hotels and their attached bars and restaurants.

★**Starbeam Bistro** INTERNATIONAL **$**
(mains K3500-7000; ⏱7am-10pm) Located close to Ananda Pahto, this garden bistro was set up by Chef Tin Myint who spent several years working with the Orient-Express hotel group. Dishes include Rakhine fish curry, market fresh specials, traditional salads such as avocado or tea leaf, and classic baguettes and sandwiches. Best washed down with a healthy blend or fresh juice.

BAGAN & CENTRAL MYANMAR OLD BAGAN

BUSES FROM BAGAN

Destinations from Bagan include the following:

DESTINATION	PRICE	DURATION	DEPARTURES
Kalaw (Taunggyi bus)	K10,000	9hr	7.30am
Magwe	K4500	4hr	7am
Mandalay	K7500-9000	4-7hr	frequent
Monywa	K3500	4hr	7.30am
Taunggyi	K10,000-11,000	10hr	7.30am
Yangon	K13,000-18,000	10hr	frequent

Be Kind to Animals the Moon
VEGETARIAN $

(off Bagan-Nyaung U Rd; mains K1500-4000; ⊘7am-10pm; 🖋) The original among the couple of vegetarian restaurants clustered near Tharabar Gate, this place offers a friendly welcome and delicious food including pumpkin and ginger soup, aubergine curry and a lime and ginger tea that the owners claim is good for stomach upsets.

Sarahba III/Gyi Gyi's
VEGETARIAN, BAMAR $

(off Bagan-Nyaung U Rd; mains K500-2000; ⊘6am-6pm) Join the crowds under a shady tree near the Tharabar Gate squatting on low chairs at green-painted tables and digging into some of Bagan's best tucker, all freshly prepared and supremely tasty. There's no sign and the name refers to what locals jokingly call the place after owner Gyi Gyi.

Golden Myanmar
BAMAR $$

(Bagan-Nyaung U Rd; buffet K3500; ⊘10am-10pm) Keep-it-real seekers (and lots of horse-cart drivers) favour this excellent roadside eatery with shaded seats on a brick floor. The 'buffet' (your pick of chicken, pork, fish or mutton curry) comes with the usual tableful of condiments. There's another location near Ananda Pahto.

Scoopy's
ICE CREAM $

(off Bagan-Nyaung U Rd; mains from K500-2500; ⊘11am-6pm) Run by the French-Burmese owners of the Black Bamboo in Nyaung U, this relaxed cafe and ice-cream parlour is something of a godsend. Toasted sandwiches, homemade muffins and treats such as Western chocolate bars are available, all great for picnic snacks while touring the temples.

Sarabha II
CHINESE, INTERNATIONAL $$

(mains K2000-8000; ⊘11am-9pm) Of the two Sarabhas back to back by the Tharabar Gate, we like the one behind best, away from the road. It's a great midday resting point for shade and its range of food (Chinese, Thai, Burmese, pizza). The food's good, and cheaper than hotel restaurants, but best are the cold towels handed out to wipe the dust off your face.

🛍 Shopping

Shwe War Thein Handicrafts Shop
HANDICRAFTS

(☑061-67032; shi@mptmail.net.mm; ⊘peak season 6am-10pm) Just east of Tharabar Gate (and well signed off the Bagan–Nyaung U Rd) is this popular treasure trove of Myanmar trinkets. The collection includes antique and new puppets, woodcarvings, chess sets, lacquerware and bronze pieces. Ask to see the antique section at the rear. Lacquerware selections are wider in Myinkaba and New Bagan.

❶ Getting There & Away

Depending on water levels, boats from Mandalay arrive in Old Bagan near the Aye Yar Hotel.

Myinkaba
မြင်းကပါ

☑061

Lacquerware lovers will want to stop at Bagan's most famous shopping zone as this otherwise sleepy village, about half a mile south of Old Bagan, which has been home to family-run lacquerware workshops for generations. At least a dozen workshops and storefronts are located around the smattering of choice *pahto* (temples) and stupas from the early Bagan period. And King Manuha, respectfully called the 'Captive King', built the poetic Manuha Paya while held here in the 11th century.

🛍 Shopping

Before splashing the cash, it's wise to stop at a handful of places to compare varying styles and prices. Workshops such as those recommended below will show you the many stages of lacquerware-making and how lacquer is applied in layers, dried and engraved. There's refreshingly little pressure to buy at any of the workshops. But quality varies; often the best stuff is kept in air-conditioned rooms at the back. Most workshops and stores keep long hours (roughly 7am to 9pm during peak season). Generally, it is possible to bargain about 10% off the quoted prices, but not much more.

Art Gallery of Bagan
LACQUERWARE

English-speaking Maung Aung Myin has two rooms and a busy workshop on the road 200yd (180m) north of Mahamuni. Apart from the full range of lacquerware, including some beautiful and pricey cabinets and casks, there are also antique and new puppets ($20 to $150).

Family Lacquerware Work Shop
LACQUERWARE

Smaller workshop off the east side of the road, here there are some contemporary styles using alternative colours such as blue and yellow with fewer layers of lacquer.

Golden Cuckoo
LACQUERWARE

Just behind the Manuha Paya, this family-run workshop spans four generations and focuses on 'traditional' designs, which are applied to some unusual objects, including a motorbike helmet ($250) and a guitar ($500).

ⓘ Getting There & Away

Pick-ups running between New Bagan, Old Bagan and Nyaung U stop here.

New Bagan (Bagan Myothit) ပုဂံမြို့သစ်
☏ 061

Not as bustling as Nyaung U, even though it's closer to the juicy temples, New Bagan sprung into existence in 1990 when the government relocated the village from the Old Bagan area. The people have done the best to make the most of their new home, with a network of shady, dusty roads away from the river. It's laid-back, friendly and definitely the site of Bagan's best midrange accommodation and riverside restaurants. The morning market offers an interesting glimpse into local life.

🏃 Activities

Amata Boutique House
SPA

(www.amataBTQhouse.com; Thiripyitsaya Quarter; spa treatments $25-90; ⊙8am-10pm) Amata Boutique House is a huge riverside complex in New Bagan that includes a restaurant and lacquerware gallery. However, we recommend the Blossom Spa here which includes 10 stylish treatment rooms to pamper that inner princess (or prince).

🛏 Sleeping

All prices quoted in New Bagan are low-season walk-in rates and include breakfast, and all places include hot water on tap.

Bagan Central Hotel
HOTEL $

(☏061-65057; Main Rd; s/d $35/40; ❄️ 🖧) These stone-clad chalets have an original look compared with other 'budget' places around Bagan. The interior switches to bamboo and the clean rooms include a wooden floor and recently renovated bathrooms. All rooms are set around a tree-shaded courtyard where breakfast is served.

Thiri Marlar Hotel
HOTEL $

(☏061-65050; thirimarlar@mptmail.net.mm; r $35-50; ❄️ 🖧) The teak walkways leading to the 15 lovely rooms are wrapped around a small pagoda-style dining room, though most guests eat breakfast on the roof deck with temple views. Spotless standard rooms are rather compact but inviting, with shiny wood floors and small rugs. Superior rooms are much more spacious and worth the extra bucks.

Bagan Beauty Hotel
GUESTHOUSE $

(☏061-65062; Main Rd; s/d $15/20; ❄️ 🖧) She's not much of a beauty these days, but this friendly, family-run guesthouse offers the cheapest rooms in New Bagan. Maybe a facelift is on the cards, but in the meantime the musty rooms do include air-con and hot water, plus free wi-fi.

Yun Myo Thu Motel
GUESTHOUSE $

(☏061-65276; 3 Khat Tar St; s/d $20/30; ❄️) Translating rather romantically as 'the lady of lacquer city', this is a typical Burmese guesthouse that sees few foreigners and is consequently pretty good value for money. The well-tended rooms include flatscreen TV, air-con and hot water, but there is little English spoken.

★ Kumudara Hotel
HOTEL $$

(☏061-65142; www.kumudara-bagan.com; superior s/d $38/44, junior ste s/d $50/56; ❄️ @ 🖧 ≋) No hotel boasts better balcony views of the mighty sprawl of red-brick temples than Kumudara. Opt for the chic junior suites and suites in a green geometrical building that fits well with the arid, desert-like setting. Inside, rooms have a mix of wood panelling, modern art and retro-style safe boxes. Kumudara also has a pool and a restaurant.

Areindmar Hotel
BOUTIQUE HOTEL $$

(☏061-65049; www.areindmarhotel.com; 1st St; s/d from $70/80; ❄️ 🖧) Set like a hacienda within private walls, the two-storey buildings surround a lush courtyard garden. The 38 rooms are beautifully decorated with sleigh beds, brass basins, polished parquet floors and traditional Burmese handicrafts. A rooftop spa is currently in the planning, to complement the open-air bar.

Thazin Garden Hotel
HOTEL $$

(☏061-65035; www.thazingardenhotel.com; r $85; ❄️ 🖧 ≋) Set down a dusty path near a clutch of small temples, this oasis of palms and flowers and shaded walkways is a charming

New Bagan (Bagan Myothit)

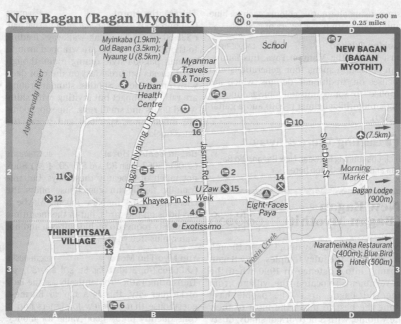

choice. The deluxe 'bungalows' are built in a paya-styled-brick complex with a sea of dark luxurious teak inside and a balcony overlooking a 13th-century pagoda within the grounds where dinner is served on the lawn in front. The 'superior' rooms are just as inviting with hanging paper umbrellas, a chess board and deck area. It has a pool, a spa and a billiards table.

Floral Breeze Hotel   HOTEL **$$**
(☑061-65309; www.hotelbze.com; Chauk Rd; r $55-65; ❄❓) Built in the classic faux-temple Bagan-style, this modern hotel offers good value rooms complete with a contemporary trim. The bathrooms include a

bathtub and reliable hot water for those needing a soak after a long day.

Crown Prince Hotel   HOTEL **$$**
(☑061-65407; www.crownprincebagan.com; Khat Tar St; deluxe $60-80, ste $80-110; ❄❓❄) A smart new hotel, the Crown Prince is reasonable value for money. Rooms are tastefully decorated and include touches such as flatscreen TV, a hairdryer and safety deposit box. Already planning ahead, a new block is under construction and a swimming pool.

Arthawka Hotel   HOTEL **$$**
(☑061-65321; arthawka.hotel@gmail.com; 160 Cherry Rd; s $55-65, d $60-70; ❄❓❄) Big

New Bagan (Bagan Myothit)

glazed clay pots and wicker chairs dot the spacious lobby of this friendly 60-room hotel. It offers spacious rooms (recently renovated) sporting wood floors and white tiled bathrooms. In the centre of the complex is a saltwater pool, shaded by palms.

★ **Blue Bird Hotel** BOUTIQUE HOTEL **$$$**
(☎061-65440; www.bluebirdbagan.com; Naratheinka 10; r $85-150; ❉@🛜🏊) An absolute charmer, the Blue Bird is one of the most homely places to stay in all of Bagan. Rooms are spacious and airy, including contemporary handicrafts and striking bathrooms with an original shower design. The lush gardens conceal a central swimming pool, perfect to cool off after a long day. The restaurant includes impressive fusion food and the best cocktails in town are shaken (and stirred) by the well-trained bar staff. Book ahead.

Bagan Lodge RESORT **$$$**
(☎061-65456; www.bagan-lodge.com; Myat Lay Rd; deluxe from $180, ste from $296; ❉@🛜🏊) New in 2013, Bagan Lodge offers something a little different from the high-end hotels of Old Bagan. Rooms are set in stone cabanas with sweeping tented roofs. Spacious and furnished in the colonial style, rooms include huge bathrooms with his 'n' hers sinks. Ongoing expansion will eventually see 80 rooms, but the owners will need the garden to keep apace to provide some shade.

🍴 Eating

New Bagan's Main Rd is lined with several Chinese and Burmese restaurants. Many foreigners grab a meal on the riverside, just west of the centre. There are several restaurants overlooking the Ayeyarwady and you can either be lost amid the tour groups or have the place to yourself. Bagan's only supermarket, and it's not very super, is Yadanar Mart on Main St.

Naratheinkha Restaurant FRENCH, INTERNATIONAL **$**
(☎09-5242420; New Bagan; K1500-5500) Blink and you'll miss it, this tiny little shopfront restaurant is well-regarded thanks to the chef-owner's extensive experience at Le Planteur Restaurant in Yangon. The menu is predominantly French-accented or Asian fusion and includes a delicious pan-fried fish with lemon butter sauce.

Mother's House BURMESE **$**
(Chauk Rd; K500-1500; ⊙7am-9pm) A tiny place on the Chauk Rd, this is the place to come and sample a traditional Burmese breakfast before exploring the temples or after catching sunrise somewhere near New Bagan. Try Shan noodles or deep-fried doughnuts.

Silver House BAMAR, ASIAN **$**
(Main Rd; mains K2000-6000; ⊙7am-10pm) A welcoming family-run restaurant that offers large, tasty portions of dishes such as traditional Myanmar chicken curry and tomato salad.

Nooch Thai Restaurant THAI, INTERNATIONAL **$**
(Main St; mains K2000-5000; ⊙7am-10pm) New Bagan's only dedicated Thai restaurant overlooks the eight faces paya. The menu includes a tour of popular Thai dishes and doubles as a drinking den by night, churning out chilled Myanmar beer.

Sunset Garden BURMESE, INTERNATIONAL **$$**
(☎061-65037; mains K2500-7500; ⊙11am-10pm; 🛜) Boasting the best riverside setting of any of the New Bagan restaurants, Sunset Garden has a huge deck above the Ayeyarwady with spectacular sunset views. Head here for a sundowner before the tour groups pile in for dinner. The menu includes a greatest hits selection of Burmese, Chinese, Thai and international dishes.

Green Elephant BURMESE, ASIAN **$$**
(mains K4000-9000; ⊙11am-4pm & 6-10pm; 🛜) The good-value and tasty Myanmar set meal (K8000) comes with a couple of curries, vegetable tempura, soup, dessert and coffee. There are small and large portions of other dishes (including local curries). But it's the setting that's the deal, with shaded tables on a lawn overlooking the Ayeyarwady River.

King Si Thu BAMAR, ASIAN **$$**
(☎061-65117; mains K2000-8000; ⊙8am-10pm; 🛜) Another riverside setting, another Myanmar restaurant mainly serving Chinese and Thai dishes such as sweet-and-sour pork, or fish with ginger. Order one hour ahead for Burmese food. There's a half-hour puppet show at 7.30pm.

🔒 Shopping

New Bagan has several good options for lacquerware – and you can watch artisans at work.

Tun Handicrafts/
Moe Moe's
LACQUERWARE

(www.tunhandicrafts.com; Main Rd; ⊙8am-9pm)
This family-run local business was one of
the first to establish itself in New Bagan and
is run by U Kan Tun and her daughter Moe
Moe. The large showroom includes a mix of
traditional and modern lacquerware, and it
is possible to see every step of the process in
an adjacent workshop.

Bagan House
LACQUERWARE

(www.baganhouse.com; 9 Jasmin Rd; ⊙8am-7pm)
Worth seeking out on the backstreets, this
stylish showroom has a mix of cheap and
higher-priced lacquerware, as well as the
usual artisans at work. Unlike other places,
it does accept credit cards if you spend more
than $100, with the usual hefty surcharge.

ℹ️ Information

Internet is available at several places along the
main street.

Exotissimo (☑061-60383; ⊙9am-6pm Mon-
Fri, 9am-noon Sat) High-end agent, which can
arrange Mt Popa tours or rent imported mountain bikes ($10 per day).

Myanmar Travels & Tours (MTT; ☑061-
65040; ⊙8.30am-4.30pm) The government-
run tourist office can help organise excursions
to visit Chin State.

ℹ️ Getting There & Around

See Nyaung U for most transport connections.
There are airline offices on Main Rd. **U Zaw Weik**
(☑061-65017; zawweik@myanmar.com.mm;
Main Rd) helps with air tickets or can arrange a
taxi around Bagan, to Mt Popa or to destinations
further afield such as Kalaw or Mandalay.

Bicycle rental starts at K2500 per day.

AROUND BAGAN

Mt Popa
ပုပ္ပါးတောင်

☑061

Like a Burmese Mt Olympus, Mt Popa is the
spiritual HQ to Myanmar's infamous '37 nat'
and thus the most popular location in the
country for *nat* worship.

Mt Popa is now the official name of the
famous Popa Taung Kalat, a towerlike 2418ft
(740m) volcanic plug crowned with a gilded
Buddhist temple accessed by 777 steps, on
the mother mountain's lower flank. The
4980ft (1500m) extinct volcano previously
known as Mt Popa has been renamed Taung
Ma-gyi or Mother Mountain to distinguish
it from the more famous Popa Taung Kalat.
Covered in lush forests protected within the
Popa Mountain Park and home to the exclusive Popa Mountain Resort, the volcano last
erupted some 250,000 years ago (some locals suggest 40 million years ago). One local
told us: 'Popa is like the sun or moon; no one
can guess how old it is.'

From the temple there are mammoth
views back towards the Myingyan Plain and
beyond. It's stunning if a little kitsch, but
only a few visitors make the half-day trip
from Bagan. Many of those who do fail to
grasp the spiritual significance of the place
find it's because they don't have a guide to
enliven the experience with stories and ex-
planations – going on a day trip to Mt Popa
without some sort of guide is like watching
a foreign-language film without subtitles.

Myanmar superstition says you shouldn't
wear red or black on the mountain, nor
should you curse, say bad things about
other people or bring along any meat
(especially pork). Any of these actions could
offend the resident *nat,* who might then re-
taliate with a spate of ill fortune, as they are
not as forgiving as Lord Buddha. And no-
one wants trouble from a mad *nat.*

◉ Sights & Activities

Mother Spirit of Popa
Nat Shrine
NAT SHRINE

(ပုပ္ပါးမယ်တော်နတ်နန်း) Before climbing
Popa Taung Kalat, drop by the tiger-
guarded shrine in the village at the foot of
the mountain (just across from the steps
guarded by elephant statues – there are
loads of critters around here). Inside you'll
find a display extending left and right from
an inner hallway door of mannequin-like
figures representing some of the 37 official
nat, plus some Hindu deities and a few nec-
romancers (the figures with goatees at the
right end of the shrine).

In the shrine there are also other *nat* not
counted among the official '37', including
three principal figures: the **Flower-Eating
Ogress** (aka Mae Wunna, or 'Queen Mother
of Popa') and her two sons (to her left and
right) **Min Gyi** and **Min Lay.**

A few other interesting *nat* here caught
our attention. The plump Pyu goddess
Shin Nemi (Little Lady) is a guardian for
children, and gets toy offerings during
school exam time. She's the cute little thing

clutching a green umbrella and a stuffed animal, midway down on the left of the shrine.

There have been a few Kyawswas in Myanmar spirit history, but the most popular is the Popa-born **Lord Kyawswa** (aka Drunk Nat), who spent his few years cockfighting and drinking. He boasts: 'If you don't like me, avoid me. I admit I'm a drunkard'. He's the guardian of gamblers and drunks and sits on a horse decked in rum and whiskey bottles, to the right. Be sure to pay your respects if you've been partying your way through Southeast Asia up until this point.

Locals pray to **Shwe Na Be** (Lady with Golden Sides) when a snake comes into their house. She's the woman holding a *naga* (serpent) near the corner to the left.

Popa Taung Kalat Temple
BUDDHIST TEMPLE

(ပုပ္ပါးတောင်ကျောင်း) From the *nat* shrine start up the steps under a covered walkway and past the usual rows of trinket and souvenir shops and shrines to a revered local medicine man, Pomin Gawng. At a steady pace it shouldn't take you more than 20 minutes to reach the summit of this impressive rocky crag crowned with a picturesque complex of monasteries, stupas and shrines. Along the way, you'll pass platoons of cheeky monkeys and a small army of locals selling drinks and endeavouring (not always successfully) to keep the steps clean of monkey poo in return for a possible tip. Families with children should take care to keep a distance from the macaques as they have large canine teeth and occasionally pilfer snacks or shiny trinkets from visitors.

The views from the top are fantastic. You may be fortunate enough to spot one of the slow-walking hermit monks called *yeti*, who wear tall, peaked hats and visit occasionally.

Popa Mountain Park
HIKING

A variety of **hiking trails** thread through the Popa Mountain Park, leading to the rim of the volcano crater and to viewpoints and waterfalls. Along the way, you'll be able to observe the difference in the vegetation. The heights capture the moisture of passing clouds, causing rain to drop on the plateau and produce a profusion of trees, flowering plants and herbs, all nourished by the rich volcanic soil. In fact, the word *popa* is derived from the Sanskrit word for flower.

> ### FRUIT OF THE PALMS
>
> On the way to or from Mt Popa, stop by at one of the several toddy and jaggery (palm sugar) operations that are set up along the road. The operators will give you a basic demo of how the alcoholic drink and sweets are made from the sap of the toddy palm. After, it is possible to sample and buy these local products.

Trekking here is best done with local guides. Ask at the turn-off, a mile or so back from Popa village (towards Bagan), or enquire at the Popa Mountain Resort, halfway up the peak. From the resort, the hike to the crater takes around four hours.

If you come by taxi, ask the driver to point out bits of **petrified forest**, which are strewn along either side of the road west of Popa village.

✱✱ Festivals & Events

Mt Popa hosts two huge **nat pwe** (spirit festivals) yearly, one beginning on the full moon of Nayon (May/June) and another on the full moon of Nadaw (November/December). Before King Anawrahta's time, thousands of animals were sacrificed to the *nat* during these festivals, but this practice has been prohibited since the Bagan era. Spirit possession and overall drunken ecstasy are still part of the celebration, however.

There are several other minor festivals, including ones held on the full moons of Wagaung (July/August) and Tagu (March/April), which celebrate the departure and return of the famous Taungbyone *nat* (Min Gyi and Min Lay). Once a year, the Taungbyone *nat* are believed to travel a spirit circuit that includes Mt Popa, Taungbyone (about 14 miles north of Mandalay) and China.

🛏 Sleeping

Most visitors find a couple of hours with Mt Popa's maddening macaques enough. There are some very basic and overpriced guesthouses in Popa village, but the range of budget accommodation on offer in Bagan is far better. There's also the lovely, lonely **Popa Mountain Resort** (☑061-69169; poparesort@myanmar.com.mm; r superior from $99, deluxe from $130; ❈@❈), owned by tycoon Tay Za, a businessman with close links to the generals. Set at 2600ft (798m) the striking

---

MOTHER SPIRIT OF MT POPA

Sometimes it's hard being a *nat*. The namesake figure of the Mother Spirit of Popa & Nat Shrine is Mae Wunna. She was famous for her love of Byat-ta, one of King Anawrahta's servants, a flower-gathering Indian with superhuman powers, who neglected his duties and was executed for it.

Their two sons, Min Gyi and Min Lay, supposedly born atop Mt Popa, followed their father's tradition. They became servants of the king (often going to China), grew neglectful of their duties, and then *they* were executed. King Anawrahta, however, ordered a shrine built at the place of their execution (at Taungbyone, north of Mandalay), now the site of a huge festival. Many worshippers come to offer a blessing to these three. Mae Wunna and her sons are the central figures facing the entry to the shrine.

---

all-wood bungalows boast a dramatic mountainside setting. Nonguests can take a dip in the infinity pool ($7) with spectacular views of Popa Taung Kalat or have a meal at the good restaurant, which overlooks the shimmering spires of Mt Popa's temples.

ⓘ Getting There & Away

Most travellers visit Mt Popa in half a day by share taxi or by organised tour from their hotel. In Nyaung U, guesthouses can usually arrange a space in a share taxi (without guide); a whole taxi is about K35,000 to K45,000 depending on the quality of the vehicle.

There is also a pick-up truck departing Nyaung U's bus station at 8.30am for Mt Popa (K3000, two hours); on the return leg, it departs Popa for Nyaung U at 1pm. Less conveniently, it is possible to take an hourly pick-up from Nyaung U to Kyaukpadaung (90 minutes) and then another to Mt Popa (45 minutes), but this takes the best part of a day.

Salay ဆားလင်း

📓 063

This Bagan-era village, 22 miles south of Bagan, is rooted in the 12th and 13th centuries, when Bagan's influence spread. It remains an active religious centre, with something like 50 monasteries shared among the fewer than 10,000 residents. Day-trippers make it here to visit a few of the 19th-century wooden monasteries and some select Bagan-era shrines, and peek at a handful of untouched British colonial buildings.

It can be paired with Mt Popa on a full-day trip, although the two are in different directions from Bagan. Eating choices tend to be better in nearby Chauk (famous for its production of the sweet tamarind flakes that are served at the end of all meals in

Bagan), but you can get noodles in the Salay market. There is currently no accommodation in Salay.

◉ Sights

An interesting feature in Salay is the faded colonial-era heritage dotted around town and some of the old buildings still feature the Royal Crown high up on their facades. Check out the market area, a few hundred metres west of the museum. This area is especially worth visiting, as few buildings in Myanmar still sport the lion-guarded crown.

Youqson Kyaung BUDDHIST MONASTERY
(ရုပ်စုံကျောင်း; admission $5; ⊙9am-4.30pm) Designed as a copy of the Crown Prince House in Mandalay, and built from 1882 to 1892, the huge wooden monastery is the best place to start a visit in Salay.

Along two of its exterior sides are detailed original carvings displaying 19th-century court life and scenes from the Jataka (stories of the Buddha's past lives) and Ramayana (one of India's best-known legends); sadly another side's pieces were looted in the 1980s. Inside, the 17th- to 19th-century pieces are behind glass cases, while the Bagan-era woodcarvings (including a massive throne backdrop) stand in open view.

The monastery was renovated twice in the 1990s and the government's Department of Archaeology runs the site; on-site staff can point you to other nearby sites in and around the town.

Bagan-Era Monuments BUDDHIST TEMPLES
Little of the history of Salay's 103 ruins is known outside a small circle of Myanmar archaeologists working with limited funds. It is said that most of the monuments in Salay weren't royally sponsored, but were built

by the lower nobility or commoners, hence there's nothing on the grand scale of Bagan's biggest structures.

In the pagoda-filled area just east of Youqson Kyaung lies **Paya Thonzu**, a small trio of brick shrines with *sikhara* (Indian-style corncob-like temple finials) and some faded murals inside. The westernmost shrine (to the left when approaching from the museum) has the most visible murals and also a narrow set of stairs leading to a small terrace. If it's locked, ask at Youqson Kyaung.

A more interesting feature is the modern makeover of the Bagan-era **Shinpinsarkyo Paya** (Temple 88), about 4 miles southwest of town via a dodgy road (and a couple of dodgy bridges). Inside the glass- and tile-filled pagoda is an original 13th-century wood Lokanat (Mahayana Bodhisattva guardian spirit). The nearby northern entrance passageway features interesting 19th-century 3D murals (some are torture to see). Original woodcarvings abound, some of which are painted afresh in original design.

Another mile or so south of Shinpinsarkyo (most taxis won't drive it, but it's an easy 15-minute walk) is **Temple 99**, an unassuming 13th-century shrine that features 578 painted Jataka scenes inside. The last 16 paintings on the left represent the '16 Dreams of King Kosala'.

Mann Paya BUDDHIST TEMPLE
In the complex about 500yd (450m) west of the Paya Thonzu, the Mann Paya is a modern pagoda housing a 20ft (6m) gold buddha made of straw lacquer. As the story goes, the buddha image was originally located near Monywa and was washed downstream during an 1888 monsoon, all the way to Salay. Ask for a peek inside from the latched door at the back.

Sasanayaunggyi Kyaung BUDDHIST MONASTERY
Half a kilometre north of the Paya Thonzu, the monastery and meditation centre of Sasanayaunggyi Kyaung, a stop-off point for day-trippers, features a lovely 19th-century glass armoire with painted Jataka panels and 400-year-old scripture in Pali inside. The monks are chatty and friendly, and will ask for a donation for their on-site school.

ⓘ Getting There & Away

Salay is 22 miles south of Bagan on a road that's often flood damaged, occasionally impassable. The route passes through the larger town of Chauk on the way. From Chauk, another road goes east to Kyaukpadaung for alternative access in combination with Mt Popa.

A hired taxi for a four- or five-hour trip to Salay from Nyaung U starts at about K40,000. A full day trip combining Mt Popa and Salay costs about K60,000. It's technically possible to come by pick-up truck from Nyaung U in three hours (not including a change in Chauk), but it's not advisable, as some sites in Salay aren't close to the drop-off point.

Pakokku ပခုက္ကူ
✓ 062

A transit point for wayward travellers on the west side of the Ayeyarwady River, Pakokku was a quiet backwater until 2007, when it found itself front-and-centre in international headlines. Monks from the Myo Ma Ahle monastery here kickstarted the nationwide protests against rising petrol prices that became the 'Saffron Revolution'. While the monks' uprising failed in the short-term, observers argue its brutal suppression was an important watershed and a key element in pushing the generals to kickstart the reform process.

Pakokku is a friendly town famed for its tobacco and *thanakha*, but few guests stay here now with the new bridge connecting it to Bagan, 16 miles south, in just 30 minutes. Should you choose to linger, there's a riverside homestay that's basic, but many guests rank as a highlight of their trip. One of the town's biggest *pwe* (festivals), **Thihoshin**, is held during Nayon (May/June).

⊙ Sights

If time is limited, the most rewarding activities in Pakokku include browsing the **market**, checking out some of the **temples** and **monasteries** – including one monastery with a giant clock tower – or just wandering amid the tropical torpor of its picturesquely decrepit side streets, which feature old homes backing onto the Ayeyarwady River.

About 17 miles northeast, on the way to Monywa, are the remains of **Pakhangyi**, a 19th-century wooden monastery. About 3 miles east of Pakhangyi (via the road behind the big modern pagoda) is the destroyed frame of **Pakhanngeh Kyaung**, which was once the country's largest wooden monastery. Many of its 332 teak pillars still stand, and the area, near the fork of the Ayeyarwady and Kaladan rivers, makes for rewarding exploration. A taxi here from Pakokku is about K30,000.

🛏 Sleeping & Eating

★ Mya Yatanar Inn
HOMESTAY $

(📞 062-21457; 75 Lanmataw St; s with shared bathroom K7000, d with bathroom K14,000; ❄) Charming, English-speaking grandma Mya Mya, her daughter and granddaughters will welcome you to their 100-year-old home on the river, a couple of blocks east of the market. Rooms are super-basic and rather rundown, but bearable once you fall under the hospitable spell of these women. Electricity is patchy by day and most rooms share the cold-water bathroom and squat toilet. Cheap meals are available and bicycles are available for K1500.

Thu Kha Hotel
HOTEL $$

(📞 062-23077; Myoma Rd; r $35-75; ❄ 🛜) New in 2013, this hotel is the smartest in Pakokku with a warm welcome to match. The spacious rooms include wooden floors, flat screen TVs and contemporary bathrooms, a rare species in this town. There is no lift, so rates drop on the higher floors. Breakfast included.

Ho Pin Myanmar Traditional Cuisine
BURMESE $

(📞 062-22979; 2 St, 11 Quarter; set meals K3500) Recommended by Bagan residents in the know who regularly travel to Pakokku on shopping runs, the Ho Pin prides itself on 'flair and care'. The kitchen is reassuringly visible to diners and hearty Burmese set meals are served up to a transient crowd. Clean bathrooms round things off.

❶ Getting There & Away

Minibuses shuttle to and from Bagan (K2000, one hour) and Monywa (K3000, three hours), leaving regularly from the corner of Tinda and Aung Taw Mu sts. From the main bus station on Myoma Rd there are three services daily to Mandalay (K6000, seven hours).

Monywa

📞 071 / POPULATION C180,000

Like its neighbour Mandalay, a visit to Monywa is not really about the town itself, but a series of interesting attractions in the surrounding countryside. Pronounced in two syllables (mon-ywa), Monywa is an engaging trade town that makes a sensible stopping point when looping north between Bagan and Mandalay. The town itself is big, hot and flat, with relatively little to see beyond the markets and the pleasant

Chindwin riverside setting, though two large, central pagoda complexes, **Shwezigon Paya** and **Su Taung Pye Zedi** are well worth a wander. It is also an embarkation point for the adventurous few who boat-hop the Chindwin to newly permit-free towns to the north.

🛏 Sleeping

Monywa Hotel
HOTEL $

(📞 071-21581; monywahotel@goldenland.com.mm; Bogyoke Rd; s $30-35, d $35-40; ❄) Set well back from the busy street amid birdsong and creeper-draped trees, this well-maintained series of multiroom cabins is popular with small tour groups. Interiors are definitely dated and the colour schemes are hideous, but even the cheaper rooms are fair-sized with effective air-conditioning, desk, fridge, piping-hot showers, satellite TV and comfy beds. It's good value as the owners have resisted the national trend of hiking prices.

Shwe Taung Tarn
GUESTHOUSE $

(📞 071-21478; 70 Station Rd; s $13-20, d $20-27; ❄) For years Shwe Taung Tarn has been Monywa's most popular budget choice. The facade looks unkempt, but better rooms lie behind a pair of newer two-storey buildings amid an unexpectedly pleasant little garden area. Rooms are some of the better value in town, but while they were once relatively stylish, many now suffer seriously scuffed floors and gob-stained walls.

★ Hotel Chindwin
HOTEL $$

(📞 071-26150; www.hotelchindwinmonywa.com; Bogyoke Rd; s $25-65, d $30-70; ❄ @ 🛜) Towering above the city centre competition, this new hotel has super smart rooms at an affordable price. Standard rooms are small but include many of the features found in the higher class rooms. Deluxe rooms are almost suites and include a spacious bathroom. Lift available and breakfast included.

Win Unity
RESORT $$

(📞 071-22438; tintinmoe@mptmail.net.mm; Bogyoke Rd; s $50-120, d $55-135; ❄ @ ❄) Easily Monywa's swankiest option, the Win Unity is a series of tile-roofed modern bungalow rooms set on the lakeside, less than half a mile north of the central area. They're all neat and comfortable, but think low-rise condo rather than colonial gem. Lake-view rooms (single/double $120/135) command

Monywa

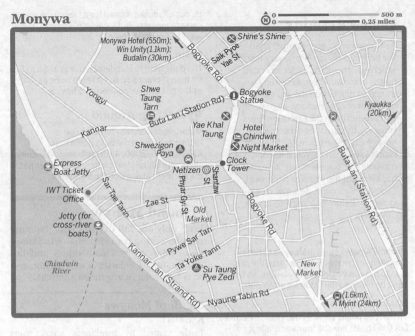

a premium that may not justify the price tag. Be aware that the 'standard' rooms are aimed more for drivers rather than for guests. The inviting pool has a swim-up bar and Jacuzzi area.

✗ Eating & Drinking

Shwe Taung Tarn has a restaurant section beside its budget hotel that cooks fine Chinese food and has an unexpectedly chic rooftop section.

Yad Khel Taung   BEER STATION $
(Bogyoke Rd; mains K1500-4000; ⊙8am-10pm) This friendly if typical draught beer station serves Shan and Chinese food, but is most remarkable for the tiny amuse-bouche plates of *namakyien,* a delicious local sesame-based hummus that arrives free with most meals. Like most Shan places, it's just a case of point and eat. Friendly locals drink beer until close and foreigners may be invited to join a toast.

Night Market   FOOD STALLS $
(Bogyoke Rd; ⊙5-10.30pm) Various cheap eats are served up nightly between the clock tower and Bogyoke (Aung San) statue. Locals flock here to pick up takeaways or chow down on plastic stools, making it a good place for people watching.

Pleasant Island   CHINESE $$
(Myakanthar Lake, Bogyoke Rd; mains K2000-10,000; ⊙7am-10pm; ⓓ) Monywa's finest restaurant occupies a tiny lake island across upper Bogyoke Rd from the Win Unity hotel. It's a photogenic spot at sunset, linked to the shore by a rickety wooden bridge. Tasty Chinese, Malay and Thai food is served at open pavilions, but it's also popular with well-to-do locals quaffing beer on a night out.

Shine's Shine   CHINESE $$
(Saik Pyoe Yae St; mains K2000-12,000; ⊙10am-10pm) Part carwash, part restaurant, the last time we saw this sort of fusion restaurant was in Kigali, Rwanda. The large compound is shaded by mature trees full of coloured lights and the restaurant serves a huge range of regional delicacies, including eel, duck and catfish.

ⓘ Information

Netizen (Shantaw St; per hr K500; ⊙8am-10pm) Comfortable downstairs room with fast internet connections. English spoken.

ⓘ Getting There & Away

AIR
The airport is 7.5m (12km_ north, off the Budalin road. Occasional Tuesdays the government's

CHINDWIN PERMITS

As Myanmar undergoes rapid change, the permit situation is also very fluid, which is particularly apt for journeys up the Chindwin River. According to transport officials on the ground, it is no longer necessary to arrange permits to travel north on the Chindwin River. However, the situation on arrival in remote Chindwin towns (eg Mawleik, Homalin or Khamti) may differ and it is possible that travellers might be sent back without the relevant paperwork. So in the meantime, do some research in Yangon before heading way up the Chindwin.

Myanma Airways stops in Monywa between Mandalay and Homalin, but as usual the decision to fly is only made the day before, so tickets can't be reserved until Monday afternoon.

BOAT

There is no public service downriver to Pakokku, but daily boats link the towns and villages of the upper Chindwin River. Foreigners no longer need permits to board these boats, but permits may still be requested in remote towns on the upper Chindwin where news travels slowly. 'Express' boats depart 4.30am daily, operated by one of several Strand Rd companies on a rotating cycle, including MGRG, Ngwe Shwe Oo or Shwe Nadi. Buy tickets one day before. Stops include Kalewa (upper/lower K18,000/7000, around 13 hours), Mawleik (upper/lower K18,000/9000, around 18 hours) and Homalin (upper/lower K18,000/12,000, around 30 hours). Departing Thursdays at 7am, the IWT (government) river ferry moves slower than political evolution. Allow up to four days from Monywa to Kalewa in the dry season. In the rainy season IWT boats become more frequent and travel further north.

BUS

Monywa's bus station is just over a mile southeast of the clock tower down Bogyoke Rd. Several companies operate hourly buses 5am to 4pm to Mandalay (K2000/3000 without/with air-con, three hours). There are also regular buses to Pakokku (K2500, three hours) with onward connections to Bagan available there, taking an extra hour. Aung Gabar Express operates a direct service to Bagan (K3500) departing at 7.30am. Buses to Shwebo (K2500, three hours) depart regularly from 5am to 1pm plus at 3pm. The attractive rural route passes

through Kyaukka, famed for its lacquerware cottage industry, but local help is needed if you want to see much there.

TRAIN

The daily train to Mandalay departs at 6am ($3, six hours) every day, but it takes twice as long as the bus in an uncomfortable box car.

ⓘ Getting Around

Motorbikes/trishaws/three-wheelers to the centre from the bus station cost K1000/1500/2000. All these transport options, along with white, plain-clothes taxis, linger near the northern Shwezigon Paya entrance.

Around Monywa

With only one full day to spare, the most popular option is to visit Hpo Win Daung caves followed by Thanboddhay and Bodhi Tataung. The latter is west-facing, and so is best seen in afternoon sunlight.

South of Monywa

A MYINT

Little visited by foreigners apart from occasional Chindwin cruise groups, A Myint is a charmingly unspoilt riverside village dominated by a series of 336 higgledy piggledy **ancient stupas** in varying stages of collapse. All are compactly arranged around a little **wooden monastery** and a few retain interior murals. Another minor attraction is the **British-era house** (62 Seidan St) of the former village chief. It's private and still owned by the charming original family, who might wind up their gramophone for you or show off their 1920s sepia photos.

A major attraction is the lovely 15-mile (24km) ride through agricultural villages from Monywa on a lane that's narrow but unusually well asphalted. Around halfway look northeast for brief, distant views.

Southeast of Monywa

When travelling by private vehicle between Mandalay and Monywa, the following sites can be conveniently visited as a short detour en route. However, for those travelling by local transport, it is wiser to visit on a return excursion from Monywa, costing around K8000/12,000 by motorbike/three-wheeler and taking around three hours.

THANBODDHAY PAYA သမ္ဗုဒ္ဓေဘုရား

The central feature of this carnivalesque **complex** (Thanboddhay Paya; admission $3) is a large mid-20th-century temple whose unique roof is layered with rows of gilt mini-stupas. Its flanks burst gaudily bright colours and are offset by 30ft-high (9m) concrete obelisks set with uncountable buddha shapes. The multi arched **temple interior** (admission $3; ☺ 6am-5pm) is plastered with so many buddha images (5,823,631 according to temple guardians), large and small, that it feels like you're walking through a buddha house of mirrors. While there is an official entry charge, nobody was collecting money during our visit. Thanboddhay's kitschfest continues in the surrounding pastel-hued monks' quarters and with two huge white concrete elephants at the site's gateway. It's 1 mile (1.5km) off the Mandalay road, 6 miles (10km) from Monywa.

BODHI TATAUNG တော်ဒိတစ်ထောင်

Another 5m miles (8km) east from Thanboddhay, the name of this vast hillside buddha-rama translates as '1000 buddhas'. However, for most visitors, only two of them really count. Opened in 2008, the glimmering 424ft (130m) **standing buddha** is claimed to be the world's tallest, and it utterly dominates the landscape for miles around. Inside the multistorey torso, seemingly interminable stairways link painted galleries; many lower ones depicting gruesome scenes from hell that are not really suitable for young children. You might hope that climbing to buddha's head would take you, artistically at least, to

Nirvana. However, so far at least, visitors' progress is blocked at the 16th floor, barely halfway up. A spiritual message? The interior closes at 5pm.

Lower down the hillside lounges a slightly smaller but still large 312ft (95m) **reclining buddha**. It's hardly refined and the dark interior contains poorly maintained tableaux: enter through the left buttock, as you do.

Note that both giant buddhas face west, so for the best light plan a visit in the late afternoon.

If you're feeling inspired, the Bodhi Tataung site hosts many other minor fascinations, including a whole **garden** of identical sitting buddhas under concrete parasols, and the gilded 430ft (130m) stupa **Aung Setkya Paya**, which has lovely views from its upper rim, reached via an inner passageway.

Carry your sandals to save your feet from the gravel on connecting roads.

North of Monywa

Wizened old neem trees and many an attractive stupa enliven the busy, well-paved road leading north from Monywa. After 19 miles, Budalin is a small junction settlement with a basic noodle shop, from which it's still rather a slog to reach the area's minor attractions. But you'll certainly be getting far, far off the tourist radar.

TWIN DAUNG

Twin Daung is one of four volcanic crater lakes in Myanmar, from whose swirling green waters Spirulina is cultivated. You can visit the lakeside Spirulina

---

AN 11TH-CENTURY LOVE TRIANGLE

In 1056 the King of Bago became a vassal of Bagan's ascendant ruler, Anawrahta, who later sent his armies to bolster Bago against the Khmers. Among the tribute gifts that symbolised the relationship was one of four Buddha hair relics sent to Bagan and now enshrined within Bagan's Shwesandaw pagoda. Another 'gift' was the King of Bago's beautiful daughter Princess Manisanda (aka Khin U). To collect these priceless prizes, Anawrahta sent his most trusted commanders, the 'four paladins', led by his son and foremost general Kyanzittha. But as they returned Kyanzittha was overcome by temptation for the future queen, kicking off a classic love triangle. Once their affair was discovered, Kyanzittha was bound and sentenced to death by his furious father. However, the magic lance that was supposed to execute him instead broke the ropes that bound him and Kyanzittha made a fairy-tale escape, grabbing the lance and fleeing in a fishing boat. After a series of similarly implausible triumphs against Anawrahta's search parties, Kyanzittha settled in Kaungbyu, before finally returning to Bagan in 1077, only to rekindle the affair with Manisanda. Today, there is some controversy as to where Kaungbyu was, but Monywa guides are adamant that it was the delightful little village of A Myint.

factory to see the concrete cultivation tanks, peer through a microscope at the algae's incredible spiral form and see a range of packaged Spirulina-based products (manufactured elsewhere and not for sale here). The palm-fronted lakeside has a certain south-sea charm and views from the crater rim are very wide without being enormously spectacular.

Access is by an 8-mile (13km) unpaved lane that doubles back to the southwest, starting just a few yards after the toll gate when arriving in Budalin from the south.

PAYAGYI

The large Payagyi stupa and its oversized *chinthe* (half-lion/half-dragon deity) face an abrupt twin-peaked hill, topped with a stupa and castle-like rocky outcrop and said to have an indelible footprint of Bagan-era King Kyanzittha at its base. Now boxed within concrete walls and tin roof, the empty front prayer hall retains its 170-year-old teak pillars. Its carved-stone floor tiles, telling Ramayana tales, have been moved for safe keeping to a museum shed: notice number 274 featuring Hanuman (the monkey god) riding a sheep and smoking a cheroot. The attractive wooden monastery building seems oversized for the handful of resident monks.

It's 19 miles (30km) from the central junction in Budalin (marked by a golden horseback Bandula statue, 1640ft (500m) north of the Twin Daung turning), where you veer left. Keep left again after 2 miles (3km) then continue 14 miles (22km) to Ta Kook Ta Nel. Turn right after the little row of teahouses then follow the track 3 miles (5km) to Payagyi. It's a long way to come for one monastery, but the rural scenes en route are very attractive, especially along the asphalted first 5.5 miles (9km) after Budalin through cottonfields, sunflowers and Palmyra palms to Nyaung Kai/Ywathar, which has a massive Shwezigon pagoda in a field at its southeast edge.

West of Monywa

HPO WIN DAUNG

Monywa's biggest draw for culture vultures, this rural **complex** (admission $2) of 492 buddha chambers was carved into a limestone hillside between the 14th and 18th centuries. None of the 'caves' are more than a few yards deep, and many

are just big enough for a single image but a few of the best (notably caves 478 and 480) have retained some colourful, well-executed murals. The area is fairly large and there's no map so some visitors prefer to engage an informal guide (around K5000) who is likely to be friendly but not especially informative. Without a guide, just head up and left from the starting point and don't worry, it isn't necessary to climb nearly as far as the hilltop stupas that loom high on the ridge above. Around the complex, cheeky monkeys are all too keen to help you gain merit by donating food to them.

Some 2000ft (700m) beyond the restaurants and souvenir stands of Hpo Win 'village' lies **Shwe Ba Taung** (admission $2), a smaller, contrastingly different set of 46 cave chambers accessed from pathways cut around 25 ft (8mt) vertically down into the limestone. The buddha images are larger and far newer than those of the main site but the intriguing overall effect is of a Buddhist Disneyland set in a miniature Petra. Squint at Hpo Win Daung as you return and you might see why locals think the hill looks like a reclining buddha.

ⓘ Getting There & Away

The fastest access to the sites from Monywa is to cross the Chindwin River by boat then continue 23km west (the caves are 6km southwest of the main Pale road). From Strand Rd in Monywa, simple open-top ferry boats take locals across the Chindwin River for K200 each but foreigners must charter a whole boat, K3000 each way for up to five people. Boats run approximately 6am to 8pm.

Once across, waiting jeeps (carrying up to six at a pinch) want K20,000 return including waiting time. Motorbike drivers on the west bank won't take foreigners due to the jeep monopoly but you can bring a bike (and driver) across with you. Renting a chauffeured motorbike costs around K10,000 return (plus boat charges).

Visiting by taxi/motor-trishaw from Monywa (K25,000/40,000 return) you'll need to cross the big Chindwin Bridge. That adds 9 extra miles (14km) but allows a stop at the brilliantly perched if brash **Shwe Taung Oo pagoda** for 360-degree river and plain views. The route also passes some apocalyptic copper-mining shack-villages backed by a vast industrial-scale open pit. By motorbike you could go out by boat, back by bridge and enjoy sunset from Shwe Taung Oo.

SPIRULINA

An algae that grows in alkaline, sub-tropical lakes, Spirulina is named for its coiled spiral (or more accurately helix) shape, which is only visible when looking through a microscope. Harvested and dried, Spirulina was once a food-source for Aztec people. Today it's a popular dietary supplement said to help reduce cholesterol, lower blood pressure and counter hay fever. In Myanmar, Spirulina is best known as an ingredient of Mandalay Brewery's popular 'anti-aging' beer.

YANGON–MANDALAY HIGHWAY

There are two routes buses and cars ply between Yangon and Mandalay: the pot-holed old Hwy No 1, which some call the 'high road' (though it runs west of the Shan Hills); and the new Yangon–Mandalay Expressway, dubbed the 'big road'. Neither are particularly gorgeous drives but both provide access to a couple of places of interest en route to the north, including the former capital of Taungoo and the modern-day 'royal capital' of Nay Pyi Taw, a visit to which plunges you into the deepest depths of the bizarre.

Taungoo   တောင်ငူ

🎵 054

A busy highway town, Taungoo (also spelled Toungoo) is a popular overnight stop for both tourists and truckers. Sporting several interesting temples, a lively central market and a pretty lake, it has more places of interest than any other town on the Yangon–Mandalay Expressway, but then there's not a lot of competition. A great guesthouse on the town's outskirts makes it easy to stay an extra day, and can also be used as a base for visiting elephant camps in the hills to the west.

King Mingyinyo founded his capital here in 1510, and his dynasty ruled the country for the next 150 years. However, WWII bombing wrecked most of Mingyinyo's Ka-tumadi Palace (only sections of the old walls and moat can still be seen). In celebration of the town's 500th anniversary in 2010 a couple of impressive new gates were built,

as well as a massive statue of the king, un-missable on the old Yangon–Mandalay road, east of the palace walls.

The Karen hills to the east are famed for their vegetables and coffee. The area is also known for its numerous areca (betel) palms. In Myanmar, when someone receives unex-pected good fortune, they are likened to a betel-lover receiving a paid trip to Taungoo.

Kayin State is less than 22 miles (35km) east and Kayah State another 40 miles (64km) further east. Karen and Kayah in-surgents have been known to operate within these areas. A dry-weather road continues east all the way to Loikaw, but any travel be-yond the Sittoung (Sittang) River a couple of miles east of Taungoo requires special per-mission through a travel agent.

◉ Sights & Activities

Apart from visiting the sights, it's fun to **hire a bike** and spend half a day pedal-ling around the town's sights and into the countryside. Bikes can be rented from My-anmar Beauty Guest House for K2000 a day.

Shwesandaw Paya   BUDDHIST TEMPLE

(ရွှေဆံတော်ဘုရား) Taungoo's grandest pil-grimage spot is situated in the centre of town, around 500m west of the main road. The central stupa, a standard-issue bell shape, is gilded and dates back to 1597; lo-cal legend says an earlier stupa on the site was built centuries before and contains sacred-hair relics. Entering from the north, to your right is a display of Taungoo kings (and a rather busty queen), and a round building housing a reclining buddha sur-rounded by *devas* (celestial beings) and monastic disciples.

Nearby, on the western side of the stupa, there's a 12ft (3.5m) bronze, Mandalay-style sitting buddha, given to the paya in 1912 by a retired civil servant who donated his body weight in bronze and silver for the casting of the image. He died three years after the cast-ing at age 72; his ashes are interred behind the image.

On the east side, there's a shrine to Thurathati – a goddess borrowed by Bud-dhists from Hindus – atop a mythical *hintha* bird. Fine-arts students come to pray to her before exams.

Myasigon Paya   BUDDHIST TEMPLE

(မြစည်းခုံဘုရား) About 820 ft (250m) south of Shwesandaw, off Pagoda St, this lovely modern pagoda features a gold *zedi* and

WORTH A TRIP

VISITING THE ELEPHANT CAMPS

Myanmar has the largest population of domesticated elephants in the world, number around 4000, and is the only country where they are still used on a large scale in industry, in particular for logging carried out under the auspices of the state-owned Myanmar Timber Enterprise (MTE). In a mountainous area of Karen villages and teakwood plantations, 35 miles (56km) northwest of Taungoo, it's possible to visit logging camps and see up close working elephants and their *oozies* (the Myanmar word for mahouts) continuing a pattern of life unchanged for centuries. It's worth noting, however, that many animal welfare organisations continue to express concerns about the methodologies used to domesticate elephants.

With at least three days' notice (two weeks is better), trips of a day or longer can be arranged to this otherwise restricted area through Dr Chan Aye (p155) of the Myanmar Beauty Guest House II/III/IV.

Day trips, starting at 6am and returning to Taungoo around 5pm, cost $120 per person for two people, with prices dropping the larger the group. Included in the rates are the necessary permits, return transport, a walk into the forest, an elephant ride, a lunch of rice and curry, and plenty of bottled water. Bamboo rafting and motor biking in the jungle can be added for additional fees.

Overnight trips with a stay in either Shwe Daung or Ngwe Daug, both Karen villages, cost $250 per person for two people; it's also possible to do this trip and continue onward to Pyay the next day for $375 per person for two people. The doctor provides free medical service to villagers in the area.

many glass mosaics. On the north side, an open building has a faded mural of Taungoo kings. A nearby squat white building is actually a **museum** (to have it opened, ask in the pagoda; it usually costs K1000). The museum has bronze images of Erawan (the three-headed elephant who serves as Indra's mount) and assorted buddha images, but is more interesting for its random secular collection of British colonial-era memorabilia, including an ancient Kodak camera, 80-year-old plates and a cream soda bottle.

Kandawgyi Lake
LAKE, PARK

(ကန်တော်ကြီး; swimming pool for 2hr K500; ☺ swimming pool 7am-6pm) This pretty ornamental lake dates from the days when Taungoo (then known as Katumadi) was capital and Bayin Naung ruled. Strolling or cycling around its perimeter, lined with shady trees, is a pleasant way to pass an hour or so.

While nobody swims in the lake itself, on its eastern (town) side, you'll find a small **swimming pool** at the Evergreen Cafe, which also has friendly owners.

On the lake's western flank, sandwiched between the old palace walls and moat, is the **Kyet Minn Nyi Naung Amusement Park**, built by the firm responsible for the neighbouring Royal Katumadi Hotel. Apart from various places to eat and drink here, you can play snooker (K1000 per hour) and

tennis (K3000 per hour) or hire the karaoke room. There's a free kids' playground, but we were told the pedal boats on the lake were 'not for foreigners'.

Kawmudaw Paya
BUDDHIST TEMPLE

(ကောင်းမှုတော်ဘုရား) One of Taungoo's oldest religious sites, this countryside temple is around 1 mile (1.5km) west of the lake through the new Sin Gate Arch. In the temple's southwest corner, look for a small pillar in a sandbox (with barefoot prints). Locals come here and walk around it to conquer personal problems.

🛏 Sleeping

★ **Myanmar Beauty Guest House II, III & IV**
GUESTHOUSE $

(☎ 054-23270; fourdoctors@mptmail.net.mm; Pauk Hla Gyi St; s $15-40, d $20-50, tr $40-60; ✱) This three-part, 20-room rural complex at the edge of town is reason enough to stop in Taungoo. The Beauty has a pick'n'mix of rustic, all-wood, bungalow-style rooms. Don't get confused by the numbers, as it comes down to buildings and the higher the number, the nicer the room. The spacious S1 and S2 rooms in building IV face the fields and have air-con and a good hot shower; III is a step down, and II is usually used by drivers and guides. Staff are super, as is the wildly local breakfast, with samosas, sticky rice and exotic fruits. It's about 1.5 miles (2.5km) south of the turnoff from the old Yangon–Mandalay Highway into the centre of Taungoo and is a K1500 to K2000 trishaw ride from the centre. **Myanmar Beauty Guest House I** (☑054-23270; 7/134 Bo Hmu Pho Kun St; r $10-15), in town, isn't worth considering.

Mother's House Hotel   HOTEL $
(☑054-24240; mhh@banganmail.net.mm; 501-502 Yangon–Mandalay Highway; s/d $30/35; ❋☎) This 33-room bungalow complex right on the highway guarantees 24-hour electricity, satellite TV and clean and comfy hotel-style rooms with wooden floors and banoffee pie colour schemes.

Hotel Amazing Kaytu   HOTEL $
(☑054-23977; www.amazing-hotel.com; 8th St Ohtkyauttan; s/d from $38/43; ❋☎) 'Hotel Amazing' and 'Simply the Best' are stretching the imagination, but the owners clearly don't lack confidence in their property. Rooms include satellite TV and clean bathrooms, plus a clock set to Spanish time in the lobby. It's just north of the main turn off from the old Yangon–Mandalay Highway into the centre of Taungoo.

Myanma Thiri Hotel   HOTEL $
(☑054-23764; mthirihotel@myanmar.com.mm; Magalar Rd; r $20-55; ❋☎☎) With a bit of TLC, this old colonial-era building could be Taungoo's answer to a boutique hotel. The cheaper rooms, set in the original building, are cavernous but decaying. There are a few deluxe rooms in separate new chalets set amid the spacious grounds. It is probably best avoided until some builders get to work.

Royal Kaytumadi Hotel   HOTEL $$$
(☑054-24761; www.kmahotels.com; Royal Kaytumadi St; r $75-150, ste $250-1000; ❋@☎☎) Hogging the west side of the lake is Taungoo's fanciest option, with superbly appointed rooms, striking decorative detail and facilities including a swimming pool and spa. The property is owned by a businessman with close links to the generals. The same businessman also bankrolled the new city gates and giant statue of Mingyinyo erected to celebrate the city's 500th anniversary.

✗ Eating
Around Taungoo's tea shops, try asking for *yo yo* (normal coffee), which should get you a cup of 'Taungoo coffee', which actually comes from the Karen mountains to the east.

At the **night market**, which convenes next to the central market, vendors specialise in chapattis and meat-stuffed *palata* (fried flatbread). On the old Yangon–Mandalay Highway, particularly to the south, are many Chinese and Myanmar restaurants; the restaurant at Mother's House Hotel is particularly inviting.

Yagon Food Villa   PAN-ASIAN $
(185 Bo Hmu Pho Kun St; mains K2000-3000; ☺8.30am-9.30pm) Colourful fake-leather sofas and chairs add a bright note to this reliable option serving the usual mix of rice and noodle dishes, with surprising cameos from international dishes such as burgers and fish and chips on the menu.

ℹ Information
Arena Net Cafe (Bo Hmu Pho Kun St; per hr K500; ☺9am-4pm) Arena is next to Myanmar Beauty Guest House 1. Internet cafes are abundant, but don't expect speedy connections.

Dr Chan Aye (☑054-23270; drchanaye@gmail. com; Myanmar Beauty Guest House II, III, IV) Runs a clinic and speaks good English.

ℹ Getting There & Away
The 62-mile (100km) unpaved logging road from Oktwin (9 miles/15km south of Taungoo) to Paukkhaung provides a shortcut to Pyay. Foreigners are not allowed to travel along this road unless on a tour; Dr Chan Aye can make this trip with you, including a one- or two-night stop in a village or jungle camp along the way (from $375 per person for two people, including accommodation, meals and transport). Road travel east across the Sittoung River, towards Loikaw, is also restricted.

BUS
Most buses leaving Taungoo originated elsewhere. Generally stops are at private bus company offices scattered along the old Yangon–Mandalay Highway, just south of the turn-off to the 'centre'. It's easiest to have your hotel arrange a seat.

Nay Pyi Taw (K2500-K3000, three hours, frequent)

Mandalay (K7500-K9000, nine hours, early morning or early evening) Air-con bus.

Yangon (K4300-K5000, six hours, frequent) Buses with and without air-con.

TRAIN
The Taungoo **train station** (☑054-23308) has a military presence, following some Karen 'attacks' on trains passing in the night. Destinations include Mandalay (ordinary/upper $7/17, nine hours, departures 3.18am, 1.04pm, 2.43pm, 7.51pm, 9.35pm and 12.04am), Nay

Pyi Taw ($2/6, three hours, departures 1.04pm, 7.51pm, 9.35pm and 12.04am), Thazi ($4/11, five hours, departures 1.04pm, 9.35pm and 12.04am) and Yangon ($5/13, seven hours, departures 2.17am, 3.27am, 5.15am, 10:56am, 10.51pm and 11.57pm).

Nay Pyi Taw   နေပြည်တော်

📍 067 / POPULATION C925,000

In 2005, following the tradition of Burma's ancient kings, the military relocated Myanmar's capital to a more strategically central location, about 240 miles north of Yangon. At untold expense (some reports have it at more than $4 billion), Nay Pyi Taw was built on scrub ground amid rice paddies, villages and small towns such as Pyinmana on the old Yangon–Mandalay Highway. Most government ministries and their staff have been relocated here, but with a couple of exceptions the diplomatic community have dug in their heels in Yangon.

Absurdly grandiose in scale, Nay Pyi Taw (one translation is 'Royal City of the Sun') is a sprawling, shoddily constructed city with eight-lane highways, 24-hour electricity, and zones for shopping, government housing and hotels, ministry buildings and generals' homes. Apart from the roadblocks that protect the roads leading to the generals' mansions, ministry buildings and the parliament, it's surprisingly open. Visits to some of its sights, including a giant gilded pagoda and a zoo and safari park, allow you to mingle freely with locals while putting a dollar or two into the private economy. All this aside, it's a soulless place, Canberra meets Brasilia with a peculiar Orwellian twist.

◎ Sights

You don't come to Nay Pyi Taw for the sights so much as for its surreal atmosphere. Besides, the city is very much a work in progress.

When approaching from the new Yangon–Mandalay Expressway, visitors enter Nay Pyi Taw along the 'hotel zone' of Yarza Thingaha Rd. At the road's northern end near the Thabyaegone roundabout (one of the city's several gigantic, grassy road hubs) is the newly built convention centre, **Maniyadanar Kyauk Sein Khanma**. This is the location of the quarterly jade and precious stones fair, Emporium, about the only time Nay Pyi Taw fills up with visitors. Next door is the Gems

Museum and northeast of the roundabout is the Water Fountain Garden.

Continue northeast from here to the Yarza Thingaha roundabout and hang a right to find the Uppatasanti Paya, Nay Pyi Taw's main sight. If approaching the city from the old Yangon–Mandalay Highway via the long-established town of Pyinmana, visitors hit the golden pagoda first.

Be careful where you point your camera in Nay Pyi Taw: photography of official buildings or military officials is prohibited. The giant **statues of three kings** (Alaungpaya, Anawrahta and Bayinnaung), seen in some publicised photos of Nay Pyi Taw, are in a military zone in the hills to the east, and are not accessible to the public.

Uppatasanti Paya   BUDDHIST TEMPLE

(ဥပ္ပါတသန္တိစေတီ) An act of merit-making by General Than Shwe and his wife, this 321ft-tall (98m) golden pagoda – 1ft (30cm) smaller than Yangon's Shwedagon Paya – is impressive from afar (especially when illuminated at night), but close up betrays its hasty construction with poor finishing. Nevertheless, the vast interior is lined with some vivid carved-stone murals depicting the life and legend of Buddha and key scenes from Myanmar's Buddhist history. Foreigners are supposed to pay a $5 entry charge, but no one asked us for it when we showed up.

At the foot of the pagoda's east side is a covered, open-sided enclosure where two fabled **white elephants** (Buddawadi and Nandawadi) stand chained and munching bamboo. Along with these two females, who are more dusky pink than white, there's also a regular pair of grey elephants for comparison. Between 10am and 4pm the elephants are unchained and disappear from public view to roam the grazing ground to the rear.

Zoological Garden & Safari Park   ZOO

(တိရိစ္ဆာန်ရုံ နှင့် ဆာဖာရီဥယျာဉ်; zoo $10, photo charge K2000, safari park $20; ⏰8.30am-8pm Tue-Sun, safari park 8.30am-4.30pm) A good 45-minute drive northeast of the hotel zone (and closer to Pyinmana) are these animal-focused attractions, both run by the government. As zoos go, it's not a badly kept place and most of its inhabitants were shifted here from Yangon's decrepit colonial-era zoo. Spread across 612 acres are more than 80 different species of animal, bird and reptile, including hippos, lions, deer,

Nay Pyi Taw

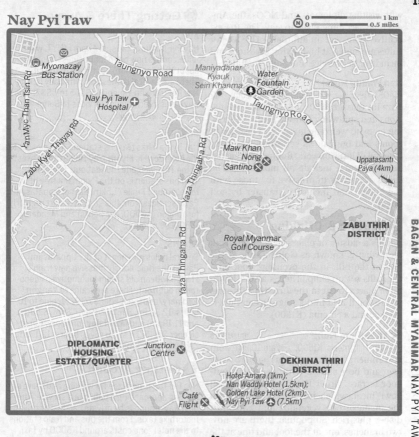

bison, crocodiles and several elephants. There's also an air-conditioned pool house for black-footed and Humboldt penguins, and a planetarium.

Next door, more wild beasts roam the **safari park**, which opened in 2011 and is toured on electric canopy-covered buggies which are quite a relief in the heat of the day. The 35-acre facility, home to zebras, rhinos, tigers and a pair of giraffes, is divided into sections showcasing the fauna of Africa, Asia and Australia.

Water Fountain Garden PARK
(admission K200, camera charge K1000; ☺8.30am-8.30pm) More or less at the heart of Nay Pyi Taw is this government-built grassy park, which boasts a viewing platform, water features (usually turned on around dusk) and cheaply constructed and already crumbling decorative structures bedecked with twinkling fairy lights at night.

🛏 Sleeping

Foreign visitors must stay in the hotel zone where new complexes have sprouted like daisies. Forced to build quickly, construction and decorative standards are often woeful, but the competition means some reasonable rates are available when compared with tourist destinations such as Yangon and Mandalay.

Golden Lake Hotel HOTEL $
(🖉067-434011; thegoldenlakehotelnpt@gmail. com; 36-37 Yaza Thingaha Rd; r $25-35; ❄🔊) One of the very few cheapies in the hotel zone, Golden Lake has standard rooms with shared bathroom or superior rooms with attached bathroom. Both include similar amenities such as satellite TV and fridge.

Hotel Amara HOTEL $$
(🖉067-422201; www.thehotelamara.com; 11 Yarza Thingaha Rd; r $70-670; ❄@🔊🌀) A favourite

with visiting diplomats and NGOs, the Amara is a welcoming place to stay. The 104 executive rooms are an affordable US$70, but suites are aimed at high-flying investors and include butler service. Breakfast included.

Nan Waddy Hotel RESORT $$
(☎067-419051; www.nanwaddyhotel.com; 12 Yarza Thingaha Rd; r $60, ste $120-250) The spacious and sprawling Nanwaddy has a striking lobby to welcome guests and a series of rooms and bungalows set around a pretty lake full of lotus flowers. Rooms are reasonable value and include all mod cons. The suites are pretty impressive for those with the budget and include a transfer by golf buggy.

✗ Eating & Drinking

There's a cluster of places to eat and drink atop what is known as Golden Hill. At the foot of the hill, in the evenings, food and tea stalls set up shop. There's also a handful of places to eat in the **Junction Centre**, where you'll also find a huge Ocean Supermarket and a cinema (K1500).

★**Maw Khan Nong** BURMESE $
(Golden Hill; meals K1500; ⊙7am-10pm) Join government workers at this superb canteen and beer station with a spacious outdoor terrace. Order the good value 'Bagan bowl' meal, which includes a choice from the menu of one vegetable and two meat dishes plus rice. So popular there are now two branches, one at the foot and one at the summit of the hill.

Santino INTERNATIONAL $$
(Golden Hill; meals K2500-10,000; ⊙7am-10pm) The menu at this appealing Western-style cafe, bakery and restaurant has something for everyone, kicking off with full American-style breakfasts and continuing with things such as burgers, club sandwiches and pizza. There is also a huge menu of Burmese, Chinese, Japanese and Thai food. Think United Nations.

Café Flight INTERNATIONAL $$
(3 Yarza Thingaha Rd; mains K2000-11,000; ⊙8am-10pm) The safest way to board a Myanma Airways plane is to board this one, parked in front of the Sky Palace Hotel, and turned into a cafe-bar serving draught Tiger beer, coffee, noodles, pasta and pizza. The plane smells more than a little musty, so most diners prefer to eat in the main restaurant behind.

❶ Getting There & Away

AIR
Nay Pyi Taw International Airport (NYT; www.nptia.com) is now open for business, located about 10 miles (16km) southeast of the city. There are several domestic flights daily linking Nay Pyi Taw with Yangon (US$65 to US$75 one way), plus international services to Bangkok several times a week.

BUSES
Nay Pyi Taw has two bus stations. The closest to the hotel zone is **Myomazay Bus Station**, west of the Thabyaegone roundabout. The Bawga Thiri bus station is on the Pyinmana side of town, around 1 mile (1.5km) east of Uppatasanti Paya; services from this station depart regularly for Yangon (K6000, five hours) and Mandalay (K5000, six hours).

TRAINS
Several miles northeast of the Uppatasanti Paya is the ridiculously massive new train station with an old steam locomotive as decoration out front. There are trains to **Yangon** (ordinary/upper/sleeper $7/19/21, nine to 10 hours, 12.36am, 8am, 12.19pm, 8pm, 8.59pm and 11.19pm) and **Mandalay** (ordinary/upper/sleeper $7/15/17, six to seven hours, 12.13am, 2.43am and 3.52pm).

❶ Getting Around

Nya Pyi Taw is no place for walking and there's nothing approaching a public bus service. The best way around is by private car, taxi or private motorbike taxis. From the bus and train stations to the hotel zone costs around K5000 by taxi. Four hours by motorbike taxi around the city from Pyinmana should cost around K10,000.
Nay Pyi Taw Taxi & Car Rental Services (☎067-414994) Run by government-affiliated Max Myanmar group. A taxi from the airport to town is about K10,000.

Meiktila

☑064
This attractive lakeside town, on the crossroads between Yangon, Mandalay, Bagan and Inle Lake, is a busy little trade centre with plenty of locals in uniform from the air-force bases outside town. Legend goes that King Anawrahta, founder of Bagan, had a pond here broadened into the current lake that looms west of town. When the king asked if the lake extended all the way to Mt Popa, the report came back: 'Lord, it doesn't go that far.'

And the bad news kept coming. Between February and March 1945, the British killed 20,000 Japanese soldiers based here in the final WWII battle for control of Burma. Much of the city was flattened. Sadly that trend has continued: town-engulfing fires devastated the city in 1974 and 1991; another big one took out several buildings in 2003.

The name has perhaps become something of a burden, as in 2013 Meiktila once again hit the headlines for all the wrong reasons when internecine rioting broke out between the Buddhist and Muslim communities. Dozens were killed and hundreds displaced and it is still possible to see scars from the violence on the outskirts of town.

◉ Sights

Lake Meiktila (မိတ္ထီလာကန်) is the town's premier attraction. There are no boating options, but you can cycle around some of it. Between the road and rail bridges, west of the city centre, you won't miss **Phaung Daw U Paya**, a temple housed in a giant floating barge shaped in the form of a golden *karaweik*, a mythical bird.

Cross the road bridge to reach the wooden pier leading to the pretty **Antaka Yele Paya**, a small pagoda perched on an island in the lake. Back on the main road is an **Aung San statue**.

A few hundred metres southwest of the bridge is a building that was once a **British colonial diplomat house**. The building was used as an interrogation centre by the Japanese in WWII, and many years later Aung San Suu Kyi and Michael Aris honeymooned here. The house is to the east of the Lakeside Wunzin Hotel.

A mile around the west end of the lake, **Shwe Kyaung** is a walled monastery on the inland side of the road with Japanese signs leading to a **WWII monument** that British and Japanese survivors erected in 1972. Monks will show you around. Just past the monument, a picturesque path leads between the lake and (usually) flooded rice fields.

Don't keep going to the south side of the lake, as the path leads into the no-go zone of a military compound.

🛏 Sleeping & Eating

Honey Hotel   HOTEL $
(☎ 064-25755; Panchan St; s/tw $30/35; ❄ 🖥) Right on the lake in the southern tip of the town centre, this converted mansion is Meiktila's leading budget option. If available, opt for room G2, which has views directly across the lake. Newly built, more expensive rooms at the front of the complex substitute fresh paint, linens and TVs for the lack of lake view.

Lakeside Wunzin Hotel   HOTEL $$
(☎ 064-23848; www.mountpleasanthotelmyamar. com; 49A Than Lwin Rd; superior/deluxe/ste $59/72/85; ❄) Showing its age these days, the more expensive suites here overlook the lake from a quiet backstreet out of the centre. Discounts are regularly available.

Staff are happy to join you for tennis on the scrappy court outside should you be travelling with a racket. It is located to the west of the town centre about 1000ft (300m) from Antaka Yele Paya.

Shwe Ohn Pin   CHINESE $$
(Mandalay-Yangon Rd; dishes K2500-4500; ⊙ 7am-10pm) This clean tiled restaurant, located in the centre, hands you an English menu for its tasty Chinese and Myanmar dishes.

Golden Rain Tea Center   TEAHOUSE $
(tea K200; ⊙ 5am-9.30pm) This popular place, just off the Mandalay–Yangon Rd, has all the usual milky, sweet drinks and filling chicken or pork steamed buns. Mix with locals at the low tables shielded by a rattan roof cover.

ℹ Getting There & Away

BUSES

Express buses zooming between Yangon and Mandalay stop on the road east of the clock tower (and not at the local bus station). Along this road you'll find half a dozen ticket-sales shops, including **Asia World** (☎ 09-4301 1348) opposite the Thiri Minglar Mosque.

Buses from Meiktila go to the following destinations: Bagan (K7000, five hours, 4pm), Mandalay (K3000, three to four hours, several daily), Nay Pyi Taw (K3000, three to four hours, several daily) and Yangon (K10,000, 10 to 12 hours, three daily).

TRAIN

There's a small train station in town, catching slow trains heading east–west.

A more useful station is in Thazi, about 16 miles (26km) east, at the crossroads of the Yangon, Mandalay and Taunggyi lines.

YANGON–BAGAN HIGHWAY

This western route north of Yangon to Bagan is less heavily trafficked than the Yangon–Mandalay route. Sometimes called the 'low road', or 'Pyay Hwy', this route is arguably more attractive than the old Yangon–Mandalay Highway. It follows the eastern bank of the Ayeyarwady River and rises over lovely hills and valleys north of Magwe. At Pyay, connections to Thandwe (and Ngapali) head west over the mountains.

Pyay (Prome) ပြည်

♪ 053

With a breezy location on the Ayeyarwady River, Pyay is the most interesting stop on the Yangon–Bagan Highway. The city's glory days date back to the ancient Pyu capital of Thayekhittaya, the partially excavated remains of which lie 5 miles (8km) east of Pyay's other stellar attraction: the dazzling Shwesandaw Paya.

Myanmar folk alternate the town's pronunciation between 'pyay' and 'pyi'. The Brits, apparently, couldn't deal with the confusion and called it Prome. The current town site became an important trading centre during the Bagan era. The Mon controlled it when King Alaungpaya conquered it in 1754. Pyay boomed, along with the British Irrawaddy Flotilla Company in the 1890s. Today, it remains an important transit point for goods between northern and southern Myanmar. Soak up its lively atmosphere along the riverfront and at the roundabout, at the centre of which is a gilded equestrian statue of Aung San.

◉ Sights

Shwesandaw Paya & Around
BUDDHIST TEMPLE

(ရွှေဆံတော်ဘုရား နှင့် အနီးဝန်းကျင်) Set on top of a hill in the town centre, the stunning Shwesandaw Paya (and the surrounding pagodas and monasteries) is not only Pyay's major point of interest, but also one of the country's biggest Buddhist pilgrimage sites. Just over 3ft (1m) taller than the main zedi at Yangon's Shwedagon (p46), the Shwesandaw stupa follows the classic Burmese design seen at Bagan's Shwezigon (p182).

Legend goes that it was built in 589 BC, and that the golden zedi houses four strands of the Buddha's hair (the Golden Hair

Relics). Atop the zedi are two hti (umbrella-like pinnacles), unusual for Myanmar. The lower, bigger one dates from Pyay's days as a Mon city. The higher, smaller one was added by King Alaungpaya as a symbol of peace between his realm and the Mon, after brutally capturing the city in 1754. In the southwest corner of the complex, the **Sacred Tooth Hall** is said to house an original tooth from the Buddha. It's in the golden bell (locked) behind the glass. The locks come off once a year for the November full-moon festivities.

The panoramic views from the pagoda are pretty great too. To the east, you'll see the **Sehtatgyi Paya** (Big Ten Storey), a giant (maybe not 10 storeys, though) seated buddha, eye-to-eye with the Shwesandaw and watching over it. The smaller gold stupa on the highest hill southeast of Shwesandaw is the **Wunchataung Paya** (Apology Mountain Pagoda), where people can say 'sorry' for misdeeds. While they're at it, they get the best view of Shwesandaw and the mountains across the river. Reach Wunchataung via Sehtatgyi Rd, east of the Shwesandaw.

Central Market
MARKET

Follow Strand Rd north of a morning to catch all the action at the lively and colourful central market which spreads over several blocks. As you approach, you'll pass an ornate **Chinese Temple** dedicated to the goddess Guan Yin on the corner of Ya Yoke Tann St. A little further on are giant clay water pots and a row of thanakha wood sellers. Continue along the riverside north of the market to find the Shwepaliamaw Paya.

Payagyi Paya
BUDDHIST TEMPLE

(ဘုရားကြီးဘုရား) Once marking one of Thayekhittaya's four corners, this towering pagoda probably dates from the 5th or 6th century AD. Three terraces encircle the slightly swollen, breastlike structure from its base; 'ladies' are not allowed on the upper one. The modern hti is lit up at night and lies a half-mile (800m) east of the bus station.

⌂ Sleeping

Myat Lodging House
HOTEL $

(☏ 053-25695; 222 Bazaar St; r with fan $5-15, with air-con $20-25; ❄) This small back-street guesthouse has simple rooms a block from the Pyay 'action'. The $5 rooms might be the cheapest in Myanmar, but are a cell with a fan and shared bathroom. Higher-priced rooms come with a private bathroom and

Pyay

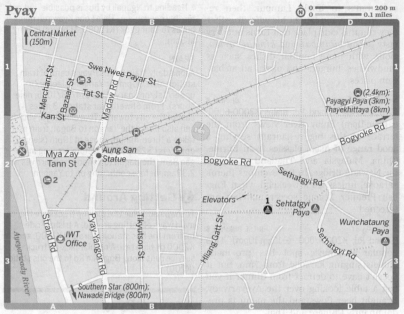

Central Market (150m)

Swe Nwee Payar St

Merchant St
Bazzar St
Tat St
Kan St
Madaw Rd

(2.4km);
Payagyi Paya (3km);
Thayekhittaya (8km)

Bogyoke Rd

Mya Zay Tann St
Aung San Statue
Bogyoke Rd
Sethatgyi Rd

Elevators
Sehtatgyi Paya

Wunchataung Paya

Sethatgyi Rd

Strand Rd
Ayeyarwady River
Pyay-Yangon Rd
IWT Office
Tikyutson St
Hlang Gatt St

Southern Star (800m);
Nawade Bridge (800m)

are set at the back of the maze of buildings. Friendly English-speaking staff give out maps of Pyay and Thayekhittaya.

Smile Motel HOTEL $
(☎ 053-22523; 10-11 Bogyoke Rd; r $24-35; ❋) The long corridor leading to the simply furnished rooms may have a shabby carpet and remind you of *The Shining*, but it's all pretty clean and the staff are nice, if a bit surprised at your existence. The $35 rooms are essentially triples if three's not a crowd.

★Lucky Dragon HOTEL $$
(☎ 053-24222; www.luckydragonhotel.com; 772 Strand Rd; r from $40-60; ❋ ⓦ ☎) Leaving all other town centre hotels in the shade, this enclave of modern, bungalow-style, wood-floored rooms across from the river is reasonably priced and has pleasant, helpful staff. Another plus is the small pool, long enough for a few cooling laps after touring Pyay's sights. Breakfast included.

Mingalar Garden Resort HOTEL $$
(☎ 053-28662; flying Tiger Garden, Aung Chan Tha Quarter; s/d standard $50/60, superior $60/70; ❋ @) Near Payagyi Paya and closer to Thayekhittaya than the Ayeyarwady River, this quiet garden complex of spacious bungalows is set in the beautifully presented

grounds of a former cheroot manufacturer. It's worth spending the extra dollars for the more modern superior rooms, all of which overlook an ornamental lake. Breakfast included lakeside.

✕ Eating & Drinking

The **night market** on Mya Zay Tann St, between the Aung San statue and the river, is atmospheric and well worth browsing for its cheap eats.

★Grandma Café KOREAN, INTERNATIONAL $
(Mya Zay Tann Rd; mains K1000-2500; ⊙ 8am-10pm) Owner Banyar Aung learned to make Korean food while working at various

restaurants in Kuala Lumpur, then returned home and taught his wife. Together they run this cute place that turns out very tasty *dolsot bibimbap* and *kimchi ramen,* along with more familiar dishes such as sandwiches, burgers and pasta, all at bargain prices.

Southern Star   CHINESE $
(☑ 053-25484; Strand Rd; mains K3000-6000; ☺ 10am-11pm) Enjoy river views from the terrace of this big restaurant serving a good range of Asian classics from Burma, China, Malaysia and Thailand, close by the Nawade Bridge. In the evenings there's karaoke, unless it's a weekend when English Premier League soccer matches are screened.

Hline Ayar   CHINESE, BURMESE $
(Strand Rd; K2000-7000; ☺ 10am-10pm) This popular live-music spot has provincial models singing karaoke from 7pm, but it doesn't have to detract from dinner if you bag a table looking over the Ayeyarwady. Draught beer flows and the menu is predominantly Chinese and Thai.

❶ Information

Cosmic (Kan St; per hr K400; ☺ 7.30am-11pm) For internet, try here. It's in the same building as the old cinema.

❶ Getting There & Away

BOAT
Routes along the Ayeyarwady River start and stop in Pyay, heading south, but few foreigners use this service.

The **IWT office** (☑ 053-24503; Strand Rd; ☺ 9am-5pm Mon-Fri) is helpful on ever-changing times for slow-going government ferries. At research time, a cargo ferry left around 3am in the middle of Tuesday night for Yangon (deck/cabin $12/24, about three days).

BUS
Pyay is located at the junction of roads to Yangon, Bagan and Thandwe (for Ngapali Beach). The highway bus station is about two miles (3km) east of the centre (just off Bogyoke Rd).

Several companies run buses to Yangon (K4500, seven hours) throughout the day, including **Asia Express** (☑ 053-28145). There are no direct buses north to Bagan from Pyay, but you can catch a bus that left from Yangon for the full Yangon–Bagan fare (K15,000 to K18,000, 12 hours). Or take the 8.30am bus to Magwe (K4100, six hours), from where there are morning departures for Bagan.

Heading to Ngapali by bus is possible, but not terribly convenient. Thile Lone Kyaw run minibuses to Taunggok (K11,000, 11 hours) leaving at 5pm.

TRAIN
A lone daily train leaves Pyay's central train station at 11.30pm for Yangon (sleeper/upper/1st/ordinary class $14/13/10/5, nine hours). From Shwethekar station, 3 miles east of the city towards Thayekhittaya, you can also board the Yangon to Bagan train as it takes a three-minute pause at 10pm (sleeper/upper/1st $28/26/23), before arriving in Bagan 8am; the Bagan to Yangon train arrives at 2.30am, before continuing on to Yangon.

❶ Getting Around

Trishaws and blue taxi pick-up trucks are the main ways of getting around. A trishaw ride to/from the bus station is around K1500, and K2000 by blue taxi. A regular pick-up truck service runs along Bogyoke Rd to the bus station (K200).

Around Pyay

Thayekhittaya   သရေခေတ္တရာ

It's no Bagan, but this ancient site, about 5 miles east of Pyay centre, makes for an enjoyble few hours of laid-back exploration, often in isolation. Known to Pali-Sanskrit scholars as Sri Ksetra (Fabulous City), Thayekhittaya is an enormous Pyu city that ruled in the area from the 5th to 9th centuries AD. Local legend links its origin to the mythical King Duttabaung, who supposedly worked with ogres and other supernatural creatures to build the 'magical city' in 443 BC. The earliest Pali inscriptions found here date back to the 5th or 6th centuries.

◉ Sights

Seeing the 5.5-sq-mile **site** (သရေခေတ္တရာ; admission $5, incl museum $10; ☺ 8am-5pm) means either walking the 7.5-mile loop around it or hopping on the back of an **ox-drawn cart** (per person K5000; ☺ 3hr) for a bumpy, dusty journey past the spaced-out temples, most just outside the oval city walls. It's a good idea to have a knowledgeable guide as well if available at the museum. Bicycles aren't permitted.

At the entrance to the site is the small, government-run **Sri Ksetra Museum** (admission $5; ☺ 10am-4pm Tue-Sat) with its posted map of the area and various artefacts from excavations, including Hindu deities, 6th-century buddha images, Pyu beads and silver coins. It is possible to cast a glance over the collection in the main hall while buying the entry ticket to visit Thayekhittaya.

Behind the museum to the south, the road soon follows the remains of the old palace walls. Ox-cart drivers – at a speed that ebbs and flows according to the mood of the ox – make a counter-clockwise loop of the following sites.

The first stop will be at a recent excavation: a large brick building that is thought to have been a palace. After 2.5 miles (4km) the road passes Rahanta Gate, where fragments of the overgrown brick gate run alongside the dirt road. Immediately south is the Rahanta cave temple, thought to date to the Bagan period and last repaired in the 1920s, with eight buddha images lined along the south wall.

About a mile (1.5km) south, the Bawbawgyi Paya (Big Grandfather Stupa) is Thayekhittaya's most impressive site: a 50yd (45m) cylindrical stupa with a golden *hti* on its top. It's among the oldest and least obviously renovated Pyu sights, dating back to the 4th century. It's the prototype of many Myanmar pagodas.

Two-hundred yards (190m) northeast is the smaller cube-shaped Bebe Paya, which has a cylindrical top and a few buddha images inside; it's thought to date to the 10th century. Just north is the squat Leimyethna Paya, which has a visible iron frame keeping it together. Inside four original buddha reliefs (a bit cracked, some faces missing) are visible. On either side of the roads around here, look out for long ruts in the ground, which were once brick moats.

A couple of hundred yards (190m) to the north is a fork in the road: to the right (north) is a tin-roofed cemetery; to the left (west), on the way to 'Thaungpye Mound', is the better (but bumpier) way back to the museum.

Take the left and after half a mile (800m) you'll pass by a gap in the 9ft (3m)-thick city walls, which has become a gate. Continue another mile, (1.5km) through a booming farming village of thatch huts, with piles of radishes and other produce. Towards the north end of the village is the 13th-century East Zegu Paya, a small four-sided temple with overgrown walls and (usually) locked doors. It's off the main road, but is worth visiting for the walk past the fields and farmers.

ⓘ Getting There & Away

The turn-off here is a couple of miles east of Payagyi Paya. A return taxi between Thayekhittaya and Pyay should cost about K10,000. No direct pick-up truck connects the Pyay town centre with the site. You can bike to the site, but not around it.

Shwedaung ရွှေတောင်

This small town about 9 miles (14km) south of Pyay, via the road to Yangon, contains the famous Shwemyetman Paya (Paya of the Golden Spectacles), a reference to the large, white-faced sitting buddha inside the main shrine. The buddha wears a gargantuan set of eyeglasses with gold-plated rims. Coming south from Pyay, the turn-off for Shwemyetman is located on the right-hand side of the road; a green-and-white sign in English reads 'Shwe Myet Hman Buddha Image – 1 Furlong'.

Spectacles were first added to the image during the Konbaung era, when a nobleman offered them to the temple in an attempt to stimulate local faith through curiosity. Word soon spread that the bespectacled buddha had the power to cure all ills, especially afflictions linked to the eyes. The first pair of spectacles was stolen at an early stage, and a second pair was made and enshrined inside the image to protect it from thieves.

An English officer stationed in Pyay during the colonial era had a third pair fitted over the buddha's eyes after his wife suffered from eye trouble and the abbot suggested such a donation. Naturally, as the story goes, she was cured. This pair is now in a small shrine to the right of the image.

On the southern side of Shwedaung, about 3 miles (5km) from Shwemyetman, is the attractive hilltop Shwenattaung Paya (Golden Spirit Mountain), which reportedly dates back to the Thayekhittaya era. Among the many images of buddha is a serene one carved from marble. A large *paya pwe* (pagoda festival) is held here each year on the full moon of Tabaung (February/March).

To get to Shwedaung, hop on a pick-up truck headed towards Yangon. Pick-up trucks leave frequently from the Pyay bus station and pass by the Aung San statue before hitting the highway.

Akauk Taung အကောက်တောင်

Carved into cliffs overlooking the Ayeyarwady, about 19 miles (30.5km) downstream from Pyay, are dozens of buddha images at Akauk Taung (Tax Mountain). The mountain is named for the crafty toll-takers from the mid-19th century, who spent the hours between taxing boats carving reclining and meditating buddhas into the steep cliff.

To get there, you'll need to taxi across the Ayeyarwady to **Htonbo** (ထုံဘိုရွာ), a village about 90 minutes by road from Pyay, then hire a boat (about K15,000) for the 45-minute look. To do so, you must bring a copy of your passport or visa to show the *strict* immigration officers in Htonbo.

For some visitors, it's too much travel for minimal payoff. A return taxi to Htonbo from Pyay (sometimes with Shwedaung thrown in) takes around two hours one-way and costs about K30,000 for the round trip.

Magwe မဂွေး

📞 063

About 155 miles (250km) north of Pyay and 93 miles (150km) south of Salay, Magwe's locale on the Ayeyarwady River is nice enough, as is the impressive 1.8-mile (3km) Magwe Bridge. Beyond this, however, it's a place of dilapidated buildings running along a confusing web of leafy streets. Still, if you're travelling along the bumpy road connecting Bagan and Pyay, you'll probably want to break your journey here and stretch your legs around the 'sights'. Famously, the capital of Magwe Division sat out of the 1988 pro-democracy marches.

◉ Sights

Magwe's chief pagoda, the 1929 **Mya Tha Lun Paya**, a mile (1.5km) north of the **Magwe Bridge**, features a gilded stupa and occupies a hilltop site with great river views.

Just across the river, about the same distance north of the bridge, is Minbu and the fun **Nga Ka Pwe Taung** (Dragon Lake), a burping pool of butane gas and mud that has (over the years) built a few acres of lunar-like terrain with bubbling pools atop four odd mounds. The sludge isn't hot; if your toes slip in, wash them off below at a small pagoda. The largest mound is named Thu Sei Ta and the second largest Nanda,

for the mythical Dragon King's daughter and son, respectively. It's about a 30-minute taxi ride here from the centre.

🛏 Sleeping & Eating

Rolex Guest House GUESTHOUSE $

(📞 063-23536; cnr Mya Than Lun Rd & Ayeyarwady Bridge; s/d with fan K8000/13,000, with air-con K15,000/30,000; 🕸) This rambling old guesthouse, on the roundabout facing the bridge entry, has ageing rooms with cold-water bathrooms attached. It's easy to find and will just about do the trick if passing through for the night.

Nan Htike Thu Hotel HOTEL $$

(📞 063-28205; www.nanhtikethu.com; Strand Rd; r $50-120; 🕸🖥🛜) Newly opened in 2013, this riverfront hotel is the best in Magwe. Superior river view rooms are $70 and all are smartly kitted out with flat screen TV, minibar and bathtubs. Facilities include a huge kidney-shaped swimming pool. Across the road on the river's edge is the Elysium Restaurant. The hotel is 1.5 miles (2.5km) south of the bridge.

★**Mona Liza 2** BURMESE, CHINESE $

(Strand Rd; mains from K1500-6000; 🕚7am-10pm) On the river, just south of the bridge, this is a very popular drinking spot that also serves great value food. We had a Burmese set lunch and the plates just kept coming, all for K1500. As the sun dips across the river, locals hit the beer and whisky for the 7pm music and dance show.

Central Restaurant CHINESE $

(Pyitawthar Rd; mains K2000-5000; 🕚7am-10pm) Handy for the bus station, this reasonably clean-looking Chinese restaurant serves the usual noodle and rice dishes, including hot and sour chicken.

ℹ Getting There & Around

Magwe's highway bus station is about 1.5 miles (2.5km) east of the central market. Buses from Magwe go to the following destinations: Nyaung U (K6000, four hours, morning), Pyay (K4100, seven hours, frequent), Yangon (K8000, 12 hours, frequent) and Mandalay (K5500, 10 hours, 6.30pm).

Motorised trishaws – with room for you and a few mates – tout their services at the bus station. A ride from the station to Nga Ka Pwe Taung and a stop at Mona Liza 2 costs about K10,000.

Temples of Bagan

Best Temple Murals

➡ Upali Thein (p174)

➡ Nandamannya Pahto (p181)

➡ Payathonzu (p181)

➡ Ananda Ok Kyaung (p174)

➡ Abeyadana Pahto (p179)

Best Sunset Spots

➡ Shwesandaw Paya (p176)

➡ Buledi (p175)

➡ Pyathada Paya (p178)

➡ Thabeik Hmauk (p177)

➡ Tan Kyi Paya (p172)

Why Go?

Marco Polo, who may have visited on his travels, described Bagan as 'one of the finest sights in the world'. Despite centuries of neglect, looting, erosion and regular earthquakes, not to mention questionable restoration, this temple-studded plain remains a remarkably impressive and unforgettable vision.

In a 230-year building frenzy up until 1287 and the Mongol invasions, Bagan's kings commissioned more than 4000 Buddhist temples. These brick and stucco religious structures are all that remain of their grand city, with the 11th- to 13th-century wooden buildings having long gone.

Many restoration projects have resulted in an archaeological site that can barely be described as ruins. Often the restorations bear little relation to the building styles and techniques used at the time of original. Still, Bagan remains a wonder. Working temples such as Ananda Pahto, give a sense of what the place was like at its zenith, while others conceal colourful murals and hidden stairways leading to exterior platforms and jaw-dropping views across the plain.

When to Go
Bagan

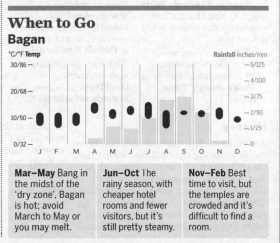

Mar–May Bang in the midst of the 'dry zone', Bagan is hot; avoid March to May or you may melt.

Jun–Oct The rainy season, with cheaper hotel rooms and fewer visitors, but it's still pretty steamy.

Nov–Feb Best time to visit, but the temples are crowded and it's difficult to find a room.

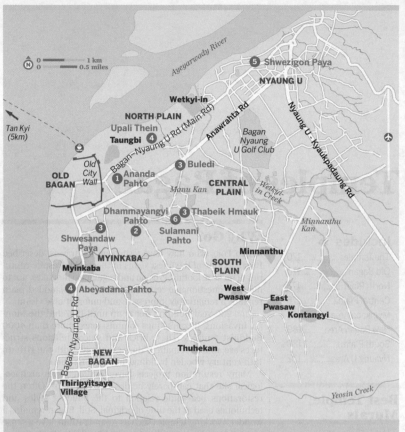

Temples of Bagan Highlights

❶ Marvel at the perfectly proportioned **Ananda Pahto** (p174), which houses four giant buddha statues carved from teak

❷ Speculate over what lies inside the bricked-up inner sanctum of mysterious **Dhammayangyi Pahto** (p176)

❸ Take in all the colours of the sunset from **Shwesandaw Paya** (p176) or **Buledi** (p175), or enjoy the spectacle, minus the crowds, at **Thabeik Hmauk** (p177)

❹ Admire the intricate murals decorating **Upali Thein** (p174) and **Abeyadana Pahto** (p179)

❺ Get acquainted with the 37 *nats* at the beautiful *zedi* **Shwezigon Paya** (p182) in Nyaung U

❻ Inspect the fine internal ornamental work of **Sulamani Pahto** (p177), a temple known as the Crowning Jewel

History

According to Pali inscriptions found here, Bagan kings apparently flirted with a couple of different city names during its heyday, including Arimaddanapura (City of the Enemy Crusher) and the less dramatic Tambadipa (Copper Land). The name Bagan may in fact derive from Pyugan, a name first written down by the Annamese of present-day Vietnam in the mid-11th century as Pukam. The British in the 19th century called the site 'Pagan' while the military junta switched it back to Bagan in 1989.

Glory Days

Bagan's two and a half centuries of temple building (from the 11th century to the 13th century) coincided with the region's transition from Hindu and Mahayana Buddhist beliefs to the Theravada Buddhist beliefs that have since characterised Myanmar. Legend has it that the main players were the monk Shin Arahan who came (sent by Manuha, the Mon king of Thaton; more on him later) to convert Bamar King Anawrahta.

To call his quest a success would be a landmark understatement. Inspired by his new faith, Anawrahta ordered Manuha to give him a number of sacred Buddhist texts and relics. When Manuha naturally refused, Anawrahta marched his army south and took everything worth carrying back to Bagan, including 32 sets of the Tripitaka (the classic Buddhist scriptures), the city's monks and scholars and, for good measure, King Manuha himself.

The self-assured Anawrahta then turned to architects to create something that befit Buddha. They built and built, and many of the greatest Bagan edifices date from these efforts, including Shwezigon Paya, considered a prototype for all later Myanmar stupas; the Pitaka Taik (Scripture Library), built to house the Pitaka (scriptures); and the elegant and distinctive Shwesandaw Paya, built immediately after the conquest of Thaton. Thus began what the Myanmar

BAGAN IN ...

Many visitors set aside just two days in Bagan even though it is easy to spend four or five days here and still leave much unexplored. Personalise the following itineraries or consider renting a bike and heading off to view thousands of other random sights – the real pleasure of Bagan comes from a leisurely soaking up of its scale and time-slip atmosphere.

One Day

Stick to the **Old Bagan** area starting at the Tharabar Gate (p172) then heading south to Bagan's most popular temple, Ananda Pahto (p174) and west to Thatbyinnyu Pahto (p172), near where it is possible to climb up the old city wall.

Just west is where King Anawrahta stored all the non-Buddhist images at Nathlaung Kyaung (p171). Back on the main road, backtrack towards Tharabar Gate and detour on the gravel road for a river view from Bupaya (p173).

In the afternoon visit lacquerware shops in **Myinkaba**, climb up the hidden stairs in modern Manuha Paya and see the bas-relief figures in Nan Paya (p178). Finish up at one of the choice sunset spots: Pyathada Paya (p178) is the adventurous option, east of Myinkaba on goat-herd trails, or play it safe with the easily accessible (hence crowded) Shwesandaw Paya (p176), near Old Bagan.

Two Days

Having followed the one-day plan, now tick off other highlights starting with Dhammayangyi Pahto (p176), Bagan's largest temple. Take the paths east to the gorgeous Sulamani Pahto (p177) and escape the crowds at its neighbouring 'mini-me' version, Thabeik Hmauk (p177), which is also a good (and generally less-crowded) place for sunset viewing.

Another lovely view can be had from the terrace of Dhammayazika Paya (p180) in the South Plain area east of Myinkaba. While out this way visit Leimyethna Pahto (p181) for its well-preserved frescoes and Pyathonzu (p181), which also houses 13th-century murals.

Four Days

On day three many itineraries will see you heading out of the immediate Bagan area to **Salay** (p146), another area sprinkled with old temples and monasteries, and/or **Mt Popa** (p144), famous for its picturesque, *nat-* (spirit-) infested hilltop temple. Both places are interesting, but if you'd rather stay closer to Bagan, schedule visits to Abeyadana Pahto (p179) and Nagayon (p179) in Myinkaba and the frescoes in **Lawkahteikpan Pahto**.

Adventurous half-day boat trips can be made down or across the Ayeyarwady (Irrawaddy) to more remote temples with the chance to sail back into town at sunset.

Temples of Bagan

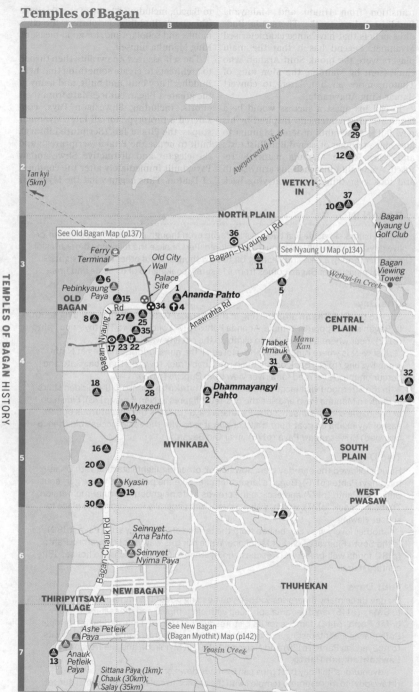

Ayeyarwady River

Tan kyi
(5km)

WETKYI-
IN

NORTH PLAIN

36

Bagan-Nyaung U Rd

See Old Bagan Map (p137)

See Nyaung U Map (p134)

Ferry
Terminal

Old City
Wall

Palace
Site

Pebinkyaung
Paya

OLD
BAGAN

6
15
1
Ananda Pahto
34 4
25
35
17 23 22

Bagan-Nyaung U Rd

Anawrahta Rd

8
27

29
12
10 37
5
11

Bagan
Nyaung U
Golf Club

Bagan
Viewing
Tower

Wetkyi-in Creek

CENTRAL
PLAIN

Thabek
Hmauk

Manu
Kan

31

18

28

Myazedi
9

Dhammayangyi
Pahto
2

26

32
14

MYINKABA

16
20

3
Kyasin
19

30

7

SOUTH
PLAIN

WEST
PWASAW

Bagan-Chauk Rd

Seinnyet
Ama Pahto

Seinnyet
Nyima Paya

THURHEKAN

THIRIPYITSAYA
VILLAGE

NEW BAGAN

See New Bagan
(Bagan Myothit) Map (p142)

Ashe Petleik
Paya

Anauk
Petleik
Paya

13

Yeosin Creek

Sittana Paya (1km);
Chauk (30km);
Salay (35km)

people call the 'First Burmese Empire', which became a pilgrimage point for Buddhists throughout Southeast Asia.

King Anawrahta's successors, particularly Kyanzittha (r 1084–1113), Alaungsithu (r 1113–67) and Narapatisithu (r 1174–1211), continued their incredible architectural output, although the construction work must have been nonstop throughout the period of Bagan's glory.

Decline

Historians disagree on exactly what happened to cause Bagan's apparently rapid decline at the end of the 13th century. The popular Myanmar view is that hordes of Mongols sent by Kublai Khan swept through the city, ransacking and looting. A contrasting view holds that the threat of invasion from China threw the last powerful ruler of Bagan into a panic. Legend has it that, after a great number of temples were torn down to build fortifications, the city was abandoned so that the Mongols merely took over an already deserted city.

Bagan scholar Paul Strachan argues in *Pagan: Art and Architecture of Old Burma* that the city was never abandoned at all. Indeed evidence suggests Bagan continued as an important religious and cultural centre into the 14th century and beyond, after which its decay can be blamed on the three-way struggle between the Shan, Mon and Bamar. People began moving back in some numbers only after the British established a presence in the area in the late 19th century, but by that point the plain of temples had fallen victim to frequent earthquakes (there were at least 16 trembles that shook Bagan between 1174 and the big one in 1975), general weathering and neglect.

Controversial Restoration

The enduring religious significance of Bagan is at the heart of the site's recent transformation from piles of picturesque ruins to a practically complete 13th-century city, minus the buildings, such as palaces, homes and monasteries, that would have been made of wood.

Dr Bob Hudson describes it as 'the most radical heritage management project in modern times', noting that, as of 2008, at least 1299 Buddhist temples, monasteries and stupas had been speculatively rebuilt from mounds of rubble since 1995, and a

Temples of Bagan

further 688 damaged buildings received major repairs.

'There are now at least 3300 "sites" in Bagan and they are still digging up new ones,' says Hudson, who points out that many international authorities have criticised the poor workmanship and historically inaccurate methods, styles and materials often being employed.

Putting this into perspective, Hudson notes that construction appears to have begun on new monuments every two weeks between 1200 and 1280. Down history these hastily built structures have been patched up, repaired and rebuilt. 'It's the ancestors of the same dodgy contractors who are doing the work today,' he quips.

A Living Religious Site

Following the 1975 quake, Unesco spent 15 years and more than US$1 million on restoration projects. But Bagan's current advanced state of restoration is mainly because of a hugely successful donations program initiated by the government in the mid-1990s and enthusiastically supported by many merit-making locals. The result, according to one Unesco official, is 'a Disney-style fantasy version of one of the world's great religious and historical sites'.

Defending the rebuilding program, Culture Minister Win Sein was quoted in *The New Light of Myanmar* as saying 'it is our national duty to preserve, strengthen and restore all the cultural heritage monuments of Bagan to last and exist forever', pointing out that the temples are 'living religious monuments highly venerated and worshipped by Myanmar people'.

This conflict of interests aside, zoning restrictions continue to be broken in the Bagan archaeological area, the most notable recent examples being the construction of the Aureum Palace's Bagan Viewing Tower at the east end of the central plain and the Bagan Golden Palace – both of which seem large and incongruous on the temple-strewn plain.

THE TEMPLES

We cover the headline acts among the thousands of temple sites that are strewn across the Bagan plain.

Old Bagan ပုဂံမြို့ဟောင်း

The most practical part of Bagan to tour on foot (with water and a hat), this roughly counter-clockwise 1-mile (1.6km) circuit takes in temples within the old city walls.

Gawdawpalin Pahto BUDDHIST TEMPLE
(ဂေါ်တော်ပလ္လင်ပုထိုး) Standing 197ft (60m) tall, Gawdawpalin is one of the largest and most imposing Bagan temples, although by no means the most inspiring, with its modernised altar and tile floors inside. Built

during the reign of Narapatisithu and finished under that of Nantaungmya, it's considered the crowning achievement of the late Bagan period. Its name means 'Platform to which Homage is Paid'. The stairs to the top terrace are closed to visitors.

The most recent homage was its heavy-duty reconstruction following terrific damage sustained in the 1975 earthquake, as it stands near the site of the quake's epicentre.

Mimalaung Kyaung
MONASTERY

(မီးမလောင်ကျောင်း) A nice set of *chinthe* (half-lion/half-dragon deity) guards the stairway leading up this small, square monastery platform, constructed in 1174 by Narapatisithu. It's about 650ft (200m) south of Gawdawpalin, on the other side of the road. In front of the monastery is a brick-and-stucco Tripitaka library next to a large acacia tree. Atop the steps, a tiered roof (with a newer gold-capped *hti*, an umbrella-like decorated pinnacle) contains a large sitting buddha.

Archaeologists discovered an intricately carved 2.5inch (6cm) votive tablet here that contained 78 sculpted figures.

Pahtothamya
BUDDHIST TEMPLE

(ပုထိုးသားများ) On the dirt road 500ft (150m)east towards the dominating Thatbyinnyu, the Pahtothamya (or Thamya Pahto) was probably built during the reign of Kyanzittha, around the turn of the 12th century, although it is popularly held to be one of five temples built by the little-known king Taunghthugyi (aka Sawrahan; r 931–64). In its prominent vertical superstructure and reconstructed lotus-bud *sikhara* (corncob-like temple finial), however, the monument is clearly beginning to move forward from the early period.

The interior of this single-storey building is dimly lit, typical of the early type of Pyu-influenced temples, with their small, perforated stone windows. With a torch you can pick out super painting remnants along the interior passages, perhaps the earliest surviving murals in Bagan. Steps lead up to a roomy viewing platform.

Nathlaung Kyaung
HINDU TEMPLE

(နတ်လှောင်ကျောင်း) Between Pahtothamya and Thatbyinnyu, this stubby building – the only Hindu temple remaining in Bagan – has a fascinating history. Named

KEY BAGAN DATES

c 950 Evidence from the remains of Pyu-style buildings is the earliest indication of a settlement on this bend in the Ayeyarwady (Irrawaddy).

1057 Temple building speeds up with the sacking of the Mon city of Thaton by Bagan's warrior king Anawrahta, a newly enthusiastic devotee of Buddhism.

c 1100-70 Temples become bigger and are better lit by broader windows, with more of an eye to vertical proportions than horizontal lines.

c 1170-1280 Bagan's late period of architecture sees more intricate pyramidical spires or adorning tile work added to the buildings, with an increased Indian influence.

1287 Bagan's decline is accelerated when the Mongols over-run the area, the Bamar having possibly abandoned the city already.

1975 An earthquake registering 6.5 on the Richter scale hits Bagan; many temples are damaged, but major reconstruction starts almost immediately with the help of Unesco.

1990 Military forcibly relocate a village that had grown up in the 1970s in the middle of the walled area of 'Old Bagan' to 2.5miles (4km) south of the main archaeological zone.

1996 Bagan placed on Unesco World Heritage Tentative List.

1998 More than US$1 million collected from local donations for the restoration of Bagan.

2008 An imaginary recreation of the 13th-century Bagan Palace is opened on a site opposite that of the original palace.

2011 Indian government pledges $22 million for the restoration of Ananda Pahto.

TAN KYI PAYA

From the Old Bagan jetty you can hire a private boat to reach Tan Kyi village, where you can arrange a taxi ride (or hike) up to **Tan Kyi Paya**, the gold stupa atop the mountain, visible from much of Bagan. Views are terrific and unique, looking back over the river to Bagan's mighty sprawl. A ride for three or four people, including wait time, is about K20,000. The trip takes three or four hours.

'Shrine Confining Nat', it's where King Anawrahta stored non-Buddhist images, particularly ones for local *nat,* as he tried to enforce Buddhism. The king himself described the temple as 'where the *nat* are kept prisoner'. Severely damaged in the 1975 earthquake, only the temple's main hall and superstructure (with seven original Gupta-style reliefs) still stand.

A sign dates it to the early 11th century. Some say it was built in 931 by Taunghthugyi; if true, this was about a century before the southern school of Buddhism came to Bagan. The temple is dedicated to the Hindu god Vishnu.

The central square of brick supports the dome and crumbled *sikhara,* and once contained freestanding figures of Vishnu, as well as Vishnu reliefs on each of the four sides. The statues were stolen by a German oil engineer in the 1890s, but the badly damaged brick-and-stucco reliefs can still be seen.

Thatbyinnyu Pahto
BUDDHIST TEMPLE

(သဗ္ဗညုပုထိုး) Named for 'omniscience', Bagan's highest temple is built of two white-coloured boxy storeys, each with three diminishing terraces rimmed with spires and leading to a gold-tipped *sikhara,* 207ft (63m) in height. Its monumental size and looming height make it a classic example of Bagan's middle period. Built in 1144 by Alaungsithu, its terraces are encircled by indentations for 539 Jataka.

Plaques were never added, leading some scholars to surmise that the monument was never consecrated. Visitors are barred from climbing Thatbyinnyu's inner passages. There are some original murals near the west entrance.

A couple of hundred yards south you can climb up on the southeastern corner of the old city wall. The small 'tally *zedi* (stupa)' just northeast of Thatbyinnyu Pahto was built using one brick for every 10,000 used in constructing the main temple.

Shwegugyi
BUDDHIST TEMPLE

(ရွှေဂူကြီး) Built by Alaungsithu in 1131, this smaller but elegant *pahto,* 650ft (200m) north of Thatbyinnyu, is an example of Bagan's middle period of temple-building, a transition in architectural style from the dark and cloistered to the airy and light. Its name means 'Great Golden Cave' and its corncob *sikhara* is a scaled-down version of the one at Ananda.

Inside are fine stucco carvings, a teak buddha and stone slabs that retell (in Pali) its history, including that it took just seven months to build. Missing from the scripts are details of its builder's demise: Alaungsithu's son brought his sick father here in 1163 to smother him to death.

Pitaka Taik
BUDDHIST LIBRARY

(ပိဋကတ်တိုက်) Following the sacking of Thaton, King Anawrahta is said to have carted off some 30 elephant-loads of Buddhist scriptures in 1058 and built this library (just northeast of Shwegugyi) to house them. The square design follows the basic early Bagan *gu* (cave temple) plan, perfect for the preservation of light-sensitive palm-leaf scriptures. It's notable for the perforated stone windows, each carved from single stone slabs, and the plaster carvings on the roof, which imitate Myanmar woodcarvings.

Tharabar Gate
ARCHAEOLOGICAL SITE

(သရပါတံခါး) Do stop on the east side of this former entrance of the original palace site. The gate is the best-preserved remains of the 9th-century wall, and the only gate still standing. Traces of old stucco can still be seen on the gateway. On either side of the arched gateway are two niches, home not to buddha images but to *nat* who guard the gate and who are treated with profound respect by locals.

To the left is Lady Golden Face, and to the right her brother Lord Handsome. Like most *nat,* Tharabar Gate's twosome had a tragic history. A king married Lady Golden Face to lure her brother Lord Handsome, whom he feared, out of hiding. When the king had Handsome burned at the stake, his sister jumped in too; only her face was saved from the fire.

Superstitious locals don't venture through the gate by motorbike, car or horse cart without first paying a one-time offering to the *nat* (usually a bunch of bananas and a couple of coconuts) to ensure protection against traffic accidents. Don't worry: bicycles are OK, blessing-free.

A number of restaurants are past the former moat, about 650ft (200m) east.

Mahabodhi Paya   BUDDHIST TEMPLE
(မဟာတေဝိဘုရား) Unlike any other Bagan temple, this monument, located on the north side of the main road 1000ft (350m) west of the gate, is modelled after the famous Mahabodhi temple in Bodhgaya, India, which commemorates the spot where the Buddha attained enlightenment. Built during the reign of Nantaungmya in 1215, the temple's unusual pyramidal spire is richly coated in niches enclosing seated buddha figures, rising from a square block. The stairway to the top is closed.

Inside is a modern makeover, with tile floor and carpet. The ruined buildings just north feature some original glazed painting fragments.

Bupaya   BUDDHIST TEMPLE
(ဗူးဘုရား) On the bank of the Ayeyarwady (reached from the Nyaung U road, about 650ft (200m) northwest of the Mahabodhi Paya), this cylindrical Pyu-style stupa, named for *bu* (gourd), is said to date back to the 3rd century, further than any Bagan temple. Most likely it was erected around the same time as the city walls (around AD 850).

What's seen now – a gold stupa above a row of crenulated terraces leading down to the water – is a reconstruction; the 1975 earthquake demolished the original.

Off the road to the southeast is the Pebinkyaung Paya, a 12th-century pagoda built in a unique Sinhalese style.

North Plain
The bulk of Bagan temples are scattered across the vast northern plain between Nyaung U, Old Bagan and New Bagan. This broad area runs between the Old Bagan walls and Nyaung U, and (mostly) between

---

LOCAL KNOWLEDGE

BAGAN'S MOST SIGNIFICANT TEMPLES

U Thein Lwin, Deputy Director General, Department of Archaeology, Bagan, recommends his most significant temples to see:

Ananda Pahto
Not only is it an outstanding example of Bagan temple architecture, Ananda is rich in decorative detail, including the four standing wooden images of Buddha, the life of Buddha is depicted in niche carvings and the Jataka series tiles.

Nagayon
This is the last restoration project that Unesco was involved in and was built in the same period as Ananda. Look for the 28 images of Buddha under the main sculpture.

Abeyadana Pahto
This is my personal favourite – inside you can see 550 Jataka mural paintings and various Hindu deities paying homage to Buddha.

Gubyaukgyi
Famous for its frescoes, this is one of the last temples built in the 11th century – apart from life-of-Buddha illustrations, you can see scenes from four Buddhist synods held in ancient times.

Lawkahteikpan Pahto
Also very important for its frescoes, including eight great miracles of Buddha's life. You can read the Jataka scenes as a complete story. You start to see a distinct Myanmar style emerge here from the Mon influence.

the two roads that connect the two. Sights are ordered (more or less) west to east.

★ Ananda Pahto
BUDDHIST TEMPLE

(အာနန္ဒာပုထိုး) With its shimmering gold, 170ft (51m)-high, corncob *hti* shimmering across the plains, Ananda is one of the finest, largest, best preserved and most revered of all Bagan temples. Thought to have been built between 1090 and 1105 by King Kyanzittha, this perfectly proportioned temple heralds the stylistic end of the early Bagan period and the beginning of the middle period.

The central square measures 174ft (53m) along each side. Upper floors are closed to visitors. The entranceways make the structure a perfect Greek cross; each entrance is crowned with a stupa finial. The base and the terraces are decorated with 554 glazed tiles showing Jataka scenes, thought to be derived from Mon texts. Look back as you enter to see the huge carved teak doors that separate interior halls from cross passages on all four sides.

Facing outward from the centre of the cube are four 31ft (9m) standing buddha statues. Only the Bagan-style images facing north and south are original; both display the *dhammachakka mudra* (a hand position symbolising the Buddha teaching his first sermon). The other two images are replacements for figures destroyed by fire in the 1600s.

All four have bodies of solid teak, though guides may claim the southern image is made of a bronze alloy. Guides like to point out that if you stand by the donation box in front of the original southern buddha, his face looks sad, while from a distance he tends to look mirthful.

The western and eastern standing buddha images are done in the later Konbaung, or Mandalay, style. If looked at from the right angle, the two lions at the eastern side resemble an ogre. A small, nut-like sphere held between the thumb and middle finger of the east-facing image is said to resemble a herbal pill, and may represent the Buddha offering *dhamma* (Buddhist teachings) as a cure for suffering. Both arms hang at the image's sides with hands outstretched, a *mudra* (hand position) unknown to traditional Buddhist sculpture outside this temple.

The west-facing Buddha features the *abhaya mudra* (the hands outstretched, in the gesture of no fear). At its feet sit two life-sized lacquer statues, said to represent King Kyanzittha and Shin Arahan, the Mon monk who initiated Anawrahta into Theravada Buddhism. Inside the western portico are two symbols on pedestals of the Buddha's footprints. Don't leave without taking a brief walk around the outside of the temple, where you can see many glazed tiles and lovely views of the spires and terraced roofs (often away from vendor hassle too).

In 1990, on its 900th anniversary, the temple spires were gilded. The remainder of the temple exterior is whitewashed from time to time.

It can feel more like a souvenir stand than a temple given the proliferation of peddlers outside selling books, postcards and oil paintings, but that shouldn't dissuade you from visiting. It's roughly 1600 ft (500m) east of Thatbyinnyu and the same distance north of Shwesandaw, and just over half a mile (1km) northwest of Dhammayangyi Pahto.

Most visitors access it from the northern side, where the highest concentration of hawkers are. For a quieter approach, enter from the east side.

Ananda Ok Kyaung
BUDDHIST CHAPEL

(အာနန္ဒာအုတ်ကျောင်း) Just west of Ananda's northern entry, this small *vihara* (sanctuary or chapel) features some detailed 18th-century murals bursting with bright red and green, showing details of everyday life from the Bagan period. In the southeast corner, you can see Portuguese figures engaged in trade. Built in 1137, the temple's name means 'Ananda Brick Monastery'.

Upali Thein
ORDINATION HALL

(ဥပါလိသိမ်) Just north of the Bagan-Nyaung U Rd, almost midway to Nyaung U, this squat mid-13th-century ordination hall houses some brightly painted frescoes depicting big scenes on the walls and ceilings from the late 17th or early 18th century. Sadly many pieces crumbled in the 1975 earthquake.

The building, named for a well-known monk from the 13th century, is often locked to protect the art, but you can see in (a bit) from the three gated doorways if the 'keyholder' isn't around. The roof battlements imitate Myanmar wooden architecture, and a small centre spire rises from the rooftop.

Htilominlo Pahto
BUDDHIST TEMPLE

(ထီးလိုမင်းလိုပုထိုး) This 150ft (45m)-high temple (built in 1218) marks the spot where King Nantaungmya was chosen (by a leaning umbrella, that timeless decider), among five brothers, to be the crown prince. It's more impressive from the outside, with its terraced design, which is similar to Sulamani Pahto. Unfortunately it's Vendor Central.

Have a walk around the 140-sq-ft base to take in the fragments of the original fine plaster carvings, glazed sandstone decorations and nicely carved reliefs on the doorways. Inside are four buddhas on the lower and upper floors, though the stairways are closed. Traces of old murals are also still visible.

Buledi
BUDDHIST TEMPLE

(ဗူးလယ်သီး) Great for its views, this steep-stepped, pyramid-style stupa looks ho-hum from afar, but the narrow terrace has become something of an alternative sunset spot. It's about 2000ft (600m) south of the Htilominlo, across Anawrahta Rd. It's also known as 'Temple 394' (not correctly labelled on some maps).

If persistent vendors are buzzing around, try the miniature version, **Temple 405**, with several glazed tiles visible, just east of Buledi.

Gubyauknge
BUDDHIST TEMPLE

(ဂူပြောက်ငယ်) Off Anawrahta Rd, almost a mile east of Htilominlo, this early

HISTORY OR LEGEND?

A lack of primary sources means the 'histories' attached to Burma's early kingdoms are often a matter of opinion and creative interpretation. 'The best way to treat any legendary story is as a legend,' says Sydney University's Dr Bob Hudson, an archaeological expert on Myanmar. He points out that some contemporary scholars have quite different interpretations of the story of Bagan.

'Michael Aung-Thwin, in his book *Mists of Rammana* (University of Hawaii Press), proposes that there was no conquest of Thaton, and that a Mon element in the population of Bagan got there because they had been pushed westward out of Thailand by the expansionist kings of Angkor. The appearance of Indian art styles at Bagan also did not need to come via Thaton. Following the conquest of Buddhist and Hindu principalities in eastern India by the image-shunning Muslims, the logical destination for an Indian artist who specialised in painting or carving human figures was the economically booming and devoutly Buddhist Bagan. The Indian art style became modified by local tastes and techniques, creating a distinctive Myanmar style.

'And the idea originally proposed by the 20th-century historian G H Luce, that the early, dark temples represent the brooding nature of the captive Mon, while the later high, airy temples show the outgoing nature of the Burmans, has an explanation that relies on architecture, not on imagined ethnic traits: the engineers of Bagan simply got better over time at using the arch, which they had adopted from India, and thus could build more spacious interiors.

'Doubt has also been cast on the tale of a Buddhist king of Bagan irreligiously tearing down temples to build fortifications against the advancing Mongols. This is more likely a "cautionary tale" about the kinds of things that kings should never, never do. And while there was certainly a Mongol invasion of the northern borders of the kingdom in the late 13th century, there is no real evidence that they attacked the capital. There is indeed a painting of a Mongol archer on a pagoda wall at Bagan, but he is cheerfully shooting at a duck, while his senior officer lounges under a tree.

'The provincial lords in the north, who actually did fight off the Mongols, were so successful that, as the economy of Bagan deteriorated under the burden of temple construction, a new series of capitals slowly grew up around Mandalay and Ava. Bagan was not so much destroyed as relegated to the second division.

'Some of these interpretations remain contentious. You might find the discussions on some of the Burma/Mon history websites highly entertaining, especially if you thought academics are all full of reasoned arguments and civilised discourse!'

Bagan-period temple has some excellent stucco carvings on the outside walls (particularly on the north side) and some original paintings visible inside.

Wetkyi-In-Gubyaukgyi
BUDDHIST TEMPLE

(ဝက်ကြီးအင်းဂူပြောက်ကြီး) Just west of Nyaung U and about 330ft (100m) east of Gubyauknge, this detailed off-the-main-circuit, 13th-century temple has an Indian-style spire, like the Mahabodhi Paya in Old Bagan. It's interesting for fine frescoes of scenes from the Jataka but, unfortunately, in 1899 a German collector surreptitiously removed many of the panels on which the frescoes were painted. Those that remain in the entry are in great shape.

Steps inside lead to four buddha images and you can see Hindu figures engraved on the spire.

Central Plain

Extending from the edge of Old Bagan, this vast and lovely plain (roughly south of Anawrahta Rd between New Bagan and Nyaung U) is home to a few must-sees everyone gets to (Shwesandaw Paya and Dhammayangyi Pahto) and many pockets of temples that few ever see. It's a great area to follow your own whims, as you'll find goatherds and a bit of village life out here, but there is nothing in the way of restaurants or lunch options. Some temples are locked but a 'keyholder' should be in the area.

This list of well-worthy sites runs west to east (towards the clearly visible Bagan Tower construction site, near Nyaung U).

Shwesandaw Paya
BUDDHIST TEMPLE

(ရွှေဆံတော်ဘုရား) Bagan's most famous sunset-viewing spot, the Shwesandaw is a graceful white pyramid-style pagoda with steps leading past five terraces to the circular stupa top, with good 360-degree views. It's located roughly midway between Thatbyinnyu and Dhammayangyi. Its top terrace is roomy, which is just as well, considering the numbers of camera-toting travellers coming by taxi or bus before sunset. If you go during the day, you'll likely be alone, making it a good spot for temple panoramas.

Shwesandaw means 'golden holy hair': legend has it that the stupa enshrines a Buddha hair relic presented to King Anawrahta by the King of Ussa Bago (Pegu) in thanks for his assistance in repelling an invasion by the Khmers. The terraces once bore terracotta plaques showing scenes from the Jataka but traces of these, and of other sculptures, were covered by rather heavy-handed renovations. The now-gilded *zedi* bell rises from two octagonal bases, which top the five square terraces. This was the first Bagan monument to feature stairways leading from the square terraces to the round base of the stupa.

The *hti*, which was toppled by the 1975 earthquake, can still be seen lying on the south side of the *paya* compound. A new one was fitted soon after the quake.

About 500ft (150m) north stands Lawkahteikpan Pahto, a small but interesting middle-period *gu* containing excellent frescoes and inscriptions in both Burmese and Mon.

★ Dhammayangyi Pahto
BUDDHIST TEMPLE

(ဓမ္မရံကြီးပုထိုး) Visible from all parts of Bagan, this massive, walled, 12th-century temple (about 1600 feet or 500m east of Shwesandaw) is infamous for its mysterious, bricked-up inner passageways and cruel history. It's said that King Narathu built the temple to atone for his sins: he smothered his father and brother to death and executed one of his wives, an Indian princess, for practising Hindu rituals. The best preserved of Bagan's temples, it features detailed mortar work in its upper levels.

Narathu is also said to have mandated that the mortarless brickwork fit together so tightly that even a pin couldn't pass between any two bricks. Workers who failed in this task had their arms chopped off: just inside the west entrance, note the stones with arm-sized grooves where these amputations allegedly happened.

After Narathu died – by assassination in 1170 – the inner encircling ambulatory was filled with brick rubble, as 'payback'. Others quietly argue the temple dates from the earlier reign of Alaungsithu, which would refute all this fun legend behind it. It's also likely that this bricking up of the passages was a crude way of ensuring the massive structure didn't collapse.

The plan here is similar to Ananda, with projecting porticoes and receding terraces, though its *sikhara* is reduced to a stub nowadays. Walking around the outer ambulatory, under ceilings so high you can only hear the squeaks of bats circling in the dark, you can see some intact stucco reliefs and paintings, suggesting the work had been completed. The mystery goes on.

Three out of the four buddha sanctums were also filled with bricks. The remaining western shrine features two original side-by-side images of Gautama and Maitreya, the historical and future buddhas (it's the only Bagan site with two side-by-side buddhas).

The temple's bad karma may be the reason it remains one of the few temples not to have undergone major restoration. Perhaps in time, one of the great architectural mysteries of Bagan will be solved.

Sulamani
Pahto
BUDDHIST TEMPLE

(စူဠာမဏိပုထိုး) This temple with five doorways is known as the Crowning Jewel and was constructed around 1181 by Narapatisithu. It is one of Bagan's most attractive temples, with lush grounds (and ample vendors) behind the surrounding walls. It's a prime example of later, more sophisticated temple styles, with better internal lighting. Combining the early period's horizontal planes with the vertical lines of the middle period, the receding terraces create a pyramid effect. The stairways to the top are closed.

The brickwork throughout is considered some of the best in Bagan. The gilded *sikhara* is a reconstruction; the original was destroyed in the 1975 earthquake. The interior face of the wall was once lined with 100 monastic cells, a feature unique among Bagan's ancient monasteries.

There's much to see inside. Carved stucco on mouldings, pediments and pilasters represent some of Bagan's finest ornamental work and is in fairly good condition. Glazed plaques around the base and terraces are also still visible, as are many big and small murals.

Buddha images face the four directions from the ground floor; the image at the main eastern entrance sits in a recess built into the wall. The interior passage around the base is painted with quite big frescoes from the Konbaung period, and there are traces of earlier frescoes.

Thabeik Hmauk
BUDDHIST TEMPLE

(သပိတ်မှောက်) Facing Sulamani from the east, and well worth visiting, this *sikhara*-topped temple looks like a miniature version of its more famous neighbour, but sees far fewer visitors (or vendors). Thabeik Hmauk means 'Boycott Temple', as it was made in response to the similarly designed Sulamani, which was ordered by the brutal king Narapatisithu. Much of its interior was damaged by the 1975 earthquake, but there are multiple stairways up to a wrap-around meditation chamber with little light.

TEMPLES OF BAGAN CENTRAL PLAIN

ℹ️ KEYHOLDERS & SOUVENIR HAWKERS

Major temples that remain active places of worship such as Ananda Pahto and Shwezigon Paya are always open during the day. At many others to get inside it is first necessary to find the 'keyholder' whose job it is to act as the caretaker of the site. Often they (or their kids) will find you first and open the gate for you. A bit of 'tea money' (say K500) is appreciated. We're told that the keyholders are assigned by the archaeology department.

The other constant of Bagan temples – even relatively remote ones – are souvenir hawkers, often selling (and sometimes creating) colourful sand paintings. Some of these replicate parts of the murals from inside the temples and are quite skilful, with prices starting at as little as K1000 for the smaller canvases, but rising sharply for more detailed and larger works; other images are pretty generic and found across all temple sites. Although some hawkers can be persistent, if you're not interested in buying, most will leave you alone.

We're told that official souvenir hawkers at the temples pay a sizeable fee for a licence, but it's likely that there are many more unofficial vendors given the potential for relatively easy money. 'Even if they only sell a few trinkets a week, it's an easy job,' said one frequent visitor to Bagan, 'as the alternative is a farm job which pays far less a day.' A guide also bemoaned that children in Bagan are starting to quit school in order to work as hawkers.

There are two outside terraces, reached by narrow stairs, with superb views.

Pyathada Paya
BUDDHIST TEMPLE

(ပြဿဒါးဘုရား) Dating from the 13th century, during the latter period of temple building at Bagan, this huge, impressive pagoda is a superb sunset-viewing spot, with a giant open terrace (Bagan's largest) atop the steps, and another small deck further up. The tour groups have discovered it so you're unlikely to have the place to yourself. It is about half a mile southeast of Sulamani, reached by dirt roads that sometimes get obscured in goat fields.

Pyathada's interior arches are still partly open to view. The architects used an inner relieving arch and a second upper arch to support the huge chambers, illustrating the point that temple styles changed in Bagan because the builders improved at arch construction. Note how the top stupa isn't centred on the top platform.

Myinkaba Area
မြင်းကပါဝန်းကျင်

The sites north and south of Myinkaba village are all just off the main road and are easy to access. These are listed in order from north to south.

Mingalazedi Paya
BUDDHIST TEMPLE

(မင်္ဂလာစေတီဘုရား; ⌂) Close to the riverbank, towards Myinkaba from Old Bagan, Mingalazedi Paya (Blessing Stupa) represents the final flowering of Bagan's architectural outburst, as displayed in its enormous bell-like dome and the beautiful glazed Jataka tiles around each terrace. Although many of the 1061 original tiles have been damaged or stolen, there are still 561 left. The smaller square building in the *zedi* grounds is one of the few Tripitaka libraries made of brick.

Gubyaukgyi
BUDDHIST TEMPLE

(ဂူပြောက်ကြီး) Situated just to the left of the road as you enter Myinkaba, Gubyaukgyi (Great Painted Cave Temple) sees a lot of visitors who are drawn by the well-preserved, richly coloured paintings inside. These are thought to date from the temple's original construction in 1113, when Kyanzittha's son Rajakumar built it following his father's death.

In Indian style, the monument consists of a large vestibule attached to a smaller antechamber.

The fine stuccowork on its exterior walls is in particularly good condition. Perforated, Pyu-style windows mean you'll need a powerful torch to see the ceiling paintings clearly. If it's locked during off-season, ask in the village for the keyholder.

Next to the monument stands the gilded Myazedi (Emerald Stupa). A four-sided pillar in a cage between the two monuments bears an inscription consecrating Gubyaukgyi and written in four languages: Pyu, Mon, Old Burmese and Pali. Its linguistic and historical significance is great, since it establishes the Pyu as an important cultural influence in early Bagan and relates the chronology of the Bagan kings as well as acting as a 'Rosetta Stone' to allow scholars to decipher the Pyu.

Manuha Paya
BUDDHIST TEMPLE

(မနုဟာဘုရား) In Myinkaba village, stands this active and rather modern-looking pagoda, even though it dates back to 1059. It is named after Manuha, the Mon king from Thaton, who was held captive here by King Anawrahta. In the front of the building are three seated buddhas; in the back is a huge reclining buddha. All seem too large for their enclosures – supposedly representing the stress and discomfort the king had to endure.

It is said that only the reclining buddha, in the act of entering *parinibbana* (final passing away), has a smile on its face, showing that for Manuha, only death was a release from his suffering. But if you climb to the top of this paya via the stairs in the back (ask for keys if it's locked), you can see the face of the sitting buddha through a window – from up here you'll realise that the gigantic face, so grim from below, has an equally gigantic smile.

Nan Paya
BUDDHIST TEMPLE

(နန်းဘုရား) Just south of Manuha Paya by dirt road, this shrine is said to have been used as Manuha's prison, although there is little evidence supporting the legend. In this story the shrine was originally Hindu, and captors thought using it as a prison would be easier than converting it to a Buddhist temple. It's worth visiting for its interior masonry work – sandstone block facings over a brick core, certainly some of Bagan's finest detailed sculpture.

Perforated stone windows are typical of earlier Bagan architecture – in fact it was probably Bagan's first *gu*-style shrine. In the central sanctuary the four stone pillars have finely carved sandstone bas-relief figures of three-faced Brahma. The creator deity is holding lotus flowers, thought to be offerings to a freestanding buddha image once situated in the shrine's centre, a theory that dispels the idea that this was ever a Hindu shrine. The sides of the pillars feature ogre-like kala-ate heads with open mouths streaming with flowers.

Legend goes that Shiva employed these creatures of Hindu legend to protect temples, but they proved too ferocious so Shiva tricked them into eating their bodies, then fed them flowers to keep their minds off snacking on worshippers. In the centre of the four pillars is an altar on which once stood a standing buddha or (some locals believe) a Hindu god. Ask at Manuha if the temple is locked.

Abeyadana
Pahto
(အပါယ်ရတနာပုထိုး) About 1300ft (400m)
BUDDHIST TEMPLE
south of Manuha Paya, this 11th-century temple with a Sinhalese-style stupa was supposedly built by Kyanzittha's Bengali wife Abeyadana, who waited for him here as he hid for his life from his predecessor King Sawlu. It's famed for its original frescoes, which were cleaned in 1987 by Unesco staff. Ask at the caretaker's house to the south if the temple is locked.

With a torch, you can make out many figures that Abeyadana, believed to be a Mahayanist, would likely have asked for: Bodhisattvas such as Avalokitesvara, and Hindu deities Brahma, Vishnu, Shiva and Indra. The inner shrine contains a large, brick, seated buddha (partly restored); surrounding walls are lined with niches, most now empty. Inside the front wall are many Jataka scenes.

Some visitors enjoy the sunset at the often-overlooked Kyasin across the road.

Nagayon
(နဂါးရုံ) Slightly south of Abeyadana and
BUDDHIST TEMPLE
across the road, this elegant and well-preserved temple was built by Kyanzittha. The main buddha image is twice life size and shelters under the hood of a huge *naga* (dragon serpent). This reflects the legend that in 1192 Kyanzittha built the temple on the spot where he was sheltered while fleeing from his angry brother and predecessor Sawlu, an activity he had to indulge in on more than one occasion.

Paintings also decorate the corridor walls. The central shrine has two smaller standing buddhas as well as the large one. The temple itself – with corncob *sikhara*, which some believe to be the Ananda prototype – can be climbed via tight stairs.

Somingyi
Kyaung
(စိုးမင်းကြီးအုတ်ကျောင်း) Named after the
BUDDHIST TEMPLE
woman who supposedly sponsored its construction, this typical late-Bagan brick monastery (about 650ft or 200m southwest of Nagayon) is thought to have been built in 1204. A *zedi* to the north and *gu* to the south are also ascribed to Somingyi. Many brick monasteries in Bagan were single-block structures; Somingyi is unique in that it has monastic cells clustered around a courtyard.

THREE TEMPLES BY THE AYEYARWADY

From Nyaung U's jetty you can negotiate a fun boat trip to see three temples just off the Ayeyarwady riverbank. Half a mile, or nearly 1km, north is 13th-century **Thetkyamuni**, with a few murals inside (hard to make out) and tight, dark steps leading up to a small terrace up top. On the hill nearby is the same-era **Kondawgyi Pahto**, with better preserved murals and views from the surrounding platform.

Another half a mile or so north is the 11th- and 12th-century **Kyauk Gu Ohnmin** cave temple, built in the side of a ravine. It's said during WWII Japanese soldiers hid out here. The inside tunnels lead to blocked-off rubble. Some locals say the tunnel was intended to go, ahem, to Pindaya Cave near Inle Lake. You can climb on top of the temple from the new steps to the right.

These sights are accessible, with more difficulty, by road. A boat trip takes about two or three hours, and the driver will show you the temples. It costs about K20,000 for three or four people.

New Bagan Area
ပုဂံမြို့သစ်

Sights are a little scarcer heading south of New Bagan towards the outskirts of the Bagan area.

Seinnyet Nyima Paya & Seinnyet Ama Pahto
BUDDHIST TEMPLE

(စိမ်းညွက်ညီမဘုရား နှင့် စိမ်းညွက်အမပုထိုး) This stupa and shrine stand side by side (about 820ft or 250m north of New Bagan) and are traditionally ascribed to Queen Seinnyet in the 11th century, although the architecture clearly points to a period two centuries later. The *zedi* rests on three terraces and is topped by a beautiful stylised umbrella.

Lawkananda Paya
BUDDHIST TEMPLE

(လောကနန္ဒာဘုရား) At the height of Bagan's power, boats from the Mon region, Rakhaing (Arakan) and even Sri Lanka would anchor by this riverside pagoda (about 820ft or 250m southeast of the New Bagan crossroads; a sign in Burmese points the way) with its distinctive elongated cylindrical dome. Built in 1059 by Anawrahta, it is still used as a place of worship and is thought to house an important Buddha tooth replica.

There are lots of benches for wide-open views of the Ayeyarwady, but it's sometimes hard to enjoy hassle-free.

Ashe (East) & Anauk (West) Petleik Paya
BUDDHIST TEMPLE

(အရှေ့ နှင့် အနောက်ဖက်လိပ်ဘုရား) Just inland to the northeast from Lawkananda Paya are the excavated remains of these twin 11th-century paya. Found in 1905, the lower parts of the pagodas are ho-hum from the outside but feature hundreds of terracotta Jataka lining the vaulted corridors (particularly impressive in Anauk Petleik Paya).

A keyholder usually appears to unlock the door and turn on the fluorescent lights.

Sittana Paya
BUDDHIST TEMPLE

(စစ်တနာဘုရား) About half a mile further south, this large, 13th-century bell-shaped stupa is New Bagan's most impressive structure. Built by Htilominlo, and showing some Hindu influences, it's set on four square terraces, each fronted by a standing buddha image in brick and stucco.

A rather rickety stairway leads up the stupa's southern side to the terraces, where you can circle the structure. At the southwestern corner is a closed-off chamber leading into an inner sanctum.

South Plain

This rural area, along Bagan's southern reaches, follows the main road between New Bagan and Nyaung U Airport, passing Pwasaw and Minnanthu villages on the way. Other than a few places, such as Payathonzu, most sights see few tourists.

Many horse-cart drivers will take in the cluster of sights north of Minnanthu and go via dirt paths towards Central Plain sights, such as Sulamani Pahto. Views west from some temples here rival any other in Bagan in terms of scope of the site.

The following sites are listed in order from west to east.

Dhammayazika Paya
BUDDHIST TEMPLE

(ဓမ္မရာဇိကဘုရား) Sitting in lush garden grounds with a gilded bell, the Dhammayazika dates from 1196. Set in the south-central end of Bagan on the main road, it also has lovely views from its highest terrace. The pentagonal *zedi* is similar to the Shwezigon but with a more unusual design.

An outer wall has five gateways. Up top, five small temples, each containing a buddha image, encircle the terraces; some of them bear interior murals added during the Konbaung era.

Watch out for ghosts here! Supposedly the stupa's construction began under a general who died before its completion. His likeness is said to appear in many photos of the site, including a fairly recent one of government officials.

It's possible, with perseverance, to cycle the thrilling dirt roads here from Dhammayangyi Pahto, a mile (1.5km) north.

Leimyethna Pahto
BUDDHIST TEMPLE

(လေးမျက်နှာဘုရား) Built in 1222, this east-facing, whitewashed temple near Minnanthu village (a couple of klicks east of Dhammayazika on the north side of the road) stands on a raised platform and has interior walls decorated with well-preserved frescoes. It is topped by a gilded Indian-style spire like that on Ananda. The jar-like structures out the front were pillars of a building toppled by the 1975 earthquake.

Tayok Pye Paya
BUDDHIST TEMPLE

(တရုတ်ပြေးဘုရား) A couple of hundred yards (200m) north of Leimyethna by dirt road, this spired temple gets attention for the views from its upper reaches, although the top level is now closed.

Payathonzu
BUDDHIST TEMPLE

(ဘုရားသုံးဆူ) Across the main road from Tayok, this complex of three interconnected shrines (the name means Three Stupas) is worth seeing for its 13th-century murals close up. It was abandoned shortly before its construction was complete.

Each square cubicle is topped by a fat *sikhara;* a similar structure appears only at Salay. The design is remarkably like Khmer Buddhist ruins in Thailand.

Enter through the middle shrine. To the right (south) are scratched-up, whitewashed walls. The other two shrines (particularly the northernmost one) are home to lovely, vaguely Chinese- or Tibetan-looking mural paintings that contain Bodhisattva figures.

Whether these indicate possible Mahayana or Tantric influence is a hotly debated issue among art historians. Some drawings are rather crudely touched up.

The three-shrine design hints at links with the Hindu Trimurti (triad) of Vishnu, Shiva and Brahma, a triumvirate also associated with Tantric Buddhism. You might also say it represents the Triple Gems of Buddhism (buddha, dhamma and sangha), except that such a design is uncommon in Asian Buddhist architecture, although it does appear in the Hindu shrines of India and Nepal.

Thambula Pahto
BUDDHIST TEMPLE

(သမ္ဘုလပုထိုး) This square temple, surrounded by crumbling walls just north of Payathonzu, is decorated with faded Jataka frescoes and was built in 1255 by Thambula, the wife of King Uzana. It's often locked, but go to the (shaded at midday) doors and peek through the gate to see into wall and ceiling murals.

A mural of a boat race can be seen from the southern entrance; good ceiling murals are seen from the north side.

Nandamannya Pahto
BUDDHIST TEMPLE

(နန္ဒပညာပုထိုး) Dating from the mid-13th century, this small, single-chambered temple has very fine frescoes and a ruined seated buddha image. It's about 650ft (200m) north of Thambula; a sign leads down a short dirt road. The murals' similarity with those at Payathonzu has led some art historians to suggest they were painted by the same hand.

Nandamannya earns its reputation from its mural of the 'Temptation of Mara', in which nubile young females (vainly) attempt to distract the Buddha from the meditation session that led to his enlightenment. The undressed nature of the females shocked French epigraphist Charles Duroiselle, who wrote in 1916 that they were 'so vulgarly erotic and revolting that they can neither be reproduced or described'.

Times change: the topless women can be seen, without blushing, on the back left wall.

Just behind the temple is the **Kyat Kan Kyaung**, a working underground monastery dating from the 11th century. Mats on the tunnel floors are used for meditation.

TEMPLE FESTIVALS

The following are Bagan's major temple festivals or *paya pwe*, listed in order of their celebration through the year. At them all expect religious chanting around the clock, religious paraphernalia stalls and music and drama performances.

Manuha Paya Held on the full moon of Tabaung (February/March).

Gawdawpalin Pahto Celebrated on the full moon of Thadingyut (September/October).

Shwezigon Paya Celebrated on the full moon of Tazaungmon (October/November).

Ananda Pahto This roughly two-week event culminating on the full moon of Pyatho (December/January) is Bagan's biggest festival, when hundreds of monks come to collect alms from thousands of merit-seeking locals.

Nyaung U Area ညောင်ဦး

The main site in this area is the superb Shwezigon Paya.

Shwezigon

Paya BUDDHIST TEMPLE

(ရွှေစည်းခုံဘုရား) At the west end of Nyaung U, this big, beautiful *zedi* is the town's main religious site, and is most famous for its link with the 37 *nat*. Lit up impressively at dusk the gilded *zedi* sits on three rising terraces. Enamelled plaques in panels around the base of the *zedi* illustrate scenes from the Jataka. At the cardinal points, facing the terrace stairways, are four shrines, each of which houses a 13ft (4m)-high bronze standing buddha. Gupta-inspired and cast in 1102, these are Bagan's largest surviving bronze buddhas.

A 4-inch (10cm) circular indentation in a stone slab, before the upwards-heading eastern steps, was filled with water to allow former Myanmar monarchs to look at the reflection of the *hti* without tipping their heads backwards (which might have caused them to lose their crowns).

The most important site here is the small yellow compound called 37 Nat (in English) on the southeast side of the site. Inside are figures of all the 37 pre-Buddhist *nat* that were officially endorsed by Bamar monarchy in a compromising gesture towards a public reluctant to give up all their beliefs for Buddhism. Ask around if the compound is locked. At one end stands an original stone figure of Thagyamin, king of the *nat* and a direct appropriation of the Hindu god Indra. This is the oldest known freestanding Thagyamin figure in Myanmar.

The site was started by Anawrahta but not completed until the reign of Kyanzittha. The latter is thought to have built his palace nearby.

A path on the north side leads down to the riverbank, where you can get some interesting views.

Kyanzittha Umin BUDDHIST TEMPLE
(ကျန်စစ်သားဥမင်) Although officially credited to Kyanzittha, this cave temple may actually date back to Anawrahta. Built into a cliff face 270yd (250m) southwest of Shwezigon, the long, dimly lit corridors are decorated with frescoes, some of which are thought to have been painted by Bagan's Tartar invaders during the period of the Mongol occupation after 1287. An attendant will usually greet you with keys to unlock the doors and a torch to lend.

It's very quiet in here, and you can actually see the 700-year-old brush strokes.

Eastern Myanmar

Best Places to Eat

➡ Thu Maung Restaurant (p207)

➡ Kyaingtong's Central Market (p210)

➡ Lin Htett Myanmar Traditional Food (p191)

Best Places to Stay

➡ La Maison Birmane (p190)

➡ Dream Villa Hotel Kalaw (p206)

➡ Pindaya Inle Inn (p203)

➡ Inle Princess Resort (p197)

➡ Amara Mountain Resort (p207)

➡ Villa Inle Resort & Spa (p197)

Why Go?

Slicing the crystal-placid waters of Inle Lake in a boat; trekking among Pa-O and Danu villages outside Kalaw; feeling like you've travelled back in time at a remote hill-tribe market in the back hills of Shan State. What do some of Myanmar's most emblematic experiences have in common? They can all be tackled in the country's east.

Eastern Myanmar is the country's most generous crossroads of the cultural and the adventurous. Unlike elsewhere in Myanmar, taking part in activities such as caving, trekking, hiking and boating involves little or no red tape. And for those who would rather establish their own trail altogether, the ethnic Tai and hill-tribe areas surrounding Kyaingtong are harder to reach, but as a result have remained distinctly untouristed, while tiny Kayah State only recently became open to independent travellers.

When to Go
Eastern Myanmar

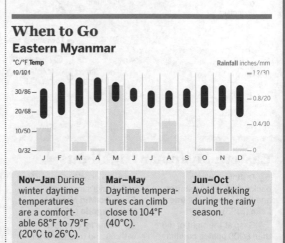

| **Nov–Jan** During winter daytime temperatures are a comfortable 68°F to 79°F (20°C to 26°C). | **Mar–May** Daytime temperatures can climb close to 104°F (40°C). | **Jun–Oct** Avoid trekking during the rainy season. |

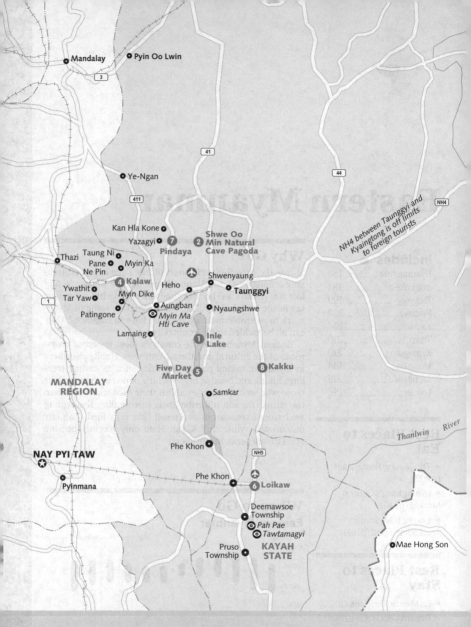

Eastern Myanmar Highlights

1 Drift around the backwaters, ruined stupas and tribal markets of **Inle Lake** (p193)

2 Gasp at the sight of more than 8000 golden buddhas

covering nearly every surface of Pindaya's incredible **Shwe Oo Min Natural Cave Pagoda** (p202)

3 Come face-to-face with Tai and traditional hill-

tribe culture in and around **Kyaingtong** (p213)

4 Hike through mountains, fields and villages on the **trek** (p196) from Inle Lake to Kalaw

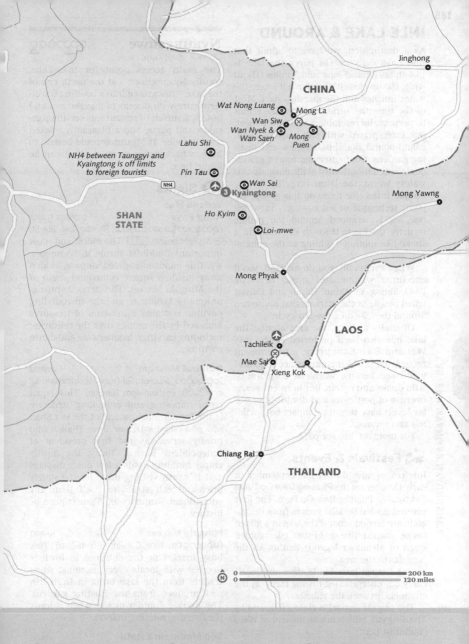

NH4 between Taunggyi and Kyaingtong is off limits to foreign tourists

5 Pick up a unique souvenir (or perhaps some unique photos) at the Inle Lake area's **Five-Day Market** (p194)

6 Be one of the first independent tourists to visit **Loikaw** (p216), the atmospheric capital of tiny Kayah State

7 Get off the beaten track on an overnight trek through the tea-tree-studded hills surrounding **Pindaya** (p202)

8 Get lost among the 2478 stupas at **Kakku** (p219)

INLE LAKE & AROUND

As a destination, we have to admit that Inle Lake delivers. On paper the lake is 13.5 miles (22km) long and 7 miles (11km) wide, but up close it's hard to tell where the water finishes and the marshes start. Most of the time the surface of the lake seems to perpetually resemble a vast silver sheet, one interspersed with stilt-house villages, island-bound Buddhist temples and floating gardens. Commuter and tourist motorboats and flat-bottomed skiffs navigate this watery world, the latter propelled by the unique Intha (for more on this group, see p331) technique of leg rowing – in which one leg is wrapped around the paddle to drive the blade through the water in a snake-like motion – adding to the ephemeral aura.

When eventually you do hit land, you'll encounter whitewashed stupas or Shan, Pa-O, Taung Yo, Danu, Kayah and Danaw tribal people at the markets that hopscotch around the lake on a five-day cycle.

Officially at least, the area around the lake has also been protected as the **Inle Wetland Bird Sanctuary**, a government recognised bird sanctuary, since 1985 and you'll see herons, warblers, cormorants, wild ducks and egrets. But in recent years, overuse of pesticides and diminishing water levels have begun to impact both wildlife and humans.

For more on this, see p373.

⭐ Festivals & Events

Inle comes alive during late September or early October for the **Phaung Daw Oo Paya Festival** at Phaung Daw Oo Paya. The four revered golden buddha images from the pagoda are ferried around the lake in a gilded barge shaped like a *hintha* (the golden swan of Myanmar legend) visiting all the pagodas in the area.

The festival lasts for 18 days and locals carry out energetic leg-rowing races on the channels between the villages.

The pagoda festival is closely followed by **Thadingyut**, which marks the end of Waso (Buddhist Lent).

ℹ Information

There is a compulsory $10 fee to enter the Inle Lake area, which you must pay on arrival at the **permit booth** (⊙ 6am-9pm), located by the bridge at the entrance to Nyaungshwe.

Nyaungshwe ည‌ောင်ရွှေ

📞 081 / POPULATION C10,000

The main access point for Inle Lake, scruffy Nyaungshwe – at the north end of the lake – has grown into a bustling traveller centre with dozens of guesthouses and hotels, a surfeit of restaurants serving pancakes and pasta, and a pleasantly relaxed traveller vibe. If Myanmar could be said to have a backpacker scene at all, it can be found here.

◉ Sights

Yadana Man Aung Paya
BUDDHIST TEMPLE

(ရတနာမာန်အောင်ဘုရား; Phoung Taw Site St; ⊙ daylight hours) **FREE** The oldest and most important Buddhist shrine in Nyaungshwe, this handsome gilded stupa is hidden away inside a square compound south of the Mingala Market. The stepped stupa is unique in Myanmar, and the surrounding pavilion contains a museum of treasures amassed by the monks over the centuries, including carvings, lacquerware and dance costumes.

Cultural Museum
MUSEUM

(ဗုဒ္ဓပြတိုက်; Museum Rd (Haw St); admission $2 or K2000; ⊙ 10am-4pm Tue-Sun) This equal parts imposing and crumbling structure is the former *haw* (palace) of the last Shan *sao pha* (sky lord), Sao Shwe Thaike, who briefly served as the first president of Independent Burma. Today, the mostly empty building holds a few dusty displays and is worth visiting more for the stately brick-and-teak structure itself than any educational summary of Shan culture or history.

Mingala Market
MARKET

(မင်္ဂလာဈေး; Yone Gyi Rd; ⊙ 5am-2pm) This busy market at the entrance to town is flooded with locals every morning, when traders from the lake bring in fresh fish and produce from the floating gardens. The market doubles in size when it hosts the five-day rotating market.

Red Mountain Estate
WINERY

(www.redmountain-estate.com; ⊙ 9am-4pm) **FREE** This winery, located in a valley within cycling distance from Nyaungshwe, is open daily for tastings (K2000 for four wines).

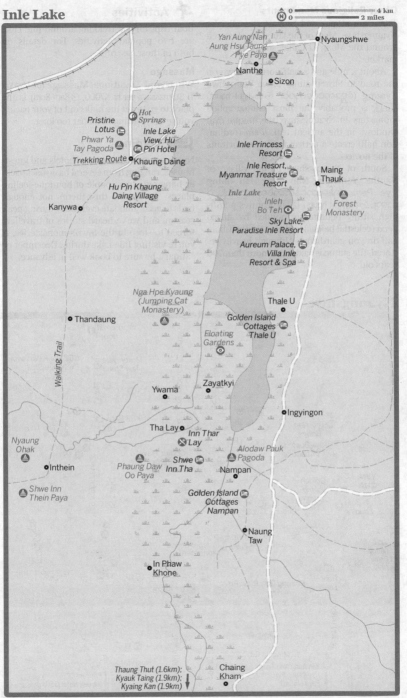

Inle Lake

Other Religious Monuments

There are stupas and monasteries all over Nyaungshwe. Most of the latter are clustered around the Mong Li Canal, southeast of the market.

About a mile and a half north of town on the road to Shwenyaung, **Shwe Yaunghwe Kyaung** (ရွှေရောင်ဝဲကျောင်း; ⊙ daylight hours) **FREE** is probably the most photographed monastery in Nyaungshwe: the unique oval windows in the ancient teak *thein* (ordination hall) create a perfect frame for portraits of the novices.

South of Nyaungshwe in the village of Nanthe, **Yan Aung Nan Aung Hsu Taung Pye Paya** (ရန်အောင်နန်အောင်ဆုတောင်းပြည့် ဘုရား; ⊙ daylight hours) **FREE** features a 26ft-high sitting buddha surrounded by stucco *deva* (celestial beings) and *chinthe* (half-lion, half-dragon guardians). Although heavily restored, the statue is said to be more than 700 years old.

🏃 Activities

Boat trips on and trekking around Inle Lake are two popular activities. For details on both of these, see p195.

Massage

Win Nyunt Traditional Massage (off Mya Wa Ti St; massage per hr K7000; ⊙ 8am-8pm) is the place to go to get the kinks out of your back if you've been sitting in a boat too long.

🛏 Sleeping

Nyaungshwe has dozens of hotels and guesthouses, ranging from several basic backpacker hang-outs to a couple of boutique-feeling places. Yet despite this, there's not enough beds to accommodate everybody during peak season, and we've heard stories of travellers forced to sleep in the town's monasteries. If you're visiting Inle Lake during December or January, be sure to book well in advance.

Nyaungshwe

As is the case elsewhere in Myanmar, rates have increased exponentially in recent years, making most of Nyaungshwe's rooms of poor value, although rates are somewhat open to negotiation (except in the high season) because of the intense competition.

Almost all rooms have bathrooms with hot showers, but few places offer air-con because of the natural cooling effect of the breeze passing over the lake. All room rates include breakfast.

★ May Guest House   GUESTHOUSE $

(☑081-209 417; 85 Mya Wa Ti St; r $20-30; @ 🖗) Minor bathroom issues (low water pressure, tiny towels) and rather thin walls aside, we love this homey, neat and friendly guesthouse. Room arc basic, but clean and cool, there's an inviting garden area and free wi-fi. Thoughtful, pressure-free staff can arrange boat trips and other travel needs.

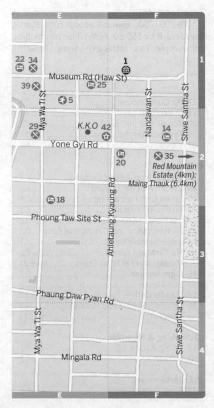

Inle Inn   HOTEL $

(☑081-209 016; inleinns@gmail.com; Yone Gyi Rd; r $30-40; 🖗) Potted plants, inviting trellises, and bamboo rooms result in a pleasing cocoon of vegetation at this budget place. Superior rooms are slightly larger and tack on a desk.

Golden Empress Hotel   GUESTHOUSE $

(☑081-209 037; www.facebook.com/goldenempress hotel; 19 Phaung Daw Pyan Rd; r $35-70; ❋@🖗) An expansive house looked after by friendly owners, the 13 rooms at this new place, attractively decked out with blond wood panelling, are reminiscent of a ski lodge. All should be equipped with air-con by the time you read this.

Aquarius Inn   GUESTHOUSE $

(☑081-209 352; aquarius352@gmail.com; 2 Phaung Daw Pyan Rd; r $18-40; ❋@🖗) The cheapest rooms here are pretty standard for this price range, and the real highlights are the family atmosphere, friendly service and the communal garden. Ten new air-con rooms should by finished by the time you read this.

Nandawunn Hotel   HOTEL $

(☑081-209 211; nandawunn@gmail.com; 80 Yone Gyi Rd; r $30-40; ❋🖗) In a residential part of town, east of the market, this tidy compound includes generally large rooms, the more expensive of which boast air-con, fridge and bathtub.

Remember Inn Hotel   HOTEL $

(☑081-209 257; www.rememberinn.jimdo.com; Museum Rd (Haw St); r $18-25, bungalows $25; ❋🖗) This place combines huge-but-plain fan-cooled rooms in the main structure and a few free-standing, air-con bungalows; the latter were being renovated when we were in town.

Nawng Kham – Little Inn   GUESTHOUSE $

(☑081-209 195; Phaung Daw Pyan Rd; r $20) The seven simple budget rooms here have fans, bathrooms and hot showers and are set in a peaceful garden.

Inle Star Hotel   GUESTHOUSE $

(☑081-209 745; 49 Kann Nar St; r $15-60) Imposing cement block with brand-new but characterless rooms next to the canal. There's only one fan-cooled cheapie, while the more expensive rooms are generally huge and come equipped with air-con.

Gold Star Hotel   HOTEL $

(☑081-209 200; goldstarhtl@gmail.com; cnr Kyauk Taing Ah Shae St Rd & Phaung Daw Pyan Rd;

r $40-55; ❄🛜) A mish-mash of divergent rooms: some tiny and with a fan, some huge and with air-con; in different buildings, so look at a few.

Ming Ga Lar Inn
HOTEL $

(📋 081-209 899; www.mingalarinn.blogspot.com; Phaung Daw Pyan Rd; r $25-70; ❄❄🛜) Rooms here range from tired budget rooms outfitted with bamboo to new but rather gaudy midrangers with air-con and attached sitting area.

Gypsy Inn
GUESTHOUSE $

(📋 081-209 084; 82 Kann Nar St; r K15,000-30,000; 🛜) Handy for accessing the canal leading to the lake, this place has an old block containing aged-feeling budget rooms with shared bathrooms, and a newer block of rooms with private baths.

Joy Hotel
GUESTHOUSE $

(📋 081-209 083; joyhotelinle@gmail.com; Jetty Rd; r $12-28; 🛜) Basic but clean: the cheaper rooms with shared bathrooms here are small and boxy, but there are better rooms with private bathrooms and hot showers.

Four Sisters Inn
GUESTHOUSE $

(📋 081-209 190; Kann Nar St; r $10-20) Located at the edge of town and boasting a homestay feel, this bright blue compound consists of a row of rather plain budget rooms.

Bright Hotel
HOTEL $

(📋 081-209 137; www.luckybrighthotel.com; 53 Phoung Taw Site St; r $20-80; ❄🛜) Being renovated when we stopped by, the cheapest rooms are fairly typical for this kind of hotel but the more inviting 'Superior' rooms have air-con, tub, TV and fridge.

★La Maison Birmane
HOTEL $$

(📋 081-209 901; www.lamaisonbirmane.com; bungalows $70-90; @🛜) Nyaungshwe's only true boutique hotel is this charming compound of 10 wooden bungalows. Rooms, which face an organic garden, are attractive and spacious, with open-feeling marble bathrooms in the more expensive ones, and beds on an elevated platform in all. There are loungeworthy communal areas, and the whole package is looked after by friendly, attentive owners. Given Nyaungshwe's generally overinflated prices, this place feels like a great value. Closed for renovation every June.

Teakwood Hotel
GUESTHOUSE $$

(📋 081-209 250; www.teakwoodgh.com; Kyaung Taw Anouk Rd; r $50-80; ❄🛜) The rooms here are simple but attractive, some boasting windows that let in lots of light and open-feeling bathrooms attractively decked out with rocks. There are a few new bungalow-type rooms, and when we stopped by, a new structure being built. The downside is that we've received reports of rather assertive sales pitches for boat trips.

Princess Garden Hotel HOTEL $$
(☑081-209 214; www.princessgardenhotel.com; r $40, bungalows $50; ☒) Located near Mong Li Canal a brief walk south from the centre of town, this place combines 12 wooden bungalows and seven rooms. All are relatively plain but comfortable, located around a shady garden that boasts Nyaungshwe's only swimming pool, and looked after by friendly, service-minded owners.

Hu Pin Hotel HOTEL $$
(☑081-209 291; www.hupinhotelmyanmar.com; 66 Kan Thar 1 St; r $80-90; ☒☎) The epitome of the bland Chinese-style hotel, the rooms here won't win any prizes for interior design, but are spotlessly clean and comfortable, if rather overpriced. Standard rooms only have twin beds, while the more expensive rooms, in an adjacent building, are larger, and include fridge and bathtub.

Pyi Guest House GUESTHOUSE $$
(☑081-209 076; pyi.nsmm@gmail.com; 35 Phaung Daw Pyan Rd; r $60-95; ☒☎) Pyi takes the form of nine new sturdy-feeling brick bungalows. Rooms are spacious and include TV, fridge, safe and air-con, but not a whole lot of interior design or charm.

Queen Inn GUESTHOUSE $$
(☑081-209 544; queen.inle@gmail.com; r $60; ☒☎) Formerly a homey-feeling budget-ranger, the Queen appears to have had hotel aspirations so the new overpriced rooms in canalside cement structures have air-con and lots of furniture. At least the nightly family-style dinners are still available (K2000, from 6pm to 9pm).

Viewpoint HOTEL $$$
(☑081-209 062; www.inleviewpoint.com; Yone Gyi Rd; r $150; @☎) Behind the restaurant of the same name is this watery plot of 20 elevated duplex bungalows. Rooms are smart and light, with lots of windows and huge balconies, some overlooking nearby rice fields. An eco theme sees the rooms built using mostly natural materials and including interesting quirks like a Shan-style wooden 'refrigerator'.

Hotel Amazing Nyaungshwe HOTEL $$$
(☑081-209 477; www.amazing-hotel.com; Yone Gyi Rd; s/d $140/150, ste $160-220; ☒☎) The more expensive rooms in this wannabe boutique hotel are attractively decorated with murals and cultural artefacts, while the cheaper rooms feel a bit tight and plain. Still, it remains among the more professional-feeling hotels in town, albeit rather overpriced during the high season.

Paradise Hotel HOTEL $$$
(☑081-209 321; www.inleparadise.com; 40 Museum Rd (Haw St); r $150-200; ☒) We can find no faults with the recently renovated bungalow-type rooms here – they're attractive, neat, spacious and come equipped with hot shower, fridge, TV and air-con – except for their insanely overpriced high-season rates.

✗ Eating

The food situation in Nyaungshwe can be pretty uninspiring. Most restaurants tend to reach far beyond their culinary capabilities, yet there are a few places that serve local food. The good news – if you're a fan of quantity over quality at least – is that serves tend to be rather large and there's an emphasis on rather gentrified Burmese- and Shan-style set meals, most starting at K3500. In this genre, **Unique Superb Food House** (3 Mya Wa Ti St; mains from K1000; ⊘8am-9pm) and the more pizza/pasta-oriented **Star Flower** (off Phaung Daw Pyan Rd; mains K3500-5000; ⊘7am-9pm; ☑) get generally good reports.

For cheap local eats, check out the **food stalls** (Yone Gyi Rd; Meals K1000; ⊘6-9am) in Mingala Market. Local specialities include *shàn k'auq-swèh* (Shan-style noodle soup) and *to-p'ù thoug* (Shan tofu salad), prepared using yellow chickpea tofu, chilli, coriander and chilli oil.

Every evening a very basic **night market** (⊘5-9pm) unfolds just off Yone Gyi Rd.

★Lin Htett Myanmar Traditional Food BURMESE $
(Yone Gyi Rd; meals from K2500; ⊘9am-9pm; ☑) Hands-down our favourite place to eat in Nyaungshwe, service at Lin Htett is as friendly as the food is delicious. If you haven't yet encountered authentic Myanmar dining, here's the drill: choose a curry or two (refer to the pictures or, better yet, have a look behind the counter), and perhaps a salad (the pennywort salad, made from a slightly bitter fresh herb, is

delicious). You'll find the accompaniments (rice, a sour soup, vegies, a fishy dip and three *balachaung*, chilli-based dips) will be supplied as a matter of course.

Lotus Restaurant
INTERNATIONAL, BURMESE $
(Museum Rd (Haw St); mains K1000-3500; ⊙10.30am-9.30pm; 🖩) Don't like to make culinary decisions? Go for the family-style Burmese dinner here, which includes soup, salad, curry and a generous fruit plate for only K3500.

Thukha Caffee
TEAHOUSE $
(cnr Lan Ma Taw St & Yone Gyi Rd; snacks from K200; ⊙5am-4pm; 🖉) Ostensibly Nyaungshwe's only Muslim teashop, this tidy place serves good tea and, in the mornings, tasty *pakoda*, deep-fried vegetable dumplings, and other tasty teashop snacks.

Everest Nepali Food Centre 2
NEPALI $
(Kyaung Taw Anouk Rd; mains K1500-3500, set meals K3500; ⊙6.30am-9pm; 🖉🖩) A branch of the longstanding Kalaw-based Nepali restaurant, the Nyaungshwe outlet does hearty set meals spanning rice, chapatti, curries and sides.

Inle Pancake Kingdom
INTERNATIONAL $
(off Phoung Taw Site St; mains K1000-2700; ⊙8am-9pm; 🖉🖩) Choose from a huge range of filled pancakes and toasted sandwiches at this cute little cabin; it's on a narrow alley north of the sports field. Follow the signs from Phoung Taw Site St.

Golden Kite Restaurant
ITALIAN $
(cnr Mya Wa Ti St & Yone Gyi Rd; pizzas from K5000, pasta from K3500; ⊙10am-10pm; 🖉🖩) If you must seek out Italian food in Nyaungshwe, consider the pizzas or pasta here. This long-standing place claims to have got its recipes via an Italian lady from Bologna (you'll most likely get the spiel) – she's also allegedly the source of the fresh basil.

Ma Tin Myint Family
BURMESE $
(Yone Gyi Rd; set meal K2500; ⊙10am-9pm; 🖩) Cheap-and-filling Burmese-style set meals.

Hu Pin Restaurant
CHINESE-BURMESE $
(Kan Thar 1 St; dishes from K1500; ⊙8am-9pm; 🖩) This bright canteen has an illustrated menu of Chinese favourites such as sweet-and-sour pork.

Green Chili Restaurant
THAI $$
(Hospital Rd; mains K2000-5500; ⊙9am-9pm; 🖩) This restaurant boasts one of the poshest dining rooms in town. On the surface, the Thai menu here is also one of the more diverse and interesting, but unfortunately the flavours are more suited to the timid tourist.

Viewpoint
SHAN, FRENCH $$$
(www.viewpoint.leplanteur.net; Yone Gyi Rd; mains $2.50-29, set meals $15-17; ⊙11am-11pm; 🖉🖩) Taking obscure local cuisines upscale is usually dangerous culinary territory, but the self-professed 'Shan nouvelle cuisine' at this – Nyaungshwe's swankiest and most ambitious restaurant – is worth investigating. On the ground floor of the same building, **Lounge-E** (get it?) does French food.

🍷 Drinking & Entertainment

Despite the nascent backpacker vibe, there's no bar scene in Nyaungshwe. The locals head to grubby beer-based restaurants such as **Kaung Kaung** (Lan Ma Taw St; ⊙9am-10pm), which has Myanmar and ABC beers on tap, while tourists head to **Min Min's** (Yone Gyi Rd; ⊙10am-10pm), where the beer costs more but where the daring can order a caipirinha, Irish coffee or pina colada.

Aung Puppet Show
PUPPET SHOW
(Ahletaung Kyaung Rd; admission K3000; ⊙show times 7pm & 8.30pm) Down the road opposite the Nandawunn Hotel, this place has two nightly shows of traditional Myanmar puppetry.

ℹ Information

There's an international ATM at **KBZ Bank** (Lan Ma Taw St); money can be exchanged at the nearby KBZ Bank **stall** (Lan Ma Taw St; ⊙9am-2pm).
Comet Travel & Internet Café (📞081-209 126; Yone Gyi Rd; ⊙8am-10pm) Books flights and buses and has a few internet terminals (per hour K1000).
Golden Island Cottages (GIC; 📞081-209 551; Phoung Taw Site St; ⊙8am-6pm) You'll need to come here to arrange guides to Kakku and Samkar, or to book a room at one of the group's hotels. Unfortunately, if manager U Ngwe isn't in, information can be nearly impossible to come by.
K.K.O (Yone Gyi Rd; per hour K1000; ⊙7am-10.30pm) Internet cafe.
Thu Thu (📞081-209 258; Yone Gyi Rd; ⊙6am-9pm; 📞) A super-friendly, no-hassle travel agent, who in addition to booking bus and plane tickets, can also arrange boat excursions and trekking guides.

ℹ Getting There & Away

The jumping-off point for Inle Lake is Nyaungshwe, but the tiny town has no bus terminal nor airport. If travelling to Inle Lake by air, you'll need to fly to Heho; if by land, to Taunggyi, hopping off in Shwenyaung, the junction leading to Nyaungshwe... It's confusing, we know; take a deep breath and take in the following.

AIR

The main airport for the Inle region is at Heho, 25 miles northwest of Nyaungshwe on the way to Kalaw.

Airlines flying out of Heho include **Air Bagan** (☑ Heho Airport 63324; www.airbagan.com), **Air KBZ** (☑ Heho Airport 63331; www.airkbz.com), **Air Mandalay** (☑ Heho Airport 63066; www.airmandalay.com), **Asian Wings** (☑ Heho Airport 63327; www.asianwingsair.com) and **Yangon Airways** (www.yangonair.com). The airline offices are in Heho and/or Taunggyi, but several Nyaungshwe-based agents can sell tickets.

The airlines have spider web–like networks of flights across the country, with many destinations only reachable via multiple transfers; be sure to double-check if your flight is direct or not.

Taxis waiting at the airport charge K25,000 to Nyaungshwe (one hour). If you're pinching pennies and have the time, a cheaper but much, much less convenient option is to hike the near mile to NH4 and wait for a pick-up truck or bus bound for Taunggyi (from K2000, 1½ hours); ask to be let off at Shwenyaung, from where you charter a *thoun bein* (motorcycle trishaw) to Nyaungshwe (K6000). You will most likely face a long wait.

BUS, MINIVAN, PICK-UP & VAN (SHARE TAXI)

To Inle Lake, any bus bound for Taunggyi can drop you at Shwenyaung – located at the junction for Nyaungshwe/Inle Lake – for the full Taunggyi fare. From Shwenyaung, *thoun bein* drivers will take you the remaining 7 miles to Nyaungshwe for around K6000.

Nyaunshwe-based travel agents such as Thu Thu (p192) can sell tickets and arrange hotel pick-up. Otherwise, if you're bound for somewhere else or those times don't work, you'll need to hop on a bus, minivan, pick-up or van (actually a share taxi) in Shwenyaung – all transport that originates in Taunggyi stops at this town on NH4.

To get to Shwenyaung, hop on any Taunggyi-bound pick-up at the **pick-up stand** (off Yone Gyi Rd) west of the market (K1000), or charter a *thoun bein* from the queue on Lan Ma Taw St (K6000). Be sure to be at the junction in Shwenyaung early so you don't miss your bus; to get an idea of the destinations, times and prices of transport from Taunggyi, see transport to/from Taunggyi (p201).

TAXI

The easiest way to find a taxi in Nyaungshwe is to ask at your hotel. Charter taxi fares include Shwenyaung (K10,000, 30 minutes), Taunggyi

(K20,000, one hour), Heho (K20,000, one hour) and Kalaw (K40,000, three hours). Taxis have room for up to four passengers.

TRAIN

The train rumbling through the hills from Shwenyaung to Thazi is slow but the scenery en route is stunning. From Shwenyaung's tiny station, trains depart at 9.30am and 10.30am, arriving in Kalaw after three hours ($3) and reaching Thazi at least another six hours later ($5). *Thoun bein* drivers go to Shwenyaung's train station for around K6000.

ⓘ Getting Around

Several shops on Yone Gyi Rd and Phaung Daw Pyan Rd rent out clunky Chinese bicycles for K1500 per day.

Motorcycle taxis at the **stand** (Lan Ma Taw St) near the market go to Shwenyaung for around K6000.

Inle Lake

☑ 081

Almost every visitor to Nyaungshwe takes a boat trip on Inle Lake. However, the lake is so large and the villages so spread out that Inle never feels too crowded.

In addition to tourist sights, Inle Lake is also home to accommodation options, often in the form of bungalows elevated directly over the water.

⊙ Sights

A longtail motorboat is the way to reach most of the sights; for sample prices, see p195.

Inthein　　　　　　　　　　　　　VILLAGE
(အင်းသိမ်) A narrow, foliage-cloaked canal winds through the reeds to the lakeside village of Inthein (also known as Indein). The *Apocalypse Now* ambience evaporates somewhat when you see the waiting tourist boats and souvenir stalls, but no matter, the pagodas on the hilltop are still incredibly atmospheric despite the crowds.

The first group of ruined stupas is immediately behind the village. Known as **Nyaung Ohak**, the crumbling stupas are choked in greenery but you can still discern some ornate stucco carvings of animals, *devas* and *chinthe*.

From Nyaung Ohak, a covered stairway climbs the hill, leading to **Shwe Inn Thein Paya**, a complex of 1054 weather-beaten *zedi* (stupas), most constructed in the 17th and 18th centuries. Some of the *zedi* lean at crazy angles while others have been reconstructed.

INLE LAKE'S FIVE-DAY MARKET

A rustic market rotates among several cities and towns in the Inle Lake region. The most touted of these is the so-called floating market at Ywama, but this has become quite touristy in recent years. The land-based options, where tribal people come down from the hills to trade livestock and produce, are generally much more interesting and 'authentic'.

Towns host the market once every five days; hotels and guesthouses can advise you where the market will be heading next. Keep in mind that markets are not held on full-moon days. For boat prices to the various destinations, see activities opposite.

Heho, Thandaung, Thaung Tho Thandaung's market is small, but accessible only via a brief walk from the lakeshore, so it's off the beaten track; larger but still rustic is the market at Thaung Tho, located at the far southern end of Inle Lake.

Taunggyi, Floating Market (Ywama) The 'Floating Market' at Ywama has emerged to become the most touristy of the circuit – consider heading elsewhere.

Maing Thauk, Kyauk Taing, Phaung Daw Oo Paya Maing Thauk is close to Nyaungshwe and reachable by land or boat; the Kyauk Taing market, located at the far southern end of Inle Lake, is largely off the tourist circuit.

Shwenyaung, Khaung Daing, Kalaw, Hmaw Be, Inthein Inthein, although popular among tourists, is still worth a visit for its sheer size and photogenic setting; Kalaw's normally tidy market spills over to the streets on market day; Hmaw Be's market, south of Inle Lake, is small but rustic and untouristed.

Nyaungshwe, Pindaya, Nampan On market day Nyaungshwe's normally sleepy market swells to several times its normal size; tiny Pindaya's central market also attracts vendors and buyers who come down from the surrounding hills.

From the pagoda, there are great views across the lake and valley. For even better views, there are two more **ruined stupas** on conical hills just north of the village, reached via a dirt path behind Nyaung Ohak. You could easily spend a few hours exploring the various ruins here.

Part of the five-day inshore circuit, the **market** at Inthein is one of the biggest and liveliest in the area.

Nga Hpe Kyaung
(Jumping Cat Monastery)
BUDDHIST TEMPLE

(ငါးဖယ်ကျောင်း; ⊙ daylight hours) FREE On the western side of the lake, the Nga Hpe Kyaung is famous for its jumping cats, trained to leap through hoops by the monks during the slow hours between scripture recitals. The monks seem happy to put on a cat-jumping show for visiting tourists and the cats get treats for their efforts, so they seem fairly happy, too. A better reason to visit the pagoda is to see the collection of ancient buddha images. The huge wooden meditation hall has statues in the Shan, Tibetan, Bagan and Inwa (Ava) styles displayed on ornate wood and mosaic pedestals.

Ywama
VILLAGE

(ရွာမ) Ywama was the first village to be developed for tourism and, as a result, it has the greatest number of souvenir shops and restaurants. It's still a very pretty village, with winding channels lined with tall teak houses, but the charm can be diminished by the crowds of tourist boats and paddling souvenir vendors. The main attraction at Ywama is the famous **floating market**, though this is a victim of its own success. Held once every five days, the market is a traffic jam of tourist boats and souvenir hawkers, with a few local farmers peddling vegetables in among the crowds.

Phaung Daw
Oo Paya
BUDDHIST TEMPLE

(ဖောင်တော်ဦးဘုရား; camera/video fee K200/300; ⊙ daylight hours) A wide channel leads south from Ywama to the village of Tha Ley and Phaung Daw Oo Paya, the holiest religious site in southern Shan State. Enshrined within the huge tiered pagoda are five ancient buddha images that have been transformed into amorphous blobs by the sheer volume of gold leaf applied by devotees.

During the annual Phaung Daw Oo festival, the images are paraded around the lake in an ornate barge shaped like a *hintha*. Local families often bring their children here as part of the ordination rites for the *sangha* (Buddhist brotherhood) – a fascinating spectacle if you happen to be there at the right time.

Nampan
VILLAGE

(နံပန်) The peaceful village of Nampan is built on stilts over the water. Its main temple, **Alodaw Pauk Pagoda**, is one of the oldest shrines on the lake, and the whitewashed stupa enshrines a fabulous gem-encrusted, Shan-style buddha. Nampan has several small **cheroot factories** and there are some decent restaurants on the edge of the village.

Floating Gardens
GARDENS

(ကျွန်းမျော) North of Nampan are these famous gardens, where Intha farmers grow flowers, tomatoes, squash and other fruit and vegetables on long wooden trellises supported on floating mats of vegetation. In the morning and afternoon, farmers paddle up and down between the rows tending their crops.

In Phaw Khone
VILLAGE

(အင်းပေါ်ခုံ) This tidy village of teak stilt houses is famous for its **weaving workshops**. Buildings across the village vibrate with the clatter of shuttles and the click-clack of shifting loom frames, and the workshops are a popular stop on the tourist circuit.

Maing Thauk
VILLAGE

(မိုင်းသောက်) Half of the village of Maing Thauk is set on dry land, while the other half sits on stilts over the water, linked to the shore by a 450yd wooden bridge. You can continue walking uphill to a peaceful forest monastery for good views over the lake.

Maing Thauk is accessible by boat and by road – you can cycle there in an hour or so along a dirt track leading southeast from Nyaungshwe.

Thaung Thut
VILLAGE

(သောင်သွတ်) At the southern end of the lake, the village of Thaung Thut, about 1½ hours from Nyaungshwe, holds an important tribal market every five days. A long walkway leads uphill from the village to a complex of whitewashed Shan **stupas**.

Further south, the village of **Kyauk Taing** is devoted to pottery-making and is also part of the market circuit. Also in the area,

Kyaing Kan specialises in weaving robes using lotus threads.

🏃 Activities
Motorboat Trips

Every morning, a flotilla of slender wooden canoes fitted with long-tailed outboard motors surges out into the lake, transporting visitors to various natural, cultural, religious, historical or commercial sites.

Every hotel, guesthouse and travel agent in Nyaungshwe can arrange motorboat trips, or you can make your own arrangements directly with the boat drivers at one of the piers or near Teik Nan Bridge – they'll most likely find you before you can find them. Prices for the standard day-long boat trip start at around K15,000 to K18,000, which typically includes visits to the famous sights in the northern part of the lake such as Phaung Daw Oo Paya in Tha Ley, the Nga Hpe Kyaung (Jumping Cat Monastery) in Nga Phe village and the floating gardens. Tacking on a trip to Inthein will raise the cost to about K18,000 or K20,000. Other destinations further afield include Thaung Thut (K20,000, 1½ hours), Hmaw Be (K35,000, two hours) and Samkar (K50,000, three hours). The fee covers the entire boat; drivers will carry up to five passengers, who get reserved seats and life jackets.

The boats have no roof, so be sure to wear sunscreen. And bring a coat or buy a blanket in the market to keep off the wind chill on boat tours around the lake.

Trekking

Inle Lake is the jumping-off point for several treks in the area. The most popular of these is the three-day walk to Kalaw; for details on this trek, see boxed text, p196. There are also some interesting day hikes and overnight treks to the east of Inle Lake, typically beginning in lowland rice paddies dotted with Shan stupa ruins and ascending to hillside Pa-O villages with panoramic views over the lake. A common option is a two-day, one-night trek, involving a short boat trip and a stay with a Pa-O family. Guides can talk you through the various treks and itineraries.

Another option is the three-day trek from Nyaungshwe to the 2478 stupas at Kakku, outside of Taunggyi. This trek crosses through predominately Pa-O territory, and must be led by a Pa-O guide. It can be arranged via Golden Island Cottages (p192).

Day hikes cost start at around K10,000 a day (per person, for groups of two or more), which includes a basic lunch of rice and curry (carry your own bottled or purified water); overnight treks run from K15,000 to K30,000 per person, per day.

Recommended Nyaungshwe-based guides include the Pyone Cho at **Lotus Tour** (☑09 4283 13717; Lotus Restaurant, Museum Rd (Haw St); ⊗10.30am-9.30pm); **Htet Naing** (☑09 4283 32317), who can also be contacted via Thu Thu (p192); or the guides at **Sunny Day Tour Services** (☑09 4283 72118; htwe.sunny@yahoo. com; cnr Lan Ma Taw St & Yone Gyi Rd; ⊗7am-8pm).

🛏 Sleeping & Eating

Although many travellers choose to stay in Nyaungshwe, there are also a number of upmarket resorts at the edge of the lake, or some cases, built on stilts over it. The majority of the Inle Lake's accommodation is near Maing Thauk, although there are a few choices at Khaung Daing.

Reservations are obligatory during the high season. All rates include breakfast. All of the hotels can arrange pick-ups and return boat trips to/from Nyaungshwe for between K8000 and K10,000.

In addition to the resorts, there are numerous tourist-oriented floating restaurants in stilt houses on the lake that offer rather overpriced Chinese and Shan food, cold beers and English-language menus. The greatest concentration of restaurants is in Ywama, but Nampan also offers some OK choices, including two branches of **Inn Thar Lay** (Tha Ley; mains K2000-4500; ⊗8am-3pm).

TREKKING FROM INLE LAKE TO KALAW

Instead of enduring yet another crowded, vomit-inducing bus ride, consider walking the distance between Inle Lake and Kalaw. There are numerous alternative routes to take you to your destination, and depending on the route that you and your guide agree upon, the journey can take between two and four days.

Although scenic, it's important to understand that this trek is more of a cultural (or even agricultural) experience than a nature walk. The only real forest you'll encounter is just outside Kalaw, and the bulk of the trek passes through relatively modern Pa-O and Danu settlements and extensive wheat, rice, tea, potato, sesame and chilli plantations. At some points you'll be walking on footpaths, while other parts of the trek are on roads (both paved and unpaved) or even along train tracks. You'll most likely spend one night with a Pa-O or Danu family and another at a Buddhist temple.

There are numerous alternate long and short routes; some choose to go by car to Lamaing and walk to Kalaw in one day, while other guides have found ways to extend the trip to four nights. Discuss the options with your guide. If you're doing the standard three-day option, you'll most likely begin at one of the lakeside villages of Inthein, Tone Le, Thandaung or Khaung Daing. In general, you can expect at least four hours of mostly level walking each day, the only truly steep part being the ascent from Thandaung at Inle Lake. The second day passes through hilly agricultural areas, and as you approach Kalaw on day three, the trek passes through tall mountains fringed with pine trees and tea plantations.

The winter months are the best time to do the trek, the only downside being that you'll almost certainly run into other trekkers – nights with as many as 50 people sleeping at the monastery have been reported. During the rainy season many of the roads are irritatingly muddy and slippery. Leeches and mosquitoes can also be a problem.

Guides can arrange to have your bags transported to a hotel in Nyaungshwe, so you carry only what you need for the walk – a towel and a torch (flashlight) are good extras to bring along.

If arranging your trek from Inle Lake, expect to pay from approximately $15 to $30 per person, per day, in groups of two or more. Rates include food, but not the cost of shipping your gear to your destination (per bag K3000), if you want to do so, and the boat fee at Inle Lake (from K8000 to K18,000).

For recommended Nyaungshwe-based guides, see above; for Kalaw-based guides, see p204.

TRANSPORT TO/FROM INLE LAKE

Air

Destinations to/from Heho include the following

Destination	Price	Duration	Frequency
Kyaingtong	$119-128	55min-2¾hr	direct 1.10pm Tue & Sat; via Mandalay or Tachileik; frequent 11.30am-4pm
Lashio	$87-98	45min-1½hr	direct 9am Mon, Wed & Fri; via Mandalay or Tachileik; frequent 11.30am-4pm
Mandalay	$50-60	30min	frequent noon-4pm
Nyaung U (Bagan)	$68-79	75min	via Mandalay; frequent noon-4pm
Tachileik	$119-129	45min-1¾hr	direct 11.30am Mon, Wed & Sat, 1.50pm Tue & Sat; via Lashio or Mandalay; frequent 11.30am-4pm
Yangon	$102-112	1hr-2¾hr	direct frequent 8.30am-5.30pm; via Mandalay & Nyaung U; 4pm

Bus

From Inle Lake, a few bus companies now make stops in Nyaungshwe. Destinations include the following:

Destination	Price	Duration	Frequency
Mandalay	K10,000-16,000	10hr	3 departures at 7pm
Nyaung U (Bagan)	K10,000-11,000	10hr	7am & 7pm
Yangon	K13,000-22,000	12hr	frequent 5.30pm-7pm

Golden Island Cottages HOTEL $$
(🖉 Nampan 081-209 390, Thale U 081-209 702; www.gicmyanmar.com; bungalows $80-140; @ 🛜) Owned by a cooperative of Pa-O tribal people, the bungalows here aren't particularly sexy or well equipped, but considering that they're the least expensive Inle Lake outfit, they come off as clean and spacious, and a relatively good deal.

The Nampan resort has a great location over open water, while the Thale U resort is closer to shore.

Inle Princess Resort BOUTIQUE HOTEL $$$
(🖉 081-209 055; www.inleprincessresort.net; bungalows $200-300; ❄ @ 🛜) Consistently the highest-ranked hotel in the Inle Lake area, the Inle Princess is honeymoon material. The stylish wooden cottages, decked out with handmade furniture, luxurious fabrics, potted plants and ethnic artefacts on the walls, would not look out of place in an Asian design magazine. The more expensive bungalows have plant-filled sun decks facing the lake.

The restaurant and staff also get positive reports.

Villa Inle Resort & Spa HOTEL $$$
(🖉 081-209 870; www.villainle.com; Maing Thauk; bungalows $300-330; ❄ @ 🛜) The 16 landbound wooden villas here eminate sophistication, boasting attractive furnishings, a spacious feel and vast inviting balconies that jut out over the lake. At these rates, it's not exactly a steal, but the friendly service, leg room and eco-conscious vibe make Villa Inle one of the few places on the lake where you feel like you're getting value for your money.

Inle Lake View HOTEL $$$
(🖉 081-209 332; www.inlelakeview.com; Kaung Daing; r $220-325; ❄ @) Behind a brick wall and edged by fruit trees and flowers, this attractive, low-key compound is our pick of the lot at Khaung Daing. The 38 rooms and villas are spacious, well equipped and tastefully furnished, and all include balconies with great views over the lake.

Inle Resort HOTEL $$$
(🖉 081-209 361; www.inleresort.com; Maing Thauk; bungalows $110-210; ❄ @ 🛜) Located on dry land near Maing Thauk, 60 elevated

bungalows and duplex villas come together in an attractive, spacious park-like setting. The more expensive bungalows here are huge and have wide balconies that border Inle Lake; the cheapest rooms feel rather tight and look out over a pond. Under foreign management, the food here gets good reports.

Shwe Inn Tha RESORT $$$

(📞09 519 2952; www.inlefloatingresort.com; Nam Pan; bungalows $170-290; ✸@📶✸) Open since 1996, Shwe Inn Tha has done a better job than most of Inle's lake-bound resorts at ageing gracefully. The 38 bungalows are still in good nick, and come equipped with air-con/heater and outdoor showers. The two 'suites' tack on TV and a dining room, while all rooms have access to one of the lake's only pools.

Pristine Lotus HOTEL $$$

(📞081-209 317; www.pristinelotussparesort.com; Khaung Daing; bungalows $200; ✸@📶) The 50 bungalow 'suites' here are on a landscaped hillside west of Inle Lake. The home-like rooms feel airy and sophisticated, with an extra bed on an elevated platform, huge bathrooms and wide balconies. There's a spa on the grounds and when we visited, another 70 bungalows were being built across the street.

Sky Lake HOTEL $$$

(📞081-209 128; www.inleskylake.com; Maing Thauk; bungalows $130-180; 📶) Although they don't exactly feel new, the above-water bungalows have a bit of leg room and come equipped with TV, safe and fridge, making them of slightly better value for money than most.

Myanmar Treasure Resort HOTEL $$$

(📞081-209 481; www.myanmartreasureresorts. com; Maing Thauk; bungalows $310-430; @📶) The high-season rates here are pretty insane, but we have to admit that Myanmar Treasure is one of the newer and nicer Inle Lake bungalow outfits. The 59 dark wood bungalows, built in 2006 and located over the lake, are handsome and functional, although the balconies are pretty skimpy. The resort is connected to the mainland via a long bridge.

Hu Pin Inle Khaung
Daing Village Resort HOTEL $$$

(📞081-209 296; www.hupinhotelmyanmar.com; Khaung Daing; r/cottage/ste $200/250/300; ✸📶) Edging the western side of the lake, we really

DON'T MISS

AROUND KHAUNG DAING BY BICYCLE

Just because you've been on a boat doesn't mean you've 'done' Inle Lake. The countryside that surrounds all that water is also worth a visit, and a half-day cycling trip to Khaung Daing, located at the northwestern corner of the lake, is an easy and worthwhile way to experience it. The attractions are admittedly low-key, and the real reason to come here is the bike ride through some beautiful countryside.

After renting a bicycle in Nyaungshwe, cross Teik Nan Bridge and follow the tree-lined, bone-shaking dirt track through the rice fields until you reach the sealed road, then turn left.

The first place you'll reach is Khaung Daing's **hot springs** (Khaung Daing; swimming pool $8, private bath $5, mixed hot pool $8; ⊙6am-6pm), to where hot water from the natural springs has been channelled into a swimming pool and a series of private bathhouses for men and women. The springs are also the start or end point of several trekking routes between Kalaw and Inle Lake.

As you approach Khaung Daing, the road is seemingly lined with gold and white-washed stupas, some perched on the tall hills to the west of the lake. Perhaps the most interesting is **Phwar Ya Thay Paya** (ဖွားရေသောဘုရား; Khaung Daing; ⊙daylight hours) FREE, located roughly behind Pristine Lotus. We were told that the name means 'Lady Monk', and refers to the temple's lone female resident. Many stairs lead to the top here, and the temple offers amazing views over the lake and countryside.

Continuing south, after a few minutes you'll reach **Khaung Daing** (ခေါင်းတိုင်), a quiet Intha village known for its tofu, prepared using split yellow peas instead of soybeans. There are some basic restaurants and teashops here.

Just past Khaung Daing, turn left into the gateway that leads to Hu Pin Inle Khaung Daing Village Resort. The road here ends in yet another **hilltop temple** with intermittent views of the lake.

like 86 somewhat quaint, old-school wooden rooms and above-water 'cottages' and 'suites' here, many offering some of the most fantastic views of Inle Lake of any of the area's accommodation. But given the equally old-school amenities, the high-season rates are asking a lot.

Taunggyi တောင်ကြီး

📞 081 / POPULATION C200,000

Taunggyi is the administrative capital for the whole of Shan State. Perched on top of a mountain, it's also a busy trading post, and the town markets are piled high with Chinese and Thai goods freighted in daily via the border crossings at Mong La and Tachileik. However, unless you've spent too much time in rural Shan State and are pining for the big city and/or consumer goods, there's really little of interest here for the average visitor.

⊙ Sights

Taunggyi has a number of historic **churches** and there are several Myanmar-style **mosques** on the alleyways southwest of the market. On the outskirts south of town, the huge white **Sulamuni Paya** (စူလာမုနိဘုရား; ⊙ daylight hours) **FREE** has a gilded corncob stupa that pays tribute to the Ananda Pahto in Bagan. You can continue a few miles uphill to the ridge-top **Shwe Phone Pye Paya** (ရွှေဘုန်းပြည့်ဘုရား; ⊙ daylight hours) **FREE** for dizzying views over Taunggyi and Inle Lake; a round-trip taxi to both temples should run to about K10,000.

Shan State Cultural Museum & Library MUSEUM
(ရှမ်းပြည်နယ်ယဉ်ကျေးမှုပြတိုက်နှင့် စာကြည့်တိုက်; Bogyoke Aung San Rd; admission $2 or K2000; ⊙ 9.30am-4pm Wed-Sun) In addition to the usual displays of local ethnic-group outfits you'll also find a handful of displays of weapons, musical instruments and jewellery, although few are accompanied by an English-language explanation.

Myanmar Vineyard VINEYARD
(www.myanmar-vineyard.com; ⊙ 9am-4pm) **FREE** Located at Aythaya, 3 miles west of Taunggyi, this vineyard – the country's first – sits at an elevation of 4290ft on well-watered, limestone-rich soils, providing good growing conditions for Shiraz, Cabernet Sauvignon, Sauvignon Blanc, Chenin Blanc and Moscato grapes. Open daily for tours and tastings.

Taunggyi

EASTERN MYANMAR TAUNGGYI

✹✹ Festivals & Events

As part of the full-moon celebrations during Tazaungmon (the eighth month of Myanmar's lunar calendar), the city holds a huge **fire-balloon festival**, when hundreds of hot-air balloons in kaleidoscopic colours

Taunggyi

and shapes are released into the sky to carry away sins. The three-day festival takes place in October or November, and accommodation can be very hard to find in Taunggyi at this time.

🛏 Sleeping

Kan-Tone Kan-Sone Hotel   HOTEL $
(☎ 081-212 3737; 31 Bogyoke Aung San Rd; r $20-30; 🖥) The showers dribble, and there are certainly newer places in town, but the kind staff here speak English, really make you feel at home, and can provide good tourism advice.

Eastern Hotel   HOTEL $
(☎ 081-212 2243; easternhotel.tgi@gmail.com; 27 Bogyoke Aung San Rd; r incl breakfast $25-42, ste incl breakfast $56-60; 🕸🖥) Located in a well-maintained villa, the predominate vibe here is tidy, a feeling that extends from the rather tight standard rooms to the larger wood-floored suites.

✗ Eating

Sein Myanmar Restaurant   BURMESE $
(Bogyoke Aung San Rd; meals from K2000; ⊘ 10am-10pm) Locals crowd into this busy restaurant for full-flavoured Burmese-style rice-and-curry sets.

Night Market   BURMESE $
(Tabin Shwe Htee St; mains from K300; ⊘ 4-10pm) Taunggyi's night market is the place to go for cheap local eats; Daw Than Kyi, at the western end, does excellent *t'ămìn jìn,* Shan-style rice (look for the rainbow-coloured plastic sheeting).

Tokyo Cafe   TEASHOP $
(Bogyoke Aung San Rd; mains from K500; ⊘ 6am-6pm) This spic-and-span teashop has an English-language menu of one-plate dishes.

🛍 Shopping

Taunggyi Gift Shop   HANDICRAFTS
(cnr Bogyoke Aung San Rd & Nan Thidar St; ⊘ 8am-6pm) A brief selection of local foods, Shan-style clothing and handicrafts.

ℹ Information

Taunggyi's **immigration office** (Bogyoke Aung San Rd) is about 1 mile south of town; a taxi here will cost about K2000.

ATMs that accept international cards can be found at **CB Bank** (Bogyoke Aung San Rd), **KBZ Bank** (Bogyoke Aung San Rd) and **United Amara Bank (UAB)** (Bogyoke Aung San Rd). Inconveniently, exchange is only available at the **stall** (27/28 Bogyoke Aung San Rd; ⊘ 9am-2.30pm) attached to the Air KBZ office.

There are a few internet cafes along Bogyoke Aung San Rd, including the following:
Cyber Planet Internet Cafe (Childers Hospital St; per hr K300; ⊘ 9am-11pm)
Cyber Point Internet Café (Bogyoke Aung San Rd; per hr K400; ⊘ 6am-10pm)

ℹ Getting There & Away

Buses, minivans, pick-ups, vans (share taxis) and taxis leave Taunggyi from several stands around town.

Most long-distance buses depart from the **Maw Cherry bus station** (Circular Rd West), about a mile north of the town centre; a taxi here will run to K2000. The **offices** (Bogyoke Aung San Rd) of companies running bus and van services to destinations such as Mandalay and Yangon are found along the west side of Bogyoke Aung San Rd, south of Kan-Tone Kan-Sone Hotel. The **office** (Nagar Pwat Kyaung St) for buses to Nyaung

U (Bagan) is on Nagar Pwat Kyaung St. Some companies, including **Shwe Taung Yoe Express** (Mya Kan Thar St), offer free transport to the bus station. Minivans to Heho and Kalaw leave from a **stop** just off Merchant St.

Pick-up trucks to Nyaungshwe (off Merchant St) wait a block or so north of Merchant St. **Pick-ups to Thazi and Meiktila** leave just south of Merchant St.

TRANSPORT TO/FROM TAUNGGYI

Destination	Bus	Minibus	Pick-Up	Van (Share Taxi)
Heho (airport)	N/A	K2000; 1hr; 1pm, 2pm & 3pm	K1000; 1hr; departs when full 6am-4pm (from stop off Merchant St)	N/A
Kalaw	K2500; 3hr; 1pm, 2pm & 3pm; from Maw Cherry bus stand	K3000; 3hr; daily 1pm, 2pm & 3pm; from Merchant St	K2000; 3hr; departs when full 6am-4pm; from stop off Merchant St	N/A
Lashio	K15,000; 12hr; daily 2pm	N/A	N/A	N/A
Loikaw	K10,000; 8hr; daily 7am; from Maw Cherry bus stand	N/A	N/A	N/A
Mandalay	K7500-13,000; 10hr; frequent 6-8pm; from stalls on Bogyoke Aung San Rd and Shwe Taung Yoe Express	N/A	N/A	K18,000-20,000; 10hr; departs when full 8.30am-8pm; from stalls on Bogyoke Aung San Rd
Meiktila	K5000; 6hr; daily 7am	N/A	K3000; 8hr; departs when full 6am-4pm; from stop off Merchant St	N/A
Nyaungshwe	N/A	N/A	K1000; 1hr; departs when full 6am-4pm; from stop off Merchant St	N/A
Nyaung U (Bagan)	K8000-10,000; 10hr; daily 6pm; from stall on Nagar Pwat Kyaung St and Shwe Taung Yoe Express	N/A	N/A	N/A
Pindaya	K3000; 4hr; daily 1pm & 1.30pm; from Maw Cherry bus stand	N/A	N/A	N/A
Thazi	N/A	N/A	K3000; 7hr; departs when full 6am-4pm	N/A
Yangon	K15,000; 12hr; frequent approx 6-8pm; from stalls along Bogyoke Aung San Rd	N/A	N/A	N/A

Taxis wait near the **corner of Bogyoke Aung San Rd and Merchant St** (cnr Bogyoke Aung San Rd & Merchant St), or **in front of the Kan-Tone Kan-Sone Hotel** (Bogyoke Aung San Rd). Destinations include Nyaungshwe (K20,000, one hour), Kakku (K35,000, 1½ hours) and Kalaw (K40,000, three hours).

Heho functions as the air hub to/from Taunggyi; for details on flights and times, see boxed text, p201. In Taunggyi, **Air Bagan** (☑ 081-212 4736; Bogyoke Aung San Rd; ☺8am-5pm Mon-Fri & 9am-2pm Sat & Sun), **Air KBZ** (☑ 081-212 4768; 27/28 Bogyoke Aung San Rd; ☺9am-5pm), **Air Mandalay** (☑ 081-212 1330; www.airmandalay. com; Bogyoke Aung San Rd; ☺8.30am-5.30pm Mon-Fri & 9am-1pm Sat & Sun), **Asian Wings** (☑ 081-205 900; www.asianwingsair.com; Bogyoke Aung San Rd; ☺9am-5.30pm) and **Yangon Airways** (☑ 081-212 3995; 134 Bogyoke Aung San Rd; ☺9am-5pm) all have offices on on Bogyoke Aung San Rd, or you can go to **Shan Pyi Thar** (☑ 081-212 4549; 8 Bogyoke Aung San Rd, no roman-script sign; ☺9am-6pm), a travel agent located roughly across from Cyber Point Internet Café. A taxi from Heho's airport to Taunggyi costs K25,000; a cheaper but less convenient option is to hike the near mile to the highwayand wait for a pick-up truck or bus to Taunggyi (K2000, 1½ hours).

Pindaya ပင်းတယ

☑ 081 / POPULATION C5000

The road to Pindaya cuts across one of the most densely farmed areas in Myanmar – at first glance, the patchwork of fields and hedges could almost be a landscape from central Europe or middle America. Yet the main reason to make this journey is to visit the famous Shwe Oo Min Natural Cave pagoda, a massive limestone cavern filled with thousands of gilded buddha statues.

◉ Sights & Activities

★ Shwe Oo Min
Natural Cave Pagoda CAVE

(ရွှေဥမင်သဘာဝလိုက်ဂူဘုရား; Shwe U Min Pagoda Rd; admission $3 or K3000, camera fee K300; ☺6am-6pm) Set on a limestone ridge above Pone Taloke Lake, this winding complex of natural caves and tunnels is filled to bursting with buddha images in an astonishing variety of shapes, sizes and materials.

The stairs leading to the cave are about 2 miles south of town on Shwe U Min Pagoda Rd, a 10- to 15-minute walk from town. A horse cart from the market to the Nget Pyaw Taw pagoda entrance will cost K1000, and a

motorcycle taxi will take you to the top for K1000.

At the latest count, the caves contained more than 8094 statues, some left centuries ago by Myanmar pilgrims and others newly installed by Buddhist organisations from as far afield as Singapore, the Netherlands and the USA. The collection of alabaster, teak, marble, brick, lacquer and cement images is still growing – pilgrims arrive in a slow but steady stream, installing new images and meditating in tiny, naturally occuring, meditation chambers in the cave walls.

A series of covered stairways climb the ridge to the cave entrance. Most people arrive via the long stairway that starts near the gleaming white *zedi* of **Nget Pyaw Taw Pagoda**, just south of the Conqueror Hotel. You can skip the last 130 steps to the cave mouth by taking the lift.

Two more covered stairways lead north from the lift pavilion. One descends gently back to Pindaya, while the other climbs to a second **cave pavilion** containing a monumental 40ft-high, gilded Shan-style sitting buddha. The steps continue along the ridge to a third chamber with a large **reclining buddha** and more shrines and pagodas along the hilltop.

Other Religious Monuments

Downhill from the main cave on the dirt path to Pone Taloke Lake, the gorgeous **Hsin Khaung Taung Kyaung** (ဆင်ခေါင်းတောင်ကျောင်း; off Shwe U Min Pagoda Rd; ☺daylight hours) **FREE** was constructed from carved teak panels in the late 19th century. The steps to the main cave start just beyond the *kyaung* (monastery) – the path is lined with ancient crumbling *zedi*.

At the north end of Pone Taloke Lake, the **Kan Tu Kyaung** (ကံတုကျောင်း; Zaw Ti Kar Yone St; ☺daylight hours) **FREE** features some heavily restored stupas and a fine teak *kyaung* with a large collection of antique buddha images on ornate plinths.

Trekking

A couple of local guides lead treks in the hill country surrounding Pindaya. Most conduct overnight treks to **Yazagyi**, an attractive and modern Palaung village located in hilly tea-plantation country about five hours' walk east of Pindaya. Some choose to extend this to two nights with a visit to **Kan Hla Kone**, a remote Danu village. It's also possible to trek from Pindaya to Kalaw, a trip of about three days. Overnight treks start at about $20 per day per person (in groups of two or more), and guides with experience in these areas include U Myint Thoung at Old Home Tour Information Centre (p203) and **Sai Win Htun** (☎081-66166; winhtun123@gmail.com; Golden Cave Hotel, Shwe U Min Padoga Rd), who can be contacted at Golden Cave Hotel.

Festivals & Events

The main annual **paya pwe** (pagoda festival) at Shwe Oo Min takes place on the full moon of Tabaung (February/March). Expect all the usual singing, dancing and hand-operated fairground rides.

Sleeping

Golden Cave Hotel HOTEL $
(☎081-66166; www.goldencavehotel.com; Shwe U Min Pagoda Rd; r $35-40; @ 📶) A comfy budget/midrange place near the steps to Shwe Oo Min. The smarter superior rooms have balconies looking towards the caves, and are also equipped with a TV and a fridge.

Myit Phyar Zaw Gyi Hotel HOTEL $
(☎081-66403; 106 Zaw Ti Kar Yone St; r $10-20) Next to the market and close to the lakeshore, Pindaya's one true budget option is tidy, friendly and good value for money.

Pindaya Hotel HOTEL $
(☎081-66189; Shwe U Min Pagoda Rd; r $40-50; ❄) The 'deluxe' rooms in the funky main structure are spacious, have lots of natural light, balconies looking over the lake, and attractive wood flooring and furnishings. The cheaper 'superior' rooms are smaller and at ground level. It's pleasant, but given the lack of amenities – no TV or fridge – feels somewhat overpriced. Located just south of 'downtown' Pindaya on Shwe U Min Pagoda Rd.

★ **Pindaya Inle Inn** HOTEL $$
(☎081-66029; www.pindayainleinn.com; Mahar Bandular Rd; r/chalets $75-120; @ 📶) Located at the entrance to town, across the lake from Shwe Oo Min Pagoda, this is a surprisingly sophisticated place to stay for a small town like Pindaya. Rooms are in either bamboo or stone cottages, in a lovingly tended garden centred on a longhouse-style restaurant and bar. The larger, more expensive 'cottages' really do feel like small homes, and come equipped with TV, fridge, huge bathrooms with tub, and fireplace.

Conqueror Resort Hotel HOTEL $$
(☎081-66106; www.conquererresorthotel.com; off Shwe U Min Padoga Rd; r $70-100; 📶 ❄) There isn't a blade of grass out of place at this immaculately maintained resort hotel near the main entrance to the caves. Rooms are set in duplex bungalows around a central restaurant and a large, inviting pool. All come equipped with TV, a minibar and balcony, and the 'suitc' rooms tack on a spacious and stylish bathroom.

Eating & Drinking

Good Morning BURMESE $
(Shwe Min U Pagoda Rd; mains K800; ⏲7am-8pm) A friendly local has put together an English-language menu of five different noodle dishes; try the 'Mandalay moun ti', thick rice noodles with bean powder, spiced oil and a side of peppery broth.

Kyan Lite Restaurant CHINESE-BURMESE $
(Zaw Ti Kar Yone St; mains from K1000; ⏲10am-9pm) On the lakeshore close to the market, Kyan Lite serves cold beers and a familiar menu of Myanmar Chinese dishes.

Green Tea Restaurant INTERNATIONAL, BURMESE $$
(Shwe U Min Pagoda Rd; mains K1800-8200; ⏲10am-9pm; 📶) Located between the market and Shwe Oo Min Pagoda, this open-air dining room looking over Pone Taloke Lake is Pindaya's poshest place to dine. The dishes don't quite live up to the setting, although the Burmese food is OK for a restaurant of this type.

Information

We're told that there is a $2 'entry fee' to Pindaya, collected at the entrance to town, although we've never been hit up for this.

There was no ATM nor currency exchange in Pindaya at research time, so bring cash.

Net Villa (off Zay Part St; per hr K400; ⏲1-11pm) At research time, Pindaya's only internet cafe. A bit tricky to find; U Myint Thoung at Old Home Tour Information Centre can probably show the way.

Old Home Tour Information Centre (☎081-66104, 081-66188; 46 Shwe U Min Pagoda Rd; ⏲9am-5pm) Located at the market intersection. Here you'll find friendly local U Myint Thoung, who sells a small selection of books and antiques, and who leads treks and day tours.

Getting There & Away

There's very little direct transport to Pindaya, so you'll probably have to make your way to

SAMKAR

Samkar (ဆမ်ကား), located south of Inle Lake, is probably best known for its Buddhist ruins. But the real reason to visit is the trip, a boat ride of about three hours that winds south through scenic lakeside villages and beautiful countryside to a second, virtually untouristed lake ringed by Shan, Intha and Pa-O villages.

Formerly the seat of a dynasty of Shan princes, today's Samkar has two parts: the old town, a land-bound Shan village home to a small plot of crumbling ruins and a market that is part of the five-day circuit, and a more modern 'floating' village. On the opposite side of the lake, **Tharkong Pagoda** is a collection of *zedi* (stupas) that date back at least 500 years. Nearby, **Tai Arkong** is a village known for alcohol production.

To visit Samkar, a Pa-O guide ($10) and entrance fee (per person $5) must be arranged through Golden Island Cottages (p192). A boat here should cost around K50,000. If you choose to stay overnight, there's attractive accommodation at **A Little Lodge in Samkar** (☑ 09 681 0445; littlesamkarlodge@gmail.com; Samkar; r $70), a short walk from Samkar's old town.

Aungban, a few miles east of Kalaw along NH4, where transport to Pindaya waits near the clock tower intersection. There, you'll find two daily pick-ups (K1000 to K2000, 1½ hours, 8am and 11am), as well as waiting motorcycles (K6000 one way, K10,000 round-trip) and taxis (K30,000 one way, K50,000 round-trip).

From Pindaya's market intersection, minibuses bound for Taunggyi depart at 5.30am and 5.45am (K2000 to K3000, three hours), as well as seriously overpacked pick-ups to Aungban at 9am, 9.30am and 12.30pm (K1000, 1½ hours).

Kalaw ကလော

☑ 081 / POPULATION C10,000

Founded as a hill station by British civil servants fleeing the heat of the plains, Kalaw still feels like a high-altitude holiday resort: the air is cool, the atmosphere is calm, the streets are leafy and green, and the surrounding hills are the only place in Myanmar where travellers can trek overnight without prior permission. In addition to foreign trekkers, Kalaw has a significant population of Nepali Gurkhas and Indian Hindus, Sikhs and Muslims, who came here to build the roads and railway line during the British period.

◉ Sights & Activities

Right in the centre of Kalaw is **Aung Chan Tha Zedi** (အောင်ချမ်းသာစေတီ; Aung Chan Thar St; ⊙ daylight hours) FREE, a glittery stupa covered in gold- and silver-coloured glass mosaics.

Kalaw's **market** (ကလောမြို့မရျေး; Min St; ⊙ 6am-5pm) is also worth a browse – several stalls sell dried fruit and local liqueurs. Every five days the market is swelled by traders from hill-tribe villages around town.

South of the market, the myriad stupas of **Hsu Taung Pye Paya** (ဆုတောင်းပြည့်ဘုရား; Aung Tha Pyay St; ⊙ daylight hours) FREE were restored from ruins using donations from visiting pilgrims. For a good view over the market area, take the steps on the north side of Union Hwy (NH4) to **Thein Taung Paya** (သိမ်တောင်ဘုရား; off Union Hwy (NH4); ⊙ daylight hours) FREE, a modest Buddhist monastery with a small congregation of friendly monks.

Trekking

Almost everyone who comes to Kalaw goes trekking in the hills. The town is surrounded by Buddhist pagodas, hilltop viewpoints and the peaceful villages of the Palaung, Danu, Pa-O, Taung Yo and Danaw tribes, all set in a gorgeous landscape of forest-capped hills.

Popular destinations for one-day treks around Kalaw include the **Myin Ma Hti Cave**, the Pa-O villages south of **Lamaing**, and the Pa-O, Danu and Taung Yo villages near **Myin Dike** train station. Another common route runs southwest from Kalaw to the Palaung villages of **Ywathit** and **Tar Yaw**, passing the **Viewpoint**, a rustic, Nepali-run restaurant with sweeping views over the hills.

The guides at Ever Smile do visits to **Pane Ne Pin** and **Myin Ka**, Palaung and Taung Yo villages respectively, located in a beautiful area north of Kalaw. Alternatively, the guides at Jungle King lead one-day treks to

Patingone, a four-hour hike south of Kalaw, where there's a Pa-O/Taung Yo traditional healer.

The most popular overnight trek is undoubtedly the two- to four-day trek to Inle Lake; for details, see p196. One Kalaw-based outfit has recently initiated two-day mountain-bike treks along a similar route; contact Naing Naing Hire Bike (p209) for details on this. A less common overnight route is the multiday trek to Pindaya, via Taung Ni. If you're interested in nature more than culture, Moteh, a guide based at Viewpoint, offers a day or overnight 'jungle' trek through a protected forest. Trekkers sleep in the woods or stay overnight at a Taung Yo village.

The level of development varies as you move from village to village. Some tribes wear traditional clothing and live without electricity or running water, while their immediate neighbours watch European football on satellite TV. The standard of living for tribal people across the region has been raised by development projects run by the UN and other international NGOs. Most villagers depend primarily on farming, but some subsidise their income by making handicrafts and providing meals and accommodation for visiting trekkers.

On single-day treks, the only equipment you need is a pair of good walking shoes.

Meals are usually included in the price of the trek, while you should buy and carry your own drinking water. Trekking goes on year-round, but expect muddy conditions during the rainy season (approximately June to October).

Trekking without a guide is not recommended – the trails are confusing, the terrain challenging and few people in the hills speak English. The going rate for a day hike is around K8000 to K9000 per person, overnight treks between K10,000 and K15,000 per person, per day, in groups of two or more.

Recommended guides leading treks around Kalaw:

Ever Smile
TREKKING
(📞 081-50683; Yuzana St; ⊙ 8am-8pm) This outfit specialises in the trek to Inle Lake, as well as day treks within Kalaw Township. Naing Naing, a guide here, gets good reports.

Rural Development Society
TREKKING
(RDS; 📞 081-50747, 09 528 0974; sdr1992@gmail.com; Min St) Founded by charity-minded Tommy Aung in 1992, this NGO also leads day and overnight treks in the area and to Inle Lake. Advance notice of three days is requested; email or call Tommy for details.

Kalaw

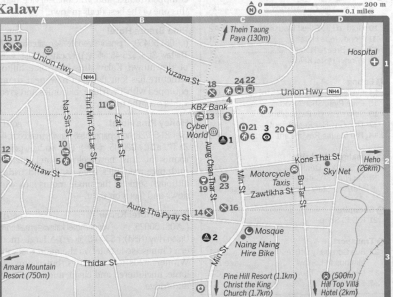

Sam's Trekking Guide TREKKING
(☑ 081-50377; Union Hwy (NH 4); ☺ 7am-7pm)
Sam and his family have years of experience leading treks, and conduct day and overnight treks in Kalaw Township, as well as multiday treks to Inle Lake and Pindaya. If nobody's at the office, head over to **Sam's Family Restaurant** (Aung Chan Tha St; mains from K1000; ☺ all day).

JP Barua TREKKING
(☑ 081-50549) JP leads day treks within Kalaw Township. He has no office, and can only be contacted via phone.

Moteh TREKKING
(☑ 09 7322 1878; Viewpoint) Based at Viewpoint, a restaurant southwest of Kalaw, Moteh leads day and overnight 'jungle' treks to a wooded area.

Jungle King TREKKING
(Golden Lily Guest House, 5/88 Nat Sin St; ☺ 7am-9pm) Based out of Golden Lily Guest House, the family here have been leading treks in the area for decades.

🛏 Sleeping

Kalaw has a generous spread of hotels and guesthouses. Few offer air-conditioning – in this climate they don't need to – but some offer heaters for the winter nights, when the temperature has been known to drop perilously close to freezing.

🏨 In Town

★ Dream Villa Hotel Kalaw HOTEL $
(☑ 081-50144; dreamvilla@myanmar.com.mm; 5 Za Ti' La St; r $40-45; 🛜) A cut above your average Myanmar hotel, the Dream Villa is a spotless, three-storey home with 24 tasteful, wood-panelled rooms attractively decorated with a few local design touches. All rooms have TV and fridge, while the more expensive have a bit more leg room and bathtubs.

Eastern Paradise Motel HOTEL $
(☑ 081-50315; 5 Thiri Min Ga Lar St; r $25-40; 🛜) A central location, large, homey and well-equipped rooms, and gracious service make this one of the best deals in town.

Pine Breeze Hotel HOTEL $
(☑ 081-50459; pinebreezehotel@gmail.com; 174 Thittaw St; r $25-45; ❄🛜) Located just west of 'downtown' Kalaw, this baby-blue hilltop structure has four floors of new, neat rooms equipped with TV, fridge, balconies and great views over the town.

Honey Pine Hotel HOTEL $
(☑ 081-50728; honeypinehotelkalaw@gmail.com; 44 Za Ti' La St; r $20-45; ❄🛜) The budget-priced rooms at this new-feeling hotel include midrange amenities such as TV and fridge, although some of the single rooms lack windows and feel a bit tight.

Winner Hotel Kalaw HOTEL $
(☑ 081-50025; winnerhotel.kalaw@gmail.com; Union Hwy (NH4); r $30-45; ❄🛜) A large, modern Chinese-style hotel on the main road, the Winner holds few surprises, but rooms are large, uncluttered and clean, and include TV and fridge.

Golden Lily Guest House HOTEL $
(☑ 081-50108; 5/88 Nat Sin St; r $7-14; @) A cha-
let mood pervades at this mazelike budget
complex. Opt for the more expensive rooms,
which are bigger, newer and nicer, and share
a wide balcony that looks over the town.

Outside of Town

Some of Kalaw's best and most atmospheric
accommodation is located outside of the city
centre.

Green Haven Hotel HOTEL $
(☑ 081-50639; greenhavenhotel@gmail.com; Oo
Min Rd; r $35-50; @☎) The 20 tidy, wood-pan-
elled rooms here are housed in two imposing, two-storey white structures. To get here,
follow Min St south, turning right at the
second intersection, or hop on a motorcycle
taxi (K1000) near the market.

Pine Hill Resort HOTEL $$
(☑ 081-50079; pinehill.kalaw@gmail.com; 151
Oo Min Rd; r & bungalows $70-100; ❄☎) Set
around a colonial bungalow, this hotel con-
sists of 32 neat rooms in concrete duplex
cottages sprawling in immaculate gardens.
'Deluxe' rooms tack on a safe, air-con and a
bathtub. To get here, follow Min St south, turn-
ing right at the second intersection, or hop on
a motorcycle taxi (K1000) near the market.

Hill Top Villa Hotel HOTEL $$
(☑ 081-50346; hilltopvillayangon@gmail.com; r &
bungalows K75,000-150,000; ☎) The park-like
atmosphere and the tidy bungalows at this
popular place are nice enough, but they don't
really justify the distance from town and the
high tariff. Located about 1.5 miles south of
town via Bu Tar St.

Amara Mountain Resort HOTEL $$$
(☑ 081-50734; www.amara-mountain.com; 10/182
Thidar St; r $140; ☎) Accommodation here is
based in two attractive mock-Tudor buildings
in a hilltop garden, one built in 2002 and
another more than a century previously, in
1909. The 11 rooms are equally spacious and
attractive regardless of age, with wood floors
and lots of natural light, some boasting large
bathtubs and fireplace, although no TV or air-
con. The only real downside is the distance,
about half a mile west of Kalaw.

Eating & Drinking

Kalaw has some good places to chow down,
many serving food with a distinctive Indian
or Nepali flavour.

★ **Thu Maung Restaurant** BURMESE $
(Myanmar Restaurant; Union Hwy (NH4); meals
from K2500; ⏱11am-9pm) One of our fave
Burmese curry restaurants in this part of
the country, Thu Maung serves rich, meaty

OFF THE BEATEN TRACK

WALKING AROUND KALAW

Although trekking in the hills around Kalaw without a guide is not recommended, there
are some interesting and easy-to-find sights just outside town that can be tackled in the
form of a self-guided, half-day walk.

Starting at the market, head south on Min St, continuing to University St and turning
southwest (right) at the roundabout-like junction (the park will be on your left). Follow-
ing the hilly, pine-lined road, and veering left at the junction after the Pine View Inn, it
should take 10 minutes or so to reach **Christ the King Church** (University Rd; ⏱day-
light hours) FREE, which was run by the same Italian priest from 1931 to 2000.

Return the way you came until you reach the intersection with Oo Min St. Turn left
and continue about 10 minutes or so until you see a group of pagodas on your left; this
is **Shwe Oo Min Paya** (ရွှေဥမင်ဘုရား; Oo Min Rd; ⏱daylight hours) FREE, a natural cave
dripping with golden Buddha statues (and also just dripping – watch your footing on the
slippery marble pathways).

After exploring the caves, continue along the road until you reach a T-junction. Turn
right and follow the wooden signs with gold letters that lead you to **Hnee Paya** (နီးဘုရား;
Hnee Pagoda St; ⏱daylight hours) FREE, home to a 500-year-old, gold-lacquered bamboo
Buddha.

After paying your respects, backtrack along Hnee Pagoda St and turn left at the in-
tersection. Continue along Circular Rd (West) until you reach the T-junction; turn right
on Saitta Thukha St and after about 10 minutes or so you'll merge with Thidar St just
behind **Hsu Taung Pye Paya**.

TRANSPORT TO/FROM KALAW

Destination	Bus	Minibus	Pick-Up	Train
Aungban (for Pindaya)	N/A	K500; 20 min; daily 6.30am, 7am & 7.30am	K500; 4-5hr; frequent 7am-6pm	N/A
Heho (airport)	N/A	K2500; 3hr; daily 6.30am, 7am & 7.30am	N/A	N/A
Loikaw	N/A	K4000; 6hr; daily 5.30am	N/A	$7-8; 11hr; daily 8.50pm
Mandalay	K7000-10,000; 7-8hr; frequent 8-10pm	N/A	N/A	N/A
Meiktila	N/A	K4000; 4-5hr; frequent 7am-noon	K3000; 4-5hr; frequent 7am-6pm	N/A
Nay Pyi Taw	K7000; 7-8hr; frequent 8.30-9pm	K5500/7-8hr; daily 9.30am	N/A	$3-8; 15hr; daily 12.49pm & 3.50pm
Nyaung U (Bagan)	K7000; 7-8hr; daily 9am & frequent 8-9pm	N/A	N/A	N/A
Shwenyaung (for Inle Lake)	N/A	K2500; 3hr; daily 6.30am, 7am & 7.30am	N/A	$1-3; 3hr; daily 10.15am & 12.30pm
Taunggyi	N/A	K2500; 3hr; daily 6.30am, 7am & 7.30am	N/A	N/A
Thazi	N/A	K5000; 4hr; frequent 7am-noon	K3000; 4hr; frequent 7am-6pm	$2-5; 7hr; daily 2pm
Yangon	K10,000-16,500; 10-12hr; frequent 5-8pm	N/A	N/A	N/A

chicken, pork, mutton and fish curries coupled with exceptionally delicious dips, sides, salads, pickles and trimmings. The tomato salad, made from crunchy green tomatoes, is a work of art. Located adjacent to the steps that lead to Thein Taung Paya; the English-language sign says 'Myanmar Restaurant'.

Ma Hnin Si Cafe   TEAHOUSE
(Bu Tar St; mains from K200; ⊙6am-6pm) There's a tiny English-language sign here, but a better locator is the crowd of locals enjoying plates of *pakoda* (vegetables fried in lentil-flour batter) and other tasty deep-fried snacks and excellent noodle dishes.

Everest Nepali Food Centre   NEPALI $
(Aung Chan Thar St; set meals K2500-3000; ⊙9am-9pm; 🛜) Relive memories of trekking in Nepal with a plate of *dhal baht* (rice served with lentils and other side dishes) at this convivial eatery run by a Nepali family.

Pyae Pyae Shan Noodle   SHAN $
(Union Hwy (NH4); mains from K500; ⊙7am-8pm) This cosy, friendly shop sells delicious bowls of the eponymous noodle, and has an English-language menu of other one-plate dishes.

Thiri Gay Har Restaurant   INTERNATIONAL, BURMESE $$
(Seven Sisters; Union Hwy (NH4); mains K2000-4500; ⊙10am-10pm; 🍴) Gentrified but relatively full-flavoured Burmese – as well as Shan, Chinese and Western – is served at this cute cottage.

Morning Star   TEAHOUSE
(Kone Thai St; snacks from K200; ⊙6am-6pm) A cuppa at this colourful teashop is accompanied by a platter of tasty Indian sweets.

Hi Snack & Drink   BAR
(Kone Thai St; ⊙5-10pm) Hi is the size of a closet and boasts a fun, speakeasy feel; if you

haven't had a rum here, you haven't been to Kalaw.

🔒 Shopping

R.D.S. Shop HANDICRAFTS

(Min St; ⊘9am-6pm) Representing the commercial wing of the Rural Development Society, this shop sells fabrics, clothing and handmade paper produced by local tribes. Profits go towards development projects in local Shan and Pa-O villages, and the organisation can also arrange treks.

ℹ️ Information

KBZ Bank (Min St) has an ATM that accepts international cards, and a currency exchange counter (9am to 2pm Monday to Saturday).

Internet is available at **Cyber World** (Aung Chan Thar St; per hr K1000; ⊘8am-11pm) and **Sky Net** (Kone Thai St; per hr K500; ⊘7am-midnight).

ℹ️ Getting There & Away

Several **bus ticket offices** (Union Hwy (NH4)) across from the market, as well as English-speaking Dev Singh at **Sun Shine** (Union Hwy (NH4); ⊘7am-9pm), book seats on the long-distance buses between Kalaw and various destinations. Air-con buses, fan-cooled minivans and pick-ups to other destinations in and around Shan State also stop along this stretch of the Union Hwy (NH4),

but it's worth noting that fares for foreigners are routinely doubled.

Small local **minibuses** bound for Taunggyi depart every morning from a stop behind the Aung Chang Tha Zedi; these buses can drop you off in Aungban (for Pindaya), Heho (airport) or Shwenyaung (for Inle Lake). Nearby, the morning **minibus to Loikaw** (Kone Thai St) departs from in front of Morning Star.

Kalaw's **train station** is a stop on the slow, winding line that links Thazi and Shwenyaung, as well as the line that links Loikaw and Nay Pyi Taw. Note that trains often leave hours behind the official departure times.

Kalaw has no airport of its own, but flights are served via Heho, about 16 miles away. For details on flights, see p197. Taxis waiting at the airport charge K20,000 to Kalaw (1½ hours); a cheaper option is to hike the near mile to the Union Hwy and wait for a westbound bus or pick-up, although you may face a long wait.

ℹ️ Getting Around

Most people choose to walk around town but **motorcycle taxis** at the corner of Kone Thai and Bu Tar Sts can run you to Hnee Paya or the Shwe Oo Min caves and back for around K3000.

Bicycles can be rented at **Naing Naing Hire Bike** (📱09 4283 12265; naing.cc@gmail.com; Min St; per day K2000; ⊘8.30am 5pm).

TRANSPORT TO/FROM THAZI

Destination	Bus	Minibus & Pick-Up	Train
Aungban (for Pindaya)	N/A	K5000; 4hr; frequent 7am-11pm	N/A
Loikaw	N/A	K7000-10,000; 10hr; daily 5.30pm	N/A
Kalaw	N/A	K5000; 5hr; frequent 7am-11pm	$2-5; 9hr; daily 6am
Mandalay	K5000; 3hr; frequent 11am-3pm	K5000; 3hr; frequent 11am-3pm	$3-7; 3hr; daily 3am, 6am & 9pm
Meiktila	N/A	K1000; 30min; frequent 4am-6pm	N/A
Nay Pyi Taw	K3000; 4hr; daily 5pm & 6pm	N/A	$3-6; 4hr; daily 11am
Nyaung U (Bagan)	K5000; 7-4hr; frequent 12.30pm	N/A	N/A
Shwenyaung (for Inle Lake)	N/A	K7000; 6hr; frequent 7am-11pm	$3-7; 5hr; daily 6am
Taunggyi	N/A	K7000; 7hr; frequent 7am-11pm	N/A
Yangon	K10,000; 9-10hr; daily 5pm & 6pm	N/A	$9-24; 11-12hr; daily 9am, 6pm & 8pm

Thazi

သာစည်

064 / POPULATION C10,000

Thazi crops up on travellers' itineraries for one reason only – the town marks the intersection of the Mandalay–Yangon rail line and the highway towards Inle Lake and the Thai border.

If you need to stay overnight, you can do a lot worse than the **Moon-Light Rest House** (09 222 5081, 064-69056; Thazi-Taunggyi Hwy; r $10-15; ❋ ☎). The basic rooms are clean, the atmosphere is wholesome, the welcome is genuine and the attached restaurant serves good food. Staff can help out with travel arrangements.

Internet (Thazi-Taunggyi Hwy; per hr K400; ⊙9am-9pm) is available across the street from Moon-Light Rest House.

Most people arrive in Thazi by train – the station is about 300yd north of the main road. Buses drop off and pick up passengers along the highway near Moon-Light Rest House. Fares are typically doubled for foreigners. To get a seat on one of the more comfortable express buses between Mandalay and Taunggyi, you'll need to make an advance reservation – the staff at the Moon-Light can help.

KYAINGTONG & BORDER AREAS

Beyond Taunggyi, the landscape rucks up into great folds, cloaked in dense forest and cut by rushing mountain rivers. This is the heartland of the Golden Triangle, where the opium trade formerly flourished and insurgent armies battled for independence for most of the last century. Ceasefires with the main rebel groups have largely allowed the region to move out of the shadow of civil war, but drug trafficking and other illegal activities are common, and travel to the border areas is still largely subject to confusing government-imposed travel restrictions.

Kyaingtong

ကျိုင်းတုံ

084 / POPULATION C20,000

The second-biggest city in Shan State, Kyaingtong, also known as Kengtung or sometimes Chiang Tung, is one of the most attractive towns in Myanmar. In culture and appearance, it feels closer to the hill towns of northern Thailand and southern China, and the vast majority of the town's residents belong to one of several Tai ethnic groups: Shan, Tai Lü, Tai Khün and Tai Nuea.

For years, Kyaingtong was caught in the crossfire between rival drug lords, but peace has returned to the quiet, pagoda-lined streets. The rugged terrain of eastern Shan State contributes to the sense of isolation – Kyaingtong is an outpost of development in a sea of largely deforested mountains, where Wa, En, Shan, Akha and Lahu tribal people follow a way of life that has changed little in centuries. Needless to say, visits to hill-tribe villages are a major attraction.

⊙ Sights

If there were many more Buddhist monasteries in Kyaingtong, people would have nowhere left to live. The town's many monasteries are called *wat* rather than *kyaung*, and local monks wear both orange and red robes, reflecting the close cultural links to Thailand.

The old British enclave in Kyaingtong was centred on **Nyaung Toung** (ညောင်တုန်း; Kan Rd), a lake popular for morning and evening strolls. There are several decaying colonial buildings above the lake shore, including the handsome **Colony House** (Mine Yen Rd). On the road leading towards Taunggyi, the **Roman Catholic Mission** (off Tachileik-Taunggyi Rd (Main Rd)) and **Immaculate Heart Cathedral** (off Tachileik-Taunggyi Rd (Main Rd)) have been providing an education for hill-tribe orphans since colonial times.

★**Central Market**   MARKET
(ဩို့ပွဲရုံး; Zeigyi Rd; mains from K500; ⊙5am-1pm) Kyaingtong's Central Market is one of our favourites in Myanmar, and plays host to an exotic mix of tribal people from the hills, heaps of fresh and unusual produce and delicious breakfast stalls. The market is closed on full-moon days.

Wat Jong Kham   BUDDHIST TEMPLE
(ဝတ်ကျုံခန်း; off Mine Yen Rd; ⊙daylight hours) The gilded stupa of Wat Jong Kham rises majestically above the centre of town. Legend dates the *wat* to a visit by Gautama Buddha, but a more likely date for the stupa is the 13th-century Thai migration from Chiang Mai.

Yat Taw Mu   BUDDHIST TEMPLE
(ရပ်တော်မူ; off Tachileik-Taunggyi Rd (Main Rd); ⊙daylight hours) Pointing dramatically towards the mountains on a ridge

Kyaingtong

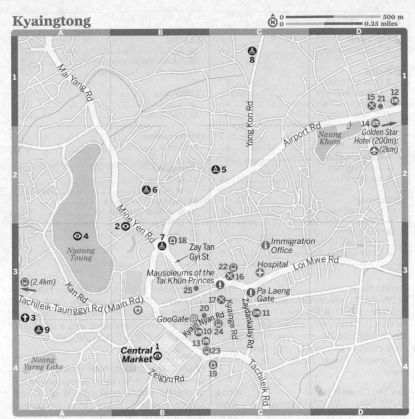

overlooking Nyaung Toung lake, the 60ft-high standing buddha statue known as Yat Taw Mu is probably the most distinctive landmark in Kyaingtong. Next to the statue is a dusty **Cultural Museum** (admission $2 or K2000; ⊙ 10am-4pm Tue-Sun) with an emphasis on costumes, as well as some farming implements and other tribal objects, some inexplicably painted silver.

Wat Mahamuni　　　　BUDDHIST TEMPLE
(ဝတ်မဟာမုနိ; Mine Yen Rd; ⊙ daylight hours) **FREE** In the middle of a traffic roundabout, Wat Mahamuni is a classic Thai-style *wat* with a richly painted interior.

Wat In　　　　BUDDHIST TEMPLE
(ဝတ်အင်း; off Airport Rd; ⊙ daylight hours) **FREE** Just north of Airport Rd, Wat In contains a stunning collection of ancient gilded wooden buddha images in all shapes, sizes and positions.

✹ Festivals & Events

Kyaingtong's Chinese community celebrate the **Chinese New Year** in early February with the usual firecracker-charged festivities.

For Buddhists, the big calendar event is the **Water Festival** in April, when everyone gets a dousing, including visitors.

🛏 Sleeping

The accommodation scene in Kyaingtong will inspire few postcards home. As is the case elsewhere in Myanmar, breakfast is included in the fee and electricity is scarce; most hotels run generators from about 7pm to 10pm.

Sam Yweat Hotel　　　　HOTEL **$**
(☏ 084-21235; www.samywethotel.blogspot.com; cnr Kyaing Lan 1 Rd & Kyaing Lan 4 Rd; r $30-35; ❋) A large concrete building holding 27 rooms, which don't have much in the way of charm, but feel new, clean and spacious.

Kyaingtong

Private Hotel
HOTEL $

(☎ 084-21438; www.privatehotelmyanmar.com; 5 Airport Rd; r $35-42; ❄ @) The rooms here surround a tidy lawn, are comfortable and well maintained, and the eccentric owner makes every effort to please. The only downside is the location, a long hike from the centre of town.

Law Yee Chain Hotel
HOTEL $

(☎ 084-23242; hotelktg.lyc@gmail.com; Kyain Nyan Rd; s/d $25/35; ❄ 🛜) Above a Chinese bakery just south of the market, the rooms here are pretty plain and verge on aged, and the only real perks are the convenient location and wi-fi.

Sam Ywet Guest House
GUESTHOUSE $

(☎ 084-21643; Airport Rd; r $10-20) It's not exactly downtown, but this is the closest Kyaingtong has to a recommendable and conveniently located cheapie. The basic rooms here are fan-cooled and have cold-water showers.

Harry's Trekking House
GUESTHOUSE $

(☎ 084-21418; harry.guesthouse@gmail.com; 132 Mai Yang Rd; r $7-20; ❄) A hodge-podge of air-con rooms with TV and attached bathroom and simple fan-cooled rooms. Treks and transport can be arranged from here. Inconveniently located 1½ miles north of the centre of Kyaingtong.

Princess Hotel
HOTEL $$

(☎ 084-21319; kengtung@mail4u.com.mm; 21 Zaydankalay Rd; r $50; ❄) The most popular mid-range choice in town, the Princess Hotel has a convenient location near the market, and capable service. The rooms are large and clean, and come equipped with a television, air-conditioning, a fridge and a phone.

Golden Star Hotel
HOTEL $$

(☎ 084-22411; goldenstarhotelktg@gmail.com; Airport Rd; r $55-65; ❄ 🛜) Kyaingtong's newest hotel has the architectural subtlety of a North Korean embassy. If you have no qualms with this particular aesthetic, the 52 rooms are spacious and generously equipped with air-con, TV, fridge and wi-fi, although it is located a fair hike outside the centre of town.

✕ Eating

Nearly all of Kyaingtong's restaurants serve Chinese food as perceived through a Burmese (ie oily) lens. For local eats, your only options are the breakfast stalls at the morning market (p210) or dinner with a generous local family.

Lod Htin Lu Restaurant
CHINESE-BURMESE $

(Kyange Rd; mains from K1500; ⏱ 10am-9pm) This longstanding restaurant features OK takes on dishes such as *mapo tofu* and other Chinese classics.

Golden Banyan Restaurant
CHINESE-BURMESE $

(Zay Tan Gyi St; mains from K1500; ⏱ 10am-9pm) Popular among tourists, the mostly Chinese-style food here is pretty standard, but the outdoor tables beneath a huge banyan tree create atmosphere.

EASTERN MYANMAR KYAINGTONG

Best Choice Restaurant   CHINESE-BURMESE **$**
(Airport Rd; mains from K1500; ☺10am-9pm) This Chinese restaurant has a cosy dining room at the back and tables under an awning in the yard.

🛍 Shopping

★U Mu Ling Ta   LACQUERWARE
(off Tachileik Rd; ☺8am-5pm) This fifth-generation, family-run shop specialises in lacquerware, from the ubiquitous multi-coloured Bagan style to the striking, black Kyaingtong style. Pieces are made on-site, so you can get a peek into the production process if you don't have the budget for a purchase (they're not cheap). The shop is located at the top of an unmarked driveway on Tachileik Rd – locals should be able to point you in the right direction.

Blacksmith   HANDICRAFTS
(off Mine Yen Rd; ☺8am-4pm) East of Wat Jong Kham is this home-bound blacksmith. The Shan family here make daggers, knives and swords, the latter used in local wedding ceremonies. You can watch the smithy at work, and all items arc available for purchase, with prices starting at around K6000.

OFF THE BEATEN TRACK

DAY TRIPS AROUND KYAINGTONG

The hills outside of Kyaingtong are dotted with the villages of the En, Lahu Akha, Palaung, Loi, Lishaw and Wa tribes, as well as those of various Tai groups. As of 2013, the local authorities have allowed overnight stays, but a guide and advance permission with the authorities in Kyaingtong are required. Recommended guides include **Sai Leng** (☎09 4903 1470; sairoctor.htunleng@gmail.com), **Freddie** (Yot Kham; ☎09 4903 1934; yotkham@gmail.com) and **Paul** (Sai Lon; ☎084-22812, 09 4903 0464), and guide fees run from $20 to $25 per day. Transport can be arranged at Princess Hotel or Harry's Trekking House.

The most popular destination is **Pin Tau**, only 9 miles north of Kyaingtong, where it's possible to visit the villages of several tribes in a single day. A round-trip taxi here will cost around K40,000.

Ho Kyim, approximately 10 miles south of town, is home to several Loi, Akha and Lahu villages. A round-trip taxi here costs around K50,000.

The area surrounding the atmospheric Tai Khün village of **Wan Sai** is home to several worthwhile sights. From Wan Sai, where many residents still live in traditional wooden homes, it's a brief walk to an Akhu village, and another 30- to 40-minute walk to **Ho Lang**, a hilltop En village. Along the same road, and with great views of the Tai Khün village of **Wan Loi** and the river valley, is **That Jom Loi**, a hilltop temple. The area is located a 45-minute drive east of Kyaingtong; a taxi trip to these destinations will run to about K40,000.

Located a 40-minute drive northwest of Kyaingtong is the jumping-off point for **Lahu Shi**, a remote Lahu village accessible only via an arduous three-hour uphill slog. Also north of town, off the road that leads to Mong La, **Wan Nyek** and **Wan Saen** are two villages where the Loi people still live in traditional longhouses. A taxi to either of these trailheads costs K40,000.

Loi-mwe, 20 miles southeast of Kyaingtong, functioned as a second-tier hill station in the British era and you can still see a number of fading **colonial buildings** and a 100-year-old Catholic **church**. The main attraction, though, is the drive up here through a landscape of hills and terraced rice fields. A taxi here should run around K55,000.

If you don't have the time or funds for a trek, a good **self-guided walk** can be had along the former road to Mong La, now colloquially known as Yang Kon Rd. The area is home to several Shan families who earn a living by making **pottery** and *khao sen* (fermented rice noodles), the latter made by a laborious process of boiling, pounding and squeezing a dough of rice flour. Your walk terminates at **Wat Yang Kin** (ဝတ်ရန်ကင်း; Yang Kon Rd; ☺daylight hours) **FREE**, known among locals for the decorative robes covering the main buddha statue.

TRANSPORT TO/FROM KYAINGTONG

Destination	Air	Bus	Pick-Up	Van (Share Taxi)
Heho	$119-154; 55min; Mon-Wed, Sat & Sun	N/A	N/A	N/A
Mandalay	$129-158; 25min-1½hr; daily (direct or via Heho)	N/A	N/A	N/A
Mong La	N/A	N/A	K5000; 4hr; frequent 7am-3pm	K15,000-20,000; 3hr; frequent 7am-3pm
Tachileik	N/A	K10,000; 4-5hr; daily 8am & 11.30am	N/A	K12,000-15,000; 3-4hr; frequent 6am-noon
Yangon	$159-198; 2hr 45min; daily (via Heho & Mandalay)	N/A	N/A	N/A

ⓘ Information

At research time, private banks with ATM/exchange hadn't yet hit Kyaingtong, and you'll have to rely on the moneychangers in the market.

GooGate (off Kyain Nyan Rd; per hr K500; ⊙9am-9pm) Conveniently located internet access off Kyain Nyan Rd.

Immigration Office (cnr Zay Tan Gyi St & Yang Kon Rd; ⊙24hr) Down an alley north of Pa Laeng Gate; issues permits for travel around Kengtung and to Mong La and Tachileik.

Sunfar Travels (☑084-28133; Kyain Nyan Rd; ⊙7am-4pm) Sells tickets for all the private airlines.

ⓘ Getting There & Away

Shwe Myo Taw Express (☑084-23145; Tachileik Rd) and **Thet Nay Wun** (Kyain Nyan Rd), with offices in town, run air-con buses to Tachileik. Vans (share taxis) bound for Tachileik or Mong La depart from from Kyaingtong's **bus station**, west of town. If you're pinching pennies, insanely crowded **pick-ups to Mong La** depart from a stand north of Zay Tan Gyi St.

ⓘ TRAVEL RESTRICTIONS

➡ At research time, foreign travellers were allowed to travel by road between Tachileik and Mong La, and by air between Kyaingtong and Tachileik and the rest of Myanmar, but the 280 miles of Union Highway (NH4) between Kyaingtong and Taunggyi remained completely off-limits.

➡ If you crossed to this part of Myanmar by land without having obtained a visa in advance, there are a few caveats; see p217 for details.

Several airlines, including **Air Bagan** (☑084-22867, in Yangon 01-513 322; www.airbagan.com; Airport Rd; ⊙9am-5pm Mon-Sat, to noon Sun), **Air KBZ** (☑084-23593, in Yangon 01-373 787; www.airkbz.com; Airport Rd; ⊙7.30am-7.30pm) and **Yangon Airways** (☑084-22798, in Yangon 01-383 100; www.yangonair.com; 36 Zay Tan Gyi St; ⊙9am-5pm) connect Kyaingtong and other destinations in northern Myanmar via a confusing, web-like flight map. Note that several flights aren't direct, with many – including flights to Yangon – involving sometimes as many as two stops. Be sure to double-check before buying your ticket. Taxis charge K5000 and *thoun bein* K3000 for the 2-mile trip to/from Kyaingtong's airport.

Mong La ဗိုင်းလား

☑(+86) 691 / POPULATION C20,000

Located on the Chinese border, Mong La lies within Myanmar, but is part of semi-autonomous Wa State, a finger of land controlled by the United Wa State Army (UWSA), an ethnic militia associated with drug production and trafficking. The Wa – former headhunters – have their own government, license plates (attached, almost exclusively, to white '90s-era sedans) and road signs. Chinese is the lingua franca in Wa State, and the Chinese yuan (Y) is the currency.

Until the border with China was closed to all but locals in 2005, Mong La was the epitome of the wild border town. Those days are over, but the abandoned casinos and bustling Chinese atmosphere provide a bizarre contrast with the largely traditional Tai Lü villages that surround Mong La.

◉ Sights & Activities

Most people come to Mong La to gamble, although most of the casinos have moved to **Wan Siw**, a village a few miles west of Mong La. The casinos aren't exactly foreigner-friendly, generally featuring games that most Western tourists aren't familiar with while also requiring gamblers to exchange a certain amount of money (usually around US$50) into non-refundable chips upon entry.

Perhaps Mong La's most infamous sight is its **central market**, a known hotspot for wildlife trafficking.

Museum in Commemoration of Opium-Free in Special Region   MUSEUM
(⊙24hr) FREE In 1997 Mong La was declared 'drug-free' by the Wa authorities, and this temple-like museum was their effort to promote this. In addition to photos, maps and paraphernalia, inside the dusty and neglected building you'll find creepy life-sized dioramas: one shows long-haired, leather-coat-wearing Myanmar youth abusing drugs before eventually, post-rehab, sporting a new haircut and a pressed *longyi*, 'come to the normal stream of life'.

That Luang Mong La   BUDDHIST TEMPLE
(သက်လောင်းမိုင်းလား; ⊙daylight hours) FREE This golden hilltop temple has views over the Chinese border post and Mong La. Inside, you'll find an immense Buddha statue and dioramas of famous religious sites across Myanmar.

Day Trips Around Mong La

There's huge potential for trekking among various ethnic groups outside Mong La, but at research time few routes had been established and overnight stays were generally not encouraged.

Destinations outside of Mong La include **Mong Puen**, a Tai Lü village a 30-minute drive east of Mong La, where there's a crumbling old Buddhist temple and where most of the 69 families live in traditional wooden houses; **Wat Nong Luang**, an old Buddhist temple accessible only via a very rough four-hour drive; and **Nam Yi**, a village home to a large Buddha image. A car and driver to most destinations around Mong La should cost around Y400 to Y500 per day.

🛏 Sleeping & Eating

Mong La's hotels are some of the grottiest and dodgiest we've seen anywhere, which

coming from a Lonely Planet author, is saying a lot.

The city's central market is the place to go for food; Chinese-style noodles and steamed buns are available at breakfast, and at lunch and dinner, open-air Chinese restaurants line the perimeter.

Kai Xuan Hotel   HOTEL $$
(🖥(+86) 691-556 8555; no roman-script sign; r Y220-260, ste Y580-680; ❋@) By far the best hotel we encountered in Mong La. Rooms are new-feeling and come equipped with thoughtful amenities ranging from a desktop computer to a flat-screen TV with a free porn channel! There's no English-language sign, but Kai Xuan is the imposing pink building opposite the northwest corner of the market.

ℹ Information

Chinese yuan is the currency in Mong La; be sure to change in advance at Kyaingtong's central market.

If entering Wa State via private vehicle, you'll need to pay at Y40 car tax at the first UWSA checkpoint. Arriving in Mong La, it's also necessary to pay the Wa State authorities for a site fee (Y36) and a service charge (Y30), payable at **Shwe Lin Star Tourism** (🖥(+86) 691-556 9331; shwelinstar@hotmail.com; ⊙7.30am-3pm).

ℹ Getting There & Away

Mong La's **bus station** is about a mile west of town. It's here that you can get a seat on infrequent vans (K15,000 to K20,000, three hours, from 6am to 5pm) or a bench on a dangerously overcrowded pick-up (K5000, four hours, from 10am to 3pm) to Kyaingtong.

ℹ Getting Around

Most of Mong La's sights are outside of the city centre, so if you don't already have one, you'll want to hire a car and driver. Hiring in Mong La, prices start at about Y400 per day.

ℹ TRAVEL RESTRICTIONS

➡ At research time, non-Chinese travellers were not allowed to cross to/from China at Mong La.

➡ If you arrived in Myanmar via land at Tachileik and left your passport at the border, a guide and permits are required to visit Mong La. If you haven't already arrived with a guide from Kyaingtong or elsewhere, you'll be required to hire one in Mong La for Y100 per day.

TRANSPORT TO/FROM TACHILEIK

Buses and vans (share taxis) depart from Tachileik's bus station, 2km and a 20 baht (B) truck ride or a K1500/50B motorcycle taxi ride from the border. At research time, a new bus station, a couple miles beyond the present one, was under construction.

Air Bagan (☑ 084-51929, in Yangon 01-513 322; www.airbagan.com; 1/11 Bogyoke Aung San Rd; ⊘ 9am-5pm)

Air KBZ (☑ 09 4903 6646, in Yangon 01-373 787; www.airkbz.com; 1/205 Bogyoke Aung San Rd; ⊘ 9am-5pm)

Asian Wings (☑ 084-53270, in Yangon 01-515 259; www.asianwingsair.com; 1/157-C Bogyoke Aung San Rd; ⊘ 9am-5pm)

Yangon Airways (☑ 01-383 100, 084-53211; www.yangonair.com; 18 Bogyoke Aung San Rd; ⊘ 9am-5pm) fly to/from Tachileik's airport, located roughly near the new bus station.

Destination	Air	Bus	Van (Share Taxi)
Heho	$119-135; 55min-1hr 15 minutes; Mon, Tue, Fri & St (direct or via Mandalay)	N/A	N/A
Kyaingtong	$62; 18min; Wed & Sun	K10,000; 4-5hr; frequent 7.30am-12.30pm	K12,000-15,000; 3-4hr; frequent 6am-noon
Lashio	$194-240; 40min-1hr 15min; Tue, Thur & Sat	N/A	N/A
Mandalay	$129; 25min-1½hr; Mon, Tue, Fri & St (direct or via Heho or Lashio)	N/A	N/A
Myitkyina	$193; 1hr 40min; Wed & Fri	N/A	N/A
Yangon	$197; 1¾hr; Tue, Wed, Fri & Sat (direct or via Mandalay & Heho)	N/A	N/A

Tachileik   တာချီလိတ်

☑ 084 / POPULATION C20,000

Facing the town of Mae Sai across the Thai-Myanmar border, this hectic town is like border towns all over Asia – it's a border post and a magnet for black-market goods, with not much else to offer.

If you're stuck overnight in Tachileik, **River Side Hotel** (☑ 084-51161; r 700-900B; ❋) is acceptable, but accommodation on the Thai side is better in every respect; the **Khanthongkham Hotel** (☑ 0 5373 4222; www.kthotel.com; 7 Th Phahonyothin; r incl breakfast 800-900B, ste incl breakfast 1200-1650B; ❋ ☎), near the border in Mae Sai, is recommended.

KAYAH STATE

Wedged between Shan State to the north and west, Kayin State to the west and south, and Thailand to the east, tiny Kayah State (ကယားပြည်နယ်) – Myanmar's smallest – is

home to a disproportionate number of tribal groups, including the Yinbaw, Bre, Kayin (Karen), the eponymous Kayah (Karenni or Red Karen), and perhaps most famously, the 'longneck' Kayan (also known as Padaung).

After years of only being open to pre-approved package tourists, Kayah State is now 'open' to Foreign Independent Travellers (FITs), although only a handful have made it to the area. This doesn't mean you can go anywhere, though; at research time, only the capital Loikaw, and parts of Deemawsoe Township, an hour southeast of Loikaw, were accessible, and only for day trips.

Loikaw   လွိုင်ကော်

☑ 083 / POPULATION C20,000

The capital of Kayah State is a tidy-feeling town on the Pilu River. There's one must-see sight in Taung Kwe Paya; other than that, it's more about exploring the surrounding areas and spending time in a low-key destination where relatively few other travellers have been.

⊙ Sights

★ **Taung Kwe Paya** BUDDHIST TEMPLE
(တောင်ကွဲဘုရား; NH5; camera fee K500; ⊗ daylight hours) Virtually rocketing from the landscape is this explosion of craggy limestone and white and gold stupas. The mountaintop Buddhist temple compound is Kayah State's most famous sight, and the *loi kaw* (Shan for 'island of mountains') are allegedly the origin of the town's name. Even if you're templed out, the wacky Buddhist Disneyland vibe is heaps of fun, and the views of the town and countryside really are breathtaking.

To the east extend a few other similar rock-topped temples, including **Tat Tapin Mont**, 'One Tree Mountain'. On ground level, the area includes a huge **reclining Buddha** and **Poke Hpayone Paya**, Kayah State's largest monastery with more than 500 monks and novices.

ⓘ GETTING TO THAILAND: TACHILEIK TO MAE SAI

As of 2013, Tachileik is one of Myanmar's newly 'open' land borders for foreign tourists. But there are a few caveats, and the following information is liable to change, so be sure to check the situation locally before you travel.

Getting to the border The border is a short walk from 'downtown' Tachileik, or just over a mile (2km) and a 20B truck ride or a K1500/50B motorcycle taxi ride from the town's bus station.

At the border If you've arrived in Kyaingtong or Tachileik via air from elsewhere in Myanmar, you can freely exit the country at Tachileik. The Myanmar border post is open from 6am to 6pm, and upon crossing to Thailand, the Thai authorities will issue you permission to stay in Thailand up to 15 days, or you can enter with a Thai visa obtained overseas. Likewise, if you're crossing from Thailand and have already procured a Myanmar visa, you'll be allowed to proceed to Kyaingtong and/or Mong La, or by air to other destinations in Myanmar.

If you're approaching from Thailand and haven't already obtained a Myanmar visa, it's relatively straightforward to cross to Tachileik for the day, and slightly more complicated to get a two-week visa and permission to visit Kyaingtong and/or Mong La. The **Thai immigration office** (☑ 05 373 1008) is open from 6.30am to 6.30pm.

After taking care of the usual formalities, cross the bridge and head to the Myanmar immigration office. There, you must pay a fee of 500B and your picture is taken for a temporary ID card that allows you to stay in town for the day; your passport will be kept at the office.

If you'd like to visit Kyaingtong and/or Mong La, proceed directly to the MTT office. There, you'll need to inform the authorities exactly where you're headed, and you'll need three photos and US$10 or 500B to process a border pass valid for 14 days; your passport will be kept at the border during this time, and you're expected to exit Myanmar at Tachileik. It's also obligatory to hire a guide for the duration of your stay. Guides cost 1000B per day. If you haven't already arranged for a Kyaingtong-based guide to meet you at the border, you'll be assigned one by MTT and will also have to pay for your guide's food and accommodation during the duration of your stay. Recommended Kyaingtong-based guides include Sai Leng, Freddie and Paul (see boxed text on p213 for more their details). Note that if you're crossing this way, advance permission from MTT is required to visit other destinations in Myanmar.

Moving on Mae Sai's bus station is 1.5km from the border; pick-ups ply the route between the bus station and Soi 2, Th Phahonyothin (15B, five minutes, from 6am to 9pm). Alternatively, it's a 50B motorcycle taxi ride to/from the stand at the corner of Th Phahonyothin and Soi 4. From Mae Sai, major bus destinations include Bangkok (673B to 943B, 12 hours, frequent from 4pm to 5.45pm), Chiang Mai (182B to 364B, five hours, nine departures from 6.15am to 4.30pm) and Chiang Rai (39B to 69B, 1½ hours, frequent from 5.45am to 6pm). For further information, head to www.shop.lonelyplanet.com to purchase a downloadable PDF of the Northern Thailand chapter from Lonely Planet's latest *Thailand* guide.

There is no direct transport to Mong La from Tachileik. See p220 for details on getting to Kyaingtong.

OPEN OR NOT?

In the months before I hit the ground to research this book, several destinations across Myanmar had been declared 'open', meaning that for the first time in decades, Foreign Independent Travellers (FITs) could visit them without a guide or prior permission from MTT in Yangon. But as I discovered firsthand, these central government missives sometimes meant little or nothing to the localities in question.

Kayah State was one such destination. I had chartered a boat from Inle Lake to Phe Khon (ဖယ်ခုံ), less than an hour by truck from Loikaw, the state capital. According to the Myanmar Ministry of Foreign Affairs, Loikaw was an 'open' area, and although Kayah State had previously seen some package tourists, only a handful of FITs had ever visited the area before I rolled in.

My decision seemed doomed from the start. Within seconds of arriving in Phe Khon I was set upon by Michael, the obligatory 'helpful' English-speaking local. Between sob stories, Michael reiterated that he would never accept any payment for his help – a surefire sign in my book that he was looking for money. No more than five minutes later – I still have no idea how these people knew that I'd arrived – a plain-clothes police officer appeared. My command of Burmese isn't great, but it was clear that he was drilling my boat drivers, asking them questions about who I was and why I was in Phe Khon. While Michael continued to explain how much he could help me, yet another plain-clothes officer appeared on the scene, followed by a brief cameo by the local homeless crazy man. Had I turned on some music and ordered some beers, we could have had a pretty wild party.

I had arranged for a Loikaw-based guide to meet me in Phe Khon, and when he eventually arrived, the plain-clothes officials escorted all of us to the home of the local immigration officer. Arriving at her home, she never spoke to me directly, but her message was clear: I was not welcome in Phe Khon and would have to go back to Nyaungshwe.

This initiated a flurry of communication: my guide called the travel agent in Nyaungshwe who claimed it was OK for me to take a boat to Phe Khon; the immigration officer called other immigration officers; my guide called an immigration office in Loikaw; there was shouting and tempers began to get heated. We shifted to Phe Khon's dusty immigration office where there were more loud phone calls, terse discussions and flipping through documents. At this point at least five people were involved, including a new arrival who did nothing but silently take notes, diligently jotting down all the phone numbers we had called.

It was at this point that I realised that, although I was responsible for all this fuss, I had essentially become irrelevant; nobody had once spoken to me or even looked in my direction. The situation had become about something greater than just me, and things were not looking good. The immigration official was not budging, and my guide had been told that the previous week she had turned three foreigners back. I assumed that the official simply wasn't aware of the new rules and didn't want to get herself in trouble, but my guide insisted that she was motivated by politics (he was NLD, she USDP) and/or fishing for a bribe.

Finally, more than two hours after I had arrived, my guide was able to get a hold of his friend, a high-ranking official in Loikaw's immigration office. After a sheepish phone conversation, the local immigration officer relinquished, allowing me to proceed only after making my guide write a handwritten letter declaring that he would never meet an FIT travelling from Nyaunshwe again – seemingly her last-ditch effort at saving face.

In the end, I made it to Loikaw, but the ordeal compounded the fact that even in the 'new' Myanmar, old paranoia, political alliances, personal connections and confounding bureaucracy remain as strong as ever – almost certainly stronger than the rule of law.

By Austin Bush, Lonely Planet author

Thiri Mingalarpon Kyaung　　BUDDHIST TEMPLE
(သီရိမင်္ဂလာပုံကျောင်း; Hawkyi Rd; admission by donation; ☉daylight hours) Dating back to 1912, this monastery formerly served as palace of Kayah *sao pha*, sky lords, until 1959. After the last *sao pha* passed away in 1987, his children donated the then-decaying structure to a local Buddhist organisation. Had they not done this the government,

at that time keen to do away with symbols of Kayah identity, would probably have allowed the building to fall into disrepair.

Christt the King Church
CHURCH

(off NH5; ⊙daylight hours) FREE Long the stomping ground of Roman Catholic missionaries, Kayah State is seemingly home to more churches than Buddhist temples. Built in 1939, this is the state's oldest remaining church, and has an attractive bell tower with a bell brought from Italy. These days, mass is held in a larger adjacent temple in Burmese, English, Kayan and Latin.

Kayah Cultural Museum
MUSEUM

(ကယားသ၍ကျေးမှုပြတိုက်; off NH5; admission $2 or K2000; ⊙9am-4pm Tue-Sun) Like most of Myanmar's regional museums, this vast hall is home to a disproportionately scant selection of dusty local relics and the usual display of mannequins wearing ethnic costumes, of which few have any English-language explanation.

🛏 Sleeping

Min Ma Haw
GUESTHOUSE $

(☑083-21451; 120 Kant Kaw Rd; r $30-40; 🌬) The 'econ' rooms here are are simple and bare, although some of the larger ones have en suite bathroom, TV and fridge. The air-con rooms are bigger and better, but not great.

Nan Ayar Inn
GUESTHOUSE $

(☑083-21306; Nat Thying Naung Rd; r $15-35) Simple but homey-feeling rooms in a bright green house by the river.

Moon Joy Inn
HOTEL $

(☑083-21618; 4 Thiri Rd; r K10,000-30,000; 🌬🖨) The 'econ' rooms in this unmissable purple house share bathrooms, while the more expensive have en suite, air-con and fridge.

Hotel Loikaw
HOTEL $$

(☑083-22946; www.hotelloikaw.com; 9 St; r $65-85; 🌬🖨) Loikaw's fanciest hotel is this new-feeling compound of rather flashy duplex bungalows that house 25 comparatively plain (but large) rooms. A five-storey annexe was being built when we were in town. Inconveniently located a long walk north of 'downtown' Loikaw.

🍴 Eating

For a tasty budget breakfast, head to the knot of **noodle stalls and teashops** (Shwe Taung Rd; mains from K500; ⊙6am-3pm) off Shwe Taung Rd.

Shan Noodle Shop
SHAN $

(NH5, no roman-script sign; mains from K500; ⊙6am-8pm) A Shan family here put together tasty bowls of *shàn k'auq-swèh*. The noodle shop is located on a corner, a block south of the monument; look for the large tree.

WORTH A TRIP

KAKKU

Arranged in neat rows sprawling over the hillside, the 2478 stupas at Kakku are one of the most remarkable sights in Shan State. According to local legend, the stupa garden was founded by the Buddhist missionaries of the Indian emperor Ashoka in the 3rd century BC. As such, the stupas at Kakku span a bewildering variety of styles, marking the prevailing architectural trends for whenever they were constructed. Some are simple and unadorned while others are covered in a riot of stucco deities and mythical beasts. Among the tall Shan-style stupas are a number of small square 'monastery style' stupas that are unique to this region. Like most ancient sites across the country, Kakku been extensively restored and modernised using donations from pilgrims, so don't expect an Indiana Jones–style ruin in the jungle.

The annual **Kakku Paya Pwe**, held on the full-moon day of the lunar month of Tabaung (March), attracts Pa-O pilgrims from across Shan State.

Kakku is surrounded by Pa-O villages and the site can be visited only with a Pa-O guide, arranged through **Golden Island Cottages** (☑21 23136; 18 Circular Rd East; ⊙6am-5pm). There's a $3 entry fee for the site and a $5 fee for the guide, and you must also arrange a taxi to the site – K35,000 from Taunggyi, including a few hours waiting at the stupas.

So far there isn't any accommodation at Kakku, but you can get a meal at the **Hlaing Konn Restaurant** (mains from K500; ⊙lunch & dinner Sep-Apr) overlooking the site.

Mingala Hin Htoke   BURMESE $

(Kant Kaw Rd, no roman-script sign; mains K500; ⊙9am-6pm) Locals come here for *hìn t'ouq*, an Intha dish of steamed banana leaf packets of rice with pork or chicken. Look for the tiny blue sign.

Shwe Let Yar   BURMESE $

(no roman-script sign; set meals from K2300; ⊙11am-7pm) Generally considered Loikaw's best curry restaurant; ask for the curry of the day and don't be afraid to try the delicious *balachaung*, a spicy dip.

❶ Information

At research time, Loikaw had neither ATM nor currency exchange; bring cash.

125 Internet Café (Kant Kaw Rd; per hr K500; ⊙9am-8pm)

Loikaw Travel Infos (☑09 4280 01621, 09 4927 8443; loikawtravel.infos@gmail.com) Natives of Loikaw, Htay Aung and Win Naing are the go-to guys for everything Kayah travel-related. They lead tours of the city and state (per day $30) and can arrange transport (per day from $50 to $80) and the permission necessary to visit areas outside of Loikaw.

❶ Getting There & Away

Loikaw's **bus station** (NH5) is located about 1.5 miles north of the centre of town on NH5; a *thoun bein* to/from here costs K1500.

Loikaw's **train station** is southeast of the centre of town, and is the terminus for a line that runs to Nay Pyi Taw. Not only are trains exceedingly slow, but station staff don't really know what to do with foreign travellers; you're better off taking the bus.

It's also possible to charter a **boat** from Phe Khon, an hour from Loikaw in Shan State, to Nyaungshwe (Inle Lake). The guys at Loikaw Travel Infos can arrange a boat, which costs at least K130,000 and takes about five to six hours. Be aware that, as of 2013, FITs travelling by boat from Nyaungshwe were routinely turned back in Phe Khon; see p218 for our experience.

Loikaw Airport (NH5) is just north of town. **Myanma Airways** (☑083-21014, in Yangon 01-246 452; www.myanmaairways.aero; NH5) conduct twice-weekly flights to/from Yangon ($63); contact a day in advance for departure/arrival times and days.

Around Loikaw

Although Kayah State had been declared 'open' only a few months before we hit the ground, visits without advance permission from MTT were limited to Loikaw, its immediate surrounding areas, and parts of Deemawsoe Township, a region 1½ hours south of Loikaw. Overnight stays outside of Loikaw are not permitted.

In **Dor Sor Bee**, just east of Loikaw, are several Kayah **animist shrines**. The towering logs, whitewashed and topped with decorations meant to symbolise the sun and moon, are gathering points during the Kayah New Year, in April. Also in the area are **Keinari Keinara**, a family-run loom making Kayah textiles, and **Pataing Hnyin**, a quiet Pa-O village. Loikaw Travel Infos include these sights on their day tour of Loikaw.

The only relatively remote area accessible without previous permission at research time was **Pah Pae**, a hilly and savagely deforested area in Deemawsoe Township that is home to five Kayan (Padaung or 'longneck') villages; for more on this ethnic group, see p332.

Rangkhu, the largest village, is also thought to be the largest Kayan village in Kayah State. On the surface at least, it appears to be a relatively modern village, but several women here still wear neck rings, and the village remains animist/Buddhist unlike its predominately Roman Catholic and Baptist neighbours. Loikaw Travel Infos requests a K10,000 donation to the villagers, and are working to reinstate overnight stays here – something not allowed since 1996. Pah Pae is about 1½ hours southeast of Loikaw; Loikaw Travel Infos can arrange permission to visit the area and car transport for $80. It's also working on ways to approach the village by foot or via boat.

At research time there were efforts to establish visits to **Tawtamagyi**, another Kayan village in Deemawsoe Township, and **Htay Ko**, a traditional tribal area in **Pruso Township**, southwest of Loikaw, but for the medium term at least, advance permission from MTT in Yangon is required to visit these areas.

Mandalay & Around

Best Religious Structures

➡ Bagaya Kyaung (p249)

➡ Mahamuni Paya (p228)

➡ Mingun Paya (p255)

➡ Pahtodawgyi (p249)

➡ Shwe In Bin Kyaung (p230)

Best Views

➡ River scenes, Ayarwaddy River View Hotel (p236)

➡ U-Bein Bridge (p248), Taungthaman Lake

➡ City panoramas, 10th-floor Skybar of Shwe Ingyin Hotel (p236)

➡ Sagaing from Shin Pin Nan Kain (p253) or Shwe-Kyet-Kya (p254)

Why Go?

For those who haven't been there – and that includes *The Road to Mandalay* author Rudyard Kipling – the mention of 'Mandalay' typically conjures up images of Asia at its most traditional and timeless. The initial reality can be a major anticlimax – a traffic-choked grid of interminable straight roads full of anonymous concrete buildings. But don't despair – though it's a relatively 'young', dynamic city, Mandalay is Myanmar's cultural capital. It's easy to escape from the fumes and architectural banalities of the main streets in quarters full of craft workshops and tree-shaded monasteries. The temple-topped Mandalay, Yankin and Yedagon Hills offer welcomed exceptions to the city's pan-flat topography, and several mini-theatres showcase traditional performing arts. Meanwhile, Mandalay is the main transport hub for northern Myanmar and offers a panoply of easy day-trip destinations, including four former royal capitals and the site of what would have been the world's biggest stupa, had it ever been finished.

When to Go
Mandalay

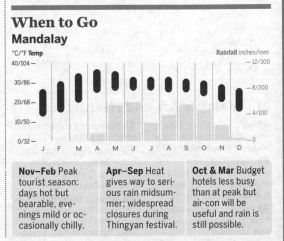

Nov–Feb Peak tourist season: days hot but bearable, evenings mild or occasionally chilly.

Apr–Sep Heat gives way to serious rain midsummer; widespread closures during Thingyan festival.

Oct & Mar Budget hotels less busy than at peak but air-con will be useful and rain is still possible.

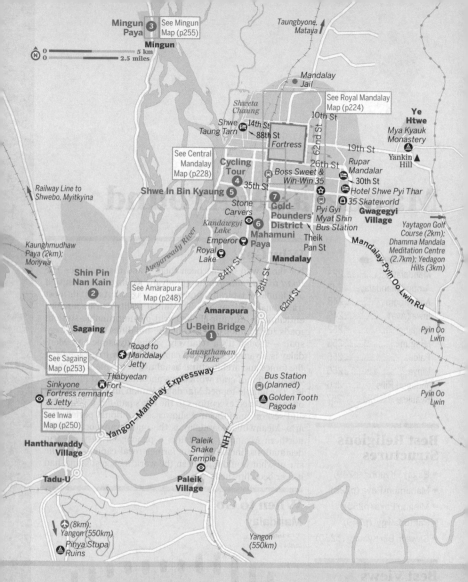

Mandalay & Around Highlights

1 Watch sunrise or sunset from the world's longest teak bridge, **U-Bein Bridge** (p248)

2 Survey Sagaing's monastery-dappled hills and gilded pagodas from **Shin Pin Nan Kain** (p253) pagoda

3 Ponder unfinished **Mingun Paya** (p255), reached by boat from Mandalay

4 Escape Mandalay's bustle with our **cycling tour** (p233)

5 Potter around Mandalay's lesser-known monasteries, including the teak masterpiece **Shwe In Bin Kyaung** (p230)

6 Arrive at **Mahamuni Paya** (p228) by 4am as attendants wash the face of the country's most famous buddha image

7 Discover crafts being made, including edible sheets of gold leaf, in the **Gold Pounders' District** (p227)

8 Witness the two-man **'elephant' dance** during an annual festival at little-visited Kyaukse (p257) or with free evening performances at Mya Nandar Restaurant (p240)

History

According to Myanmar myths, the Buddha himself visited Mandalay Hill and, in an earlier incarnation, had scuttled up the riverside bluff Shwe-kyet-kya (p254) in the guise of a chicken. In less legendary epochs, the Mandalay region hosted several of Burma's post-Bagan capitals. New kings often sought to create a legacy by founding a new capital, transporting whole buildings with them such that little remained at older sites. The longest-lasting of these capitals was Inwa (p249), known to Europeans as Ava. Mandalay itself only took shape as a city from 1857 and its brief, if momentous, period as a tailor-made capital city lasted less than 25 years from 1861. Despite powerful fortress walls that enclosed the gigantic royal city, the British had little trouble ejecting Mandalay's elite from their teak houses in 1885. They deported King Thibaw and demolished part of the original city to create a parade ground, turning the centrepiece palace complex into a governor's residence and club. Much later, during fierce WWII fighting in March 1945, the palace was ravaged by fire, leaving nothing of the original. New Mandalay grew outside the original walls into the vast concrete grid city you see today. The area within the walls was left as a vast tree-shaded army camp, and remains a strange military-controlled dead-zone, out of bounds to foreigners apart from the central palace. This was completely rebuilt in the late 1990s, reputedly using forced labour.

MANDALAY

02 / POPULATION C1,100,000 / ELEVATION 244FT

Hot, busy and not immediately beautiful, Mandalay is primarily used by travellers as a transport and day-trip hub. But even amid the central grid of lacklustre concrete-block ordinariness lurk many pagodas, striking churches, Indian temples and notable mosques. West of centre towards the fascinating Ayeyarwady (Irrawaddy) riverside, shadier backstreets link countless little-visited monasteries. And there's plenty of fascination to be found delving into a range of craft workshops and arts performances.

◉ Sights

Several of Mandalay's top attractions are covered by a K10,000 Archaeological Zone ('combo') ticket valid for one week from first purchase. Currently the ticket is only checked (and sold) at Mandalay Palace. Shwenandaw Kyaung, two sites at Inwa (Ava) and one minor one in Amarapura.

◉ Royal Mandalay

★ **Mandalay Hill** LANDMARK

(Map p224; camera fee K1000)
To get a sense of Mandalay's pancake-flat sprawl, climb the 760ft hill that breaks it. The barefooted walk up covered stairways on the hill's southern slope is a major part of the experience, passing through and around a colourful succession of prayer and shopping opportunities. The climb takes a good 30 minutes, but much longer if you allow for stops en route. The summit viewpoint is especially popular at sunset when young monks converge on foreigners for language practice.

➡ **South Routes**

There are two southern stairways. The most obvious starts between two giant **chinthe** (half-lion, half-dragon guardian deities) with 1729 steps. More interesting for glimpsed views, albeit harder on the feet, there's also an alternative southeastern stairway. The two routes converge then climb to a

---

NAVIGATING MANDALAY

Central Mandalay city streets are laid out on a grid system. East–west streets are numbered from 1st to 49th with 12th/26th as the north/south edges of the fortress moat. North–south streets are numbered over 50th, starting from the main Pyin Oo Lwin road in the east but becoming slightly confused west of diagonal 86th where some roads are more crooked and un-numbered.

A street address that reads '66th (26/27)' means a location on 66th St between 26th and 27th Sts. Corner addresses are given in the form '26th at 82nd'. The 'downtown' area runs roughly from 21st St to 35th St, between 80th St and 88th St. Across the railway tracks, 78th St 33/34 has the main new shopping malls while 30th, 35th and 73rd are all developing as busy commercial streets.

shrine building containing a large **standing Buddha** (Map p224), whose outstretched arm points towards the royal palace. This gesture evokes the legend in which the historical Buddha supposedly visited Burma, accompanied by his disciple Ananda, and on climbing Mandalay Hill prophesied that a great city would be founded below after 2400 years. Scholars calculated that to mean 1857 AD, the year that King Mindon did indeed decree the capital's move from Amarapura to Mandalay.

Further up, behind the forgettable **Myatsawnyinaung Ordination Hall** (Map

Royal Mandalay

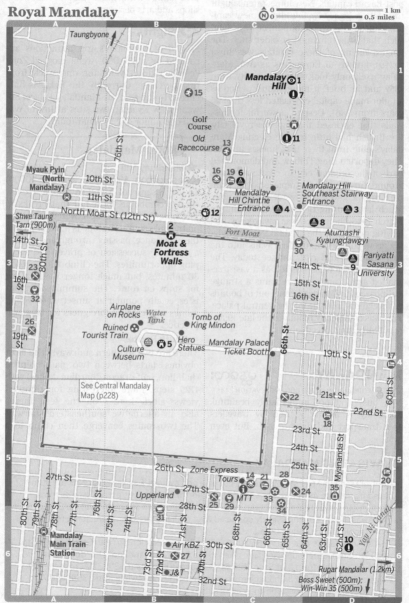

See Central Mandalay Map (p228)

p224) are the windowless ruins of a three-storey stone fortress retaken from the Japanese by Britain's Royal Berkshire Regiment in a March 1945 battle.

Near the summit, on the east side facing the penultimate stupa, a contemporary statue depicts ogress **San Dha Mukhi** (Map p224) offering forth her severed breasts. That's the sort of display that might have alarmed a more squeamish man, but according to legend, her bizarre feat of self-mutilation impressed the Buddha so much that he ensured her reincarnation 2400 years later as King Mindon.

➡ **Other Stairways**

Steeper stairways lead up from the north (25 minutes) or west (15 minutes) but there's little to see en route apart from canoodling couples (south) or lounging monks (west). Wear shoes for these stairways and, near the top of the south route, be prepared to clamber across/between a trio of pipes.

➡ **Vehicles**

It's possible to drive most of the way up Mandalay Hill. From the upper car park both a lift and an escalator tower should whisk you up to the hilltop. However, as both are often broken you'll probably need to walk the last five minutes by stairways.

From 10th St at 68th St, shared pick-up route 16 (per person K1000) shuttles to the car park. Motorcycle taxis typically charge K3000 up, K2000 down (even though the down route is much further due to a long one-way loop).

Shwenandaw Kyaung BUDDHIST MONASTERY
(ရွှေနန်းတော်ကျောင်း ; Golden Palace Monastery; Map p224; admission K10,000 combo ticket) Lavished in carved panels, this fine teak monastery-temple is noted for its carvings, particularly the interior gilded Jataka scenes (past-life stories of the Buddha). The building once stood within the Mandalay Palace complex as the royal apartment of King Mindon, who died inside it in 1878.

Reputedly unable to cope with Mindon's ghost, his successor, King Thibaw, had the building dismantled, carted out of the palace complex and reassembled outside the fortress walls, where it was converted into a monastery (1880). It's a good thing he did, as all other palace buildings were later lost to WWII bombs.

Kyauktawgyi Paya BUDDHIST TEMPLE
(ကျောက်တော်ကြီးဘုရား; Map p224; 12th St, 66/68; ⊙5am-8pm) FREE At the heart of this large 19th-century complex is a 900-tonne Buddha, 26ft tall and dressed in royal

attire. Carved from a single block of marble, it reputedly took 10,000 men 13 days to transport it from a canal to the present site before its dedication in 1865.

Outer halls are edged in mirror tiles. A little subshrine in the southeast courtyard displays a giant marble 'alms bowl' and colourful renderings of King Mindon's 1865 visit. The October temple festival is so big that stallholders start erecting evening food stalls along the eastern approach roads some two weeks before it starts.

★ Moat & Fortress Walls   FORTIFICATIONS
(Map p224) FREE Viewable only from the outside, a 230ft-wide moat and well over 4 miles of crenellated 26ft-high walls form a vast square around the site of the former Mandalay fortress/citadel. Reconstructed in the original 1857 style, the walls are punctuated at regular intervals with gatetowers topped by pyramidal creations of fancifully carved woodwork. Artful photography can make much of these scenes, but the overall effect isn't quite as impressive as you might anticipate, partly due to the sheer length and regularity of the walls.

Mandalay Palace   PALACE
(မန္တလေးနန်းတော်; Map p224; admission K10,000 combo ticket; ⊙ entry 7.30am-4.30pm) The glittering 1990s reconstruction of Mandalay's royal palace complex is impressive for its scale, with more than 40 timber buildings constructed to resemble the 1850s originals. Climb the curious spiral, timber-walled watchtower for a good general view. The palace's most striking structure is a soaring multi-

layered pyramid of gilt filigree above the main throne room, in front of which a series of royal paraphenalia are displayed. Few other halls have much inside but the westernmost building within the palace oval contains a minor culture museum where the most intriguing exhibit is King Thibaw's dainty, glass-pillared four-poster bed.

Palace access for foreigners is only via the fortress's east gate. If cycling or motorcycling you must dismount as you pass through the gate and, due to army sensibilities, you are required to stay on the direct access way and palace loop road. From this road you can see (but technically should not approach) the tomb of King Mindon, a large drum-tower, sheds containing over 600 stone inscription slabs and a small airplane on some rocks in the trees.

Peshawar Relics   BUDDHIST
(Map p224; U-Khanti Monastery; admission by donation; ⊙ 8am-6pm) Three tiny shards of bone, believed to be Buddha relics, were discovered in 1908 by British archaeologists at the site of a once-great ancient stupa at Peshawar (in today's Pakistan). For years they were displayed on Mandalay Hill but after thefts of associated gemstones alerted authorities to their vulnerability, the relics were moved to a loveable little museum room in the U-Khanti Monastery.

On request the monk will bring out the little reliquary, place it in a hexagonal light stand and offer the pilgrim a magnifying glass with which to examine in suitable awe the crystal phial within which the bones are almost invisibly housed.

WHITE ELEPHANTS

Legend has it that before giving birth to her auspicious son, the Buddha's mother dreamt of a white elephant presenting her with a lotus flower. In certain Buddhist countries this led to the idea that rare albino elephants were sacred and could not be put to work. Effectively of no practical use, yet expensive to feed, white elephants were thus seen by 19th-century Western observers to be the embodiment of financial extravagance. The term 'white elephant' eventually came to mean as much in standard English. However, in Burma/Myanmar and Siam/Thailand, the possession of white elephants was (and is) a potent symbol of kingship. Certain Burmese monarchs referred to themselves as 'golden-footed lord of the white elephant'. In 1885 when one of King Thibaw's white elephants died, it was interpreted as an omen foretelling the king's imminent demise at the hands of a British invasion force. And the Brits' insensitive decision to drag the elephant's carcass unceremoniously out of Mandalay Palace so horrified the pious city folk that the act helped spark 10 years of guerilla resistance.

Zoo

ZOO

(Map p224; main entrance on 12th St; foreigner/local/monk K2000/1000/200; ⊙8am-5pm) The 53-acre Yatanapon Zoological Gardens are attractively laid out and richly stocked, but the conditions of the tigers and sun bears are upsettingly cramped and elephants, often chained to the spot, are made to perform a show at weekends (2pm).

◉ Central Mandalay

Eindawya Paya

DUDDHIST TEMPLE

(အိမ်တော်ရာဘုရား; Map p228; Eindawya St, 88/89) **FREE** Ranged around a sizeable stupa glowing with gold leaf, Eindawa was founded in 1847 by King Pagan Min, whose princely palace once stood here.

In 1919, Eindawa was the site of a notable cultural battle when a group of Europeans defied the Buddhist ban on shoe-wearing and were forcibly evicted. For their pains, four of the monks who ejected the insensitive foreigners were convicted by a colonial court, one receiving a life sentence. So please take your shoes off!

Setkyathiha Paya

BUDDHIST TEMPLE

(မဟာသက်ျသိဟာဘုရား; Maha Thakya Thiha Paya; Map p228; 30th St, 85/86) **FREE** Mostly hidden behind shopfronts, this large elevated pagoda complex includes a 'golden rock' look-alike and a sacred bodhi tree planted by U Nu, Myanmar's first post-independence prime minister. However, it is best known for an impressive 17ft-high seated bronze Buddha, cast in 1823 by King Bagyidaw.

Shwekyimyint Paya

BUDDHIST TEMPLE

(ရွှေကျီးမြင့်ဘုရား; Map p228; 24th St, 82/83) **FREE** Founded in 1167 by Prince Minshinzaw, exiled son of King Alaungsithu, Shwekyimyint considerably predates Mandalay itself. Minshinzaw himself consecrated the central sitting Buddha image, that's roughly life-sized and crusted with gold and jewelled raiments, in an intimately hushed little prayer chamber. The pagoda also hosts other images collected by later Myanmar kings, relocated here for safe keeping after the British occupied Mandalay Palace.

Gold-Pounders' District

WORKSHOPS

(Map p228; 36th St, 77/79) **FREE** Those one-inch-square gold-leaf sheets that worshippers piously place onto sacred buddha images are laboriously hand-pounded in dozens of specialist workshops in this two-block area. Two main street souvenir-shop showrooms, **King Galon** (Map p228; 36th St, 77/78; ⊙8am-6pm) and **Golden Rose** (Map p228; 36th St, 78/79; ⊙7am-9pm) have English-speaking staff who'll patiently talk you through the process while musclebound gold-beaters demonstrate. It's free and fascinating, and there's no sales pressure, though several souvenir options might well prove tempting.

Sri Ganesh Temple

HINDU TEMPLE

(Map p228; 27th St, 80/81) **FREE** This temple's colourful, sculpture-strewn *gopuram* (monumental tower) might excite you if you've never been to southern India or Singapore.

Jade Market

MARKET

(Map p228; 87th St, 39/40; admission $1; ⊙8am-4pm) This heaving grid of cramped walkways is a shoulder-to-shoulder mass of jade traders. You don't need to pay the $1 entry (not always enforced) to observe interesting scenes of craftsmen cutting and polishing jade pieces just outside along the market's eastern flank (87th St). Or retreat to the octagonal **Unison Teahouse** (Map p228; 38th St at 88th St; tea K300; ⊙5am-1am) to watch furtive-looking jade merchants discussing deals over a cuppa.

Beware that there are proposals afoot to move the jade market way south of town.

THE WORLD'S BIGGEST BOOK

Around the beautiful gilt-and-gold stupa of the mid-19th-century **Kuthodaw Paya** (ကုသိုလ်တော်ဘုရား; Map p224; ⊙24hr) **FREE**, you'll find 729 text-inscribed marble slabs, each housed in its own small stupa and together presenting the entire 15 books of the Tripitaka. Another 1774 similarly ensconced marble slabs (collected in 1913) ring the nearby **Sandamuni Paya** (Map p224; ⊙8.30am-5pm) **FREE** with Tripitaka commentaries. Collectively these slabs are often cited as the 'World's Biggest Book'. Producing the Kuthodaw set alone required an editorial committee of over 200. When King Mindon convened the 5th Buddhist Synod here he used a team of 2400 monks to read the book in a nonstop relay. It took them nearly six months.

Central Mandalay

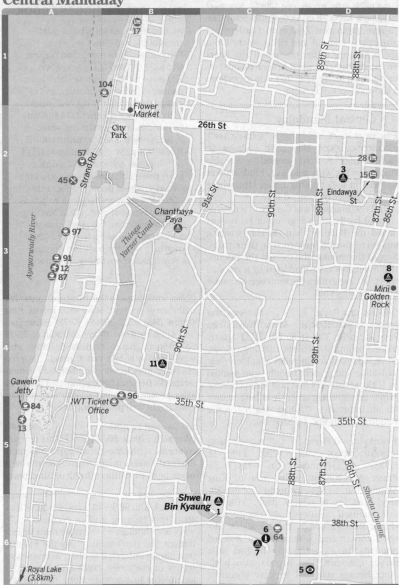

104

Flower Market

City Park

26th St

57
Strand Rd

45

Ayeyarwady River

97

91
12
87

Chanthaya Paya

Thinga Yarzar Canal

91st St

28

3
15

Eindawya St

90th St

89th St

87th St
86th St

8

Mini Golden Rock

89th St

90th St

11

Gawein Jetty

84

IWT Ticket Office

96

35th St

35th St

13

Shwe In Bin Kyaung
1

6
64

7

88th St

87th St

86th St

Shweta Chaung

38th St

5

Royal Lake (3.8km)

Cultural Museum & Library MUSEUM
(Map p228; 80th St, 24/25; foreigner K5000;
⏰ 9.30am-4.30pm Tue-Sat) This dowdy, poorly
lit three-room collection displays archaeological finds, buddhas and a bullock cart. It's
ludicrously overpriced.

⊙ Greater Mandalay

★**Mahamuni Paya** BUDDHIST TEMPLE
(မဟာမုနိဘုရား; 83rd St; ⏰ complex 24hr, museum sections 8am-5pm) **FREE** Every day, thousands of colourfully dressed faithful venerate

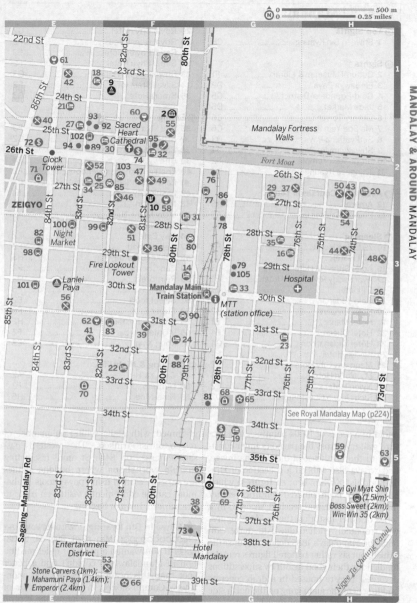

Mahamuni's 13ft-tall **seated Buddha**, a nationally celebrated image that's popularly believed to be some 2000 years old. Centuries of votary gold leaf applied by male devotees (women may only watch) has left the figure knobbly with a 6-inch layer of pure gold...

except on his radiantly gleaming face, which is ceremonially polished daily at 4am.

The statue was already ancient in 1784 when it was seized from Mrauk U by the Burmese army of King Bodawpaya. The epic story of how it was dragged back to Mandalay is

Central Mandalay

retold in a series of 1950s paintings in a **picture gallery** across the pagoda's inner courtyard, to the northeast of the Buddha image. Bodawpaya also nabbed a collection of Hindu-Buddhist **Khmer bronze figures**, which had already been pilfered centuries earlier from Angkor Wat, and reached Mrauk U by a series of other historical thefts. Many figures were reputedly melted down to make cannons for Mandalay's 1885 defence against the British, but six rather battered figures remain, fondled for their good health by superstitious devotees. They're housed in a drab concrete building near the giant gong on the north side of the northwest inner courtyard.

Near Mahamuni's outer northeast exit you'll find a merrily kitsch clock tower and the rather odd **Maha Buddhavamsa Museum of World Buddhism**.

From the central shrine with its multi-tiered golden roof, long concrete passageways leading in each cardinal direction are crammed with stalls selling all manner of religio-tourist trinkets. The western passage emerges on 84th St amid fascinating **marble workshops** where buddha statues are expertly crafted using power tools. Mahamuni can be conveniently visited en route to Amarapura, Inwa or Sagaing.

★ **Shwe In Bin Kyaung** BUDDHIST MONASTERY
(ရွှေအင်ပင်ကျောင်း; Map p228; 89th St, 37/38) **FREE** If you wanted a place for quiet meditation in Mandalay, you couldn't find a better spot than this beautifully carved teak monastery. Commissioned in 1895 by a pair of wealthy Chinese jade merchants, the central building stands on tree-trunk poles and the interior has a soaring dark majesty. Balustrades and roof cornices are covered in detailed engravings, a few of them mildly humorous.

Ma Soe Yein Kyaung BUDDHIST MONASTERY
(မစိုးရိမ်ကျောင်း; Map p228; 39th St, 87/88) **FREE**
Across the creek from Shwe In Bin, the city's

largest monastery lacks ancient historical pedigree but does sport a 'Big Ben' clock and a unique six-storey octagonal **library tower** (Map p228) topped with a great viewpoint, along with a shrine shaded by artificial mango and *ptao* trees. The monastery has long been noted for the politically forthright views of its monks, and it's the base of controversial monk Ashin Wirathu, figurehead of the 969 movement.

Thingaza Kyaung   BUDDHIST MONASTERY
(သာလိာကျောင်း; Map p228; 92nd St, 34/35) **FREE** This appealingly lived-in monastery has some photogenically dilapidated buildings and, tucked behind the *tagondain* (pillar topped with golden duck) is a shaded open-air trio of sinuous buddha figures that have been weathered into almost abstract ghosts.

Skinny Buddha   STATUE
(Dokara Sariya; Map p224; 30th St, 60/62) **FREE** Built in 2011, this remarkable 75ft-tall seated Buddha is a 'meditation image' that falls stylistically somewhere between manga cartoon and Cubism.

Yankin Hill   BUDDHIST TEMPLES
(ရန်ကင်းတောင်) **FREE** Staring distantly towards Mandalay Palace, merrily temple-topped Yankin Hill is mostly worth climbing for views of greater Mandalay's rice-field setting and of the Shan foothills behind. After a 10-minute climb via the obvious covered stairway you're likely to encounter a couple of **domesticated stags** – feeding them supposedly brings Buddhist merit. Pagoda walkways turn south along the ridgetop, eventually ducking down into a **rocky cleft** where devotees splash water on tacky gold fish statues that lie at the feet of a Buddha image.

Cars and motorbikes can drive almost to the hill top from the southeast. Some pick-up 5 (၅) services terminate near the 19th St stairway. Around 300yd back towards Mandalay then 300yd north, **Mya Kyauk monastery** has a dazzlingly distinctive brassy stupa and is famed for its water (see p235).

Activities

Behind the zoo, the outdoor, Olympic-sized **Yatanaban Swimming Pool** (Map p224; admission K2000; ⏲6am-6pm) is OK, but don't use the diving board or you'll pike yourself into a stagnant fountain puddle. For a fee nonguests can use attractive outdoor pools at hotels Mandalay City ($5), **Mandalay Swan** (Map p224; guest/nonguest free/$5; ⏲7am-8pm) and Mandalay Hill Resort ($15).

Asia Centre Driving Range GOLF
(Map p224; ☎02-64583; K2000 plus K700-2000 per 60 balls, club rental K1000, coaching per hr K5000; ⏲6am-6pm) Central driving range.

Shwe Mann Taung Golf Club GOLF
(Map p224; ☎02-75898; green fee/caddy/clubs $30/10/15; ⏲5am-6pm) Manicured 18-hole course handily close to Mandalay Hill.

Yaytagon Golf Resort GOLF
(☎09 203 4052; green fee/caddy/clubs/buggy $30/10/20/15; ⏲5am-7pm) Beautifully set 18-hole course at the base of the Yedagon Hills.

Oriental Ballooning BALLOON RIDES
(http://orientalballooning.com; per person US$320; ⏲pre-sunrise, Nov-Mar) Pre-dawn balloon flights depart daily in season, weather permitting. Departure points vary.

Courses

Dhamma Mandala MEDITATION CENTRE
(☎09 204 4348; www.mandala.dhamma.org) Rural centre near the base of the Yedagon Hills offering bilingual 10-day vipassana courses roughly once a month on a donation basis. Book ahead via website. No visa support.

Festivals & Events

Traditional *pwe* (festivals), big and small, happen all the time, blocking streets or jazzing up pagoda precincts with all-night music and lively street stalls. Cycle around enough and you'll likely stumble into one.

Mingun Nat Festival SPIRIT FESTIVAL
(⏲Feb/Mar) Pays homage to the brother and sister of the Teak Tree, who drowned in the river while clinging to a trunk. Fifth to 10th days of the waxing moon of Tabaung.

Waso BUDDHIST FESTIVAL
(⏲Jun/Jul) The Sagaing Waso festival and then the big Paleik festival take place in the two weeks following the Waso full moon.

Taungbyone Nat Pwe SPIRIT FESTIVAL
(⏲Aug) This massive and camply chaotic festival is held about 12 miles north of Mandalay honouring two famous Bagan-era *nat*. Celebrations culminate on the five days leading up to the full moon of Wagaung. A week later worshippers move on to Irinaku (Yadanagu) south of Amarapura.

Thadingyut BUDDHIST & ELEPHANT FESTIVALS
(⏲Oct) On the full moon of Thadingyut, Myanmar's lights-festival celebrates Buddha's return from the celestial sphere. At the south base of Mandalay Hill, the big temple festival at Kyauktawgyi Paya (p225) builds for two weeks beforehand. One day before full moon, Kyaukse (25 miles south of Mandalay) has its famous two-man elephant dance competition.

Sleeping

None of Mandalay's very cheapest local guesthouses take foreigners. Unless otherwise stated, all room rates include breakfast. In smaller hotels air-con generally goes off during power cuts as generators can't cope.

Royal Mandalay

Hotel Emperor HOTEL $$
(Map p228; ☎02-68743; www.hotelemperormandalay.com; 74th St, 26/27; r Oct-Mar $80-100, Apr-Sep $50-80) Lashings of wood panelling, pretty foliage and the odd carving enliven this super-friendly new family-style hotel. Rooms aren't big and some windows stare straight at a wall, but beds are firm, the air-con works well, rooms have fridge, hair dryer, kettle, toiletries etc, and there's decent wi-fi. A modern bistro next-door does cocktails and international meals. Bicycle rental $5.

Peacock Lodge GUESTHOUSE $$
(Map p224; ☎09 204 2059, 02-61429; www.peacocklodge.com; 60th St, 25/26; r standard/deluxe $35/50; ❄) One of Myanmar's great homestay-style inns; the Peacock's main 1960s house is set in a tree-shaded yard complete with fairy lights, parasol seating and an old horsecart. Dated, if fair-sized, standard rooms overlook a lotus-filled canal but far better are the contrastingly boutiquey new 'deluxe' rooms: choose the prized upper ones with balcony.

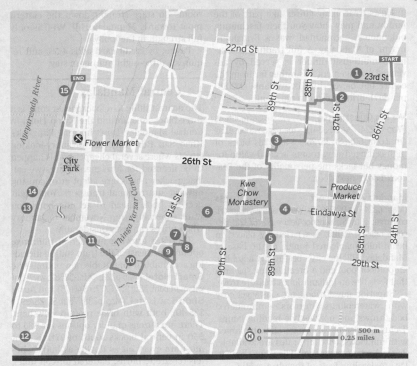

Cycling Tour
West Mandalay

START 23RD ST AT 86TH ST
FINISH AYARWADDY RIVER VIEW HOTEL
LENGTH 2.2 MILES; ONE TO THREE HOURS

Pedalling Mandalay's web of shaded lanes you'll pass many unvisited monasteries and have ample chances for encounters and real-life insights. This is just one possible route.

Turning off bustling 86th St can feel as if you've entered a village. If 23rd St is flooded beyond the redbrick-towered ❶ **Christ Cathedral** substitute the street a block further south (24th St). Briefly follow 87th St, then opposite the spired, pink ❷ **St Michael's Catholic Church** turn west, zigzagging through residential alleys to 88th St.

West of the T-junction 25th St sports a few remnant timber and bamboo-weave homes and one of Mandalay's ❸ **jaggery workshops**. Visit grand ❹ **Eindawya Paya** then veer west off shady 89th St just before a ❺ **crocodile bridge** representing Ngamoe Yeik, the servant of tragic Burmese-chronicle hero Min Nandar.

Take the narrow east–west lane between wooden and colonial-style monastery residences. After ❻ **Khin Makantaik** wind past ❼ **Asumtaik** and ❽ **Sakutaik** monasteries and spot a ❾ **house-workshop** that creates rice-puff snacks in big sweet-smelling woks. Where 91st St makes a dogleg, a mosaic colonnade leads into ❿ **Chanthaya Paya**, where the most precious buddha image supposedly dates back to the reign of Indian emperor Ashoka. Chanthaya's golden stupa looks particularly photogenic in afternoon light. The best viewpoints are across a long ⓫ **teak footbridge** which could be touted as Mandalay's own mini U-Bein Bridge were it not for the smell of rubbish.

Sweep around the impressively colourful ⓬ **Jin Taw Yan Chinese Temple** emerging onto Strand Rd where the Ayeyarwady River offers a series of boat berths, with fascinating cargo bustle beyond 26th St. Enjoy the riverside scenes with a meal and show at ⓭ **Mya Nandar**, or a chilled beer at ⓮ **Cafe YMH** or a rooftop cocktail at ⓯ **Ayarwaddy River View Hotel**.

Hosts treat many guests like part of the family, and may show you their fascinating old photos – 'granddad' was a British-era mayor of Mandalay. A full traditional Burmese multi-dish dinner is served by advanced arrangement. It's rather far from the centre but bicycle hire is available (K2000 per day). Bring mosquito repellent.

Ma Ma Guesthouse
GUESTHOUSE $$

(Map p224; 02-33411; mamaguesthouse11@ gmail.com; 60th St, 25/26; r $40) This block of high-ceilinged new rooms is good value for money but lacks the personality of the Peacock Lodge next door.

Mandalay Hill Resort
HOTEL $$$

(Map p224; 02-35638; www.mandalayhillresort. com.mm; 10th St; superior/deluxe $276/322, discount rates $170/190;) Handily placed in beautifully manicured jungle at the base of Mandalay Hill, the city's best resort hotel has an outdoor pool and a breathtaking spa area that feels like an Indiana Jones treasure trove.

'Superior' guest rooms are classy yet cosy with watercolours, mirrors, embroidered bed-throws and nozzle-style reading lamps. 'Deluxe' versions are very slightly larger, with hill views. Discount rates are available, depending on occupancy. The $1200 spa villas are dazzling feats of the ultra-exotic.

Hotel by the Red Canal
BOUTIQUE HOTEL $$$

(Map p224; 02-61177; www.hotelredcanal.com; 22nd St at 63rd St; r $288-324 Oct-Mar, $186-216 Apr-Sep;) Neotraditional roof gables make this intimate 26-room hotel feel like a cosy oriental palace. Teak floorboards, toiletries in potion bottles, tasteful Asian knick-knacks and little extras like tea-time snacks and complimentary cocktail hour add to the keen service. An artificial stream gurgles past the best 'Chin' rooms. Slightly less pricey 'Kachin' rooms compensate for low natural light with tropical outdoor showers.

'Rakhine' rooms lack balconies. All in all it's a lovely place but the high-season prices seem extremely steep. Look for online bargains.

Sedona Mandalay
HOTEL $$$

(Map p224; 02-36488; www.sedonahotels.com. sg; 26th St at 66th St; r from $240;) Stroll across ponds through a temple-style gateway to a grandly airy lobby, which overlooks a large open-air swimming pool in a lush semi-jungle setting. Room decor doesn't always quite live up to expectations, but better

rooms do stare straight down the eastern moat towards Mandalay Hill. Wi-fi is only full strength in the lobby.

Paying by credit card adds 4.5% and requires a three-night minimum stay.

Central Mandalay

The nearest thing to a 'backpacker zone' is a three-block area around the Nylon Hotel in Central Mandalay. Don't imagine Bangkok's Khao San Rd. These are ordinary-looking streets where several cheaper hotels happen to be licensed for foreigners. Places we call 'backpacker hotels' are adept at organising onward and regional transport. You might need to book ahead to get the hotel you want, especially from November to January when prices can rise considerably.

There's a growing number of midrange options northeast of the train station including acceptable if forgettable new options like **Smart Hotel** (Map p228; 02-32682; www.stayatsmart.com; 28th St, 76/77; r $40-75) and **Aung Shun Lai Hotel** (Map p228; 76th St, 28/29; r $35-40), both with basic rooftop view bars. There are dozens of older options for $35 to $50 in central blocks south of 27th St, but most are every bit as dowdy as budget hotels (cigarette burns, battered air-con units, musty bathrooms) despite perhaps having a lift and relatively glitzy foyer. Expect many brand-new options within a year or two.

★ Rich Queen Guesthouse
BACKPACKER HOTEL $

(Map p228; 02-60172; off 87th St, 26/27; s fan/air-con $15/20, d/tr $25/35;) This friendly new hotel is one of Mandalay's best-value retreats, especially if you score a front-corner room with giant windows, fridge, high ceilings and piping-hot showers. Avoid the few dark box-rooms at the back. It's near the market on a quiet narrow alley, along which monks often pass while you're enjoying a generous local breakfast. Bicycle rental is K2000.

Don't confuse this with the double-priced Rich Queen Hotel 3km east along 26th, where several rooms lack windows altogether.

AD1 Hotel
BACKPACKER HOTEL $

(Map p228; 34505; Eindawya St, 87/88; s/d $10/20, with air-con $15/24;) About the cheapest deal in town for single travellers, AD1 offers rooms that are simple and ageing, if functionally clean. It's just off vibrant 'onion market street' in the eastern approach lane to Eindawya Pagoda. Beware if asking a taxi to take you here – to local ears 'AD 1' sounds very much like '81' (ie 81st St).

ET Hotel
BACKPACKER HOTEL $

(Map p228; ☑02-66547, 02-65006; ethotelmdy@ mandalay.net.mm; 83rd St, 23/24; s/d fan $18/20, air-con $20/25, without bathroom $12/18; ❋ ☎) Above a brightly modernised foyer, the ET remains a good-value backpacker favourite. Bare fluorescent bulbs on pastel-blue corridor walls can feel a little soulless but rooms are clean and mostly spacious with warm showers, fans and new air-con units in some.

Power points are in short supply but wi-fi is available in several common areas. Bicycle rental is K1500. Odd-numbered rooms have more natural light. The cheapest options, on the roof, have shared bathrooms.

Hotel Mahar
HOTEL $

(Map p228; ☑02-22854; hotelmahar@mdy.net. mm; 24th St, 83/84; s/d/tr $18/25/35 Oct-Mar, $12/22/27 Apr-Sep; ❋@☎) At first glance this new, skinny seven-storey tower offers more than you'd expect for the price: in-room wi-fi, power-surge control plugs (very necessary), scurrying staff, new air-con and basic toiletries. Singles are very small with OK if sometimes drain-scented bathrooms, but the best veranda doubles have a private balcony, desk and stocked minibar. However there are cleaning niggles, breakfast is comically minimal and English is limited.

Nylon Hotel
BACKPACKER HOTEL $

(Map p228; ☑02-33460; 25th St at 83rd St; s/d fan $12/15, air-con $20/25; ❋@☎) Mandalay's long-term backpacker standby is a no-frills five-floor tower (no lift, breakfast on the top floor).

Better air-con doubles are fair sized with new ceiling moldings, but others can be cramped and a little musty, albeit more likely to have windows than at the similarly priced Garden Hotel next door. Solar-heated showers, and wi-fi in the dingy lobby.

Royal Guest House
BACKPACKER GUESTHOUSE $

(Map p228; ☑02-65697, 02-31400; 25th St, 82/83; s/d $17/22, with shared bathroom $12/15; ❋☎⊞) This compact warren of little rooms is enlivened by foliage frontage, multiple pastel colours and little box-balcony windows in better rooms. However, bed quality can prove inconsistent and the cheaper rooms can be windowless and seriously small.

Sabai Phyu Hotel
BACKPACKER HOTEL $

(Map p228; ☑02-64506; 81st St, 25/26; s/d $16/20, shared bathroom $8/16; ❋) This last resort cheapy has tiny 1st-floor rooms that are as glamorous as padlocked prison cells. The 3rd-floor air-con rooms are more acceptable and owners are friendly. Cold showers.

Hotel Yadanarbon
HOTEL $$

(Map p228; ☑02-71058; www.hotelyadanarbon. com; 31st St at 76th St; r $45-80, ste $150; ❋☎) Brand new in 2013, all 58 rooms have a Thai sense of style with fine linens, bed sashes, parquet floors and a vague colonial style to the bathroom doors. Even the cheapest 'standard' rooms (only four) are fair sized, with fridge, safe, small sitting space, flat-screen TV and bathtub. The location is handy for the train station and there's a wealth of street food right outside.

Royal City Hotel
HOTEL $$

(Map p228; ☑02-28299, 02-31805; royalcity@ winmaxmail.net.mm; 27th St, 76/77; s $30-35, d $35-40, tr $45; ❋@☎) The best feature of this traveller-oriented lower-midrange hotel is the lovely roof garden. Room decor and bathrooms are looking somewhat tired (tubs in superior rooms) but upper-floor rooms are being revamped with attractive carved mirrors. The lift works when electricity allows.

WONDERFUL WATER

Modern **Mya Kyauk monastery** (မြေကျောက်ကျောင်း) near the base of Yankin Hill is graced by a grandly sparkling gilded stupa. But its fame revolves around a subterranean source of moderately alkaline mineral drinking water found by faith-led digging in 1998. The water supposedly 'promotes IQ and ameliorates diabetes, constipation, gout and morning sickness'. By day it's available to the faithful from faucets at the monastery's front gates. More interestingly, with a translator's help, you can seek an audience with head monk Bhaddanta Khaymar Sarya, who might deign to give you a bottle of the special H_2O. Before opening, try holding the bottle up to the sunlight. At the right angle, light projects an image reminiscent of a stupa onto the back of the label. 'Magic', claim the locals – or at least good bottle design.

Gold Yadanar
HOTEL $$

(Map p228; ☑ 02-71048; www.goldyadanarhotel. com; 34th St, 77/78; d/tw/ste/tr $50/60/70/80; ✳@⚘🛜) For a 40-room hotel, a large chandelier dangling from a two-story foyer might seem a little excessive but it's stylishly done. The brand-new rooms are impeccably tidy and well equipped, and the chunkily rounded wooden furniture looks durable. Some rooms have very limited natural light.

Mandalay City Hotel
HOTEL $$

(Map p228; ☑ 02-61911, 02-61700; www.mandalay cityhotel.com; 26th St, 82/83; r $85-95; ✳@⚘🛜) Walking past you'd never guess that this enticing palm-shaded oasis lay just behind all the dreary buildings of 26th St. The airy, tiled lobby is entered across a fish pond and there's an attractive outdoor pool (nonresidents $5). Statuettes and local paintings add some sparse interest to rooms that are comfortable but not luxurious. If possible choose 'garden view': the rear rooms have frosted-glass windows with no view whatsoever.

Hotel Queen
HOTEL $$

(Map p228; ☑ 02-71562; www.hotelqueenmanda lay.com; 81st St, 32/33; standard/superior/ste Oct-Mar $45/55/65, Apr-Sep $35/50/60; ✳@🛜) Good value among midrange towers of its kind; even the smaller rooms have sitting areas. Superior rooms are more spacious. The foyer is attractive, staff are energetic and a rooftop bar is planned, but some stained corridor carpets and cloth headboards need replacing.

Silver Star Hotel
HOTEL $$

(Map p228; ☑ 02-66786, 02-33394; www.silver starhotelmandalay.com; 27th St at 83rd St; r $40-50; ✳@🛜) Never really stylish, the Silver Star is now starting to age, with half the lightbulbs out on landings, but it's better than many similar options and worth considering if you get a half-price online deal.

Royal Power Hotel
HOTEL $$

(Map p228; ☑ 02-24676; www.hotelroyal.com.mm; 80th St, 27/28; d $45-50, tr $80) A glass elevator climbs to business-style rooms that are plain and have somewhat scuffed parquet floors. If you score a north-facing 9th-floor room the views up the palace moat are impressive.

79 Living Hotel
HOTEL $$

(Map p228; ☑ 02-32277; 79livinghotel@gmail.com; 79th St, 29/30; d/family $35/60; ✳🛜) Sensibly priced new lower-midrange hotel, handily placed behind the train station, has gleaming clean floors, high ceilings, minibar, lift and maybe a (fake) welcome rose on the bed.

My World Hotel
HOTEL $$

(Map p228; ☑ 02-30841; 30th St, 73/74; tw $40-50; ✳🛜) Opened in 2013, the 31 rooms have boutiquey modern design ideas and the little 5th-floor roof 'garden' has appealing views down busy 30th St towards the station. However, some finishing touches seem rushed, corridor carpets already need attention and some cheaper rooms are windowless.

Shwe Ingyinn Hotel
HOTEL $$$

(Map p228; ☑ 02-73464; http://shweingyinnhotel. com; 30th St at 78th St; d $100-120, ste $250) Built in 2012, Shwe Ingyin has far more style than you'd expect from a hotel outside a major station. A carved wooden receptionist 'island' dominates the lobby, lantern-lamps and potplants enliven corridors and a 10th floor rooftop 'Skybar' has some of the best city views in town. However, the fake wooden flooring is practical rather than pretty, and bathrooms feel a little lacklustre for the price, except in the suites.

Choose rooms 03 or 04 on all floors for the most attractive room layout with curving window frontage. Kettle and safe in all rooms.

Kyi Tin Hotel
HOTEL, BUNGALOWS $$$

(Map p228; ☑ 02-23715; www.kyitinhotel.com; 80th St, 31/32; d bungalow/deluxe $100/150, promotional rates $55/65) Kyi Tin's defining feature is its series of balcony-fronted bungalows set in a large yet very central lawn-and-fountain garden. Brand new but designed in a relatively simple Burma-colonial style with black laquered wooden floors, they're fair value at promotional rates.

Less interesting 'deluxe' rooms with subdued cream-brown colours are in a part-finished modern block.

🏨 Greater Mandalay

★ Ayarwaddy River View Hotel
HOTEL $$

(Map p228; ☑ 02-64946, 02-72373; www.ayarwaddy riverviewhotel.com; Strand Rd, 22/23; d $70-110, ste $170; ✳@⚘🛜) Luxurious for the price, this sizeable 2011 hotel has tasteful, restrained decor in large, fully equipped rooms sporting parquet floors and fashion-neutral bathrooms. Price (four categories) depends on size and view. And what a view! Upper-floor front-facing rooms look across the river towards distant Mingun, rear-upper ones overlook the city, Mandalay Hill and the Shan uplands. Enjoy the lot, all 360 degrees, from the rooftop bar where marionette shows are staged in season.

Shwe Taung Tarn BOUTIQUE HOTEL **$$**
(☑ 02-75405; www.shwetaungtarnhotel.webs.com; 14th St at 88th St; d/tr $80/105; ❄ 🎧 ❄) The most affordable of Mandalay's new boutique hotels; a great attraction of this 14-room delight is the little swimming pool part-shaded by palms. It's overlooked from the roof terrace and the more appealing B-block, where the buttresses look almost churchlike and the rooms have wing-doored balconies with wooden loungers. A-block rooms are nearer the road and lack balconies.

All rooms have smart, locally flavoured decor touches and corner bathtubs. The location is peaceful if out of the way, on a curious stretch of 14th St near the better-known Emerald View Inn.

Golden Mandalay HOTEL **$$**
(Map p224; ☑ 09 4025 18896, 02-61488; shwemdy 1974@gmail.com; 60th St at 19th St; r $35; ❄) Attractively set amid palms with a small dining terrace perched above a canal, this 10-room 'family paradise' is a cluster of relatively simple bungalow-style rooms, festooned on the outside with bamboo patchwork designs, temple-style steps, polished stones and carved totem-like designs. It's sweetly unique but lights could be brighter, bathrooms aren't modern, beds are spongy and wi-fi is very limited.

Rupar Mandalar BOUTIQUE RESORT **$$$**
(☑ 02-61555; www.ruparmandalarresort.com; 53rd St at 30th St; d/ste $300/650; ❄ @ 🎧 ❄) This stunning all-teak low-rise complex is set in tropical foliage melding timeless neo-traditional features with modern design flair. Family suites sleep six in three fully equipped en-suite sub-bedrooms, which share two extensive lounges and a kitchenette. The outdoor swimming pools are remarkably spacious and guests qualify for a free 15-minute Thai massage in the appealing spa.

It's hidden away in the far eastern semi-rural suburbs, so you'll need wheels to get virtually anywhere. Local travel agencies offer discounted room rates from $190.

Hotel Shwe Pyi Thar HOTEL **$$$**
(☑ 02-74402; www.hotelshwepyithar.com; 51st St, 31/32; r $250-300, ste $600-2500) All the carvings, marble, polished parquet, greenery, views and black lacquered bedsteads don't necessarily compensate for the design flaws and isolated out-of-town location of this 91-room, six-storey complex.

✖ Eating

There's no single area to look for restaurants; indeed many of the better choices require cycling down seemingly endless dark roads. South of the moat, 27th St is one such road. But if you persist for a few minutes in any direction you're likely to find at least a couple of good street-food areas. For inexpensive barbecue snacks (notably spicy whole fish for around K2500) washed down with K600 draft beers go to one of the countless beer stations (see p240).

✖ Royal Mandalay

★ Green Elephant BURMESE **$$**
(Map p224; ☑ 02-61237; www.greenelephant -restaurants.com; 27th St, 64/65; mains K5000-8000, set menus K8000-10,000, service tax 15%; ⊙11am-2pm & 6-9pm; 🎧 🍴) It's hard to do better for Burmese cuisine than with Green Elephant's attractively presented multi-dish set menus. While these are aimed at tour groups, individuals can usually get a slightly adapted version on request. Ours featured six dishes, including tasty

---

TASTE SENSATIONS
....

Something different? Mandalay has plenty of tourist-frightening culinary curiosities:

➡ seasonal fried crickets or grasshoppers (pe yit) sold from **street vendors** (Map p228; 86th St, 24/25), mostly June to October.

➡ cheese-topped cream puffs: a baffling sweet-savory counterpoint at Chewy Junior (p239)

➡ goat brain or fighting ball (ie testicle) curry at **Lakshmi Indian Restaurant** (Map p228; 32nd St, 73/74; veg/nonveg curry set K1500/2500; ⊙11am-9pm) or Pan Cherry (p239)

➡ barbecued chicken anus at Mr BarBQ (p240)

roast-aubergine salad and a scrumptiously tangy mango-pork curry – one of our best meals in Myanmar.

Service is very obliging and a few tables are tucked within an air-conditioned Pyin Oo Lwin–style colonial-era building full of period relics (ask). Others spill out into a bamboo-tufted garden lit by lanterns and a less impressive pavilion space beside it.

Café City   WESTERN $$

(Map p224; ☑02-61237; East Moat Rd, 20/22; meals K6100-8500, burgers K2900, draught beer K1500; ⊙9am-10.30pm; 🛜📶) Twanging country music, red 'leather' booth-seats and classic vintage signs add to the feeling of a comfortable, latter-day American diner. The menu ranges from steaks and English triangular sandwiches to 'lobster' and delicious coconut-basted fish kebabs. Oh, and its coffee is possibly Mandalay's best (espresso K1900). It's popular with wealthy local families.

Koffie Korner   MULTICUISINE $$

(Map p224; ☑02-68648; 27th St at 70th St; mains K3500-7500; ⊙9am-11pm; 🛜📶) This spacious, gently buzzing lounge-style cafe-restaurant is set behind palms, alluringly lit at night. The predominantly Western menu includes quesadillas, Russian salad, pasta, steak and some brilliantly imaginative sauce flavour combinations like lime-caper-butter, spicy raisin-orange or garlic-mint. There's coffee (K1500 to K2500) and cocktails (K2500 to K6000).

Ko's Kitchen   THAI $$

(Map p224; ☑02-69576, 02-31265; 80th St at 19th St; soups & dishes K3560-5000; ⊙11.30am-2.30pm & 5.30-9pm; 📶) Authentic northern Thai food served in an attractive art-deco building with simple, almost Mediterranean peach decor. Eat early to avoid evening tour groups, which can overwhelm this relatively modest-sized place.

STREET DINING

Along with beer-station barbeques, the best-value dining is usually at street stalls, many of which plonk down their plastic stools for only a few hours a day. Certain corners or street sections have culinary specialities, but knowing which is where takes some insider knowledge.

Morning Only

➡ *Baosi* dumplings – **Yong Xing** (Map p228; 83rd St, 30/31; *baosi* K350; ⊙5am-7.15am).

➡ Shan noodles with *dofubyo* – 29th St, 80/81 before 10am.

➡ *Mohinga* – Mandalay's best breakfast *mohinga* from a three-wheel street-trolley stall at 32nd St at 81st St, from 6.30am to 9.30am only.

Daytime

➡ Point-and-pick multi-curries – several inexpensive family snack outlets are dotted along an unnamed lane between 74th and 75th Sts. Our favourite here is the furthest east – unsigned, super-cheap **Mtay Myint Thar** (Map p228; 74th-75th link-lane 28/29; meal K500; ⊙10am-7.30pm), a traditional wooden shack house decked with contorted roots and plants.

➡ Burmese sweets – take away from near 85th St at 27th St in Zeigyo Market.

➡ sweet tea and fresh *nanbya* (tandoor bread) – **Min Thiha** (Map p224; 28th St at 72nd St; tea/*nanbya* K300/250; ⊙5am-5pm) or Unison Teahouse (p227).

Nighttime Only

➡ Indian chapatti and curry – 28th St at 82nd St or **Nay** (Map p228; 27th St at 82nd St; curry/chapatti K1200/150; ⊙5pm-11pm).

➡ Indian/savoury 'pancakes' and biryanis – **Karaweik** (Map p228; 26th St at 83rd St; ⊙5.30pm-midnight).

➡ Chinese food stalls – 34th St at 76th St with a night market (vegetables) stretching along 34th St.

Golden Duck CHINESE $$
(Map p224; ☑02-72921, 02-36808; 80th at 16th; veg/nonveg dishes from K1450/3150, shark-fin soup K45,550; ⊘10.30am-2.30pm & 6-9.30pm; ⊠⊞) Large, bustling Chinese restaurant that's a veritable local institution. Brisk service, views across the moat from the air-con upper floor and rooftop. Most tables seat six.

✕ Central Mandalay

Ruby NEPALI, VEGETARIAN $
(Map p228; 28th St, 81/82; thali K1500; ⊘7am-9pm; ☑) Organic vegetarian Indian/Nepali meals served up in a small shop-room box-restaurant by a friendly family from Mogok. Nearby **Nepali Food** (Map p228; 81st St, 26/27; thali K2000; ⊘8am-9pm) is similar.

Lashio Lay SHAN $
(Map p228; 23rd St, 83/84; per plate K500-1300; ⊘10am-9.30pm) Simple long-running shop-restaurant with consistently excellent pre-cooked Shan food. Point and pick, pay per dish. Two dishes plus rice make an ideal meal.

Super 81 CHINESE $
(Map p228; 81st St, 38/39; mains K3500-7500; ⊘9.30am-11pm) Excellent, beautifully presented Chinese food in very generous portions, as well as typical barbeques and cheap draft beer in frosted glasses. Downstairs is a convivial beer station but prices are the same upstairs in the pleasantly appointed air-con restaurant section. Handy while awaiting a Moustache Brothers performance (see p241).

Rainforest THAI $
(Map p228; ☑09 4316 1551; lane off 27th St, 74/75; mains K2000-4500; ⊘10am-10pm; ☎☑⊠) Climb through a treasure-packed family 'antique' shop to a covered balcony with tinkling wind chimes and assorted handicrafts, to dine on Thai food that's creamy and mildly spiced for Western palates.

Aye Myit Tar BURMESE $
(Map p228; 81st St, 28/29; full meal K2000-4700; ⊘8.30am-9.30pm; ⊠) Brightly lit, this simple but historic thick-walled colonial-era merchant's building now houses a popular multi-curry eatery. Choose the main dish and four sides; four condiments, soup, rice and salad come with it for free.

Pan Cherry INDIAN $
(Map p228; 81st St, 26/27; curry meal K1500-4000; ⊘9am-9pm) Sit at pink plastic chairs in a floral-ceilinged box room for great-value if somewhat unsophisticated meals complete with dhal, condiments, veg side, rice and poppadom.

Chewy Junior CREAM PUFFS $
(Map p228; www.chewyjunior.com.sg; 31st St, 80/81; puffs K850-950; ⊘9am-9pm; ☎⊠) Laid out like an American doughnut cafe, this comfy Singaporean franchise sells brilliant 'cream puffs' – light, semi-sweet custard in a bun-shaped ball of choux pastry that's chewier than an eclair. Toppings range from chocolate to fruit conserves to grated cheese. Inexpensive fresh fruit juices and instant coffee, too.

Too Too Restaurant BURMESE $
(Map p228; 27th St, 74/75; meal; K2800-4000; ⊘10am-8.30pm) Respected home-style local fare, pre-cooked and served in a bright bland box-room. Pick your main curry (prawn recommended) from the display and two sides, two condiments, soup and rice come free.

Pakkoku Dawlaymay BURMESE $
(Map p228; 73rd St, 27/28; full meal K2000-3000; ⊘10am-8.30pm; ⊠) This basic, archetypal local restaurant is a garage-style room with whirring fans and light-panels that indicate (in Burmese) which of 35 possible curries are available that day (printed list usually available in English on request). Any curry comes with a panful of rice and eight plates of accompaniments, usually including salad-herbs, tomato-bean curry, peanut salad and a semi-sweet dhal.

V Café/Skybar INTERNATIONAL $$
(Map p228; ☑02-24688; 25th St at 80th St; mains/burgers K5000/2000, espresso/draught beer/cocktails K800/1000/3000; ⊘9am-10.30pm; ☎⊠) V's prices are noticeably cheaper than most of Mandalay's air-conditioned Western cafe-bars. While the dangling hearts and mood-lit flower cut-outs are more cutesy than trendy, there's a top-floor rooftop bar with close-up views of the moat and fortress walls.

Marie-Min VEGETARIAN $$
(Map p228; off 27th St, 74/75; mains K1500-2500; ⊘9am-10pm, closed Jun; ☑⊠) An all-vegetarian menu fits the owners' stated principle: 'Be kind to animals by not

eating them.' Highlights include tofu curry, a meal-sized aubergine 'dip' and avocado milkshakes (K1500) that are as 'fabulous' as promised.

BBB INTERNATIONAL $$
(Map p228; 76th St, 26/27; 🖉) A Mandalay classic, undergoing a fashionable refit by the Café City owners.

Cafe House CHINESE, THAI, EUROPEAN $$
(Map p228; 37th St, 78/79; mains K1500-6000; ⊘8am-10pm; 🖉) Easily missed in the goldpounders' area, Cafe House is comfy with forgettable decor but strong air-con. The big draw here is the superb fried wanton wheel with ginger sauce (K3500), a great snack for two to share.

🍴 Greater Mandalay

Mr BarBQ BEER STATION $
(Map p224; 71st St at 31st St; barbecue K300-4000; ⊘11am-11pm) This unusually open, garden-style beer station is hard to beat for quality barbecue, with many less common options including whole squid and delicious fish-wrapped prawns.

Mya Nandar BURMESE, CHINESE $$
(Map p228; 🖉02-66110; www.amazing-hotel.com/index.php/the-restaurant.html; Strand Rd, 26/28; mains K4000-10,000; ⊘9am-11pm; 🖉) Smart open-sided pavilions in a great tree-shaded riverside location. Food is good and varied but the bigger draws (October to February) are the free puppet shows (1pm) and traditional dances (7.30pm to 9pm), performed even when tour groups fail to show up. Bring mosquito repellent.

Royal Lake LUXURY BEER STATION
(🖉09 9100 9445; Kandawgyi Lake; mains K4000-7000; ⊘9am-11pm, music from 7pm) This lakeside complex has a boardwalk seating area with stage for live music. What's far more remarkable, however, is a gilded wooden 'royal barge' moored 650ft around the shore. Once a feature of the central moat, the barge is far more boatlike than the bigger, concrete Yangon version (p72). When things are quiet, you can just have a beer without eating a full meal.

🍺 Drinking & Nightlife

Cafes with angular lines, strong air-con and wide-ranging international menus include comfortably hip **Cafe JJ** (Map p224; www.cafejj.com; 26th St at 65th St; coffee K1000-2300,

cocktails K2900-6100; ⊘9am-10.30pm; 🕾), upscale diner style Café City (p238), good value, cutesy V Cafe (p239) and loungey Koffie Korner (p238). Each mix cocktails, but for a drink with a sunset view it's hard to beat the rooftop bar of the Ayarwaddy River View Hotel (p236).

For ice-cold K600 beers in frosty glasses, head to one of the many beer stations. Some lack English signs but are easy to spot from the Myanmar or Dagon Beer awnings. If you can't spot one, handy examples in the backpacker zone include **Pyi Taw Win** (Map p228; 81st St, 24/25; barbecue items K200-1800; ⊘8am-10.30pm) and part-restaurant **Rainbow** (Map p228; 83rd St at 23rd St; beer K600, barbeque/mains from K500/2000; ⊘10am-11pm). Further afield are pleasantly garden-like **Shwe Lettyar** (Map p228; 31st St at 82nd St; ⊘8am-11pm) or Mr BarBQ (p240), convivial **Mya Yi Nandar** (19th St, 65/66; draft beer/stout K600/750) with its mature palm trees, bustling **Uncle Chan** (Map p228; 35th St, 72/73; barbecue items K300-2500, mains K3000-4000; ⊘8am-10pm) and basic but wi-fi equipped **Nine-Nine** (Map p228; 74th St, 34/35; draft beer/stout K600/750; ⊘9am-11.30pm) in the 35th St area.

Choose **Cafe YMH** (Ya Mone Hlaing; Map p228; Strand Rd, 26/28; draft beer K500; ⊘9am-9pm) for river views, **Golden Lion** (Map p224; 66th St, 12/13; draft beer K600; ⊘10am-10pm) for sunset moat views, albeit across a busy road.

Mandalay has no real nightclubs; if locals suggest 'dancing' they probably mean witnessing a 'model show' – a popular local entertainment where young women sing to a karaoke-style recorded backing tape. Shows typically start around 7.30pm and there's no cover charge beyond beer and food costs.

Great examples include **Boss Sweet** (35th St at 60th St; draft beer K1000; ⊘7-11.30pm) and **Yatanaban Restaurant** (Map p224; draft beer K800) beside Yatanaban swimming pool.

Several more places, plus cafes and restaurants, form an alternative entertainment district that's strung out along Kandawgyi Pat Rd, the causeway road across the northern side of Kandawgyi Lake.

Hunters BAR-CAFE
(Map p228; 167 27th St, 80/81; beer K1800-2000, cocktails K2500-4500; ⊘7.30am-late Nov-Feb, 11am-late Mar-Oct; 🕾) This Kiwi-run expat favourite is a low-key, high-ceilinged bar serving wicked espresso martinis. Upstairs there's a pool table, dartboard and different event nights including a mini disco (Saturday 10pm to midnight).

Central Park BAR, BARBEQUE
(Map p224; 27th St, 68/69; beer K850-1700, cocktails K2800-4500; ☺10am-11pm) This convivial open-sided bar-pavilion cleverly combines the best points of a beer-and-barbecue station with a low-key, musically eclectic cocktail bar, adding a tourist-friendly food menu to boot. It's a sociable place to unwind and some of the decorative local artefacts are a century old. Two-for-one happy-hour cocktails 6.30pm to 7.30pm.

MR2 Pub COCKTAIL BAR
(Map p224; 80th St, 16/17; espresso/juice/cocktails K1000/1600/3500; ☺9am-11pm) The animated youthful clientele don't seem quite poised enough for the cutting-edge music and design of this smooth bar, which softens its neo-Bauhaus architecture with fountain pool, coloured lights and giant floral paintings. Restaurant by day.

Emperor BEER STATION
(Kandawgyi Pat Rd at 85th St; draft beer K1000) This simple beer station comes to life after dark when the trees are lit with orange paper lanterns. Snooker tables available; live acoustic music sets from around 7pm.

☆ Entertainment

Minglar Diamond Cineplex CINEMA, CONCERTS
(Map p228; facebook.com/minglarcinemas; 5th fl, Diamond Plaza, rear bldg, 33rd St, 78/77; tickets K1200-3500) Hidden on the 5th floor of this big shopping centre are a three-screen cinema, several fast-food eateries and a concert hall with occasional Myanmar rap and pop gigs.

35 Skateworld ROLLERSKATING
(35th St, 51/52; per hr K1000, skate/skateboard rental K1000/1500; ☺7am-10pm) Local teenagers rollerskate to music with a Euro-pop bass line that's powerful enough to blowdry their hair.

A-nyeint

A-nyeint is a form of vaudeville folk opera with dance, music, jokes and silly walks. Typically it's performed on temporary street stages during local community festivals (especially November and December).

Moustache Brothers COMEDY
(Map p228; 39th St, 80/81; admission K8000; ☺8.30pm) This classic *a-nyeint* group became world famous in the 1990s when their jokes and rants against the Myanmar government brought them a string of prison sentences, as well as a name-check from Hugh Grant's character in the movie *About a Boy*. The show, now entirely in English, doesn't please everyone but it remains a classic Mandalay must-see.

It takes a series of classical Burmese dance snippets and weaves them together with endless quips from irrepressable Lu Maw, whose sheer delight in pronouncing English colloquialisms is often funnier than the jokes he tells. His word-boards add comic effect while helping listeners

---

MOUSTACHE BROTHERS – FROM SLAPSTICK TO SATIRE

In 1996 the internationally celebrated Moustache Brothers performed an Independence Day show at Aung San Suu Kyi's Yangon compound, telling politically tinged jokes about Myanmar generals. For two of the three 'brothers' (Par Par Lay and Lu Zaw), the result was arrest and seven years' hard labour. Several Hollywood comedians (including Rob Reiner and Bill Maher) wrote to the government in protest while the third brother, Lu Maw, kept the Mandalay show going with the help of his wife.

After their release in 2002, the reunited Moustache Brothers remained 'blacklisted' from playing at outside events (marriages, funerals, festivals and so on). However, they played a series of gala performances at home attended – inevitably – by government agents, nicknamed 'KGB' by Lu Maw. The regional commander soon summoned Par Par Lay and demanded that all performances stop, even in his house. But when Par Par Lay got home, some Westerners had already gathered for that night's show. Imaginatively, the troupe decided to go ahead without costumes and makeup, arguing that a costumeless show would be a 'demonstration' not a real 'performance'. Somehow, it worked. Following the September 2007 troubles, the group's original leader Par Par Lay (who passed away in August 2013) suffered another month in jail. But the shows – now entirely in English – have never stopped. Costumes have reappeared, at least for the dancers, adding colour to the concrete box theatre room that's adorned with photos of the brothers' glory days and their many celebrity encounters.

to decipher his thick accent. There's plenty of slightly indulgent self-promotion and many love-hate gags involving Lu Maw's wife – cover star of a 1990s Lonely Planet *Myanmar (Birmania)* guide (Italian edition). A fair few 'KGB' and corruption jokes still pepper the lighter-hearted wisecracking. (See box on p241).

Dance, Music & Puppet Shows

Evening shows, professionally performed but aimed squarely at tourist audiences, have helped rekindle interest in traditional dance and puppetry. The most authentic performances are set to a six-piece 'orchestra' led by a distinctively wailing *hneh* (an oboe-like instrument). The other musicians are percussionists, playing gamelan-style arrangements on gongs and tuned circles of mini-drums known as *saiwai*. As well as the listings here, you can also see a selection of performances during dinner shows at several upmarket hotels, and at Mya Nandar (p240) riverside restaurant.

Mandalay Marionettes   PUPPET SHOW
(Map p224; www.mandalaymarionettes.com; 66th St at 27th St; admission K10,000; ⊘8.30pm) On a tiny stage, colourful marionettes expressively recreate snippets of traditional tales. Occasionally a sub-curtain is lifted so that you can briefly admire the deft hand movements of the puppeteers (one an octogenarian), who have also performed internationally.

Mintha Theater   DANCE
(Map p224; www.minthatheater.com; 27th St, 65/66; admission K8000; ⊘8.30pm Jul-Mar) Colourfully costumed dancers perform around 10 dances from a larger repertoire. Some give human form to many traditional stories, others are oddballs – perhaps a swan-necked harp recital, a comedy drunkard or the jokily incompetant moustachioed U Shwe Yoe, tumbling off the stage as he fails to impress his beau.

Win-Win 35   LIVE MUSIC
(35th St, 60/62; ⊘9am-11pm, music from 7.30pm) A small stage in the garden of this spacious beer station provides live music from talented local bands. The show we enjoyed featured Hotel California-esque chords and a singer with a Joe Cocker rasp. No cover, cheap beer and sizzler-plate meals where the main vegetable is roast garlic.

Shopping

Mandalay is a major arts and crafts centre. It's probably the best place in Myanmar for traditional puppets and handwoven tapestries. Beware: items may be deliberately scuffed or weathered to look older than they are. Handicraft places generally have to pay commissions to drivers or guides, so prices may prove better if you visit alone.

Puppets are sold at Moustache Brothers and Mandalay Marionettes. **Monks' accoutrements** (alms bowls, robes, fans etc) are sold in the street west of Eindawya Paya. Some gold-leaf-pounding workshops have a selections of **souvenir items**.

Shwe Pathein   SOUVENIRS
(Map p228; 141 36th St, 77/78; ⊘8am-5pm) Pathein-style parasols. Next door there's a leather-workshop and a gold-leaf shop.

Rocky   SOUVENIRS
(Sein Win Myint; Map p224; 27th St, 62/63; ⊘8am-9pm) Various handicrafts including stuffed 'gold-thread' appliqué tapestries, plus gems and jade.

Sut Ngai   FABRIC
(Map p228; 33rd St, 82/83; ⊘8am-8pm Mon-Sat) Sells Kachin fabrics and costumes, aimed mainly at Kachins themselves rather than tourists.

Zegyo   MARKET
(Zaycho; Map p228; 84/86th, 26/28th) The 25-storey tower that brutally overpowers the Mandalay skyline balances atop one of three horrendous, neighbouring concrete 'malls', stiflingly crammed full of fabric sellers. However, the surrounding older market areas are fascinating places to wander amid piles of dried fish, sacks of chilli and giant bunches of bananas.

Aurora   HANDICRAFTS
(Map p228; 78th St, 35/36) Handicrafts gallery.

Ocean Super Center   SUPERMARKET
(Map p228; Diamond Plaza basement, 78th St, 33/34; ⊘9am-9pm) Central Mandalay's best-stocked supermarket is in the basement of the city's biggest shopping mall.

Around Mandalay

There are numerous **silk workshops** and handicraft emporia along the main Sagaing road in Amarapura. Good-value souvenirs can be found in the approach passages to Mahamuni Paya and from

TRANSPORT TO/FROM MANDALAY

DESTINATION	BUS	TRAIN	AIR	BOAT
Bagan	9hr, $10	8hr, $4-10	$60-68	10-14hr, $15-45
Bhamo	N/A	N/A	$58-134	34-72hr, $9-100
Hsipaw	5-6hr, $4-5	11hr, $4-9	$95-108 Lashio +2hr taxi	N/A
Inle Lake	11-13hr, $12-25	N/A	$75 via Heho +1hr taxi	N/A
Katha	$80	13½hr to Naba +1hr bus, $10-25	N/A	1-2 days. $36-80
Mytkyina	N/A	16-20hr, $10-45	$70-150	4-6 days
Nay Pyi Taw	5hr, $8	10hr, $7-21	$100-120, twice weekly	N/A
Yangon	9-10hr, $12-20	15½-16½hr, $11-33	$79-150	N/A

peddlers around Inwa. Mingun has numerous 'art' galleries, mostly inexpensive.

ⓘ Information

INTERNET ACCESS

Wi-fi is available in better cafe-bars and in the lobbies of most foreigner-licensed accommodation. Internet cafes are dotted every two or three blocks throughout the city centre. Speeds may improve but for now connection is annoyingly slow almost everywhere. Forget downloads or streaming.

MONEY

Pristine euro, US dollar and Singapore dollar banknotes can be changed for excellent rates at at Mandalay Airport, at downtown moneychangers including **Faith** (Map p228; 26th St, 81/82; ⊘9am-6pm) and at several branches of **KBZ Bank** (Map p228; 34th St at 78th St; ⊘9.30am-3pm Mon-Fri) and **CB Bank** (Map p228; 26th St, 84/86). Both banks have 24-hour ATMs for Visa, MasterCard, Maestro, Plus and UnionPay. **Zone Express** (Map p224; www.myanmarzonetravel.com; 68th St, 26/27; ⊘8am-8pm) has good rates for US dollars and euros, bearable rates for Thai baht and, if you're desperate, will change UK pounds, Aussie and Hong Kong dollars and Japanese yen at utterly dreadful rates. As yet, very few businesses accept credit cards.

POST

DHL (Map p228; Hotel Mandalay, 78th St, 37/38; ⊘8.30am-5.30pm Mon-Fri, 8.30am-12.30pm Sat) International courier.

Main Post Office (Map p228; 22nd St, 80/81; ⊘10.30am-4pm)

TELEPHONE

Local/national calls cost K100/200 per minute from PCO street stands. Mobile-phone SIM cards typically cost around $140 from ever-multiplying phone shops.

CTT (Map p228; 25th St, 80/81; ⊘8.30am-7pm Mon-Fri, 9am-5pm Sat & Sun) Sweaty, anonymous-looking room for international calls (per minute to Thailand/Europe/North America K1500/3000/3000).

TOURIST INFORMATION & TRAVEL AGENCIES

MTT (Myanmar Travel & Tours; Map p224; ✆02-60356; www.myanmartravelsandtours. com; 68th St at 27th St; ⊘9.30am-4.30pm) The government-run travel company doubles as a tourist office, giving away multi-city maps as well as selling transport tickets and permit-needing tours – notably to Mogok (two weeks required to apply for permit).

Nice Style (Map p228; ✆30709, 02-64103; www.nicestyletravel.com; 25th St, 82/83; ⊘9am-5pm Mon-Fri, to 3pm Sat & Sun; ☎) Professional travel and tour agent.

Seven Diamond (Map p228; ✆02-30128, 02-72868; www.sevendiamondtravel.com; 82nd St, 26/27; ⊘8.30am-6pm) Helpful, major agency that can pre-book flights and hotels by email request and organise airport-bound shared taxis.

ⓘ Getting There & Away

AIR

All flights use Mandalay International Airport (www.mandalayairport.com), which is just over 20 miles south of the city. The more central Chanmyathazi Airport is essentially mothballed and has no scheduled commercial flights.

International

Mandalay's international connections are likely to grow in coming years. Currently you can fly to the following:

➡ Kunming at least daily on **China Eastern** (Map p228; ✆02-76333; Hotel Mandalay, 78th St, 37/38)

➡ Bangkok with **Air Asia** (Map p228; www. airasia.com; 26th St, 78/79), **Thai Smile** (www. thaismileair.com) and **Bangkok Airways** (Map p228; ☑02-36323; www.bangkokairways. com; 78th St, 33/34). Note that Air Asia uses Bangkok's old Don Mueang Airport – don't underestimate connection times if you have to swap Bangkok airports. ThaiSmile flights can be combined with Thai Airways longhaul flights.

➡ Gaya (India) thrice weekly November to April using government-run MAI (Myanma Airways International; Map p228; ☑02-69551; www. maiair.com) at 27th St; ☺9am-5.30pm Mon-Fri, to 1pm Sat & Sun) on flights primarily used by Buddhist pilgrims.

➡ Singapore ($195) on Golden Myanmar via Yangon, but note that the direct flight is outbound only. Returning you'll spend a night in Yangon.

➡ Imphal (Manipur, northeast India) – in November 2013 Golden Myanmar operated a one-off Mandalay–Imphal flight. If this route becomes regular it could become a game-changer in offering a whole new route between Myanmar and northeastern India.

Domestic

The government-run Myanma Airways has a lacklustre reputation and sells its own tickets directly, sometimes only at short notice. For other domestic flights, we have often found that travel agencies offer prices that are competitive or even better than buying direct from airline offices, so do shop around. However, Golden Myanmar does offer online pre-booking discounts to Yangon ($36 to $85). See table for other fares.

Airlines

Air Mandalay (Map p228; 78th St, 29/30)

Asian Wings (Map p228; ☑02-74791; www. asianwingsair.com; 30th St at 78th St; ☺9am-5pm Mon-Fri, 9am-2pm Sat-Sun)

Air Bagan (Map p228; www.airbagan.com; 78th St, 27/28; ☺9am-5pm Mon-Fri, to 1pm Sat)

Golden Myanmar (www.gmairlines.com)

Air KBZ (Map p224; www.airkbz.com; 30th St, 71/72)

Myanma Airways (MA; Map p228; ☑02-36221; 81st St, 25/26; ☺8.30am-3pm)

Yangon Airways (Map p228; 78th St, 29/30)

BOAT

Taking a boat on the Ayeyarwady River is one of Mandalay's delights. Flits to Mingun or all-day rides to Bagan are most popular, though the new afternoon return service to Inwa is a great alternative. Pre-booking one day ahead is usually fine for Bagan or Bhamo – bring plenty of drinking water. For Mingun and Inwa just show up 30 minutes before departure. Passort required. The following companies operate:

IWT Ferries (Map p228; ☑02-36035; www. mot.gov.mm/iwt; Gawein Jetty) Slow boats to Bhamo and Bagan plus the more picturesque Hantharwaddy Bagan-bound cruiser depart from Gawein Jetty.

Malikha (Map p228; ☑02-72279; www.malikha-rivercruises.com) Three Malikha boats do the Bagan run; Malikha 3 is the most elegant. Buy tickets through hotels/agencies.

MGRG (Map p228; ☑09 505 7685; http:// mgrgexpress.com; Strand Rd) Bagan express ferries (October to March). Tickets from a booth at the jetty.

Nmai Hka (Map p228; ☑09 40270 0072; www. nmaihka.com; A-15, 2nd fl, train station) Shwei Keinnery ferries to Bagan (tourist season) and Bhamo (summer), plus seasonal Tharlarwaddy

MANDALAY DOMESTIC AIR ROUTES

These are sample fares with peak-season schedules. Abbreviations: AM (Air Mandalay); AW (Asian Wings); AB (Air Bagan); GM (Golden Myanmar); K7 (Air KBZ); MA (Myanma Airways); YH (Yangon Airways).

DESTINATION	PRICE ($)	FREQUENCY	AIRLINES
Bhamo	115-130 (54)	Tue, Thu, Fri, Sun	AB, AW (MA)
Heho	56-64	several daily	AB, AM, AW, K7, YH
Homalin	155 (89)	Sat (Tue, Thu)	AW (MA)
Kalaymyo	105-118	Mon, Wed, Sat	AB
Kyaingtaing	145	Wed, Sun (via Tachileik)	YH
Khamti	75	Wed, Sat	MA
Lashio	77-83	Wed, Fri, Sat, Sun	AW, YH
Myitkyina	126-135 (66)	Sun, Fri (Tue, Fri)	AB, AW (MA)
Nay Pyi Taw	76	Wed, Fri	AW
Nyaung U (Bagan)	56-64	twice daily	AB, AM, AW, K7, YH,
Putao	135-149	Tue, Fri, Sun	AB (permits required)
Tachileik	145	daily	YH
Yangon	75-135	several daily	AB, AM, AW, GM, K7, MA, YA

MANDALAY FERRY OPTIONS

If you want a full cruise there are plenty of very upmarket options, notably with **Paukan** (Map p228; www.ayravatacruises.com), **Amara** (Map p228; www.amaragroup.net/de/river/river-de) and **Orient Express** (www.orient-express.com/web/rtm/voyages_in_myanmar.jsp) boats. Exact offerings change every year so consult the websites and count on spending thousands of dollars.

DESTINATION	PRICE	DURATION (HRS)	DEPARTURES	BOAT
Bagan	$40	10	7am daily Oct-Mar only	Nmai Kha, MGRG
Bagan	$40	10	7am daily Oct-Mar then sporadic	Malikha
Bagan	$30	11	6am Mon & Fri	IWT Hanthawaddy
Bagan	$15	14	5.30am Wed & Sun	IWT slow boat
Bhamo	$9	45	6am Mon, Thu & Sat	ITW slow boat
Bhamo	$9	45	6am Wed & Sun	ITW cargo boat
Bhamo	$100	34	7am thrice weekly Jul-Sep	Nmai Kha
Inwa	$8	1	noon daily Oct-Mar	Nmai Kha
Katha	$80	22	7am thrice weekly Jul-Sep	Nmai Kha
Katha	K36,000	14	5am daily	Pan Lon Express
Mingun	K5000	1	9am daily Oct-Mar	Tourist Boat Association
Mingun	$6	1	8.30am daily Oct-Mar	Nmai Kha

to Mingun and Inwa. Ticket office is 100yd east of IWT. Departures from Gawein Jetty.

Pan Lon (Map p228; Strand Rd; ☺ticket office 5am-6pm) Express boats to Katha. Change there for Bhamo or Shwegu.

Tourist Boat Association (Mayan Chan Jetty; Map p228) Departs for Mingun at 9am from a jetty at the end of 26th St. No pre-booking; just show up.

BUS & SHARED TAXI

Two of Mandalay's three major bus stations are infuriatingly distant from the city centre and there are proposals to move the main highway bus station even further south. **Thiri Mandalar bus station** is relatively central. Buses for Monywa, Shwebo and Bhamo leave from here (though foreigners currently may not take Bhamo services). **Pyi Gyi Myat Shin bus station** is 2 miles east of the centre and has buses for Hsipaw and Lashio. **Kwe Se Kan Highway bus station** is 6 miles south of centre, and it can take 45 minutes for the K3000/6000 motorbike/taxi ride from central Mandalay, even more by pick-up 10. Allow plenty of time once you're there to find the right bus in the mayhem.

Pre-booking bus tickets for longer-distance routes (over four hours) is wise. Booking through backpacker hotels will usually incur a commission but that's rarely more than the motorbike-taxi fare you'd incur when buying your own. Alternatively, use a city-centre ticket agency. There are many, especially on 32nd St where **Ko Htay/Shwe Mann Thu** has a particularly wide choice of destinations and offers several

transfer buses ('ferries') to the main bus station, most costing K1000 per person. Ko Htay has a second branch beside My World Hotel.

Bus company and ticket agency contacts include the following:

Aung Yedana (Map p228; ☎ 09 4711 0564; 79th St, 27/28)

Cherry Myay (Map p228; ☎ 02-73571; 27th St at 83rd St; air-con car/minivan per person K5000/6000; ☺ 6.30am-4pm)

Duhtawadi (Map p228; ☎ 02-61938; 31st St, 81/82)

Kazein (Map p228; ☎ 02-32068, 09 5262 227; 32nd 80/81)

Lwin Mann (Map p228; ☎ 09 6500 767, 02-60151; 27th 82/83; back/front seat K6000/7000; ☺ 6am-5pm)

Meisho Mann (Map p228; ☎ 09 4027 11451; 79th 30/31)

Ko Htay/Shwe Mann Thu (Map p228; ☎ 02-22365; 32nd St, 82/83; ☺ 8am-9pm)

Long-distance shared taxis, where available, are worth considering. Most offer door-to-door service, saving potentially long trips to/from bus stations at either end of your journey.

TRAIN

As the train station is relatively central rail travel has the advantage of saving a long commute to an outlying bus station. Just inside the main ground-floor entrance, the **MTT sub-office** (Map p228; train station, near south door; ☺ 9.30am-6pm) can sell tickets (with commission) if the queues upstairs look too daunting. Passport required.

MANDALAY TRAIN ROUTES

Sample foreigner fares (ordinary/upper class/sleeper):

DESTINATION	PRICE ($)	DURATION (HR)	DEPARTURE
Hsipaw	4/9/-	11	4am
Monywa	2/-/-	5¼	2.30pm
Myitkyina	10/27/30	20	2.10pm, 4.20pm
	14/31/36	17/24	4.30am/7.40pm
	-/18/45	16	1pm
Naba (for Katha)	6/17/18	13½	4.30pm
Nyaung U (Bagan)	4/10/-	8	9pm
Pakkoku	3/-/-	11	6pm
Yangon	11/30/33	15½-16½	6am, 3pm, 5pm

❶ Getting Around

TO/FROM THE AIRPORT

Much of the one-hour drive into town from Mandalay Airport is through fields and scrubland swaying with mango trees and palmyra palms and liberally dotted with gilded pagodas. If you're arriving in Myanmar for the first time it's a great first taste.

There are free shuttle buses for Air Asia customers (9am from 79th St, 26/28) and Golden Myanmar customers (5.30am from Sedona Hotel, picking up at Hotel Mandalay 5.45am). Otherwise there's no airport bus.

Several taxi companies with booths in the arrivals area offer shared taxis at K12,000/4000 per vehicle/seat. These include **Shwe Myanmar** (☑ 02-72325; 34th St, 79/80), **Great Taxi** (☑ 02-32534), **Bardo** (☑ 02-24561) and **Seven Diamond Express** (Map p228; ☑ 02-22365; 32nd St, 82/83). Even if you choose the K4000 'shared' option you'll still be collected/dropped at your hotel as long as it's reasonably central. Coming from town, book one day ahead if possible. Cheaper guesthouses will order you an airport car for about the same price as a shared taxi, but big hotels ask far more. Taxis on the street typically want double, as they'll find it hard to get a return ride.

BICYCLE & MOTORCYCLE RENTAL

On foot, Mandalay's vast size can rapidly become overwhelming. If you're not intimidated by the traffic, renting a bicycle or moped can be a great solution. Several rental agents in the central backpacker area charge K1500/10,000 per day for bicycles/motorbikes including long-established **Mr Jerry** (Map p228; 83rd St, 25/26; ☺8am-8pm) plus **Mann Restaurant** (Map p228; 83rd St, 25/26), **Mr Bean** (Map p228; 83rd St, 24/25) and **Morris's Bikes** (Map p228; 25th St, 82/83). Several hotels rent bicycles, too. Cyclists are advised to carry a head torch at night.

To go further afield, expat-run **Mandalay Motorcycle** (Map p228; ☑ 09 4440 22182; www.mandalaymotorbike.com; 32nd St, 79/80; city/trail bike per day K12,000/40,000) has 125cc and 150cc trail bikes. The office is only staffed by appointment and supply is limited so call ahead to book a bike. And do discuss route plans before you head out, as some routes are out of bounds or need permits.

MOTORCYCLE TAXI

Motorcycle taxis lurk near hotels and on many a city corner. Expect to pay K1000 for a short hop, K1500 across the centre, and K10,000 all-day hire within Mandalay (or K15,000 including Amarapura, Inwa and Sagaing). These drivers speak decent English:

Aung-Aung (☑ 09 4026 48306) Friendly, helpful driver.

Ko Zaw (☑ 09 4025 12327; mandalay.city.tour@gmail.com) Thoughtful, English-speaking motobike taxi driver.

Zimi (☑ 09 4315 9591) Daughter of Moustache Brother Lu Maw, Zimi is probably the only female motorcycle taxi driver in Mandalay.

PICK-UPS

The public transport system uses pick-up trucks that make regular lengthy stops, rarely leaving till jammed full. Route numbers are displayed above the cab in Burmese script. Different coloured boards sometimes denote variant routings.

From 25th/83rd diagonally opposite Nylon Hotel: ➡ ၁ (1), ၅ (5), ၁၉ (19) via 78th St, south to the train station, east on 30th, then 5 and 19 head east on 19th while 1 heads north up 62nd

➡ ၁၆ (16) to the base of Mandalay Hill; blue sign goes via train station

From 84th St at 29th St: ➡ ၈ (8) passes Mahamuni Paya en route to Amarapura

➡ ၁၀ (10) to the Highway bus station

MANDALAY BUS & ROAD TRANSPORT

Bus stations: TM (Thiri Mandalar bus station); PGMS (Pyi Gyi Myat Shin bus station); Main (Kwe Se Kan Highway bus station). Agents: AY (Aung Yedana); ChM (Cherry Myay); Duh (Duhtawadi); LM (Lwin Mann); MM (Meisho Mann); ShMT (Ko Htay/Shwe Mann Thu). For shared taxis have your hotel book by phone and get picked up at your door.

DESTINA-TION	TYPICAL FARE (K)	DURA-TION	DEPARTURE TIME	DEPARTURE POINT	AGENT	TYPE
Amarapura	500	45min	frequent	84th at 29th	N/A	pick-up
Bagan	8500	8hr	8.30am, 4.30pm, 10pm	Main	ShMT	(air-con) bus
Bagan	8000	8hr	7.30pm	Main	ShMT	bus
Hsipaw	4000	6hr	5am, 6am	PGMS	Duh	bus
Hsipaw	5000	6hr	2.30pm	PGMS	Duh	(air-con) bus
Hsipaw	18,000	5hr	8am	hotel	Duh	shared taxi
Inle Lake	10,000	11hr	7.30pm, 8pm	Main	ShMT	bus
Inle Lake	25,000	10hr	8am, 9am	hotel	AY	shared taxi
Kalaw	10,000	8hr	use Taunggyi buses	Main	N/A	bus
Kyaukse	4000	4½hr	1pm	PGMS	Kazein	(air-con) bus
Lashio	6,000	11hr	6pm	PGMS	various	bus
Lashio	23,000	7hr	8am, 9am	hotel	AY	shared taxi
Monywa	2000	3½hr	hourly 7am-4pm	TM	N/A	bus
Nay Pyi Daw	6000	4hr	many 7am-9pm	Main	ShMT	bus
Shwebo	2000	3½hr	hourly 8am-3pm	TM	N/A	bus
Pyin Oo Lwin	7000	2hr	6am-4pm	hotel	LM, ChM	shared taxi
Pyin Oo Lwin	2000	2½hr	as full 'til mid-afternoon	83rd at 28th	N/A	pick up
Sagaing	500	1hr	around 3 per hour till 7pm	84th at 30th	N/A	pick-up
Taunggyi	10,000	11hr	many 6pm-7.30pm	Main	ShMT	bus
Taunggyi	10,000	11hr	6 daily 7am-noon	hotel	MM	shared taxi
Taungoo	8000	6hr	9pm	Main	ShMT	bus
Yangon	10,500	8hr	many 7.30am-9.30am & 7.30pm-10pm	Main	many	bus
Yangon	16,500	8hr	many 9pm	Main	many	luxury bus

TRISHAW

Traditionally the main form of city transport, pedal trishaws are now relatively rare except around the markets. Fares include city centre to base of Mandalay Hill for K4000 return and all-day hire from around K10,000.

English-speaking drivers include eloquent **Ko Re** (koore6070@gmail.com) and **Mr 'Take it Easy'** (myintshin15@gmail.com; 27th St, 80/81).

AROUND MANDALAY

For many visitors, the historic sites around Mandalay trump anything in the city itself. Iconic attractions include U-Bein Bridge in Amarapura, Sagaing's temple-studded hills and horse-cart rides around the rural ruins of Inwa.

Entry to Inwa's two main sites and Amarapura's Bagaya Kyaung are included in Mandalay's K10,000 'combo' ticket. A separate K3000 ticket for Mingun and Sagaing is patchily enforced. No one checks for tickets at the other sites.

A popular option is to combine Amarapura, Sagaing and Inwa into a full-day trip by motorcycle taxi (K15,000) or taxi (K30,000 to K50,000).

For most taxi drivers and the **J&T Minibus Tour** (Map p224; 09 4253 13392; jandt. mdy@gmail.com; 69 33rd St, 71/72; per person/car K17,000/40,000), 'Inwa' means dropping you at the Myitnge ferry assuming you'll cross then tour by horse cart. However,

Myanmar Upperland (Map p224; ☏02-65011; www.myanmarupperland.com; 27th St, 71/72; ◷9am-6pm Mon-Sat) offers an all-day tour by air-con minibus (K18,000 per person, hotel pickup 8.30am) that includes driving into and around Inwa as well as sunset at U-Bein Bridge, lunch, water and several interesting workshop visits.

Motorbike taxis typically add around K2000 to drive around the Inwa ruins (if you insist). Add another K2000 to see Paleik en route, and K5000 more to include Mingun, too. Beware that doing the whole lot in one very long day will feel very rushed. Ideally, make two or three more modest day trips. There are two foreigner-licensed hotels are in Sagaing.

Amarapura
အမရပူရ

☏02 / POPULATION C35,000

Myanmar's penultimate royal capital, Amarapura (pronounced amuRA-puRA) means 'City of Immortality', though its period of prominence lasted less than 70 years (from 1783). Starting from 1857, King Mindon began dismantling most of the palace buildings and shipping them 7 miles north to Mandalay, which was to become the new capital according to a Buddhist prophecy.

These days Amarapura is essentially a spread-out suburb of Mandalay, but it's leafy and attractively set on a wide, shallow lake, named for an ogre who supposedly came looking for the Buddha here. The lake is crossed by an iconic wooden footbridge which is the main attraction. Several other minor sights are widely scattered and would sensibly require a bike or taxi to see them all.

⊙ Sights

★U-Bein Bridge WOODEN FOOTBRIDGE
(ဦးဘိန်းတံတား) The world's longest teak footbridge gently curves 1300yd across shallow **Taungthaman Lake**, creating one of Myanmar's most photographed sites. In the dry season it feels surreally high and mostly crosses seasonal vegetable gardens. But after the summer rains, the whole area becomes a big lake and water laps just below the floor planks. Just a few of the 1086 poles on which it stands have been replaced by concrete supports.

A great time to visit the bridge is just after sunrise when hundreds of villagers and monks commute back and forth across it. The light is often best around an hour before sunset, but by then there will be a large number of tourists and trinket sellers. A popular visiting tactic is to walk

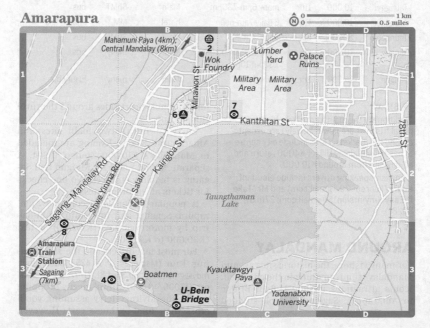

Amarapura

across the bridge then return by paddle-boat (K5000) as the sun is setting. However, as boats are usually only available at the bridge's western end (where tour buses arrive), you'll need to make return pick-up arrangements before you walk across. Or simply ask your taxi/motorbike driver to drop you at the eastern end.

Maha Ganayon Kyaung
BUDDHIST MONASTERY

FREE Just west of U-Bein Bridge, this sprawling monastery is a pleasantly meditative place for most of the day. But at about 11am, busloads of tourists arrive to gawp while the whole monastery sits down to eat, their silence pierced by the endless rattle of camera shutters. Worth avoiding.

Shwe Sin Tai
SILK WORKSHOP

(⊙7am-6pm) **FREE** Hand-worked silk weaving workshop that welcomes visitors without sales pressure.

Kyo Aung Sanda
BUDDHIST MONASTERY

FREE Little visited, this curious latterday monastery features a mini 'Golden Rock', prayerhall full of monk-posture statues and several surreal Alice in Wonderland-style staring Tweedledum and Owl figures.

Pahtodawgyi
BUDDHIST STUPA

(ပုထိုးတော်ကြီး) **FREE** This vast bell-shaped pagoda, erected by King Bagyidaw in 1820, is the tallest structure for miles around (185ft). It's still slightly damaged from the 2012 earthquake, but once repairs are complete men (only!) should once again be allowed to climb half-way to the upper terrace to appreciate views over the plethora of *hti* (stupa pinnacles) glittering through Amarapura's lush treescape.

Shwe Linmin Paya
STUPA

(Kanthitan St) Attractive 19th-century square-based stupa with gold spire and white/ice-blue lower sections from a 2006 makeover. It's set in a nursery of flowering shrubs beside the lake-road.

Bagaya Kyaung
BUDDHA MUSEUM

(ဘားကရာကျောင်း; admission by combo ticket) If you're trying to squeeze full value out of your Mandalay 'combo' ticket, you might head to this 1996 concrete-pillared reconstruction of an early-19th-century monastery. It has plenty of flying wooden filigree roofwork and contains a substantial ancient library of Pali scripts, plus a museum of 19th-century Buddha images, but few travellers are greatly impressed. Nearby there are several distinctive **tobacco drying barns**, a fascinating little **foundry** where giant woks are cast, and, further east, the hefty but forgettable ruins of two former **palace** buildings.

✖ Eating

Near either end of U-Bein Bridge there are eateries and food stalls where you can buy noodles, tea and roasted crab.

Renaissance Cafe
BURMESE, THAI

(therenaissancetrading@gmail.com; 3 Salain; set meals K7500-13,000) Partly a showcase for the company's attractive modern rattan furniture and tableware, this charming restaurant is the smartest in Amarapura and offers a variety of multi-dish Thai, Burmese or European meals; your guide or driver eats for free. Almost next door the 'lost-in-the-jungle' Amarapura Restaurant looks delightful but food quality is less reliable.

ℹ Getting There & Away

Crammed-full pick-up 8 from 84th St at 29th St in Mandalay (K500, 45 minutes) passes along the main Sagaing road. For U-Bein Bridge, get off just after it crosses the railway and walk east or take a horse cart (K2000).

Inwa (Ava)
အင်းဝ

Since 1364, Inwa (Ava) has taken four turns as royal capital. Indeed, upper Burma was often referred to as the 'Kingdom of Ava', even well after the royal court finally abandoned Inwa for Amarapura in 1841. Despite its rich history, the site today is a remarkably rural backwater sparsely dotted

Inwa

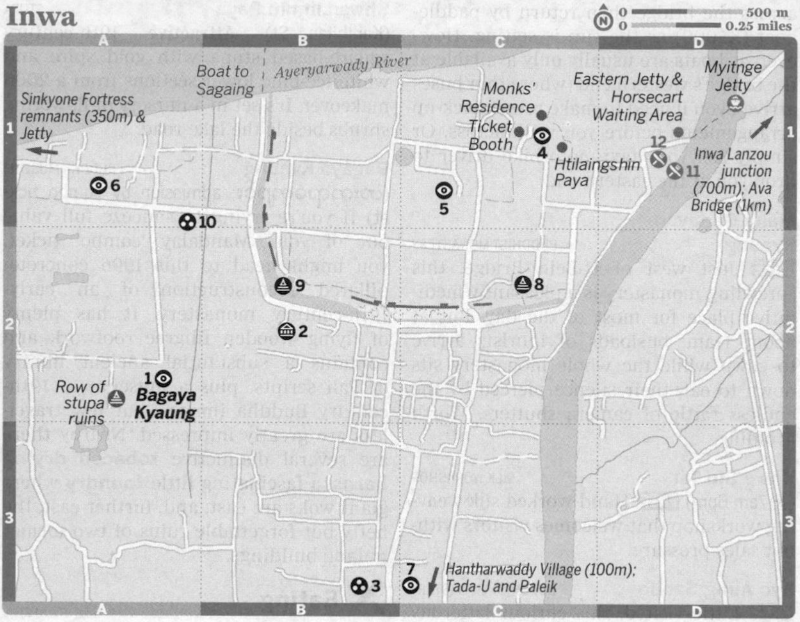

with ruins, monastic buildings and stupas. It's a world away from the city bustle of Mandalay. For many visitors, exploring by horse cart is part of the charm, though cycling around allows more flexibility, village stops and human interactions.

The Mandalay 'combo ticket' (p223) is theoretically required to visit Inwa, but it's only checked for those entering Bagaya Kyaung and Maha Aungmye Bonzan.

Inwa

Top Sights

1 Bagaya Kyaung A2

Sights

2 Inwa Archaeological Museum B2
3 Le-htat-gyi Paya B3
4 Maha Aungmye Bonzan (OK Kyaung) C1
5 Nanmyin C1
6 Nogatataphu Paya A1
7 Sandamuni Paya C3
8 Shwe Myauk Taung C2
9 Shwezigon Paya B2
10 Yedanasimi Paya A1

Eating

11 Ave Maria D1
12 Small River Restaurant D1

Sights

The major sites are plagued by tenaciously persistent drinks vendors and postcard peddlers. But much of Inwa's charm is in simply finding your own viewpoint or village encounter amid the pagodas.

★ Bagaya Kyaung WOODEN MONASTERY

(ဘားကရာကျောင်း; combo ticket required) Despite unpromising red corrugated roofing, this lovely 1834 teak monastery is Inwa's most memorable individual attraction. It's supported on 267 teak posts, the largest 60ft high and 9ft in circumference, creating a prayerhall that's cool, dark and feels genuinely ancient. Stained timbers are inscribed with repeating peacock and lotus-flower motifs. Despite the constant flow of visitors, this remains a living monastery with globes hung above the little school section to assist in the novices' geography lessons. Beware of protruding floorboard nails.

Nanmyin WATCHTOWER

(အင်းဝမျှော်စင) All that remains of King Bagyidaw's palace complex is this 90ft 'leaning tower of Inwa', shattered but patched up and still standing after the 1838 earthquake. The tower is neither beautiful nor especially high, but wide views from the top are great for getting your bearings amid the widely scattered sights; at least if it's open. Damaged timbers meant that it was closed for safety reasons during the time of research.

Maha Aungmye Bonzan (OK Kyaung) MONASTERY

(မဟာအောင်မြေဘုံစံ) Built, unusually, of stucco-covered brick, this 1822 royal monastery temple is a rare survivor from the Ava era. The faded, sturdy structure looks very attractive in cleverly taken photographs, but in the harsh midday sun the main attraction is the cool afforded by its ultra-thick walls and the bats flitting through its empty undercroft. Directly east, forming a fine background, is **Htilaingshin Paya**, an attractive array of gilded stupas, some dating back to the Bagan period.

Behind, near the crumbling former monks'-residence building, a footpath leads to seasonally flooded river gardens and views to Sagaing.

Yedanasimi Paya STUPA RUINS

This small but photogenic ensemble brings together three sitting buddhas and a handful of old brick stupas shaded by a giant flame tree.

✖ Eating & Drinking

There are basic local tea-shops at Maha Aungmye Bonzan, Nogatataphu, each of the villages and at the main (eastern) jetty, where there are two appealing tourist-friendly options:

Small River Restaurant MULTICUISINE $$

(mains K3500-7000; ⏰10am-3pm) A popular tourist retreat near Inwa jetty, Small River has tables dotted through a tree-shaded garden backing onto a modest colonial-era wooden house (not part of the restaurant).

Ave Maria CHINESE, BURMESE $

(mains K2000-4000; ⏰6am-5pm) Follow the signs to this slightly hidden garden restaurant with attractive river views.

ℹ Getting There & Away

Sagaing-Mandalay pick-ups can drop you at Inwa Lanzou junction just west of Ava Bridge. From there it's a 15-minute walk or a 10-minute trishaw ride (K200) to the Myitnge river crossing. A covered wooden longboat shuttles across to Inwa's eastern jetty (two minutes, K800 return) around every 15 minutes according to demand, last at 6pm. One or two motorbikes could physically be bundled aboard but ticket sellers refuse to let tourists take their bikes across westbound. However, bringing them back *from* Inwa is OK.

Unless you specify otherwise, most taxis and motorbike taxis will also drop you at the

---

ALTERNATIVE INWA

Get a little off the beaten track at some of the following minor sights and viewpoints:

➡ the row of disintegrating brick stupas west of Bagaya Kyaung leading towards a mysterious array of overgrown temple ruins (accessible dry-season only).

➡ the view of the **Shwezigon Paya** golden stupa across the moat from near the ludicrously overpriced two-hall **Archaeological Museum** (foreigner/local K5000/200; ⏰9am-4.30pm Tue-Sun).

➡ tree-framed views of several small pagodas from the rough track that gives a false short cut between gigantic **Nogatataphu Paya** (Lawkatharupha Paya) and the Sagaing Ferry jetty

➡ the short restored sections of city wall near the three whitewashed pagodas of **Shwe Myauk Taung**: best viewed across the moat looking north

➡ Ayeyarwady River views from the square inner bastions of the 1874 **Sinkyone Fortress** and numerous stupas down weather-damaged lanes directly south.

Fascinating **Hantharwaddy Village**, starting around a mile south of the moat, has countless stupas including the large, gilt bell-shaped **Sandamuni Paya** (Maha Myamuni) and the four-storey stub of the once huge **Le-htat-gyi Paya** (လေးထပ်ကြီးဘုရား), now dangerously fissured by earthquakes. A charmingly uncommercial laquerware company **Myanma Nwe Sin** in the back streets makes monks' alms bowls.

Myitnge jetty. However, motorbikes can drive right into Inwa via two possible routes off the airport highway. One route starts directly west of the big river bridge at milepost 357.8, to the southwest of Amarapura. An alternative access lane starts across the roundabout from the Paleik road junction at milepost 357. From the latter head north then turn right at the first T-junction, sidestepping the broken bridge on a bike-wide track and replacement pontoon. Both of these routes wind through fascinatingly stupa-speckled Hantharwaddy Village.

Mandalay-Inwa Boat

For the first time in 2013–14, Nmai Kha ran a tourist-season ferry direct from Gawein Jetty ($8 return, no extra charge for bicycles) leaving Mandalay at 12.30pm (one hour) and returning from Sinkyone Fortress at 4pm (two hours). While giving only a limited time in situ, it offers a great way of getting to/from Inwa by bicycle. Indeed for now, arriving without a bike means a long walk to the main Inwa sites. Once the horse-cart cartel catches on to this boat service, however, doubtless carts will start meeting the boat. The boat's return journey delightfully passes Sagaing's golden stupas at sunset.

Sagaing-Inwa Boat

Very rarely used by foreigners are the few daily longboat ferries to Sagaing from Apyinsanyar village (per person/boat K200/2000). They leave when full.

ⓘ Getting Around

There are no taxis or motorbike taxis (unless you bring your own from Mandalay). The most popular way to visit Inwa is by horse cart (one-/two-hour tours K6000/9000 for one or two people). Dozens of carts await at Inwa's eastern jetty. As yet finding a horse cart at Sinkyone is hit and miss. Horse-cart tours are a major part of the Inwa experience, carriages avoid noise pollution and create picturesque scenes along the tree-lined tracks. However, cart drivers typically stick to a fairly fixed route so bringing your own bicycle or motorbike from Mandalay can prove an attractive alternative if you want to explore more thoroughly. Walking can prove uncomfortably sweaty.

Sagaing   စစ်ကိုင်း

📷 072 / POPULATION C40,000

As you cross the Ayeyarwady on the busy new bridge, Sagaing's uncountable white-and-gold stupas shimmer on waves of low green hills. No individual pagoda stands out as a particular must-see, but taken together the whole scene is enthralling – like a hilly green Bagan. A highlight is walking the (sometimes steep) covered stairways that lead magically past monasteries and nunneries, to viewpoints from which you can survey the river and yet more stupas.

History

Named for the trees hanging over the river, Sagaing became the capital of an independent Shan kingdom around 1315. The fall of Bagan had thrown central Myanmar into chaos and though Pinya had emerged as the new regional capital, its ruler's son set up Sagaing as a rival power centre.

Its first period of importance lasted around half a century: in 1364 the founder's grandson, Thado Minbya, moved the capital to Inwa. From 1760 Sagaing enjoyed just four more years as capital, but the town's significance from then on became more spiritual than political. Today it is home to thousands of monks and nuns, and is a place where many Myanmar Buddhists go to meditate when stressed.

◉ Sights

◉ Sagaing Hill   စစ်ကိုင်းတောင်

Stupa-topped hillocks coalesce into Sagaing Hill, a long tree-dappled north–south ridge that starts around 1½ miles north of the market area. A narrow, driveable lane winds up, or take the 350-step stairway from One Lion Gate.

Sagaing

Pon Nya Shin Paya

BUDDHIST TEMPLE

(ဆွမ်းဦးပုညရှင်ဘုရား; camera fee K300) This 'early offering shrine', full name Soon U Pon Nya Shin Paya, is the most important of the temples on Sagaing Hill's southern crown and the first you'll come to on climbing the One Lion stairway. Notice the bronze frogs that serve as a collection box in the rather gaudy buddha hall – the hill was originally thought to resemble a giant toad, a superstitious blessing which inspired Sagaing's development in the 14th century. The central 97ft-high gilded stupa was originally conceived in 1312.

Legends claim that the stupa magically appeared overnight, built by the local king's faithful minister Pon Nya in a superhuman flurry of activity inspired by a magical Buddha relic that he'd found in a betel-nut box. The myth fancifully claims that Pon Nya himself was of supernatural parentage, his father having 'flown' to Sagaing from the Himalayas millennia before, arriving to a curious communion with the Buddha, seven hermits and a flower-bearing orang-utan. (Burmese genealogy is never boring.)

Umin Thounzeh

BUDDHIST TERRACE

(ဥမင်သုံးဆယ်) Around 10 minutes' walk north of Pon Nya Shin, Umin Thounzeh (literally 30 Caves) is famed for its crescent-shaped colonnade of 45 buddha images.

Around Sagaing Hill

Shin Pin Nan Kain

PAGODA

Shin Pin Nan Kain's brass-clad stupa sits on a hilltop that's lower than Sagaing Hill but has even better panoramas. Resident monk Bhikku Tilawka speaks decent English and delights in showing guests the best viewpoints.

Lejunman Aung Paya

STUPA

Contemporary stupa with gilt details and a white corncob spire.

Sagaing

THE MISSING KING

After Inwa-based King Hsinbyushin sacked the then Thai capital, Ayuthaya, in 1767, he returned with thousands of prisoners who were resettled around Mandalay. These included skilled artisans (credited with kick-starting many of Mandalay's great craft traditions) and even the Ayuthayan ex-King Uthumphon who lived locally for nearly 30 more years as a monk. His final resting place has long been disputed, but in 2013 archaeologists claimed 'with 90% certainty' to have identified the grave in **Lin Zin Kone Cemetery**. It's currently just a pile of old bricks backing onto rubbish-strewn waste ground, but according to press reports a Thai-funded $3 million restoration has been mooted.

Tilawkaguru
CAVE TEMPLE

(တိလောကကုရှ) Accessed from a dead-end road at the southwest base of Sagaing Hill, this mural-filled cave complex dates originally from 1672. Opening times are sporadic and finding the key-holder can be challenging.

Sitagu Buddhist Academy
UNIVERSITY

Set up in 1994 to educate the brightest young monks, the academy's centrepiece is a Sanchi-style hemispherical stupa, gilded and embossed with dharma-wheel patterns. In the surrounding arcade are photos of Asia's great Buddhist sites, often shown as holiday-style snaps featuring the university's founder-monk U-Nyan Nate Tara.

Thakya Dita Nunnery
NUNNERY

Modern nunnery with a 16ft, 6in gilded woven-cane Buddha figure in an air-conditioned glass chamber.

Town Centre

The flat market area has little charm but further south it's pleasant to cycle along Strand Rd with a few old **colonial-era buildings** lining its north side and views across to Inwa from the Ayeyarwady riverfront.

Htuparyon Paya
STUPA

This gigantic stupa, originally built in 1444, is unusual for having three circular storeys each incorporating arched niches. Across Say Yon Gyi St, a garden of garish statues includes a particularly fearsome red cobra.

Ayeyarwady Bridges

Linking Sagaing and Amarapura are two parallel bridges, each with multiple metal-framed spans. The 16-span 1934 **Ava Bridge** was partly demolished in 1942 to deny passage to advancing WWII Japanese troops. It wasn't repaired until 1954. The big new Sagaing Bridge was completed in 2005.

Shwe-kyet-kya
STUPAS, VIEWPOINT

One of the best places from which to appreciate Sagaing is from across the river at this little bluff with a cascade of small stupas. It's part of a pair with the bigger Shwe-kyet-yet on a gentle rise across the road. The name, meaning Golden Fowl's Run, relates to various curious legends from one of Buddha's supposed past lives...as a chicken.

Northwest of Centre

Kaunghmudaw Paya
STUPA

(Monywa Hwy) Five miles northwest of central Sagaing, Kaunghmudaw Paya is a vast gilded pudding of a stupa rising 150ft high. It was built in 1636 to commemorate Inwa's re-establishment as the royal capital. According to local tradition, the king agonised interminably over how to shape the stupa. His queen, tired of hubby's indecisiveness, ripped open her blouse and, pointing to her breast, said: 'Make it like this!'

Less romantic scholars claim it was actually modelled after the vast Suvarnamali Mahaceti (Ruwanwelisaya) stupa in Anuradhapura, Sri Lanka. Kaunghmudaw is distantly visible from Sagaing Hill and easy to spot as you drive past en route to Monywa. The surrounding area has many other stupas and is well known for silversmiths.

Ubamin Silverware
SILVER WORKSHOP

(☑ 09 203 1564, 072-21304; www.ubaminsilverware.com; Monywa Highway) Behind their shop (2 miles northeast of Sagaing market), Ubamin's artisans hammer, tap and polish remarkable detail into silver pots, repoussage vases and animal figures. Fascinating, and no sales pressure.

🛏 Sleeping & Eating

Only two hotels have foreigner licenses though a third was under (re)construction at the time of research.

Shwe Pyne Sone   HOTEL $$
(☎ 072-21942; shwepyaesonehotel.sgg@gmail.com; 20 Aoe Tan Lay Rd; r $20-40; ❄🖥) New, fresh rooms, most bright and with high ceilings, lead off generously spacious common sitting areas on each landing. Wifi in the lobby, bicycle/motorbike rental K4000/10,000.

Sein Pann Myaing   GUESTHOUSE $
(Tha Dhamma St; r $15-35) Ageing and very musty; a last resort.

Minsuyek   BEER STATION $
(Strand Rd; draft beer K500; ⊙8am-9pm) It's scruffy and slightly disreputable but this stilted riverside beer station has great views towards Inwa.

❶ Getting There & Away

Pick-ups from Mandalay (K500, one hour) drop off passengers in the market area, but return from outside Aye Cherry Restaurant by the Ava Bridge's south sliproad.

Small **longboats** (Strand Rd; K200/2000 per person/boat) will shuttle you across to Inwa from the end of Zeya St. Charter or be prepared to wait hours.

Mingun   မင်းကွန်း

♫ 072 / POPULATION C1000

Home to a trio of unique pagodas, Mingun is a compact riverside village that makes a popular half-day excursion from Mandalay. The journey is part of the attraction, whether puttering up the wide Ayeyarwady or rollercoastering along a rural lane from Sagaing.

A Sagaing-Mingun fee (K3000) is half-heartedly collected on the east side of Mingun Paya. In peak season this might be checked at the Mingun Bell but we weren't asked for it at all.

From November to February little Mingun can feel overloaded with visitors (especially before 1pm, when most tourist boats return to Mandalay). But drinks sellers and oil-painting vendors are easily avoided by simply walking around behind the monuments on the dusty paths to the west. Views from these paths are most attractive in the afternoon when sunlight illuminates the west-facing side of Mingun Paya.

◉ Sights

Mingun Paya   STUPA RUIN
(မင်းကွန်းဘုရား) Started in 1790, Mingun Paya (or Pahtodawgyi) would have been the world's biggest stupa had it been finished. In fact, work stopped when King Bodawpaya died in 1819. That left only the bottom third complete. But the result is still a huge structure – a roughly 240ft cube on a 460ft lower terrace. It is often described as the world's largest pile of bricks.

For added drama, there are several deep cracks caused by the massive 1838 earthquake. The November 2012 earthquake caused further damage, meaning that climbing to the top is currently forbidden for safety reasons.

Pondaw Paya   STUPA
To see what Mingun Paya would have looked like had it ever been completed, have a quick look at diminutive Pondaw Paya, 200yd south at the end of the tourist strip.

Chinthe Ruins   RUIN
Across the road from Mingun Paya lie two house-sized brick-and-stucco ruins. These are just the haunches of what would have

Mingun

MANDALAY & AROUND MINGUN

been truly gigantic *chinthe* (the pagoda's half-lion, half-dragon guardian deities).

Mingun Bell   GIANT BELL

(မင်းကွန်းခေါင်းလောင်း) In 1808 Bodawpaya continued his biggest-is-best obsession by commissioning a bronze bell weighing 55,555 *viss* (90 tonnes). It's 13ft high and over 16ft across at the lip and was the world's biggest ringable bell for many decades, albeit now surpassed by the giant bell of Pingdingshan, China. You can duck beneath and stand within the bell while some helpful bystander gives it a good thump.

Hsinbyume Paya   BUDDHIST STUPA

(ဆင်ဖြူမယ်ဘုရား) Built in 1816, possibly using materials pilfered from Mingun Paya, this unusual pagoda rises in seven wavy, whitewashed terraces representing the seven mountain ranges around Mt Meru – the mountain at the centre of the Buddhist universe.

✖ Eating

There are half a dozen snack shacks around Mingun Paya entrance. **Point** (mains K2000-3500), near the ferry jetty, has a river view and serves draft Spirulina beer (K700).

❶ Getting There & Away

Mingun is a pleasant 35-minute drive from Sagaing, easily added to an 'ancient capitals' motorbike or taxi tour from Mandalay.

But it's more popular to go by boat (one hour out, 40 minutes back, passport required). From Mandalay's 26th St 'tourist jetty' (Mayan Chan), boats depart at 9am (foreigner/bicycle K5000/500 return) returning at 1pm. Alternatively Nmai Hka's *Tharlarwaddy* ($6 return, bicycles free) departs 8.30am from Gawein Jetty, returning 11.30am. For $8 extra, the latter boat continues to Inwa. Don't waste money on 'upper class' tickets which uselessly provide a bed but no other luxury.

Another option is taking a bicycle on the boat then riding down to Sagaing (roughly two hours). There are no major hills en route but there are plenty of undulations that can be a little testing for gearless rental bikes. Sagaing–Mandalay pick-ups will transport you and your bike back to Mandalay for K2000 or less.

Paleik   ပုလဲ

♫ 02 / POPULATION C2500

Modest and rather kitschy, Paleik's **Yadana Labamuni Hsu-taung-pye** is widely known as the **Snake Pagoda** (Hmwe Paya)

due to three resident giant pythons. They appeared from the nearby forest in 1974 and never left. Predictably much of the statuary now celebrates Buddha getting cosy with snakes but the main attraction is the pythons' 11am daily washing and feeding ceremony. Off-season it's delightfully low key, attracting a handful of local families. But the whole atmosphere changes dramatically when, as commonly occurs in peak season, a tourist bus arrives.

Less than five minutes' walk south of the snake pagoda is Paleik's 'mini-Bagan', an almost entirely overlooked collection of over 300 close-packed **stupas** in varying states of repair. Many date from the Konbaung period.

Paleik is about 12 miles south of Mandalay. Riding a motorbike along the busy Mandalay–Yangon road is an unpleasant chore, mitigated slightly by a brief stop at the gigantic 1996 **Golden Tooth Pagoda**, which looks especially impressive when floodlit at night. There are contrastingly pleasant, well-asphalted rural lanes running cross-country to Inwa and, with a brief double-back, to Sagaing: turn west at Newday Petrol just north of the big river bridge.

Pinya

Possibly Myanmar's most forgotten ancient capital, Pinya rose to prominence in 1303 in the aftermath of the last wave of Mongol attacks. Its founder was upstart governor-king Thihathu, whose son, Athingaraza Sawyun, soon set up a rival kingdom across the river in Sagaing. The two coexisted for half a century, creating Bagan-style buildings, but today all that remains of old Pinya is a trio of large brick stupa ruins. Two of them are significantly overgrown but each has buddha images still visible within. The trio isn't worth a special trip but the site makes an easy 10-minute detour en route to/from Mandalay Airport.

Yedagon Hills

One of Mandalay's loveliest motorcycle excursions heads east on a rural lane starting just south of 35th St's eastern end. The ride starts with an avenue of rain trees between paddy fields that glow emerald green in October. Cross the big canal and continue past the **Yaytagon Golf Resort**

(☏ 09 203 4052; green fees/caddy/clubs/buggy $30/10/22/15; ⊘ 5am-7pm) and the second of two similarly named Dhamma Mandala meditation centres (p232), and the road appears to end at an abrupt green massif. In fact, a small lane to the right winds high up into these steep hills for super views, accessing a series of stupas, mini-monasteries and hermitages perched on and into crags and clefts, partly hidden in the lush foliage. The most eye-catching

feature is the **Denggangaya (500 monk) stairway** with a seemingly endless procession of 8ft-tall red-robed concrete statues descending the mountain from **Tharwadaitar shrine**.

Kyaukse

☐ 066 / POPULATION C50,000

Bagan was not the only place to benefit from King Anawrahta's remarkable 11th-century building spree. According to legend, one of Anawrahta's relic-carrying elephants took a liking to Webu Hill, above today's Kyaukse. The king took that as a sign to found a city at its base, starting with an irrigation system created using a stone dam (*kyauk se*). Nearly a millennium later the attractive small town (around 40 miles south of Mandalay) remains elephant mad. Naive elephant masks and toys are sold at numerous kiosks, white elephant statues guard the **gigantic golden Buddha** halfway up Webu Hill's north slope, and a nationally famous **elephant dance** competition forms the centrepiece of Kyaukse's main festival. Dancing 'elephants' are actually two humans in wonderfully idiosyncratic elephant costumes. The competition is held once day before Thadingyut full moon (October), but for a day or two beforehand you might see 'elephants' practice-prancing around town.

WHICH CAPITAL WHEN

Capital	From
Pinya (Myinsaing dynasty)	1303
Sagaing (co-existing with Pinya)	1315
Inwa (Ava)	1364
Taungoo	1555
Inwa (Ava)	1636
Shwebo (then called Mokesbo)	1752
Sagaing	1760
Inwa (Ava)	1764
Amarapura	1783
Inwa (Ava)	1823
Amarapura (following the 1838 earthquake)	1841
Mandalay	1861

Northern Myanmar

Best Places to Stay

➡ Hotel Pyin Oo Lwin (p264)

➡ Mr Charles Guest House (p271)

➡ Malikha Lodge (p290)

➡ Hotel Madira (p277)

➡ Friendship Hotel (p281)

Best Places to Eat

➡ Club Terrace (p265)

➡ Jing Hpaw Thu (p278)

➡ Aung Padamyar (p264)

➡ Shamie Restaurant (p281)

➡ Shwe Lawon (p275)

Why Go?

Rugged and remote, northern Myanmar offers a fascinating mix of ethnic minority peoples and the prospect of travel through some of the least-visited areas of the country. While much of this vast region remains off-limits, two main routes are accessible. One climbs rapidly from Mandalay to the British-era summer capital of Pyin Oo Lwin, and then continues across the rolling Shan Plateau to Lashio. The crisp evenings are a great relief from the heat of the plains, while hikes take visitors into timeless Palaung and Shan hill-villages.

The other option is taking a ride along the mighty Ayeyarwady (Irrawaddy) River. You'll need close on a week if you want to stop off along the way from Bhamo to Mandalay, but shorter itineraries are possible starting from Katha, the setting of George Orwell's *Burmese Days*. The lazy, meandering journey downstream provides great opportunities for genuine interaction with the locals. Far beyond Myitkyina lie the rarely seen, snow-capped peaks of Myanmar's Himalayas.

When to Go
Northern Myanmar

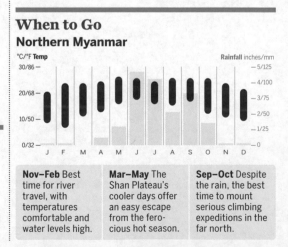

°C/°F Temp — Rainfall inches/mm

Nov–Feb Best time for river travel, with temperatures comfortable and water levels high.

Mar–May The Shan Plateau's cooler days offer an easy escape from the ferocious hot season.

Sep–Oct Despite the rain, the best time to mount serious climbing expeditions in the far north.

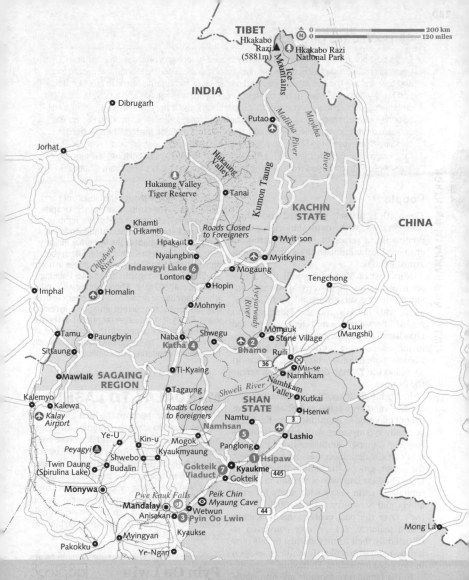

Northern Myanmar Highlights

1 Walk to unspoilt Shan and Palaung villages from **Hsipaw** (p268), a laid-back plateau town with royal connections

2 Spend lazy days drifting down the mighty Ayeyarwady River starting from pretty **Bhamo** (p280) and taking in little-visited towns on the way

3 Enjoy the cool air and colonial architecture of **Pyin Oo Lwin** (p260), the British summer capital of Myanmar

4 Explore George Orwell connections in sleepy **Katha** (p283)

5 Head to the remote hills of northern Shan State and visit

the tea-growing, ridge-top town of **Namhsan** (p273)

6 Brave the rough road to serene **Indawgyi Lake** and mystical **Shwe Myitsu Pagoda** (p280)

7 Ride a bouncing train across the mighty **Gokteik Viaduct** (p267), Myanmar's longest railway bridge

❶ TRAVEL RESTRICTIONS

Large portions of the north are essentially closed to foreign visitors without special permission. The main exceptions are areas along or close to the Mandalay–Lashio road and towns along the Ayeyarwady between Mandalay and Bhamo. You can link Mandalay and Myitkyina by railway but not by road, unless you have a guide and a private car. With suitable permits (allow several weeks' preparation), and if the stars are right, additional options include expensive fly-in tours to the Himalayan foothill area around Putao. You can also drive, accompanied by a guide, from Lashio to Mu-se for the Chinese border crossing. Travel between Myitkyina and Bhamo, whether by boat or road, is impossible for foreigners (and difficult even for the locals thanks to ongoing fighting). Foreigners are seriously discouraged from visiting the jade-mining sin city of Hpakant (Pakkan).

People

The north is sparsely populated and ethnically complex, with many minority groups dominating a series of pro- and anti-government local administrations and regional armed militias.

Northeast of Mandalay you'll find many Shan people (as in eastern Myanmar), divided into five sub-groups all prefixed 'Tai', along with the Wa and the Palaung, who regard themselves semi-religiously as the guardians of Burmese tea production. Lashio and several other border areas have large Chinese populations, who speak Mandarin as well as the Yunnan dialects spoken across the frontier.

In Kachin State, north of Mandalay, 'minorities' (notably Kachin and Shan) form an overall majority. As an ethnic term, Kachin is generally synonymous with speakers of the Jingpaw (Jingpo) language. But by Myanmar's official definition it also covers at least five other groups, including Rawang and Lisu. The Lisu language is written in a sci-fi capitalised Latin script with many inverted letters and 'vowel-free' words (hello is 'hw hw'). Over the past century, many Kachin and a majority of Lisu have converted to Christianity, their former animist beliefs now largely reduced to colourful folklore as seen in two great festivals at Myitkyina.

In the Himalayan foothills are minuscule populations of various Tibetan tribal peoples including the Taron, Asiatic pygmies who now number less than 10 and are limited to Naungmun in Myanmar's northernmost tip.

❶ Dangers & Annoyances

Since Burma's independence, the north has witnessed a smorgasbord of low-level uprisings and ethnic separatist movements. Tourists aren't allowed too close to any flashpoints so for most visitors these are a political curiosity rather than a serious danger, although the closure of parts of the region is an obvious annoyance. Despite ongoing efforts to broker ceasefires, fighting continues between the Kachin Independence Army and the Tatmadaw, the Myanmar military, especially in eastern Kachin State. Shan rebels and the United Wa State Army are active in northern Shan State, along with the smaller Palaung State Liberation Front. Who's fighting who and where can change dramatically, so check with locals to see what the current situation is in remote areas. Foreigners are never targeted, but there is always the chance of being in the wrong place at the wrong time. The Tatmadaw do not take kindly to travellers wandering into conflict zones.

MANDALAY TO LASHIO

For an easy escape from the heat and hussle of Mandalay, do what the colonial Brits did – nip up to Pyin Oo Lwin. And as you've come this far, why not continue further across the rolling hills of the Shan Plateau to discover some of Southeast Asia's most satisfying hill treks from Kyaukme or Hsipaw. But bring a decent fleece: while days are warm, it gets chilly after dark and can be downright cold at 5am when buses depart and markets are at their candlelit best.

Pyin Oo Lwin ပြင်ဦးလွင်

📞 085 / POPULATION C70,000 / ELEV 3445FT

Founded by the British in 1896, the town was originally called Maymyo ('May-town'), after Colonel May of the 5th Bengal Infantry, and was designed as a place to escape the Mandalay heat. Following the Indian-raj terminology for such places, it has been known ever since as a 'hill station', although in fact it's fairly flat (just at a raised elevation). After the construction of the railway from Mandalay, Maymyo became the summer capital for the British colonial administration, a role it held until the end of British rule in 1948. The name was changed after the British departed but numerous colonial structures, ranging from impressive mansions to churches, remain. So too do the descendants of the Indian and Nepali workers who came here to lay the railway line.

In later decades, Pyin Oo Lwin was famous mostly for its fruit, jams, vegetables and fruit wines, as well as for the huge military academies that train the officers of the Tatmadaw (Myanmar Army). Now, with the rise of the

Pyin Oo Lwin

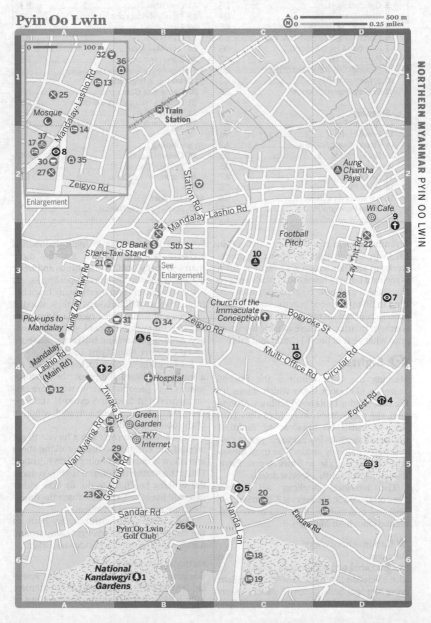

Pyin Oo Lwin

◎ Top Sights
1 National Kandawgyi Gardens B6

◎ Sights
2 All Saints' Church A4
3 Candacraig Hotel D5
4 Chan Tak D4
5 Former Croxton Hotel C5
6 Maha Aung Mye Bon Thar Pagoda B4
7 Number 4 High School D3
8 Purcell Tower A2
9 Seventh Day Adventist Church D3
10 Shwezigone Paya C3
11 Survey Training Centre C4

⬮ Sleeping
12 Aureum Palace A4
13 Bravo Hotel A1
14 Cherry Guesthouse A2
15 Dahlia Motel D5
16 Grace Hotel 1 .... A5
17 Grace Hotel 2 .... A2
18 Hotel Pyin Oo Lwin C6
19 Kandawgyi Hill Resort C6
20 Royal Parkview Hotel C5

21 Ruby Hotel A3

⊗ Eating
22 Aung Padamyar D3
23 Club Terrace A5
24 Daw Khin Than B3
25 Family Restaurant A1
26 Feel B6
27 La Yone A2
28 Sain Mya Ayar D3
29 San Francisco B5

◎ Drinking & Nightlife
30 December Cafe A2
31 Golden Triangle Café & Bakery B4
32 Win Thu Zar A1
33 Woodland C5

⬗ Shopping
34 Central Market B4
35 Liqueur Corner A2
36 Pacific World Curio B1

❶ Transport
37 Crown Bicycle Rental A2

Myanmar version of the nouveau riche, Pyin Oo Lwin is once again becoming a popular weekend and hot-season getaway. The town is seeing a burst of investment, roads are getting busier and new construction is beginning to fill up the once generous tree-shaded spaces between mansions in the wealthy southern quarter. Get here quickly to experience what's left of the old charm and calm.

◎ Sights

Marking the town centre is the **Purcell Tower**, a 1936 clock tower which thinks it's Big Ben, judging by its hourly chimes. Around 6am, the pretty **Maha Aung Mye Bon Thar Pagoda** insists on broadcasting Buddhist lectures through its loudspeakers just in case you weren't already awake. The most important central pagoda is **Shwezigone Paya**, though it's not worth a special detour.

The red-brick, Anglican **All Saints' Church** (Ziwaka St; ⊘ services at 8.30am Sun, 7am Wed) was originally built in 1912 as the regimental church for Maymyo.

★ National Kandawgyi Gardens   PARK
(အများသားကန်တော်ကြီးဥယျာဉ်; Nandan Rd; adult/child under 12yr/camera $5/3/1; ⊘7am-6pm, aviary 8am-5pm, orchid garden & butterfly museum 8.30am-5pm, Nan Myint Tower lift operates till 5pm)

Founded in 1915, this lovingly maintained 435-acre botanical garden features more than 480 species of flowers, shrubs and trees. For casual visitors, its most appealing aspect is the way flowers and overhanging branches frame views of Kandawgyi Lake's wooden bridges and small gilded pagoda. Admission includes the swimming pool, visits to the **aviary**, **orchid garden** and **butterfly museum** and the bizarre **Nan Myint Tower**.

Looking like a space rocket designed for a medieval Chinese Emperor, the 12-storey tower offers panoramic views which are better appreciated from the external staircase than through the grease-smeared windows of the observation deck.

Annoyingly, you can't use a bicycle to get around the grounds so bring walking shoes and allow around two hours to do it justice. Using the southern entrance slightly reduces the walking you have to do. By 6pm either gate will likely be locked so watch the time – there are no closure warnings.

The garden's two entrances are both on the eastern side of Kandawgyi Lake, around a mile south of smaller Kandawlay Lake.

National Landmarks Garden   MUSEUM
(adult/child $4/2; ⊘8am-6pm) This extensive hilly park is dotted with representations of

landmarks from around Myanma. Some are pretty tacky. The entrance is across the road from National Kandawgyi Gardens, a little to the north of its southern (main) entrance. There is also an **amusement park** just to the north; one ticket gets you into both sites.

Colonial Buildings COLONIAL BUILDINGS

Most of Pyin Oo Lwin's trademark colonial-era buildings are dotted amid the southeastern woodland suburbs on and off Circular Rd. Many look like classic 1920s British homes, while the biggest have the feel of a St Trinian's–style boarding school. There are also a number of decaying but still impressive mansions on Nan Myaing St heading towards the Naval College.

Check out the splendid **Former Croxton Hotel** (Gandamar Myaing Hotel; Circular Rd), as well as the **Number 4 High School** (Circular Rd) and the **Survey Training Centre** (Multi-Office Rd). Up near the Shan Market, a fine half-timbered mansion is now a **Seventh Day Adventist Church** (Cherry St).

Chan Tak CHINESE TEMPLE

(134 Forest Rd) This large, classically styled, if mostly modern, Chinese temple comes complete with ornate stucco dragons, rock gardens, a vegetarian buffet restaurant, landscaped ponds and a seven-layered Chinese-style pagoda.

Candacraig Hotel HISTORIC BUILDING

(Thiri Myaing Hotel; ☑ 085-22047; Anawrattha Rd; s/d $42/48) Formerly the British Club, this classic colonial pile comes complete with side turrets and is set in attractively manicured gardens. There's a slightly spooky air to the place – many locals believe it's haunted – and it sees comparatively few guests, despite the seven huge, if old-fashioned, rooms available here. There's a restaurant but, sadly, no raj-redolent bar.

🏃 Activities

The 18-hole **Pyin Oo Lwin Golf Club** (☑ 085-22382; Golf Club Rd; green fee $10, caddy $5, club hire $6, shoe hire $1; ⊙ 6am-6pm) is one of Myanmar's better courses and popular with the many army officers based in town. There's a strict dress code – collars, caps and no jeans – and a caddie is compulsory. You can hire clubs and golf shoes.

🛏 Sleeping

Some of Pyin Oo Lwin's cheaper hotels aren't licensed to accommodate foreigners.

Staying in the leafy gardens area south of the centre is a distinctively Pyin Oo Lwin experience, but consider renting a bike and you'll need a torch; the pot-holed roads get very dark at night. Staying centrally is less atmospheric, but more convenient for transport, restaurants, shops and internet cafes. Unless otherwise stated, breakfast is included in quoted rates.

🛏 Town Centre

Ruby Hotel HOTEL $

(☑ 085-21909; rubyhotel@gmail.com; Block 4, 32/B Mingalar St; r $30; ✳ 🛜) Tucked down a quiet side street, but close to the centre of town, this Muslim-owned newcomer has nice, bright, well-kept rooms with decent bathrooms. Prices drop out of season.

Grace Hotel 2 GUESTHOUSE $

(☑ 085-22081; 46/48 Mandalay-Lashio Rd; r $5-20) For the money, the best deal in town. The rooms are compact and the cheapest are without windows and bathrooms, but the doubles with shower are acceptable.

Cherry Guesthouse GUESTHOUSE $

(☑ 085-21306; 19 Mandalay-Lashio Rd; s/d $10/20; 🛜) Breezy place, even if the small singles without bathrooms are nothing to shout about. Pay more and the room quality jumps dramatically.

Bravo Hotel HOTEL $

(☑ 085-21223; www.bravo-hotel.com; Mandalay-Lashio Rd; s/d/tr $20/30/40; ✳ 🛜) Earthenware amphorae, ornate teak chests and carved gilded panel-work reveal that some thought has gone into the design here, although the rooms are a little musty for boutique status. A solid midrange option with helpful staff.

🛏 Palace Hill

Aureum Palace HOTEL $$$

(☑ 085-21902; www.aureumpalacehotel.com; off Mandalay Hwy; bungalows/ste $99/250; ✳ 🛜) Owned by tycoon Tay Za, this painstakingly precise recreation of the former British governor's mansion is a considerable achievement. However, only five suites are within the main half-timbered mansion, with the remaining accommodation being in stylish but modern bungalows at the bottom of the extensive grounds (electric buggy links).

📖 Gardens Area

Grace Hotel 1
GUESTHOUSE $

(☑085-21230; 114A Nan Myaing Rd; s/d/tr $15/25/36) The high-ceilinged rooms with solid wooden furniture mirror Pyin Oo Lwin's retro colonial vibe. Comfortable beds, obliging staff and a pleasant garden with fading sun-loungers. Bike hire is K2500 a day.

Dahlia Motel
GUESTHOUSE $

(☑085-22255; 67 Eindaw Rd; s/d/tr $20/35/45; ✳) A clump of concrete buildings offering the cheapest beds in the leafy 'burbs, the Dahlia is short on atmosphere but has pleasant staff. Rooms differ in quality; check them first.

★ Hotel Pyin Oo Lwin
HOTEL $$

(☑085-21226; www.hotelpyinoolwin.com; 9 Nandar Rd; r $120-150; ✳@🛜🏊) Stylish new place with 18 bungalows scattered around a 5-acre site that feels like a suburban cul-de-sac and comes with a mini-version of the Purcell Tower. The big, comfortable bungalows all have terraces and working fireplaces. Efficient, English-speaking staff, Asian fusion restaurant and a heated, indoor swimming pool.

Royal Parkview Hotel
HOTEL $$

(☑085-22641; www.royalparkviewpyinoolwin.com; 107 Lanthaya St; r $45-60; ✳🛜) Still one of Pyin's best midrange options, there's neither royalty nor park views here, but long ceiling drapes create a fashionable edge to the restaurant and the wide range of rooms are attractive, comfortable and come with mini-terraces.

ℹ WANDERING BY WAGON IN PYIN OO LWIN

Clip-clopping around town in the picturesque, colourfully painted horse-drawn carriages that stand in for taxis here is a long-established Pyin Oo Lwin tradition. Known locally as 'wagons', they congregate close to the market and the clock tower. Wandering the mansion-lined streets of the southern part of town by wagon is especially evocative, and they can also be positioned artfully to act as foreground props for photos.

Increasing traffic, though, means the wagons are less plentiful than they once were. Some of the drivers, too, have adopted the 'fleece the tourist' tactics of Yangon taxis. Always establish the price before you set off and pick a driver who speaks some English.

Kandawgyi Hill Resort
HOTEL $$

(☑085-21839; www.myanmartreasureresorts.com; Nandar Rd; d/tr $80/75) Splendid setting, with five of the 15 rooms inside a 1921 British-era house whose key asset is a delightful terrace commanding a large sweep of garden leading down to the lakefront road. The rest are well-spaced, well-appointed bungalows. It's one of very few hotels to have heating (important in January).

🍴 Eating

Pyin Oo Lwin's culinary choices reflect its different communities, with Indian- and Chinese-themed places, as well as many restaurants serving a fusion-like mix of dishes. Standard, cheap teahouses and eateries are scattered throughout the city centre, both along the main road and around the Central Market, where a night market fills three blocks of Zaigyo St with **snack-food stands** (snacks from K200; ⊙5.30-9pm), as well as close to the Shan Market. But if you're willing to spend a little more, a handful of stand-out restaurants can make dining in Pyin Oo Lwin a real pleasure.

★ Aung Padamyar
INDIAN $

(44, Block 28 Thumingalar; curries K3500; ⊙11am-7pm) The finest Indian in town: a secluded, friendly, family-run joint with a range of curries, all of which come with side dishes to create a veritable feast. To find it, take the first right off Circular Rd after the Shan Market and then the first left down a small alley. Look for the red sign. Only kyat is accepted here.

Family Restaurant
BURMESE, THAI $

(off Mandalay-Lashio Rd; curries from K2800; ⊙9.30am-9pm) The decor is bland and there's no alcohol served, but the delicious curry spread comes with complimentary veggie side dishes, salad, rice, soup, pappadams and chutneys and dips.

Daw Khin Than
BURMESE $

(Mandalay-Lashio Rd; curries K3000; ⊙7am-7pm) With so many foreign-themed eateries in town, proper Bamar food is hard to find. This place satisfies lunchtime curry cravings, as well as offering Shan noodles for breakfast.

La Yone
CHINESE $

(Zeigyo Rd; mains from K3000; ⊙8am-9pm; 🖬) Almost every restaurant in Pyin Oo Lwin features Chinese-influenced dishes, but La Yone is run by immigrants from Fujian and so the flavours are far more authentic. At night, it also acts as an unofficial beer station.

San Francisco
SOUTHEAST ASIAN $

(Golf Club Rd; noodles/mains from K2000/3000; ⊙5.30am-9.30pm; 🖋) A long way from the Bay Area, this airy joint attracts many locals with its mix of Chinese and Thai dishes, along with a few Kachin and Western specialities. Equally good for a beer; the servings are big here.

Sain Mya Ayar
CHINESE $

(Zay Thit Rd; dim sum & noodles from K500; ⊙ 6am-8pm) Cute Chinese-style, open-air restaurant run by a Shan family serving tasty dim sum in the front yard of a modest half-timbered colonial-era house. They do noodle dishes and juices too.

★ Club Terrace
SOUTHEAST ASIAN $$

(🖋23311; 25 Golf Club Rd; noodles from K2500, mains from K4000; ⊙8am-10pm; 🖋) Pyin Oo Lwin's most romantic restaurant occupies a gorgeous half-timbered colonial bungalow with tables spilling out onto the garden terrace. The food favours a scrumptious combination of Thai and Chinese flavours, as well as a small selection of Shan and Western options. Extensive wine selection, including local fruit vintages, and the best service in town.

Feel
EUROPEAN, PAN-ASIAN $$

(🖋22083; off Nandar Rd; mains from K3000; ⊙8.30am-9pm; 🖋) The upmarket yet casual lakeside setting is an obvious attraction, while the menu spans Europe and a fair chunk of Asia (this is the only place in town for Japanese if you're craving sushi). Reservations are occasionally advisable for dinner. The waterside terrace is a relaxed spot for coffee (from K800) or a drink.

🍸 Drinking & Nightlife

Woodland
BAR

(53 Circular Rd; cocktails from K3300; ⊙11am-11pm; 🖋) Electric-blue panelling, a glass wall that reveals an aviary, as well as a spacious garden area, make this a stylish if self-conscious venue for an evening libation. There's live music, cocktails, foreign beers and an extensive menu of Asian and Western favourites.

Golden Triangle Café & Bakery
CAFE

(Mandalay-Lashio Rd; Coffee & tea from K1000, sandwiches & pizzas from K2500; ⊙7am-10pm) This upbeat Western-flavoured cafe occu-

---

IRRAWADDY DOLPHINS

The Irrawaddy dolphin is one of Myanmar's most endangered animals. This small cetacean has a short, rounded snout like a beluga whale and hunts using sonar in the turgid waters of lakes and rivers. In the past, dolphins and humans were able to coexist quite peacefully – there are even reports of dolphins deliberately herding fish into nets – but the use of gill nets and the poisonous run-off from gold mining has driven the dolphin onto the critically endangered list. Only an estimated 58 to 72 remain in the river for which they are named. Yet sightings do still occur, and a 45-mile stretch of river south of Kyaukmyaung has been designated as a dolphin protection zone.

---

pies a column-fronted, late-colonial building full of ceiling fans and big blackboard menus. It serves a range of coffees and juices, as well as cakes, sandwiches and pizzas.

Win Thu Zar
BEER STATION

(Mandalay-Lashio Rd; beer K500; ⊙9am-9pm) Standard male-dominated beer hall notable purely because it serves tastily smooth Spirulina 'anti-ageing' beer on draught.

December Cafe
CAFE

(Zeigyo Rd; ⊙6am-9pm) Popular with officer cadets – wear green to blend in – this place occupies the ground floor of an old colonial building and has good cheap coffee (K300), juices, milkshakes and Burmese-style snacks.

🛍 Shopping

Central Market
MARKET

(Zeigyo Rd; ⊙6.30am-5.30pm) Sample Pyin Oo Lwin's famous (if seasonal) strawberries and other fruit, fresh, dried or as jams and wine. Also has cheap Western clothes and *longyi*. There are tailors on the 1st floor if you need alterations or something knocked up.

Liqueur Corner
ALCOHOL

(Zeigyo Rd; ⊙8.30am-8.30pm) Local fruit wines (bottles from K5000), as well as rotgut whisky and beer.

Pacific World Curio
ANTIQUES, CRAFT

(Mandalay-Lashio Rd; ⊙8am-7pm) Decent selection of Shan puppets, as well as other 'antiques' and local craft items. Haggle hard.

TRANSPORT TO/FROM PYIN OO LWIN

DESTINATION	BUS	SHARED TAXI	PICK-UP TRUCKS	TRAIN
Mandalay	K2000, 7am & 8am, 2hr	K6000/7000 back/front seat, frequent, 2hr	K2000, frequent until 6pm, 2-3hr	ordinary/1st/upper class $4/8/9, 1 daily 5.40pm, 6hr
Hsipaw	K5000, air-con 7.30am & 4pm, 3hr	N/A	N/A	$3/5/6, 1 daily 8.22am, 7hr
Kyaukme	K4000, air-con 7.30am & 4pm, 2hr	N/A	N/A	$2/4/5, 1 daily 8.22am, 5hr
Lashio	K5500, air-con 7.30am & 4pm, 5hr	N/A	N/A	$4/8/10, 1 daily 8.22am, 11hr
Yangon	K11,500, frequent 5.30am-6pm, 11hr	N/A	N/A	N/A
Nay Pyi Taw	K5800, 2 daily 10.30am & 5.30pm, 6hr	N/A	N/A	N/A

❶ Information

There are internet places all over town, although connection speeds vary. Pristine dollars can be changed at the **CB Bank** (Mandalay-Lashio Rd; ⊘10am-3pm Mon-Fri).

Green Garden (9/10 Ziwaka St; per hr K400; ⊘7am-9pm; 🛜) Snacks and drinks and free wifi.

TKY Internet (Ziwaka St; per hr K400; ⊘10am-10pm) Handy for Grace Hotel 1.

Wi Cafe (Circular Rd; per hr K500; ⊘6am-9pm; 🛜) Hipster teahouse with attached internet cafe and free wifi.

❶ Getting There & Away

Yangon and Nay Pyi Taw buses leave from the inconvenient main bus station Thiri Mandala, 2 miles east of the Shan Market.

All other buses leave from behind the San Pya Restaurant, 600m south of the bus station, as do some shared taxis and pick-ups to Mandalay.

Pick-ups to Mandalay leave from near the gas station at the roundabout at the entrance to town, as well as less frequently from outside the train station – north of the town centre.

Shared taxis to Mandalay leave from 4th St.

❶ Getting Around

MOTORCYCLE TAXIS

Easy to find close to the Central Market and the Bravo Hotel. Expect to pay K1500 to Kandawgyi Gardens. For longer hires, consider engaging English-speaking **Jeffrey** (✆09 4025 10483), who acts as a guide and motorcycle driver. Rates are $20 for a full day.

BICYCLE

Crown Bicycle Rental (Mandalay-Lashio Rd; ⊘7.30am-7pm) rents bicycles (K3000 for 24 hours) and motorbikes (K10,000 for 24 hours).

THREE-WHEEL PICK-UPS

These congregate outside the market; around K2000 to Kandawgyi Gardens.

'WAGONS'

Pyin Oo Lwin's signature horse-drawn buggies can be found near the Central Market. Reckon on K1500 to K2000 for a short trip across town, K15,000 for an all-day tour.

Around Pyin Oo Lwin

Towards Mandalay

ANISAKAN FALLS   အန်းစခန်းရေတံခွန်

About 1.5 miles north of Anisakan village, the plateau disappears into an impressive, deeply wooded amphitheatre, its sides ribboned with several waterfalls. The most spectacular of these is the gorgeous three-step **Dat Taw Gyaik** whose last stage thunders into a shady splash pool beside a small pagoda on the valley floor. It's best visited, and photographed, in the early morning or late afternoon.

To get here from Pyin Oo Lwin take the main Mandalay highway (a motorbike taxi is K6000 return). In Anisakan town take the second asphalted turn right (signposted) and keep right past the first large pagoda. At the end of this road a pair of basic shack-restaurants mark the start of a steep, twisting, rocky forest trail about 40 minutes' trek from the waterfall. It's treacherous in the rainy season (wear proper walking shoes), although you'll get to see the falls in magnificent, full flow. Local girls will follow you with drinks; they make good guides (K1000).

Towards Kyaukme

If you're driving to Kyaukme/Hsipaw, none of the following is more than a 2-mile detour from the main road but visiting via public transport is awkward. A round-trip half-day tour by motorcycle-taxi to all of the above from Pyin Oo Lwin should cost around K12,000. Sites are reviewed from west to east.

AUNG HTU KAN THA PAYA
အုံထူးကံသာဘုရား

Although only finished in March 2000, this dazzling pagoda is by far the region's most impressive religious building. It enshrines an enormous 17-ton white marble Buddha statue that fell off a truck bound for China in April 1997. After several attempts to retrieve the Buddha failed, it was decided that the statue 'had decided to stay in Myanmar'.

Eventually cranes were used to yank him up the hill and a dazzling new golden pagoda was built for him. He is now draped in gilt robes and sits in a temple interior that's an incredible overload of gold. The pagoda is on a hilltop, just south of the Lashio-bound highway, around 15 minutes' drive beyond Pyin Oo Lwin's vast Defense Forces Technological Academy compound. If you reach the toll gates you've gone half a mile too far.

PWE KAUK FALLS
ပွေးကောက်ရေတံခွန်

Called Hampshire Falls in British times, **Pwe Kauk** (admission K500, camera fee K300; ☉ 6am-7pm) is a series of small weirs and splash pools, linked by wooden bridges, rather than an actual waterfall. The forest glade setting is pretty, although the souvenir stands undermine any sense of natural serenity. It's a two-minute drive down a steep, easily missed lane off the Hsipaw road that starts directly north of Aung Htu Kan Tha Paya.

MYAING GYI
မြိုင်ကြီး

After descending a loop of hairpins, the Hsipaw road reaches Myaing Gyi where a rickety monastery climbs a wooded hillside. Two minutes' drive further on, the roadside **Wetwun Zaigone Monastery** is more photogenic with a fine array of stupas and Balinese-style pagodas behind a giant old banyan tree.

PEIK CHIN MYAUNG
ပိတ်ချင်းမြောင်

About 5 miles east of Myaing Gyi is this Buddhist cave complex. Many similar caves are little more than rocky niches or overhangs but **Peik Chin** (camera fee K300; ☉ 6.30am-4.30pm) **FREE** is much more extensive. It takes around 15 minutes to walk to the cave's end, following an underground stream past a series of colourful scenes from Buddhist scriptures interspersed with stupas and Buddha images.

There are a few sections where you'll need to bend over to get beneath dripping rocks but most of the cave is high-ceilinged and adequately lit so you don't need a torch. It can feel sweaty and humid inside. No shorts or footwear permitted.

The access road is around 2½ miles east of Myaing Gyi, just beyond the green sign announcing your arrival in Wetwun town. Turn right through a lion-guarded gateway arch then descend inexorably for another 2 miles to the large parking area thronged with souvenir stalls.

NORTHERN MYANMAR AROUND PYIN OO LWIN

THE GOKTEIK VIADUCT

A highlight of the long, slow Mandalay–Lashio train ride is the mighty Gokteik Viaduct (ဂုတ်ထိပ်ပိတ်တား), about 34 miles northeast of Pyin Oo Lwin. Built in 1901 by contractors from the Pennsylvania Steel Company it bridges the Gokteik Gorge, a densely forested ravine that cuts an unexpectedly deep gash through the otherwise mildly rolling landscape. At 318ft high and 2257ft across, it was the second-highest railway bridge in the world when it was constructed, and remains Myanmar's longest. Trains slow to a crawl when crossing the viaduct to avoid putting undue stress on the ageing superstructure, which, despite some 1990s renovation work, still creaks ominously as trains edge their way across. In either direction, the best views are from north-facing windows, that is the left side if you're heading towards Lashio. It's also visible through the trees for some time as the train winds down from the plateau and there are fine views from parts of Gokteik station (near the viaduct's western end) but beware that the train only stops there very briefly. Theoretically taking photographs of the viaduct is banned for 'security reasons', but nobody seems to care if you do.

Kyaukme ကျောက်မဲ

082 / POPULATION C85,000 / ELEV APPROX 900M

Pronounced 'Chao-may', Kyaukme is a low-rise, bustling market town with a smattering of colonial-era architecture, bracketed by monastery-topped hills, each only 15 minutes' walk away using steep, covered stairways. The main attraction here is hiking into surrounding Shan and Palaung hill villages. Although Kyaukme is rather bigger than Hsipaw, the town sees far fewer travellers and there's only one foreigner-licensed guesthouse. Kyaukme means 'black stone'; local legend has it that its citizens were dishonest traders of precious (or not so precious) gems.

🛏 Sleeping & Eating

There's a strip of Yunnan-style Chinese restaurants close to the cinema, three blocks south of Shwe Phi Oo Rd, as well as eating possibilities in the market.

A Yone Oo Guest House   GUESTHOUSE $
(082-40183; Shwe Phi Oo Rd; r $6-28; ❄) The only option for foreigners, the cheapest rooms are grim. For $10 you get bearable digs with OK shared bathroom and shower. The best rooms have air-con and private bathrooms.

Thiri Pyitsaya   BURMESE-CHINESE $
(4/54 Shwe Phi Oo Rd; dishes from K500; ⊙ 7am-9pm; 🗐) Amiable place for basic noodle and rice dishes, as well as juices and beers.

❶ Getting There & Away

Buses leave from the southwest corner of the market. Minibuses pick up from A Yone Oo Guesthouse (which can book tickets). Other Lashio- and Mandalay-bound buses can be caught on the main highway (a K1500 motorbike taxi ride away).

TREKKING FROM KYAUKME

Typical walking destinations have an unspoilt charm that challenge even those around Hsipaw. But Kyaukme itself is pretty spread out so most treks start with a motorcycle ride to a suitable trailhead. This is typically included in guide fees, which cost around K30,000 for a couple. For longer motorbike trails you'll need to add K10,000 per day for bike rental plus petrol.

Naing-Naing (09 4730 7622; naingninenine@gmail.com), nicknamed '9-9', is Kyaukme's best-known guide. He speaks good English, has a fascinating background and an extensive knowledge of the entire area. He prefers to take groups of four.

There are no shared taxis from Kyaukme.

The train station is a 10-minute walk northwest from the guesthouse

Hsipaw သီပေါ

082 / POPULATION C54,000 / ELEV APPROX 700M

More foreigners are finding their way to delightful Hsipaw (pronounced 'see-paw' or 'tee-bor'), drawn by the possibility of easily arranged hill treks that are more authentic than those around Kalaw or in northern Thailand. Many people, though, find the town's laid-back vibe and intriguing history (it was once a Shan royal city) as much of an attraction and spend far longer here than they intended. With just enough tourist infrastructure to be convenient, Hsipaw remains a completely genuine northern Shan State town.

TRANSPORT TO/FROM KYAUKME

DESTINATION	BUS	MINIBUS	TAXI	TRAIN
Mandalay	K3500, 4 daily 4.30am-7am, 5½hr	K6500/7500 back/front seat, 2 daily 7-8am, 4½hr	K60,000-70,000, book privately, 4hr	ordinary/1st/upper class $3/7/8, 1 daily 11.25am, 11½hr
Hsipaw	K1000, 3 daily 7am, 11am, 4pm, 1hr	N/A	N/A	$1/2/3, 1 daily 1.50pm, 3hr
Lashio	K3000, 1 daily, 7am, 3hr	K5500/6500 back/front seat, 2 daily noon-1pm, 3hr	N/A	$2/3/4, 1 daily 1.50pm, 6hr
Yangon	K14,500, 1 daily 2pm, 15hr	N/A	N/A	N/A

⊙ Sights

The present town centre, Tyaung Myo, dates back only to the early 20th century. The main monasteries, stupas and former palace lie on higher ground around a mile further north in Myauk Myo.

Central Riverfront
NEIGHBOURHOOD

Hsipaw's riverside **produce market** (⊙4.30am 1pm) is most interesting before dawn when the road outside is jammed with hill-villagers (Shan, Palaung, Lisu) selling their wares: all are gone by 7am. Between here and the large **central market** (⊙8am-5pm) are four column-fronted 19th-century **godowns** (warehouses) and a **banyan tree** worshipped by locals as a *nat* (spirit) shrine.

Mahamyatmuni Paya
BUDDHIST TEMPLE

(Namtu Rd) South of the central area, Maham-yatmuni Paya is the biggest and grandest pagoda in town. The large brass-faced Buddha was inspired by the famous Mahamuni Buddha in Mandalay. He's now backed by an acid-trip halo of pulsating coloured lights that would seem better suited to a casino.

Myauk Myo
NEIGHBOURHOOD

At the northern edge of town, Hsipaw's oldest neighbourhood has a village-like atmosphere, two delightful teak monasteries and a collection of ancient brick stupas known lo-cally as **Little Bagan**. The wooden **Madahya Monastery** looks especially impressive when viewed from across the palm-shaded pond of the **Bamboo Buddha Monastery** (Maha Nanda Kantha). The 150-year-old Buddha is made from lacquered bamboo strips, now hidden beneath layers of gold.

Around and behind lie a few clumps of ancient brick stupas, some overwhelmed by vegetation in vaguely Angkor Wat style. The nickname for this area, Little Bagan, blatantly overplays the size and extent of the sites but the area is undoubtedly charming.

To get here cross the big bridge on Nam-tu Rd heading north. Turn first left at the police station, then first right and fork left. Take this lane across the railway track then follow the main track as it wiggles.

To return by an alternative route, take the unpaved track east behind the Bamboo Buddha monastery, rapidly passing **Eissa Paya** (where one stupa has a tree growing out of it). You'll emerge near **Sao Pu Sao Nai**, a colourful shrine dedicated to the guardian *nat* of Hsipaw. Rather than turning left into the shrine, turn right and you'll reach Namtu Rd a little north of the railway.

Sunset Hill
VIEWPOINT

For sweeping views across the river and Hsipaw, climb to **Thein Daung Pagoda**, also known as Nine Buddha Hill or, most

---

DON'T MISS

HSIPAW'S SHAN PALACE

Hsipaw was ruled by a *sawbwa* (sky prince) until the advent of the military junta that seized power in 1962 ended the centuries-old tradition of the different regions of Shan State being run as separate kingdoms by 32 sky princes. The last *sawbwa* of Hsipaw disappeared during the army takeover (the book *Twilight over Burma; My Life as a Shan Princess*, written by his wife Inge Sargent, describes the tragic events), leaving his nephew Mr Donald in charge of the family palace. Imprisoned himself for a number of years and then placed under effective house arrest, during which time the palace was closed, Mr Donald is now free thanks to the reforms Myanmar has undergone since 2011, and people can once again visit the palace.

In truth, it's not a palace in the traditional sense. Built in 1924, it's a fading, although still impressive, English-style mansion set in rundown grounds. But if the building is infused with a melancholic air, then the charming Mr Donald and his wife Fern make very gracious hosts. They welcome visitors in their sitting room decorated with family photos and will relate the fascinating history of their ancestors and the sad fate of the last *sawbwa*.

While there is no admission fee, a donation (given respectfully) is expected and goes towards maintaining the palace. Mrs Fern is also a keen reader and always appreciates new books in English. In theory, the palace is open for a few hours each day (9am to noon and 4pm to 6pm; if the gates are chained, they're not receiving visitors). To reach it, cross the bridge at the northern end of Namtu Rd, turn right at the police station and then left at the monastery. The palace is up the track past the immigration office.

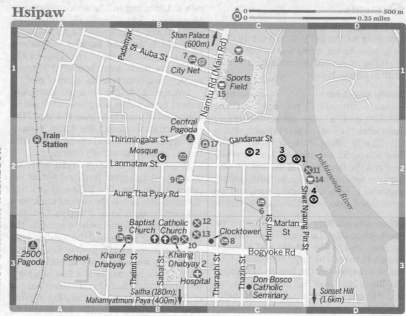

Hsipaw

popularly, Sunset Hill. It's part of a steep ridge that rises directly behind the Lashio road, around 1½ miles south of Hsipaw.

Cross the new river bridge, follow the main road left then take the laterite track that starts with a triple-crowned temple gateway around 300m beyond. There's a small English sign at the gateway. The climb takes around 15 minutes.

Bawgyo Paya
BUDDHIST TEMPLE

(ဘော်ကြိုဘုရား) Five miles west of Hsipaw, beside the Hsipaw–Kyaukme road (you'll get a brief glimpse of it from the right-hand side of any Kyaukme- or Mandalay-bound bus), this pagoda is of great significance to Shan peo-

ple and gets overloaded with pilgrims who arrive en masse during the annual **Bawgyo Paya Pwe** culminating on the full moon day of Tabaung (February/March).

The pagoda's current incarnation is an eye-catching 1995 structure of stepped gilded polygons, within which the dome supposedly incorporates genuine rubies. The name translates loosely as 'Dad come and get me', and the original pagoda was built centuries earlier by a heartbroken Shan king who had married off his daughter, warrior-princess Saw Mun La, to the Burmese king as part of a Shan-Burma peace deal. The Burmese king adored her but, as the seventh wife in his harem, her presence

Hsipaw

⊚ Sights
1 Banyan Tree Nat Shrine	C2
2 Central Market	C2
3 Godowns	C2
4 Produce Market	D2

⊜ Sleeping
5 Golden Doll/Mr Kid	B3
6 Lily Guesthouse	C2
7 Mr Charles Guest House	B1
8 Nam Khae Mao	C3
9 Yee Shin Guesthouse	B2

⊗ Eating
10 Ah Kong Kaik	B3
11 Club Terrace	D2
12 Law Chun	B3
13 San	B3

⊙ Drinking & Nightlife
14 Black House Coffee Shop	D2
15 La Wün Aung	C1
16 Pontoon	C1

⊜ Shopping
17 Mr Book Book Stall	B2

and growing favour caused trouble. Jealous concubines set about denouncing her as a spy. The king didn't fall for the lies but realised that he'd better get her out of his court before the other wives murdered her. The plan should have worked, but on the long, arduous route back to her father's court she fell ill. The Shan king was sent for but arrived to find her already dead of a mystery sickness. The point where she died became the site of a pagoda to underline Shan-Burmese friendship.

🏃 Activities

Hiking

Each of the guesthouses can organise guides (around K10,000 per day, K20,000 for an overnight trek) to take you on a range of fascinating walks into the hills above town visiting Shan and Palaung villages. Mr Charles Guest House is especially well organised and most evenings there'll be guides sitting on the front terrace to answer questions about the various options. Generally a next-day departure is possible if you don't want anything too adventurous. Trekking without a guide is less satisfying (very few villagers speak English) but it is possible – get someone to write down your destination in local script before departing. Most villages have motorcycle tracks too, so it may be possible to pay a villager to drive you back if you're fed up, although finding a bike isn't always straightforward.

Workshop Visits

If you don't fancy trekking, there are various workshops and mini **factories** around town, where you can see locals carrying out cottage industries like weaving, noodle-making, cheroot rolling and even popcorn popping. All these are marked on the map in the reception at Mr Charles Guest House. Or find a guide to combine a few workshop visits with, perhaps, a field-stroll to Parpeit village and hot springs.

🛏 Sleeping

⭐ **Mr Charles Guest House**   HOTEL $
(☎082-80105; www.mrcharleshotel.com; 105 Auba St; dm $7, r $9-55; ❄🛜) Still the most efficient,

---

DON'T MISS

TREKKING AROUND HSIPAW

The Palaung and Shan villages dotted in the hills surrounding Hsipaw are perhaps the main reason to visit the area, and treks to them are deservedly popular. The most visited village is **Pankam**, a Palaung settlement nestled on a ridge about five hours' walk from Hsipaw. It's a gentle trek that takes you through a number of timeless Shan villages with stilt-houses. Note how each hamlet has a *kin-gyiao*, a wooden phallus placed above a buried urn of vegetable oil to ensure fertile fields. Gateways with crossed wooden knife symbols are present to protect the settlements from evil spirits. Pankam itself has a fascinating shrine commemorating the 12th-century legend of how a powerful *nat* spirit bestowed tea seeds on the Palaung. Tea remains the principal source of income for the Palaung, who regard themselves as the guardians of tea cultivation in Shan State.

Pankam can be visited as part of a multiday trek, hiking out and back in two days, or you can hitch a lift one-way on a motorbike (K4000 from Hsipaw, but K8000 coming back) if you don't want to stay overnight. Going with a guide will enable you to communicate with the locals, but you can do the trek on your own. Take the road to Mandalay for a mile and then branch right where the main road swerves sharp right at the far edge of Hsipaw. After that, keep on asking the way!

But with Pankam now firmly on the tourist route, some travellers are seeking alternative treks to more remote locations. Options include a two-day hike to **Kyaukme** that takes you through fields and forests. Much more strenuous and adventurous is the three-day trek up to little-visited **Namhsan**, a Golden Palaung tea-growing town high up in the hills. It's a journey that starts in the soy bean and maize fields of the Shan villages, before you ascend to the tea plantations of the Palaung areas. Along the way you'll stay in villages that have seen very few, if any, foreigners. Bear in mind that some of these treks are only possible between October and March; during the rainy season, the trails become very difficult.

If you want something less arduous, then the guides at Mr Charles Guest House can take you to local waterfalls, or arrange combined trekking and boat trips, which will spare your knees.

MOGOK

Long closed to foreigners, the ruby-mining town of Mogok is now open. With 90% of the world's rubies coming from Myanmar, Mogok and the surrounding area is a key hub of the ruby trade, with much of the mining done by hand.

As well as rubies, you'll find blue sapphires and lapis lazuli and other semi-precious gems on sale in the markets. Many of the traders are Chinese or Indian. If you're interested in purchasing any stones be sure you know what you are doing; this isn't a place for rookie gem-buyers.

In addition to rubies, Mogok has a significant Shan population, as well as Palaung and Lisu. There are a number of eye-catching pagodas and a WWII cemetery containing the remains of British soldiers who died fighting nearby.

Although Mogok is 110km northwest of Kyaukme along a rough road, at the moment it can only be visited on government-arranged tours from Mandalay with a guide. Official travel agencies can arrange permits ($40) in a few days, but add in the guide and car and it is a pricey trip. There are a couple of guesthouses licensed for foreigners.

comfortable and traveller-friendly guesthouse in town, the ever-expanding Mr Charles operation encompasses everything from simple mattresses on the floor in the dorms, to swish suites with heating and air-con. Expect to pay $16 to $22 for a room with its own bathroom, but book ahead in peak periods.

The helpful staff at this Shan-owned guesthouse can arrange transport, treks and tours. There's bicycle (K2000 per day) and motorbike (K10,000 per day) hire and communal upstairs balconies where guests swap travel stories late into the evening. Breakfast is included.

Lily Guesthouse   GUESTHOUSE $

(☏082-80318; namkhaemaoguesthouse@gmail.com; 108 Aung Tha Pyay Rd; s/d with shared bathroom $10/15, d $30-35; ❄@☎) An offshoot of the Nam Khae Mao operation, rooms here are bright, spacious and clean and the staff obliging. Treks can be organised and there's bike hire (K2000 per day).

Nam Khae Mao   GUESTHOUSE $

(☏082-80077; namkhaemaoguesthouse@gmail.com; 134 Bogyoke Rd; r with shared bathroom $7, d & tr $30; ❄@☎) The cheapest rooms are a little bleak and plain, but the ones with bathrooms are sizeable and come with air-con and hot water. Internet is K500 per hour.

Golden Doll/Mr Kid   GUESTHOUSE $

(☏082-80066; 124 Mandalay-Lashio Rd; s & d K10,000, with shared bathroom K4000-6000) Family-run and friendly, but also basic and rather rundown. The wood-panelled rooms are box-like with concrete floors and lumpy beds, while the shared bathrooms are downstairs and across the yard.

Yee Shin Guesthouse   GUESTHOUSE $

(☏082-80711; Namtu Rd; r $7) Chinese-owned and centrally located, the rooms here are tiny. But they're clean and so are the shared bathrooms located outside.

🍴 Eating & Drinking

Hsipaw's dining options have improved as the number of visitors has increased. While there are many simple places strung out along Namtu Rd, more sophisticated restaurants are beginning to pop up.

Street vendors sell *moun-ou-khalei* (rice-flour balls) and *kauk-pout* ('cow-po'), rounds of pounded sticky brown rice that are barbecued then sprinkled with jaggary and sesame.

San   SHAN, CHINESE $

(Namtu Rd; mains from K1500, barbecue from K200; ⊘8am-11pm; 📶) With its retro interior and small terrace, San is popular with travellers who come for the many barbecue options and the Chinese-style mains. Dali beer from China is K800.

Law Chun   CHINESE $

(Mr Food; Namtu Rd; mains from K1000; ⊘7am-9pm; 📶) With Chinese dishes for Burmese and Western palates (so light on the spices), 'Mr Food' stands out from the pack thanks to its bright and breezy interior. There's Dagon beer on tap.

Ah Kong Kaik   BURMESE $

(cnr Namtu & Bogyoke Rds; curries K2000; ⊘9am-8pm) The best place in town for authentic Bamar food. Curries come with an array of side dishes. Do as the locals do and sample them at lunchtime when they are fresh.

★ **Club Terrace** SOUTHEAST ASIAN $$

(35 Shwe Nyaung Pin St; mains from K3500; ⊙10am-10pm; 📱) Dine by the river in a gorgeous 90-year-old teak house with a lovely terrace. The menu mixes Thai and Chinese flavours, with a few Shan dishes like minced chicken curry with basil leaves. Decent wine list, splendid service and a peaceful, evocative setting. It's an offshoot of the restaurant of the same name in Pyin Oo Lwin.

Pontoon CAFE

(Pontoon Rd; ⊙8am-6pm) Great coffee and fine ciabatta sandwiches, as well as salads, cakes and banana pancakes. It's located in a refurbished traditional wooden house.

La Wün Aung TEAHOUSE

(Namtu Rd; dishes from K800; ⊙24hr) One of several teahouse bars that hide the sports field but make amends by screening international football matches. It never closes and they rent motorbikes for K8000 a day.

Black House Coffee Shop CAFE

(23 Shwe Nyaung Pin St; coffee from K800, banana & chocolate cake K500; ⊙6am-6pm) An airy, 75-year-old teak shophouse backed by a wide river-facing yard, this is an easy place to linger over a coffee made from Shan-grown beans, or a late-afternoon beer.

❶ Information

The guesthouses are the best sources of reliable advice about things to do and see. Another mine of local information and history is Ko Zaw Tun,

who is known as Mr Book, as he runs a small **book stall** (Namtu Rd; ⊙7am-8.15pm) opposite the entrance to the Central Pagoda (which his family helped to build).

City Net (Auba St; per hr K500; ⊙8.30am-11pm) The only reliable internet cafe in town. The connection is best in the morning.

❶ Getting There & Away

Buses and minibuses leave from a variety of locations: the two Khaing Dhabyay bus stands on the Mandalay–Lashio road close to Mr Kid's Guesthouse, the Yee Shin Guesthouse and the Duhtawadi Cafe on Lammataw St opposite the market.

Lashio-bound buses can be picked up from the Mandalay–Lashio road opposite the Khaing Dhabyay bus stands.

The train station is in the west of town.

❶ Getting Around

Trishaw rides start from K500; trishaws wait by the market. Bicycles can be rented at Mr Charles, Lily and Nham Khae Mao guesthouses. Motorbikes can be rented from Mr Charles and La Wun Aung for between K8000 and K10,000 per day.

Around Hsipaw

Namhsan နှန်ဆန်

☑ 082 / POPULATION C32,000 / ELEV 5249FT

High in the Shan Hills, Namhsan is an atmospheric, scrappy, ridge-top town that

TRANSPORT TO/FROM HSIPAW

DESTINATION	BUS	MINIBUS	SHARED TAXI	TRAIN
Mandalay	K4500-6000, 6 daily, 5.30am, 7am, 8am, 10am, 7pm & 8pm, 5½hr	K8000, 2 daily 7am & 9am, 5hr	K12,000/14,000 back/front seat, whole car K50,000	ordinary/1st/upper class $4/8/9, 1 daily 9.40am, 13hr
Pyin Oo Lwin	K5000, 2 daily 7pm & 8pm, 3hr	N/A	N/A	$3/5/6, 1 daily 9.40am, 7hr
Kyaukme	K1000, 2 daily noon & 3.30pm, 1hr	K1500, 1 daily 7am	N/A	$1/2/2, 1 daily 9.40am, 3hr
Namhsan	K6000, 1 daily 9.30am, 5hr	N/A	N/A	N/A
Lashio	N/A	N/A	K40,000 private hire	$2/3/4 1 daily 3.15pm, 4hr
Yangon	K14,500-16,500, 7 daily, 15hr	N/A	N/A	N/A
Taungyi	K15,000, 1 daily 3.30pm, 12hr	N/A	N/A	N/A

looks out over a sea of rucked-up mountain ridges and plunging ravines. Spread out along one steep street that climbs and twists along the ridge, the population is a fascinating mix of Golden Palaung, Shan and Burmese, as well as a few Chinese from nearby Yunnan Province. Hardly any foreigners make it here (and there's very little English spoken), so expect some stares.

The surrounding slopes are covered by the Palaung tea plantations that are the mainstay of Namhsan's economy, as well as pagodas and monasteries. Two possible one-day return hikes take you up to superb viewpoints at Taung Yo monastery and atop Loi San ('Ruby Mountain'). The scenic (if very rough) journey from Hsipaw to Namhsan is an attraction in itself, while trekking back again to Hsipaw (two nights and three days) is an ideal way to stay in little-seen villages en route. Hsipaw's Mr Charles Guest House can help suggest guides.

Namhsan is periodically closed due to fighting between the Palaung State Liberation Front and the Myanmar military. Check the current situation before setting off.

🛏 Sleeping & Eating

There is only one guesthouse in Namhsan. A few Chinese-style restaurants and teahouses are scattered along the main street. All close by 8pm.

Shwephetaunggtan
Co-operate Guesthouse GUESTHOUSE $
(☑ 082-89032; Main St; per person K5500) Very basic (and overpriced) rooms, all without bathrooms, although there is a hot shower in the courtyard that the owner is inordinately proud of.

U Shwe Tun CHINESE-SHAN $
(Main St; mains from K1000; ⊙ 7am-8pm) Run by the descendants of Chinese immigrants, this place has a good selection of Yunnan-style dishes, with a few local Shan ones too.

ℹ Getting There & Away

In theory, shared pick-ups run to Namhsan (K6000, five to six hours) at least five times a week from Kyaukme bus stand, picking up passengers in Hsipaw (same price) by pre-arrangement on ☑ 09 4730 6067. Ask your guesthouse to call for you. From Hsipaw, renting your own jeep will cost around K60,000.

Hiring a motorbike is the best way to reach Namhsan, but it's not a journey for novices. The road is mostly an unsealed, pot-holed, rocky track and it's a knee-jarring, back-breaking, arms-aching four-hour ride. The consolations for the pain are the stunning views along the way and the chance to stop off in Palaung hamlets.

There's also a very local bus that runs from Namhsan to Lashio and then onto Mandalay (K10,000, 15 hours) every other day. Foreigners are normally barred from taking it, but only a masochist would consider it anyway.

OFF THE BEATEN TRACK

MENSEN MARKET TOWN & ONWARD TO LASHIO

If you're frustrated with visiting markets where camera-toting foreigners are almost as prevalent as locals, then Mensen is the place for you. Slumbering for five days a week, Mensen wakes up on Wednesdays and Fridays, when the town's population triples as Palaung, Shan and even some Kachin descend from the hills to sell their produce and to shop.

It's a fun and photogenic market that spreads across much of Mensen's main street and people are overwhelmingly friendly. Mensen is about two hours' drive by motorbike from Hsipaw along a reasonable road. You won't be allowed to stay here, but visiting for a few hours is no problem. Like all markets, the earlier you get here, the more you'll see.

Mensen lies also along a much more scenic route to Lashio than the main Mandalay–Lashio highway. Starting from Hsipaw, you'll first reach Panglong (where you turn left into the hills for Namhsan) and then Mensen. After that, take the right-hand fork off the main road at the end of Mensen; Lashio is 32 miles further on along a road that winds through Shan villages and maize fields.

Technically, this road is out of bounds for foreigners. At the time of writing, though, there were no checkpoints and travellers could use the route, making a Hsipaw–Namhsan–Lashio loop possible. Take local advice before trying this.

Lashio

☏ 082 / POPULATION C130,000 / ELEV 2805FT

Lashio (pronounced '*lar*-show') is a booming and sprawling market town with a significant Chinese population. You're most likely to come here for the airport – the nearest to Hsipaw – or, if you've managed to organise the necessary permits, to meet your guide for the four-hour drive to the Chinese border at Mu-se.

Once the seat of an important Shan *sawbwo* (prince), Lashio played a pivotal role in the fight against the Japanese in WWII as the starting point of the Burma Road, which supplied food and arms to Chiang Kai-Shek's Kuomintang army. Little evidence of that evocative history remains today, thanks to a disastrous 1988 fire that destroyed most of the city's old wooden homes.

🛏 Sleeping & Eating

Most hotels in Lashio are Chinese-owned and overpriced; room rates don't include breakfast. Food stalls serving Shan noodles, hotpots and barbecue can be found at the junction of Theinni Rd and Bogyoke St. Many more appear after 5pm when the busy **night market** (5pm to 9pm) gets going. There's also an internet cafe close to the market on Theinni Rd. Three-wheel pickups and motorbike taxis charge K300 to K1000 for short hops around town.

Ya Htaik   HOTEL $

(☏ 082-22655; Bogyoke Rd; s without bathroom $15, tw/d $35/40, tr $50-55; ❄ 🛜) The only place where you'll find a budget bed. The cheapest rooms are perfectly acceptable, but the shared bathrooms have squat toilets and tiny showers. More expensive rooms are decent-sized.

Thi Da Aye   HOTEL $

(☏ 082-22165; Thiri Rd; r $30-45; ❄ 🛜) Large, clean and bland rooms, with proper showers. They're still not worth the money but you're close to the night market.

Golden Hill Hotel   HOTEL $$

(☏ 082-23656; goldenhillhotel.lashio@gmail.com; cnr Bagan St & Hnin Si St; r $45-85; ❄ 🛜) The newest and best hotel in town. Soulless, but spotless and bright rooms and efficient staff. It's perched on a hill very close to the Mahamyatmuni Paya.

Shwe Lawon   CHINESE $

(Theinni Rd; mains from K2500; ⊙ 9am-9pm; 🍴) The 2nd-floor terrace is swish by Lashio standards and the locals rate it as the best Chinese food in town. Big selection of meat, fish and veggie dishes.

❶ Getting There & Away

The main bus station is a mile north of the city centre. Minibuses and shared taxis leave from here too.

Lashio's miniature train station is 2 miles northwest of the market.

The airport is 3 miles north of town. A taxi costs K3000 to the airport; K5000 if you're coming from it.

MYITKYINA & THE UPPER AYEYARWADY

Snaking across Kachin State like a fat yellow python, the mighty Ayeyarwady River provides the main transport route between

TRANSPORT TO/FROM LASHIO

Destination	Bus	Minibus	Shared Taxi	Air	Train
Mandalay	K6000, 6 daily, 8hr	K10,000, 4 daily, 7½hr	K15,000/17,000 back/front seat, frequent, 7hr	$84, 3 weekly, 45min	ordinary/1st/upper class $5/10/12, 1 daily 5am, 16hr
Mu-se	K2500, frequent, 4hr	N/A	N/A	N/A	N/A
Hsipaw	K2000, 6 daily, 3hr	N/A	K15,000/17,000 back/front seat, frequent, 2hr	N/A	$2/4/5, 1 daily 5am, 4hr
Pyin Oo Lwin	K5500, 6 daily, 6hr	N/A	K15,000/17,000 back/front seat, frequent, 5hr	N/A	$4/8/10, 1 daily 5am, 11hr
Nay Pyi Taw	K9000, 3 daily 5pm, 6pm & 7pm, 12hr	N/A	N/A	N/A	N/A
Taungyi	K15,000, 1 daily 2pm, 14hr	N/A	N/A	N/A	N/A
Yangon	K14,500, 2 daily 2pm & 4pm, 15hr	N/A	N/A	$157, 4 weekly, 1¾hr	N/A

a series of gently interesting port towns, isolated villages and gold-panning camps. While no individual sight is jaw-dropping, the journey itself involves an immersion in local life that many visitors find unforgettable. Unlike boat rides from Mandalay to Bagan, ferries on the upper Ayeyarwady are used almost entirely by locals and the slow days drifting along the river provide an opportunity to interact with people in a way that is often impossible on dry land. A phrase book and a bottle of Grand Royal whiskey can be useful tools to help break the ice.

Note that the Ayeyarwady isn't scenically dramatic in the way of, say, the Nam Ou in neighbouring Laos, but the landscape does reach several modest crescendos as rolling fields and distant sand banks alternate with forest-dappled 'defiles'.

Myitkyina မြစ်ကြီးနား

♪ 074 / POPULATION C40,000

The capital of Kachin State, Myitkyina lacks much in the way of real sights. Nonetheless, it's an engaging, multicultural place, home to Kachin, Lisu, Chinese and Burmese, and hosts two of Myanmar's most important 'ethnic' festivals. A low-rise town with a fair scattering of part-timber houses, its residents seem keen to assist visitors, with

local Christians particularly eager to practise their English. Quiet at the best of times, the town is especially sleepy on Sundays when the churches fill up. Few foreigners make it here; those who do are mostly missionaries or NGO workers.

◉ Sights & Activities

Produce Market MARKET
(⊗5am-5pm) This riverside market specialises in colourful heaps of Chinese fruit and local vegetables. Many of the latter arrive by canoe and are then lugged up the rear stairway on shoulder poles. At dawn, this creates an unforgettable spectacle with boats gliding in across shimmering golden water backed by a rising sun.

Directly southwest is the architecturally drab **main market** (⊗8.30am-5pm).

Hsu Taung Pye Zedidaw BUDDHIST TEMPLE
(ဆုတောင်းပြည့်စေတီတော်) This gilded 'wish-fulfilling' pagoda is the town's most eye-catching religious building, sitting on the banks of the Ayeyarwady River at the north end of Zaw John (Strand) Rd. Opposite its stupa, a 98ft-long **reclining buddha** and nearby standing equivalent were funded by a Japanese soldier who served here in WWII, in part to commemorate 3400 of his comrades who died.

Kachin State Cultural Museum   MUSEUM
(ကချင်ပြည်နယ်ယဉ်ကျေးမှုပြတိုက်; Yon Gyi St; admission $2; ⊘9am-4pm) Displays Kachin and Shan costumes and the usual assortment of instruments, farming tools and ethnological artefacts. There are English captions.

Aung Ze Yan Aung Paya   PAGODA
(အောင်ဇေရန်အောင်ဘုရား) Just east of the airport, this pagoda is noteworthy for its arcing ranks of around 1000 little buddhas sitting in the grounds.

⫷ Tours

Snowland Tours   TOURS
(☑23499; snowland@mptmail.net.mm; Wai Maw St) Two blocks east of the station, this helpful agency with English-speaking staff can book flights and arrange customised tours.

🎇 Festivals & Events

Lisu New Year   CULTURAL
Started in 2011, this big three-day bash unites Lisu folks from all across Kachin State and Xishuangbanna (China) in a very colourful, if comfortably slow-moving, fair. The event is entirely untouristy, unless you count the many costumed Lisu villagers snapping photos of one another – varied regional Lisu costumes being markedly different.

Highlights include barefoot climbing of a knife tower and have-a-go stalls to try out your prowess on a traditional crossbow. Held before the February full moon.

Manao Festival   CULTURAL
Originally a way to propitiate the local *nat*, this is now a nationally important gathering of the six Kachin tribes for feasting and costumed dances, performed in Manao park (north of centre) where the large Native American–style totem poles remain in place year-round. Accommodation will be stretched at this time.

Observers get into the festival mood by drinking copious quantities of rice beer. Held on and around 10 January, Kachin State Day.

🛏 Sleeping

In Myitkyina, nowhere named 'Guesthouse' accepts foreigners. Apart from the YMCA and the rather sorry New Light Hotel (singles/doubles $20/35), all other options are variations on the typical Chinese-style hotel.

Xing Xian Hotel   HOTEL $
(☑074-22281;   yadanarpaing@mptmail.net.mm; 127 Shan Su North; r $15-30; ❊) Two giant vases welcome you into this quiet, friendly, long-standing and centrally located hotel. The 'superior' options are roomy, well equipped and the best deal in town at $20.

YMCA   HOSTEL $
(☑074-23010;   mka-ymca@myanmar.com.mm; YMCA St; r $8-36; ❊) Low prices and helpful English-speaking staff mean the 10 rooms here book up fast. Conditions, though, are pretty basic. The cheapest rooms, without bathrooms or air-con, are especially grungy.

Hotel United   HOTEL $
(☑074-22085; hotelunitedmyitkyina@gmail.com; 38 Thit Sa St; s/d/tr $30/35/45; ❊) Well-kept rooms, with small bathrooms, and more refined than many of the other options in town. Some English spoken.

★ Hotel Madira   HOTEL $$
(☑074-21119; madira.hotel.mka@gmail.com; 510 Pyayhtaungsu Rd; r $45-55; ❊🛜) Kachin-owned, this new place offers quality rooms and service (as well as intermittent wi-fi) not available anywhere else in town. The rooms are big, bright and fresh. Breakfast is included.

🍴 Eating

Traditionally, Kachin food uses relatively little oil in contrast to Burmese cuisine. Classic dishes include *chekachin* (steamed chicken pasted with spices and wrapped in a banana leaf), *sipa* (mixture of freshly steamed vegetables sprinkled with sesame powder)

ℹ MYITKYINA TRAVEL RESTRICTIONS

At the time of writing, travel to and from Myitkyina was severely restricted due to ongoing fighting between the Kachin Independence Army and the Myanmar military. Foreigners are barred from taking both buses and boats to or from Myitkyina, meaning the only way in or out of the town is by train or plane (unless you are prepared to hire an expensive private car and guide). That situation will hopefully change, allowing travellers to once more catch a boat south to Bhamo. We've included details of the journey in the hope that happens soon.

and *nakoo-che* (hot-sour fish with bamboo shoots). Wash it down with *kaung-ye,* a cloudy semi-sweet pink-brown beer made from sticky rice.

As well as the places reviewed here, there is a wide range of accessible (if fairly standard) eateries along Zaw Gyi St west of the rail tracks.

Orient Restaurant KACHIN, JAPANESE $
(YMCA St; mains from K2000; ☉7am-9pm, closed Sun Morning; 🖻) A meeting place for Myitkyina's tiny foreign community, the menu here is an intriguing blend of local dishes, Western faves and sushi and ramen (the Kachin owner lived in Japan previously).

Kiss Me BURMESE $
(Zaw John Rd; dishes K500-1500; ☉6am-9pm; 🖻) A hotspot for Myitkyina's fashionable youth, this riverside pavilion turns out some fine food. Try the *gyin tok,* a crunchy ginger salad; there are curries and fine shakes and juices too.

River View CHINESE $
(Riverside; dim sum K400-700; ☉6am-10pm) Get your morning nourishment from this riverside terrace joint with the tastiest dim sum in town. Popular for coffee and tea too, it's directly south of the main vegetable market.

Night Market STREET FOOD $
(Aung San Rd & Wai Maw St; dishes from K500; ☉4.30-9.30pm) Stalls with Shan hotpots and noodles, as well as barbecue and curries.

★ Jing Hpaw Thu KACHIN $$
(Riverside; dishes from K1500; ☉9am-10pm) Make sure to head out to this attractive riverside restaurant, considered the top spot for real Kachin food. Superb, tangy dried beef with a spicy dipping sauce, as well as the fish dishes and chicken or pork served in a banana leaf, are specialities here. No Eng-lish spoken, so just point at the dishes that take your fancy. A three-wheeler will charge K4000 return from the centre of town.

Mya Ayer CHINESE $$
(71 Shan Su North; mains from K3500; ☉6am-10pm; 🖻) The most authentic Chinese option in a town with a sizeable Chinese population. Big menu, with the hot and sour dishes especially good. A great place to dine in communal Chinese style.

Bamboo Field Restaurant CHINESE $$
(313 Pyi Htaung Su Rd; dishes from K3000, burgers K2500; ☉9am-10pm; 🖻) On the main airport road, this barn-like place has a rotating crew of singers belting out Burmese pop songs every night. The menu mixes (overpriced) Chinese dishes with Western classics. Draft beer is K600 and they show the football here.

❶ Information

Tolerable maps are available at the YMCA and Xing Xian Hotel. Dollars can be changed at the New Light Hotel (just north of the clock tower). There are a number of internet cafes but connections are deadly slow.

Buddy Internet Cafe (Butayone St; per hr K400; ☉8am-11pm) Close to the main police station and the most reliable connection.

❶ Getting There & Away

At the time of writing, foreigners were only allowed to arrive and leave Myitkyina by plane or train, or by private car with a guide.

Myitkyina's airport is a couple of miles from the town centre. A three-wheeler/motorbike taxi costs K3000/3500. On arrival at the airport, you'll be half-heartedly quizzed by the immigration police.

The train station is close to the clock tower in the centre of town.

NAVIGATING MYITKYINA

The town sprawls for miles but the central area is a manageably compact grid. Walking out of the train station, Waing Maw St heads east reaching the river bank in five short blocks. Parallel but four blocks further north is Zei Gyi Rd, the junction marked by one of Myitkyina's two clock towers. Zei Gyi runs east to the market and river, west across the tracks passing very close to the YMCA (follow the tracks north), the Hotel United (second block then north) and plentiful restaurants. Parallel to Ze Gyi four blocks further north, Si Pin Thar Yar St also crosses the railway. The main road then swerves northwest to become Pyi Htaung Su Rd, the road to the airport and Sinbo ferry jetty. But if you instead continue in a northerly sweep on Thakhin Phay Net St, you'll reach the museum and, eventually, Manao Park and Jing Hpaw Thu restaurant.

TRANSPORT TO/FROM MYITKYINA

DESTINATION	AIR	TRAIN	BUS	FAST BOAT
Mandalay	$115, daily, 1hr 10min	$10-45 depending on class, 4 daily, 24hr	N/A	N/A
Sinbo	N/A	N/A	N/A	K10,000, 1 daily 8.30am, 5hr
Naba (for Katha)	N/A	$6-14, 4 daily, 12hr	N/A	N/A
Shwebo	N/A	$11-29, 1 daily, 20hr	N/A	N/A
Bhamo	$90, twice weekly, 1hr	N/A	N/A	N/A
Hopin (for Indawgyi Lake)	N/A	$3-7, 3 daily, 5hr	N/A	N/A
Yangon	$180, daily, 2hr 40min	N/A	N/A	N/A
Putao (with permits)	$90, 3 daily, 1hr	N/A	N/A	N/A

Boats leave from the Talawgyi Pier, a K5000 ride from town in a three-wheeler.

ⓘ Getting Around

Motorised three-wheelers (called *thonbeecars*: *thoun* means 'three', *bein* means 'wheel') carrying up to four people charge K3000 to/from the airport, K6000 to the boat jetty for Sinbo.

Bicycles (K2000 per day) and motorbikes (K20,000 per day) can be rented at the Orient Restaurant next to the YMCA.

Myit-Son & Jaw Bum
မြစ်ဆုံ နှင့် ကျော်ဘန်တောင်

About 27 miles north of Myitkyina, Myit-Son marks the point where the Mayhka and Malikha Rivers come together to form the Ayeyarwady. It's considered a local 'beauty spot', though 'intriguing' describes the ravaged scene better than 'beautiful'. The confluence point is distantly overlooked by a series of rough snack- and teahouses, a big dumpling-shaped golden pagoda and a traditional Kachin longhouse rebuilt as a 'cultural emblem'. However, more interesting is the nearby purgatory of gold-panning outfits churning up the muddy stream in accompanying Tang Phray village, using semi-mechanised bamboo-tower conveyor belts.

The road north of Myitkyina (bound eventually for Putao) has been partly rebuilt, but the last 11km to Myit-Son are horrendously bumpy. You'll need a photocopy of your passport and visa to hand to a police checkpoint en route. A motorbike/taxi from Myitkyina costs around K20,000/50,000 return (1½ hours each way). For a token extra fee you can detour 1 mile off the main road at Nawng Nang village to comically named Jaw Bum. Its name translates as 'praying mountain' but it's really only a fairly modest hill, a sacred site for Kachin and Lisu Baptists. In spite of its religious connections, most visitors here are amorous local couples who climb a repulsively ugly six-storey concrete viewing tower to observe and drop litter on a sweep of rural scenery.

Myitkyina to Bhamo

Travelling by boat, the first day is through low-lying scenery that is not immediately memorable but has the bonus of a forced stay in appealing Sinbo, a village that's wonderfully unspoilt apart from the piles of riverside rubbish that mar almost every habitable area along the route. The Sinbo to Bhamo section, on smaller (25 plank-seat) longboats, spends most of the route traversing the Ayeyarwady's first defile where the river cuts through hills shaggy with forest-bamboo mix, the boat stopping at isolated sandbanks to pick up gold-panners, rattan harvesters and cantilever fishermen. In the dry season, access to Bhamo can be complicated by the boat having to weave through a maze of very shallow sandbars.

Sinbo   ဆင်ဘို

POPULATION C1700

Taking the river route between Myitkyina and Bhamo, you'll be forced to spend a night in this delightfully car-less riverside village. Though conditions aren't luxurious, the stop is actually a blessing in disguise – for some travellers one of the highlights of the river trip. Founded as a teak station for the Scottish firm Steel Brothers, Sinbo is a neat grid of unpaved streets, the mostly wood and part-timber houses set amid coconut and

NORTHERN MYANMAR BHAMO (BANMAW)

WORTH A TRIP

INDAWGYI LAKE

About 110 miles southwest of Myitkyina, placid Indawgyi (အင်းတော်ကြီးကန်) is the largest natural lake in Myanmar and one of the most special, serene places in the entire country. The lakeshore is ringed by rarely visited Shan villages, and the surrounding **Indawgyi Wetland Wildlife Sanctuary** provides a habitat for more than 120 species of birds, including shelducks, pintails, kingfishers, herons, egrets and the Myanmar peacock. Very remote and tranquil, it's a great place to kick back for a few days.

The mystical **Shwe Myitsu Pagoda**, on an island off Nam Tay village, seems to float on the surface of the lake. The central, gilded stupa was constructed in 1869 to enshrine Buddha relics transported here from Yangon. Pilgrims visit in droves for the Shwe Myitsu Pwe, held during the week before the full moon of Tabaung (March), at which time the lake waters are low enough for a walk along a seasonal causeway to the pagoda. Boatmen ask K15,000 for a return trip to the pagoda; a day trip around the lake will set you back K50,000 to K60,000.

During festival time you might be allowed to camp or bed down at **Nam Tay monastery**. At other times, however, the only licensed guesthouse is 12 miles away in Lonton. **Indawmaha** (per person K7000) is near the end of the village close to the army checkpoint and has eight very simple rooms in a stilt building right at the water's edge.

Two doors north of the guesthouse, kayaks can be hired (K15,000 per day) from the Inn Chit Thu Tourism Group, a locally run organisation that puts its profits into community projects. The kayaks are a great way to explore the lake. You can also rent bicycles here (K7000 per day); the picturesque village of **Lwemun** is a good destination to bike to. Close by are a few teahouse restaurants where you can get simple meals cooked on a wood stove; fish curry is a favourite here.

Three of the daily Myitkyina–Mandalay trains stop in **Hopin**, which is roughly halfway between Myitkyina and Katha. From Hopin, overloaded pick-ups leave a couple of times a day (last departure around 2pm) for the excruciatingly uncomfortable but scenically stunning 28-mile trip to Lonton (K4000, 3½ hours). The alternative, chartering a 4WD for a three-day, two-night trip from Myitkyina, will likely cost several hundred dollars. There's a very rough road that continues all the way to Khamti via the casino-filled jade-mining boom town of **Hpakant** (Pakkan) but foreigners can't go anywhere beyond **Nyaung Bin** without very hard-to-score permits.

toddy palms. There are no must-see sights but river views are mesmerising from the muddy lane that climbs between the trio of old stupas and the 1919 British Officers' Bungalow (now fenced and out of bounds for military use) at the south end of town. On arrival from Myitkyina, boats are usually met by **Hla Tun**, the manager of the one ultra-simple **guesthouse** (bed/dinner/breakfast K3000/2000/1500). It has eight hardboard-separated sleeping spaces over a party dining room featuring portraits of Buddha, Jesus and Avril Lavigne. Delicious dinners are cooked by Hla Tun's wife on a simple wood-stove out back.

Bhamo (Banmaw) ဗန်းမော်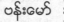

♪ 074 / POPULATION C25,000

For many travellers, Bhamo ('ba-more'; Banmaw), is just a staging post on the river journey to Myitkyina or Mandalay. But if you take the time to stop for a few days, you'll discover one of Myanmar's most relaxed and attractive towns. The central **riverfront** (Kannar Rd) is especially lively on Friday, when villagers flood in for the market. It's lined with several old stained-teak houses and is overhung with magnificent mature 'rain trees', so named because their lovely pink flowers bloom in the monsoon season. At the southern end of this riverfront are dealerships selling great stacks of clay-pots including simple water carriers from Shwegu and giant glazed amphorae from Kyaukmyaung. Two short blocks east then one north on Lammataw Rd brings you to the main market (Thiri Yadana) from which Sinbyushin St leading west becomes the main road to Myitkyina and China. It quickly passes Post Office St (for Grand Hotel, turn right after one block), the **pre-dawn** vegetable market and Letwet Thondaya Rd (for the Friendship Hotel, turn left after the second block). Around 500m further is the large, photogenic complex of **Theindawgyi Paya** featuring an elongated golden bell-shaped gilded stupa. It's best admired from the southeast across a pond lined with concrete monk statues.

About 3 miles north of town, beyond the military enclave, the much more historic **Shwe Kyina Pagoda** has two gold-topped stupas and marks the site of the 5th-century Shan city of **Sampanago** (Bhamo Myo Haung, Old Bhamo). Almost nothing remains of the old city, though locals remember numerous remnant bricks and posts remaining into the 1950s. If you know what you're looking for you can still make out a section of 10ft-high mud rampart where the lane around the monastery cuts through it to the east, but you'll probably need a guide and the site is hardly memorable. Far more impressive is the awesome **bamboo bridge** (return toll with bicycle K300) that allows you to make your precarious way across the wide Tapin River. A nice cycle ride is to continue over the bridge for half an hour west through timeless **Sinkin** village and on to a brickworks from which a 10-minute stairway climb takes you up **Theinpa Hill** past a meditation hall to a stupa with very attractive **panoramas**.

🛏 Sleeping

Only three places accept foreigners.

★ Friendship Hotel   HOTEL $
(📞074-50095, in China 0086-692 687 6670; Letwet Thondaya Rd; s/d/tr $25/30/40, with shared bathroom $10/20/30; ✳@) Large, comfortable and excellent value for money. Even the shared bathrooms are well maintained, while the better rooms have decent mat-

tresses and all qualify you for one of the best buffet breakfasts in Myanmar. Helpful manager Moe Naing speaks fluent English and offers a useful free map.

Hotel Paradise   HOTEL $
(📞074-50136; hotelparadisebanmaw@gmail.com; Shwe Kyaung Kone St; s/d/tr $15/30/35; ✳@) All the rooms here are a decent deal: reasonably sized and clean with OK bathrooms. It's past the southern end of the riverfront on a strip of lively restaurants.

Grand Hotel   HOTEL $
(📞074-50317, in China 0086-692 688 1816; Post Office Rd; r $20-35; ✳) Grand indeed is its modern lobby and blue-glass facade, but the rooms are altogether more down-to-earth and rather austere. Keen staff and some English spoken.

🍴 Eating

There's a popular beer station on the short diagonal street cutting behind the Friendship Hotel (fine for football-watching), basic teahouses along the riverfront, and a cafe attached to the Hotel Paradise that is good for coffee and smoothies.

Shamie Restaurant   BURMESE $
(Mingone Junction; curries K2000; ⏱7am-10pm) Excellent spot for proper curry spreads, with eight different types available (including beef, a rarity in Buddhist Myanmar). They come with rice and veggies and fantastic home-made tamarind chutney.

Sein Sein   CHINESE $
(Kannar Rd; mains from K2000; ⏱9am-9pm; 📶) The rough round tables and beer-poster decor promise little. But the reliable Chinese food is considered the best in town and there's draught Dagon beer (K500). It's near the IWT office.

NORTHERN MYANMAR BHAMO (BANMAW)

ℹ GETTING TO CHINA: MU-SE TO RUILI

At the time of writing, it was expected that sometime in 2014 Mu-se–Ruili would become a permit-free, standard border crossing, making it much easier to travel to China. Check the current situation before you depart.

Getting to the border While no documents are required to travel to Mu-se itself, people planning to cross the border need a permit (which takes two weeks to arrange through Myanmar Tours & Travel), and a pre-booked guide and car ($200) to make the four-hour journey from Lashio to Mu-se.

At the border You must have a Chinese visa already; they are not available at the border.

Moving on From Ruili, four buses run daily to Yunnan's capital Kunming (14 hours).

Sut Ngai KACHIN $

(Sinbyushin St; mains from K1500; ⊙9am-9pm)
Popular with the locals, there's fine barbecue, as well as Kachin specialities like lime-
flavoured pork served in a banana leaf and
draft Tiger beer (K700). No English spoken;
point at what others are eating.

❶ Information

Free town maps are available for guests at the
Friendship Hotel. They are extremely useful, if
misleadingly out of scale towards the edges.

The prefix ☑0086-692 denotes 'China numbers', which should be dialled from another
China-line phone (☑0086-692 numbers) to
avoid paying international call rates.

Ever Internet Cafe (off Sinbyushin St; per hr
K500; ⊙9am-9pm) Slow connection. It's four
blocks north of the market off the main road to
the right.

❶ Getting There & Away

At the time of writing, foreigners were not allowed to enter or exit Bhamo by bus.

IWT ferries leave from a jetty 2½ miles south
of town. Fast boats leave from a pier on the
central riverfront.

The airport is a 10-minute ride from the centre
of town. Immigration police will interview you
briefly on arrival.

A Bhamo-Katha railway is allegedly under
construction.

❶ Getting Around

Motorcycle/three-wheeler taxis cost
K1000/2000 to the airport, K2000/3000 to the
IWT ferry dock.

Rent bikes from **Breeze Coffee & Cold** (Letwet
Thondaya Rd; per day K2000; ⊙8.30am-7pm),
a small shop almost opposite Friendship Hotel.

Bhamo to Katha

Between Bhamo and Shwegu, the scenery
reaches a modest climax in the short second
defile where the Ayeyarwady passes through
a wooded valley with a rocky cliff face at one
section (often described misleadingly as a
gorge).

Shwegu ရွှေကူ

☑074 / POPULATION C15,000

Every year around a dozen foreign travellers
jump ship at historic Shwegu, a long ribbon
of township that stretches for three miles
along the Ayeyarwady's southern bank. It's
best known for its elegantly unfussy **pottery**
and for the fabled Shwe Baw Kyune monastery on mid-river Kyundaw ('Royal') Island.
Few locals speak English.

⊙ Sights

Shwe Baw Kyune BUDDHIST MONASTERY

(ရွှေဘောကျွန်း) At first glance this monastery looks 20th-century. Historians, though,
say it was built in the 13th century while
monastic fables suggest it was founded two
millennia ago when an Indian prince turned
up with seven holy bone fragments of the
Buddha. These are now encased within
small Buddha statuettes decorated over the
centuries with layers of gold leaf.

While they form the monastery's priceless
main treasure (dattaw), for non-Buddhists
the monastery is far more interesting for
its extraordinary array of over 7000 closely
packed stupas, ancient and modern, which
fill the eastern end of the island. Some are
whitewashed, others gilded and many more
are mere piles of antique bricks with just

TRANSPORT TO/FROM BHAMO

DESTINATION	AIR	IWT FERRY	FAST BOAT
Mandalay	$115, 4 weekly, 50min	$12/60 deck/cabin, 3 weekly Mon, Wed & Fri, 40-48hr	N/A
Myitkyina	$90, 2 weekly, 1hr	N/A	K15,000, 1 daily, 31hr (overnight stop)
Sinbo	N/A	N/A	K8000, 1 daily, 5hr
Shwegu	N/A	$5, 3 weekly Mon, Wed & Fri, 6hr	K3000, 1 daily, 3hr
Katha	N/A	$10, 3 weekly Mon, Wed, Fri, 12hr	K6000, 1 daily, 6hr
Kyaukmyaung	N/A	$12, 3 weekly Mon, Wed & Fri, 24hr	N/A
Yangon	$180 (via Mandalay), 3 weekly, 2½hr	N/A	N/A

traces of former stucco detail. Most appear to have been suffocated for years by foliage, Angkor Wat style. The bushes were recently cut back to reveal the spectacle, but getting to the outlying stupas is very uncomfortable barefoot given all the stubble and thorns (carry your sandals).

Hidden here and there are dozens of tiny buddha statues and the odd brick-and-stucco lion. The whole scene is made even more photogenic by a series of *pyatthat* (stepped towers) that flank the monastery's central golden-tipped stupa. And the island setting, with its tree-shaded village of wooden stilt houses, makes for a wonderfully peaceful environment. There's a big local festival here in the week leading up to full moon of Tabaung.

Old Shwegu NEIGHBOURHOOD
Around 400m west of the central jetty is a stretch of relatively old wooden houses. Further inland is an area of tree-shaded footpaths and alleys that forms an intriguing pottery district. Here, in household compounds, Shwebo's archetypal *tau ye-u* (drinking water pots) and *subu* (football-sized piggy banks) are formed and fired in kilns of carefully heaped rice-husks.

An Daw Paya BUDDHIST TEMPLE
(အံတော်ဘုရား) This eye-catching ornate pagoda lies in a rural mainland field, directly across the river from Shwe Baw Kyune and around 2 miles east of central Shwegu. Motorcycles charge K1000 to get there but finding one to come back can be tricky.

🛏 Sleeping & Eating

Only one guesthouse accepts foreigners. **Sag Guesthouse** (☎ 074-52647; s with/without bathroom K16,000/6000) is opposite where the Bhamo–Mandalay buses stop and behind the Mingala Monastery. The rooms are small, with hard beds and cold showers, but this is your only option. It's a 10-minute motorbike ride (K1000) from the jetty. There are teahouses and simple restaurants clustered near the jetty.

ℹ Getting There & Away

IWT ferries leave Monday, Wednesday and Friday for Katha ($5). Foreigners are technically barred from the fast boats that leave daily between 11am and noon (K7000), but you may be allowed on here. An afternoon bus to Mandalay via Katha leaves at 2pm but won't take foreigners.

RIVER SHOPPING

Even if you don't get off at some of the places the boats stop at, you'll have no problem meeting the people who live there. The IWT ferries and fast boats are the principal source of income for many people residing along the banks of the Ayeyarwady, and the moment they hove into sight, villagers jump into their wooden longboats laden with eveything from home-cooked curries, grilled fish and beer to cigarettes to sell to the passengers. Others wade out to the ferries, their wares balanced precariously on their heads. Not only do these impromptu markets make great photo opportunities, what's on offer is generally cheaper and tastier than the monotonous diet of noodles and oily curries sold on board the IWT ferries. And you'll soon get used to shopping on water.

ℹ Getting Around

From a logging jetty 300m west of An Daw Paya, an open longboat ferries passengers across to Shwe Baw Kyune (K500/4000 per person/boat, four minutes). A much more convenient option is to charter your own boat directly from Shwegu's central jetty, taking around 15 minutes each way. A K10,000 return charter should include several hours' wait while you explore the island.

Katha ကသာ

☑ 074 / POPULATION C12,000

Literature lovers and boat bums will enjoy this small but lively Ayeyarwady port town, the setting for George Orwell's *Burmese Days*. It makes a pleasant break from the IWT ferry, and there's a rail link to Mandalay if you're fed up with the river altogether. The guesthouses and various boat ticket sales booths are close together along three short central blocks of Strand Rd, the attractive curving riverside road.

◉ Sights

In 1926 and 1927, Katha was home to British colonial police officer Eric Blair, better known by his pen name George Orwell. Much of *Burmese Days* is based on Orwell's time here and several buildings that feature in the book are still standing. None, though, are marked as such or are commercial tourist attractions (although hints from the local government suggest that may change in the near future), so ask politely before trying to barge in. The half-timbered former **British Club**, now used as an association office (and much re-built since Orwell's time), is tucked away 100m behind the 1924 **Tennis Club** on a street appropriately called Klablan (Club St). A block north, the 1928 **DC's House** was actually completed just after Orwell's stay but its unmistakable style would fit McGregor. Three families now live there and Daw Wei Wei Dwin sometimes shows visitors into the original (much decayed) drawing room. Two blocks south, Orwell would have lived at the comfy, two-storey **police commissioner's house**, which is still used as such (so it's not advisable to knock on the door). Directly northwest, the Orwell-era **St Paul's Anglican Church** collapsed in 2007 and has been replaced by a new church part-sponsored by troops from the Princess of Wales's Royal Regiment in appreciation of the hospitality they received in Katha during Christmas 1944.

There are several attractive temples at the southern end of town near the prison.

🛏 Sleeping

Only three of Katha's guesthouses accept foreigners. The two on the riverfront are basic without private bathrooms. They're within 60m of each other and are best (albeit noisy) if you can score one of a handful of rooms with river views.

Eden Guesthouse　　　　　GUESTHOUSE $
(☑ 074-25429; Shwe Phone Shein St; r K20,000; ❀☂) The newest and smartest place in town and the only spot with wi-fi. It's above the cafe of the same name and close to the cluster of Orwell-related sites.

Ayarwady Guest House　　　　GUESTHOUSE $
(☑ 074-25140; Strand Rd; s/d K6000/10,000; ❀) An old wooden house with hardboard room dividers. The best double has air-con. Bathroom facilities are primitive. Some English spoken.

Annawah Guest House　　　　GUESTHOUSE $
(☑ 074-25146; Strand Rd; r K6000) Mostly patronised by locals, the downstairs rooms are dark, the upstairs ones include some truly minuscule spaces. The pot-bellied owner bears a few similarities to Orwell's villain U Po Kyin.

🍴 Eating & Drinking

Sein Family Restaurant　　　　CHINESE $
(Strand Rd; dishes from K1500; ⊙7am-8pm; 🍴) Run by the descendants of Chinese immigrants and serves consistently good Chinese fare; opposite the riverfront.

Shwe Sisa　　　　　　　BEER STATION
(Strand Rd; draught beer K600; ⊙9am-10pm) Brew with a view. Perched over the riverside a block southwest of the guesthouses, Shwe Sisa is fine for a beer or barbecued 'Slavia' fish.

ℹ Getting There & Away

At the time of writing, foreigners were not allowed on buses to or from Katha.

IWT ferry tickets are only available an hour before departure and can be bought from opposite the main jetty.

Buy tickets for the Katha–Mandalay express boat a day before departure from the office on the riverfront.

The nearest train station on the Mandalay–Myitkyina line is at Naba, 16 miles west of Katha. A daily train connects Katha–Naba ($2, 2pm), while there are two afternoon buses to Naba (K1000, 2pm & 5pm).

TRANSPORT TO/FROM KATHA

DESTINATION	IWT FERRY	EXPRESS BOAT	TRAIN
Mandalay	$9/45 deck/cabin, 3 weekly Mon, Wed & Fri, 5pm, 24-40hr depending on the season	K25,000, 1 daily 5am, 14hr	$6-14, 4 daily, 12hr
Kyaukmyaung	$5, 3 weekly Mon, Wed & Fri, 5pm, 12hr	N/A	N/A
Shwegu	$5, 3 weekly Mon, Wed & Fri, 5pm, 6hr	N/A	N/A
Bhamo	$5/25 deck/cabin, 3 weekly Tue, Fri & Sun, 9pm, 16hr	N/A	N/A
Myitkyina (via Naba)	N/A	N/A	$6-14, 4 daily, 12hr

Katha to Kyaukmyaung

IWT ferries tend to sail the section south of Katha in the dark, but this stretch has some of the Ayeyarwady's more appealing landscapes with several pagoda-topped hills and thatched villages. The first stop is **Ti Kyaing** (pronounced 't'chine'; Htigyaing), where a double row of riverfront thatched wooden stilt houses leads north from the jetty, a monastery hill rises directly above and there's a large reclining Buddha on the next hill northeast.

Further south the landscape becomes more monotonous towards **Tagaung**, which gave its name to a whole era of Burmese history, but hasn't got much left to show for it.

Kyaukmyaung
ကျောက်မြောင်း

📄 075 / POPULATION C10,000

The last major IWT stop before Mandalay is Kyaukmyaung (pronounced 'Chaomiao'), famous for its distinctive glazed pottery. That is produced in the delightful **Ngwe Nyein** district, a 20-minute stroll south along the riverside from central Kyaukmyaung's attractive triple-stupa, **Nondo Zedi**. Traffic en route is mainly a procession of ox carts carrying faggots or rice husks for pot-firing.

Beyond **Letyway Kyaunggyi** monastery you'll see almost every open space filled with large amphorae waiting to be shipped on river barges. Homes, many of them old wooden affairs with distinctive portalarches, double as storefronts selling vases, jugs and mustard pots (from K200). While some are vivid green (notably big owlfigure vases), archetypal Kyaukmyaung designs are usually glazed a rich glossy brown that's casually daubed with swirls of beige-yellow, the latter apparently taking its colour from old batteries.

The pottery district stretches nearly a mile further south, to and beyond the brutal gash of the new Ayeyarwady bridge site. En route are a few crumbling old stupas, while a block or two inland several 'factories' are housed in bamboo thatched barns. These can shelter as many as 60 potters working at hand-turned or foot-turned wheels. Visitors are generally welcome to nose around and you'll also see kilns, drying yards and piles of rough clay being chopped.

🛏 Sleeping & Eating

Kyaukmyaung has one ultra simple **guesthouse** (per person K1500) but it isn't licensed for foreigners so you'll normally be expected to sleep in nearby Shwebo, 18 miles west. However, the local police will usually make exceptions if your ferry happens to arrive at an antisocial late hour. The guesthouse, unmarked in English, is down an alley just inland from the main junction (riverside and Shwebo roads). Almost at the ferry jetty, the restaurant marked with a diamond graphic is run by local character Sein Win who speaks some English.

ℹ Getting There & Away

Southbound Katha–Mandalay express boats usually get here around 2pm, arriving at a central jetty three minutes' walk north of Nondo Zedi. IWT river ferries stop here mid-afternoon too. Pick-ups meet the boats and charge K500 for the 45-minute ride to Shwebo, where buses leave for Mandalay hourly (K2000, three hours).

Shwebo
ရွှေဘို

📄 075 / POPULATION C40,000

Between 1752 and 1755, the leader of little Moksobo village, Aung Zeya, revived Burmese prestige by fighting off both Manipuri and Bago-Mon armies. Rebranding himself King Alaungpaya (or Alaungmintayagyi), his short reign transformed formerly obscure Moksobo into glittering Shwebo ('Golden Leader'), which became, until his death in 1760, the capital of a newly reunified Burma. These days, Shwebo makes relatively little of its royal history and few foreign tourists bother making a special excursion to see its recently reconstructed palace. However, if you're jumping off an Ayeyarwady ferry at Kyaukmyaung, Shwebo makes a pleasant enough staging point from which to reach Bagan (via Monywa and Pakokku) without returning to Mandalay. Shwebo is locally famed for snakes and *thanakha* and some visitors consider it good luck to take home some earth from 'Victory Land', as Shwebo has been known since Alaungpaya's time.

👁 Sights

Shwe Daza Paya　　　BUDDHIST TEMPLE
(ရွှေတန်ဆာဘုရား) As you approach from the south, central Shwebo's skyline is given a very alluring dazzle by a collection of golden pagoda spires. These cluster around the extensive, 500-year-old Shwe Daza Paya. Close

up, however, the complex feels a little anti-climactic. Across the road, the dilapidated **Chanthaya Paya** was undergoing repairs at the time of writing.

Shwebon Yadana   PALACE

(ေရွှဘုံရတနာ; admission incl Hanlin $5; ☺ 7.30am-5pm) The city's most striking buildings are a pair of towering gold-painted wooden throne rooms, nine tiers high, once part of King Alaungpaya's 1753 palace. What you see today, though, are reconstructed, empty structures; the exhibits formerly on display are now in the National Museum in Nay Pyi Taw. The main reason to come here is to pick up your ticket for Hanlin.

Old City Moat   NEIGHBOURHOOD

During its 18th-century heyday, the palace was at the heart of an enormous walled city. The walls are now almost entirely gone but some parts of the wide **moat** are well-preserved. The most attractive is the section around 2 miles north of town near **Maw Daw Myin Tha Paya**, a pagoda built by Alaungpaya and guarded by giant *chinthe*.

🛏 Sleeping

Win Guest House   HOTEL $

(☎ 075-22049; Aung Zeya St; r with/without bathroom $20/10; ✳) Well-kept guesthouse in a convenient location close to the market. Rooms with bathrooms come with air-con and are a big step up from the ones with shared, but clean, bathrooms.

Shwe Phyu Guest House   HOTEL $

(☎ 075-22264; Yan Gyi Aung St; d K15,000-20,000, with shared bathroom K8000) Noisy and over-priced, the shared bathrooms here are basic. Better rooms are cleaner and the bathrooms tolerable. Some English spoken.

🍴 Eating & Drinking

Open-air food stands set up shop around the market, especially after dusk. There's a sprinkling of restaurants along Aung Zeya St, with many beer stations in the northern quarter and along Yan Gyi Aung St.

Eden Culinary Garden   CHINESE $

(Aung Zeya St; dishes from K1200; ☺ 6am-9pm; 🖥) The staff fall over themselves at the sight of a foreigner, and the courtyard setting is pleasant, even if the standard Chinese fare isn't very exciting. Draft Tiger is K700.

Shwe Paing   BURMESE-CHINESE $

(Yan Gyi Aung St; mains from K1300; ☺ 6am-9pm) Airy, neighbourhood Chinese joint with a Burmese flavour to the generous dishes, which come with soup and salad.

Melody Music Garden   BEER STATION

(Yan Gyi Aung St; draft Tiger beer K700; ☺ 9am-10pm) Ice-cold beer and partially obscured moat views. Bring mosquito repellent.

ℹ Information

SBO Internet (per hr K400; ☺ 8am-11pm) Swish, for Myanmar, place with snacks and a reasonable connection.

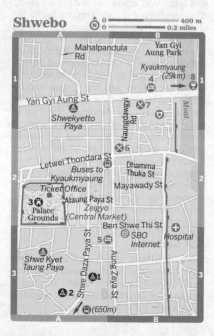

Shwebo

TRANSPORT TO/FROM SHWEBO

DESTINATION	TRAIN	BUS	PICK-UP TRUCK
Mandalay	$2-5, 3 daily, 4hr	K2000, 15 daily 5am-3pm, 3hr	N/A
Myitkyina	$11-37, 3 daily, 14-16hr	N/A	N/A
Monywa (for Bagan)	N/A	K1500, hourly 5am-3pm, 3½hr	N/A
Kyaukmyaung	N/A	K500, 2 daily 2pm & 3pm, 45min	K500, frequent until 4pm, 45min

❶ Getting There & Away

The main bus station is a mile south of the town centre.

The train station is in the west of town.

❶ Getting Around

A trishaw or motorbike ride from either station to the centre costs around K1000. Hotel staff can often arrange informal bicycle hire.

Hanlin ဟန်လင်း

POPULATION C4000

An almost imperceptible rise means that the attractive village of Hanlin (Halingyi, Halin, Halim) sits very slightly above the pan-flat surrounding plains. For centuries this geographical advantage was deeply significant and the site was home to a large city over 1600 years ago. The few visitors who brave seriously rough roads to get here come to explore the area's various archaeological remains. But unless you're desperately interested in the subject, Hanlin is an underwhelming experience, mainly because the site is poorly run and signposted. Before leaving Shwebo, be sure to visit Shwebon Yadana and warn the archaeological office there that you will be visiting Hanlin. Even so, you will likely have to go in search of the various key-holders to the sites yourself.

⦿ Sights

Archaeological Zone ARCHAEOLOGICAL SITES
(admission $5, free with Shwebon Yadana ticket) The 32 excavation sites here date back to the Pyu era (4th to 9th centuries AD). The sites rise above Hanlin village and survey the plains for a surprising distance; archaeologists have found large, low sections of brickworks that once formed part of a **wall** enclosing a complex that was 2 miles wide and 1 mile long. Many of the sites have yielded pottery and coins.

Several of the excavated **grave sites** can be visited. To nonspecialists, they look relatively similar (metal-roofed barns covering in-situ skeletons whose depth is a guide to their antiquity). If you don't want to spend hours seeing everything, consider making a beeline for **Site 29** where you can still see the ornaments and weapons with which the bodies were buried.

The excavations are scattered over several square miles, so you'll need wheels. An archaeology department fixer might be willing to accompany you but more likely you'll be on your own. The key-holders at each sub-site expect a tip (K1000), which is a good way of benefiting the local community (your $5 entry fee goes to the government's archaeology department).

Hanlin Village VILLAGE
Coming all this way without visiting the archaeological sites would be inexplicable, but Hanlin village is a magical place in its own right. Unpaved ox-cart tracks link an incredible plethora of decaying old stupas that create the feeling of an untouched mini-Bagan. It's best appreciated when the area is viewed from behind **Maung San Monastery** with its obvious golden *zedi*.

Near the market is a collection of **inscribed steles** and stone slabs in

---

SHWEBO THANAKHA

Wherever you go in Myanmar you'll find hawkers selling *thanakha*, the sandalwood-like logs that are ground to a paste and smeared on the skin as ubiquitous sun-block. Shwebo's *thanakha* is considered the country's sweetest-smelling and forms the subject of a famous folk song, and if you want a gift to delight guesthouse grandmas elsewhere in Myanmar, you won't do better. It's sold on the southern approach cloister to Shwe Daza Paya.

AYEYARWADY RIVER TRIP PLANNING

At the time of writing, foreigners were barred from taking fast boats, with the exception of the daily express from Katha to Mandalay, and all local boats. Foreigners are not allowed to travel to or from Myitkyina by boat. Several companies offer luxury cruise trips along the Ayeyarwady, albeit rarely more than a few times a year. See p26 for details.

Which Boat?

Travellers cruising the Ayeyarwady used to be able to choose between the slow IWT ferries or the much quicker fast boats, or alternate between the two. But since an overloaded fast boat sank two minutes after leaving Bhamo in 2012, foreigners have been officially banned from taking the speedier boats.

This being Myanmar, the rule is not enforced rigidly. While you'll have no luck getting on a fast boat in Bhamo, you may be allowed on one in smaller ports such as Shwegu and Kyaukmyaung. Foreigners are still able to take the Katha–Mandalay express boat.

While the ban is annoying if you're in a rush, in truth the fast boats are more uncomfortable than the IWT ferries and often dangerously overcrowded. The moral is that if you decide to travel the Ayeyarwady, be prepared to take your time.

IWT Ferries

These two-/three-storey craft are the cheapest option and the best for interacting with locals but they're slow, unreliable and not very comfortable for long journeys.

Routes They run three times a week between Bhamo and Mandalay (Monday, Wednesday and Friday) with stops in Shwegu, Katha, Ti Kyaing, Tagaung and Kyaukmyaung. Ferries can be a day or more late so don't be in a hurry.

Tickets Ticket-purchasing procedures vary by port but foreigners always need to pay with pristine US dollar bills, sometimes at the relevant IWT office. Agency bookings aren't possible and there are no seat reservations, indeed no seats whatever, just cold metal decks.

Comfort & Provisions You'll generally need to sleep aboard at least one night, maybe three nights northbound from Mandalay to Bhamo. A few simple cabins are available ($60, shared toilet) but most folk travel deck class (maximum fare $12) for which you'll need your own mat and bedding. Snacks and drinks are sold onboard, but are comparatively pricey. Food can also be bought at the boat stops.

Fast Boats

Long covered motorboats carrying between 30 and 80 passengers. Departures are regular.

Routes Fast boats make daily one-day hops on the following sections, always travelling by day (each sector will be in a different boat): Myitkyina–Sinbo, Sinbo–Bhamo, Bhamo–Shwegu–Katha and Katha–Mandalay.

Tickets Usually purchased just before departure, or one day before for Katha–Mandalay.

---

now-forgotten Pyu script. Within the **Nyaung Kobe Monastery**, a museum room displays various ancient, but unlabelled, archaeological finds. Another minor attraction is the little **hot spring area** where villagers collect water from circular concrete-sided well-pools and bathe in two bigger basin-pools.

❶ Getting There & Away

Hanlin is about 12 butt-kicking miles southeast of Shwebo. There are two routes here. One follows the canal beside the bus station for 6 miles to Bo Tè village. From there, turn left (across the canal) on the first significant road. This soon degenerates into an outrageously rutted ox-cart track that is slowly being upgraded. Fork left at the only other junction. The other, quicker route takes you south of the bus station, before turning left and travelling for 6 miles down an unsealed rocky track that leads to Site 29 and the village. Going either way by car or three-wheeler would be excruciatingly uncomfortable. It's marginally less painful by motorcycle: with a driver you'll pay at least K10,000 return from Shwebo.

Comfort & Provisions The wooden bench seats are small and often partly broken. Life jackets may not be available. You'll need to sleep at local guesthouses, which are very basic in Sinbo, Shwegu and Katha. Bring plenty of drinking water. You can buy food at the brief intermediate halts.

When to Go?
Boats run all year between Mandalay and Bhamo.

➡ Journeys are fastest in autumn when water levels are high. By February, sandbanks mean that the IWT ferry will have to moor overnight, adding up to a day to southbound journey times.

➡ April is difficult with boats packed full of local travellers and ferries seriously overloaded.

➡ In summer, rain and high winds can make the passage very uncomfortable.

Where to Start/Finish?
North of Mandalay there are currently only three realistic start/finish points for foreigners on the Ayeyarwady adventure:

Bhamo No rail or road link to Mandalay or Myitkyina, so the only way in is by air. But accommodation is good and Bhamo to Katha is the most popular single section of river trip due to the (brief) drama of the second defile. Shwegu, in between Bhamo and Katha, is an offbeat highlight.

Katha Popular for its George Orwell connections but guesthouses are basic. Three daily trains connect to Mandalay, albeit at antisocial times and from a railhead 18 miles away. River scenery south of Katha is initially lovely but there's no easy jump-off point till Kyaukmyaung.

Kyaukmyaung Getting off at this interesting pottery town makes sense if you're heading for Bagan, which you can reach across country via Shwebo, Monywa and Pakokku. Continuing by boat to Mandalay you'll pass Mingun but IWT ferries won't stop there.

How Long Will It Take?
The minimum time from Bhamo to Mandalay by IWT ferry will be two to three days, assuming the boats are running to schedule. You can save time by jumping ship at Katha and catching the express boat to Mandalay. Bear in mind that it takes two days longer to travel northbound, upriver, than it does going in the other direction.

How Much Will It Cost?
IWT ferries are far cheaper than the other options. A deck ticket from Bhamo to Mandalay is $12, whereas the express boat from Katha to Mandalay alone costs K25,000.

THE FAR NORTH

Myanmar's far northern range of Himalayan 'Ice Mountains' is one of the world's least-known 'last frontiers'. Hkakabo Razi (19,295ft), the nation's loftiest summit, is over a half a mile higher than Mont Blanc and had never been climbed until 1996. Perhaps that's not surprising given that the trek to reach its base camp took almost a month. The surrounding Hkakabo Razi National Park is considered a treasure trove of biodiversity. Landscapes here are similar to those found in the Indian state of Arunachal Pradesh – steep forests, ridges of peaks bursting through the snowline and deep valleys carved by fast-flowing mountain rivers. Further south is the Hukaung Valley Tiger Reserve (www.panthera.org/programs/tiger/tigers-forever/Myanmar), which, at 6748 sq miles, is larger than all of India's tiger reserves put together, although reports suggest that the number of tigers has dropped dramatically in recent years thanks to unregulated logging and mining in the area.

The far north has sparse populations of Kachin, Rawang, Lisu and even a handful of Taron, the only known pygmy group in Asia. Set well back from the higher peaks, the only settlement of any size is Putao, an oddly diffuse place that has a market but no other real sense of a town centre. This was the site of the isolated British WWII military outpost, Fort Hertz, though there's no fortress to visit.

Today the region still feels (and genuinely is) entirely cut off from the rest of Myanmar. This may change as the airport runway gets extended and new tourism facilities are being developed. But for now, to get even the briefest possible glimpse, you'll have to do an organised 'tour', costing from around $600 per person for the shortest four-day option. That will get you to one or two photogenic suspension footbridges and some unspoilt rural villages, though the latter aren't markedly different from similar settlements elsewhere in rural north Myanmar. Unless you trek for many days further, the Himalayan horizon will remain fairly distant, and might stay hidden altogether by rain clouds. So is it worth the trouble? That really depends on how you value exclusivity. If you're comparing tourist numbers, Putao makes Bhutan look like a veritable Benidorm.

The best time to visit is from October to April, when daytime temperatures are quite pleasant and nights are cold but rarely freezing.

Tours

Foreigners are periodically barred from travelling to Putao and the far north, as they were at the time of writing. When travel is allowed, the only way to visit is on a pre-arranged tour. Allow ample time for organising practicalities as your agency will need to obtain permits that take between 10 days and two weeks to issue, often much longer. The cheapest tours usually cost from around $150 per person per day (minimum four days) plus flights to Putao. Tour package fees generally include food, permits and excursions and/or treks.

In the dry season, an appealing part-day activity is a boat trip along sections of the deep green Malikha River alternating between rapids and calm pebble-bottomed shallows and passing beaches, sculpted rocks, unspoilt villages and rainforest jungle-sections. When water levels are higher, white-water rafting is a possibility. This might be combined with an interesting excursion to Machanbaw (40 minutes' drive from Putao). With an attractive setting beside the mirror-calm Malikha River,

Machanbaw was the district's former colonial administrative centre and retains a well-spaced scattering of older British-era buildings.

Tours typically include some trekking. Even for just a two-day walk you'll probably get porters, a good cook and accommodation provided en route whether camping or in a very basic village homestay or cabin. Longer treks include a 14-day hike to the peak of 11,926ft Mt Phon Kan Razi, for views over the Myanmar Himalaya and the Mishimi Hills of neighbouring Arunachal Pradesh. For an excellent visual impression of the route's attractions and challenges see www.hsdejong.nl/myanmar/putao.

Don't underestimate the rigour of hiking here. Even the shortest loop includes long days of fairly strenuous gradients and a high chance of leeches, and you'll need to be prepared for damp, cold weather.

Sleeping & Eating

In coming years, a major expansion in facilities can be expected if Putao is developed into Myanmar's ecotourism gateway. For now, however, unless you're allowed to stay at the basic 'army' guesthouse (www.traveltomyanmar.com/hotel_putao.htm), all tours start and finish with at least one night at either the stunning but massively expensive Malikha Lodge (www.malikhalodge.net; r for two nights $3000), around an hour's drive from Putao, or at the more affordable Putao Trekking House (www.putaotrekkinghouse.com), a perfectly decent place but with some inconsistencies and indifferent food served in a glaringly lit dining hall. The cabin rooms are designed so that the small verandahs face a central lawn rather than the distant mountain horizon.

Getting There & Away

AIR

Twice-weekly Air Bagan flights to Putao cost around $170 from Yangon, $120 from Mandalay and $90 from Myitkyina but without tour permits you won't be allowed to board the plane. Tours can be organised through Malikha Lodge, **Journeys** (www.journeysmyanmar.com), MTT and assorted Yangon agencies.

Road transport from Myitkyina would be appallingly rough but isn't permitted anyway for foreigners. There are a limited number of vehicles in the Putao area, almost all trucks or WWII-era jeeps.

Western Myanmar

Best Places to Stay

➡ Yoma Cherry Lodge (p294)

➡ Shwe Thazin Hotel (p307)

➡ Royal City Guest House (p307)

➡ Pleasant View Resort (p295)

➡ Sandoway Resort (p295)

➡ Noble Hotel (p300)

Best Places to Eat

➡ Aung (p300)

➡ Htay Htay's Kitchen (p296)

➡ Pleasant View Islet Restaurant (p296)

➡ Kaung Thant (p308)

Why Go?

Even as more of the country's remote areas become 'open' and tourist numbers increase, Myanmar's westernmost states remain staunchly untouristed.

The handful of tourists who make it to Rakhine State tend to confine themselves to the relaxing resorts of Ngapali Beach, and understandably so: the pristine sand and the turquoise waters of the Bay of Bengal are some of the country's best. Yet those with more adventurous aspirations can head to the state's scrappy, atmospheric capital Sittwe and the old Rakhine capital of Mrauk U, an amazing archaeological site, studded with hundreds of temples.

And for the even more daring, looming to the north is elusive, underdeveloped Chin State, where if you're willing to deal with the red tape and lack of infrastructure, a richly traditional area of mountains, forests and culture awaits.

When to Go
Western Myanmar

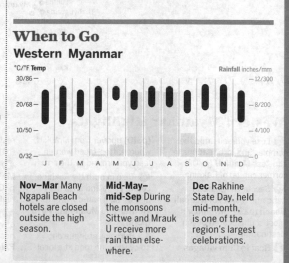

Nov–Mar Many Ngapali Beach hotels are closed outside the high season.

Mid-May–mid-Sep During the monsoons Sittwe and Mrauk U receive more rain than elsewhere.

Dec Rakhine State Day, held mid-month, is one of the region's largest celebrations.

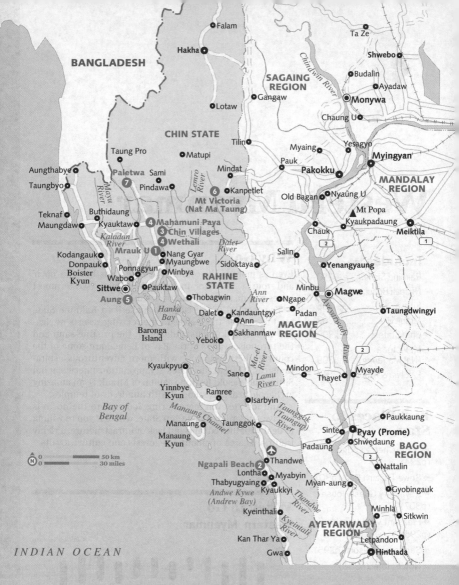

Western Myanmar Highlights

1 Lose yourself amid the temples and fortifications in timeless **Mrauk U** (p302), former capital of Rakhine

2 Savour the seafood, sand and resorts of **Ngapali Beach** (p293), Myanmar's most sophisticated beach destination

3 Boat to **Chin villages** (p310) upriver from Mrauk U, where tattoo-faced women lead you around by the arm

4 Take in both the Rakhine countryside and ancient history on a half-day trip to **Wethali** and **Mahamuni Paya** (p308)

5 Burn your tongue on spicy Rakhine food at a local restaurant such as **Aung** (p112)

6 Get a permit to climb **Mt Victoria** (Nat Ma Taung; p309), the country's second-highest peak

7 Be among the handful of visitors to the remote heartland of Chin culture in **Paletwa** (p310)

RAKHINE STATE

The interchangeable terms Rakhine (sometimes spelled Rakhaing) and Arakan refer to the people, the state and dialect of Myanmar's westernmost state. Isolated from the Burmese heartland, but in an ancient crossroad that has been the seat of at least four kingdoms, and home to a geography that spans both mountains and coastline, it's not a surprise that the inhabitants of Rakhine State remain staunchly proud of their unique identity.

History

Even today there remains a debate over whether the Rakhine are actually Burmans with Indian blood, Indians with Burmese characteristics or a separate race (as is sometimes claimed locally). Although the first inhabitants of the region were a dark-skinned Negrito tribe known as the Bilu, later migrants from the eastern Indian subcontinent developed the first Hindu-Buddhist kingdoms in Myanmar before the first Christian millennium. These kingdoms flourished before the invasion of the Tibeto-Burmans from the north and east in the 9th and 18th centuries. The current inhabitants of the state may thus be mixed descendants of all three groups: Bilu, Bengali and Burmese.

Regardless, Rakhine's historical roots are linked to those of northern India, which held political and cultural sway over the region for centuries before the land fell under Bagan's dominance during medieval times. In 1430 the local king Naramithla returned after three decades in exile in the Bengali city of Guar to establish a new capital at Mrauk U from where Rakhine was ruled for the next 400 years. When the British annexed the state in 1826, the capital was moved to Sittwe.

In 2012, sectarian riots in Sittwe led to the expulsion of that city's Muslim community (known in the western press as the Rohingya). The unrest was seen as at least partially responsible for sparking widespread anti-Muslim sentiment across Myanmar; for background on the Rohingya see p335.

Ngapali Beach
ငပလီကမ်းခြေ

📙 043

'Getting away from it all' isn't exactly why most people come to Myanmar, but if the need strikes, Ngapali's idyllic palm-lined beach is *the* place to do it. With its pristine white sands, the clear blue waters of the Bay of Bengal, and a host of sophisticated accommodation, Ngapali – some say named by a wayward Italian reminiscing about Napoli years ago – has a justified reputation as the country's premier beach getaway.

But this is Myanmar, and despite the jet-setters and accolades, Ngapali continues to maintain a charming fishing-village vibe, as evidenced by the small boats heading out day and night to catch a bounty that is later served up superfresh in restaurants and hotels. Ox-drawn carts amble along the beach as locals find the sand-ways a smoother ride than the rough one-lane road. And although Ngapali is currently experiencing something of a construction boom, fewer than two dozen bungalow-style resorts spread across more than 15 miles of coast means that there's still a lot of space on the beach.

Peak season is from November to March, yet even at the height of the season, Ngapali is a snoozy, early-to-bed place. Things are almost comatose during the rainy season (June to October) when flights dip to once a week and most hotels either shut up shop or keep open only a handful of rooms.

◉ Sights & Activities

South of the hotels, and easily reached barefoot by the beach, is the rustic fishing village of **Gyeik Taw**, where small fish are dried on bamboo mats across the beach. Even further south is the bigger village of **Lontha** and an inlet of the same name, backed by a sweeping curve of mangrove and sand facing south.

On a bayside hill east of Lontha is a modest white **stupa**. It's worth seeing for its glorious panoramic views – and for the adventure to reach it. To get there, turn left at the town junction (near the market). The road runs parallel to the boat-filled bay and quickly degenerates into a path too sandy to ride

---

ℹ TRAVEL RESTRICTIONS

Much of Rakhine State is now open to foreign independent travellers, although the southern half of the state is the only part that foreign tourists can reach by bus, as well as by air. The northern part of the state, home to the capital Sittwe, must be accessed by air or boat.

Ngapali Beach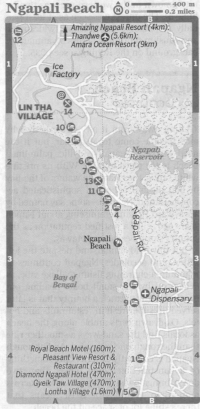

0 — 400 m
0 — 0.2 miles

Ngapali Beach

🛌 Sleeping
1	Amata Resort & Spa	B4
2	Aureum Palace	B2
3	Bayview Beach Resort	A2
4	Jade Marina Resort	B2
5	Laguna Lodge	B4
6	Lin Thar Oo Lodge	A2
7	Memento Resort	A2
8	Ngapali Bay Villas & Spa	B3
9	Sandoway Resort	B3
10	Silver Beach Hotel	A2
11	Thande Beach Hotel	A2
12	Yoma Cherry Lodge	A1

🍴 Eating
	Catch	(see 3)
13	Green Umbrella	A2
14	Htay Htay's Kitchen	A1
	Lili's Bar	(see 5)
	Sandoway Resort Restaurant	(see 9)

WESTERN MYANMAR NGAPALI BEACH

Map labels: Amazing Ngapali Resort (4km); Thandwe ✈ (5.6km); Amara Ocean Resort (9km); Ice Factory; LIN THA VILLAGE; Ngapali Reservoir; Ngapali Beach; Bay of Bengal; Ngapali Rd; Ngapali Dispensary; Royal Beach Motel (160m); Pleasant View Resort & Restaurant (310m); Diamond Ngapali Hotel (470m); Gyeik Taw (470m); Lontha Village (1.6km)

on; if you're on a bike, leave it with a local. About five minutes or so after passing a small bridge, you reach the hill steps to the stupa.

Four-hour **snorkelling trips** (per person incl boat, mask & snorkel K20,000), arranged by any hotel or directly with boat owners on the beach, usually depart at 7am or 8am to catch the day's clearest water. Most trips take in a few spots around (private) 'Pearl Island' off the south end of the beach. The coral's not super, but there are plenty of bright red and blue fish to follow. Some snorkellers bring along fishing rods to drop a line.

🛌 Sleeping

When we stopped by, Ngapali was undergoing a pretty serious construction boom and there were several yet-unfinished resorts. Names to look for by the time you read this include **Ashin Villa** and **Max Myanmar**, both north of the airport; **Eden Resort**, **Hotel at the Rocks** and **Thingaha Ngapali Resort**

Hotel, all located along the strip directly south of the airport; and **Jade Marina Resort** (☏ 043-42430; www.jademarinaresort.com; r $200-350) and **Ngapali Bay Villas & Spa** (☏ 043-42301; www.ngapalibay.com; bungalow $305-525), south of Lin Tha Village.

If there's somewhere you particularly want to stay, be sure to plan ahead; during high season (from November to March) some hotels can get booked out, sometimes way in advance. The vast majority of places, including nearly all of the upscale resorts, are closed during the rainy season (from June to October).

Nearly all hotels include airport transfer and breakfast in their rates. Where there isn't 24 hour electricity we note the times the power kicks in.

★ Yoma Cherry Lodge
HOTEL $$
(☏ 043-42339; www.yomacherrylodge.com; off Ngapali Rd; r $80-100; 🌀 🛜) Virtually alone on the secluded bay just north of Lin Tha Village, this new place takes the form of a garden compound with handsome, Burmese-influenced, thatched-roof structures. Rooms are modern-feeling and huge, with equally spacious balconies and attractive furniture, and best of all, the rates are refreshingly approachable. Electricity is available 24 hours, although air-con is allowed only between 6pm and 6am.

Royal Beach Motel
HOTEL $$
(☏ 043-42411, in Yangon 01-544 484; www.royalbeachngapali.com; Ngapali Rd; r $75-100; 🌀) Cosier and more personable than other mid-

range places, this place boasts an almost village-like atmosphere. The 23 rooms are overwhelmingly comfortable and inviting, many sporting huge balconies. Yet given the lack of amenities (there's no TV or wi-fi), it must be said that the high-season rates are asking a bit much.

Laguna Lodge HOTEL $$
(☑043-42312, in Yangon 01-501 123; www.laguna lodge-myanmar.com; Ngapali Rd; r $50-70) For a 'house on the beach' feel, the 20-room Laguna, run by a German chef, goes rustic with dark-wood, open-shuttered windows and huge balconies. Mosquito nets hang over the big beds and a giant circular window in the bathrooms provides views through your room to the beach.

Memento Resort HOTEL $$
(☑043-42441, in Yangon 01-228 556; www.nga palimementoresort.com; Ngapali Rd; r $30-90; 🌊) The beachfront rooms at this longstanding budget/midrange place can't be described as sexy or new, but they are spacious and comfortable, and are located steps from a particularly rocky and scenic strip of beach. Cheaper rooms without sea views – Ngapali's only real budget option – offer only a bed, a cold-water shower and a fan. Power is available from 6pm to 6am.

Lin Thar Oo Lodge HOTEL $$
(☑043-42322, in Yangon 01-503 721; www.lin tharoo-ngapali.com; Ngapali Rd; r $30-90; 🌊) When we stopped by, furious construction meant that the 31 rooms at this midrange-feeling place were a rather eclectic mix of new and old duplex bungalows, the former

the more desirable with minibar, a TV and air-con. Electricity is on from 6pm to 6am.

Silver Beach Hotel HOTEL $$
(☑043-42652, in Yangon 01-381 898; www.silver beachngapali.com; Ngapali Rd; r/ste $100/150; 🌊@) At the beach's north end, Silver Beach is the cheapest way to go for 24-hour electricity. The prim, red-roofed duplex cottages conjure up the look of a 1950s British holiday camp, with dated furnishings and facilities to match.

Diamond Ngapali Hotel RESORT $$
(☑09 7310 4399; www.diamondngapali.com; Ngapali Rd; r $85-150; 🌊🌊) Located at the scrappy southern end of Ngapali's main beach, the 24 new but simple cement bungalows here alternate between pool and sea views.

Pleasant View Resort RESORT $$$
(☑043-42222, in Yangon 01-393 086; www.pvr ngapali.com; Ngapali Rd; r $130-160, bungalows $180-335; 🌊@🌐) The Pleasant View lives up to its name with an pleasing location at the far southern end of the beach. Accommodation ranges from free-standing and duplex bungalows to rooms in a two-storey structure, all of which are spacious and simply but chicly decorated with a TV, minibar and hot-and-cold shower. The power is on from 2pm to 8am.

Sandoway Resort RESORT $$$
(☑043-42233, in Yangon 01-294 612; www. sandowayresort.com; Ngapali Rd; r & bungalows $190-410; 🌊@🌐🌊) Along with palm-shaded walkways leading past well-tended gardens and ponds, the highlight at this Italian–Myanmar joint venture are the free-standing two-storey 'villas' and 'cottages' that feature

---

WORTH A TRIP

KAN THAR YA BEACH

If Ngapali's ever-expanding resort scene is too slick for you, try **Kan Thar Ya** (ကမ်းသာယာ ကမ်းခြေ), an almost entirely undeveloped beach area 64 miles south. The sand isn't as fine as Ngapali's, and a location between the mouths of two rivers means the water isn't always clear, but if you've ever dreamt of having a quiet beachside town to yourself, this is it.

The only foreigner-approved place to stay is **Maw Shwe Chai Resort** (☑09 5985 28191, in Yangon 01-510 381; www.mawshwechairesort.com; r incl breakfast $40-60), located at a small private beach outside Gwa, approximately 30 minutes south of Kan Thar Ya. The bungalow-style rooms are simple but stylish, and are found in an attractive grove of coconut palms.

To reach Kan Thar Ya, hop on the daily fan-cooled bus that runs from Thandwe to Yangon via Gwa and tell the driver to let you off at Maw Shwe Chai Resort (K12,000, about six hours, 11am).

lofty ceilings and appealing craft details. You get no TV, but there's a massive communal screening room for movies, comfortably set out with padded armchairs for nightly screenings.

Amara Ocean Resort
RESORT $$$

(☑in Yangon 01-721 869; www.amaragroup.net; bungalows $290-400; ❄ @ ☎ ☒) Fancy 3 miles of almost entirely undeveloped, white sand beach? If you can afford one of the 26 beautiful teak villas at this resort north of the airport, then it's all yours. Rooms are steps from the beach and can all claim sea views, in addition to modern amenities and spacious bathrooms.

Aureum Palace
RESORT $$$

(☑043-42360, 01-399 341; www.aureumpalacehotel.com; Ngapali Rd; bungalows $389; ❄ @ ☎ ☒) How's this for decadent: 42 free-standing bungalow suites interspersed throughout a jungly, isolated-feeling compound, and equipped with handsome wood and stone furnishings and private Jacuzzi. The only thing more ostentatious is the hotel's single 'Executive Room', complete with a private pool.

Amata Resort & Spa
RESORT $$$

(☑043-42177, in Yangon 01-665 126; www.amataresort.com; r $200-230, bungalows $305-460; ❄ @ ☎ ☒) Owned by a Yangon sea captain, this swish complex of gorgeous two-storey cabanas and rooms (request rooms 701 and 702 for their brilliant beach views), set back from the beach in lush gardens, is quite possibly Ngapali's most stylish. In addition to the eponymous spa, it's also home to Ngapali's lone tennis court ($7).

Amazing Ngapali Resort
RESORT $$$

(☑043-42011, in Yangon 01-203 500; www.amazing-hotel.com; r $260-570; ❄ ☎ ☒) The spacious and well-equipped 36 double-storey villas at this resort get both rave reviews and repeat visitors, although we weren't crazy about the rather frumpy furnishings. The resort's formerly isolated location near the airport is set to change substantially due to large-scale resort projects on either side.

Bayview Beach Resort
RESORT $$$

(☑043-42299, in Yangon 01-504 471; www.bayviewmyanmar.com; Ngapali Rd; r $150-396; ❄ @ ☒) The luxurious Bayview occupies a nice strip of beach, with a rare on-the-beach bar. The 33 'bungalows' are actually linked rooms with an inviting, attractive layout, modern amenities (TV, minibar, safe), semi-outdoor shower, lots of space, and lounge chairs on the private deck. Guests can rent out windsurfers, kayaks and catamarans (per hour $5 to $10).

Thande Beach Hotel
RESORT $$$

(☑043-42278, Yangon 01-546 225; www.thandebeachhotelmyanmar.com; Ngapali Rd; r $125-270; ❄ @ ☎ ☒) The least stylish of the upmarket resorts, the Thande is nevertheless a pleasant place to bunk, offering duplex bungalows and rooms in a two-storey building surrounded by gardens, all located in a handy mid-beach location.

🍴 Eating & Drinking

A dozen or so indistinguishable seafood restaurants cluster in two strips: one running south of Silver Beach Hotel and another running south from Sandoway Resort. All have practically identical English-language menus and prices: a dish of crab, squid or barracuda starts from K2000 or K2500, barbecued tiger prawns are K3500 to K5000, and lobster is K15,000 and up.

There's also a strip of sand-in-your-toes-type beach restaurants between Memento Resort and Thande Beach Hotel. Of these, Green Umbrella (mains from K2000; ☻10am-10pm; 🗈) gets the best reports, although it was closed when we visited during the rainy season.

And the top-end hotel restaurants also offer a culinary alternative – particularly if you're looking for western-style food. The Sandoway Resort Restaurant's (Sandoway Resort, Ngapali Rd; mains $6-48; ☻7am-10pm; 🗈) Italian co-owners ensure that the pasta is *al dente*, and the German management at Catch (Bayview Beach Resort, Ngapali Rd; mains $5-24; ☻7am-11pm) ensure a decent schnitzel, among other dishes.

Htay Htay's Kitchen
BURMESE $$

(Ngapali Rd; mains K2000-5000; ☻7am-11pm; 🗈) At the north end of the beach, this handsome restaurant and gift shop is run by a very friendly couple. Expect tasty, if gentrified, Rakhine-style food.

Pleasant View Islet Restaurant
SEAFOOD $$

(Pleasant View Resort, Ngapali Rd; mains K4000-10,000; ☻11am-10pm; 🗈) Set on a rocky islet at the beach's south end (you may have to wade through knee-deep surf to get to it), this stylish eatery serves Western-influenced seafood dishes at a better price than most hotel restaurants. It's also perfect for sunset cocktails and nibbles.

Lili's Bar INTERNATIONAL $$
(Laguna Lodge, Ngapali Rd; meals $4-6; ⊘7am-11pm) A cute spot in the palm-shaded sand with a lazy dog or two lolling around, fake turtles, generous plates of pasta and K2000 cocktails.

ⓘ Information

Ngapali Dispensary (☑043-42233; off Ngapali Rd; ⊘9am-noon & 1-4pm) is a charity-built clinic with English-speaking staff.

Some upscale hotels allow nonguests to use their **internet** (per 30 minutes/hour $3/6), or there's an **internet cafe** (Ngapali Rd; per hr K500; ⊘7am-7pm) next door to Htay Htay's Kitchen.

ⓘ Getting There & Away

AIR

Thandwe airport is named for the town 4 miles inland, but is closer to Ngapali village. Hotel buses meet planes, typically offering free transport.

Asian Wings (☑043-42037, in Yangon 01-515 259; www.asianwingsair.com; 112 Ngapali Rd), **Air Bagan** (☑043-42429, 01-513 322; www.airbagan.com; 407 Ngapali Rd), **Air KBZ** (☑in Yangon

01-373 787; www.airkbz.com), **Air Mandalay** (☑043-42404, in Yangon 01-501 520; www.airmandalay.com) and **Yangon Airways** (☑in Yangon 01-383 100; www.yangonair.com) serve Yangon ($100 to $120, 55 minutes to two hours 15 minutes, daily), sometimes via Sittwe ($80 to $110, 45 minutes, daily). Connections can dwindle to once a week from approximately May through September.

BOAT

Taunggok, 50 miles or so north of Thandwe, is the jumping-off point for travellers catching boats to Sittwe. Carriers include **Shwe Pyi Tan** (☑043-65130, in Taunggok 043-60704) with departures at 6.30am on Monday, Tuesday and Friday ($35, 10 to 11 hours); and **Malikha Travels** (☑in Taunggok 043-60127), leaving at 6.30am on Monday, Wednesday and Saturday ($30, 10 to 11 hours).

WESTERN MYANMAR NGAPALI BEACH

OFF THE BEATEN TRACK

THANDWE

Located about 4 miles inland to the northeast of Ngapali Beach, **Thandwe** (သံတွဲ) fills a hilly valley with its low-key streets. It's been a key Rakhine town for many centuries. When the British stationed a garrison here around the turn of the 20th century – indeed, the former colonial jail is today Thandwe's central **market** (သံတွဲဈေး; ⊘6am-4pm) – they twisted the name into Sandoway.

While not a major destination, Thandwe makes for a nice visit if you're staying at Ngapali Beach and fancy a change of scene.

Three golden stupas stand on hilltops around Thandwe, each offering excellent viewpoints of the town's tin roofs, peeking out of a sea of palms and hills. The tallest, **Nandaw Paya** (နန်းတော်ဘုရား; ⊘daylight hours) FREE, a mile west of the market, was supposedly erected in AD 761 by King Minbra to enshrine a piece of a rib of the Buddha. The long shrine facing the stupa to the south houses some nice wood-carving reliefs of Buddha's life.

Just east of town, right across a small river about half a mile from the market, **Sandaw Paya** (ဆံတော်ဘုရား; ⊘daylight hours) FREE was supposedly built in AD 784 by Rakhaing King Minyokin to house a Buddha hair, and was rebuilt by the Burmese in 1876.

Across the river (north past the bus station and east on a stone road about 1.3 miles from the market), **Andaw Paya** (အံတော်ဘုရား; daylight hours) FREE is the lowest stupa but offers revealing glimpses of the river's fork from the hills east. It claims to house a Buddha molar relic and dates from AD 763.

Pick-up trucks to/from Ngapali run every 45 minutes from 6am to 6pm (K500).

Pick-ups to Taunggok depart from Thandwe's bus station (K1500 to K3500, three to four hours, every two hours from 4.30am to 4.30pm).

BUS

Aung Thit Sar (☑ 043-65363) run daily air-con buses to Yangon (K14,000, about 14 hours) via Thandwe and Pyay (Prome); you'll pay the same if you only go as far as Pyay (about 10 hours). Tickets are sold by hotels in Ngapali Beach, and the bus will pick you up from your accommodation around 11am (they depart from Thandwe at 1pm). The road – particularly between Taunggok and Pyay – has the reputation of being one of Myanmar's hardest, bounciest, most stomach-churning trips. Bring warm clothes, as the ride over the mountains at night gets cold.

Allegedly faster and smoother are the daily fan-cooled buses to Yangon that ply a newer route via Gwa (K12,000, about 10 hours, 11am).

❶ Getting Around

Pick-up trucks run frequently from Thandwe to Ngapali Beach and on to Lontha village (K500, every 45 minutes from 6am to 6pm). Catch one in either direction on the main road.

Bicycles can be rented from most hotels for K3000 per day and a few motorbikes are available for K10,000.

Sittwe စစ်တွေ

☑ 043 / POPULATION C180,000

Rakhine State's capital Sittwe sits in an incredible spot where the wide, tidal Kaladan River kisses the big fat Bay of Bengal. Despite this, sectarian violence in 2012 (see p312) and the town's generally scrappy vibe mean that most visitors approach the city as little more than the transit point for the ruins at Mrauk U.

History

Prior to the Burmese invasion of the Mrauk U kingdom in 1784, there was little more than a village here. Fifty years later, Sittwe's economy underwent a boom when British forces took over during the First Anglo-Burmese War. The British moved the state capital here from Mrauk U and named the place Akyab after the nearby Akyattaw Ridge.

Incoming wealth from cargo trade with Calcutta fuelled the construction of some fine colonial mansions, but much of the grace was lost under heavy WWII fighting between the British and Japanese forces.

Today, the town's economy is set to benefit from the construction of a new harbour,

a joint venture between Myanmar and India, next to the municipal market.

◉ Sights

Most of Sittwe's action runs along the Main Rd, which parallels the Kaladan River. Along this route, don't miss the **Fruit Bat Trees** (Main Rd), where, during the day, hundreds of noisy fruit bats fight with equally noisy crows before heading off at dusk – there's a great view of their migration from the roof of the Shwe Thazin Hotel.

Central Market MARKET

(၍, ပ၀ဈ; Strand Rd; ⊙6am-6pm) Focussed on the 1956 municipal market building, there's lots going on here from dawn up to noon and beyond – it's well worth popping by before your boat or plane leaves. Head straight past *longyi*, fishing-net and vegetable stands to the fish and meat area, where stingrays and gutted eels and drying sharks make quite a scene. In the bay, small boats jostle for space to unload their catch.

A few blocks north is the **Rice Market** (ဆန်ဈေး), with tiny lanes between the water and Strand Rd filled with simple wood homes, where traders hawk brown and sticky rice – some bound for Bangladesh.

Sittwe

◉ Sights
1 Central Market	C3
2 Fruit Bat Trees	B3
3 Jama Mosque	C3
4 Rakhine State Cultural Museum	C3
5 Rice Market	D2
6 Shwezedi Kyaung	A1

🛏 Sleeping
7 Mya Guest House	B4
8 Noble Hotel	B3
9 Prince Guest House	C1
10 Shwe Thazin Hotel	B4

🍴 Eating
11 Aung	C3
12 Móun·di Stand	A4
Mya Teahouse	(see 7)
13 River Valley Seafoods Restaurant	C4

❶ Transport
14 Air Bagan	C2
15 Air KBZ	B1
16 Air Mandalay	B1
17 Shwe Pyi Tan	C1

View Point
LANDMARK

(စစ်တွေ့ကျူးရှုရှိင့်; Strand Rd) **FREE** The riverside Strand Rd leads about 1.5 miles south to a smashing location called the View Point, where you can sip on a beer or eat at the somewhat overpriced **Point Restaurant** (Strand Rd; mains 1000-6000K; ☉9am-9pm; 📷) as the sun sets over the Bay of Bengal. Just west, in front of a closed naval base, is **Sittwe Beach**, a broad, grey-brown strip of sand.

It would make a long but pleasant walk, otherwise auto rickshaws, known locally as *thoun bein,* will take you there and back for 5000K, taxis for 10,000K.

Rakhine State Cultural Museum
MUSEUM

(ရခိုင်ပြည်နယ်ယဉ်ကျေးမှုပြတိုက်; Main Rd; K2000; ☉9.30am-4.30pm Tue-Sat) This museum features two floors of Rakhine cultural goodies that benefit from just barely enough English subtitles. On the first floor are displays on local customs, such as models showing off some of the 64 traditional Mrauk U royal hairstyles, and drawings illustrating key moves you may need for Rakhine wrestling. The second floor features diagrams and artefacts that detail Rakhine's origins (around 3000 BC) and four key periods (Dhanyawadi, Vesali, Lemro and Mrauk U), complete with useful renderings and models.

Maka Kuthala Kyaungdawgyi
MUSEUM

(မဂ္ဂကုသလကျောင်းတော်ကြီး; Main Rd; ☉6am-7pm) **FREE** Monk U Bhaddanta Wannita spent 49 years collecting old coins and buddha images from monasteries to protect them from thieves. Some of his collection is displayed in his former monastery, which is housed in a grand, century-old British colonial mansion just north of the centre. The dusty, eclectic museum contains cases of old banknotes, buddhas and votives (candleholders) and coins from the Mrauk U and other ancient periods, plus many bone relics of head monks, kept in small tins.

Sittwe

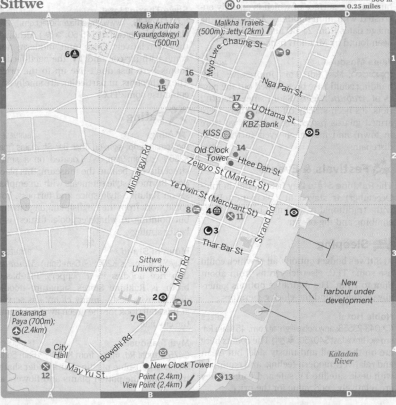

0
0
500 m
0.25 miles

Maka Kuthala Kyaungdawgyi (500m)

Malikha Travels (500m); Jetty (2km)

Myo Lwe Chaung St

6

9

16
15

Nga Pain St

17
U Ottama St
KBZ Bank

KISS @

5

Old Clock Tower
14
Htee Dan St
Zeigyo St (Market St)

Minbargyi Rd

Ye Dwin St (Merchant St)

8   4   11

Strand Rd

1

3
Thar Bar St

Sittwe University

Main Rd

2

10

New harbour under development

Lokananda Paya (700m); (2.4km)

7

City Hall

May Yu St

Bowdhi Rd

12

New Clock Tower Point (2.4km); View Point (2.4km)

13

Kaladan River

Shwezedi Kyaung
BUDDHIST TEMPLE

(ရွှေစေတီကျောင်း; U Ottama St; ⊙ daylight hours) **FREE** Partly housed in a picturesque, ramshackle colonial-era building on a backstreet, this was the monastery of U Ashin Ottama (1880–1939), a leader of the Burmese independence movement during British colonial rule, who died during imprisonment for his political activities. In September 2007, monks at this monastery followed in his footsteps and took part in the protest marches then happening across the country. More recently, in 2012, the monastery served as a shelter for those displaced by the anti-Muslim riots.

Lokananda Paya
BUDDHIST TEMPLE

(လောကနန္ဒာဘုရား; May Yu St; ⊙ daylight hours) **FREE** You can't miss this big golden pagoda between the airport and the centre. Its gilded, cavernous worship hall held aloft by decorated pillars is pretty spectacular.

On the west side of the compound is a small ordination hall, which houses the intriguing Sachamuni Image, a bronze buddha, the surface of which is entirely encrusted with mini-buddhas. Apparently the image dates from 24 BC and is said to have been found by Mrauk U fishermen.

Jama Mosque
MOSQUE

(ဂျမားပလ္လီ; Main Rd) This impressive 1859 building could have been ripped out the pages of *Arabian Nights*. Sadly, since the 2012 riots, it's been strictly off-limits (there were armed guards protecting it when we were in town) and has fallen even further into disrepair.

🎊 Festivals & Events

The **Rakhine State Day** (a Saturday in mid-December) is staged at Lokananda Paya, with traditional wrestling, bamboo pole climbing and tug-of-war.

🛏 Sleeping

At Sittwe's budget options, all of which could use some TLC, electricity runs from about 6pm to 11pm. The midrange options generally include round-the-clock generators.

Noble Hotel
HOTEL $

(☏ 043-23558; anw.noble@gmail.com; 45 Main Rd; s/d incl breakfast $40/50; ❄ 🛜) The rooms here are on the small and musty side, but clean and relatively modern-feeling, and equipped with desk, satellite TV, safe and fridge. They are relatively good value for the price.

Mya Guest House
HOTEL $

(☏ 043-23315, 043-22358; 51/6 Bowdhi Rd; s/d $20/30) Tucked just off Sittwe's busy main road, this basic cement building has simple, spacious rooms with fans and private bathrooms (no hot water).

Prince Guest House
GUESTHOUSE $

(☏ 043-22539; 27 Main Rd; r without bathroom $7-15) Rather dingy rooms (small, with a fan and a mosquito net and coil) with shared bathrooms. Check out a few rooms before choosing – some are better than others.

Royal Sittwe Resort
RESORT $$

(☏ 043-23478, in Yangon 01-544 484; www.royalsittweresort.com; r incl breakfast $80-85; ❄ 🛜 🏊) This formely state-run hotel has been taken over and spiffed up by a local entrepreneur. Well, except the pool, which was green and half full. The rooms, although tidy and comfortable, are overpriced, but are the only ones in town that boast a beach view. The Royal Sittwe is a 1.5 miles south of town, so staying here only makes sense if you've got a driver.

Shwe Thazin Hotel
HOTEL $$

(☏ 043-23579; www.shwethazinhotel.com; 250 Main Rd; r incl breakfast $45-60; ❄ 🛜) Although they're relatively clean and modern, and come with air-con and TV, the aged-feeling rooms here just don't live up to the price. The bathrooms, in particular, are smelly and could use some TLC.

🍴 Eating

★ Aung
BURMESE $

(no roman-script sign; off Thar Bar St; mains from K2500; ⊙ 10am-9pm; 📵) Located on a small street directly behind the museum, this place does Burmese-style set meals with an emphasis on Rakhine-style spice and tartness. You could work from the English-language menu, but pointing to whatever looks tastiest is a better strategy.

Móun-di Stand
BURMESE $

(May Yu St; mains K200; ⊙ 6am-6pm) *Móun-di,* thin rice noodles in a peppery, fish-based broth, is Rakhine State's signature noodle dish. Sittwe's best – many claim – is served at this stall (look for the green awning) facing the city hall.

Mya Teahouse
TEAHOUSE $

(51/6 Bowdhi Rd; mains from K200; ⊙ 6am-5pm) Sit on bright-blue plastic chairs under shady trees amid the potted plants and flowers at this delightful teahouse. Good for a breakfast of fried rice or *mohinga*, too.

River Valley Seafoods Restaurant CHINESE, BURMESE **$**
(5 Main Rd; mains K1500-3500; ⊘7am-10.30pm)
Popular among foreign visitors and the local gentry, Sittwe's fanciest restaurant offers open-air space overlooking the harbour and a menu with many seafood options.

ⓘ Information

During the rainy season, clouds can sometimes cut telephone communication.

Sittwe's **hospital** (☐043-23511; Main Rd) and **post office** (May Yu St) are both near the new clock tower.

KBZ Bank (Main Rd; ⊘9.30am-3pm Mon-Fri)
Bank offering foreign exchange.

KISS (Main Rd; per hr K500; ⊘noon-9pm)
Internet cafe with plenty of terminals.

ⓘ Getting There & Away

Overland routes between Sittwe and Yangon (as well as to Mrauk U) are generally closed to foreigners. Note that the information we provide is for the dry season – schedules are different in the wet season and vary from year to year, so double check everything well in advance.

AIR

Sittwe's airport is about 1.5 miles west of the centre. *Thoun bein* (K3000 to K4000) and taxis (K6000 to K7000) await flights.

In peak season, **Air KBZ** (☐043-22779, in Yangon 01-373 787; www.airkbz.com; U Ottama St; ⊘8am-5pm), **Air Mandalay** (☐043-21638, in Yangon 01-501 520; www.airmandalay.com; U Ottama St; ⊘8am-6pm) and **Air Bagan** (☐09 852 2256, in Yangon 01-513 322; www.airbagan. com; Htee Dan St; ⊘9am-5pm) connect Sittwe with Yangon ($120 to $146, one hour 15 minutes) and Thandwe ($80 to $110, 45 minutes). During the rainy season (from July to October), schedules can drop to one or two times a week.

Although foreign travellers are still allowed to visit the city, the sectarian violence that erupted in Sittwe in 2012 (see p312) has had a huge impact, effectively turning the city into a predominately Burmese, quasi police state overnight. When we were in town, Sittwe's former Muslim quarter, virtually empty, was strictly off-limits, and like the town's oldest mosque, was protected by armed guards. A loosely-enforced 10pm to 5am curfew was also in place.

BOAT

Sittwe's **jetty** is 1 mile north of town, a K2000 ride in a *thoun bein*.

To Mrauk U

Unless you've already been granted permission in advance, the only way to/from Mrauk U for foreigners is by boat. There are a few options.

The slowest option is the double-decker boats to Mrauk U run by the government's **Inland Water Transport** (IWT; ☐043-23382). There's an office west of Sittwe's jetty, though there's no need to buy tickets in advance. Ferries depart Sittwe Tuesday and Friday at 8am, and return from Mrauk U on Wednesday and Saturday at 8am ($5, four to seven hours). There's also a **private ferry service** leaving Sittwe on Monday, Thursday and Sunday at 7am, and returning on Tuesday, Friday and Sunday at 7am ($15, four to seven hours).

Slightly faster is a chartered **private boat** (K150,000, four to seven hours), a simple tarp-covered boat with flat deck, a few plastic chairs and a very basic toilet. Generally a boat can fit four to six people, with a driver who will wait at Mraul U with the boat for two or three nights.

By far the fastest option are the 'speedboats' run by Shwe Pyi Tan (p302), with departures from Sittwe on Wednesday and Sunday at 7am, and from Mrauk U on Monday and Thursday at 7am ($20, two hours).

WESTERN MYANMAR SITTWE

WORTH A TRIP

DAY TRIPS FROM SITTWE

Have a day to spare? Consider taking one of the following boat trips. The most potentially interesting is to the weaving village **Wabo**, a 90-minute boat ride from Sittwe, where you can see Rakhine-style *longyi* being made; the Rakhine are known in Myanmar as skilled weavers who can produce intricate designs in their cloths. The other is to hilly **Baronga Island**, across the wide Kaladan River, to see a typical fishing village. Boat hire to either will run about K60,000, and you'll also need a guide, such as Sittwe-based **Naing Naing** (☐09 4217 46111; mr.theinnaing.f4@gmail.com), to arrange and lead your trip (per day $15).

To Taunggok

Fast boats to Taunggok, the jumping-off point for Ngapali Beach, are run by **Malikha Travels** (☎ 043-24037, 043-24248; Main Rd; ⏱ 9am-5pm), with departures on Monday, Thursday and Saturday at 6am ($30, 10 to 11 hours), and **Shwe Pyi Tan** (☎ 09 4959 2709; cnr Main Rd & U Ottama St, no roman-script sign; ⏱ 7am-9pm), with departures on Tuesday, Wednesday, Saturday and Sunday at 6am ($35, 10 to 11 hours).

Mrauk U မြောက်ဦး

☎ 043 / POPULATION C50,000

'Little Bagan?' Not by a long shot. Myanmar's second-most-famous archaeological site, Mrauk U (pronounced 'mraw-oo') is different in just about every way. The temples – previously mistaken for forts due to thick bunker-style walls built against the fierce Rakhine winds – are smaller and younger, and unlike Bagan's, are predominately made from stone, not brick. Also un-

like Bagan, Mrauk U's temples are dispersed throughout a still-inhabited and fecund backdrop of busy villages, rice fields and rounded hillocks. And best of all, you're likely to have them to yourself: in a good year, only about 5000 foreign visitors visit. The site's remote location, a four to seven hour boat ride up a creek of the Kaladan River, plus the lack of government promotion, means this is unlikely to change in the short term.

History

Mrauk U (meaning, bizarrely, Monkey Egg) was the last great Rakhine capital for 354 years, from 1430 to 1784, when it was one of the richest cities in Asia. In its heyday, it served as a free port, trading with the Middle East, Asia, Holland, Portugal and Spain. The Portuguese Jesuit priest, A. Farinha, who visited in the 17th century, called it 'a second Venice' while other visitors compared it to London or Amsterdam. Little remains of the European quarter, Daingyi Phat (about

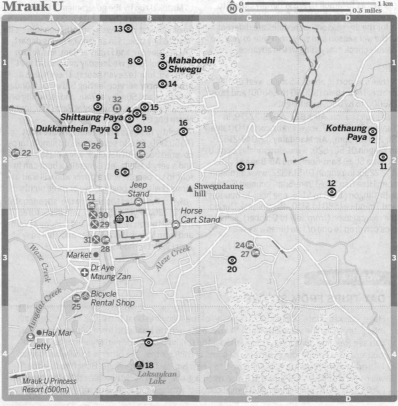

Mrauk U

3 miles south of Mrauk U's current centre), other than ruins and a Hindu temple.

The Mrauk U dynasty was much feared by the peoples of the Indian subcontinent and central Myanmar. Japanese Christians fleeing persecution in Nagasaki were hired as bodyguards for the king. At Mrauk U's peak, King Minbin (1531–53) created a naval fleet of some 10,000 war boats that dominated the Bay of Bengal and Gulf of Martaban. Many of Mrauk U's finest temples (Shittaung, Dukkanthein, Laymyetnha and Shwetaung) were built during his reign.

Mrauk U was a successor to three earlier kingdoms in the area: Dhanyawady (circa 1st to 6th centuries AD); Wethali (3rd to 11th centuries AD), the remains of which are still visible to the north; and Lemro (11th to 15th centuries AD). All four kingdoms blended elements of Theravada and Mahayana Buddhism with Hinduism and Islam. In the late 18th century, the Konbaung dynasty asserted its power over the region and Mrauk U was integrated into the Burmese kingdoms centred on Mandalay.

After the First Anglo-Burmese War of 1824–26, the British Raj annexed Rakhine and set up its administrative headquarters in Sittwe, thus turning Mrauk U into a political backwater virtually overnight.

◎ Sights

The original site of Mrauk U is spread over 17.5 sq miles, though the town today and the bulk of the temples to visit cover a 2.7-sq-mile area. Most of the temples in the North Group and all of the Palace Site can be reached by foot, but you'll most likely want to hire a bike or jeep to see the more remote temples in the North Group or those in the East Group.

The sights are not always marked – in English or any other language – and this is where an experienced guide can come in handy. Not only do many of the guides in the **Regional Guides Society – Mrauk U** (☑ 09 4217 20168, 09 4217 20296; www.facebook. com/rgs.mrauku; per day $20) speak English well and have a good grasp on local history and culture, but they're also locally based, work independently and are dedicated to the principles of community-based tourism.

A torch is necessary to see some of the more interesting stone carvings – in particular those at Dukkanthein Paya, Andaw Paya and Mahabodi Shwegu.

◎ North Group

For many, this area is the pick of the litter for Mrauk U, with all sites within walking distance. There are a couple of food stalls and a gift shop below Shittaung Paya.

★ **Shittaung Paya**   HISTORICAL SITE
(ရှစ်သောင်းဘုရား; admission K5000; ⊘7am–5pm) The usual starting point is at this, Mrauk U's most complex temple. Shittaung means 'Shrine of the 80,000 Images', a reference to the number of holy images inside. King Minbin, the most powerful of Rakhine's

kings, built Shittaung in 1535. It's a frenzy of stupas of various sizes; some 26 surround a central stupa. Thick walls, with windows and nooks, surround the two-tiered structure, which has been highly reconstructed over the centuries – in some places, rather clumsily.

➡ **Outside the temple**

Beside the southwest entrance stairway, and inside a locked mint-green building, is the much-studied **Shittaung Pillar** (⊙daylight hours) FREE, a 10ft sandstone obelisk brought here from Wethali by King Minbin. Considered the 'oldest history book in Myanmar' (by the Rakhine at least), three of the obelisk's four sides are inscribed in faded Sanskrit. The east-facing side likely dates from the end of the 5th century. The western face displays a list dating from the 8th century, outlining Rakhine kings from 638 BC to AD 729 (King Anandacandra).

Lying on its back next to the pillar is a cracked, 12ft-long **sandstone slab** featuring an engraved lotus flower (a Buddhist motif) growing from a wavy line of water and touching an intricately engraved *dhammacakka* (Pali for 'Wheel of the Law').

Along the outer walls, several **reliefs** can be seen (some are hard to reach); a few on the south side are rather pornographic.

➡ **Inside the temple**

Inside the temple's prayer hall you'll see several doors ahead. Two lead to passageways that encircle the main buddha image in the cave hall (which can be seen straight ahead).

The far left (southwest) doorway leads to the **outer chamber**, a 310ft passageway with sandstone slabs cut into six tiers. Over 1000 sculptures show a lot of detail of Rakhine customs (eg traditionally dressed dancers, boxers and acrobats), beasts of burden, and hundreds of Jataka (scenes from Buddha's past 550 lives). At each corner are bigger figures, including the maker King Minbin and his queens at the southwest cor-

ner. The passage opens in the front, where you can step out for views.

Next to the outer chamber entry is a coiling **inner chamber** leading past scores of buddha images in niches, passing a Buddha footprint where – it's said – Buddha walked during his post-enlightenment. Once you get to the dead end, double back to the hall, and see if you can feel the passageway becoming cooler. Some claim it does, symbolising the 'cooling effect' of Buddhist teachings.

Andaw Paya   HISTORICAL SITE

(အံတော်ဘုရား; ⊙daylight hours) FREE Andaw Paya takes the form of an eight-sided monument with a linear layout: rectangular prayer hall to the east, multispired sanctuary to the west. Sixteen *zedi* (stupas) are aligned in a square-cornered U-shape around the southern, northern and western platforms. Two concentric passageways are lined with buddha niches; in the centre of the shrine, an eight-sided pillar supports the roof.

The original construction of the shrine is ascribed to King Minhlaraza in 1521. King Minrazagyi then rebuilt Andaw in 1596 to enshrine a piece of the Buddha tooth relic supposedly brought from Sri Lanka by King Minbin in the early 16th century.

★ Dukkanthein Paya   HISTORICAL SITE

(ထုတ်ခံသိမ်ဘုရား; ⊙daylight hours) FREE Built by King Minphalaung in 1571, Dukkanthein Paya smacks of a bunker (with stupas). Wide stone steps lead up the south and east side of the building considered to be an ordination hall; take the east side steps to reach the entrance.

The interior features spiralling cloisters lined with images of buddhas and common people (such as landlords, governors, officials and their spouses) sporting all of **Mrauk U's 64 traditional hairstyles.** The passageway nearly encircles the centre three times before reaching the sun-drenched buddha image.

The poorly restored **Laymyetnha Paya** (⊙daylight hours) FREE, 90yd north, looks a bit like a squashed-up version of the Dukkanthein, but was actually built 140 years earlier, making it the oldest temple of the Mrauk U period.

★ Mahabodhi Shwegu   HISTORICAL SITE

(မဟာဗောဓိရွှေဂူ; ⊙daylight hours) FREE The highlight of this squat, little-visited temple is its passageway with bas-relief illustrations of the tribumi – Buddhist visions of

---

ⓘ FEES

For foreign visitors to Mrauk U there's an archaeological site entry fee of K500; this is usually collected at the Shittaung Paya or at the boat jetty. On the government ferry you'll be asked to show proof of payment before leaving.

heaven, earth and hell – including acrobats, worshippers and animals. At the end there's a 6ft central buddha and four buddhas in niches; the throne of the former includes some erotic carvings.

Mahabodhi Shwegu is largely hidden behind shrubbery on a hilltop northeast of Ratanabon Paya. To get here, proceed up the barely discernible uphill path that starts behind the covered water well.

Directly south, **Ratana San Rwe and Ratana Hman Kin** (ရတနာစံရွှေဘုရား၊ ရတနာမှန်ကင်းဘုရား; ⊙ daylight hours) FREE, two adjacent hilltop stupas, are the result of recent and extensive restoration.

Ratanabon Paya
(ရတနာပုံဘုရား; ⊙ daylight hours) FREE This massive stupa (sometimes called Yadanapon) is ringed by 24 smaller stupas. It was apparently built by Queen Shin Htway in 1612. During WWII a bomb nailed it, but it had already been picked at by treasure hunters attracted by the name, which means 'accumulation of treasure'. Renovations later repaired the enormous bomb-made crack and reinserted the tall *chattra* (spire).

Laungbanpyauk Paya
(လောင်ပွန်းပြောက်ဘုရား; ⊙ daylight hours) FREE This octagonal, slightly leaning *zedi* was built by King Minkhaungraza in 1525. An unusual feature is its outer wall, adorned with Islamic-inspired glazed tiles in the shape of large flowers.

Pitaka Taik
(ပိဋကတ်တိုက်; ⊙ daylight hours) FREE This compact, highly ornate stone building is one of the seven Mrauk U libraries left out of the original 48. Today protected by a blue-and-maroon shelter, it was built in 1591 by King Minphalaung as a repository for the Tripitaka (Three Baskets; the Buddhist canon), which was received from Sri Lanka in the 1640s. It's wee – only 13ft long and 9ft high.

⊙ East Group
This area stretches about a mile east of the palace walls.

★ Kothaung Paya
(ကိုးသောင်းဘုရား; ⊙ daylight hours) FREE One of Mrauk U's highlights, Kothaung Paya is also Mrauk U's largest temple. It was built in 1553 by King Minbin's son, King Mintaikkha, to outdo his pop's Shittaung by 10,000 images ('Kothaung' means 'Shrine of 90,000 Images').

Kothaung Paya is located a mile or so east of the palace; follow the road directly north of the market, veering left on the much smaller road before the bridge.

Much of Kothaung Paya was found in fragments. Legends vary – that lightning or an earthquake in 1776 destroyed it, jewel-seekers overturned walls, or that it was built with inferior stones by a superstitious king bent on beating a six-month timeline. Regardless, the structure as it looks today is the result of a rather heavy-handed 1996 reconstruction. Recalling Borobudur in Indonesia, the exterior is coated with bell-like stone stupas. The 90,000 images in question line the outer passageway, the entrances to which are guarded by grimacing ogres. Stairways lead up to a top terrace, once dotted with 108 stupas.

Peisi Daung Paya
(ပေစီတောင်ဘုရား; ⊙ daylight hours) FREE On a hilltop sits this unrestored four-door pagoda thought to predate the Mrauk U period. Climb to the top, push your way past the rubble and cobwebs and inside you'll find four sandstone buddha images, three of which have marble eyes – ostensibly added later by merit-seeking monks. The view from the top, of seemingly endless hillocks that allegedly were each home to some sort of Buddhist monument, puts Mrauk U's former wealth and glory in perspective.

Pharaouk Paya
(ဘုရားအုပ်ဘုရား; ⊙ daylight hours) FREE The name of this hilltop temple can be interpreted as meaning 'holding control of the people', and its 29 niches with sitting buddha statues are a reference to Mrauk U's 29 former townships.

Sakyamanaung Paya
(သကျမာန်အောင်ဘုရား; ⊙ daylight hours) FREE Roughly half a mile northeast of the palace walls, and behind Shwegudaung hill, this graceful Mon-influenced *zedi* was erected in 1629 by King Thirithudhammaraza. At this later stage, stupas were built more vertically and ornately than before.

The lower half of the well-preserved 280ft *zedi* features a multitiered octagonal shape as at Laungbanpyauk Paya, but beyond this the bells revert to a layered circular shape mounted by a decorative *hti* (umbrella-like top). You'll see brightly painted, half-kneeling giants at the west gate.

LOCAL KNOWLEDGE

U AUNG KYAW ZAN: GUIDE

How long have you been a guide at Mrauk U?

I was the first guide! At that time, there were only scholars visiting, two or three every year.

What are your early childhood memories of the temples?

They were all overgrown, even Shittaung [Paya]. When I was about 10, we went into Shittaung [Paya] and had to take a big torch with kerosene. There were so many small headless buddhas, but they'd all been taken away. Even back then, none of the Buddha statues had heads, all were cut off.

Ever find anything valuable?

So many things! But my wife says that the things I found are cursed and that's the reason I was poor and working as a teacher.

How do you feel about the restoration of Mrauk U?

We don't want restoration. We'd rather have conservation, but this requires training.

Best sunrise view?

Shwetaung Paya (p307) – it's the highest, so you have the biggest scope.

Best sunset view?

Haridaung Paya (p306) – it has a panoramic view of the entire area.

Best for stone carvings?

In my view, the best stone carvings are those in the museum at Mahamuni Paya (p306). They're more like Khmer style – very ancient and beautiful.

Most interesting Buddha statue?

The most marvellous is the Sanda Muhni (p307). I believe it was originally in the palace because the colour and texture suggest that the amount of gold used was generous.

Looking over Shwegudaung hill (back to the west) **Ratanamanaung** (⊙ daylight hours) **FREE** offers fine views.

👁 Palace Site & Around

Just east of the main strip of Mrauk U village, the one-time royal palace of Mrauk U now is mostly crumbling walls (though the outer walls still stand 11.5ft high).

According to the legend, King Minbin's astrologers advised a move here in 1429 after the palace at Launggret had been invaded by 'poisonous snakes and evil birds'. His representatives witnessed some strange things at this spot – an old guy playing a flute pointed to a cat-chasing rat and then a snake-biting frog – apparently suggesting its soil as being worthy of a king. Construction began in 1430 (though some sources say it didn't start until 1553).

Palace Museum   MUSEUM

(နန်းတော်ပြတိုက်; admission K5000; ⊙10am-4pm Sun-Tue) Just inside the palace's western walls is the Department of Archaeology's insufficiently illuminated but worthwhile

museum. Inside, you'll find an interesting selection of buddha images, inscribed stone slabs, cannons, floor tiles, Wethali-era coins and a helpful model of the Mrauk U site. Old photos on the walls include a pre-restoration shot of Ratanabon's crack. Items are signed in English, although foreign scholars note that the dates on some pieces should be taken with a pinch of salt.

Haridaung Paya   HISTORICAL SITE

(ဟာရီတောင်ဘုရား; ⊙ daylight hours) **FREE** Built around 1750, this small white temple with particularly good westward views, is on a hilltop just north of the palace walls. It's a good place to get your bearings or to view sunset.

👁 South Group

South of the palace site and across the river are evocative, easy-to-lose-your-way back lanes through thatched-hut villages and a host of pagodas. About half a mile south, the **Laksaykan Gate** leads to the eponymous lake, a source of clean water.

Sanda Muhni Phara Gri Kyaung Taik
BUDDHIST TEMPLE

(စန္ဒာမုနိဘုရားကြီးကျောင်းတိုက်; ⊙ daylight hours) **FREE** The highlight at this hilltop monastery, and the temple's namesake, is the **Sanda Muhni**, a buddha statue said to have been cast from the precious metal leftover from making the Mahamuni Buddha. Legend has it that this 4ft image was encased in cement in the 1850s to protect it from pillaging British troops, and then forgotten about for over a century. In April 1988 one of the glazed eyes dropped out, revealing the metal statue below.

The **main hall** is packed with more ancient buddha images that the monks will happily explain to you. They will also point out a large copper roof tile (now used as a table top), saved from Mrauk U's palace after the Burmese carted the rest off to Mandalay back in the 18th century.

Next door, a small elevated structure – not open to the public – is home of Buddha's many scattered molars, a **relic** brought here from Sri Lanka in the 16th century.

Shwetaung Paya
HISTORICAL SITE

(ရွှေတောင်ဘုရား; ⊙ daylight hours) **FREE** Southwest of the palace, the 'Golden Hill Pagoda' is the highest in Mrauk U. Built by King Minbin in 1553, it's accessed by a few trails largely lost under thick vegetation. This is a good spot from which to view the sun rise.

⚒ Festivals & Events

One of the most interesting times to visit Mrauk U is during the huge weeklong **paya pwe** (pagoda festival) held near Dukkanthein Paya in mid-May. It includes music, dance, traditional wrestling and boat racing.

🛏 Sleeping

Generators keep power going most of the day and night at some guesthouses, and unless mentioned otherwise, all offer breakfast. At research time, only the Mrauk U Princess Resort could boast an internet connection, although a few places claimed they were in the process of getting online.

★ **Royal City Guest House** HOTEL **$**

(☑ 043-24200, 09 850 2400; r $25, bungalows s/d $35/40; ❋) Clean, comfortable, attractive fan-cooled rooms in the main building for the budget set, and new, air-con (available from 5pm to 11pm) bungalows across the road for those who can afford a bit more,

all in a homey atmosphere looked after by a team of charming, friendly staff. We wish every town in Southeast Asia had one of these.

Mrauk U Palace HOTEL **$**

(☑ 09 4217 51498; www.mraukupalaceresort.com; r $30-40; ❋) The town's newest accommodation takes the form of 18 identical yellow duplex bungalows equipped with fridge, hot-water showers and small balconies; the rate is determined by whether or not you choose to turn on the air-con.

Golden Star Guest House
BACKPACKER GUESTHOUSE **$**

(☑ 09 4967 4472; r K8000-18,000) Mrauk U's longstanding backpacker crash pad offers 13 fan-cooled rooms, some with en suite, all needing a fair bit of TLC.

Prince Hotel GUESTHOUSE **$**

(☑ 043-24200, 09 4958 3311; r $25-45; ❋) Located half a mile southeast of the market, an ongoing renovation sees the larger, more expensive rooms given a bit of life, but in general, 'rustic' is the operative word here.

Waddy Htut Guest House GUESTHOUSE **$**

(☑ 043-50240; r with shared bathroom K2500-20,000) The novelty of paying the local rate is almost enough reason to stay here. But as the locals could probably tell you, what you get for this price is little more than hot, humid closets with shared bath.

★ **Shwe Thazin Hotel** HOTEL **$$**

(☑ 043-50168, 09 850 1844; www.shwethazinhotel.com; r $55-80; ❋) Built in 2010, this meticulous, handsome compound offers Mrauk U's best balance of price, comfort and location. The 23 chalet-style rooms feel spacious and comfortable, and all are en-suite with a satellite TV, fridge, tub and 24-hour electricity.

Nawarat Hotel HOTEL **$$**

(☑ 043-24200, in Yangon 01-578 786; reservation@nawarathotel.com; r $38-60; ❋) It's neither new nor sexy, but we liked this competent compound of semi-detached concrete bungalows located a short walk from Mrauk U's big sights. All rooms come equipped with satellite TV, fridge, and balcony, and the price depends on how many people are staying per room and how many hours of electricity you want.

Vesali Resort Hotel HOTEL **$$**

(☑ 043-50008, 09 858 6426; vesaliresort@gmail.com; r $45-60; ❋) Though somewhat

WETHALI & MAHAMUNI PAYA

A half-day trip to the unrestored ruins of the former kingdom of Wethali and the ancient buddha image at Mahamuni Paya is a low-key but worthwhile way to see the Rakhine countryside and learn about local history and legend.

About 7 miles north of Mrauk U are the barely discernible remains of the kingdom of **Wethali** (ဝေသာလီ; ☉daylight hours) FREE. According to the Rakhine chronicles, Wethali was founded in AD 327 by King Mahataing Chandra; archaeologists believe that the kingdom lasted until the 8th century. Today, in addition to the walls of the 1650ft by 990ft central palace site, the main attraction for visitors is the so-called **Great Image of Hsu Taung Pre**, a 16.5ft Rakhine-style sitting Buddha. It's said to be carved from a single piece of stone and date to AD 327 (but most visitors argue the features look more modern).

The elevated track that runs adjacent to Wethali is in fact an **abandoned railway line**. A rare incidence of the former military government bowing to popular opinion occurred here in late 2010 when a few brave locals protested against the planned route of a new railway linking Sittwe with Minbu, the construction of which was damaging temples and sites within the archaeological area. The project was halted and the railway's route changed.

Continuing north, just beyond the former ancient capital of Dhanyawady, is **Mahamuni Paya** (မဟာမုနိဘုရား; ☉daylight hours) FREE, the alleged first home of the buddha image now housed in the temple of the same name in Mandalay. The legend goes that that the image was cast when Buddha visited the area in 554 BC. Yet even today, some Rakhine recount, with fresh, fiery passion, how the Burmese King Bodawpaya sent soldiers to dismantle and remove the Mahamuni Buddha in 1784. Today, 'Mahamuni's brother' – a smaller statue allegedly cast from the same materials – is now one of three fine golden images resting inside. A replica of the original, commissioned 100 years ago by a wealthy resident of Sittwe, sits to the left. The temple structure dates from the 19th century, as earlier ones were destroyed by fire. Down the steps, near the south walls of the shrine, is a **museum** (admission $5) with a couple of dozen relics and some beautiful engraved stones.

There is a strip of good **Burmese restaurants** across from Mahamuni Paya, so it's a clever idea to combine this trip with lunch. The trip can be arranged via the Regional Guides Society – Mrauk U (p303). It spans about half a day, and car hire runs about K46,000, plus $20 for a guide.

inconveniently removed from the bulk of the temples and town, the Vesali's 28 semi-detached bungalows make up for this with dark-wood floors, vaulted ceilings, private decks, modern bathrooms and 24-hour electricity. An ongoing restoration promises air-con and TV in all rooms.

Mrauk U Princess Resort HOTEL $$$
(☎043-50232, 09 850 0556; www.maruukoo princessresort.net; bungalows $320; ❄@) Mrauk U's most luxurious digs, the Princess offers 23 handsome and large, if somewhat empty-feeling wooden villas. We liked the vast, tub-equipped bathrooms, and the attractive gardens and ponds that make up the grounds, but given the lack of TV, fridge or other modern amenities, it all feels more than a little overpriced. Closed July to August.

✖ Eating

Mrauk U's culinary options are pretty limited. There are a few local restaurants serving basic Chinese-style food to the west of Mrauk U's market, while for something more upscale, consider the Gamone Phyu restaurant at Mrauk U Princess Hotel or the restaurant at the Vesali Resort Hotel.

Kaung Thant BURMESE $
(no roman-script sign; meals from K1500; ☉10am-10pm) A bare-bones Burmese-style curry shop at the foot of the bridge just north of the market, 'Good and Clean' does Rakhine-style set meals served by a cheeky local family.

For You CHINESE, BURMESE $
(mains K1000; ☉8am-10pm) The best bang for your kyat, For You serves vast plates of fried noodles and huge bowls of noodle soup.

Happy Garden
CHINESE, BURMESE $

(mains K1000-3000; ⊙7am-11pm) This beer garden–style place has an English menu of mostly Chinese-sounding dishes, or you could go for the Burmese-style set meal (from K1500).

🛍 Shopping

Stalls outside the Shittaung Paya sell some souvenirs.

L'amitie Art Gallery
ART GALLERY

(⊙7am-7pm) This simple hut is hung with attractive canvases in oils and pastels created by the ex–civil servant, Shwe Maung Thar, the same artist who painted the ceiling panels in the central hall of Shittaung Paya, and and his son, Khine Minn Tun.

ℹ Information

In case of an emergency, the hospital at Sittwe is your best bet. For minor bruises and stomach upsets, friendly **Dr Aye Maung Zan** (✆043-24200, 043-50032), south of the market, speaks English.

Mrauk U's only **internet** connection is at the Mrauk U Princess Hotel ($4 per hour).

ℹ Getting There & Away

BOAT
Mrauk U's **jetty** is about half a mile south of the market. Go here, or to the adjacent **Hay Mar** teashop, where Aung Zan can assist in buying tickets. See p301 for details on getting away from Mrauk U by boat.

ℹ Getting Around

Although you'll see lots of them around town, foreigners are allegedly banned from riding on Mrauk U's *thoun bein* due to an accident involving a foreign tourist in 2011. This may have changed by the time you're in town.

HORSE CART
Horse-cart rides around the temples, arranged at the **stand** east of the palace gate, cost about K15,000 per day.

4WD
Aged 4WDs can be hired from the **stand** on the north side of the palace site. A day hire, taking in the sites within the confines of our map, should cost about K38,000.

BICYCLE
Bicycles can be hired from the **shop** (per day K2000; ⊙7am-5pm) south of the bridge leading to the central market.

CHIN STATE

Hilly, sparsely populated and severely lacking infrastructure, Chin State (ချင်းပြည်နယ်) is also one of Myanmar's remotest, least developed and – according to the United Nations Development Programme – poorest states. The state shares a border with Bangladesh and India, and in addition to the eponymous Chin, a Tibeto-Burman group who have largely adopted Christianity and who constitute approximately half of the population, it is home to several obscure hill tribes and a relatively small Burmese contingent.

Mt Victoria (Nat Ma Taung)
ဝိတိုရိယတောင်(နတ်မတောင်)

The most accessible destination in Chin State is **Mt Victoria (Nat Ma Taung)**, roughly 80 miles west of Bagan. The 10,016ft (3053m) mountain, Myanmar's second highest, stands amid a 279 sq mile national park and is a prime spot for **birdwatching**. It's

---

ℹ TRAVEL RESTRICTIONS

In 2013, Myanmar's central government declared several destinations in Chin State – including Kanpetlet, Mindat, Mt Victoria, and the state capital Hakha, among others – 'open', meaning that permission from MTT is no longer necessary to visit these areas. However, like many of Myanmar's remote destinations, the reality on the ground is that many local authorities still expect to see permits and a licensed guide, and Foreign Independent Travellers (FITs) without these will be regarded with suspicion and stand a risk of being turned back.

If this sounds like too much hassle, keep in mind that there are a couple of options for mingling with Chin people just outside Chin State that don't require government permits: the villages north of Mrauk U in Rakhine State and a flight from Mandalay to Kalaymyo (Kalay), a half Chin town in Sagaing Region just northeast of Chin State.

WORTH A TRIP

CHIN VILLAGES

An interesting contrast to the temples at Mrauk U is a day trip to the Chin villages along the Lemro River.

These boat trips don't reach Chin State, but seven or so of the traditional Chin villages along this stretch of the river have dwindling contingencies of elderly women who have tattooed faces, a Chin practice that ended a couple of generations ago.

You may feel ambivalent about taking their photos but the women we met didn't seem to mind posing, having made a conscious decision to use their unique and soon-to-disappear looks as a way of attracting tourists and earning money for the betterment of their communities. Simple handicrafts are sold in the villages and without tourist donations (you should plan on donating school supplies, medicine or a few thousand kyat) it's highly unlikely that remote, impoverished villages such as **Pan Paun** would have a new school building, let alone salaries for the teachers who work there.

In addition to the Chin villages, there's the busy morning market at the village of **Pan Mraung**.

Typical trips, which the Regional Guides Society – Mrauk U (p303) or your hotel can help arrange, include a half-hour car transfer to the jetty, an approximately two-hour boat trip upstream, and an hour or so at a couple of villages. Car transfer will run about K38,000 and the boat another K48,000. You'll also need a guide – about $20. There's not much in the way of food or drink to buy in the Chin villages so pack any food and water you'll need.

best visited in November when the rhododendron bushes that cover the slopes are in full bloom.

Visiting Mt Victoria is done via Nyaung U, and begins with a eight- to nine-hour jeep ride on rough roads to Mindat town. From here, options include a short trek to the peak, followed by camping on Mt Victoria, or staying at a village at the base of the mountain.

From the village on the opposite side of the peak, Kanpetlet, it's a seven- to eight-hour ride back to Nyaung U.

Permits are no longer required to visit Mt Victoria, but for all intents and purposes, a guide is, which means that everybody approaches Mt Victoria in a guided tour. A typical trip to Mt Victoria spans from four to six days, and is generally only possible from approximately October to May. The cost for two people, including accommodation and transportation, will run to about $1200.

Several tour agencies have itineraries covering Mt Victoria, including the Yangon-based **Tours Myanmar** (☑09 4200 60272; www.toursmyanmar.com), which offers both vehicle and bicycle tours to the area led by experienced guide Mr Saw; and Bike World Explores Myanmar (p393), with both trekking and cycling tours.

Paletwa & Around

Another generally accessible destination in Chin State is **Paletwa** (ပလက်ဝ), a predominately Chin town on the banks of the Kaladan River, approximately 10 miles west of the border with Bangladesh.

The countryside surrounding Paletwa is home to traditional Chin villages and a few still visible remnants of World War II fighting, including bomb craters and even a few burnt-out tanks. Head upstream another half day and you'll reach **Taung Pro** (တောင်ပြို), an even more remote, traditional Chin outpost.

Visiting Paletwa takes a minimum of five days, and is best done during the winter, from approximately November to February. You'll need advance permission from MTT in Yangon, and you'll also need an experienced guide. Sittwe-based Naing Naing (p301) has been to the area several times and can arrange the necessary permits.

Accessing Paletwa is done from Mrauk U, in Rakhine State, and begins by hiring a car to the jetty at Kyauktaw (K46,000, two hours). After overnighting there, Paletwa is a six or seven hour boat trip upstream (about K200,000). Taugro is another six or so hours upstream (K200,000). Guide fees, accommodation and food will run to a total of about $70 per day.

Understand Myanmar (Burma)

Myanmar (Burma) Today

Following political and economic reforms, sanctions have been dropped and the world is now eager to engage with Myanmar, which for nearly 50 years has borne international isolation. Some changes have been momentous but they cannot mask the toxic problems still plaguing the country, including ethnic and religious conflicts, human rights abuses and a flawed constitution that, if it remains unamended, diminishes the chances of a democratic result in the 2015 general election.

Best in Print

Golden Parasol
(Wendy Law-Yone; 2013) Yone's fascinating memoir provides an insider's view on key events in modern Myanmar's history; her father, Ed Law-Yone, an influential newspaper editor, was exiled from the country in the 1960s.

Burma/Myanmar: What Everyone Needs to Know
(David I Steinberg; 2013) Make sure you get the updated second edition of this essential primer on Myanmar.

Best in Film

Kayan Beauties
(2013; www.kayanbeauties.com) Thriller about four Kayan girls who travel from their village to Taunggyi, where one of them gets kidnapped by human traffickers.

Youth of Yangon
(2013; http://vimeo.com/ondemand/youthofyangon) Beautifully shot 12-minute documentary about Yangon's tiny skateboarding community and the struggles they face pursuing their passion.

Yangon Calling
(2013; www.yangoncalling.com) Documentary about Myanmar's punk rock scene directed by Berlin-based filmmakers Alexander Dluzak and Carsten Piefke.

Asean Chair 2014

'Now is Myanmar's time in the sun,' went the narration for a promotional film screened in Bandar Seri Begawan, Brunei's capital, in October 2013, as President Thein Sein accepted his nation's role as chair of the Association of Southeast Asian Nations (Asean). When the chance last came around in 2006 to lead the regional power bloc, Myanmar was skipped over amid fears that non-Asean countries would boycott meetings in a nation run by a military junta that brutally suppressed its people.

Thein Sein's reforms since the elections of 2010 blew away such concerns. By-elections in April 2012 saw a landslide victory for National League for Democracy (NLD) candidates including Aung San Suu Kyi, who is now a member of the national parliament and de facto leader of the opposition. The economy is developing rapidly as foreign investors rush to gain a foothold in a market largely cut off from the world for nearly half a century. The easing of censorship has witnessed an explosion in new media, largely unafraid to document the country's multiple failings as well as its successes.

Plight of the Rohingya

Of particular international concern has been treatment of the Rohingya. During 2012 this minority Muslim group living in Rakhine State found themselves under attack from the majority Rakhine Buddhist population. Arson sprees reduced entire Muslim quarters to smoldering ash. Government estimates put deaths on both sides at fewer than 100. But Human Rights Watch uncovered evidence of four mass grave sites in the state and labelled the attacks as 'ethnic cleansing'.

It's reckoned that, following the violence, around 125,000 Rohingya were effectively ousted from cities and pushed into squalid, makeshift camps guarded by troops. Local media outlets, seizing new-found press freedoms, have covered the events in detail and global rights organisations have rallied to the Rohingya defense. Even US President Barack Obama, in his first visit to Myanmar in 2012, implored Myanmar's citizens to acknowledge that the Rohingya 'hold within themselves the same dignity as you do.'

Buddhists vs Muslims

Obama's words fly in the face of the rise in the local Buddhist fundamentalist movement 969, led by Ashin Wirathu, a radical Buddhist monk. Stickers sporting the 969 logo are now ubiquitous across the nation; the numbers symbolise the virtues of Buddha, Buddhist practices and the Buddhist community. Among other things, 969 calls for a boycott of Muslim-owned businesses and restrictions on marriages between Muslims and Buddhists.

Such is the respect accorded to monks in Myanmar – even radical ones such as Wirathu, who was jailed under the military regime for inciting hatred – that when *Time* published a story about the Mandalay-based preacher under the headline 'The Face of Buddhist Terror' in July 2013, that edition of the magazine was banned by the government. Among the few locals to speak out publicly against the violence and preaching of hate towards Muslims are members of No U Turn, a popular punk rock band.

In September 2013 Buddhist versus Muslim mob violence spread down the Rakhine coast to Thandwe, beside the country's prime beach resort Ngapali. The following month the International Crisis Group (www.crisisgroup.org) released a report stating that 'unless there is an effective government response and change in societal attitudes, violence against Myanmar's Muslim communities could spread.'

Nationwide Ceasefire Agreement

The flare in conflict between Buddhists and Muslims comes at the same time as there has been an increase in small terrorist bomb attacks across Myanmar, including one at the Trader's Hotel in Yangon in October 2013 that injured a guest.

Amid these worrying developments, a glimmer of hope is an end to the civil wars that have plagued Myanmar in the modern era. Since the 2010 elections the government has been pushing for a Nationwide Ceasefire Agreement (NCA) with the rebel ethnic groups. In November 2013, 17 of these groups signed an agreement conditionally supporting the NCA. Even so, according to the Myanmar Peace Monitor (www.mmpeacemonitor.org) there remain 'contradictions' in the government's peace strategy, citing claims by rebel groups of continued attacks and provocations by the military.

At the time of writing talks were underway to achieve the NCA. Should it be achieved, the plan is to move forward towards the creation of a federal

POPULATION: **55.17 MILLION**

AREA: **676,578 SQ KM**

GDP PER CAPITA: **$1400**

GDP GROWTH: **6.5%** (2012)

INFLATION: **7.3%**
(AUG 2013, WORLD BANK)

POLITICAL PRISONERS: **64**
(NOV 2013; SOURCE WWW.AAPPB.ORG)

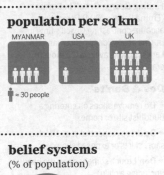

population per sq km

MYANMAR   USA   UK

≈ 30 people

belief systems
(% of population)

89
Buddhist

4
Muslim

4
Christian

3
Animist & Other

if Myanmar (Burma) were 100 people

68 would be Bamar
9 would be Shan
7 would be Kayin (Karen)
4 would be Rakhaing

3 would be Chinese
2 would be Indian
2 would be Mon
5 would be other

Best Travel Literature

The Trouser People
(Andrew Marshall; 2012) The new edition includes Marshall's eyewitness account of the 2007 Saffron Revolution.

Golden Earth
(Norman Lewis; 1952) What's amazing about Lewis's vivid account of travelling in the turbulent Burma of 1951 is how little some things have changed.

Finding George Orwell in Burma
(Emma Larkin; 2004) Perceptive account contrasting Orwell's time in Burma as a colonial policeman with Larkin's own travels in the modern era.

Dos & Don'ts

➡ **Do** remove shoes on entering a Buddhist site or home.

➡ **Do** dress respectfully: no shorts, short skirts or exposed shoulders.

➡ **Don't** touch somebody on the head (including a child).

➡ **Don't** pose with or sit on Buddha images.

➡ **Don't** point your feet at anyone or anything – apologise if you accidentally brush someone with your foot.

➡ **Don't** speak politics with locals unless they raise the subject first.

➡ **Do** ask before you photograph anyone.

union in which ethnic minority regions would gain a greater degree of autonomy. The Myanmar Peace Centre has been set up to organise seminars and conferences on peacemaking and confidence building – something sorely lacking between the Tatmadaw and the rebel groups. Also up for debate is the military reducing its political power in government.

Changing the Constitution

This last point could prove to be the stickiest to overcome, because of its impact on the next general election, scheduled for 2015. For any changes in the constitution to be approved they must have the support of more than 75% of parliament. However, the same constitution dictates that 25% of parliamentary seats be held by military appointees.

Speaking to the EU foreign ministers in Luxembourg in October 2013, Aung San Suu Kyi said that without the constitution being amended Myanmar is 'still very, very far away from a genuine democratic form of government.' The Nobel Prize winner, who has made clear her ambitions for the country's presidency, has a personal stake in such changes, as the constitution stipulates the president not only must have military experience but also cannot have a spouse, children or even children's spouses who are citizens of another country. Suu Kyi, the widow of British citizen Michael Aris, has two British sons denied their Burmese citizenship by the former regime.

In January 2014 Thein Sein backed changing the constitution so that 'any citizen' could become president. But even with his support, securing such an amendment is far from certain as the current president's control over parliament, dominated by the Union Solidarity & Development Party (USDP) and the military, is limited.

History

A succession of major ethnic groups have held sway down the ages across the territory that now makes up Myanmar, with the Bamar only coming into prominence in the 11th century. Civil war erupted between minority groups after independence from British colonial rule in 1948; on the fringes of the nation the unrest continues today. A 'deeply flawed' election in 2010 saw 48 years of military rule and repression replaced by a quasi-civilian government and glimmers of democratic hope.

Pre-Colonial Burma

The Earliest Inhabitants

Archaeologists believe humans have lived in the region as far back as 75,000 BC.

In 2003 the BBC reported the finding of a 45-million-year-old fossil (possibly the anklebone of a large ape-like animal) in central Myanmar that might just prove the area to be the birthplace of *all* humans. The implication of this research, written up in an academic paper by palaeontologist Laurent Marivaux of the University of Montpellier II, is that our primate ancestors may have had Asian rather than African origins. Not surprisingly, the military government was happy to embrace this interpretation.

There's no debate that 2500 years ago the area was a key land link between traders from China, India and the Middle East. Ancient Greeks knew of the country too.

The First Burmese Empire

Bagan was nearly 200 years old when its 'golden period' kicked off – signalled by an energetic, can-do King Anawrahta taking the throne in 1044. His conquest of the Mon kingdom and the adoption of Buddhism inspired a creative energy in Bagan. It quickly became a city of glorious temples and the capital of the First Burmese Empire.

Anawrahta's successors (Kyanzittha, Alaungsithu and Htilominlo) lacked his vision, and the kingdom's power slowly declined. In 1273 King Narathihapate made the diplomatic mistake of offending the growing

The limestone Padah-Lin Caves in western Shan State contain paintings that could be 13,000 years old, and there's evidence that local farmers had domesticated chickens and made bronze by 1500 BC.

TIMELINE	850 BC	3rd century BC	1st century BC
	According to Burmese chronicles, Abhiraja of the Sakyan clan from India founds Tagaung, 127 miles north of Mandalay; his son travels south and founds a kingdom at Rakhine (Arakan).	The Mon, who migrated into the Ayeyarwady Delta from present-day Thailand (and from China before that), establish their capital, Thaton, and have first contact with Buddhism.	Possible founding of Beikthano (named after the local word for Vishnu), a Pyu town east of current-day Magwe; it's believed to have flourished for about 400 years.

power of Kublai Khan by executing his envoys. When the Mongols invaded in 1287, Narathihapate fled south to Pyay (Prome) where he committed suicide.

In the ensuing chaos, Shan tribes (closely related to the Siamese) from the hills to the east grabbed a piece of the low country, while the Mon in the south broke free of Bamar control and re-established their own kingdom.

The Second Burmese Empire

It would be another 200 years before the Bamar were able to regroup to found their second empire. During this time a settlement of Bamar refugees in central Taungoo survived between the Mon to the south and the Shan to the north and east, by playing the larger forces off against each other.

In the 16th century a series of Taungoo kings extended their power north, nearly to the Shan's capital at Inwa, then south, taking the Mon kingdom and shifting their own capital to Bago. In 1550 Bayinnaung

Remembered as *tayokpyay min*, or 'the king who ran away from the Chinese', Narathihapate was also known for his gluttonous appetite, demanding 300 varieties of dishes at his banquets.

ORIGINAL KINGDOMS

Four major precolonial ethnic groups peppered Burma's flatlands with their kingdoms for centuries, while smaller ethnic groups lived – mostly untouched – in the remote hills beyond. The early histories that are attached to these groups are a mix of fact and legend.

Pyu Arriving from the Tibeto-Burman plateau and/or from India around the 1st century BC, the Pyu established the first major kingdom of sorts, with city-states in central Myanmar including Beikthano, Hanlin and Sri Ksetra (Thayekhittaya). In the 10th century Yunnanese invaders from China had enslaved or scared off most Pyu.

Rakhine Also known as Arakanese, these people claim their kingdom was well under way by the 6th century BC. Certainly it was in full force by the 15th century, when their Buddhist kingdom was based in Mrauk U and their navy controlled much of the Bay of Bengal.

Bamar Also known as Burmans, these people arrived from somewhere in the eastern Himalaya in the 8th or 9th century, supplanting the vanquished Pyu and establishing the cultural heartland of Myanmar as it's still known. Centuries of conflict with the Mon erupted after their arrival. Although the Bamar came out on top, the result was really a merger of the two cultures.

Mon This race, who may have originated from eastern India or mainland Southeast Asia, settled fertile lowlands on the Ayeyarwady (Irrawaddy) River delta across Thailand to Cambodia. They developed the area as Suvannabhumi (Golden Land), with their Burmese kingdom, centred around present-day Thaton, coming into existence around the 9th century.

AD 754	849	1044	1057
Nanzhao soldiers from Yunnan, China, conquer the hill tribes in the upper reaches of the Ayeyarwady River and challenge the Pyu who ruled from the city of Sri Ksetra.	Bagan is founded on the site of a once-thriving Pyu city; its first name may have been Pyugan, something recorded 200 years later by the Annamese of present-day Vietnam.	Anawrahta slays his brother, takes the throne in Bagan and starts organising his kingdom to kick off the 'golden period' of the First Burmese Empire.	Having subdued the Shan Hills, Anawrahta's armies sack the ancient Mon city of Thaton and bring back 30,000 people to Bagan, including the Mon king, Manuha.

came to the throne, reunified all of Burma and defeated the neighbouring Siamese so convincingly that it was many years before the long-running friction between the two nations resurfaced.

Following Bayinnaung's death in 1581 the Bamar's power again declined. The capital was shifted north to Inwa in 1636. Its isolation from the sea – effectively cutting off communication around the kingdom – ultimately contributed to Myanmar's defeat by the British.

The Third Burmese Empire

With all the subtlety of a kick to the groin, King Alaungpaya launched the third and final Burmese dynasty by contesting the Mon when the latter took over Inwa in 1752. Some say Alaungpaya's sense of invincibility deluded the Burmese into thinking they could resist the British later on.

After Alaungpaya's short and bloody reign, his son Hsinbyushin charged into Thailand and levelled Ayuthaya, forcing the Siamese to relocate their capital to what would eventually become Bangkok. Hsinbyushin's successor, Bodawpaya (another son of Alaungpaya), looked for glory too, and brought the Rakhine under Burmese control. This eventually led to tension with the British (who had economic interests in Rakhine territory) that the dynasty would not outlive.

Colonial Burma

Wars with the British

With eyes on fresh markets and supply sources in Southeast Asia, Britain wrested all of Burma in three decisive swipes. In the First, Second and Third Anglo-Burmese Wars they picked up Tanintharyi (Tenasserim) and Rakhine in 1824, Yangon and southern Burma in 1853, and Mandalay and northern Burma in 1885.

The first war started when Burmese troops, ordered by King Bagyidaw, crossed into British-controlled Assam (in India) from Rakhine to pursue refugees. General Maha Bandula managed some minor victories using guerrilla tactics, but eventually was killed by cannon fire in 1824. Burmese troops then surrendered. The Treaty of Yandabo, helped by the missionary translator Adoniram Judson (whose name is still on many Baptist churches in Myanmar), gave Rakhine and Tenasserim to the British.

Two Burmese kings later, Bagan Min started his reign in the same manner that many did: with mass executions to rid the capital of his potential rivals. An 1852 incident involving the possible kidnapping of two British sea captains (some argue it never happened) gave the British a welcome excuse for igniting another conflict, and an opportunity for more land. The British quickly seized all of southern Burma,

Published in 1925, GE Harvey's *History of Burma* gives a chronological rundown of Myanmar's kingdoms from the Pyu era until 1824, faithfully recounting many fanciful legends along the way.

Thant Myint-U's *River of Lost Footsteps* is a must-read historical review that recounts kings' blunders and successes, while adding occasional family anecdotes of Burma's early days of independence.

1084	**1273**	**1290s**	**1315**
Kyanzittha continues the reforms started by his father, Anawrahta, including developing the Burmese written language; he's succeeded in 1113 by his grandson Alaungsithu, who rules until 1167.	In a curious gesture of diplomacy against far-superior forces to the north, the Burmese in Bagan slay Tartar ambassadors, prompting a peeved Kublai Khan to invade 14 years later.	Marco Polo becomes possibly the first Westerner to travel in central Burma (then known to foreigners as Mien), and publishes an account of his travels in 1298.	After the collapse of Bagan, Sagaing becomes the capital of a Shan kingdom. The capital moves to Inwa in 1364 and stays there intermittently until 1841.

including Yangon and Pathein (Bassein). They then marched north to Pyay (Prome), facing little opposition.

The Final Two Kings

The 1885 conflict between Burma and Britain is sometimes called 'the war over wood', as Britain's victory allowed it to secure rights to Burma's plentiful teak forests.

The unpopular Bagan Min was ousted in favour of the more capable and revered Mindon Min, who moved the capital to Mandalay. Palace intrigues, including the murder of Mindon's powerful half-brother by Mindon's own sons, stayed the king's hand in naming his successor. When Mindon suddenly died following an attack of dysentery in 1878, the new (rather reluctant) king, Thibaw Min, was propelled to power by his ruthless wife and scheming mother-in-law. The following massive 'massacre of kinsmen' (79 of Thibaw Min's rivals) made many British papers. Alas, previous kings hadn't had to face the consequences of world media attention, and this act did little to generate public backlash in the UK against Britain's final, decisive war against the Burmese.

In 1885 it took Britain just two weeks to conquer Upper Burma, exile Thibaw and his court to India and establish control over all the country. Direct colonial rule was implemented only where the Bamar were the majority (ie in the central plains). The hill states of the Chin, Kachin, Shan, Kayin and Kayah were allowed to remain largely autonomous – a decision that would have ramifications in the run-up to independence in 1948 and beyond.

THREE KINGS

Lording it over a military parade ground in Myanmar's capital of Nay Pyi Taw are giant statues of the three kings considered the most important in Burmese history:

➡ **Anawrahta** (1014–77) The creator of the First Burmese Empire ascended the throne in Bagan in 1044. He unified the Ayeyarwady Valley and held sway over the Shan hills and Rakhine at the same time as introducing key religious and social reforms that form the basis of modern Burmese culture.

➡ **Bayinnaung** (1516–81) Aided by Portuguese mercenaries, this king of Taungoo is famed for unifying Burma for its 'second empire' and conquering Ayuthaya, the capital of Siam (Thailand), in 1569. Since 1996 his likeness has ominously looked over Thailand from near the border at Tachileik.

➡ **Alaungpaya** (1714–60) With no royal roots, this hometown hero of Mokesebo (Shwebo) founded the Konbaung dynasty and created the second largest empire in Burmese history. His reign lasted only eight years, ending when he died – some say from poisoning – on retreat from Siam, after being turned back by rains.

1433	1472	1527
Rakhine's ruler, Naramithla, establishes a new capital at Mrauk U, which, over the course of the next few centuries, grows into a grand city of temples and international commerce.	The great Mon King Dhammazedi takes the throne, unifies the Mon, moves the capital from Inwa to Bago (Pegu), and sets up diplomatic contact with Europe.	The Shan, who had exercised increasing control over the area following the fall of Bagan, defeats the kingdom at Inwa and rules Upper Burma for 28 years.

ROMANA CHAPMAN / GETTY IMAGES ©

➡ Buddha statue, Mrauk U

The Impact of British Rule

Burma was henceforth administered as part of 'British India'. Indian immigrants flooded into the country, acting like second colonisers: building businesses and taking rare, low-level government jobs from the hostile indigenous population. In 1927 the majority of Yangon's population was Indian. Chinese immigration was also encouraged, further subjugating and marginalising the Burmese people.

Cheap British imports poured in, fuelled by rice profits. Many key cities and towns were renamed by the British with Yangon becoming Rangoon, Pyay becoming Prome and Bagan renamed Pagan.

Much of Burma was considered a hardship posting by British colonial officials, who found the locals difficult to govern. On the other hand, many of the British officials were incompetent and insensitive, and refused to honour local customs such as removing shoes to enter temples, thus causing grave offence to the majority Buddhist population. Inflamed by opposition to colonial rule, unemployment and the undercutting of the traditional educational role of Buddhist monasteries, the country had the highest crime rate in the British Empire.

One of the biggest meteor showers in modern history filled Burma's sky in 1885. Locals saw it as an omen of the end of their kingdom.

Rise of Nationalism

Burmese nationalism burgeoned in the early days of the 20th century, often led by Buddhist monks. University students in Yangon went on strike on National Day in 1920, protesting elitist entrance requirements at British-built universities. The students referred to each other as *thakin* (master), as they claimed to be the rightful masters of Burma. One *thakin* – a young man called Aung San – was expelled from university in 1936 for refusing to reveal the author of a politically charged article.

Growing demands for self-government and opposition to colonial rule eventually forced the British to make a number of concessions. In 1937 Burma was separated administratively from India and a new legislative council including elected Burmese ministers was formed. However, the country continued to be torn by a struggle between opposing political parties and sporadic outbursts of anti-Indian and anti-Chinese violence.

Built during British rule of Burma, Yangon's infamous Insein prison was the Empire's largest penitentiary. It is still in use and has been the unwelcome home of political dissidents including, on three occasions, Aung San Suu Kyi.

Aung San & WWII

More famous in the West as Aung San Suu Kyi's father, Bogyoke (General) Aung San is revered as a national hero by most Myanmar people and his likeness is seen throughout the country. Aung San Suu Kyi, who was only two when he died, called him 'a simple man with a simple aim: to fight for independence'.

1540	1551	1599	1760
Lower Burma is reunified after Tabinshwehti, the ambitious and young king of Taungoo, defeats the Mon kingdom at Bago – helped by Burmans fleeing the Shan in Inwa.	Bayinnaung becomes king and, having conquered the Shan in 1557, reunifies all of Myanmar as the Second Burmese Empire; his forces take the Siam capital of Ayuthaya in 1569.	Following his defeat of Bago, the King of Rakhine grants the Portuguese mercenary Filipe de Brito e Nicote governorship of the port of Syriam (Thanlyin), which he controls until 1613.	Burmese King Alaungpaya, having conquered Inwa, Pyay (Prome), Dagon (which he renames 'Yangon') and Tenasserim (Tanintharyi), fails to take Ayuthaya in Siam and dies during the retreat.

WWII Sites in Myanmar

Start of Burma Rd, Lashio, Northern Myanmar

Taukkyan War Cemetery, North of Yangon

Thanbyuzayat War Cemetry, Mon State

Meiktila, Central Myanmar

Aung San was an active student at Rangoon University: he edited the newspaper and led the All Burma Students' Union. At 26 years old, he and the group called the 'Thirty Comrades' looked abroad for support for their independence movement. Although initially planning to seek an alliance with China, they ended up negotiating with Japan and receiving military training there. The 'Thirty Comrades' became the first troops of the Burmese National Army (BNA) and returned to Burma with the invading Japanese troops in 1941.

By mid-1942 the Japanese had driven retreating British-Indian forces, along with the Chinese Kuomintang (KMT), out of most of Burma. But the conduct of the Japanese troops was starting to alienate the Burmese. Aung San complained at Japan's 15th Army headquarters in Maymyo (now Pyin Oo Lwin): 'I went to Japan to save my people who were struggling like bullocks under the British. But now we are treated like dogs.'

Aung San and the BNA switched allegiance to the Allied side in March 1945. Their assistance, along with brave behind-enemy-lines operations by the 'Chindits', an Allied Special Force, helped the British prevail over the Japanese in Burma two months later. Aung San and his colleagues now had a chance to dictate post-war terms for their country.

Independent Burma: 1947–62

Towards Independence

In January 1947 Aung San visited London as the colony's deputy chairperson of the Governor's Executive Council. Meeting with British Prime

---

REVOLUTIONARY MONKS

In 1919, at Mandalay's Eindawya Paya, monks evicted Europeans who refused to take off their shoes. The British, sensing that this 'Shoe Question' was the start of a nationalist movement, sentenced the monk leader, U Kettaya, to life imprisonment. This would not be the last involvement of the *sangha* (Buddhist brotherhood) in politics.

U Ottama, a monk who had studied in India and returned to Burma in 1921, promoted religious liberation as a way to bring the independence movement to the attention of the average local Buddhist. After numerous arrests, U Ottama died in prison in 1939. Another monk, U Wizaya, died in prison in 1929 after a 163-day hunger strike, which began as a protest against a rule that forbade imprisoned monks from wearing robes.

In the footsteps of these martyrs to the nationalist cause strode the brave monks who, risking arrest and worse, marched the streets in 2007. Monks currently account for 256 of Burma's 1994 political prisoners and include the 31-year-old U Gambira, one of the organisers of the 2007 protests, who is serving a sentence of 68 years.

1784	1813	1826	1852
Alaungpaya's son Bodawpaya defeats Rakhine, hauling off the revered Mahamuni Buddha image (supposedly cast during Buddha's legendary visit to the area in 554 BC) to Inwa.	Adoniram Judson, a Baptist missionary from Massachusetts, arrives to convert souls and translate the Bible; thanks to his influence, Myanmar has the third-largest number of Baptists worldwide.	The Treaty of Yandabo concludes the First Anglo-Burmese War that had begun two years previously; the British annex Rakhine and Taninthayi (Tenasserim) and demand an indemnity of £1 million.	Britain uses several minor offences to kick-start the Second Anglo-Burmese War for control of Lower Burma; Mindon Min overthrows his half brother and sues for peace.

Minister Clement Attlee, a pact was agreed, under which Burma would gain self-rule within a year.

A month later, Aung San met with Shan, Chin and Kachin leaders in Panglong, in Shan State. They signed the famous Panglong Agreement in February 1947, guaranteeing ethnic minorities the freedom to choose their political destiny if dissatisfied with the situation after 10 years. The agreement also broadly covered absent representatives of the Kayin, Kayah, Mon and Rakhine.

In the elections for the assembly, Aung San's Anti-Fascist People's Freedom League (AFPFL) won an overwhelming 172 seats out of 225. The Burmese Communist Party took seven, while the Bamar opposition, led by U Saw, took three. (U Saw was Burma's prime minister between 1939 and 1942, and was exiled to Uganda for the rest of WWII for secretly communicating with the Japanese following a failed attempt to gain British agreement to Burmese home rule.) The remaining 69 seats were split between ethnic minorities, including four seats for the Anglo-Burman community.

On 19 July 1947 32-year-old Aung San and six aides were gunned down in a plot ascribed to U Saw. Some speculate that the military was involved, due to Aung San's plans to demilitarise the government. Apparently U Saw thought he'd walk into the prime minister's role with Aung San gone; instead he took the noose, when the British had him hanged for the murders in 1948.

U Nu & Early Woes

While Myanmar mourned the death of a hero, Prime Minister Attlee and Aung San's protégé, U Nu, signed an agreement for the transfer of power in October 1947. On 4 January 1948, at an auspicious middle-of-the-night hour, Burma became independent and left the British Commonwealth.

Almost immediately, the new government led by U Nu had to contend with the complete disintegration of the country, involving rebels, communists, gangs and (US-supported) anticommunist Chinese KMT forces.

The hill-tribe people, who had supported the British and fought against the Japanese throughout the war, were distrustful of the Bamar majority and took up armed opposition. The communists withdrew from the government and attacked it. Muslims from the Rakhine area also opposed the new government. The Mon, long thought to be totally integrated with the Burmese, revolted. Assorted factions, private armies, WWII resistance groups and plain mutineers further confused the picture.

In early 1949 almost the entire country was in the hands of a number of rebel groups, and there was even fighting in Yangon's suburbs. At one stage the government was on the point of surrendering to the

Armed Forces Day (27 March) commemorates the Burmese soldiers' resistance against the Japanese army in WWII.

The Burman (1882) and *Burma: A Handbook of Practical Information* (1906) by colonial adventurer Sir J George Scott remain in print today and still provide an insight into the nation's culture.

1857	1862	1866
Mindon Min moves Upper Burma's capital from Inwa to a newly built city at the foot of Mandalay Hill, thus fulfilling a purported 2400-year-old prophecy by Buddha.	Bahadur Shah Zafar, the last emperor of India, is exiled with his family to Yangon, which the British call Rangoon. He dies in 1858, and is buried in secrecy.	Mindon's sons conspire against the heir apparent – beheading him in the palace – prompting Mindon to pick Thibaw, who showed no interest in the throne, as his successor.

JOHN ELK / GETTY IMAGES ©

→ Kuthodaw Paya, Mandalay

communist forces, but gradually fought back. Through 1950 and 1951 it regained control of much of the country.

With the collapse of Chiang Kai-Shek's KMT forces to those of Mao Ze-dong, the tattered remnants of the KMT withdrew into northern Burma and mounted raids from there into Yunnan, China. But being no match for the Chinese communists, the KMT decided to carve their own little fiefdom out of Burmese territory.

Following Ne Win's military coup in 1962, the country started closing off the outside world, limiting foreign-ers' visits to just 24-hour visas, later extended to a week.

The First Military Government

By the mid-1950s the government had strengthened its hold on the coun-try, but the economy slipped from bad to worse. U Nu managed to re-main in power until 1958, when he voluntarily handed the reins over to a caretaker military government under General Ne Win. Considering the pride most of the country had in the Burmese army, which had helped bring independence, this was seen as a welcome change.

Freed from the 'democratic' responsibilities inherent in a civilian gov-ernment, Ne Win was able to make some excellent progress during the 15 months his military government operated. A degree of law and order was restored, rebel activity was reduced and Yangon was given a massive and much-needed cleanup.

According to Thant Myint-U, Ne Win's first period of government was 'the most effective and efficient in modern Burmese history'. Sadly, the same would not be true for the general's second, much more extended, stint at Burma's helm.

The Junta Years: 1962–2010

The Burmese Road to Socialism

As many as 250,000 people of Indian and Chinese descent left Burma in the 1960s. Anti-Chinese riots in Yangon in 1967 also resulted in hundreds of Chinese deaths.

Free elections were held in December 1960 and the charismatic U Nu regained power with a much-improved majority, partly through a policy of making Buddhism the state religion. This, and politically destabilising moves by various ethnic minorities to leave the Union of Burma, resulted in an army coup in March 1962.

U Nu, along with his main ministers, was thrown into prison, where he remained until he was forced into exile in 1966. Ne Win established a 17-member Revolutionary Council and announced that the country would 'march towards socialism in our own Burmese way', confiscat-ing most private property and handing it over to military-run state corporations.

Nationalisation resulted in everyday commodities becoming available only on the black market, and vast numbers of people being thrown out of work. Ne Win also banned international aid organisations, foreign-language publications and local, privately owned newspapers and politi-

1885	1886	1920	1937
The Third Anglo-Burmese War results in the end of the Burmese monarchy, as Britain conquers Mandalay, sending Thibaw and his family into exile in India.	Burma becomes an administrative province of British-ruled India, with its capital at Ran-goon; it takes several years for the British to successfully suppress local resistance.	Students across Burma strike in protest against the new University Act, seen as helping to per-petuate colonial rule; the strike is celebrated today by National Day.	A new constitution for Burma sets up a legislative council, giving locals a larger role in the running of the country; it's not enough to stem calls for independence.

cal parties. The net result was that by 1967, a country that had been the largest exporter of rice in the world prior to WWII was now unable to feed itself.

Riots & Street Protests

Opposition to Ne Win's government eventually bubbled over into a strike by oil workers and others in May 1974 and, later that same year, riots over what was seen as the inappropriate burial of former UN secretary-general U Thant in Yangon. Responding with gunfire and arrests, the government regained control and doggedly continued to run the country – further impoverishing the people with successive demonetisations.

In late 1981 Ne Win retired as president of the republic, retaining his position as chair of the Burmese Socialist Programme Party (BSPP), the country's only legal political party under the 1974 constitution. But his successor, San Yu, and the government remained very much under the influence of Ne Win's political will.

In 1988 the people again took to the streets en masse, insisting that Ne Win had to go. Public protests reached a climax on the auspicious date of 8 August 1988 (8-8-88), after which the government steadily moved to crush all opposition, killing an estimated 3000 and imprisoning more. Tens of thousands, mainly students, fled the country.

Slorc Holds an Election

In September 1988 a military coup (widely thought to have had the blessing of Ne Win) saw the formation of the State Law & Order Restoration Council (Slorc) and the promise to hold a multiparty election within three months.

Although 235 parties contested the election (which was delayed until May 1990), the clear front runner from the start was the National League for Democracy (NLD). The NLD was led by several former generals, along with Aung San Suu Kyi (daughter of hero Aung San), who had made such a public impression at rallies during the 1988 protests.

In the run-up to the election, Slorc tried to appease the masses with construction programs, adding a coat of paint to many buildings in Yangon and abandoning socialism in favour of a capitalist economy. In 1989 it changed the name of the country to Myanmar, then placed Aung San Suu Kyi under house arrest and detained many other prodemocracy leaders.

Convinced it had effectively dealt with the opposition, the government went ahead with the country's first election in 30 years. The voter turnout – 72.59% – was the highest in Myanmar's history. The result was a resounding victory for the NLD, which took 392 of the 485 contested

U Nu, Burma's first prime minister, was also a devout Buddhist who banned the slaughter of cows after winning the 1960 election. His autobiography *Saturday's Son* was published in 1975.

Patricia Elliott's *The White Umbrella* (www.whiteumbrella.com) is the fascinating true story of Shan royal Sao Hearn Hkam, wife of Burma's president and founder of the Shan State Army.

HISTORY THE JUNTA YEARS: 1962–2010

1939	1941	1945	1947
Still under British watch, the leader of Burma's government, U Saw, holds office until his arrest by the British in January 1942 for communicating with the Japanese.	After training with the Japanese, Aung San – Aung San Suu Kyi's father – founds the Burmese Army, and marches into Burma with his benefactors to oust the British.	Aung San turns his army against the Japanese to support the British; later he forms the Anti-Fascist People's Freedom League (AFPFL) to fight for Burmese independence.	Having gained independence from Britain and rallied ethnic groups to a 10-year deal where they could secede from Burma by 1958, Aung San and six colleagues are assassinated by rivals.

seats (or about 60% of the vote), with the military-backed National Unity Party gaining just 10 seats with just over 25% of the vote.

NLD Under Attack

Slorc barred the elected members of parliament from assuming power, decreeing that a state-approved constitution had to be passed by national referendum first. In October 1990 the military raided NLD offices and arrested key leaders. Five years later Slorc deemed it safe enough to release Aung San Suu Kyi; at the same time many other high-level dissidents, including the NLD's Tin U and Kyi Maung, were also released from prison.

In May and September 1996 a congress of NLD members was held in a bold political gambit to show that the party was still an active force. The military junta responded by detaining hundreds who attended the congress; the street leading to Suu Kyi's residence was also blockaded, prohibiting her from making speeches at her residence.

In 1998 Suu Kyi attempted to leave Yangon to meet with supporters, but was blocked by the military and forcibly returned to the city. A second attempt to drive to Mandalay in September 2000 again saw the Lady (as she is affectionately known) detained at a military roadblock and

The 1988 demonstrations were sparked by a students' fight at the Rangoon Institute of Technology (that's right, RIOT) that ended with police intervening and some students being killed.

MIXED FEELINGS ABOUT THE TATMADAW

'Born of the people and one with the people': that's how former Senior General Than Shwe describes Myanmar's army, the Tatmadaw. Other commentators, including the academic and former diplomat Andrew Selth, author of *Burma's Armed Forces: Power Without Glory*, call it a 'state within a state'.

From a small and disunited force at the time of independence, the army has grown to nearly half a million soldiers. It takes care of its troops and their dependants by providing subsidised housing and access to special schools and hospitals. The military also owns two giant corporations – the Union of Myanmar Economic Holdings (UMEH) and Myanmar Economic Corporation (MEC) – whose dealings extend into nearly every corner of the economy.

Small wonder that for many families, having a son (it's rarely a daughter, although there are some roles for women in the army) who is a solider results in much appreciation for the financial security it brings. Many other people in Myanmar live in fear of the army, but there are others who continue to respect the institution for the role it originally played in securing independence for the nation.

Summing up such divided feelings is none other than Aung San Suu Kyi who, in an interview for the *Financial Times* said, 'I was brought up to be fond of the military, to believe that everybody in military uniform was, in some way or other, my father's son. This is not something that you can just get rid of. It stays with you.'

1948	1958	1962	1964
On 4 January the country gains independence as the Union of Burma with U Nu as the prime minister; immediately it is destabilised by various ethnic and political conflicts.	A split in the AFPFL causes parliamentary chaos; U Nu barely survives a no-confidence vote and invites General Ne Win to form a 'caretaker government' which lasts until 1960.	Following the coup by Ne Win, a peaceful student protest at Rangoon University is suppressed by the military, with over 100 students killed and the Student Union building dynamited.	All opposition political parties are banned, commerce and industry are nationalised and Ne Win begins the process of isolating Myanmar from the rest of the world.

later placed under house arrest. Save for barely a year (between 6 May 2002 and 30 May 2003), she would spend the next decade shut away from the public.

Than Shwe Takes Over

Due to the tourism boycott launched by the NLD and others there was a disappointing turnout for the junta's official 'Visit Myanmar Year 1996'. Increased sanctions from the West led the government to seek other sources of income: namely from trade with China, India and Thailand.

Khin Nyunt, feared head of military intelligence, became Prime Minister in 2003. The man known as the Prince of Darkness took the lead on the junta's seven-step 'roadmap towards discipline-flourishing democracy'. But only a year later hard-liner Senior General Than Shwe ousted Khin Nyunt and many of his fellow intelligence officers; at a secret trial Khin Nyunt was sentenced to 44 years in jail.

Than Shwe initially promised to continue the transition to democracy, but instead his activity showed a focus on negotiating multimillion-dollar trade deals with China, India and Thailand, and importing weapons and military know-how from Russia and North Korea.

In 2005 an entirely new capital city was created in the arid fields near Pyinmana. The junta named the city-in-the-making Nay Pyi Taw (Royal Capital), leaving little doubt that Than Shwe's strategies and inspirations were aligned less with the modern world than with Burmese kings of centuries past.

The 'Saffron Revolution'

In mid-2007 natural gas prices rose by 500% (and petrol by 200%), leading to price hikes for everything from local bus tickets to rice. In late August a group of '1988 generation' protestors were arrested for staging a march against the inflation. On 5 September, when monks denounced the price hikes in a demonstration in Pakokku, the protests escalated. The military responded with gunfire and allegedly beat one monk to death.

In response, the All Burma Monks Alliance (ABMA) was formed, denouncing the ruling government as an 'evil military dictatorship' and refusing to accept alms from military officials. By 17 September daily marches began, swelling in numbers across major cities including Yangon, Mandalay, Meiktila and Sittwe.

Unexpectedly, monk-led crowds were allowed to pray with Aung San Suu Kyi from outside her house gates on 22 September. Two days later anything from 50,000 to 150,000 protestors marched through the streets of Yangon in what would become known as the 'Saffron Revolution'. All the while the government watched, photographing participants.

Than Shwe: Unmasking Burma's Tyrant by Benedict Rogers is an unauthorised biography of the secretive senior general who, many believe, still calls the shots in Myanmar.

Karma can come around for Myanmar's former rulers. Ne Win died, disgraced and living in obscurity, in 2002. His protégé Khin Nyunt was charged with corruption and placed under house arrest until January 2012 when released as part of the amnesty on political prisoners; he now runs a gallery in Yangon.

HISTORY THE JUNTA YEARS: 1962–2010

1978	1988	1990	1995
General San Yu succeeds Ne Win as Burma's president but Ne Win remains the ultimate ruler, even after his resignation from the Burmese Socialist Programme Party in 1988.	Civilian unrest grows as living standards continue to fall. On 8 August huge nonviolent marches end with the military killing over 3000 protestors; the military promises to hold democratic elections.	In May the National League for Democracy (NLD), led by Aung San Suu Kyi, conclusively wins the first nationwide election in three decades, but the military refuses to relinquish power.	Aung San Suu Kyi is released from house arrest. The government uses forced labour to ready some sites for 'Visit Myanmar Year'; NLD and other activist groups launch a tourism boycott.

On 26 September the army began shooting protestors and imposed a curfew. By the end of the week monasteries had been raided, around 3000 people had been arrested and more than 30 were dead, including a Japanese photographer whose killing in central Yangon was captured on video.

According to research by Asean and the UN Cyclone Nargis caused 84,537 deaths and 53,836 missing people – 138,373 in all, 61% of whom were female. Other estimates are even higher, suggesting 300,000 were lost. Children, unable to withstand the inflow of water, were most vulnerable to drowning.

Cyclone Nargis

In the aftermath of the 2007 demonstrations, Than Shwe finalised the long-delayed new constitution, which had been under discussion since 1993, and announced a national referendum for it on 10 May 2008. But on 2 May Cyclone Nargis – the second-deadliest cyclone in recorded history – tore across the Ayeyarwady Delta.

Cyclone Nargis' 121mph winds, and the tidal surge that followed, swept away bamboo-hut villages, leaving more than two million survivors without shelter, food or drinking water. Damages were estimated at $2.4 billion. Yangon avoided the worst, but the winds (at 80mph) still overturned power lines and trees, leaving the city without power for two weeks.

The government was widely condemned for its tepid response to the disaster. Outside aid groups were held up by a lack of visas and the Myanmar military's refusal to allow foreign planes to deliver aid. Locals stepped into the breach, heroically organising their own relief teams. In the meantime, the government kept the referendum more or less on schedule, outraging many locals and outside observers.

Constitutional Referendum

Even before the cyclone, activist groups and NLD members had urged the public to vote 'no' at the referendum to change the constitution. They feared that it would enshrine the power of the generals. Others worried that not voting would only deepen the military hold on the government and leave no wiggle room for other political parties to contribute.

A DIFFERENT KIND OF REVOLUTION

As David Steinberg points out in *Burma/Myanmar: What Everyone Needs to Know*, the Saffron Revolution was neither saffron nor a revolution. Burmese monks wear maroon (not saffron) coloured robes for a start. The revolutionary part of the events of 2007 was that, for the first time, they were broadcast via smuggled-out videos on satellite TV or the internet. 'For the first time in Burmese history, violent suppression by the state was not simply a matter of rumour but was palpably visible', writes Steinberg. For a nail-biting account of how such incendiary video evidence was captured, watch the Oscar-nominated documentary *Burma VJ* (www.burmavjmovie.com).

1997	2000	2002	2003
US and Canada impose an investment ban on Myanmar. State Law & Order Restoration Council (Slorc) changes name to the State Peace & Development Council. Myanmar joins Asean.	The EU intensifies its economic sanctions against Myanmar, citing continued human rights abuses in the country. Aung San Suu Kyi again under house arrest until May 2002.	In March Ne Win's son-in-law and three grandsons are arrested for plotting to overthrow the junta; Ne Win is placed under house arrest and dies 5 December, aged 91.	Aung San Suu Kyi and NLD members are attacked by pro-government mobs in northern Myanmar; up to 100 are killed. 'The Lady' is again placed under house arrest.

Voting took place in two rounds during May 2008, while a reported 2.5 million people still required food, shelter and medical assistance. The military announced that 98.12% of those eligible had voted and that 92.48% had approved the new constitution – even though very few would have even seen the document in advance of the referendum.

With Than Shwe's 'roadmap towards discipline-flourishing democracy' in place, and yet another reason found to keep his nemesis, Aung San Suu Kyi, under house arrest (beyond her scheduled release in 2009), Myanmar's first general election in 20 years went ahead in November 2010.

Myanamar Post-Election 2010
Thein Sein for President

More than 30 different political parties jumped through a considerable number of hoops to contest the 2010 election, including the National Democratic Force (NDF), a breakaway group from the NLD that, unlike its parent party, decided to participate in the poll. As expected, the USDP triumphed in an election the UN called 'deeply flawed'. Not surprisingly, many considered the change of government to be little more than 'new wine in old bottles', but one good result was that, with victory in the bag, Aung San Suu Kyi was released from house arrest and was permitted contact with the international media.

Everything is Broken by Emma Larkin is an eye-opening account of the regime's response to the worst natural disaster to befall Myanmar in modern history.

THE 2008 CONSTITUTION

Under the 2008 constitution Myanmar is divided into seven regions (where the Bamar are in the majority) and seven states (minority regions, namely Chin, Kachin, Kayah, Kayin, Mon, Rakhine and Shan States). In addition there are six ethnic enclaves (Danu, Kokang, Naga, Palaung, Pa-O and Wa) with a degree of self-governance.

A quarter of the seats both at the national and state level are reserved for unelected military candidates; this gives the military a casting vote on any constitutional change because these require a parliamentary majority of more than 75%. In four of the seven state legislatures (Chin, Kayin, Rakhine and Shan) ethnic parties hold over 25% of the seats, theoretically allowing them to call special sessions or initiate impeachment proceedings against local public officials.

There are provisions that the military cannot be legally held to account for crimes against the population committed during their governing period. Key cabinet positions are reserved for serving military and the Commander in Chief of the armed forces has far-reaching reserve powers.

Most controversially, there are the conditions that must be met for a person to assume the office of president; these clauses effectively bar Aung San Suu Kyi from leading the country should the NLD win the 2015 election.

2004	2006	2007	2008
Having brokered a ceasefire agreement with Karen insurgents, Prime Minister Khin Nyunt, the moderate voice in the military who outlined a seven-point 'roadmap' for democracy, is arrested.	General Than Shwe and the government move the capital from Yangon to Nay Pyi Taw, a new city in central Myanmar.	Following fuel price hikes, monk-led protests hit Myanmar's streets; after 50,000 march in Yangon in September the government brutally cracks down on this 'Saffron Revolution', killing at least 31.	Cyclone Nargis tears across the delta, killing an estimated 138,000 and leaving many more without homes. Two days later (sticking to schedule), a referendum on constitutional reform takes place.

In February 2011 a quasi-civilian parliament convened for its initial sessions, replacing the military regime's State Peace and Development Council (SPDC). A new president, former general and old prime minister Thein Sein, was 'chosen' by the elected reps to take over from Senior General Than Shwe, Myanmar's supreme ruler for the past two decades. Than Shwe has since quietly faded into the background.

Myanmar's national parliament is made up of the 440-seat People's Assembly (*Pyithu Hluttaw*) and the 224-seat Upper House (*Amytha Hluttaw*). There are also seven state legislatures.

Roadmap to Democracy

When the new parliament was sworn in at the end of March and a new head of the military, Min Aung Hlaing, was announced, a tick appeared against the seventh, and final, step on the junta's 'roadmap to democracy'. Given how glimmers of democratic hope for Myanmar had been so cruelly snubbed in the recent past, many could be forgiven for taking with a pinch of salt Thein Sein's inaugural address, which promised meaningful reforms for the country, including tackling corruption and poverty.

However, a year later, after the president had met with Aung San Suu Kyi, started to release political prisoners, diminished state censorship and enacted various laws to start liberalising the economy (including allowing the kyat to float), it was becoming clear that positive changes really were afoot in Myanmar. As international sanctions were dropped and world leaders flew into Yangon, it seemed the country might well be on the way to coming in from the cold.

A ceasefire in 2012 with Karen rebels also provided a hiatus to the longest-running insurrection in contemporary history. However, inter-ethnic and religious violence in Rakhine State and central Myanmar has since tempered the feel-good factor about Myanmar's reforms, reminding everyone that there are significant difficulties for the country to overcome.

Outrage: Burma's Struggle for Democracy by Bertl Lintner is one of several works by the long-time Bangkok-based foreign correspondent and Burma expert, exploring the machinations of Myanmar's military government.

2010	2011	2012	2013
NLD boycott the October elections but many other parties decide to take part; few are surprised when the military-backed USDP wins. Aung San Suu Kyi released in November.	Myanmar achieves seventh and final step on 'roadmap to democracy' when former general Thein Sein is sworn into office as president, heading up a quasi-civilian government.	Aung San Suu Kyi and 42 other NLD candidates win parliamentary seats in by-elections. Clashes between Buddhists and Muslims in Rakhine State leave hundreds dead and tens of thousands of Rohingya displaced.	On a visit to the US, Thein Sein is praised by President Obama for 'leading Mynamar in a new direction'. Inter-ethnic tensions continue with deadly clashes spreading to central Myanmar.

People & Religious Beliefs of Myanmar (Burma)

Multicultural Myanmar is more salad bowl than melting pot. The government recognises 135 distinct ethnic groups that make up eight official 'major national ethnic races': Bamar, Shan, Mon, Kayin (Karen), Kayah, Chin, Kachin and Rakhine.

Freedom of religion is guaranteed under the country's constitution. However, Buddhism is given special status. Myanmar's ethnic patchwork of people also embraces a variety of other faiths, among which Islam and Christianity are the most popular.

Main Ethnic Groups

Historically, Myanmar's diverse ethnic make-up has been delineated by its topography. The broad central plain, with the Ayeyarwady (Irrawaddy) River and Myanmar's most fertile soil, has been populated by whichever group was strongest – usually the Bamar (Burmese) in the past few hundred years. Most ethnic groups continue to live in some sort of troubled isolation in the mountains lining much of Myanmar's international borders, notably the Shan, Kayah and Kayin in the east; the Kachin to the north; and the Chin and Rakhine to the west.

As in many other ethnically (and religiously) diverse countries, feelings of pride and prejudice cause friction between Myanmar's ethnic groups. Ask a Bamar (or a Shan or a Kayin) their opinion about their countryfolk of different ethnic or religious backgrounds and you'll get an idea of what kinds of challenges governments in Myanmar down the ages have faced in their efforts to keep the peace and preserve the borders.

Bamar

Also known as Burman or Burmese, the Bamar make up the majority (69% according to 1983 census data) of the population. Thought to have originally migrated from the Himalaya, the Bamar ruled much of what is now Myanmar from Bagan (Pagan) by the 11th century. When the British conquered Myanmar in the 19th century, it was the Bamar who had to relinquish the most. Many ancient court customs and arts were lost when the Bamar monarchy was abolished.

Despite an enduring attachment to older animist beliefs in *nat* (spirits), the Bamar, from trishaw drivers to senior generals, are devout Buddhists. Monks are highly respected and the media reports daily on the merit-making of top officials at the country's principal Buddhist places of worship – continuing a tradition of patronage started by Burmese monarchs.

Saw Myat Yin, author of *Culture Shock! Burma*, expresses a viewpoint common among Myanmar women, who see their role as equal but 'supportive and complementary...rather than in competition', and that 'if they accept a role a step behind their menfolk, they do so freely and willingly.'

Khin Myo Chit's English-language *Colourful Myanmar* highlights many customs and traditions of Myanmar life and is available in many Yangon bookshops.

TRADITIONAL LIFE & DEATH IN MYANMAR

About three-quarters of Myanmar's population are rural dwellers, so much of local life revolves around villages and farming the countryside. Here, national politics or dreams of wealth can pale in comparison to the season, the crop or the level of the river (used for bathing, washing and drinking water). Everywhere, people are known for helping each other when in need, and call each other 'brother' and 'sister' affectionately.

Families tend to be large; you might find three or four generations of one family living in a two- or three-room house. The birth of a child is a big occasion. Girls are as equally welcomed as boys, if not more so, as they're expected to look after parents later in life. Some thatched huts in the countryside have generators, powering electric bulbs and pumping life into the TV a couple of hours a night; many don't. Running water outside the cities and bigger towns is rare.

In *Finding George Orwell in Burma,* Emma Larkin recounts how a Mandalay cemetery worker saved dirt from a moved gravesite so that just in case the family ever returned they could have 'some soil from around the grave'. Death, of course, is a big deal, though mourned for less time than in much of the West. To miss a funeral is an unimaginable faux pas. If a heated argument goes too far, the ultimate capper is to yell: 'Oh yeah? Don't come to my funeral when I die!'

Coming of age (*shinbyu*) is a major event in Bamar/Buddhist culture with parades around villages and towns for boys about to enter monasteries as novice monks, and both girls and boys having their ears pierced.

The military and current government stopped short of making Buddhism the state religion (as Prime Minister U Nu did in 1960). However, nation-building efforts have included establishing the Bamar language (Burmese) as the language of instruction in schools throughout Myanmar, so most non-Bamar speak Burmese as a second language.

Chin

Of Tibeto-Burman ancestry, the Chin people call themselves Zo-mi or Lai-mi (both terms mean 'mountain people'), and share a culture, food and language with the Zo of the adjacent state of Mizoram in India. Making up 2.2% of Myanmar's population they inhabit the mountainous region (mostly corresponding with Chin State) that borders India and Bangladesh to the west. Outsiders name the different subgroups around the state according to the district in which they live, for instance Tidam Chin, Falam Chin and Haka Chin.

In the past the Chin, as with most highland dwellers, led labour-intensive lives, and their relatively simple traditional dress reflected this. Men wore loincloths in the warmer months and draped blankets over themselves when the weather turned cool. The women wore poncho-like garments woven with intricate geometric patterns. These garments and Chin blankets are highly sought after by textile collectors today.

Traditionally the Chin practise swidden (slash-and-burn) agriculture. They are also skilled hunters, and animal sacrifice plays a role in important animistic ceremonies: the state has the largest proportion of animists of any state in Myanmar. Even so, some 80% to 90% of Chin are believed to be Christian, mainly following the efforts of American missionaries during the British colonial period. However, with the present-day activities of government-sponsored Buddhist missions in the region, the traditional Zo or Chin groups are fading fast. Many Chin have also fled west to Bangladesh and India.

Visit Karenni Homeland (www.karennihomeland.com) to find out more about the people living in one of the poorest and least accessible parts of Myanmar.

The Chin National Front (www.chinland.org) would like to create a sovereign 'Chinland' out of parts of Myanmar, India and Bangladesh.

Intha

Although they follow Buddhism and wear modern Burmese costume, the Intha people of Inle Lake are culturally quite distinct from their Shan neighbours.

The ancestors of the Intha are thought to have migrated to Inle from Dawei in southern Myanmar. According to the most popular legend, two brothers from Dawei came to Yaunghwe (the original name for Nyaungshwe) in 1359 to serve the local Shan *sao pha* (sky lord). The chieftain was so pleased with the hard-working Dawei brothers that he invited 36 more families from Dawei; purportedly, all the Intha around Inle Lake, who number around 70,000, are descended from these migrant families.

A more likely theory is that the Intha fled southern Myanmar in the 18th century to escape wars between the Thais and Bamar.

Kachin

Like the Chin, the Kachin (1.4% of the population) are part of the Tibeto-Burman racial group. Based mainly in Kachin State, they are divided into six ethnic sub-groups (Jingpaw, Lawngwaw, Lashi, Zaiwa, Rawang, Lisu), among which the Jingpaw are the most numerous. Also traditionally animist, the Kachin were heavily targeted by Christian missionaries during colonial times (about 36% of the population are Christian, mostly Baptist and Catholic).

As much of Kachin State lies above the tropic of Cancer, the climate is more extreme – stifling hot in the summer months and downright cold in the winter – and the Kachin seem to have abandoned their traditional dress for Western clothes that can be easily changed to suit the seasons.

About the only vestige of Kachin dress still commonly worn are men's *longyi* (sarong-style lower garment) of indigo, green and deep-purple plaid. During festive occasions Kachin women sport finely woven wool skirts decorated with zigzag or diamond patterns, and dark blouses festooned with hammered silver medallions and tassels.

Following independence from Britain, Kachin relations with the Burmese-run government were increasingly precarious. After the military coup in 1962, the Kachin Independence Army (KIA) was formed under the Kachin Independence Organisation (KIO). These two organisations effectively ran the state on an economy based on smuggling and narcotics until a cease-fire agreement was struck in 1994.

In July 2011 fighting with the Tatmadaw broke out in the state again; as of 2013, over 100,000 people have been displaced by the conflict and are currently living in refugee camps.

Kayah

Also known as the Karenni or Red Karen, the Kayah are settled in the mountainous isolation of Kayah State.

Conservationist and author Alan Rabinowitz relates much about the local life in the Kachin hills in his fascinating *Life in the Valley of Death*.

PEOPLE & RELIGIOUS BELIEFS OF MYANMAR (BURMA) MAIN ETHNIC GROUPS

THE WOMEN WITH TATTOOED FACES

The most extraordinary (but no longer practised) Chin fashion was the custom of tattooing women's faces. Chin facial tattoos vary according to tribe, but often cover the whole face – starting at just above the bridge of the nose and radiating out in a pattern of dark lines that resemble a spider's web. Even the eyelids were tattooed. A painful process, the tattooing was traditionally done to girls once they reached puberty.

Legend has it that this practice was initiated to keep young Chin maidens from being coveted by Rakhine princes whose kingdom bordered the southern Chin Hills. But it's just as likely that the tattoos were seen as a mark of beauty and womanhood. One proud old Chin woman we met told us that she was just seven when she started pestering her parents to have her own facial inking.

Efforts by Christian missionaries and a government ban on facial tattoos in the 1960s has resulted in the practice dying out. But in some Chin villages (particularly in the more traditional southern areas) live a handful of tattooed grannies.

As with many of Myanmar's ethnic groups that traditionally practised animism, the Kayah were targeted for conversion to Christianity by Baptist and Catholic missionaries during the colonial period. The name 'Red Karen' refers to the favoured colour of the Kayah traditional dress and the fact that their apparel resembles that of some Kayin (Karen) tribes – a resemblance that caused the Kayah to be classified by colonisers and missionaries as 'Karen'.

Today the Kayah make up a very small percentage of the population of Myanmar – perhaps less than 0.5% – and the vast majority lead agrarian lives. A significant number of Kayah also live in Thailand's Mae Hong Son Province.

Kayin (Karen)

No one knows for sure how many Kayin (also known as Karen) there are in Myanmar. This ethnic group numbers anything between four and seven million and is linguistically very diverse, with a dozen related but not mutually intelligible dialects. Originally animists, it's now reckoned that the majority are Buddhists, with around 20% Christian and a small percentage Muslim.

The typical dress of both the Kayin men and women is a *longyi* with horizontal stripes (a pattern that is reserved exclusively for women in other ethnic groups). A subgroup of the Kayin live on both sides of the Thai-Myanmar border.

The only major ethnic group to never sign peace agreements with the Myanmar military, the Kayin are an independent-minded people; the Karen National Union (KNU) is the best known of the insurgency groups. However, the sheer diversity of the many Kayin subgroups has made it impossible for them to achieve any real cohesion. Buddhist Kayin often side with the Buddhist Bamar against their Christian Kayin kin; also in the 2010 election a variety of ethnic parties managed to secure 43.5% of the state legislature.

Kayan

Perhaps the most recognisable – and enigmatic – of Myanmar's ethnic groups is the Kayan. Known in English as 'longnecks' and in Burmese as Padaung (actually a Shan term meaning 'wearing gold' – a moniker generally considered pejorative by the Kayan), the tribe is best known for the women's habit of wearing brass rings around their necks. Over time, the rings lower the women's collarbones and

Little Daughter: A Memoir of Survival in Burma and the West is the autobiography of Zoya Phan (written with Damien Lewis), a Kayin woman who is the international coordinator of the UK Burma Campaign and who spent many years as a child living in refugee camps.

ribcage, making their necks appear unusually long. A common myth claims if the coils are removed, the women's necks will fall over and the women will suffocate. In fact the women attach and remove the coils at will and there is no evidence that this deformation impairs their health at all.

Nobody knows for sure how the coil custom got started. One theory is that it was meant to make the women unattractive to men from other tribes. Another story says it was so tigers wouldn't carry the women off by their throats. Most likely it is nothing more than a fashion accessory.

In recent years some claim that the rings are applied with a different purpose – to provide women from impoverished hill villages with the means to make a living posing for photographs. We've heard reports that some souvenir shops on Inle Lake employ Kayan women to lure passing tourist boats, although we haven't encountered this ourselves. And there are claims that Kayan women have been ferried across the border to villages in neighbouring Mae Hong Son, in Thailand, to provide a photo opportunity for visiting tour groups. These villages are often derided as human zoos, but are actually refugee camps that also function as rural markets, with the women earning money by selling souvenirs and drinks.

At research time, the bulk of Myanmar's accessible 'traditional' (ie ring-wearing) Kayan villages in Kayah State were in Deemawsoe Township, southwest of Loikaw. The operators leading visits to the villages in this area request that visitors pay a K10,000 entrance fee, which appears to go directly to the villagers. Although tourists have been visiting this area for decades, we saw no evidence of exploitation, and the villagers seemed content to host us.

Moken

Also known as sea gypsies, or Salon in Burmese, the Moken live a nomadic life drifting on the ocean winds around the Myeik Archipelago, Tanintharyi (Tenasserim) Division. Numbering around 2000 to 3000 individuals, scientists believe they have been floating around these islands since at least 2000 BC.

Totally at home on the water, Moken families spend almost all their time on wooden boats, called *kabang*. As the boys come of age they build their own boats, and as the girls come of age and marry, they move away from their parents' boat.

Breathing through air hoses held above the water surface, the Moken dive to depths of up to 200ft in search of shellfish. For all their skill, this can be a lethal activity with divers dying in accidents each year, mainly from the bends caused by rising too quickly to the surface.

Mon

The Mon (also called the Tailing by Western historians) were one of the earliest inhabitants of Myanmar and their rule stretched into what is now Thailand. As happened with the Cham in Vietnam and the Phuan in Laos, the Mon were gradually conquered by neighbouring kingdoms and their influence waned until they were practically unknown outside present-day Myanmar.

As in Thailand, which also has a Mon minority, the Mon have almost completely assimilated with the Bamar and in most ways seem indistinguishable from them. In the precolonial era, Mon Buddhist sites including Yangon's Shwedagon Paya were appropriated by the Bamar (though the Golden Rock is still in Mon State), and Mon tastes in art and architecture were borrowed as well.

A 2011 report by the Netherlands-based Transnational Institute (www.tni.org/briefing/burmas-longest-war-anatomy-karen-conflict) concludes that the KNU 'has lost control of most of its once extensive 'liberated zones' and has lost touch with most non-Christian Karen communities. Already greatly weakened militarily, the KNU could be ejected from its last strongholds, should the Burma Army launch another major offensive.'

Today the Mon make up just over 2% of the population of Myanmar – find out more about them at Independent Mon News Agency (http://monnews.org).

PEOPLE & RELIGIOUS BELIEFS OF MYANMAR (BURMA) MAIN ETHNIC GROUPS

Naga

The Naga are mainly settled in a mountainous region of eastern India known as Nagaland, but significant numbers live in the western Sagaing Region between the Indian border and the Chindwin River.

When the British arrived in the mid-19th century, the Naga were a fragmented but fearsome collection of tribes. Headhunting was a tradition among them and for many decades they resisted British rule, though a lack of cooperation between the tribes hindered their efforts to remain independent. After nearly 17,000 Naga fought in WWI in Europe, a feeling of unity grew, which led to an organised Naga independence movement.

The Naga sport one of the world's most exotic traditional costumes. Naga men at festival time wear striking ceremonial headdresses made of feathers, tufts of hair and cowry shells, and carry wickedly sharp spears. Several tour companies organise trips to the region during the Naga new year in January when such ceremonies are performed.

Rakhine

The Rakhine (also spelled Rakhaing and formerly called Arakanese) are principally adherents of Buddhism; in fact, they claim to be among the first followers of Buddha in Southeast Asia. Their last ancient capital was centred at Mrauk U in Rakhine State, which borders Bangladesh.

The Rakhine language is akin to Bamar but, due to their geographical location, they have also absorbed a fair amount of culture from the Indian subcontinent. In the eyes of most Bamar, the Rakhine are a Creole race – a mixture of Bamar and Indian – a perception that Rakhine strongly resent. It is true though that the local culture exhibits a strongly Indian flavour, particularly when it comes to food and music. The Rakhine are skilled weavers and are known in Myanmar for their eye-catching and intricately patterned *longyi*.

Rakhine State also has a minority population of Muslim Rakhine, as well as the Rohingya, another Muslim people not recognised as citizens of Myanmar by the government.

Shan

The biggest ethnic group in Myanmar after the Bamar, the Shan account for around 8.5% of the population. Most Shan are Buddhists and call themselves Tai ('Shan' is actually a Bamar word derived from the word 'Siam'). This name is significant, as the Shan are related ethnically, culturally and linguistically to Tai peoples in neighbouring Thailand, Laos and China's Yunnan Province. In fact, if you've spent some time in northern Thailand or Laos and learned some of the respective languages, you'll find you can have a basic conversation with the Shan.

Traditionally, the Shan wore baggy trousers and floppy, wide-brimmed sun hats, and the men were known for their faith in talismanic tattoos. Nowadays Shan town-dwellers commonly dress in the Bamar *longyi,* except on festival occasions, when they proudly sport their ethnic costumes.

In former times the Shan were ruled by local lords or chieftains called *sao pha* (sky lords), a word that was corrupted by the Bamar to *sawbwa.* Many Shan groups have fought the Bamar for control of Myanmar, and a few groups continue a guerrilla-style conflict in the mountains near Thailand.

Wa

The remote northeastern hills of Shan State – the homeland of the Wa – are off limits to tourists. During British colonial times, these

Rakhine Cultural Relics

Temple ruins, Mrauk U

Mahamuni Buddha image, Mandalay

Rakhine State Culture Museum, Sittwe

To find out more about the Shan and issues in Shan State read the Shan Herald Agency for News (http://panglong.org).

In recent years there's been a massive influx of Chinese people into northern Burma, evident in Mandalay and certainly in border towns such as Mong La, where the yuan is the local currency.

tribal people – living in fortified villages, speaking dozens of dialects and having a reputation for being permanently unwashed and frequently inebriated – were hated and feared: a status they have yet to throw off.

The British distinguished two main groups of Wa according to how receptive they were to the colonisers' attempts to control them. The 'Wild Wa' were headhunters, and decorated their villages with the severed heads of vanquished enemies to appease the spirits that guarded their opium fields. (Apparently they only stopped the practice in the 1970s!)

The so-called 'Tame Wa' allowed the colonisers to pass through their territory unimpeded, yet the area inhabited by the Wa – east of the upper Thanlwin (Salween) River in northern Shan State – was never completely pacified by the British.

For decades the 30,000-strong United Wa State Army (UWSA) has controlled this borderland area, gathering power and money through the production of opium and methamphetamine; the US labelled the UWSA a narcotics trafficking organisation in 2003. Nevertheless, the

> Myanmar's constitution has set aside 'self-administered zones' for the Naga, Danu, Pa-O, Palaung, Kokang and Wa peoples.

THE ROHINGYA

Even in a nation synonymous with ethnic strife, the Rohingya stand out as perhaps Myanmar's most besieged and beleaguered group. They are, in United Nations' parlance, among the 'most persecuted minorities in the world'. However, to Myanmar's lawmakers, the general public and even the prodemocracy avant-garde, the Rohingya don't even exist.

Myanmar's officialdom are loathe to use the term 'Rohingya'. Instead, this contingent of 800,000 destitute Muslims are considered invaders from neighboring Bangladesh, who also reject them. Myanmar officials routinely describe them as pests, though they constitute as much as 20 percent of the population of coastal Rakhine State.

Animosity against the Rohingya runs so deep that even basic details of their origins and demographics are hotly disputed. Broadly speaking, the Rohingya have darker complexions than their Buddhist neighbours and generally speak a dialect of the Bengali language readily understood in Chittagong, Bangladesh's major seaport.

Those lucky enough to possess government identification are classified as 'Bengali', the dominant ethnicity in Bangladesh. But this tends to rile Rohingya activists, who resent the implication that they are wholly indistinct from their cousins across the border. Rohingya scholars cite historical evidence — including the logs of European explorers — that suggests a Rohingya presence in modern-day Myanmar that dates back centuries.

Along with various other groups of South Asian Muslims, many Rohingya descend from families led to Myanmar in the 19th century by the British Empire. During colonisation, historical borders were blurred, mass migration ensued and many Muslims (Bengali and otherwise) were brought over to toil on farms or serve as second-tier administrators.

For hardline Myanmar nationalists, the Rohingya are an undesirable outcome of colonial occupation that needs correcting. Myanmar's current citizenship law, widely derided by global human rights groups, seeks to rewind time and deny citizenship to any group who arrived after (or because of) British invasion.

This thinking is crucial to understanding widely held beliefs in Myanmar that the Rohingya are a fictitious ethnicity. An extremist screed titled Rohingya Hoax, written by a former Myanmar foreign diplomat, describes the word 'Rohingya' as a Bengali Muslim linguistic invention designed to convince the world that they are native to Myanmar. They have 'gussied up their claim in fancy and finesse,' he writes, 'distorting nebulous events of history convenient for the Rohingya chicanery.'

As the violence that has exploded across Rakhine State in 2012 and 2013 between Buddhists and Rohingya Muslims sadly shows, this disdain for Rohingya is hardly limited to rhetoric.

Patrick Winn, senior Southeast Asia correspondent for GlobalPost (www.globalpost.com)

UWSA struck a ceasefire deal with the military regime in 1989 and the territory under their control looks set to be designated a special autonomous region for the Wa under Myanmar's new constitution.

For more about ethnic and religious conflicts in Myanmar see p348.

Women in Myanmar

In *Letters From Burma*, Aung San Suu Kyi writes that a baby girl is as equally celebrated as a baby boy, as they're believed to be 'more dutiful and loving than sons'. Girls are educated alongside boys and, by university age, women outnumber men in university and college enrolment. Most white-collar professions grant women six weeks paid maternity leave before birth and one or two months afterwards.

Myanmar women enjoy equal legal rights to those of men, can own property, do not traditionally change any portion of their names upon marriage and, in the event of divorce, are legally entitled to half of all property accumulated during the marriage. Inheritance rights are also equally shared.

Rights on paper, however, don't always translate into reality. In the current parliament only 20 out of 659 members are women, and it's rare that you'll find women in other positions of power in Myanmar including, crucially, in the military. Speaking in 2013 Suu Kyi, herself now one of those 20 parliamentarians, said 'the constitution was drawn by the military government, and by male military parliamentarians, so it should be amended to reduce gender discrimination.'

When it comes to religion, women also take a back seat. Many people in Myanmar – women as well as men – believe the birth of a girl indicates less religious merit than the birth of a boy, and that only males can attain *nibbana* (for a woman to do so, she first has to come back as a man!). Buddhist shrines, including Mandalay's Mahamuni Paya and Yangon's Shwedagon Paya, have small areas around the main holy image or stupa that are off limits to women.

Just as boys between the ages of five and 20 usually undergo a pre-puberty initiation as temporary novice monks, girls around the same age participate in an initiatory ear-piercing ceremony (often called 'ear-boring' in Burmese English). Some also become temporary nuns at this age, but nuns are not as venerated in Myanmar as monks.

When Myanmar locals go on holiday it's often in the form of a pilgrimage. Ma Thanegi describes one such trip in *The Native Tourist: In Search of Turtle Eggs*.

Religion & Belief

Faith and superstition go hand in hand in Myanmar. About 89% of the people of Myanmar are Buddhist, but many also pay heed to ancient animist beliefs in natural spirits *(nats)*. Locals are proud of their beliefs and keen to discuss them. Knowing something about Buddhism in particular will help you better understand life in the country.

Buddhism

The Mon were the first people in Myanmar to practice Theravada (meaning Doctrine of the Elders) Buddhism, the oldest and most conservative form of the religion. King Asoka, the great Indian emperor, is known to have sent missions here (known then as the 'Golden Land') during the 3rd century BC. A second wave is thought to have arrived via Sinhalese missionaries between the 6th and 10th centuries.

By the 9th century the Pyu of northern Myanmar were combining Theravada with elements of Mahayana (Great Vehicle) and Tantric Buddhism brought from their homelands in the Tibetan Plateau. During the early Bagan era (11th century), Bamar king Anawrahta decided that the Buddhism practised in his realm should be 'purified' from all

Officially Myanmar is 1% animist, 1.5% Hindu, 4% Christian and 4% Muslim; others believe that non-Buddhists may account for 30% of the population.

> ## BUDDHA'S HAND SIGNS
> At temples and shrines, look out for the following hand signs of buddha images, each with a different meaning:
>
> **Abhaya** Both hands have palms out, symbolising protection from fear.
>
> **Bhumispara** The right hand touches the ground, symbolising when Buddha sat beneath a banyan tree until he gained enlightenment.
>
> **Dana** One or both hands with palms up, symbolising the offering of *dhamma* (Buddhist teachings) to the world.
>
> **Dhyana** Both hands rest palm-up on the buddha's lap, signifying meditation.
>
> **Vitarka or Dhammachakka** Thumb and forefinger of one hand forms a circle with other fingers (somewhat like an 'OK' gesture), symbolising the first public discourse on Buddhist doctrine.

non-Theravada elements. It never completely shed Tantric, Hindu and animist elements, but remains predominately Theravada.

Theravada vs Mahayana

Theravada Buddhism (also followed in Cambodia, Laos, Sri Lanka and Thailand) differs from Hinduism, Judaism, Islam and Christianity in that it is not centred around a god or gods, but rather a psycho-philosophical system. Today it covers a wide range of interpretations of the basic beliefs, which all start from the enlightenment of Siddhartha Gautama, a prince-turned-ascetic and referred to as the Buddha, in northern India around 2500 years ago.

In the Theravada school, it's believed that the individual strives to achieve *nibbana* (nirvana), rather than waiting for all humankind being ready for salvation as in the Mahayana (Large Vehicle) school. The Mahayana school does not reject the other school, but claims it has extended it. The Theravadins see Mahayana as a misinterpretation of the Buddha's original teachings. Of the two, Theravada Buddhism is more austere and ascetic and, some might say, harder to practise.

Buddhist Tenets

Buddha taught that the world is primarily characterised by *dukkha* (suffering), *anicca* (impermanence) and *anatta* (insubstantiality), and that even our happiest moments in life are only temporary, empty and unsatisfactory.

The ultrapragmatic Buddhist perception of cause and effect – *kamma* in Pali, *karma* in Sanskrit, *kan* in Burmese – holds that birth inevitably leads to sickness, old age and death, hence every life is insecure and subject to *dukkha*. Through rebirth, the cycle of *thanthaya* (*samsara* in Pali) repeats itself endlessly as long as ignorance and craving remain.

Only by reaching a state of complete wisdom and nondesire can one attain true happiness. To achieve wisdom and eliminate craving, one must turn inward and master one's own mind through meditation, most commonly known in Myanmar as *bhavana* or *kammahtan*.

Devout Buddhists in Myanmar adhere to five lay precepts, or moral rules (*thila* in Burmese, *sila* in Pali), which require abstinence from killing, stealing, unchastity (usually interpreted among laypeople as adultery), lying and intoxicating substances.

In spite of Buddhism's profound truths, the most common Myanmar approach is to try for a better future life by feeding monks, donating

During the U Nu period, Buddhism functioned as a state religion, as embodied in such catchphrases as 'the Socialist Way to Nibbana'.

DHANA

to temples and performing regular worship at the local paya (Buddhist monument) – these activities are commonly known as 'merit making'. For the average person everything revolves around the merit (kutho, from the Pali kusala, meaning 'wholesome') one is able to accumulate through such deeds.

Monks & Nuns

Myanmar's monkhood, numbering around 500,000, is collectively known as the Sangha. Every Buddhist Myanmar male is expected to take up temporary monastic residence twice in his life: once as a samanera (novice monk) between the ages of 10 and 20, and again as a hpongyi (fully ordained monk) sometime after the age of 20. Almost all men or boys aged under 20 'take robe and bowl' in the shinpyu (novitiation ceremony).

All things possessed by a monk must be offered by the lay community. Upon ordination a new monk is typically offered a set of three robes (lower, inner and outer). Other possessions a monk is permitted include a razor, a cup, a filter (for keeping insects out of drinking water), an umbrella and an alms bowl.

In Myanmar, women who live the monastic life as dasasila ('10-precept' nuns) are often called thilashin (possessor of morality) in Burmese. Nuns shave their heads, wear pink robes and take vows in an ordination procedure similar to monks. Generally, nunhood isn't considered as 'prestigious' as monkhood, as nuns generally don't perform ceremonies on behalf of laypeople, and keep only 10 precepts – the same number observed by male novices.

Temples & Monasteries

Paya (pa-yah), the most common Myanmar equivalent to the often misleading English term 'pagoda', literally means 'holy one' and can refer to people, deities and places associated with religion. Often it's a generic term covering a stupa, temple or shrine.

There are basically two kinds of paya: the solid, bell-shaped zedi and the hollow square or rectangular pahto. A zedi or stupa is usually thought to contain 'relics' – either objects taken from the Buddha himself (pieces of bone, teeth or hair) or certain holy materials.

The term pahto is sometimes translated as temple, though shrine would perhaps be more accurate as priests or monks are not necessarily in attendance. Mon-style pahto, with small windows and ground-level passageways, are also known as a gu or ku (from the Pali-Sanskrit guha, meaning 'cave').

In mornings, you'll see rows of monks and sometimes nuns carrying bowls to get offerings of rice and food. It's not begging. It's a way of letting locals have the chance of doing the deed of dhana, thus acquiring merit.

FOUR NOBLE TRUTHS & THE EIGHTFOLD PATH

The Buddha taught four noble truths:	The eightfold path consists of:
1 Life is dukkha (suffering).	1 Right thought
2 Dukkha comes from tanha (selfish desire).	2 Right understanding
3 When one forsakes selfish desire, suffering will be extinguished.	3 Right speech
4 The 'eightfold path' is the way to eliminate selfish desire.	4 Right action
	5 Right livelihood
	6 Right exertion
	7 Right attentiveness
	8 Right concentration

Both *zedi* and *pahto* are often associated with *kyaung* (Buddhist monasteries), also called *kyaungtaik* and *hpongyi-kyaung*. The most important structure on the monastery grounds is the *thein* (a consecrated hall where monastic ordinations are held). An open-sided rest-house or *zayat* may be available for gatherings of laypeople during festivals or pilgrimages.

Nat Worship

One of the most fascinating things about Myanmar is the ongoing worship of the *nat* (spirit being). Though some Buddhist leaders downgrade the *nat*, the *nat* are very much alive in the lives of the people of Myanmar and you'll often finding them sharing space with Buddha in their own *nat-sin* (spirit house) at temples.

History

Worship of *nats* predates Buddhism in Myanmar. *Nats* have long believed to hold dominion over a place (natural or human-made), person or field of experience.

Separate, larger shrines were built for a higher class of *nat*, descended from actual historic personages (including previous Thai and Bamar kings) who had died violent, unjust deaths. These suprahuman *nat*, when correctly propitiated, could aid worshippers in accomplishing important tasks, vanquishing enemies and so on.

Early in the 11th century in Bagan, King Anawrahta stopped animal sacrifices (part of *nat* worship at Mt Popa) and destroyed *nat* temples. Realising he may lose the case for making Theravada Buddhism the national faith, Anawrahta wisely conceded the *nat's* coexistence with Buddha.

There were 36 recognised *nat* at the time (in fact, there are many more). Anawrahta sagely added a 37th, Thagyamin, a Hindu deity based on Indra, whom he crowned 'king of the *nat'*. Since, in traditional Buddhist mythology, Indra paid homage to Buddha, this insertion effectively made all *nat* subordinate to Buddha. Anawrahta's scheme worked, and today the commonly believed cosmology places Buddha's teachings at the top.

Worship & Beliefs

In many homes you may see the most popular *nat* in the form of an unhusked coconut dressed in a red *gaung baung* (turban), which represents the dual-*nat* Eindwin-Min Mahagiri (Lord of the Great Mountain Who is in the House). Another widespread form of *nat* worship is exhibited through the red-and-white cloths tied to a rear-view mirror or hood ornament; these colours are the traditional *nat* colours of protection.

Some of the more animistic guardian *nat* remain outside home and paya. A tree-spirit shrine, for example, may be erected beneath a particularly venerated old tree, thought to wield power over the immediate vicinity. These are especially common beneath larger banyan trees *(Ficus religiosa)*, as this tree is revered as a symbol of Buddha's enlightenment.

A village may well have a *nat* shrine in a wooded corner for the propitiation of the village guardian spirit. Such tree and village shrines are simple, dollhouse-like structures of wood or bamboo; their proper placement is divined by a local *saya* (teacher or shaman), trained in spirit lore. Such knowledge of the complex *nat* world is fading fast among the younger generations.

Spirit possession – whether psychologically induced or metaphysical – is a phenomenon that is real in the eyes of locals. The main fear is not simply that spirits will wreak havoc on your daily affairs, but

PEOPLE & RELIGIOUS BELIEFS OF MYANMAR (BURMA) RELIGION & BELIEF

Bright red robes are usually reserved for novices under 15, darker colours for older, fully ordained monks.

Buddhism Websites

DharmaNet (www.dharma net.org)

Access to Insight (www.access toinsight.org)

World Dharma (www.world dharma.com)

Buddhist Studies (www.buddha net.net)

rather that one may enter your mind and body and force you to perform unconscionable acts in public.

Nat Festivals

The written Burmese word *nat* is likely derived from the Pali-Sanskrit *natha*, meaning lord or guardian.

On certain occasions the *nat* cult goes beyond simple propitiation of the spirits (via offerings) and steps into the realm of spirit invocation. Most commonly this is accomplished through *nat pwe* (spirit festivals), special musical performances designed to attract *nat* to the performance venue.

To lure a *nat* to the *pwe* takes the work of a spirit medium, or *nat-gadaw* (*nat* wife), who is either a woman or, more commonly, a male transvestite who sings and dances to invite specific *nat* to possess them. The *nat* also like loud and colourful music, so musicians at a *nat pwe* bang away at full volume on their gongs, drums and xylophones, producing what sounds like some ancient form of rock and roll.

Every *nat pwe* is accompanied by a risk that the invited spirit may choose to enter, not the body of the *nat-gadaw*, but one of the spectators. One of the most commonly summoned spirits at *nat pwe* is Ko Gyi Kyaw (Big Brother Kyaw), a drunkard *nat* who responds to offerings of liquor imbibed by the *nat-gadaw*. When he enters someone's body, he's given to lascivious dancing, so a chance possession by Ko Gyi Kyaw is especially embarrassing.

Once possessed by a *nat,* the only way one can be sure the spirit won't return again and again is to employ the services of an older Buddhist monk skilled at exorcism – a process that can take days, if not weeks. Without undergoing such a procedure, anyone who has been spirit possessed may carry the *nat* stigma for the rest of their lives. Girls who have been so entered are considered unmarriageable unless satisfactorily exorcised.

Superstition & Numerology

Those with a general fear of *nat* will avoid eating pork, which is thought to be offensive to the spirit world.

Superstitions run deep in Myanmar. Many people consult astrologers to find mates and plan events. According to Benedict Rogers, author of a biography of Than Shwe, the retired senior general has seven personal astrologers at his call, several of whom are tasked with focussing their darker arts on his chief nemesis, Aung San Suu Kyi.

On a less dramatic level, Myanmar astrology, based on the Indian system of naming the zodiacal planets for Hindu deities, continues to be an important factor in deciding proper dates for weddings, funerals,

THE WATER FESTIVAL

Occurring at the height of the dry and hot season, around the middle of April, the three-day Thingyan (Water Festival) starts the Myanmar New Year. As in Thailand's Songkran, the event is celebrated in a most raucous manner – by throwing buckets of cold water at anyone who dares to venture into the streets. Foreigners are not exempt!

On a spiritual level, Myanmar people believe that during this three-day period the king of the *nat* (spirit beings), Thagyamin, visits the human world to tally his annual record of the good deeds and misdeeds humans have performed. Villagers place flowers and sacred leaves in front of their homes to welcome the *nat*. Thagyamin's departure on the morning of the third day marks the beginning of the new year, when properly brought-up young people wash the hair of their elder kin, buddha images are ceremonially washed, and *hpongyi* (monks) are offered particularly appetising alms food.

Although the true meaning of the festival is still kept alive by ceremonies such as these, nowadays it's mainly a festival of fun. In cities, temporary stages called *pandal* (from the Tamil *pendel*) are erected along main thoroughfares, with water barrels ready to douse all passersby.

ordinations and other events. Burma became independent at 4.20am on 4 January 1948, per U Nu's counsel with an astrologer.

Numerology plays a similar role, with both eight and nine being auspicious numbers. The Burmese word *ko* (nine) also means 'to seek protection from the gods'. General Ne Win was fascinated with numerology, especially that relating to the cabalistic ritual Paya-kozu (Nine Gods). In 1987 he introduced 45-kyat and 90-kyat notes, because their digits' sum equalled nine.

Islam

Although official statistics say that 4% of Myanmar's population follow Islam, according to a 2006 US government report on religious freedom in Myanmar, local Muslim leaders believe the more accurate figure is approximately 20%. Either way, Muslims have been part of Myanmar's religious fabric from at least the 9th century, and possibly as far back as the 6th century in Rakhine State.

Waves of Indian immigration under British colonial rule boosted the local Muslim population. This was slashed during WWII when many Indians fled the country, and again from the start of military rule in 1962 when ethnic Indians were expelled from the army and marginalised in society.

In subsequent years Muslims – in particular the Rohingya – have been targeted as illegal immigrants, stirring up ethnic and religious intolerance that continues to linger dangerously in Myanmar society.

Christianity

The CIA World Fact Book says 4% of Myanmar's population are Christians. Anglican, Baptist and Catholic missionaries have been active in Myanmar for over 150 years. Going even further back there were communities of Christians among the Japanese who fled to Arakan (Rakhine State) in the 16th century and the Portuguese Catholics (and later Dutch and French mercenaries and prisoners of war) who arrived in the early 17th century.

The Catholic community in Myanmar is reckoned to number around 450,000 and is divided into 13 dioceses and three arch dioceses.

Other Religions

Hinduism is practised among locals of Indian descent who settled in the country during colonial times. However, the religion's influence and reach in Myanmar stretch back many centuries, as Hindu temples in Bagan attest. Burmese adaptations of Hindu deities are worshipped as *nat*.

Other faiths you'll come across include the various traditional religions of Chinese immigrants, and animism among the small tribal groups of the highlands.

Yangon has a tiny Jewish community of about 20 people. The Jewish community in pre-WWII Rangoon numbered around 2500 and the city once had a Jewish mayor (as did Pathein). Burma was also the first Asian country to recognise Israel in 1949. However, the military coup and its aftermath encouraged most to leave. Even so, the city's 19th-century Moseah Yeshua Synagogue is beautifully maintained.

Ethnic groups that traditionally practised animism have proved more receptive to conversion to Christianity, especially the Kayin, Kachin and Chin.

PEOPLE & RELIGIOUS BELIEFS OF MYANMAR (BURMA) RELIGION & BELIEF

Aung San Suu Kyi

Free, free at last: Aung San Suu Kyi, who for 15 of the 21 years between 1989 and 2010 was a prisoner of conscience, is now a member of Myanmar's parliament. Chairperson of the National League for Democracy (NLD), she has been compared to Nelson Mandela and Mahatma Gandhi for her patient, nonviolent activism, her life story a source of inspiration not only for the oppressed and disenfranchised in Myanmar but people battling injustice around the world.

Family & Influences

Aung San Suu Kyi was born just two years before the assassination in July 1947 of her father, Aung San, leader of the Burma Independence Army and the key architect of the country's independence. Aung San had met Suu Kyi's mother, Ma Khin Kyi, a nurse, while recuperating from malaria in Rangoon General Hospital in 1942.

Her father's premature death was not the only family tragedy: in 1953 Suu Kyi's elder brother Lin drowned accidentally at the age of eight (there was also an elder sister Chit, but she had died when only a few days old in 1946, a year before Suu Kyi's birth). Later, Suu Kyi would become estranged from her eldest brother Aung San Oo, an engineer who emigrated to the US; in 2001 he unsuccessfully tried to sue her for a share of their mother's home – 54 University Ave, Yangon (Rangoon),

AUNG SAN SUU KYI IN WORDS & PICTURES

Freedom from Fear (1991) is a collection of writings by Suu Kyi and her supporters on topics ranging from her father to the Nobel Prize acceptance speech delivered by her son Alexander. *Letters from Burma* (1997) features a year's worth of weekly essays Suu Kyi wrote on Burmese culture, politics and incidents from her daily life for the Japanese newspaper *Mainichi Shimbun*.

The Lady and the Peacock: The Life of Aung San Suu Kyi of Burma (2011) by Peter Popham is the most up-to-date of several biographies of the Lady; it's comprehensive and includes extracts from Suu Kyi's private diaries. Justin Wintle's *The Perfect Hostage* (2007) is also an impressively researched account of her life and times, and of modern Burmese history, which paints a very believable, likeable 'warts and all' portrait of Suu Kyi.

On the cinematic front, Luc Bresson's *The Lady* is a biopic released in 2011 based on Suu Kyi's life between 1988 and 1999 when her husband Michael Aris died; it stars Malaysian actress Michelle Yeo as Suu Kyi.

Covering similar ground, but in documentary format, is *Lady of No Fear* (www.lady ofnofear.com), directed by Anne Gyrithe Bonne, which was finished before Suu Kyi's release in 2010 and includes interviews with close friends and colleagues about the famously private woman.

The BBC documentary *Aung San Suu Kyi: The Choice* (www.bbc.co.uk/programmes/b01n2wfw), filmed during 2011 and 2012, includes long interviews with Suu Kyi herself as well as with Hillary Clinton and other friends and family; you can find it on YouTube.

where Suu Kyi has spent the many years of her house arrest.

Her parents' political activism and example of public service had an enormous influence on Suu Kyi. 'When I honour my father, I honour all those who stand for the political integrity of Burma,' she writes in the dedication to her book *Freedom from Fear*. In the essay *My Father*, she says he was 'a man who put the interests of the country before his own needs' – something Suu Kyi has also done.

Suu Kyi's mother was also a prominent public figure in newly independent Burma, heading up social planning and policy bodies, and briefly acting as an MP, before being appointed the country's ambassador to India in 1960. Suu Kyi finished her schooling in New Delhi, then moved to the UK in 1964 to study at Oxford University. It was in London at the home of Lord Gore Booth, a former ambassador to Burma, and his wife that Suu Kyi met history student Michael Aris.

Beautiful Love Story

Luc Bresson, director of the biopic *The Lady*, calls Suu Kyi and Aris's courtship and marriage 'probably the most beautiful love story I've heard since Romeo and Juliet.' When Aris went to Bhutan in the late '60s to work as a tutor to the royal family and continue his research, Suu Kyi was in New York, working at the UN; they corresponded by post. After their marriage on 1 January 1972 in London, Suu Kyi joined him in Bhutan. Five years later they were back in Oxford, Aris teaching at the university, Suu Kyi a mother to two boys – Alexander and Kim.

In the essay she contributed to *Freedom from Fear*, her friend Anna Pasternak Slater remembers the future leader of Burma's democracy movement from that period as a thrifty housewife, 'laboriously pedallling back from town, laden down with sagging plastic bags and panniers heavy with cheap fruit and vegetables' or 'running up elegant cut-price clothes' on her sewing machine. Historian and author Thant Myint-U also recalls dropping by the Aris' home in 1984: 'Michael sat contentedly and quietly smoking his pipe, their kids playing in the room nearby' while Suu Kyi gave him 'polite and somewhat schoolmarmish' advice on his educational options. 'In later years', he writes, 'I felt I had a sense of the happy life both she and Michael had given up.'

Pasternak Slater, like many others since, recognised Suu Kyi's 'courage, determination and abiding moral strength' – qualities that were already in evidence in some of the 187 letters Suu Kyi wrote to Aris in the eight months before their marriage. In one she asks '...that should my people need me, you would help me do my duty by them.' That moment came in March 1988. Suu Kyi's mother had suffered a stroke.

AUNG SAN SUU KYI TIMELINE

19 June 1945
A baby girl is born in Yangon and named after her father (Aung San), paternal grandmother (Suu) and mother (Khin Kyi); the name means 'a bright collection of strange victories'.

1960
Daw Khin Kyi is appointed Burma's ambassador to India. Suu Kyi accompanies her mother to New Delhi, where she continues her schooling.

1964
Suu Kyi moves to the UK to study at Oxford University. Meets future husband, Tibetan scholar Michael Aris, at London home of her 'British parents', Lord Gore Booth and his wife.

1967
Graduates with a third-class degree in politics, philosophy and economics. Daw Khin Kyi retires to Yangon.

1969–71
Moves to New York for postgraduate studies, but ends up working for the UN alongside family friend and 'emergency aunt' Ma Than E and Secretary-General U Thant.

1972
Marries Aris and joins him in Bhutan, where he is tutoring the royal family. Suu Kyi works as research officer in Bhutan's Royal Ministry of Foreign Affairs.

1973–77
The couple return to the UK for the birth of their first son, Alexander. They take up residence in Oxford, where their second son, Kim, is born in 1977.

Return to Burma

Suu Kyi immediately packed her bags to return to Yangon, and Aris had 'a premonition that our lives would change would for ever'.

Meanwhile there was growing turmoil in Burma as students and others took to the streets calling for a change of government. Back in Yangon, where injured protestors were brought to the same hospital her mother was in, it was something Suu Kyi could not ignore, especially when political activists flocked to her mother's home on Inya Lake to seek her support.

It was at this point, as the street demonstrations continued to mount, that Suu Kyi decided to join the movement for democracy. Her speech at Shwedagon Paya on 26 August 1988, with her husband and sons by her side, electrified the estimated crowd of half a million, and sent ripples of excitement and hope throughout the country. Elegantly attired, the trademark flowers in her hair, the 43-year-old Suu Kyi brought a hitherto-unseen sophistication to Myanmar politics as she launched what she called 'the second struggle for national independence'.

The brutal reaction of the military brought the protests to an end a month later.

According to local custom, Aung San Suu Kyi's name, like that of all Burmese, should be spelled out in full. It's also commonly preceded by the honorific title Daw. We follow the international convention of shortening her name to Suu Kyi.

Braving the Generals

Suu Kyi, however, was just getting started, and in September 1988 she joined several former generals and senior army officers (including Tin Oo, army chief of staff in the 1970s, who had been jailed for his role in an abortive coup in 1975) to form the NLD. As the party's general secretary, she travelled around the country attending rallies.

Her assistant at the time, Win Htein, a former army captain, recalls how she had 'a real ability to connect to the people', while a diplomat quoted in the *New York Times* said her very name was 'magic' among the public. In April 1989, while campaigning in the town of Danubyu, she came up against soldiers who threatened to shoot her and her supporters; with great courage she continued to move forward and calmly asked that they be allowed to pass. Only at the last minute did a senior officer step in and order the men to lower their guns (it's a scene reimagined in the movie *Beyond Rangoon*).

In July 1989 Aung San Suu Kyi, who by now had become the NLD's primary spokesperson, was placed under house arrest for publicly expressing doubt about the junta's intentions of handing over power to a civilian government, and for her plans to lead a march in Yangon to celebrate Martyr's Day. Her status as Aung San's daughter saved her from the fate of many other NLD members, who were imprisoned in the country's notorious jails.

Suu Kyi's interviews in 1995 and 1996 with journalist and former Buddhist monk Alan Clements, described in *The Voice of Hope* (www.world dharma.com/ wd/products/ voicehope.html), often intermingle politics and Buddhism.

With her husband and sons by her side, Suu Kyi went on a hunger strike for 12 days to gain an assurance that her jailed supporters would not be tortured. None of this stopped the NLD from decisively winning the general election of May 1990.

A Prisoner of Conscience

Aris left Yangon with their sons on 2 September 1989. Suu Kyi would note see either Alexander or Kim for over two and a half years. Her husband was allowed to spend one more fortnight with her over Christmas in 1989, a time he described as 'among the happiest memories of our many years of marriage'.

At any moment during her years of arrest, Suu Kyi knew that the authorities would let her walk free to board a flight to return to her family in the UK. But once she left Burma she knew she would never be allowed to return, and she would not accept permanent exile. It was a sacrifice in which her family supported her, acting as her proxies to accept from the European Parliament in January 1991 the Sakharov Prize for Freedom of Thought, and the Nobel Peace Prize in October of the same year.

As the international honours stacked up (the Simón Bolivar Prize from Unesco in June 1992; the Jawaharlal Nehru Award for International Understanding in May 1995), Suu Kyi maintained her strength and spirits by meditating, reading (in *Letters from Burma* she writes how she loves nothing more than relaxing over a detective story), exercising, practising piano, and listening to news on the radio. From May 1992 until January 1995 she was also permitted regular visits from her husband and sons.

Five Years of Freedom

Much to the joy of her supporters at home and abroad, as well as her family, the government released Suu Kyi from house arrest in July 1995. She was allowed to travel outside Yangon with permission, which was rarely granted. During her subsequent five years of freedom, she would test the authorities several times with varying degrees of success.

The last time she would see her husband was in January 1996. A year later he was diagnosed with prostate cancer, which would prove to be terminal. Despite appeals from the likes of Pope John Paul II and UN Secretary General Kofi Annan, the generals refused to allow Aris a visa to visit his wife, saying that Suu Kyi was free to leave the country to tend to him. Aris died in an Oxford hospital on 27 March 1999, his 53rd birthday; over the telephone he had insisted Suu Kyi remain in Burma where many political prisoners and their families also relied on her support.

The following decade was marked by more extended periods of house arrest punctuated by shorter spells of freedom. A couple of intercessions by UN special envoys resulted in talks with military leaders and the release of hundreds of political prisoners, but no real progress on the political front – nor release for the woman who had become the world's most famous prisoner of conscience.

Run-Up to Elections & Release

On 22 September 2007, at the height of the failed 'Saffron Revolution', the barricades briefly came down along University Ave, allowing the protestors to pass Aung San Suu Kyi's house. In a powerful scene, later recounted by eyewitnesses and captured on mobile-phone footage, the jailed NLD leader was briefly glimpsed at the gate of her compound, tears in her eyes, silently accepting the blessing of the monks.

A couple of meetings with a UN envoy, Ibrahim Gambari, and members of the military later that year failed to result in Suu Kyi's release. Her house arrest was extended by a year in 2008 and then by a further 18 months in August 2009 following her encounter with John Yettaw (see p346).

1985–87
At Kyoto University Suu Kyi researches her father's time in Japan; she also registers at London's School of Oriental and African Studies for a doctorate in Burmese literature.

1988
Returns to Yangon in March to care for her mother, who has suffered a stroke; in September becomes secretary-general of National League for Democracy (NLD).

1989
At her mother's funeral in January she swears to serve the people of Burma until her death. Stands for election in February; placed under house arrest in July.

1991
Wins Nobel Peace Prize; sons accept it on her behalf. Pledges she will use $1.3 million prize money to establish health and education trust for Burmese people.

1995
Released from house arrest, resumes campaigning for the NLD, but her movements are restricted. At year's end she sees Aris for what will be the final time.

1996
In November her motorcade is attacked in Yangon, the windows of the car she is travelling in are smashed by a mob; despite presence of security forces no one is arrested.

1999
Suffering terminal prostate cancer, Aris is refused entry to Burma and dies in the UK. After his funeral, sons Kim and Alexander are allowed to visit their mother briefly.

Six days after the 2010 election, the regime finally saw fit to release her, announcing in the *New Light of Myanmar* that she had been pardoned for 'good conduct'. Ten days later she was reunited with her son Kim, who brought her a puppy as a present. Kim returned again in July of 2011 to accompany his mother on a trip to Bagan, her first outside of Yangon since 2003.

Reconciliation & Election

The Daw Aung San Suu Kyi Pages (www. dassk.org) gathers together links to many online features about the Lady and Myanmar, including videos.

Emerging from house arrest, Suu Kyi addressed a jubilant crowd. 'I'm going to work for national reconciliation. That is a very important thing', she said, adding, 'There is nobody I cannot talk to. I am prepared to talk with anyone. I have no personal grudge toward anybody.'

Initially, Suu Kyi's offer fell on deaf ears. However, in August 2011 the regime began to take a more conciliatory approach. Suu Kyi had talks with President Thein Sein and the government began to release political prisoners and legalised trade unions. In November 2011 the NLD announced its intention to re-register as a political party so it could contest the by-elections of April 2012 – Suu Kyi would be one of 45 NLD candidates.

In the run-up to the poll, Suu Kyi greeted a steady stream of international dignitaries to Yangon, including US Secretary of State Hillary Clinton in December 2011 and UK Foreign Minister William Hague in January 2012. She also toured the country campaigning for the NLD, battling exhaustion and ill health. The effort was rewarded by an almost clean sweep in the April election for the NLD, giving the opposition party an 8% block in the national parliament.

However, before they could take their seats, Suu Kyi and her NLD colleagues were faced with a dilemma: whether to swear an oath to 'safeguard' the very constitution they had been campaigning against. On 2 May political pragmatism won out as all the NLD MPs made the oath to become lawmakers.

International Accolades & the Future

If any further sign was needed of how much the mood had changed in Myanmar, the woman who for 24 years refused to leave the country for fear she would not be allowed to return and packed her bags for a series of high-profile international visits. First off, in May, was Bangkok, to speak at the World Economic Forum, followed by a mini European tour in June. This included visits to Oslo to accept her Nobel

THE SWIMMER

On 3 May 2009 John Yettaw, a 53-year-old Vietnam vet, retired bus driver and Mormon, strapped on homemade flippers and paddled his way across Inya Lake to the democracy leader's home. Yettaw had attempted a meeting the year before with Suu Kyi, but had been blocked that time by her two housekeepers. This time, however, Suu Kyi took pity on the exhausted American and allowed him to stay, even though she knew such a visit violated the terms of her house arrest.

Speaking to a reporter for the *New Yorker* in 2010, she said 'I felt I could not hand over anybody to be arrested by the authorities when so many of our people had been arrested and not been given a fair hearing.' When he left two days later, Yettaw was fished out of the lake by government agents. Following a trial, he was sentenced to seven years in prison, only to be released a few days later to return to the US. Aung San Suu Kyi and her two housekeepers, meanwhile, were sentenced to three years of hard labour, commuted to 18 months of house arrest – sufficient to keep the NLD leader out of the way during the 2010 elections.

Peace Prize, 21 years after winning it; her old home Oxford, to accept an honourary degree; and to London for a historic address to both Houses of Parliament. At every stop she was treated as if she was the visiting head of state.

It's not all been plain sailing. Suu Kyi's refusal to speak up for the persecuted Rohingyas has drawn criticism, the *Economist* noting how Suu Kyi's halo had slipped in the eyes of human rights advocates over the issue. She has made it plain that her goal is the presidency of Myanmar in 2015, but to achieve this ambition will require reform of the current constitution which, in turn, could mean sophisticated political dancing with the military – again, something unpalatable to many of her supporters.

Freed from captivity, Suu Kyi faces, in the words of Oxford academic Timothy Garton Ash, 'a life sentence in politics' filled inevitably with 'compromises and disappointments' as much as future triumphs.

2000

Begins second period of house arrest in September; a month later starts secret talks with the junta, facilitated by UN special envoy Rizali Ismail.

2002

Released in May; returns to campaigning around Yangon and in late June makes a triumphant visit to Mandalay, her first trip to Myanmar's second-largest city since 1989.

2003

In May, while touring northern Myanmar, Suu Kyi and 250 NLD members are attacked by a pro-junta mob; at least 70 people are killed. Another period of house arrest follows.

2007

In September she makes a fleeting appearance, greeting protesting monks at her gate. In October a meeting with UN envoy Ibrahim Gambari is followed by talks with NLD and regime reps.

2011

Freed from house arrest in November 2010, Suu Kyi commences talks with the government during 2011 leading to the release of political prisoners and recognition of the NLD.

2012

In April Suu Kyi is elected to the the lower house of the Burmese parliament, representing the constituency of Kawhmu. In June she accepts her Nobel Peace Prize in Oslo.

Government & Human Rights

'I would not say that it is a democracy yet,' said Tomás Ojea Quintana, the UN Special Rapporteur on human rights in Myanmar in an interview in October 2013, 'but it is a civilian government that is progressively gaining respect.' Here we look at who is part of that government; what separates it from the military dictatorship in charge for the previous 50 years; and how, if at all, it is tackling the country's poor record on human rights.

David Steinberg's *Burma/Myanmar: What Everyone Needs to Know* sheds light on many aspects of the country's complex situation via a series of concise and understandable Q&As on history and culture.

Political Scene

They may have been, in the UN's words, 'deeply flawed', but there's no arguing that the 2010 elections changed the political landscape in Myanmar. After decades of military dictatorship, there is now a quasi-civilian reform-minded government and many new political parties, including ones which represent ethnic minorities. By-elections in 2012 also saw participation by the National League for Democracy (NLD), which won 43 of 44 parliamentary seats it contested, confirming it as the country's main opposition force.

The USDP & Military

Over the last 50 years, Myanmar's rulers (aka the military) have adopted a variety of guises. They started out as the Burma Socialist Programme Party (BSPP) in 1962, which morphed into the State Law and Order Restoration Council (Slorc) in 1988, which was then renamed the State Peace and Development Council (SPDC) in 1997. In the run-up to the 2010 election many in the upper echelons of the military, including President Thein Sein, resigned their posts to become candidates for the military-backed Union Solidarity and Development Party (USDP), which, to nobody's surprise, was the victor at the polls.

The 2010 election resulted in over 80% of MPs coming from the military or pro-military parties; out of 440 seats in the lower house of parliament the USDP hold 213 and the military have a block of 110. No wonder there was much skepticism about whether the new government would be anything different from the old. However, as events have partly demonstrated, it has been surprisingly far from business as usual in Myanmar in recent years. Perhaps the most unexpected evolution has been that of Thein Sein, described by *Time* as 'Burma's own Gorbachev', for spearheading a path of economic and political reform that has included reconciliation with the NLD.

The 2008 constitution contains provisions to stop attempts to prosecute former general Than Shwe and other top military brass for crimes committed under their watch.

Not everyone has been convinced. 'If international law was applied to Burma, then Thein Sein could be standing trial at the International Criminal Court in the Hague,' said Mark Farmaner, Director of Burma Campaign UK, following the president's visit to the UK in July 2013. The campaigning group has produced a report detailing the president's past involvement in human rights abuses in Myanmar.

Thein Sein, who suffers from poor health, has ruled out standing for president again in 2015. His USDP colleague Shwe Mann, speaker of the lower house of parliament and previously number three in the military junta hierarchy, has declared his intentions to run for the post. It was also Shwe Mann who revealed at a press conference in October 2013 that former military chief Than Shwe was 'worried about things that shouldn't happen in today's Burmese politics.'

Conventional wisdom in Myanmar still has it that military hardliners such as Than Shwe continue to influence government from behind the scenes; regardless of whether this is true or not, there is a very open alliance of USDP, serving military and former government cronies, who have little to no interest in seeing reform go any further in Myanmar.

National League for Democracy

Founded on 27 September 1988, the National League for Democracy (www.nldburma.org) is the best known of Myanmar's pro-democracy organisations, thanks to its leader Aung San Suu Kyi. It won the 1990 election in a landslide victory that the ruling junta ignored; many of its members were subsequently thrown into prison; others went into self-imposed exile.

Unhappy with the revised constitution pushed through by the government in 2008, the NLD called for a boycott of the October 2010 elections, in turn causing the military junta to declare the party illegal. This decision caused a division within the NLD that resulted in senior members of the organisation, Dr Than Nyein and Khin Maung Swe, leaving to form the National Democratic Force (NDF), a party that did contest the 2010 poll. Since 2010 the NDF has splintered with some members rejoining the NLD.

In November 2011 the NLD decided to register as a political party so it could contest the 2012 elections. This move was approved by the election commission and in April 2012 the party went on to secure a landslide victory at the by-election, including securing a seat for Aung San Suu Kyi. Out of 45 contested seats, the NLD only lost out on two: one in eastern Shan State to the locally strong Shan Nationalities Democratic Party, and one to the USDP in northwest Sagaing Division where the NLD candidate had been disqualified.

Guy Delisle's *Burma Chronicles* is a graphic account of the year that the Canadian cartoonist spent in Myanmar with his wife, an administrator for Medecins Sans Frontières (MSF). It's both amusing and horrifying, covering topics ranging from electricity outages to the heroin shooting galleries in Chinese-owned jade-mining towns.

2014 CENSUS

'Facts are negotiated more than they are observed in Myanmar', writes David Steinberg in *Burma/Myanmar: What Everyone Needs to Know*. 'Statistics are often imprecise or manipulated, caused by internal political considerations or insufficient data, and biased externally by a lack of access to materials.' Under such circumstances, economic policy becomes pretty much guesswork.

Although recent government reforms are beginning to rectify this situation, even a basic figure such as Myanmar's population has long been elusive. The Chinese news agency Xinhua quotes the government's 2009 official figure of 59.12 million, the CIA World Factbook says 55.17 million and the Asian Development Bank has it at 61.12 million. Sean Turnell, an expert on Myanmar's economy at Sydney's Macquarie University, isn't surprised by this spread. 'The last full census was back in 1913,' he says.

In March 2014 a national census was carried out under the auspices of the United Nations Fund for Population Activities (myanmar.unfpa.org). In a country with over 135 ethnic groups, at least 19 major languages and areas where armed conflicts could still be in progress, undertaking such a survey is no simple exercise. At the time of writing, the census results were expected to be ready by August 2014.

In this book, where we give population figures, they should only be taken as estimates that try to gauge the relative size of different towns and cities.

Including MPs rejoining the party post the 2010 election, the NLD currently have 38 seats in the lower house of parliament and four in the upper house, making them the largest elected opposition force in Myanmar at the national level.

Other Political Parties & Opposition Groups

After the NLD, the next largest opposition party in parliament is the Shan Nationalities Democratic Party with 22 seats across both houses. This ethnic minority party is stronger at the local level, with 31 seats out of 143 in the Shan State parliament. The same pattern is repeated with the respective ethnic parties in Chin, Kayin and Rakhine state parliaments.

Mostly representing reactionary, old-guard interests, the National Unity Party, with 17 seats in parliament's combined houses, is next in line, followed by the Rakhaing Nationalities Development Party (RNDP) with 14 seats, and the NDF who, following resignations, have dropped to eight elected members.

Other parties with single-figure representation in the national parliament include the All Mon Region Democracy Party (AMRDP), Chin National Party and Chin Progress Party (CPP), the Pa-O National Organisation and the Wa Democratic Party.

In addition to the main parties, there are numerous other ethnic parties who either didn't win seats, chose not to contest the 2010 election, or are unregistered opposition groups. All of this is an indication of how complicated and potentially divisive ethnic politics is in Myanmar.

What's Changed?

The Economy

Myanmar's economy remains profoundly dysfunctional and underperforming. The country is rich in natural resources – including gas, oil, teak, and precious metals and gems – yet its people are the poorest in Southeast Asia, most struggling to get by on an income of less than $2 a day.

Myanmar continues to be the only country in Southeast Asia to spend more on the military than health and education combined – according to a Unicef report in 2012–13 about 29% of the country's $7.13 billion budget went to the defense forces, compared to 5.7% for health care, 11% for education and 0.3% for social welfare. The military's favourite method of financing such budgets was to print money, says Sean Turnell, an expert on Myanmar's economy at Sydney's Macquarie University, hence the galloping inflation of the past.

Inflation is currently running at around 7% (over three times the rate in Thailand), and the country had a budget deficit of K3526 billion in 2012, or around 7.7% of GDP. On the bright side the World Bank projected economic growth for the country in 2013–14 at 6.8%. The economy is also benefiting from the dropping of sanctions, the floating of the kyat and the passing in November 2012 of a new foreign investment law. Such reforms, according to Turnell, 'represent a seminal break from Burma's past.'

However, the economist notes that 'the real challenge is to make this a genuine transformation of the capabilities and freedoms enjoyed by the Burmese people.' He also points to the stultifying effect of having dominant parts of the economy still owned by cronies who 'have already demonstrated that they are a force in resisting reform.'

As previously noted, Myanmar is not short on economic assets. A report by the Harvard Ash Centre in 2013 on Burma's economy notes that 'if the reasonable tax proceeds from all natural resources

The Transnational Institute (www.tni.org) has many scholarly articles and reports about the political situation and ethnic conflict in Myanmar.

Nowhere to Be Home, edited by Maggie Lemere and Zoë West, presents 22 oral histories of Myanmar citizens gathered from those living in the country and those in exile. The stories are often heartbreaking, and the book includes very useful appendices on current affairs, history and politics.

including natural gas, jade, copper and hydroelectricity were added to gold, gems, timber and other minerals, there could be billions of dollars a year more for investments than there are now.' There is much work still ahead before Myanmar fully reaps the economic dividends of increased political stability.

Bribery & Corruption

Bribery is part of nearly *all* business in Myanmar. The owners of one private guesthouse owner told us they have to bribe their tax official. 'We pay the tax man 25% of the taxes we would have paid. He's a very rich man.' In a country where providing 'tea money' or 'gifts' to facilitate goods and services is pretty much par for the course, it's no surprise that Myanmar consistently ranks close to the bottom of Transparency International's Corruption Perception Index.

The Anti Corruption Resource Centre (www.u4.no) goes further in its assessment of the situation: 'the scale of [Myanmar's] informal and illicit economy suggests strong links between the ruling elite and organised crime activities, such as drugs and human trafficking, and illegal logging.'

President Thein Sein has launched a high-profile anti-corruption campaign, publicly acknowledging that governance falls far below international standards; the first major investigation in January 2013 by the Home Ministry and auditor general covered about 50 individuals and civil servants connected to the telecommunications ministry. Maplecroft, a UK-based research and strategic forecasting company, has also issued a report citing Myanmar Post and Telecommunications (MPT) as 'one of the most corrupt institutions in Myanmar.'

Aiming to make a change to this culture is the Yangon-based Myanmar Centre for Responsible Business (www.myanmar-responsiblebusiness.org). A joint initiative of the Institute for Human Rights and Business (IHRB) and the Danish Institute for Human Rights (DIHR), the centre was set up in 2013 and has the promotion of human rights across business in Myanmar as one of its core values. Impact assessments on specific industry sectors are being prepared including oil and gas, tourism, information and communications technologies (ICT), and agriculture.

Around 70% of Myanmar's population lives in rural areas and relies on farming for its livelihood. A third of the population lives below the poverty line.

MYANMAR'S SHADY GEM BUSINESS

Myanmar generates considerable income from the mining of precious stones – including rubies, jade and sapphire – and metals such as gold and silver. There is controversy surrounding this mining, however, with reports of forced labour and dangerous working practices.

A Reuters report in September 2013 from Hpakant, ground zero for Myanmar's billion-dollar jade industry, found 'an anarchic region...where Chinese traders rub shoulders with heroin-fuelled' prospectors working in horrific conditions.

The US ban on imports of Myanmar jade and rubies remains in place because of concerns that their mining most benefits the military and its cronies and fuels corruption and human rights abuses in ethnic minority regions that have endured armed conflict for decades.

Such sanctions have little impact on the industry, according to one Bangkok-based gem supplier interviewed by the *Wall Street Journal*, who says 'We don't need Americans. There's falling supply and the real buyers are in China. Besides, the generals are not hurt by the sanctions anyway. It mostly hurts small traders.'

UNIONS

Media Censorship

In August 2012 the government abolished pre-publication censorship of the country's media – something that had been routine since the military takeover in 1962. Even though many laws still exist under which journalists can be punished for writing material which angers or offends the government, this move has radically changed the media landscape. Previously exiled media organisations including the Democratic Voice of Burma (www.dvb.no), the *Irrawaddy* (www.irrawaddy.org) and Mizzima (www.mizzima.com) have all established bureaus back in Myanmar – one of the clearest indications of an improved reporting environment.

It's not a clear-cut improvement though. In June 2013 the government banned an edition of *Time* magazine that carried a feature on the radical monk Ashin Wirathu and the 969 movement. The amnesty given to jailed reporters comes with conditions that many have found difficult or impossible to reconcile with their profession. Reporters at DVB staged a strike in 2012 to protest against senior editors' decision to hold a training session with MRTV, the government's mouthpiece broadcaster. One of DVB's board members, Myanmar expert and journalist Bertil Lintner, resigned over the affair.

And even though it has reached its best ever position, in 2013 Myanmar still ranked 151 out of 179 nations on Reporters Without Borders' index on media censorship. Reporters Without Borders also joined the chorus of critics of the new Printing and Publishing Enterprises law as in its present form it fails to 'meet international standards on protection of the media.'

Print

The dissolution of the censorship board meant that private daily newspapers could be published for the first time since the early 1960s. Thirty-one companies gained licences to print daily newspapers; not all of them survived the year – as of October 2013, the *Irrawaddy* reported that daily newspapers were down to 10.

Apart from the well-established English-language weekly the *Myanmar Times*, which runs bold news items, there's the new English-language *Myanma Freedom Daily*. Even the notorious propaganda sheet *New Light of Myanmar* is having to move with the times; it's been partially privatised and its staff were sent to Tokyo to be trained by Kyodo News in improved news standards ahead of the relaunch of the paper at the end of 2013.

TV & Radio

Free-to-air TV channels in Myanmar include MRTV, Myawady TV and Myanmar International, but many locals prefer to get their news from overseas radio broadcasts by the BBC's World Service, VOA (Voice of America) and RFA (www.rfa.org) or from satellite-TV channels such as BBC World, CNN and DVB.

Internet

Relaxation in press censorship has also had a dramatic impact on access to the internet. Previously blocked international and exile media news sites are now freely available, as is access to blogs.

In 2012 Nay Phone Latt, recipient of the PEN/Barbara Goldsmith Freedom to Write award, was released from jail after spending four years behind bars for blogging. He has since founded the independent Myanmar Bloggers Society and the Myanmar ICT for Development Organization

---

For further information on Myanmar's economy read the reports compiled by the Harvard Ash Centre (http://www.ash. harvard.edu/ash/ Home/Programs/ Institute-for-Asia/Myanmar-Program).

In 2011 unions became legal for the first time since 1962. Employers also now have to comply with agreements made before a conciliation body. But with penalties for non-compliance being a maximum fine of $100 or less than a year in jail, critics claim the law has no teeth.

(MIDO), which disseminates information about the internet and holds training sessions on how to blog.

Such education is necessary if internet liberalisation is to have any real and lasting impact in Myanmar. Less than 0.5% of Myanmar's population currently has access to the internet and, outside of Yangon, very few people can read English.

With the launch of two new mobile phone networks imminent, the spread of internet access is set to expand across Myanmar. The new telecommunications law that has enabled this development also contains provisions for prison sentences of seven to 15 years for sending over the internet materials deemed by officials as sensitive or a threat to security. This has raised concerns among journalists, bloggers and rights activists.

The Committee to Protect Journalists has also reported that local journalists have told them that they work under the assumption that the government continues to monitor their online activities.

Land Confiscation

Democracy and human rights groups concerned with Myanmar point to land confiscation as one of the biggest problems the country needs to tackle. As Myanmar's economy has opened up, there has been an increase in grabs of resource-rich land by the military, corrupt officials and business cronies, particularly in border areas where ethnic communities report being dispossessed by a variety of industrial development projects.

Amnesty International says that two new laws relating to land ownership enacted in 2012 'fail to provide adequate protection for farmers from having their land requisitioned by the authorities'. Among the cases that it has reported on recently are those of the coconut farmers near the beach resort of Ngwe Saung seeing their plantations destroyed as new facilities were built in the lead up to SEA Games in November 2013, and the land grabs associated with the expansion of the Letpadaung copper mine in Monywa township. In March 2013 the Karen Human Rights Group (www.khrg.org) published a report detailing land conflicts in eastern Myanmar.

In September 2013 the government convened the Land Utilisation Management Central Committee to discuss the 745 complaints it had received about land confiscation and had promised to solve the issues before the end of its term of office in 2015 as well as prevent land disputes in the future.

Fiery Dragons: Banks, Moneylenders and Microfinance in Burma by Sean Turnell explains how Myanmar went from one of the richest countries in Southeast Asia to one of its poorest within the space of a century.

POLITICAL PRISONERS

The last time we researched this guide in 2011 it was estimated there were more than 2000 political prisoners in Myanmar. Following a succession of amnesties and pardons, the government claims that they have met President Thein Sein's pledge that all prisoners of conscience in Myanmar would be released by the end of 2013.

However, the Assistance Association for Political Prisoners (www.aappb.org), which keeps a running tally of the detainees, believes as of January 2014 around 33 political prisoners remain in Myanmar's jails with around another 136 facing charges linked to their political activities. The discrepancies are because of continued detentions of political activists by the government, the lack of transparency in Myanmar's prison and judicial system, and disagreements between government and opposition groups on who counts as a political prisoner.

Pro-democracy groups point out that the much-hailed 'right to protest' law introduced in 2012 is actually being used to arrest political activists as it only grants the right to protest under strict conditions and with local authorities' permission. Under the new law unauthorised gatherings of just two people are illegal.

Ethnic Conflicts

Potentially the most significant transformation within grasp of the current government is the end to what has been described as the longest-running war in modern history. Fighting between different ethnic groups within Myanmar began in 1948 after the nation's independence. 'It is not one war,' says historian Thant Myint-U, 'but a palimpsest of conflicts featuring a bewildering array of combatants, from Chinese-backed communist insurgents and ethnic minority armies battling for self-determination to opium warlords and democratic revolutionaries.'

Clashes haven't entirely stopped but, remarkably, as we go to press, Myanmar is as close as it has ever been to a meaningful ceasefire, including setting up joint monitoring mechanisms, agreed codes of conduct and freedom of movement across front lines. At a meeting in November 2013 facilitated by the government-backed Myanmar Peace Centre, representatives of political parties and exiled ethnic rebel groups met for the first time to build trust ahead of further peace discussions.

The stakes are high. Many of the most egregious human rights abuses levelled at Myanmar, including massive displacement of people, rape, the use of forced labour and child soldiers and torture, are inextricable from the conflicts between ethnic groups and the army. At the same time there are entrenched interests in maintaining the status quo on both sides, not least because of the billion-dollar black economy fuelled by smuggling and drug running in the war-torn areas.

Religious Conflicts

Since 2011, battles between religious groups in Myanmar have flared up, as witnessed particularly in Rakhine State where the government's non-recognition of the Muslim Rohingya minority is the flash point (see p335).

Relations between the religions hasn't been helped by the fact that within government Buddhists tend to attain higher rank more easily than non-Buddhists. There has also been a program of building pagodas in border regions, including the Christian area of Kachin State bordering China and the Muslim areas of Rakhine State bordering Bangladesh.

In its annual report for 2013, the US Commission on International Religious Freedoms, a bi-partisan advisory board appointed by the US president and congress, concluded that the reforms in Myanmar had 'yet to significantly improve the situation for freedom of religion and belief.'

A view widely held within Myanmar is that some of these religious conflicts have been stoked, if not instigated, by the security forces with the aim of slowing down or stalling the process of reform. According to country experts such as Sean Turnell, it's 'a scenario that can hardly be ruled out.'

Where China Meets India – Burma and the New Crossroads of Asia by Thant Myint-U is about the historic and current connections between the three countries.

Human Rights Updates

Amnesty International (www.amnesty.org)

Burma Campaign UK (www.burma campaign.org.uk)

Network Myanmar (www.network myanmar.org)

US Campaign For Burma (http:// uscampaign forburma.word press.com)

Eating in Myanmar (Burma)

Burmese food suffers from a bad rap – a rather unjustified bad rap in our opinion. While it can be oily, and lacks the diversity of that of neighbouring Thailand, with a bit of pointing in the right direction and some background knowledge we're confident you'll return from Myanmar having savoured some truly tasty and memorable meals.

A Burmese Meal

T'ămìn (rice), also written as *htamin,* is the indisputable core of any Burmese meal. Second in importance, and providing the grains with some flavour, are *hìn,* Burmese-style curries. Those who've been burned by the spiciness of Thai food will be pleased to learn that Burmese curries are probably the mildest in Asia. The downside is that Burmese curries are often oily, largely due to a cooking process that sees them cooked until the oil separates from all other ingredients and rises to the top. The Burmese term for this cooking method is *s'i pyan* (oil returns), and the process ensures that the rather harsh curry paste ingredients – typically chilli, turmeric, tomatoes, ginger, garlic, onions and shrimp paste – have properly amalgamated and have become milder. Some restaurants also add extra oil to maintain the correct top layer, as the fat also preserves the underlying food from contamination by insects and airborne bacteria while the curries sit in open, unheated pots for hours at a time.

Food is so enjoyed in Myanmar that standard greetings to friends and foreigners include *sà pyi bi la?* (have you eaten your lunch yet?) and *ba hin ne sà le?* (what curry did you eat?).

Accompanying the curries is a unique repertoire of side dishes that blend Burmese, Mon, Indian and Chinese influences, predominantly plant- and seafood-based ingredients, and overwhelmingly savoury, salty and sometimes tart flavours. Indeed, one of the pleasures of eating an authentic Burmese meal is the sheer variety of things to eat at a single setting. Upon arriving at any *Myanma sà thauq sain* (Burmese restaurant), and after having chosen a curry, a succession of sides will follow. One of these is invariably soup, either an Indian-influenced *peh·hìn·ye* (lentil soup, or dhal), studded with chunks of vegetables, or a tart, leaf-based broth. A tray of fresh and par-boiled vegetables, fruits and herbs is another obligatory side dish; they're eaten with various dips, ranging from *ngăpí ye* (a watery, fishy dip) to *balachaung* (a dry, pungent combination of chillies, garlic and dried shrimp fried in oil). Additional vegetable-based salads or stir-frys, unlimited green tea and a dessert of pickled tea leaves and chunks of jaggery (palm sugar) are also usually included.

Burmese Specialities

One of the culinary highlights of Burmese food is undoubtedly *ăthouq* – light, tart and spicy salads made with vegetables, herbs, fruit or meat tossed with lime juice, onions, peanuts, roasted chickpea powder or chillies. Among the most exquisite are *maji·yweq thouq,* made with tender young tamarind leaves, and *shauq·thi dhouq,* made with a type

DOS & DON'TS

➡ A fork is held in the left hand and used as a probe to push food onto the spoon; you eat from the spoon.

➡ Locals tend to focus on the flavours, not table talk, during meals.

➡ If you're asked to join someone at a restaurant, they will expect to pay for the meal. Expect to do likewise if you invite a local out for a meal.

of lemon-like citrus fruit. In fact, the Burmese will make just about anything into a salad, as *t'ămìn dhouq,* a savoury salad made with rice, and *nan·gyi dhouq,* a salad made with thick rice noodles, prove.

A popular finish to Burmese meals, and possibly the most infamous Burmese dish of all, is *leq·p'eq* (often spelled *laphet*), fermented green tea leaves mixed with a combination of sesame seeds, fried peas, fried garlic, peanuts and other crunchy ingredients. A popular variant of the dish is *leq·p'eq thouq,* in which the fermented tea and nuts are combined with slices of tomato and cabbage and a squeeze of lime. The salad is a popular snack in Myanmar, and the caffeine boost supplied by the tea leaves makes the dish a favourite of students who need to stay up late studying.

Regional & Ethnic Variations

Burmese cuisine can be broadly broken down into dishes found in 'lower Myanmar' (roughly Yangon and the delta), with more fish pastes and sour foods; and 'upper Myanmar' (centred at Mandalay), with more sesame, nuts and beans used in dishes.

In Mandalay and around Inle Lake, it is fairly easy to find Shan cuisine, which is relatively similar to northern Thai cuisine. Rice plays an important role in Shan cuisine, and in addition to Shan-style rice noodles, *ngà t'ămìn jin* (rice kneaded with turmeric oil and topped with fish) is worth seeking out.

Mon cuisine, most readily available in towns stretching from Bago to Mawlamyine, is very similar to Burmese food, with a greater emphasis on curry selections. While a Burmese restaurant might offer a choice of four or five curries, a Mon restaurant will have as many as a dozen, all lined up in curry pots to be examined. Mon curries are also more likely to contain chillies than those of other cuisines.

Rakhine food is often likened to Thai food for its spiciness. *Ngăyouq·thì jiq,* a 'dip' of grilled chillies mashed with lime and shrimp paste, is an obligatory side that embodies this, and sour soups and seafood-based curries are also constants. The region's signature noodle dish is *móun·dì,* thin rice noodles served in a peppery fish-based broth, often with a side of a spicy chilli paste.

In towns large and small throughout Myanmar you'll find plenty of Chinese restaurants, many of which do a distinctly Burmese (ie oily) take on Chinese standards. Despite being the most ubiquitous type of dining in Myanmar (upcountry this is often the only kind of restaurant you'll find), it's probably the least interesting.

Indian restaurants are also common, although much more so in the big cities than elsewhere. Most are run by Muslim Indians, a few by Hindus. Excellent chicken *dan·bauq* (biryani), as well as all-you-can-eat vegetarian *thali* served on a banana leaf, can be found in Yangon and Mandalay.

CUISINE

One of the seminal works on Myanmar cuisine is *Cook and Entertain the Burmese Way,* by Mi Mi Khaing, available in Yangon bookshops.

Sweets

The typical Burmese dessert is often little more than a pinch of pickled tea leaves or a lump of palm sugar (jaggery). More substantial sweet dishes, generally referred to as *móun* (sometimes written *moun* or *mont*), are regarded as snacks in Myanmar, and are often taken with equally sweet tea in the morning or afternoon.

Prime ingredients for Burmese sweets include grated coconut, coconut milk, rice flour (from white rice or sticky rice), cooked sticky rice, tapioca and various fruits. Some Burmese sweets have been influenced by Indian cooking and include more exotic ingredients such as semolina and poppy seeds. In general, Burmese sweets are slightly less syrupy-sweet than those of neighbouring Thailand, and often take a cake-like, seemingly Western form, such as *bein móun* and *móun pyit thalet,* Burmese-style 'pancakes' served sweet or savoury.

An Introduction to Myanmar Cuisine (2004) by Ma Thanegi is an excellent source of Myanmar recipes, both sweet and savoury.

Drinks

Nonalcoholic Drinks

Black tea, brewed in the Indian style with lots of milk and sugar, is ubiquitous and cheap, costing K200 per cup at the time of research. Most restaurants and teashops also provide as much free Chinese tea as you can handle.

The end of Western sanctions means that Pepsi and Coke are now available across the country; indigenous pop brands include Fantasy, Lemon Sparkling, Max, Star, Fruito and Crusher. They taste pretty much the same as their Western counterparts.

Real coffee is limited to a handful of modern Western-style cafes in Yangon and other large cities. As a result, coffee drinkers will find themselves growing disturbingly attached to the 'three in one' packets of instant coffee (the 'three' being coffee, creamer and sugar), which you can have in teahouses for about K250.

Alcoholic Drinks

In the past the people of Myanmar were not big drinkers. This was due to a lack of disposable income, but also to the consumption of alcohol being looked down upon by the many Burmese Buddhists who interpret the fifth lay precept against intoxication very strictly. However, with the advent of 'beer stations' – places that serve cheap draught beer – the number of urban locals who can afford a few glasses of beer after work is on the rise.

Beer

Apart from international brands such as Tiger, ABC Stout, Singha, San Miguel and other beers brewed in Thailand and Singapore (typically costing K1700 for a 375mL can or bottle), there are a couple of Myanmar brews. These include long-established, joint-venture Myanmar Beer, which is slightly lighter in flavour and alcohol than other Southeast Asian beers (to the palate of at least a couple of researchers). Among the locals, Myanmar draught is the favourite; a glass of it will set you back only K500 or so. Some fine, newer brands brewed in Myanmar include Dagon and Skol.

The website hsa*ba (www.hsaba.com), written by cookbook author Tin Cho Chaw, includes a blog that regularly features Burmese recipes.

Liquors & Wines

Very popular in Shan State is an orange brandy called *shwe leinmaw*. Much of it is distilled in the mountains between Kalaw and Taunggyi. It's a pleasant-tasting liqueur and packs quite a punch. Near Taunggyi

A BURMESE NOODLE PRIMER

Myanmar's noodle dishes, known generally as *k'auq·s'wèh*, are quite unlike those found elsewhere in Southeast Asia. Often eaten for breakfast or as snacks between the main meals of the day, they can be divided into three general categories:

'Dry' Noodles

➡ *S'i jeq* Meaning 'cooked oil', this refers to noodles (rice or wheat) slicked with oil, topped with roast meat, and served with a side of broth and small salad of cucumber (in Yangon) or onions (in Mandalay).

➡ *Nàn·gyì dhouq/móun·di* These two, virtually identical, dishes consist of thick, round rice noodles served with chicken, slices of fish cake, par-boiled bean sprouts and sometimes slices of hard-boiled egg. The ingredients are seasoned with toasted chickpea flour, drizzles of turmeric and/or chilli oil, and served with sides of pickled vegetables and a bowl of broth.

➡ *Nàn·byà·gyì thouq* In Mandalay, this is a dish similar to the above, but made with flat, wide wheat noodles.

'Soup' Noodles

➡ *Kya·zin hìn* Mung bean vermicelli served in a clear broth with wood-ear mushrooms, lily flowers, slices of fish cake, and pork or chicken. Typically garnished with hard-boiled egg, coriander, chilli flakes and thinly sliced shallots, and seasoned with lime juice and fish sauce.

➡ *Kyè òu* Meaning 'copper pot', this dish with Chinese origins combines thin rice noodles, egg, pork, seasoned pork balls, pork offal and greens in a hearty broth.

➡ *Móun·hìn·gà* The most ubiquitous noodle, and Myanmar's unofficial national dish, consists of fine, round rice noodles served in a thick fish- and shallot-based broth. Made hearty with the addition of pith from the stalk of the banana tree, the dish is often served topped with crispy deep-fried veggies or lentils.

➡ *Óun·nó k'auq·s'wèh* This dish unites pale wheat noodles, a mild coconut-milk–based broth, shredded chicken, slices of hard-boiled egg, deep-fried crispy bits and a drizzle of chilli oil. Served with sides of chopped green onion, thinly sliced shallots and lime.

➡ *Shàn k'auq·s'wèh* Possibly the most famous Shan dish, this takes the form of thin, flat rice noodles in a clear broth with chunks of marinated chicken or pork, garnished with toasted sesame and a drizzle of garlic oil, and served with a side of pickled vegetables. A dry version, in which the broth is served on the side, is also common.

➡ *Rakhine móun·di* This state's signature dish unites thin rice noodles, flaked fish and a peppery broth. Served with a spicy condiment of pounded green chilli.

Somewhere In-Between

➡ *To·hù nwe k'auq·s'wèh* Literally 'warm tofu', this dish is similar to *shàn k'auq·s'wèh*, except that the clear broth is replaced by a thick porridge made from chickpea flour. The mixture is supplemented with pieces of marinated chicken or pork, a drizzle of chilli oil, and sides of pickled veggies and broth.

➡ *Myì shay* Thick rice noodles served with chicken or pork and par-boiled bean sprouts, and united by a dollop of sticky rice 'glue' (actually the same batter used to make the noodles). The dish is seasoned with chilli oil and vinegar (in Mandalay) or tamarind (in Mogok), and served with sides of pickled veggies and broth.

there's a couple of vineyards making wine and in Pyin Oo Lwin there are several sweet strawberry-based wines.

There are also stronger liquors, including *ayeq hpyu* (white liquor), which varies in strength from brandylike to almost pure ethyl; and *taw ayeq* (jungle liquor), a cruder form of *ayeq hpyu*. Mandalay is well known for its rums, and there is also the fermented palm juice known as toddy.

Where To Eat & Drink

Myanmar has three dining/drinking scenarios: what's in Yangon (including many expat-oriented, high-end choices); what's in other oft-visited places, including Mandalay, Bagan, Inle Lake and Ngapali Beach (many traveller-oriented menus, with Thai and pizza); and everywhere else.

Food can be quite cheap (from K1200 or K2500 for a full stomach) if you stick to roadside restaurants with their curry-filled pots or pick-and-point rice dishes. It's worth mentioning that these restaurants, though cheap, don't always meet international hygiene standards. That said, you're usually looking at K3000 to K5000 for a meal. In many midsized towns there are basic stands and maybe a Chinese restaurant or two – and that's it.

Restaurants

The bulk of Myanmar eateries are basic, with concrete floors, assertive fluorescent lighting and occasionally a menu in barely comprehensible English.

Burmese curry-based eateries are busiest (and many say freshest) at lunch. No menus are necessary at these; just go to the line of curries and point to what you want. A meal comes with a tableful of condiments, all of which are automatically refilled once you finish them. An all-you-can-eat meal can cost as little as K1500.

Chinese restaurants are found in most towns and most have similar sprawling menus, with as many as 50 rice or noodle and chicken, pork, lamb, fish, beef or vegetable dishes, almost always without prices indicated. Veggie dishes start at around K800 or K1000; meat dishes at about K1200 or K1500.

More upmarket restaurants – some serving a mix of Asian foods, others specialising in one food type, such as pizza or Thai – can be found in Bagan, Mandalay, Inle Lake and especially Yangon. Also, most top-end hotels offer plusher eating places, sometimes set around the pool. Such comfort is rarer to come by off the beaten track.

Most restaurants keep long hours daily, usually from 7am to 9pm or until the last diner wants to stumble out, their belly full of curry or beer.

Quick Eats

Like most Southeast Asians, the people of Myanmar are great grab-and-go snackers. Stands at night markets, selling a host of sweets and barbecued meals and noodles, get going around 5pm to 8pm or later. Generally you can get some fried noodles, a few pieces of pork, or sticky rice wrapped in banana leaf for a few hundred kyat.

Myanmar's fruit offerings vary by region and season. Don't miss Pyin Oo Lwin's strawberries and Bago's pineapples. Mango is best from March to July; jackfruit from June to October.

DRINKING WATER

Drink water in Myanmar only when you know it has been purified – which in most restaurants it should be. You should be suspicious of ice, although we've had lots of ice drinks in Myanmar without suffering any ill effects. Many brands of drinking water are sold in bottles and are quite safe, but check the seal on the bottle first. A 1L bottle, usually kept cool by ice or refrigerator, costs about K300 or K400 at most hotels.

BURMESE TEAHOUSES

Myanmar's numerous teahouses are not just places to have cups of sweet milky tea and coffee or pots of Chinese tea while sitting on a tiny plastic stool. They're places to catch up with a friend. They're where gossip is passed around, deals made and, in the past government spies were rampant. They're a place of employment for thousands of 'teaboys', cheeky pre-teen male service staff. And they're a fun slice of Burmese life that all visitors should investigate.

When visiting a teashop in Myanmar, abandon any preconceived notions of a fragrant cuppa served in a dainty China cup; in Myanmar, tea means strong, often bitter shots of black brew served in minuscule glass mugs with a dollop of sweetened condensed milk and a splash of tinned milk. Depending on the size of your sweet tooth and your caffeine tolerance, to order tea in Myanmar you'll need a short language lesson:

➡ *lǎp'eq·ye* – black tea served sweet with a dollop of condensed milk – the standard

➡ *cho bawq* – a less sweet version of *lǎp'eq·ye*

➡ *kyauq padaung* – very sweet; the phrase comes from a famous sugar-palm-growing region near Bagan

➡ *cho kya* – strongest tea, also served with condensed milk

Teahouses are also your best bet for breakfast, a light snack or sweet. Ethnic Burmese-run teahouses often emphasise noodles. *Móun·hin·gà* is usually available as a matter of course, but other more obscure noodle dishes include *óun·nó k'auq·swèh* (thin wheat noodles in a mild coconut-milk-based broth), *myì shay* (thick rice noodles served with chicken or pork and a dollop of sticky rice 'glue') and *nàngyì dhouq* (a salad of wide rice noodles seasoned with chickpea flour). Teahouses that serve these dishes are also likely to serve fried rice and *t'ǎmìn dhouq* (rice salad), also great for breakfast. Indian Muslim-owned teahouses often specialise in deep-fried dishes such as the ubiquitous samosas and *poori* (deep-fried bread served with a light potato curry), as well as oil-free breads such as dosai (southern Indian-style crepes) and *nanbyá* (nan bread), the latter often served with a delicious pigeon pea-based dip. And Chinese-style teahouses often feature lots of baked sweets as well as meaty steamed buns and *yum-cha*–like nibbles.

Drinking Venues

Outside of the big cities, you'll be hard-pressed to find anything resembling the Western concept of a bar or pub. Most drinking is done at open-air barbecue restaurants, often called 'beer stations' in Burmese English. Opening hours are therefore the same as for restaurants. All but Muslim Indian restaurants keep cold bottles of Tiger and Myanmar Beer handy (charging from K1700 in basic restaurants and up to K3000 or so in swankier ones). It's perfectly fine to linger for hours and down a few beers.

Servers in teahouses around Myanmar are 'tea boys', poor kids from the countryside who bring snacks and drinks to tables. They work daily in exchange for room, board and several dollars a month. One told us: 'Some day I hope to be a tea maker or a teahouse manager.'

Teahouses

In addition to being a convenient place to grab a cuppa or a quick snack, teahouses are an important social institution in Myanmar, a key meeting place for family, friends or business associates. 'Morning teahouses' typically open from 6am to 4pm, while evening ones open from 4pm or 5pm and stay open till 11pm or later.

Vegetarians & Vegans

Vegetarians will be able to find at least a couple of meat-free options at most restaurants in Myanmar. Many Burmese Buddhists abstain from eating the flesh of any four-legged animal and, during the Buddhist rain retreat around the Waso full moon, may take up a 'fire-free' diet that includes only uncooked vegetables and fruit. Some Indian or Nepali restaurants are vegan, and even meaty barbecues have a few skewered vegetables that can be grilled up. The easiest way to convey your needs is saying '*ăthà măsà nain bù*' (I can't eat meat).

Habits & Customs

At home, most families take their meals sitting on mats around a low, round table. In restaurants, chairs and tables are more common. The entire meal is served at once, rather than in courses. In Burmese restaurants each individual diner in a group typically orders a small plate of curry for himself or herself, while side dishes are shared among the whole party. This contrasts with China and Thailand, for example, where every dish is usually shared.

Traditionally, Burmese food is eaten with the fingers, much like in India, usually with the right hand. Nowadays, it's also common for urban Myanmar people to eat with a *k'ăyìn (*or *hkayìn;* fork) and *zùn* (spoon). These are always available at Burmese restaurants and are almost always given to foreign diners.

If you eat at a private home, it's not unusual for the hostess and children to not join you at the table.

Food Glossary
Typical Burmese Dishes

ămèh·hnaq	အမဲနှပ်	beef in gravy
ceq·thà·ăc'o·jeq	ကြက်သားအချိုချက်	sweet chicken
ceq·thà·gin	ကြက်သားကင်	grilled chicken (satay)
ceq·thà·jaw jeq	ကြက်သားကြော်ချက်	fried chicken
hìn	ဟင်း	curry
ămèh·dhà·hìn	အမဲသားဟင်း	beef curry
ceq·thà·hìn	ကြက်သားဟင်း	chicken curry
ăthì·ăyweq·hìn/ thì·zoun·hìn·jo	အသီးအရွက်ဟင်း ၊ သီးစုံဟင်းချို	vegetable curry
hìn·jo	ဟင်းချို	soup (clear or mild)
s'an·hlaw·hìn·jo	ဆန်လျော်ဟင်းချို	sizzling rice soup
s'éh·hnămyò·hìn·jo	ဆယ့်နှစ်မျိုးဟင်းချို	'12-taste' soup
móun·di	မုန့်တီ	*mount-ti* (Mandalay noodles and chicken/fish)
móun·hìn·gà	မုန့်ဟင်းခါး	*mohinga* (noodles and chicken/fish)
móun·s'i·jaw	မုန့်ဆီကြော်	sweet fried-rice pancakes
móun·zàn	မုန့်ဆန်း	sticky rice cake with jaggery (palm sugar)
myì shay	မြီးရှည်	Shan-style noodle soup
ngà·dhouq	ငါးသုပ်	fish salad
ngà·baùn·(douq)	ငါးပေါင်း(ထုပ်)	steamed fish (in banana leaves)
t'ămìn	ထမင်း	rice
kauq·hnyìn·baùn	ကောက်ညှင်းပေါင်း	steamed sticky rice

PREGNANCY

Pregnant women, stay away from bananas! According to local beliefs, your baby will be born overweight if you indulge while pregnant.

oùn·t'ămìn	အုန်းထမင်း	coconut rice
t'ămìn-gyaw	ထမင်းကြော်	fried rice
t'ădhì·móun	ထန်းသီးမုန့်	toddy-palm sugar cake
weq·thăni	ဝက်သနီ	red pork

Meat & Seafood

ămèh·dhà	အမဲသား	beef
ceq·thà	ကြက်သား	chicken
k'ăyú	ခရု	shellfish
ngă	ငါး	fish
ngăk'u	ငါးခူ	catfish
ngăshín	ငါးရှဉ့်	eel
ngăthălauq·paùn	ငါးသလောက်ပေါင်း	carp
pin·leh·za/ye·thaq·tăwa	ပင်လယ်စာ ၊ ရေသတ္တဝါ	seafood
pyi·jì·ngà	ပြည်ကြီးငါး	squid
weq·thà	ဝက်သား	pork

Vegetables

bù·dhì	ဘူးသီး	zucchini/gourd
ceq·thun·ni	ကြက်သွန်နီ	onion
gaw·bi·douq	ဂေါ်ဖီထုပ်	cabbage
hìn·dhì·hìn·yweq	ဟင်းသီးဟင်းရွက်	vegetables
hmo	မှို	mushrooms
ngăpyàw·bù	ငှက်ပျောဖူး	banana flower
kălăbèh	ကုလားပဲ	chick peas
k'ăyàn·dhì	ခရမ်းသီး	eggplant/aubergine
k'ăyàn·jin·dhì	ခရမ်းချဉ်သီး	tomato
moun·la·ú·wa	မုန်လာဥဝါ	carrot
pàn·gaw·p'i	ပန်းဂေါ်ဖီ	cauliflower
p'ăyoun·dhì	ဖရုံသီး	pumpkin
pèh·dhì	ပဲသီး	beans
pyaùn·bù	ပြောင်းဖူး	corn (cob)

Fruit

| àw·za·thì | သြဇာသီး | custard apple ('influence fruit') |
| ceq·mauq·thì | ကြက်မောက်သီး | rambutan ('cocksomb fruit') |

Burma: Rivers of Flavour (2012), by Naomi Duguid, is the most expansive book on Burmese food to have been published in English.

Rudyard Kipling famously referred to *ngapi*, the Burmese fermented fish condiment, as 'fish pickled when it ought to have been buried long ago'.

cwèh·gàw·dhì	ကျဲကောသီး	pomelo
dù·yìn·dhì	ဒူးရင်းသီး	durian
lain·c'ì·dhì	လိုင်ချီးသီး	lychee
lein·maw·dhì	လိမ္မော်သီး	orange
meq·màn·dhì	မက်မန်းသီး	plum (damson)
măji·dhì	မန်ကျည်းသီး	tamarind
nănaq·thì	နာနတ်သီး	pineapple
ngăpyàw·dhì	ငှက်ပျောသီး	banana
oùn·dhì	အုန်းသီး	coconut
pàn·dhì	ပန်းသီး	apple ('flower fruit')
shauq·thì	ရှောက်သီး	lemon
t'àw·baq·thì	ထောပတ်သီး	avocado ('butter fruit')
than·băya·dhì	သံပရာသီး	lime
thiq·thì/ăthì	သစ်သီး ၊ အသီး	fruit
thăyeq·dhì	သရက်သီး	mango
thìn·bàw·dhì	သင်္ဘောသီး	papaya ('boat-shaped fruit')

Cooking Myanmar Food (www.cook myanmar food.wordpress. com) features recipes for most of the more famous Burmese dishes.

Spices & Condiments

ceq·thun·byu	ကြက်သွန်ဖြူ	garlic
gyìn	ဂျင်း	ginger
hnàn	နှမ်း	sesame
hnìn·ye	နှင်းရည်	rose syrup
kălà·t'àw·baq	ကုလားထောပတ်	ghee
kùn·ya	ကွမ်းယာ	betel quid
meiq·thălin	မိတ်သလင်	galangal (white gingerlike root)
mye·bèh·(jaw)	မြေပဲ(ကြော်)	peanuts (fried)
nan·nan·bin	နံနံပင်	coriander
ngan·pya·ye	ငံပြာရည်	fish sauce
ngăyouq·thì	ငရုတ်သီး	chilli
ngăyouq·ye	ငရုတ်ရည်	chilli sauce
oùn·nó	အုန်းနို့	coconut cream
p'a·la·zé	ဖါလာစေ့	cardamom
paun·móun	ပေါင်မုန့်	bread
pèh·ngan·pya·ye	ပဲငံပြာရည်	soy sauce
t'àw·baq	ထောပတ်	butter
tha·gu	သာကူ	sago/tapioca

If you're having issues with onion breath in Myanmar, it's because the Burmese allegedly consume the most onions per capita of any country in the world.

t'òun	ထုံး	lime (for betel)
s'à	ဆား	salt
s'ănwìn	ဆနွင်း	turmeric
sha·lăka·ye	ရှာလကာရည်	vinegar
thăjà	သကြား	sugar
to·hù/to·p'ù	တိုဟူး ၊ တိုဖူး	tofu (beancurd)

Cold Drinks

ăyeq	အရက်	alcohol
bi·ya/tăbălìn	ဘီယာ ၊ တစ်ပုလင်း	beer
can·ye	ကြံရည်	sugarcane juice
lein·maw·ye	လိမ္မော်ရည်	orange juice
nwà·nó	နွားနို့	milk
oùn·ye	အုန်းရည်	coconut juice
p'yaw·ye/ã·è	ဖျော်ရည် ၊ အအေး	soft drink
s'o·da	ဆိုဒါ	soda water
t'àn·ye	ထန်းရည်	toddy
than·băya·ye	သံပရာရည်	lime juice
ye-	ရေ	water
ye·thán	ရေသန့်	bottled water ('clean water')
ye·è	ရေအေး	cold water
ye·jeq·è	ရေကျက်အေး	boiled cold water
ye·nwè	ရေနွေး	hot water

Hot Drinks

kaw·fi	ကော်ဖီ	coffee
dhăjà·néh	သကြားနဲ့	with sugar
nó·s'i·néh	နို့ဆီနဲ့	with condensed milk
nwà·nó·néh	နွားနို့နဲ့	with milk
lăp'eq·ye·jàn/ye·nwè·jàn	လက်ဖက်ရည်ကြမ်း ၊ ရေနွေးကြမ်း	green tea (plain)
leq·p'eq·ye	လက်ဖက်ရည်	tea (Indian)

FOOD POVERTY

Although Myanmar is a food surplus producer, the World Food Programme estimates that approximately three million people in Myanmar are 'food poor'.

Architecture & Arts

For centuries the arts in Myanmar (Burma) were sponsored by the royal courts, mainly through the construction of major religious buildings that required the skills of architects, sculptors, painters and a variety of artisans. Such patronage was cut short during British colonial rule and has never been a priority since independence. Even so, traditional art and architecture endures in Myanmar, mainly in the temples that are an ever-present feature of the landscape. There's also a growing contemporary art scene.

Architecture

It is in architecture that one sees the strongest evidence of Myanmar artistic skill and accomplishment. Myanmar is a country of *zedi*, often called 'pagodas' in English. Wherever you are – boating down the river, driving through the hills, even flying above the plains – there always seems to be a hilltop *zedi* in view. Bagan is the most dramatic result of this fervour for religious monuments – an enthusiasm that continues today, as the mass rebuilding of temples at the site attests.

Traditionally, only places of worship have been made of permanent materials. Until quite recently all secular buildings – and most monasteries – were constructed of wood, so there are few original ones left to be seen. Even the great royal palaces, such as the last one at Mandalay, were made of wood. All the palaces you see today are reconstructions – often far from faithful – such as the Bagan Golden Palace made of concrete and reinforced steel.

Even so, there are still many excellent wooden buildings to be seen. The people of Myanmar continue to use teak with great skill, and a fine country home can be a very pleasing structure indeed.

Zedi Styles

Early *zedi* were usually hemispherical (the Kaunghmudaw at Sagaing near Mandalay) or bulbous (the Bupaya in Bagan). The so-called Mon-style *pahto* is a large cube with small windows and ground-level passageways; this type is also known as a *gu* or *ku* (from the Pali-Sanskrit *guha*, meaning 'cave'). The more modern style is much more graceful – a curvaceous lower bell merging into a soaring spire, such as the Shwedagon Paya in Yangon or the Uppatasanti Paya in Nay Pyi Taw.

The overall Bamar concept is similar to that of the Mayan and Aztec pyramids of Mesoamerica: worshippers climb a symbolic mountain lined with religious reliefs and frescoes.

Style is not always a good indicator of the original age of a *zedi*, as Myanmar is earthquake-prone and many (including the Shwedagon) have been rebuilt again and again. In places such as Bagan and Inthein near Inle Lake, ruined temples have been rebuilt from the base up with little or no respect for what the original would have looked like. In Bagan, for example, all *zedi* would have been traditionally covered with white or painted stucco, not left as the bare brick structures they are today.

30 Heritage Buildings of Yangon by Sarah Rooney is packed with current and historical photographs and uncovers the stories behind some of the former capital's grandest edifices.

Best Buddhist Temples

Shwedagon Paya, Yangon

Ananda Pahto, Bagan

Shwenandaw Kyaung, Mandalay

Shwesandaw Paya, Pyay

Shittaung Paya, Mrauk U

MYANMAR'S SPORTING LIFE

Martial arts are perhaps the longest-running sports that the people of Myanmar have patronised: the oldest written references to kickboxing in the country are found in the chronicles of warfare between Burma and Thailand during the 15th and 16th centuries. The British introduced football (soccer) in the 19th century and it remains Myanmar's most popular spectator sport.

Football

The Myanmar National League (MNL) was launched in 2009 and currently consists of 12 teams; Yangon United were the 2013 champions. A US embassy cable released by WikiLeaks revealed that Senior General Than Shwe had thought it would be politically more popular to instruct crony businesses to create this league rather than spend US$1 billion on buying Manchester United, as his grandson had advised. Local TV broadcasts European games and teashops are invariably packed when a big match is screened.

Martial Arts

Myanma let-hwei (Myanmar kickboxing) is very similar in style to *muay thai* (Thai kickboxing), although not nearly as well developed as a national sport.

The most common and traditional kickboxing venues are temporary rings set up in a dirt circle (usually at *paya pwe* rather than sports arenas). All fighters are bare-fisted. All surfaces of the body are considered fair targets and any part of the body except the head may be used to strike an opponent. Common blows include high kicks to the neck, elbow thrusts to the face and head, knee hooks to the ribs and low crescent kicks to the calf. Punching is considered the weakest of all blows and kicking merely a way to soften up one's opponent; knee and elbow strikes are decisive in most matches.

Before the match begins, each boxer performs a dancelike ritual in the ring to pay homage to Buddha and to Khun Cho and Khun Tha, the *nat* whose domain includes Myanmar kickboxing. The winner repeats the ritual at the end of the match.

Chinlone

Also known as 'cane ball', *chinlone* is a game in which a woven rattan ball about 5in in diameter is kicked around. It also refers to the ball itself. Informally, any number of players can form a circle and keep the *chinlone* airborne by kicking or heading it soccer-style from player to player; a lack of scoring makes it a favourite pastime with locals of all ages.

In formal play six players stand in a circle of 22ft circumference. Each player must keep the ball aloft using a succession of 30 techniques and six surfaces on the foot and leg, allotting five minutes for each part. Each successful kick scores a point, while points are subtracted for using the wrong body part or dropping the ball. The sport was included in the South East Asian Games held in Myanmar in December 2013.

A popular variation – and the one used in intramural or international competitions – is played with a volleyball net, using all the same rules as in volleyball except that only the feet and head are permitted to touch the ball.

Old Myanmar Paintings in the Collection of U Win is one of the illustrated publications of the Thavibu Gallery (www.thavibu. com) specialising in Burmese art.

Colonial & Contemporary Architecture

While many buildings erected during the British colonial period have been demolished or are facing the wrecking ball, those that survive are often well worth seeking out. They range from the rustic wood-and-plaster Tudor villas of Pyin Oo Lwin to the thick-walled, brick-and-plaster, colonnaded mansions and shophouses of Yangon, Mawlamyine and Myeik.

Yangon in particular is stocked with spectacular, if often crumbling, colonial gems such as the Secretariat, seat of British colonial power, and the Lokanat Gallery Building. Some such as the Strand Hotel and the

Moseah Yeshua Synagogue have been spruced up either by commercial investment or private donations and overseas grants.

The military junta turned its back on the city to build a new capital at Nay Pyi Taw, but there are signs in the post-2010 era that the authorities may be having a change of heart. The Yangon Heritage Trust, set up in 2012, has had high-level meetings aimed at getting a conservation zone up and running in the city along with statutory guidelines to protect historic buildings (see p59). Around 180 key buildings have been recognised by Yangon municipality as heritage buildings, but this list has no legal binding and falls far short of the 2500 sites campaigners say should be afforded protection.

At the forefront of contemporary architecture in Myanmar are the husband-and-wife team of Stephen Zawmoe Shwe and Amelie Chai, partners in SPINE Architects (www.spinearchitects.com). Most of their work, which includes residential and commercial projects, can be seen in Yangon – the Yuzana Tea Shop on Na Wa Day St and the Union Bar & Grill are good examples of their style. They also designed the Amata Resort & Spa in Ngapali and the Bay of Bengal Resort at Ngwe Saung Beach.

Amazing Wood Structures

Shwenandaw Kyaung, Mandalay

U Bein's Bridge, Amarapura

Bagaya Kyaung, Inwa

Youqson Kyaung, Salay

Pakhanngeh Kyaung, Pakokku

Sculpture & Painting

Early Myanmar art was always a part of the religious architecture – paints were for the walls of temples, sculpture to be placed inside them. Many pieces, formerly in paya or *kyaung,* have been sold or stolen and, unfortunately, you'll easily find more Myanmar religious sculpture for sale or on display overseas than in Myanmar.

In the aftermath of the 1988 demonstrations, the government forbade 'selfish' or 'mad art' that didn't have clear pro-government themes. One artist, Sitt Nyein Aye, spent two months in custody for sketching the ruins of the former student union, which Ne Win had blown up in 1962. Subsequently many artists chose to play safe with predictable tourist-oriented works.

Censorship of art exhibitions has dropped off significantly since 2010, allowing artists more freedom of expression and a mini-boom of galleries in Yangon. Myanmar artists are now attracting global attention. The couple Wah Nu and Tun Win Aung, who create paintings, video art and installations based on their memories of growing up under the socialist-military regime, have been written about in the *New York Times* and had their work purchased by the Guggenheim Museum. Nge Lay and Po Po represented Myanmar at the 2014 Singapore Biennale with pieces about education and spirituality.

Traditional Crafts

Apart from the following, other Myanmar crafts you may come across are paper parasols, silver- and metal-ware, and wood carvings.

Kammawa & Parabaik

Kammawa (from the Pali *kammavacha*) are narrow, rectangular slats painted with extracts from the Pali Vinaya (the Pitaka, concerned with monastic discipline); specifically, these are extracts to do with clerical affairs. The core of a *kammawa* page may be a thin slat of wood, lacquered cloth, thatched cane or thin brass, which is then layered with red, black and gold lacquer to form the script and decorations.

The *parabaik* (Buddhist palm-leaf manuscript) is a similarly horizontal 'book', this time folded accordion-style, like a road map. The pages are made of heavy paper covered with black ink on which the letters are engraved.

Yangon-based art researcher Nathalie Johnson has created the website Myanmar Evolution (www.myanmartevolution.com) to support the growth of contemporary arts in the country

ARCHITECTURE & ARTS SCULPTURE & PAINTING

Lacquerware

The earliest lacquerware found in Myanmar can be dated to the 11th century and sported a very Chinese style. The techniques used today are known as *yun,* the old Bamar word for the people of Chiang Mai, from where the techniques were imported in the 16th century (along with some captured artisans) by King Bayinnaung. An older style of applying gold or silver to a black background dates back to, perhaps, the Pyay era (5th to 9th centuries) and is kept alive by artisans in Kyaukka, near Monywa.

The bronze Mahamuni Buddha, in Mandalay's Mahamuni Paya, may date back to the 1st century AD and is Myanmar's most famous Buddhist sculpture.

Many lacquerware shops include workshops, where you can see the lengthy process involved in making the bowls, trays and other objects. The craftsperson first weaves a frame (the best-quality wares have a bamboo frame tied together with horse or donkey hairs; lesser pieces are made wholly from bamboo). The lacquer is then coated over the framework and allowed to dry. After several days it is sanded down with ash from rice husks and another coating of lacquer is applied. A high-quality item may have seven to 15 layers altogether.

The lacquerware is engraved and painted, then polished to remove the paint from everywhere except from within the engravings. Multicoloured lacquerware is produced by repeated engraving, painting and polishing. From start to finish it can take up to five or six months to produce a high-quality piece of lacquerware, which may have as many as five colours. A top-quality bowl can have its rim squeezed together until the sides meet without suffering any damage or permanent distortion.

Tapestries & Textiles

Tapestries *(kalaga)* consist of pieces of coloured cloth of various sizes heavily embroidered with silver- or gold-coloured thread, metal sequins and glass beads, and feature mythological Myanmar figures in

ZARGANAR

Myanmar's most popular comedian is Maung Thura, better known by his stage name Zarganar (also spelled Zargana) meaning tweezers. Born into an intellectual and politically active family he trained as a dentist in Yangon in the 1980s, a period during which he also worked as a volunteer literary teacher in Chin State, and formed part of a comedy troupe of students performing *a-nyeint* skit routines. Such was his success in the last role that he ended up on television, where he took astonishing risks for the time with his satirical material lampooning the military rulers.

His first stint in jail followed the 1988 street protests in Yangon. There were several other prison terms leading up to his last incarceration in 2008 when he criticised the government for its poor response to the tragedy of Cyclone Nargis. For this he was sentenced to 35 years in jail. *This Prison Where I Live* (http://thisprisonwhereilive.co.uk), a documentary by Rex Bloomstein, includes interviews with Zarganar filmed in 2007 before he was imprisoned. During his time in jail Zarganar was awarded the inaugural PEN Pinter Prize for his writing.

After November 2011, when Zarganar was released, *This Prison Where I Live* was updated to include footage of him meeting with German comedian Michael Mittermeier, who also features in the documentary. Bloomstein also made a BBC radio documentary entitled *Burma's Zarganar: The Man Who Laughed at the Generals*.

Since his release Zarganar has met with former US Secretary of State Hillary Clinton in the US to discuss the political situation in Myanmar. Having made many films as an actor and director, Zarganar is also one of the people behind the House of Media and Entertainment (HOME), a Yangon-based centre to train and support young filmmakers as well as encourage a new generation of fearless comedians.

padded relief. The greatest variety is found in Mandalay, where most tapestries are produced.

Good-quality *kalaga* are tightly woven and don't skimp on sequins, which may be sewn in overlapping lines, rather than spaced side by side, as a sign of embroidery skill. The metals used should shine, even in older pieces; tarnishing means lower-quality materials.

Tribal textiles and weavings produced by the Chin, Naga, Kachin and Kayin can also be very beautiful, especially antique pieces. Among traditional hand-woven silk *longyis, laun-taya acheik,* woven on a hundred spools, are the most prized.

Dance & Theatre

Myanmar's truly indigenous dance forms are those that pay homage to the *nat* (spirit beings). Most classical dance styles, meanwhile, arrived from Thailand. Today the dances most obviously taken from Thailand are known as *yodaya zat* (Ayuthaya theatre), as taught to the people of Myanmar by Thai theatrical artists taken captive in the 18th century.

The most Myanmar of dances feature solo performances by female dancers who wear strikingly colourful dresses with long white trains, which they kick into the air with their heels – quite a feat, given the restrictive length of the train.

Pwe is the generic word in Myanmar for theatre or performance and it embraces all kinds of plays and musical operas as well as dancing. An all-night *zat pwe* involves a re-creation of an ancient legend or Buddhist Jataka (story of the Buddha's past lives), while the *yamazat pwe* pick a tale from the Indian epic Ramayana. In Mandalay, *yamazat* performers even have their own shrine.

Myanmar classical dancing emphasises pose rather than movement and solo rather than ensemble performances. In contrast the less common, but livelier, *yein pwe* features singing and dancing performed by a chorus or ensemble.

Most popular of all is the *a-nyeint,* a traditional *pwe* somewhat akin to early American vaudeville, the most famous exponents of which are Mandalay's Moustache Brothers and the satirist and film actor and director Zarganar.

Marionette Theatre

Youq-the pwe (Myanmar marionette theatre) presents colourful puppets up to 3.5ft high in a spectacle that some consider the most expressive of all the Myanmar arts.

Developed during the Konbaung period, it was so influential that it became the forerunner to *zat pwe* as later performed by actors rather than marionettes. As with dance-drama, the genre's 'golden age' began with the Mandalay kingdoms of the late 18th century and ran through to the advent of cinema in the 1930s.

The people of Myanmar have great respect for an expert puppeteer. Some marionettes may be manipulated by a dozen or more strings. The marionette master's standard repertoire requires a troupe of 28 puppets including Thagyamin (king of the gods); a Myanmar king, queen, prince and princess; a regent; two court pages; an old man and an old woman; a villain; a hermit; four ministers; two clowns; one good and one evil *nat;* a Brahmin astrologer; two ogres; a *zawgyi* (alchemist); a horse; a monkey; a *makara* (mythical sea serpent); and an elephant.

It's rare to see marionette theatre outside tourist venues in Yangon, Mandalay or Bagan.

The beautifully painted little parasols you see around Myanmar are often made in Pathein – in fact they're known as *Pathein hti* (Pathein umbrellas).

ARCHITECTURE & ARTS DANCE & THEATRE

MARIONETTES

The Illusion of Life: Burmese Marionettes by Ma Thanegi gives readers a glimpse of the 'wit, spirit and style' of this traditional Burmese performance art.

Music

Much of classical Myanmar music, played loud the way the *nat* like it, features strongly in any *pwe*. Its repetitive, even harsh, harmonies can be hard on Western ears at first; Myanmar scales are not 'tempered', as Western scales have been since Bach. Traditional Myanmar music is primarily two dimensional, in the sense that rhythm and melody provide much of the musical structure, while repetition is a key element. Subtle shifts in rhythm and tonality provide the modulation usually supplied by the harmonic dimension in Western music.

Classical Music

Classical-music traditions were largely borrowed from Siam musicians in the late 1800s, who borrowed the traditions from Cambodian conquests centuries earlier. Myanmar classical music, as played today, was codified by Po Sein, a colonial-era musician, composer and drummer who also designed the *hsaing waing* (the circle of tuned drums, also known as *paq waing*) and formalised classical dancing styles. Such music is meant to be played as an accompaniment to classical dance-dramas that enact scenes from the Jataka or from the Ramayana.

Musical instruments are predominantly percussive, but even the *hsaing waing* may carry the melody. These drums are tuned by placing a wad of *paq-sa* (drum food) – made from a kneaded paste of rice and wood ash – onto the centre of the drum head, then adding or subtracting a pinch at a time till the desired drum tone is attained.

In addition to the *hsaing waing,* the traditional *hsaing* (Myanmar ensemble) of seven to 10 musicians will usually play: the *kye waing* (a circle of tuned brass gongs); the *saung gauq* (a boat-shaped harp with 13 strings); the *pattala* (a sort of xylophone); the *hneh* (an oboe-type instrument related to the Indian *shanai*); the *pa-lwe* (a bamboo flute); the *mi-gyaung* (crocodile lute); the *paq-ma* (a bass drum); and the *yag-win* (small cymbals) and *wa leq-hkouq* (bamboo clappers), which are purely rhythmic and are often played by Myanmar vocalists.

Myanmar dance scholars have catalogued around 2000 dance movements, including 13 head movements, 28 eye movements, eight body postures and 10 walking movements.

Folk

Older than Myanmar classical music is an enchanting vocal folk-music tradition still heard in rural areas where locals may sing without instrumental accompaniment while working. Such folk songs set the work cadence and provide a distraction from the physical strain and monotony of pounding rice, clearing fields, weaving and so on. This type of music is most readily heard in the Ayeyarwady Delta between Twante and Pathein.

Pop, Rock & Rap

Classical dance-drama is performed nightly at Mandalay's Mintha Theater and occasionally at the National Theatre in Yangon.

Western pop music's influence first came in the 1970s, when singers such as Min Min Latt and Takatho Tun Naung sang shocking things such as Beatles cover versions or 'Tie a Yellow Ribbon Round the Old Oak Tree'. This led to long-haired, distorted-guitar rock bands such as Empire and Iron Cross (aka IC) in the 1980s. Over two decades later, Iron Cross are still rocking – try to see them live (you're sure to see them on videotape at teashops or on all-night buses). Another long-running band is Lazy Club, who played concerts in the US in 2009.

Bands can have a stable of several singers who split stage time with the same backing band. Iron Cross, for example, features one of Myanmar's 'wilder' singers, Lay Phyu, but it can also tone it down as a backing band for the poppier stuff of other singers. One local aficionado explains: 'There's no competition between a band's many singers. They

TRADITIONAL BURMESE MUSIC CDS

· ·

Mahagitá *Harp & Vocal Music from Burma* (2003; Smithsonian Folkways)

Music of Nat Pwe: Folk & Pop Music of Myanmar (2007; Sublime Frequencies)

Pat Waing *The Magic Drum Circle of Burma* (1998; Shanachie)

U Ko Ko *Performs on the Burmese Piano* (1995; Ummus)

Various artists *Burma: Traditional Music* (2009; Air Mail Music)

White Elephants & Golden Ducks *Enchanting Musical Treasures from Burma* (1997; Shanachie)

help each other. Our rock singers don't throw TVs out the windows. On stage they jump around and all, but offstage they're very good-natured.'

Female singers like Sone Thin Par and actor Htu Aeindra Bo win fans for their melodies – and looks – but the most interesting is rapper Phyu Phyu Kyaw Thein, a sort of 'Sporty Spice', who has fronted both Iron Cross *and* Lazy Club. Other rappers include Min Min Latt's son, Anega, now busting beats with other big-name rappers Barbu, Myo Kyawt Myaung and heart-throb Sai Sai. Songs often deal with gossip, or troubles between parents and kids. Thxa Soe is a popular hip-hop singer whose 2007 hit 'I Like Drums' merged *nat* music with trance.

Current darlings of the local pop scene are the Me N Ma Girls, a toned-down Spice Girls–style troupe. Although dismissed initially as pre-packaged pop, the Girls have gone on to somewhat distinguish themselves by clinching an international record deal and playing a show at New York's Lincoln Center in 2013.

Yangon is the best place to catch a show; look out for advertisements in local publications and on billboards and leaflets.

Literature

Religious texts inscribed onto Myanmar's famous *kammawa* (lacquered scriptures) and *parabaik* (folding manuscripts) were the first pieces of literature as such, and began appearing in the 12th century. Until the 1800s, the only other works of 'literature' available were royal genealogies, classical poetry and law texts. A Burmese version of the Indian epic Ramayana was first written in 1775 by poet U Aung Pyo.

The first Myanmar novel *Maung Yin Maung Ma Me Ma,* an adaptation of *The Count of Monte Cristo,* by James Hla Kyaw, was published in 1904. Eric Blair (aka George Orwell) worked in Myanmar from 1922 to 1927 as a policeman, an experience that informed his novel *Burmese Days,* first published in 1934. Sharply critical of colonial life in the country, it is one of the few English-language books still widely available in Myanmar (unlike Orwell's *1984* and *Animal Farm,* political works that are not to the generals' tastes).

More recently, Myanmar-born Nu Nu Yi Inwa, one of the country's leading writers with at least 15 novels and over 100 short stories to her name, made the shortlist for the 2007 Man Asian Literary Prize with *Smile As They Bow.* The story, set at the Taungbyon Festival held near Mandalay, follows an elder gay transvestite medium who fears losing his much younger partner to a woman in the heat of the week-long festivities. Also check out the poetry of Ko Ko Thett (www.kokothett. webs.com) and the novels of Wendy Yone-Law.

To catch up on the latest in local literature, visit the site of the Irrawaddy Literature Festival (http://irrawaddylitfest.com), which in 2014 was held in Mandalay.

Bones Will Crow: 15 Contemporary Burmese Poets, co-edited by James Byrne and Ko Ko Thett, is the first anthology of Burmese poetry ever to be published in the West.

Cinema

Myanmar has had a modest film industry since the early 20th century and it continues today producing low-budget, uncontroversial action pics, romances and comedies that are a staple of cinemas, village video-screening halls and DVD sellers across the country. There's even an annual Academy Awards ceremony that is one of the country's biggest social events.

You'll mostly need to look to film-makers outside Myanmar for movies and documentaries that tackle some of the country's more controversial topics. Among recent documentaries available on video or doing the festival rounds are Nic Dunlop's *Burma Soldier* (www.breakthru films.org/burma-soldier), the moving story of a military recruit who loses two limbs to land mines and switches sides to become a democracy activist; Rex Bloomstein's *This Prison Where I Live* (http://this prisonwhereilive.co.uk) about the Burmese comic and political activist Zargana; the Oscar-nominated *Burma VJ*; and *Youth of Yangon* (http://vimeo.com/ondemand/youthofyangon) about the country's nascent skateboard scene.

John Boorman's *Beyond Rangoon*, a political tract/action flick set during the 1988 uprisings, had Georgetown, Penang, do a credible turn as the nation's then-turbulent capital. It starred several Myanmar actors, including Aung Ko, who plays an elderly guide to Patricia Arquette's American tourist galvanised into political activist. Another Myanmar actor, Win Min Than, was cast opposite Gregory Peck in 1954's *The Purple Plain*, the most credible of several WWII dramas set in Myanmar.

Fighting more recent wars is Sylvester Stallone, who returned to one of his most famous roles in *Rambo* (2008). This time Vietnam Vet John Rambo takes on the Tatmadaw, a whole platoon of which he mows down at the movie's climax with a jeep-mounted machine gun!

Luc Bresson's *The Lady* is a biopic about Aung San Suu Kyi, staring Michelle Yeo in the title role. Picking up attention at film festivals around the world is the thriller *Kayan Beauties* (www.kayanbeauties. com), which paints a generally realistic portrait of Kayan life in Myanmar. All of the characters in the film are played by Kayan actors.

Winner of the Aung San Suu Kyi Award at the Human Rights, Human Dignity International Film Festival in Yangon in 2013 was *Survival in Prison*, Yee Nan Theik's feature-length documentary about the political prisoner San Zaw Htway, who spent 12 years in jail.

Environment & Wildlife

Snow-capped mountains, steamy jungles, coral reefs, and open grasslands – you name it, Myanmar's environment has it. Scientists continue to discover new species amid the abundant biodiversity, but at the same time, the country's poor record on environmental laws and enforcement is killing off many others. Armed insurgencies, rampant resource extraction and unchecked infrastructure development are among the many dire threats to Myanmar's natural heritage.

Geography

A bit bigger than France and slightly smaller than Texas, Myanmar covers 261,228 sq miles and borders (clockwise from the west) Bangladesh, India, Tibet, China, Laos and Thailand, with 1199 miles of coastline facing the Bay of Bengal and the Andaman Sea. The country's south is similar to Malaysia and its north to northern India. The centre is an overlap of the two, producing 'zones' whose uniqueness is manifest in the scenery and creatures that hop around in it.

The area southwest of Yangon is a vast delta region notable for its production of rice. Paddy fields are also an ever-present feature of Myanmar's central broad, flat heartland, known as the 'dry zone' for its lack of rain. This area is surrounded by protective mountain and hill ranges (*yoma* in Burmese). Most notable are the rugged Kachin Hills, which serve as the first steps into the Himalaya to the north; Hkakabo Razi, on the Tibetan border, which at 19,295ft is Southeast Asia's highest mountain; and Mt Victoria (Nat Ma Taung), west of Bagan in Chin State, which rises to 10,016ft.

Three major rivers – fed by monsoon downpours and melted Himalayan snows – cut north to south through the country:

Ayeyarwady (Irrawaddy) River This 1240-mile-long waterway is one of Asia's most navigable big rivers, feeding much of the country's rice fields. It connects lower Myanmar (based around Yangon) with upper Myanmar (around Mandalay).

Chindwin River Originating in the Hukawng Valley of Kachin State, this 850-mile-long river connects the northern hills with the Myanmar's central zone, joining with the Ayeyarwady between Mandalay and Bagan.

Thanlwin (Salween) River Rising on the Tibetan Plateau, this river flows into Myanmar in its northeastern corner at China and empties into the Gulf of Mottama, near Mawlamyine.

Also, the Mekong River passes by on the short border with Laos.

Flora & Fauna

Myanmar, which sits on a transition zone between the plants and creatures of the Indian subcontinent, Southeast Asia and the Himalayan highlands, is a biodiversity hotspot. However, the troubled politics of the country over the last century have made it difficult for researchers to gain an accurate picture of the current state of the country's wildlife.

According to the Asean Centre for Biodiversity (www.asean-biodiversity.org), Myanmar is home to 300 species of mammal, 400 species of reptile and around 1000 bird species.

One end of the 1860-mile-long Himalaya mountain chain, formed when the Indian and Eurasian tectonic plates collided 140 million years ago, extends to Myanmar's Kachin State.

Animals

When Marco Polo wrote about Myanmar in the 13th century, he described 'vast jungles teeming with elephants, unicorns and other wild beasts'. Though Myanmar's natural biodiversity has no doubt altered considerably since that time, it's difficult to say by just how much.

The Wild Animals of Burma, published in 1967, is the most 'recent' work available and even this volume simply contains extracts from various surveys carried out by the British between 1912 and 1941, with a few observations dating to 1961. The US-based Wildlife Conservation Society (www.wcs.org) has engaged in a number of localised surveys, primarily in the far north, over the past few years, but currently nobody is attempting a full nationwide stocktake of plants and animals.

As with Myanmar's flora, the variation in Myanmar's wildlife is closely associated with the country's geographic and climatic differences. Hence the indigenous fauna of the country's northern half is mostly of Indo-Chinese origin, while that of the south is generally Sundaic (ie typical of Malaysia, Sumatra, Borneo and Java). In the Himalayan region north of the Tropic of Cancer (just north of Lashio), the fauna is similar to that found in northeastern India. In the area extending from around Myitkyina in the north to the Bago Mountains in the central region, there is overlap between geographical and vegetative zones – which means that much of Myanmar is a potential habitat for plants and animals from all three zones.

Distinctive mammals found in dwindling numbers within the more heavily forested areas of Myanmar include leopards, fishing cats, civets, Indian mongooses, crab-eating mongooses, Himalayan bears, Asiatic black bears, Malayan sun bears, gaur (Indian bison), banteng (wild cattle), serow (an Asiatic mountain goat), wild boars, sambar, barking deer, mouse deer, tapirs, pangolin, gibbons and macaques. Sea mammals include dolphins and dugongs.

The documentary *Of Oozies and Elephants* (http://vimeo.com/77426318) and an episode of the BBC's *Wild Burma: Nature's Lost Kingdom* feature the vet Khyne U Mar, known as 'the elephant lady of Burma' for her studies of captive working elephants in Myanmar. Her research is supported by the Rufford Foundation (http://www.rufford.org/rsg/projects/khyne_mar).

ENVIRONMENT & WILDLIFE FLORA & FAUNA

MYANMAR'S ECO TREASURE CHEST

Myanmar has long intrigued scientists, who believe that many critically endangered species, or even species that are new to science, might be living in closed-off parts of the country. As remote parts of the country have opened up, the scientists' hopes have been proven correct.

Myanmar snub-nosed monkey In 2010 the BBC reported the discovery of this new species of colobine monkey. It's estimated there's a population of between 260 and 330 of these primates living by the Mekong and Thanlwin Rivers in Kachin State.

Arakan forest turtles In 2009 a team of World Conservation Society scientists discovered five of these critically endangered species, less than a foot long and with a light brown shell, amid thick stands of bamboo in a sanctuary set up originally to protect elephants. In modern times, researchers had only previously seen a handful of captive examples.

Kitti's hog-nosed bat Prior to 2001, when it was located in Myanmar, the species that is also known as the bumblebee bat was thought to live only in a tiny part of western Thailand. At a length of 1.25in to 1.5in and weighing in at just 0.07oz this is the world's smallest bat.

Gurney's pitta This stunningly bright, small bird underwent a dramatic decline during the 20th century, until only a single population in Thailand was known. However, it was also discovered in Myanmar in 2003, giving hope that it may also be able to survive.

Leaf deer Also known as the 'leaf muntjac', this 25lb, 20in-tall mammal was confirmed in northern Myanmar in 1999. Its name was given because it can be wrapped up in a large leaf.

PLIGHT OF MYANMAR'S TIGERS

'There are no more tigers left.' This was the bleak assessment of Bawk Jar, as reported by the *Irrawaddy* in November 2012, based on the environmentalist and Kachin civil rights activist's own experiences and interviews with local trackers in the Hukaung Valley Tiger Reserve. Covering 8452 sq miles, the reserve was established in 2001 by the ruling junta with the support of Dr Alan Rabinowitz, executive director at the Wildlife Conservation Society (WCS) at the time and now president and CEO of the US-based NGO Panthera.

In a 2008 interview in the *Myanmar Times*, Rabinowitz applauded the government for creating the park. 'If tourists come and spend money to see wildlife, then the local people start feeling that wildlife is more valuable alive than dead', he said. The problem has been that tourism has never taken off in this region blighted by conflict between the Kachin Independence Organisation (KIO) and the Myanmar military. The *Irrawaddy* also reported how the Yuzana Corporation, owned by Htay Myint, a member of parliament for the USDP, has been chopping down trees in the park, destroying the environment not only of the tiger but several other endangered species. In June 2012, Rabinowitz, interviewed by AFP, laid part of the blame for the big cats' plight on the indigenous people for 'killing off tigers' to sell to China and was also downbeat on the chances of saving the few that perhaps still survive in the region.

One small flicker of hope is the Tiger Corridor, a joint initiative between Panthera and the Wildlife Conservation Society to create a 4660-mile-long 'genetic corridor' for tigers stretching from Bhutan to Malaysia, with a large part of the corridor passing through Myanmar. In addition, an expedition to Myanmar sponsored by the Smithsonian Institute and filmed by the BBC in its *Wild Burma* programme found evidence of tigers in two separate parts of the country.

Reptiles and amphibians include 27 turtle species (of which seven are found exclusively in Myanmar), along with numerous snake varieties, of which at least 39 are venomous, including the common cobra, king cobra (hamadryad), banded krait, Malayan pit viper, green viper and Russell's viper. Myanmar is rich in birdlife, with an estimated 687 resident and migrating species. Coastal and inland waterways of the delta and southern peninsula are especially important habitats for Southeast Asian waterfowl.

Endangered Species

Of some 8233 known breeding species (of which 7000 are plants) in Myanmar, 132 of these (animals, birds and plants) are endangered, including the flying squirrel, tiger, Irrawaddy dolphin and three-striped box turtle. There are believed to be as few as 1130 wild Asian elephants throughout Myanmar, according to a symposium convened by the Smithsonian in 2004. Paradoxically, domesticated or captive elephants – of which Myanmar is believed to have around 15,000 – are widely used by the logging industry to knock down the forests on which their wild cousins depend. Both the one-horned (Javan) rhinoceros and the Asiatic two-horned (Sumatran) rhinoceros are believed to survive in very small numbers near the Thai border in Kayin State. The rare red panda (or cat bear) was last sighted in northern Myanmar in the early 1960s but is thought to still live in Kachin State forests above 6500ft.

Deforestation poses the greatest threat to wildlife, but even in areas where habitat loss isn't a problem, hunting threatens to wipe out the rarer animal species. Wildlife laws are seldom enforced and poaching remains a huge problem in Myanmar.

The most comprehensive wildlife survey of Myanmar available was undertaken by the Bombay Natural History Society between 1912 and 1921 and published as the Mammal Survey of India, Burma and Ceylon.

Plants

As in the rest of tropical Asia, most indigenous vegetation in Myanmar is associated with two basic types of tropical forest: monsoon forest (with a distinctive dry season of three months or more) and rainforest (where rain falls more than nine months per year). It's said there are over 1000 plant species endemic to the country.

Monsoon forests are marked by deciduous tree varieties, which shed leaves during the dry season. Rainforests, by contrast, are typically evergreen. The area stretching from Yangon to Myitkyina contains mainly monsoon forests, while peninsular Myanmar to the south of Mawlamyine is predominantly a rainforest zone. There is overlapping of the two – some forest zones support a mix of monsoon forest and rainforest vegetation.

In the mountainous Himalayan region, Myanmar's flora is characterised by subtropical broadleaf evergreen forest up to 6500ft; temperate semi-deciduous broadleaf rainforest from 6500ft to 9800ft; and, above this, evergreen coniferous, subalpine snow forest and alpine scrub. Along the Rakhine and Tanintharyi coasts, tidal forests occur in river estuaries, lagoons, tidal creeks and along low islands. Such woodlands are characterised by mangroves and other coastal trees that grow in mud and are resistant to seawater. Beach and dune forests, which grow along these same coasts above the high-tide line, consist of palms, hibiscus, casuarinas and other tree varieties that can withstand high winds and occasional storm-sent waves.

The country's most famous flora includes an incredible array of fruit trees, more than 25,000 flowering species, a variety of tropical hardwoods and bamboo. Cane and rattan are also plentiful.

According to a report in the August 2012 edition of *Science Magazine* 14 of Myanmar's 36 protected areas lack staff altogether, while the rest have too few rangers for effective patrolling and management.

National Parks

By an optimistic account, about 7% of Myanmar's land area is made up of national parks and forests, wildlife sanctuaries and parks, and other protected areas. However, such protection on paper is rarely translated into reality without the backing of adequate funds and effective policing.

Environmental Issues

Recycling and making use of every little thing is part of most people's daily life in Myanmar, disposability only being a luxury of the rich. This said, the country is facing many challenges with regard to treatment of its precious environment. Essentially no environmental legislation was passed from the time of independence in 1948 until after 1988. Since

A 2009 report by environmental watchdog Global Witness found a dramatic decrease in the illegal timber trade between Myanmar and China, but notes smuggling still continues.

MAJOR PARKS & RESERVES

PARK	SIZE (SQ MILES)	FEATURES	BEST TIME TO VISIT	PERMIT NEEDED?
Hkakabo Razi National Park	1472	highest mountain in Myanmar; forests; rare species such as takin, musk and black barking deer, and blue sheep	Oct–Apr	yes
Indawgyi Wetland Wildlife Sanctuary	299	one of Southeast Asia's largest lake; 120 species of birds	Jan–Apr	no
Inle Wetland Bird Sanctuary	642	floating agriculture; birdlife, otters, turtles	year-round	no
Moeyungyi Wetlands	40	125 species of birds	Nov–Apr	no
Mt Victoria (Nat Ma Taung) National Park	279	second-highest mountain in Myanmar; rare birds and orchids	Nov–Mar	no
Popa Mountain Park	50	extinct volcano; unique dry-zone ecosystem; monkeys	Nov–Mar	no

then, government dictums, such as efforts to 'green the dry zone' and protect wildlife, were more words than action.

Slowly, things may be changing. Previously off-limit topics related to Myanmar's environment are now covered in the media, leading, occasionally, to reviews of government policy. President Thein Sein's decision to suspend construction of the Myitsone Dam in September 2011 is one example of this. The new foreign investment law passed in 2012 requires environmental impact statements for all major investment projects and a new environmental conservation law has also been introduced.

Deforestation

Myanmar supposedly contains more standing forest, with fewer inhabitants, than any other country in Indochina. That said, it's also disappearing faster than almost anywhere else in Asia, and Myanmar's forests remain the most unprotected in the region. Much of Myanmar's forest has fallen to the axe – for fuel and for timber exports (both legal and illegal) or due to clearing for farming. One of the most troubled areas is the so-called 'dry zone', made up of heavily populated Mandalay, lower Sagaing and Magwe divisions. Little of the original vegetation remains in this pocket (which is about 10% of Myanmar's land, but home to one-third of the population), due to growth in the area's population and deforestation.

In August 2013 Shan State Minister for Forestry and Mines U Sai Aik Paung told the *Myanmar Times* that illegal logging was particularly difficult to combat in parts of the state due to a lack of stability and threats to forestry officers by armed gangs of smugglers. The problem isn't new. Much of Britain's 19th-century industrialisation, as well as the train tracks made here in Myanmar, were built from Burmese timber. Following the 1988 putting down of the pro-democracy protests, the government relaxed timber and fishing laws for short-term gain, ultimately causing more long-term problems.

Equally important is tackling the day-to-day consumption of wood as a fuel source. According to Win Myo Thu, founder of the Myanmar NGO Ecodev (www.ecodev-mm.com), 90% of Myanmar's population relies on firewood for cooking and each household consumes some 3 tons of wood a year – all of which is putting pressure on Myanmar's forests, particularly in the dry zone. To tackle the problem, the A1 stove, an energy-efficient cooking stove developed by Myanmar's Forest Research Institute (FRI), has been distributed in the dry zone by Ecodev. The stoves cost around $2 each and cut a household's consumption of firewood by 1 ton a year.

Water Pollution & Inle Lake

Uncontrolled gold and other mining means that the release of pollutants into rivers and the sea is steadily increasing. The most noticeable aspect of pollution to travellers will be the piles of non-biodegradable waste, such as plastic bags, dumped at the edge of towns and villages and seen fluttering across the fields. Bans on the production and sale of polythene bags and cord exist in both Yangon and Mandalay but they are not strictly enforced.

Environmental experts are also concerned about the excessive use of chemical fertilisers and pesticides in agriculture and the run-off of these pollutants into the water supply. This has become an acute problem over recent years at Inle Lake, where there's been exponential growth in the number of commercial floating farms producing vegetables. Combined with pollution from chemical dyes used in textile processing and garbage related to increased tourism, the effect has been to turn placid Inle into a toxic pool in which fish die or struggle to survive.

For in-depth coverage of the major environmental issues facing Myanmar download the report published by the Burma Environment Working Group (www.bewg.org), a coalition of environmental organisations and activists working in the country.

DRY ZONE

Since 2009 the Korea International Cooperation Agency (KOICA) has been supporting a reforestation project across Myanmar's dry zone (www.dryzonegreening.gov.mm/eng).

ENVIRONMENT & WILDLIFE ENVIRONMENTAL ISSUES

A February 2012 report by the Department of Fisheries recorded adverse pH values across the lake, prompting U Mg Mg Pyone, secretary of the Biodiversity and Nature Conservation Association (BANCA), to state the lake's water is not safe for consumption. On top of all this, the expansion of rice cultivation near the lake and the building of more hotels is draining the water supply to Inle, causing it to shrink. In November 2012 a report entitled *Inlay Lake Conservation Project: A Plan for the Future* was released by the Institute for International Development-Myanmar (www.iid.org/myanmar.html). It outlines proposals to rehabilitate the lake by 2025, but also notes that an unchecked rise in tourism in the area is likely to put further strain on Inle's fragile environment.

Dams

In the past decade authorities have embarked on a series of hydroelectric dam projects along the country's major rivers, creating a crescendo of economic, social and environmental problems. In a nod to public opinion in September 2011 the government called a halt (for the time being) on controversial Myitsone Dam at the headwaters of the Ayeyarwady River in Kachin State, a project that was being developed in conjunction with China. Pressure remains to restart construction of the 6000 mega-wat generating dam.

In September 2013 the Indian government also cancelled its deal with Myanmar over the building of the Thamanthi Dam on the Chindwin River; if it had gone ahead the construction of this dam would have flooded parts of Tamanthi Wildlife Sanctuary and Hukaung Tiger Reserve, the habitats of several endangered species, including tigers, elephants and the very rare Burmese roofed turtle.

Mining, Oil & Gas

In November 2012, locals protesting about the environmental and social impact of the Letpadaung copper mine in Sagaing Region, a joint venture between a Chinese company and a Myanmar military enterprise, were subjected to a brutal police crackdown. Mining was subsequently suspended pending the investigation and conclusion of a parliamentary commission, chaired by Aung San Suu Kyi. The commission's recommendation was that the mining company resume operations, but only after taking steps to minimise its most harmful aspects. The mine was up and running again in October 2013 but there were concerns about whether the company was meeting its end of the agreement; the results of its environmental impact assessment are yet to be made public.

Such democratic levels of transparency are something new for Myanmar's extractive industries, which also include major gas and oil projects in the Bay of Bengal. In July 2013 the Shwe Gas Movement (www.shwe.org) issued a report slating the existing regulatory regime as woefully inadequate to address the social and environmental concerns facing the country; pending changes, it recommended that further extractive projects 'should be put to a halt.' The Shwe Gas Project, a joint venture between the Myanmar military and Indian and South Korean companies, includes the underwater extraction of natural gas and its piping across Myanmar to China.

ENVIRONMENT & WILDLIFE ENVIRONMENTAL ISSUES

GAS

According to a report by the Asian Development Bank, Myanmar has more than 8.1 trillion cubic feet of proven natural gas reserves and nearly 490 million tons of estimated coal reserves. There are also 37 oil blocks in operation, with 66 more open for exploration.

In February 2013 the Mandalay Region Legislative Assembly Committee set up the Irrawaddy River Conservation Commission, prompting environmentalists to call for the creation of a similar commission covering all of Myanmar's rivers.

Survival Guide

Directory A–Z

Accommodation

Myanmar has hundreds of privately run hotels and guesthouses licensed to accept foreigners. To get the licence they supposedly must keep at least five rooms and reach a certain standard. In fact many are simple family-run guesthouses or mini-hotels, sometimes with just a mosquito net, a fan that turns off at midnight (when the generator does) and a cold shower down the hall.

In key destinations (for example Yangon, Bagan, Inle Lake, Mandalay, Ngapali Beach) you'll find high-end hotels. In between (but closer to budget in quality) are modern, hit-or-miss Chinese-style hotels that follow familiar templates: tiled rooms with air-con, a refrigerator and a private bathroom with hot water.

Nearly all accommodation choices include a simple breakfast in their rates. Staff at most can also change money, arrange laundry service (starting at K1000 per load at budget guesthouses), rent bikes, arrange taxis, sell transport tickets and find you local English-speaking guides.

All accommodation options must fill in police forms on behalf of all guests, which include the details of your passport and visa. Hotels will not have to keep your passport.

Prices

Most hotels and guesthouses quote prices in either US dollars or kyat; you can usually pay in either currency. Prices quoted at budget and midrange hotels include all taxes; top-end hotel prices often don't include up to 20% in taxes and service charges. Only a few hotels currently accept credit cards.

There are lower rates or it's possible to bargain a little at most hotels during the low season (March to October).

Children

Travelling with children in Myanmar can be very rewarding as long as you come well prepared with the right attitude, the physical requirements and the usual parental patience. Lonely Planet's *Travel with Children* contains useful advice on travelling with kids on the road. Special attention is paid to travel in developing countries.

People in Myanmar love children and in many instances will shower attention on your offspring, who will find ready playmates among their local counterparts.

It may be confusing for some children (and distressing to adults) seeing children working at restaurants and teahouses. Sadly this is an unavoidable fact in what remains a poor country.

Practicalities

➡ Due to Myanmar's overall low level of public sanitation, parents ought to lay down a few ground rules with regard to maintaining their children's health – such as regular hand-washing – to head off potential medical problems.

➡ Children should especially be warned not to play with animals they encounter, as a precaution against rabies.

➡ Nappies (diapers) are hard to come by outside the major cities; come prepared if your

---

SLEEPING PRICE RANGES

Our listings are ordered by author preference and divided into three groups with regard to the price for a double room or dorm bed:

$ less than $50 (under K48,600)

$$ $50–150 (K48,600–145,800); in Yangon $50–200 (K48,600–194,400)

$$$ more than $150 (K145,800); in Yangon more than $200 (K194,400)

travels will take you off the beaten track.

➡ Most high-end hotels and restaurants will have highchairs available.

➡ When travelling with children, it may be more comfortable getting about by private car.

Sights & Activities

➡ Rides on trishaws and in horse carts.

➡ Boat trips on Inle Lake in dugout canoes.

➡ Big Buddhist sights and ancient ruins can make for good learning experiences, including Yangon's Shwedagon Paya, the reclining buddhas in Bago, or the 10-storey buddha in Pyay. You can climb into the back of the lacquered buddha image at Nan Paya in Salay.

➡ Some kids might dig ruins of old palace walls and moats, which you can see at places like Bagan and Mrauk U.

➡ Indulge in some face painting by trying on *thanakha* (yellow sandalwood-like paste), which is sold and applied from sidewalk stands around the country.

➡ There are zoos in Yangon, Nay Pyi Taw and Mandalay as well as excellent bird-watching at the Moeyungyi Wetlands near Bago.

➡ Traditional puppet shows are performed in Yangon, Bagan and Mandalay as well as other places.

➡ Beaches at Ngapali, Chaung Tha and Ngwe Saung and Southern Myanmar.

➡ Myanmar's festivals, such as Thingyan in mid-April with its throwing of water, and Taunggyi's fire-balloon festival in October or November, can be a lot of fun.

Customs Regulations

For the vast majority of visitors, clearing customs is a breeze, but it's important to be aware of the restrictions; for further details see www.myanmarcustoms.gov.mm.

Any foreign currency in excess of $2000 is supposed to be declared upon entry. Besides personal effects, visitors are permitted to bring duty free:

➡ 400 cigarettes

➡ 50 cigars

➡ 250g of tobacco

➡ 2L of alcoholic liquor

➡ 150ml of perfume. It's not a problem to bring a camera, video camera, laptop or mobile phone. You cannot bring in antiques, pornographic materials or narcotic drugs (obviously).

Export Restrictions

A wide variety of antiques cannot legally be taken out of the country, including the following:

➡ prehistoric implements and artefacts

➡ fossils

➡ old coins

➡ bronze or brass weights (including opium weights)

➡ bronze or clay pipes

➡ inscribed stones

➡ inscribed gold or silver

➡ historical documents

➡ religious images

➡ sculptures or carvings in bronze, stone, stucco or wood

➡ frescoes (even fragments)

➡ pottery

➡ national regalia and paraphernalia.

Electricity

Power outages occur everywhere, Yangon and Mandalay included. Many smaller towns have short scheduled periods for electricity, usually a few hours in the afternoon and evening (power always seems to be available if Myanmar TV is airing a premiership soccer game!). Many hotels and shops run generators 24 hours, others keep them on only a few hours (eg 6pm to midnight, and a few hours in the morning).

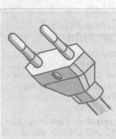

230V/50Hz

230V/50Hz

EATING PRICE RANGES

The following price ranges refer to a two-course meal with a soft drink.

$ less than $5 (K4850)

$$ $5–15 (K4850–14,580)

$$$ more than $15 (K14,580)

Embassies & Consulates

Most foreign embassies and consulates are based in Yangon. Check the government's Ministry of Foreign Affairs (www.mofa.gov.mm) for more information.

Australian Embassy (Map p40; ☑01-251 810; www.burma. embassy.gov.au; 88 Strand Rd, Kyauktada)

Bangladeshi Embassy (Map p50; ☑01-515 275; 11B Than Lwin Rd, Kamayut)

Cambodian Embassy (Map p54; ☑01-549 609; 34 Kaba Aye Pagoda Rd, Bahan)

Canadian Embassy (☑+66-02 636 0540) At the time of writing an embassy in Yangon was in the process of being set up.

Chinese Embassy (Map p50; ☑01-221 281; http:// mm.china-embassy.org/eng; 1 Pyidaungsu Yeiktha Rd, Dagon)

French Embassy (Map p44; ☑01-212 520; www. ambafrance-mm.org; 102 Pyidaungsu Yeiktha Rd, Dagon)

German Embassy (Map p50; ☑01-548 951; www.ran-gun.diplo.de; 9 Bogyoke Aung San Museum Rd, Bahan)

Indian Embassy (Map p40; ☑01-243 972; www.indiaembassyyangon.net; 545-547 Merchant St, Kyauktada)

Indonesian Embassy (Map p44; ☑01-254 465; http://kbri-yangon.org; 100 Pyidaungsu Yeiktha Rd, Dagon)

Israeli Embassy (Map p54; ☑01-515 155; http://embassies. gov.il/yangon/Pages/default. aspx; 15 Kabaung Rd, Hlaing)

Italian Embassy (Map p50; ☑01-527 100; www.ambyangon.esteri.it/ambasciata_yangon; 3 Inya Myaing Rd, Bahan)

Japanese Embassy (Map p50; ☑01-549 644; http://www. mm.emb-japan.go.jp; 100 Nat Mauk Rd, Bahan)

Korean Embassy (Map p54; ☑01-527 142; http://mmr.mofa. go.kr/english/as/mmr/main/ index.jsp; 97 University Ave Rd, Bahan)

Lao Embassy (Map p44; ☑01-222 482; A1 Diplomatic Quarters, Taw Win St, Dagon)

Malaysian Embassy (Map p44; ☑01-220 249; www.kln. gov.my/web/mmr_yangon/ home; 82 Pyidaungsu Yeiktha Rd, Dagon)

Netherlands Embassy (☑+66-02 254 7702) Affairs handled by German embassy or Netherlands embassy in Bangkok.

New Zealand Embassy (Map p40; ☑01-230 5805; 43 Inya Miyang Rd, Bahan)

Philippine Embassy (Map p40; ☑01-558 149; www. philembassy-yangon.com; 7 Gandamar St, Yankin)

Singapore Embassy (Map p50; ☑01-559 001; http://www. mfa.gov.sg/content/mfa/overseasmission/yangon.html; 238 Dhama Zedi Rd, Bahan)

Sri Lankan Embassy (Map p44; ☑01-222 812; 34 Taw Win St, Dagon)

Thai Embassy (Map p50; ☑01-226 721; www.thaiembassy.org/yangon/en; 94 Pyay Rd, Dagon)

UK Embassy (Map p40; ☑01-256 438, 01-370 863; www.gov. uk/government/world/burma; 80 Strand Rd, Kyauktada)

US Embassy (Map p54; ☑01-535 756, 01-536 509; http:// burma.usembassy.gov; 110 University Ave, Kamayut)

Vietnamese Embassy (Map p50; ☑01-511 305; www. vietnamembassy-myanmar.org/ vi; 72 Than Lwin Rd, Bahan)

Food

➡ For more about eating and drinking in Myanmar, see p355.

Gay & Lesbian Travellers

➡ Homosexuality is seen as a bit of a cultural taboo, though most locals are known to be tolerant of it, both for men and women.

➡ 'Carnal intercourse against nature' is legally punishable with imprisonment of up to 10 years. The law is rarely enforced, but it renders gays and lesbians vulnerable to police harassment; in July 2013 a dozen gay men were arrested and subjected to police abuse in Mandalay.

➡ Gay and transgendered people in Myanmar are rarely 'out', except for 'third sex' spirit mediums who channel the energies of *nat* spirits.

➡ Some Buddhists believe that those who committed sexual misconducts (such as adultery) in a previous life become gay or lesbian in this one.

➡ Public displays of affection, whether heterosexual or homosexual, are frowned upon; a local woman walking with a foreign man will raise more eyebrows than two same-sex travellers sharing a room.

➡ Check Utopia-Asia (www. utopia-asia.com) for some Yangon scene reports; it also publishes a gay guide to Southeast Asia, including Myanmar.

➡ Agencies offering gay-friendly trips to Myanmar

include **Purple Dragon** (www.purpledrag.com) and **Mandalay Travel** (www.mandalaytravel.com).

Insurance

A travel-insurance policy is a very wise idea, though not all companies cover travel to Myanmar. There is a wide variety of policies and your travel agent will have recommendations.

Worldwide travel insurance is available at www.lonelyplanet.com/travel_services. You can buy, extend and claim online anytime – even if you're already on the road.

Internet Access

Online access has improved, with wi-fi becoming the norm in big cities – most hotels, guesthouses, restaurants and cafes will have this and it's usually free. We even found internet access in relatively remote locations such as Mrauk U.

However, with tightly squeezed bandwidth and power outages it can often be a frustrating exercise to send and receive emails or check the internet, particularly in rural areas. Forget about streaming or big downloads.

Legal Matters

You have absolutely no legal recourse in case of arrest or detainment by the authorities, regardless of the charge. If you are arrested, you would most likely be permitted to contact your consular agent in Myanmar for possible assistance.

If you purchase gems or jewellery from persons or shops that are not licensed by the government, you run the risk of having them confiscated if customs officials find them in your baggage when you're exiting the country.

Forming public assemblies of over two people without the prior permission of the authorities is illegal. Drug trafficking crimes are punishable by death.

Maps

The best available is the 1.2,000,000 Periplus Editions *Myanmar Travel Map*, a folded map with plans for Mandalay, Yangon and the Bagan area, or the ITMB 1:1,350,000 *Myanmar (Burma)*. Another choice is the 1:1,500,000 Nelles *Myanmar*, a folded map on coated stock. Good places to buy maps online include International Travel Maps and Books (www.itmb.com) and East View Map Link (www.maplink.com).

Myanmar-based **Design Printing Services** (DPS; www.dpsmap.com) prints useful tourist maps of Myanmar, Yangon, Mandalay and Bagan; sometimes these maps are sold locally for about K1000 or given away by tour agencies, at hotels and international gateway airports.

Meditation Courses

Several monasteries around the country (in particular in Yangon and Mandalay) run courses on *satipatthana vipassana* (insight-awareness meditation), where foreigners are welcome. Beginners are typically expected to sign up for a 10-day residential course to learn the basics. Longer stays (and special visas covering them) are also available. Expect the following:

➡ The courses are open to all and free; voluntary donations according to your means are accepted at the end of retreats.

➡ Meditators must follow eight precepts including abstaining from food after noon and leading an austere lifestyle (no smoking or drinking; sleeping on basic beds often in shared accommodation).

➡ You will be expected to keep a 'noble silence' for most of the 10 days, save for interviews with meditation teachers.

➡ Daily practice begins at 3am; breakfast is at 5.30am and lunch at 10am.

Money

Banks & ATMs

The most useful of the local banks (which are open 9.30am to 3pm Monday to Friday) are CB and KBZ, both of which now issue and accept Mastercard and Visa cards and have ATMs in which you can use overseas-issued cards for a K5000 charge per transaction. You'll find these ATMs all across Yangon and in other major cities and tourist spots.

BRING NEW BILLS!

We cannot stress enough the need to bring pristine 'new' US dollar bills to Myanmar – that means 2006 or later bills that have colour and are in absolutely perfect condition: no folds, stamps, stains, writing marks or tears. Anything else may be rejected when you come to pay.

While $100 bills get the best exchange rates, it's also a good idea to bring lots of small dollar bills – ones, fives and 10s – and use them to pay for your hotel and other charges directly.

Black Market

Since the exchange rate has been stablised, Myanmar's black market for changing money should be avoided. Do not change money with people on the street – there are frequent reports of scam artists conning tourists in places such as downtown Yangon and Mandalay.

Cash

Myanmar remains a predominantly cash economy. The national currency, the kyat (pronounced 'chat'), is divided into the following banknotes: K1, K5, K10, K20, K50, K100, K200, K500, K1000, K5000 and K10,000; you'll rarely come across the smaller denominations and if you do they're often in tatters.

The US dollar acts as an alternative currency with most guesthouses and hotels quoting prices and accepting payment in the greenback. Prices in our reviews alternate between kyat (K) and US dollars ($), depending on the currency in which prices are quoted.

Items such as meals, bus tickets, trishaw or taxi rides, bottles of water or beer and market items are usually quoted in kyat.

These days most places will accept either currency but a few government-run services (such as archaeological sites, trains and IWT ferries) continue to insist on payment in dollars. You'll also be expected to pay for flights with dollars.

Also, when paying in US dollars, check your change carefully. Locals like to unload slightly torn bills that work fine in New York, but will be worthless for the rest of your trip in Myanmar.

Credit Cards & Travellers Cheques

Credit cards and travellers cheques remain largely useless. However, the situation is rapidly changing and in Yangon and other major tourist spots you'll increasingly find credit cards accepted by top-end hotels, restaurants and some shops.

Moneychangers

You'll find official bank and private licensed exchange booths at places such as Yangon and Mandalay airports, Bogyoke Aung San Market and Shwedagon Paya in Yangon.

Never hand over your money until you've received the kyat and counted them. Honest moneychangers will expect you to do this. Considering that K10,000 is the highest denomination, you'll get a lot of notes. Moneychangers give ready-made, rubber-banded stacks of a hundred K1000 bills. It's a good idea to check each note individually. Often you'll find one or two (or more) with a cut corner or taped tears, neither of which anyone will accept.

Many travellers do the bulk of their exchanging in Yangon, then carry the stacks of kyat around the country. Considering the relative safety from theft, it's not a bad idea, but you *can* exchange money elsewhere and the spreading of ATMs is making such a strategy increasingly unnecessary.

Tipping, Donations & Bribes

Tipping is not customary in Myanmar, though little extra 'presents' are sometimes expected (even if they're not asked for) in exchange for a service (such as unlocking a locked temple at Bagan, helping move a bag at the airport or showing you around the sights of a village). Given the low level of wages, too, it's a good idea to leave change for waiters in restaurants.

Have some small notes (K50, K100, K200) ready when visiting a religious temple or monastery, as donations may be requested and you may wish to leave one even if it's not.

The government has vowed to fight corruption, but it's a fact that bribes remain an ingrained feature of large sections of Myanmar's economy. You may find that a small amount of 'tea money' is need to expedite certain services – use sense and discretion if you find yourself in such a situation.

Opening Hours

Opening hours are generally as follows:

➡ government offices, including post offices and telephone centres, 9.30am to 4.30pm Monday to Friday

➡ shops 9.30am to 6pm or later Monday to Saturday

➡ restaurants 8am to 9pm

➡ internet cafes noon to 10pm.

Photography

There's no problem bringing a camera or video camera into Myanmar. Photo-processing shops and internet cafes can burn digital photos onto a CD, but you should have your own adapter. Colour film – Fuji and Kodak – is available.

Avoid taking photographs of military facilities, uniformed individuals, road blocks, and strategic locations such as bridges.

Most locals are very happy to be photographed, but always ask first. If you have a digital camera with a display screen, some locals (kids, monks, anyone) will be overjoyed to see their image. It's also very easy and cheap to get digital photos turned into prints that can then be given to people as presents.

Some sights, including some paya and other reli-gious sites, charge a camera fee of K100 or so. Usually a video camera fee is a little more.

For tips on how to shoot photos, pick up Lonely Planet's *Travel Photography*.

Post

Most mail out of Myanmar gets to its destination quite efficiently. International-postage rates are a bargain: a postcard is K500, a 1kg package to Australia/UK/US K16,200/18,900/20,700.

Post offices are supposed to be open from 9.30am to 4.30pm Monday to Friday but you may find some keep shorter hours.

DHL (Map p44; ☏01-215 516; www.dhl.com; 58 Wadan St, Lanmadaw; ☺8am-6pm Mon-Fri, 8am-2pm Sat) is a more reliable but expensive way of sending out bigger packages.

Public Holidays

Major public holidays.

Independence Day 4 January

Union Day 12 February

Peasants' Day 2 March

Armed Forces Day 27 March

Workers' Day 1 May

Martyrs' Day 19 July

National Day 27 November

Christmas 25 December

Safe Travel

For the vast majority of visitors, travel in Myanmar is safe and should pose no serious problems.

Bugs, Snakes, Rats & Monkeys

Mosquitoes, if allowed, can have a field day with you. Bring repellent from home, as the good stuff (other than mosquito coils) is hard to come by. Some guesthouses and hotels don't provide mosquito nets.

Myanmar has one of the highest incidences of death from snakebite in the world. Watch your step in brush, forest and grasses.

Family-run guesthouses, like regular homes, might have a rodent or two. Wash your hands before sleeping and try to keep food out of your room. If you trek in Shan State and stay in local accommodation, you may hear little footsteps at night.

In a few sites, such as Hpo Win Daung Caves, near Monywa or Mt Popa near Bagan, you'll have monkeys begging for snacks. Take care as bites are possible.

Crime

All over Myanmar, police stations have English signs up that ask: 'May I help you?' It's easy to smirk at, but some of the restrictions to travel around Myanmar are based on the government's desire to keep foreigners out of harm's way.

Locals know that the penalties for stealing, particularly from foreigners, can be severe. Most travellers' memories of locals grabbing their money are of someone

GOVERNMENT TRAVEL ADVICE

The following government websites offer travel advisories and information on current hot spots:

Australia (www.smarttraveller.gov.au)

Canada (www.voyage.gc.ca)

New Zealand (www.safetravel.govt.nz)

UK (www.gov.uk/foreign-travel-advice)

USA (travel.state.gov/travel)

SAFETY GUIDELINES FOR HIKING

We've heard about some travellers finding new paths and staying in the hills for a week or more. Most, however, stick with day trips. Here are a few points to consider before lacing up the boots:

➡ Hike with at least one companion; in most cases it's best to hire a guide.

➡ Do not venture by foot into areas restricted to foreigners; ask around before taking off.

➡ Camping in the hills is not technically legal, as foreigners must be registered nightly with local authorities by owners of 'licensed accommodation'.

➡ Trail conditions can get slippery and dangerous, especially in the rainy season.

➡ Walk only in regions within your capabilities – you're not going to find a trishaw out there to bring you back.

chasing them down to return a K500 note they dropped. If someone grabs your bag at a bus station, it's almost certainly just a trishaw driver hoping for a fare.

Insurgents & Bombs

In recent years, including in 2013, there have been a handful of bombings, usually linked with insurgent groups, in Yangon and elsewhere.

Ceasefire agreements between the government and many insurgent groups are making it easier to travel to previously off-limits parts of the country. However, the situation can and does change rapidly so check current travel advisories. Land mines on the Myanmar side of the Thai border are another threat.

The presence of Shan and Wa armies along the Thai-Myanmar border in northern Mae Hong Son makes this area dangerous. The Wa have reportedly sworn off drug production, but there's still plenty of amphetamines and opium crossing some border areas.

Politics

Even though open discussion of politics is now not such a dangerous act in Myanmar, it's still best to allow locals to take the lead on the subject and proceed to talk with discretion if they do.

Scams & Hassle

Myanmar touts are pretty minor league in comparison with others in the region. Most hassle is due to commissions. These small behind-the-scenes payments are made, like it or not, for a taxi, trishaw driver or guide who takes you to a hotel, to buy a puppet or even to eat some rice.

When arriving at a bus station, you're likely to be quickly surrounded by touts, some of whom will try to steer you to a particular hotel that offers them a commission.

Be wary of claims that your chosen place is 'no good', though in some cases we found that trishaw drivers who had warned us that 'foreigners can't stay there' ended up being correct. If you know where you want to go, persist and they'll take you.

This said, a few travel-related businesses and touts do go to creative lengths or use hard-sell techniques to rustle up customers, so do try to keep your wits about you.

Be wary of fanciful offers of jade or other gems as some are filled with worthless rock or concrete mixture. And never buy gems on the street.

Many people may approach to say 'hello' on the street. In some cases, they're just curious or want to practise some English. In other cases the conversation switches from 'what country you from?' to 'where you need to go?' It's all pretty harmless.

Do not change money on the street.

Spies

In the more off-the-beaten-track places, where authorities are less used to seeing foreigners, the chances are that you will be kept an eye on.

Transport & Road Hazards

The poor state of road and rail infrastructure plus lax safety standards and procedures for flights and boats means that travelling can sometimes be dangerous. Government-operated Myanma Airways (MA) has a sketchy safety record. The rickety state of Myanmar's railway also doesn't inspire much confidence. It's not much better on the roads, where safety often seems to be the last consideration of both drivers and pedestrians.

Proceed with caution when crossing any road, particularly in cities where drivers are unlikely to stop if they are involved in an accident with a pedestrian.

Traffic drives on the right in Myanmar, but the majority of cars are right-hand-drive imports, which add to the chance of accidents occurring. Factor in the poor state of roads and the even poorer state of many clapped-out vehicles and you have a recipe for potential disaster.

Telephone

Local Calls

Most business cards in Myanmar list a couple of phone numbers, as lines frequently go dead and calls just don't go through.

Local call stands – as part of a shop, or sometimes just a table with a phone or two on a sidewalk – are marked by a drawing of a phone and can be found all over Myanmar. A local call should be K100 per minute.

To dial long distance within Myanmar, dial the area code (including the '0') and the number.

A useful resource is the Myanmar Yellow Pages (www.myanmaryellowpages.biz).

International Calls

Internet cafes using Skype and other VOI protocols, official telephone (call) centres and top-end hotels are sometimes the only way to call overseas, though sometimes this can be done on the street through vendors offering use of their mobile phones.

Generally, it costs about $5 per minute to call Australia or Europe and $6 per minute to phone North America.

To call Myanmar from abroad, dial your country's international access code, then ☑95 (Myanmar's country code), the area code (minus the '0'), and the five- or six-digit number.

Mobile Phones

Mobile phone numbers begin with ☑09.

The mobile phone industry in Myanmar is rapidly changing. In June 2013 the government awarded Telenor Mobile Communications of Norway and Ooredoo of Qatar 15-year concessions to create new mobile phone networks. These will start to come online in 2014, expanding the range and quality of mobile communications in the country as well as impacting the cost of SIMs and calls.

At the time of research, international roaming for mobile phones was limited to a handful of Asian networks. Temporary local SIM cards

costing K20,000 and lasting one month before expiring had been in circulation during 2013 but were sold out by August of that year. Permanent SIM cards costing K1700 had also been available via lottery. Top-up cards for calls come in amounts of K5000 and K10,000.

The only easy option we found for visitors was rental of a SIM or a SIM and handset at Yangon Airport from Yatanarpon. The cost, starting at $60 for five days not including call charges, was prohibitive.

Time

The local Myanmar Standard Time (MST) is 6½ hours ahead of Greenwich Mean Time (GMT/UTC). When coming in from Thailand, turn your watch back half an hour; coming from India, put your watch forward an hour. The 24-hour clock is often used for train times.

LIVING ON MYANMAR TIME

Chances are that your bus or train will roll in late, but much of Myanmar actually does work on a different time system. Burmese Buddhists use an eight-day week in which Thursday to Tuesday conform to the Western calendar but Wednesday is divided into two 12-hour days. Midnight to noon is 'Bohdahu' (the day Buddha was born), while noon to midnight is 'Yahu' (Rahu, a Hindu god/planet). However, it's rare that the week's unique structure causes any communication problems.

The traditional Myanmar calendar features 12 28-day lunar months that run out of sync with the months of the solar Gregorian calendar. To stay in sync with the solar year, Myanmar inserts a second Waso lunar month every few years – somewhat like the leap-year day added to the Gregorian February. The lunar months of Myanmar are Tagu, March/April; Kason, April/May; Nayon, May/June; Waso, June/July; Wagaung, July/August; Tawthalin, August/September; Thadingyut, September/October; Tazaungmon, October/November; Nadaw, November/December; Pyatho, December/January; Tabodwe, January/February; Tabaung, February/March.

Traditionally, Burmese kings subscribed to various year counts. The main one in current use, the *thekkayit*, begins in April and is 638 years behind the Christian year count. Therefore, the Christian year of 2014 is equivalent to the *thekkayit* of 1376. If an ancient temple you see sounds way too old, it may be because locals are using the *thekkayit*.

Another calendar in use follows the Buddhist era (BE), as used in Thailand, which counts from 543 BC, the date that Buddha achieved *nibbana*. Hence AD 2011 is 2554 BE.

BOOK YOUR STAY ONLINE

For more accommodation reviews by Lonely Planet authors, check out http://lonelyplanet.com/hotels/. You'll find independent reviews, as well as recommendations on the best places to stay. Best of all, you can book online.

Toilets

➡ Apart from most guesthouses, hotels and upscale restaurants, squat toilets are the norm. Most of these are located down a dirt path behind a house.

➡ Usually next to the toilet is a cement reservoir filled with water, and a plastic bowl lying nearby. This has two functions: as a flush and for people to clean their nether regions while still squatting over the toilet.

➡ Toilet paper is available at shops all over the country, but not often at toilets. Some places charge a nominal fee to use the toilet.

➡ Sit-down toilets are not equipped to flush paper. Usually there's a small waste basket nearby to deposit used toilet paper.

➡ It's acceptable for men (less so for women) to go behind a tree or bush (or at the roadside) when nature calls.

➡ Buses and smaller boats usually don't have toilets.

Tourist Information

Myanmar Travels & Tours (MTT; www.myanmartravel-sandtours.com), part of the Ministry of Hotels & Tourism, is the main 'tourist information' service in the country. MTT offices are located in Yangon, Mandalay, New Bagan and Inle Lake. Other than at Yangon, these offices are pretty quiet, and often the staff have sketchy knowledge on restricted areas.

Travellers who want to arrange a driver, or have hotel reservations awaiting them, would do well to arrange a trip with the help of private travel agents in Yangon and other major cities; see p27 for recommendations. Many Myanmar 'travel agents' outside Yangon only sell air tickets.

Travellers with Disabilities

With its lack of paved roads or footpaths (even when present the latter are often uneven), Myanmar presents many physical obstacles for the mobility-impaired. Rarely do public buildings (or transport) feature ramps or other access points for wheelchairs, and hotels make inconsistent efforts to provide access for the disabled.

For wheelchair travellers, any trip to Myanmar will require a good deal of planning. Before setting off, get in touch with your national support organisation (preferably with the travel officer, if there is one). Also try the following:

Accessible Journeys (☑800-846 4537; www.disabilitytravel.com) In the US.

Mobility International USA (☑541-343 1284; www.miusa.org) In the US.

Nican (☑02-6241 1220; www.nican.com.au) In Australia.

Tourism for All (☑0845 124 9971; www.tourismforall.org.uk) In the UK.

Visas

All nationalities require a visa to visit Myanmar, and to get one your passport must be valid for six months beyond the date of your arrival.

Note that Myanmar doesn't recognise dual nationalities.

Applications

All visas are valid for up to three months from the date of issue. Starting the process a month in advance is the safe bet; these days the processing can take anything between a day and a week.

VISA FEES

The vast majority of visitors should apply for a tourist visa. Former Myanmar citizens and their blood relatives are eligible for 'social' visas, which can be extended at the Immigration Department in Yangon for $36 for up to six months. The following table lists fees, which are converted into local currency depending on which embassy you apply at.

VISA TYPE	FEE	VALIDITY OF VISA
tourist (single entry)	$22	28 days
social (single entry)	$30	28 days
social (multiple entry)	$150	6 months
work (single entry)	$30	10 weeks
work (multiple entry)	$150	10 weeks
meditation (single entry)	$30	3 months

There are slight differences between the application procedures at Myanmar embassies in different countries. Some require two passport photos, others only one. Postal applications are usually OK, but it's best to check first with your nearest embassy about its specific application rules.

There is no need for you to conceal your profession on the visa application form if you're a journalist or involved in the media.

Extensions & Overstaying Your Visa

Tourist visas can be extended for two weeks for $36 and for a month for $72. Business visas can also be extended.

You may have difficulties with some hotels and domestic airport officials if you've overstayed your visa and not officially extended it. If you do overstay, it's wise to stick with land routes and places within easy access of Yangon, as there have been cases in the past of tourists being instructed to leave the country immediately when discovered by the authorities.

If you haven't extended your visa, you will have to pay a fine of $3 per day, plus a $3 registration fee, at the airport or land border as you exit the country. The fine can be paid in kyat if you don't have dollars.

Volunteering

Official opportunities to volunteer are limited. Don't let this sway you. Everyone in Myanmar wants to learn English, and few can afford to. Ask in

---

VISA ON ARRIVAL

At the time of our research, a visa on arrival was available at Yangon, Mandalay and Nay Pyi Taw international airports for business visas and *only* if you arrive with a letter of invitation from a sponsoring company and proof of your company registration or business.

Tourist visas on arrival are available only if you've made prior arrangements with a travel agency qualified to apply for visas, such as **Oway** (Map p50; ☏01-230 4201; www.oway.com.mm; 2nd floor, Bldg 6 Junction Square, Pyay Rd, Kamayut). You will need to apply at least 10 working days before your flight and bring two passport photos and the visa approval letter issued by the agent with you for the visa to be fully processed on arrival.

---

towns or villages to sit in at an English class.

A list of NGOs that may have volunteering opportunities can be found on www. ngoinmyanmar.org, although mostly its postings are for specific experienced workers (often in medicine). You can also browse the links at Burma Volunteer Program (http://burmavolunteers.org).

Women Travellers

As in most Buddhist countries, foreign women travelling in Myanmar are rarely hassled on the road as they might be in India, Malaysia or Indonesia. However, we have heard a few reports of sexual harassment. Dressing modestly should help reduce this risk: wear a local *longyi* instead of a skirt above the knee, and a T-shirt instead of a spaghetti-strap singlet.

Few Myanmar women would consider travelling without at least one female companion, so women travelling alone are regarded as

slightly peculiar by the locals. Lone women being seen off on boats and trains by local friends may find the latter trying to find a suitably responsible older woman to keep them company on the trip.

If you didn't bring tampons, one good place to find them is Yangon's City Mart Supermarket.

'Ladies' (per the posted signs in certain areas) cannot go up to some altars or onto decks around stupas, including the one affording a close-up look at the famous Golden Rock at Kyaiktiyo, or apply gold leaf on the Buddha image at Mandalay's Mahamuni Paya. Also, women should never touch a monk; if you're handing something to a monk, place the object within reach of him, not directly into his hands.

Most locals tend to visit teahouses, restaurants or shops with members of the same sex. Asian women, even from other countries, travelling with a Western man may encounter rude comments.

Transport

GETTING THERE & AWAY

Flights, tours and rail tickets can be booked online at lonelyplanet.com/bookings.

Entering the Country

If you have your visa ready and a valid passport with at least six months of validity from the time of entry in hand, you should have no trouble entering Myanmar either by air or land.

There is no requirement for you to show an onward ticket out of the country in order to enter Myanmar.

Air

Airports & Airlines

International flights arrive at Yangon (Rangoon; RGN; www.ygnia.com), Mandalay (MDL; www.mandalayairport.com) and Nay Pyi Taw (NPT; www.nptia.com) airports. The most common route to Yangon is via Bangkok, though there are regular direct flights with several other regional cities including Singapore and Kuala Lumpur.

Land

Arriving and departing by land from China and Thailand is possible – see boxes in the region's chapters for full details.

Regular tourists are not allowed to enter Myanmar by land or sea from Bangladesh, India or Laos.

Overland links could change at some point in the future. Most of Myanmar's neighbours actively covet Myanmar ports and are planning on investing for infrastructure projects to eventually criss-cross Myanmar by road. This may mean connections from Danang, Vietnam (through Laos and Thailand) to Mawlamyine, and up through central Myanmar, across the Indian border at Morei to New Delhi.

GETTING AROUND

In unrestricted areas, travel methods are remarkably open to visitors. No set itineraries are required and you can pick and choose how you go as you go – taking a bus, plane or train, or crammed pick-up, or hopping onto a giant ferry that drifts at ox-like speed. Reaching some isolated towns such as Kengtung or Sittwe require jumps by air or boat.

Restricted Areas

In January 2013 government bans on travel to restricted areas of the country, including places in Chin, Kayah, Kayin, Shan and Kachin states, were partially lifted.

However, confusion over the new rules has led to some travellers still being turned back from some areas so make thorough inquiries before you set out. You're likely to have much greater success in visiting newly accessible areas if you're in the company of a Burmese speaker.

Some restrictions still apply to the following destinations. With permission and a guide from Myanmar Travels & Tours (MTT), which may take up to two months to secure, you may gain access to some of them:

Chin State: Tiddim, Ton Zang, Falam, Tlangtlang and Hakka

Kachin State: Hpakant, Putao, Machanbaw, Mansi, Momauk and Waingmaw

Kayah State: Demoso and Hpruso

Kayin State: Kawkareik and Hlaingbwe

Mandalay Region: Mogok

Air

Myanmar's domestic air service features a handful of overworked planes that have busy days, sometimes landing at an airport, leaving the engine on, unloading and loading, and taking off in 20 minutes! This doesn't yield a spot-free safety record.

Between the main destinations of Yangon, Mandalay, Heho (for Inle Lake), Nyaung

Major Transport Routes

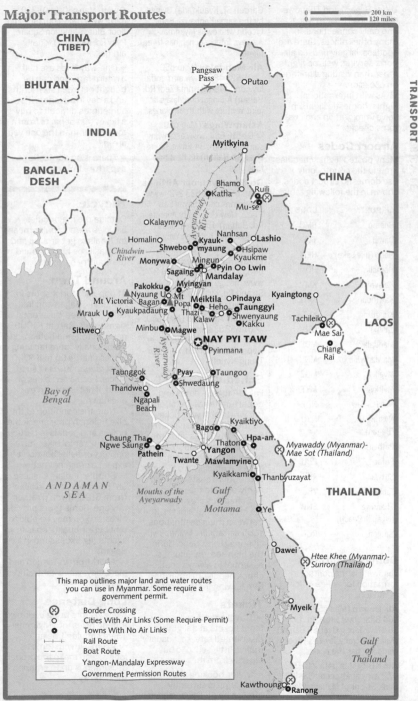

0   200 km
0   120 miles

CHINA (TIBET)

BHUTAN

INDIA

BANGLA-DESH

Pangsaw Pass

○Putao

Myitkyina

Bhamo ○Ruili ⊗

Katha ●

Mu-se ⊗

CHINA

○Kalaymyo

Homalin○

Nanhsan ○Lashio

Kyauk-myaung

Shwebo●

Hsipaw○

Kyaukme●

Chindwin River

Monywa○

Mingun●

Pyin Oo Lwin

Sagaing▲

Mandalay

Pakokku●

Myingyan●

Mt ○Pindaya

Nyaung U○ Popa▲

Meiktila●

Kyaingtong ○

Mt Victoria▲

Bagan▲

Heho●

Taunggyi

Mrauk U○

Kyaukpadaung●

Thazi●

Shwenyaung●

Kalaw●

Kakku●

Tachileik○ ⊗

Sittwe○

Minbu○ **Magwe**●

★NAY PYI TAW

Mae Sai

LAOS

●Pyinmana

Chiang Rai

Ayeyarwady River

Taunggok●

Pyay● ○Taungoo

Thandwe○

Shwedaung●

Ngapali Beach●

Bay of Bengal

Bago○

Kyaiktiyo●

Chaung Tha●

Thaton● **Hpa-an**●

Myawaddy (Myanmar)-Mae Sot (Thailand) ⊗

Ngwe Saung●

Pathein●

Thaton●

Yangon●

○Twante

Mawlamyine○

Kyaikkami● ●Thanbyuzayat

ANDAMAN SEA

Mouths of the Ayeyarwady

Gulf of Mottama

THAILAND

●Ye

Dawei●

Htee Khee (Myanmar)-Sunron (Thailand) ⊗

Myeik●

Gulf of Thailand

Kawthoung⊗ **Ranong**●

This map outlines major land and water routes you can use in Myanmar. Some require a government permit.

⊗   Border Crossing

○   Cities With Air Links (Some Require Permit)

●   Towns With No Air Links

├─┼─┤   Rail Route

- - -   Boat Route

═══   Yangon-Mandalay Expressway

───   Government Permission Routes

U (for Bagan) and Thandwe (for Ngapali Beach), you'll find daily connections. In many other places, there are spotless, largely unused airports serving, well, no flights other than visiting dignitaries on occasion.

As with international flights, domestic flights involve immigration and customs checks.

Airport Codes

Many posted flight schedules around the country only use domestic airport codes, shown in the following table.

AIRPORT	CODE
Bhamo	BMO
Dawei	TVY
Heho (Inle Lake)	HEH
Homalin	HOX
Kalaymyo	KMV
Kawthoung	KAW
Kengtung	KET
Lashio	LSH
Mandalay	MDL
Mawlamyine	MNU
Myeik	MGZ
Myitkyina	MYT
Nay Pyi Taw	NPT
Nyaung U (Bagan)	NYU
Pathein	BSX
Putao	PBU
Sittwe	AKY
Tachileik	THL
Thandwe (Ngapali Beach)	SNW
Yangon	RGN

Domestic Airlines

Following is the contact information for airline offices in Yangon.

Air Bagan (Map p50; 01-504 888; www.airbagan.com; 56 Shwe Taung Gyar St, Bahan) Owned by crony Tay Za's Htoo company; has five planes.

Air KBZ (Map p40; 01-372 977; www.airkbz.com; 33-49 Bank St, cnr of Mahabandoola Garden St, Kyauktada) Owned by the same Kanbawza Bank tycoon who owns Myanmar Airways International; has three planes.

Air Mandalay (Map p50; 01-525 488; www.airmandalay.com; 146 Dhamma Zedi Rd, Bahan) A Singapore-Malaysia joint venture with three planes.

Asian Wings (Map p50; 01-516 654; www.asianwingsairways.com; 34 Shwe Taung Gyar St, Bahan) Its fleet has four planes.

Golden Myanmar Airlines (Map p54; 01-533 272; www.gmairlines.com; Sayar San Plaza, New University Avenue Rd, Bahan) Has two planes flying routes between Yangon, Mandalay and Singapore

Myanma Airways (MA; Map p40; 01-373 828, 01-374 874; www.mot.gov.mm/ma; 104 Strand Rd, Kyauktada) Government airline.

Yangon Airways (Map p50; 01-652 533; www.yangonair.com; 166, Level 5, MMB Tower, Upper Pansodan Rd, Mingalar Taung Nyunt)

Schedules

For MA flights, dates and departure times are often not written on your ticket, so the airline doesn't have to honour the dates and times for which reservations were originally made. (In some cases, if officials are flying somewhere seats may suddenly open to the public.)

Schedules are more reliable on the other airlines, and between main destinations such as Yangon, Mandalay, Nyaung U and Heho, during the high season – but it's essential to always double-check departure times before leaving for the airport.

Tickets

➡ Travel agents sell flight tickets at a slightly discounted rate, so it usually makes little sense to buy directly from the airlines.

➡ Online booking and e-ticketing is currently offered by Air Bagan and

Oway (Map p50; 01-230 4201; www.oway.com.mm; 2nd floor, Bldg 6 Junction Square, Pyay Rd, Kamayut) for all airlines.

➡ One-way fares are half a return fare, and can be bought between six months and a day in advance. It's sometimes difficult to buy a ticket that departs from a town other than the one you are in.

➡ There is no domestic departure tax.

Bicycle

Outside the major cities bicycles are a popular means for locals to get around and can easily be hired around the country by visitors.

Around Town

At popular tourist spots in Mandalay, Bagan and Inle Lake you'll see 'bike rental' signs; rates start at K1000 per day; top-end hotels and occasionally more far-flung places charge up to K4000. Most guesthouses in such places keep a few bikes on hand; if not, staff can track one down.

Note the condition of the bike before hiring; check the brakes and pedals in particular. Many rental bikes have baskets or bells, but don't expect a crash helmet!

Sturdier Indian, Chinese or Thai imports are available (from $100) if you'd rather buy one. Some tours provide bikes, so you may be able to rent better-quality ones from agents (eg Exotissimo in New Bagan).

Apart from in Yangon and Mandalay, vehicular traffic is quite light.

Long Distance

A few visitors bring their own touring bikes into Myanmar. There shouldn't be any problem with customs as long as you make the proper declarations upon entering the country.

Gradients are moderate in most parts of Myanmar that are open to tourism. Frontier regions, on the other hand, tend to be mountainous, particularly Shan, Kayin, Kayah and Chin States. You'll find plenty of opportunity everywhere for dirt-road and off-road pedalling. A sturdy mountain bike would make a good alternative to a touring rig, especially in the north, where main roads can resemble secondary roads elsewhere.

Some of the key routes around Myanmar:

➡ Thazi to Inle Lake via Kalaw

➡ Pyin Oo Lwin (Maymyo) to Lashio via Hsipaw

➡ Mandalay to Bagan via Myingyan

➡ Mandalay to either Monywa, Pyin Oo Lwin, Sagaing, Inwa (Ava) or Amarapura.

November to February is the best time to cycle in terms of the weather.

There are basic bicycle shops in most towns, but they usually have only locally or Chinese-made parts to equip single-speed bikes. You can also buy lower-quality motorcycle helmets here; many are disturbingly adorned with swastikas – a fad, not a political alliance. Bring reflective clothing and plenty of insurance. Don't ride at night.

Travellers on a bike may end up needing to sleep in towns few travellers make it to, and a lack of licensed accommodation may be an issue. Technically, you will need permission from local immigration to stay at such places. Be patient. Most cyclists get permission from local authorities to stay one night, but the paperwork (coming with some frowns) may take an hour or so to arrange.

It's possible to store your bicycle in the undercarriage storage on buses, though you may have to pay a little extra. On smaller buses it's pos-sible you'll be asked to buy a 'seat' for your bike.

Some bike tours connect the dots of Myanmar's greatest hits – going, for example, up the Pyay highway to Bagan then Mandalay, and back to Yangon via Meiktila and Taungoo. It's more rough going, but nicer riding, to reach some mountainous areas, like Inle Lake.

Recommended tour companies:

Bike World Explores Myanmar (BWEM; ☑in Yangon 01-527 636; www.cyclingmyanmar.com) Yangon-based company that also sells and rents bikes and can offer touring advice. It has eight itineraries from easy day trips around Yangon (from $140) to 10-day adventures in Chin State (from $1128).

Exotissimo (☑in Yangon 01-860 4932; www.exotissimo.com; 147 Shwegonedine Rd, Bahan) Runs high-end cycle tours covering Mandalay to Bagan, the Shan Hills and sights in Mon State.

Spice Roads (☑in Bangkok 02-381 7490; www.spiceroads.com) Bangkok-based operation, offering two 14-day itineraries (including eight days of riding) from $2150 per person. One follows part of the old Burma Road from Pyin Oo Lwin to Mandalay.

Think Asia Travel & Tours (☑01-230 1293; www.thinkasia-tours.com/; 3rd floor, 14 Mar Ga Rd, Ahlone) Yangon-based agency offering bike tours at Inle Lake, Kalaw and Mandalay.

Boat

A great variety of boats – from creaky old government-run ferries to swanky private cruise ships – ply Myanmar's waterways; for more details see p25.

Rapidly changing sand-banks and shallow water during the dry season mean the skillful captains and pilots have to keep in constant touch with the changing pattern of the river flows.

In addition to the rivers, it's possible to travel along the Bay of Bengal between Sittwe and Taunggok (north of Ngapali Beach).

Cargo Ships

Myanma Five Star Line (Map p40; ☑01- 295 279; www.mfsl-shipping.com; 132-136 Thein Byu Rd, Botataung), the government-owned ocean transport enterprise, is only

---

BORDER CROSSINGS

There are currently entry and exit points from Myanmar's land borders at five points detailed here. No bus or train service connects Myanmar with another country, nor can you travel by car or motorcycle across the border – you must walk across. Have your visa ready before you get to the border.

➡ Mae Sai in northern Thailand to/from Tachileik in Shan State.

➡ Mae Sot in Thailand to/from Myawaddy in Kayin State.

➡ Ranong in Thailand to/from Kawthoung at far southern end of Tanintharyi Region.

➡ Sunron in Thailand to/from Htee Khee in Tanintharyi Region.

➡ Ruili in Yunnan Province, China to/from Mu-se in Shan State.

cargo now, but you can try to see about jumping on a boat to Thandwe, Taunggok or Sittwe, or south to Dawei, Myeik or Kawthoung, at some point in the future.

Ferries & Private Boats

The government-run **Inland Water Transport** (IWT; www.iwt.gov.mm) boats tend to be rather rundown and ramshackle, but provide remarkable glimpses into local river life. Many of the passengers on the long-distance ferries are traders who make stops along the way to pick up or deliver goods.

Along the heavily travelled 262-mile-long Yangon–Pyay–Mandalay route, there are 28 ferry landings, where merchants can ply their trade. IWT offices are usually near the jetty. They can offer information, schedules and fare details, and usually tickets. IWT offices, officially, accept US dollars only.

Some short trips are handled with small covered wooden ferries that fit about 25 people. Often there are smaller, private boats you can negotiate to use with the driver. We include private boat services whenever

possible. However, because of their size it's not always as safe riding with private boats compared with bigger government ferries. In 2004 a small private boat between Sittwe and Mrauk U capsized during a storm and several Italian tourists were killed.

Luxury Boats

Several luxury ferries travel the upper and lower reaches of the Ayeyarwady River; for details see p26.

Bus

Almost always faster and cheaper than trains, Myanmar buses range from luxury air-con express buses, less luxurious but nice buses (without air-con), local buses, and mini 32-seaters. Most are operated by private companies.

Classes & Conditions

Many long-haul trips allow the greatest comfort, with new(ish) air-conditioned express buses – some of which are quite nice. For several long-distance routes, many services leave between 4pm and 10pm or later, and arrive

at the final destination in the wee hours (often 5am or 6am). There are a couple of reasons for this: local people can't afford to waste a working day on a bus so prefer to travel overnight; and the buses don't overheat as much by avoiding the punishing midday sun.

If you want extra air-con comfort but don't want to go the whole way on one of these routes, you usually have to pay the full fare (eg going from Mandalay to Taungoo you pay the full fare to Yangon) and will have to deal with the middle-of-the-night arrival time. Similarly, by paying the full fare for the route, you can jump on a bus at a stop along the way, for example catch the Mandalay-to-Yangon bus at Meiktila. Staff at your guesthouse or hotel should be able to help with this.

Similar-sized but older buses, with no air-conditioning, make shorter-haul trips, such as direct links from Yangon to Pyay or Taungoo to Yangon.

Local 32-seat minibuses bounce along the highways too. These tend to use the aisles, if not for people, for bags of rice, vegies or (worst)

SURVIVING LONG-DISTANCE BUS TRIPS

Heed the following points and your long-distance bus trip will, possibly, be more comfortable:

➡ Bring snacks and drinks by all means but don't worry too much about this. A bottle of water is often handed out on better-quality buses. There are usually no bathrooms on the bus, but frequent toilet-and-refreshment stops (where everyone must get off the bus to prevent anything being stolen) punctuate journeys.

➡ Often the TV blares for much of the trip – usually sticking with Myanmar-made concerts or movies detailing things such as, oh, protagonists dying bloody deaths in car crashes, but the occasional Raiders of the Lost Ark slips in.

➡ Take a jacket or blanket (preferably both) as temperatures can drop substantially at night; air-con can also make it chilly. And consider earplugs and an eye-mask as well if you plan to grab a little shut-eye between toilet stops.

➡ Myanmar superstition says that when you're on a journey you shouldn't ask anyone 'How much longer?', or 'Brother, when will we arrive?', as this is only tempting fate.

➡ Try not to become alarmed when you see how some local passengers hold their breath whenever a bus approaches a particularly dodgy looking bridge.

dried fish. Sometimes the floor in front of you is filled too, so you'll find your knees to your chin for some bouncy hours. Getting up to stretch your legs while moving just isn't an option. (Try to sit in the front couple of rows, which sometimes have fewer bags stored, and better visibility.)

Trip durations for all forms of public road transportation are very elastic and buses of all types do break down sometimes. Older buses often stop to hose down a hot engine. Some roads – one-lane, mangled deals (read: *very* rough) – don't help matters, and tyre punctures occur too.

Costs

Bus fares are in kyat and foreigners will pay more than locals – and on occasion the price is 'set' on the spot. Generally minibuses, local 32-seaters, express buses with no air-con, and air-con luxury jobbies charge roughly the same on overlapping routes.

Reservations

From November to February it's wise to pre-book buses a couple of days in advance for key routes, such as Bagan–Inle Lake. Seat reservations are made for all buses – you should be able to check the seating plan with the reservation agent.

Car & Motorcycle

Hiring a car and driver for part or all of a trip is a good way to go, though not cheap. To drive one yourself, permission must be arranged via the government-run MTT and **Road Transport Administration Department** (RTAD; ☎01-36113), *and* you must be accompanied by a local at all times. (Some expats bypass this with registration from the RTAD.)

Driving conditions can be poor but are often better than on many roads in Viet-

ROAD DISTANCES (miles)

	Yangon	Mawlamyine	Nay Pyi Taw	Nyaungshwe	Mandalay	Myitkyina	Sittwe	Ngapali Beach	Hpa-an	Pyay	Pathein	Nyaung U
Mawlamyine	185											
Nay Pyi Taw	265	335										
Nyaungshwe	420	430	200									
Mandalay	420	500	185	175								
Myitkyina	795	900	515	465	350							
Sittwe	430	590	620	610	605	915						
Ngapali Beach	200	380	460	465	450	760	205					
Hpa-an	155	70	310	480	470	785	565	355				
Pyay	170	355	365	350	335	655	255	120	330			
Pathein	140	315	390	565	615	925	380	165	295	280		
Nyaung U	390	505	195	175	170	495	485	330	470	215	490	
Taunggyi	415	485	200	15	175	495	605	450	445	340	545	175

Approximate distances only

nam, Cambodia and Laos – and outside of the major cities traffic is comparatively light compared to Thai or Vietnamese roads. Of the 15,000 miles of roads in Myanmar, about half are paved; the remainder are graded gravel, unimproved dirt or simple vehicle tracks.

Hiring a Car & Driver

The best place to arrange a driver, perhaps for a full trip, is in Yangon, but it's possible to track down a 'taxi' or 'private car' from most travel agencies and guesthouses around the country, particularly in popular destinations such as Bagan, Mandalay and Inle Lake.

When trying to find a car with driver, consider there are three unofficial types of cars:

Tourist cars – these are reasonably new, air-conditioned cars run by a company that provides back-up or repairs in the event they break down. These are the most comfortable – and that air-con is handy when it's dusty and hot out – but the most expensive, running to about $200 to $400 a day, depending on the length of the trip. This price includes petrol for up to 12

hours' driving per day and all of the driver's expenses.

Taxis – a midrange option; these days there are plenty of taxis with working air-con on Yangon's roads and hiring one runs to about $60 to $80 per day.

Private cars – run by entrepreneur drivers, these go with windows down (ie no air-conditioning), vary in condition and price dramatically, and there's less chance that you'll have any sort of replacement if the engine goes out midway between Bago and Taungoo. Rates for these also range from $60 or $80 per day.

There are no car-rental agencies per se, but most travel agencies in Yangon, Mandalay and Bagan – as well as guesthouses and hotels elsewhere – can arrange cars and drivers.

Among the most popular and reliable rental cars in the country are secondhand, reconditioned Toyota Corona hatchbacks imported from Japan. A slightly better quality car is the Toyota Chaser. Myanmar also assembles its own Mazda 'jeeps' (MJs) using 85% local parts. Though mostly a government monopoly, these jeeps make decent off-road vehicles.

The old US-made, WWII-era Willys Jeeps that once characterised outback Myanmar travel are becoming few and far between.

Petrol & Tolls

Petrol costs K4200 per gallon. In rural parts of the country you'll find roadside stalls selling bottles of petrol.

Another cost to consider when travelling by car is the customary K50 or K100 'toll' collected upon entering many towns and villages throughout Myanmar. Many drivers are adept at handing these to the toll collectors while barely slowing down.

The toll for private cars using the expressway from Yangon to Mandalay is K4500, while to Nay Pyi Taw it's K2500.

Motorcycle & Mopeds

It's occasionally possible to rent a motorbike or moped, though few locals advertise this – and the authorities frown on it since they don't want to deal with the complications of visitors involved in accidents. In Mandalay and Myitkyina, for example, it's K10,000 per day to rent a motorbike. Unlike cyclists, you're required to wear a helmet in most towns.

Note that motorbikes and mopeds are banned in Yangon.

Hitching

Hitching is never entirely safe in any country in the world, and we don't recommend it. Travellers who decide to hitch should understand that they are taking a small but potentially serious risk. People who do choose to hitch will be safer if they travel in pairs and let someone know where they are planning to go.

One extra reason to avoid hitching in Myanmar is that local drivers may not know which areas are off limits to foreigners and may unwittingly transport them into such areas. In such cases the driver will probably be punished.

Local Transport

Larger towns in Myanmar offer a variety of city buses (*ka*), bicycle rickshaws or trishaws (*saiq-ka*, for sidecar), horse carts (*myint hlei*), ox carts, vintage taxis (*taxi*), more modern little three-wheelers somewhat akin to Thai *tuk-tuks* (*thoun bein*, meaning 'three wheels'), tiny four-wheeled 'blue taxi' Mazdas (*lei bein*, meaning 'four wheels') and modern Japanese pick-up trucks (*lain ka*, meaning 'line car').

Small towns rely heavily on horse carts and trishaws as the main mode of local transport. However, in big cities (Yangon, Mandalay, Pathein, Mawlamyine and Taunggyi) public buses take regular routes along the main avenues for a fixed per-person rate, usually K25 to K100.

Standard rates for taxis, trishaws and horse carts are sometimes 'boosted' for foreigners. Generally a ride from the bus station to a central hotel – often a distance of 1.25 miles or more – is between K1000 and K1500. Short rides around the centre can be arranged for between K500 and K1000. You may need to bargain a bit. Sometimes first-time offers are several times higher than the going rate.

Pick-up Trucks

Japanese-made pick-up trucks feature three rows of bench seats in the covered back. Most pick-ups connect short-distance destinations, making many stops along the way to pick up people or cargo. They are often packed (yet somehow never 'full' according to the driver). Pick-ups trace some useful or necessary routes, such as from Mandalay to Amarapura, from Myingyan to Meiktila, from Bagan to Mt Popa, and up to the Golden Rock at Kyaiktiyo. Unlike buses, they go regularly during the day.

Fares are not necessarily cheaper than those charged for local bus trips of the same length, and prices often go up more after dark. You can, however, pay 25% to 50% extra for a seat up the front. It's often worth the extra expense, if you don't want to do scrunch duty. Sometimes you may share your spot with a monk riding for free; usually you get exactly what you pay for ('the whole front'), unlike in some other parts of Southeast Asia.

Pick-ups often start from the bus station (in some towns they linger under a big banyan tree in the centre) and then, unlike many buses, make rounds through the central streets to snare more passengers.

ROAD RULES: TO THE RIGHT!

All Myanmar traffic goes on the right-hand side of the road. This wasn't always so. In an effort to distance itself from the British colonial period, the military government instigated an overnight switch from the left to the right in 1970. Many cars either date from before 1970, or are low-cost Japanese models, so steering wheels are perilously found on the right-hand side – this becomes particularly dicey when a driver blindly zooms to the left to pass a car!

Tours

Many high-end hotels and tour companies offer day tours. We list sources for less-expensive, private guides.

Train

There are as many opinions of Myanmar's oft-maligned train service as there are people riding it. For some a train ride on narrow-gauge tracks is like going by horse, with the old carriages rocking back and forth and bouncing everyone lucky enough to have a seat on the hard chairs – sleep is practically impossible; others dig it, as some routes get to areas not reached by road and the services provide a chance to interact with locals. 'It's not as bad as some people say, not as good as you hope,' one wise local told us.

What's certain is that compared to bus trips on the same routes, taking the train means extra travel time, on top of which likely delays (over 12 hours is not unheard of) have to be factored in. It also means extra expense. A 1st-class seat between Yangon and Mandalay is $33; a bus ticket on an air-conditioned bus is about $20.

The Network

First introduced by the British in 1877 with the opening of the 163-mile line between Yangon and Pyay, Myanmar's rail network now has over 3357 miles of 3.3ft-gauge track and 858 train stations. Extensions to the network, adding another 2264 miles of track, are currently under construction from Sittwe in the west to Myeik in the south.

The 386-mile trip from Yangon to Mandalay, via Bago, Nay Pyi Taw and Thazi, is the most popular train ride visitors take. Others worth considering:

➡ Bagan to Yangon via Taungoo and Kyaukpadaung

➡ Mandalay (or Pyin Oo Lwin) to Lashio (or Hsipaw), which takes in hilly terrain the roads miss (Paul Theroux managed to do this back when foreigners weren't supposed to, as described in his book *The Great Railway Bazaar*)

➡ Yangon to Mawlamyine via Bago, Kyalktiyo and Mottawa

➡ Pyinmana to Kyaukpadaung (31 miles south of Bagan)

➡ Thazi to Shwenyaung (7 miles north of Inle Lake)

➡ Yangon to Pyay.

An express line connects Bagan (Nyaung U) with Mandalay from where there are three other branch lines: one running slightly northwest across the Ava Bridge and up to Ye-U, one directly north to Myitkyina in Kachin State and one northeast through Pyin Oo Lwin to Lashio in the northern part of Shan State.

Note trains are classified by a number and the suffix 'Up' for northbound trains or 'Down' for southbound trains. Train numbers are not always used when purchasing tickets.

Classes & Facilities

Express trains offer two classes of passage – upper class and ordinary class; long-distance trains also offer sleepers. The main difference between ordinary and upper is that the seats recline and can be reserved in the latter, while ordinary class features hard upright seats that can't be reserved. Some trains also offer another class of service called 1st class, which is a step down from upper in comfort.

Sleeper carriages accommodate four passengers, have air-conditioning that may or may not work, linens and blankets and their own toilet. We had one to ourselves from Bagan to Yangon but it was also sealed off with no through corridor to the rest of the train. If you'd prefer to move around the train and meet fellow passengers, an upper-class seat will be better.

Long-distance trains have dining cars accessible to passengers in 1st, upper and sleeper class. The food isn't bad – fried rice and noodles. Attendants can also take your order and bring food to your seat or pass it through the window.

Trains stop pretty often too, with vendors on platforms offering all sorts of snacks. Bathrooms are basic; there are also sinks to wash hands and brush teeth. Attendants sometimes hire out bamboo mats to spread on the floor in aisles or under seats if you can't sleep upright. It can get cold at night, so bring a jacket and/or a blanket.

The express trains are far superior to the general run of Myanmar trains. Other trains are late, almost by rule – taking one 12-hour train trip that ends up running as much as 15 hours late is enough for most travellers. The Mandalay to Myitkyina route, though scheduled to take around 24 hours, can take up to 40 hours. Even on the far-more-travelled Yangon–Mandalay route delays are common, particularly in the rainy season when the tracks are prone to flooding.

TOURS

Many foreign-run companies book package tours to Myanmar. In most instances, more money will reach the local people if you travel on your own or arrange a driver and guide from a locally based agent ; for some recommendations see p27 and the destination chapters.

CLIMATE CHANGE & TRAVEL
. . . .

Every form of transport that relies on carbon-based fuel generates CO_2, the main cause of human-induced climate change. Modern travel is dependent on aeroplanes, which might use less fuel per mile per person than most cars but travel much greater distances. The altitude at which aircraft emit gases (including CO_2) and particles also contributes to their climate change impact. Many websites offer 'carbon calculators' that allow people to estimate the carbon emissions generated by their journey and, for those who wish to do so, to offset the impact of the greenhouse gases emitted with contributions to portfolios of climate-friendly initiatives throughout the world. Lonely Planet offsets the carbon footprint of all staff and author travel.

Reservations

For most major routes you should be able to buy tickets directly at the train stations, using the same ticket windows as the locals. Payment is usually required in US dollars. Smaller stations sometimes require some perseverance to get a ticket, as agents aren't used to foreigners climbing on.

A day or two's notice is usually enough to book a seat, but if you desire a coveted sleeper, you'll need at least a couple of days' notice – longer during the high season (November to March). If you hold a seat on a train pulling a sleeper car, you can try to upgrade to a berth after you board by paying the additional fare directly to the conductor.

If you're having trouble buying a ticket or making yourself understood at a train station, try seeking out the stationmaster (*yonepain* in Burmese) – the person at the station who is most likely to speak English and most inclined to help you get a seat.

Health

The following advice is a general guide only and does not replace the advice of a doctor trained in travel medicine.

BEFORE YOU GO

➡ Pack medications in their original, clearly labelled containers.

➡ Carry a signed and dated letter from your physician describing your medical conditions and medications, including their generic names.

➡ If you have a heart condition bring a copy of your ECG taken just prior to travelling.

➡ Bring a double supply of any regular medication in case of loss or theft.

➡ Take out health insurance.

Vaccinations

Proof of yellow fever vaccination will be required if you have visited a country in the yellow-fever zone (ie Africa or South America) within the six days prior to entering Myanmar. Otherwise the World Health Organization (WHO) recommends the following vaccinations for travellers to Myanmar:

Adult diphtheria and tetanus Single booster recommended if none in the previous 10 years.

Hepatitis A Provides almost 100% protection for up to a year. A booster after 12 months provides at least another 20 years' protection.

Hepatitis B Now considered routine for most travellers. Given as three shots over six months. A rapid schedule is also available, as is a combined vaccination with hepatitis A.

Measles, mumps and rubella (MMR) Two doses of MMR are required unless you have had the diseases. Many young adults require a booster.

Polio There have been no reported cases of polio in Myanmar in recent years. Adults require only one booster for lifetime protection.

Typhoid Recommended unless your trip is less than a week and only to developed cities. The vaccine offers around 70% protection, lasts for two to three years and comes as a single shot. Tablets are also available but the injection is usually recommended as it has fewer side effects.

Varicella (chickenpox) If you haven't had chickenpox, discuss this vaccination with your doctor.

Websites & Further Reading

Lonely Planet's *Healthy Travel – Asia & India* is packed with useful information. Other recommended references include *Travellers' Health* by Dr Richard Dawood and *Travelling Well* by Dr Deborah Mills. Online resources:

Centres for Disease Control and Prevention (CDC; www.cdc.gov)

MD Travel Health (www.mdtravelhealth.com)

World Health Organization (www.who.int/ith/)

HEALTH ADVISORIES

Consult your government's website on health and travel before departure:

Australia www.smartraveller.gov.au

Canada www.phac-aspc.gc.ca

New Zealand www.safetravel.govt.nz

UK www.dh.gov.uk

USA wwwnc.cdc.gov/travel/

IN MYANMAR

Availability of Health Care

Myanmar medical care is dismal, and local hospitals should be used only out of desperation. Contact your embassy for advice, as staff will usually direct you to the best options. Be aware that getting Western-style health care may not come cheap.

If you think you may have a serious disease, especially malaria, do not waste time – travel to the nearest quality facility to receive attention. It is always better to be assessed by a doctor than to rely on self-treatment.

Buying medication over the counter is not recommended in Myanmar, as fake medications and poorly stored or out-of-date drugs are common.

Infectious Diseases

The following are the most common for travellers:

Dengue Fever Increasingly problematic throughout Myanmar. The mosquito that carries dengue bites day and night, so use insect avoidance measures at all times. Symptoms can include high fever, severe headache, body ache, a rash and diarrhoea. There is no specific treatment, just rest and paracetamol – do not take aspirin as it increases the likelihood of haemorrhaging.

Hepatitis A This food- and water-borne virus infects the liver, causing jaundice (yellow skin and eyes), nausea and lethargy. All travellers to Myanmar should be vaccinated against it.

Hepatitis B The only sexually transmitted disease (STD) that can be prevented by vaccination, hepatitis B is spread by body fluids, including sexual contact.

Hepatitis E Transmitted through contaminated food and water and has similar symptoms to hepatitis A, but is far less common. It is a severe problem in pregnant women and can result in the death of both mother and baby. There is currently no vaccine, and prevention is by following safe eating and drinking guidelines.

HIV Unprotected heterosexual sex is the main method of transmission.

Influenza Can be very severe in people over the age of 65 or in those with underlying medical conditions such as heart disease or diabetes; vaccination is recommended for these individuals. There is no specific treatment, just rest and paracetamol.

Malaria While not noted in Yangon or Mandalay, malaria (which can be fatal if untreated) is very much present throughout the rest of rural Myanmar in altitudes below 1000m. Before you travel, seek medical advice on the right medication and dosage for you; note that some areas of the country have strains of the disease resistant to Mefloquine-based drugs. Wherever you are, wear long pants and sleeves and spray insect repellent to prevent bites. Also sleep in air-con or screened rooms with bednets.

Rabies A potential risk, and invariably fatal if untreated, rabies is spread by the bite or lick of an infected animal (most commonly a dog or monkey). Pretravel vaccination means the postbite treatment is greatly simplified. If an animal bites you, gently wash the wound with soap and water, and apply iodine-based antiseptic. If you are not prevaccinated you will need to receive rabies immunoglobulin as soon as possible.

Typhoid This serious bacterial infection is spread via food and water. Symptoms include high and slowly progressive fever, headache, a dry cough and stomach pain. Vaccination, recommended for all travellers spending more than a week in Myanmar and other parts of Southeast Asia, is not 100% effective so you must still be careful with what you eat and drink.

Traveller's Diarrhoea

By far the most common problem affecting travellers is usually caused by a bacteria. Treatment consists of staying well hydrated; use a solution such as Gastrolyte. Antibiotics such as Norfloxacin, Ciprofloxacin or Azithromycin will kill the bacteria quickly.

Loperamide is just a 'stopper', but it can be helpful in certain situations, eg if you have to go on a long bus ride. Seek medical attention quickly if you do not respond to an appropriate antibiotic.

DRINKING WATER

→ Never drink tap water.

→ Check bottled water seals are intact at purchase.

→ Avoid ice.

→ Avoid fresh juices – they may have been watered down.

→ Boiling water is the most efficient method of purifying it.

→ Iodine, the best chemical purifier, should not be used by pregnant women or those who suffer with thyroid problems.

→ Ensure your water filter has a chemical barrier, such as iodine, and a pore size of less than 4 microns.

Amoebic dysentery is very rare in travellers; one sign is if you have blood in your diarrhoea. Treatment involves two drugs: Tinidazole or Metronidazole to kill the parasite in your gut, and then a second drug to kill the cysts.

Giardiasis is relatively common. Symptoms include nausea, bloating, excess gas, fatigue and intermittent diarrhoea. The treatment of choice is Tinidazole, with Metronidazole being a second option.

Environmental Hazards

Air Pollution

Air pollution, particularly vehicle pollution, is an increasing problem, particularly in Yangon. If you have severe respiratory problems speak with your doctor before travelling to any heavily polluted urban centres. This pollution also causes minor respiratory problems, such as sinusitis, dry throat and irritated eyes. If troubled by the pollution, leave the city for a few days and get some fresh air.

Diving

Divers and surfers should seek specialised advice before they travel to ensure their medical kit contains treatment for coral cuts and tropical ear infections, as well as the standard problems. Divers should ensure their insurance covers them for decompression illness. Have a dive medical examination before you leave your home country – there are certain medical conditions that are incompatible with diving, and economic considerations may override health considerations for some dive operators in Myanmar.

Food

Rather than being overly concerned at street stalls, where food is freshly cooked to order, note that eating in restaurants is the biggest risk factor for contracting traveller's diarrhoea. Avoid shellfish, and food that has been sitting around in buffets. Peel all fruit, cook vegetables and soak salads in iodine water for at least 20 minutes. Eat in busy restaurants with a high turnover of customers.

Heat

Many parts of Myanmar are hot and humid throughout the year. It can take up to two weeks to adapt to the hot climate. Swelling of the feet and ankles is common, as are muscle cramps caused by excessive sweating. Prevent these by avoiding dehydration and excessive activity in the heat.

Dehydration is the main contributor to heat exhaustion. Symptoms include feeling weak; headache; irritability; nausea or vomiting; sweaty skin; a fast, weak pulse; and a normal or slightly elevated body temperature. Treat by getting out of the heat, applying cool wet cloths to the skin, lying flat with legs raised and rehydrating with water containing a quarter of a teaspoon of salt per litre.

Heatstroke is a serious medical emergency. Symptoms come on suddenly and include weakness, nausea, a hot dry body with a body temperature of over 41°C, dizziness, confusion, loss of coordination, fits and eventual collapse and loss of consciousness. Seek medical help and commence cooling by getting the person out of the heat, removing their clothes, and applying cool wet cloths or ice to their body, especially to the groin and armpits.

Prickly heat – an itchy rash of tiny lumps – is caused by sweat being trapped under the skin. Treat by moving out of the heat and into an air-conditioned area for a few hours and by having cool showers. Creams and ointments clog the skin so they should be avoided.

Insect Bites & Stings

Bedbugs Don't carry disease but their bites are very itchy. They live in the cracks of furniture and walls and then migrate to the bed at night to feed on you. You can treat the itch with an antihistamine.

Bees or wasps If allergic to their stings, carry an injection of adrenaline (eg an EpiPen®) for emergency treatment.

Jellyfish In Myanmar waters most are not dangerous. If stung, pour vinegar onto the affected area to neutralise the poison. Take painkillers and seek medical advice if your condition worsens.

Leeches Found in humid rainforest areas. Don't transmit any disease but their bites can be itchy for weeks afterwards and can easily become infected. Apply an iodine-based antiseptic to any leech bite to help prevent infection.

Lice Most commonly inhabit your head and pubic area. Transmission is via close contact with an infected person. Treat with numerous applications of an antilice shampoo, such as Permethrin.

Ticks Contracted after walking in rural areas. If you are bitten and experience symptoms such as a rash at the site of the bite or elsewhere, fever, or muscle aches, see a doctor. Doxycycline prevents tick-borne diseases.

Skin Problems

Fungal rashes are common in humid climates. There are two common fungal rashes that affect travellers. The first occurs in moist areas that receive less air, such as the groin, the armpits and between the toes. It starts as a red patch that slowly spreads and is usually itchy. Treatment involves keeping the skin dry, avoiding chafing and using an antifungal cream such as Clotrimazole or Lamisil. *Tinea versicolor* is also common – this fungus causes small, light-coloured patches, most commonly on the back, chest and shoulders. Consult a doctor.

Cuts and scratches easily become infected in humid climates. Take meticulous care of any cuts and scratches to prevent complications, such as abscesses. Immediately wash all wounds in clean water and apply antiseptic. If you develop signs of infection (increasing pain and redness) see a doctor. Divers and surfers should be particularly careful with coral cuts as they easily become infected.

Snakes

Myanmar is home to many species of both poisonous and harmless snakes. Assume all snakes are poisonous and never try to catch one. Always wear boots and long pants if walking in an area that may have snakes. First aid in the event of a snakebite involves pressure immobilisation with an elastic bandage firmly wrapped around the affected limb, starting at the bite site and working up towards the chest. The bandage should not be so tight that the circulation is cut off, and the fingers or toes should be kept free so the circulation can be checked. Immobilise the limb with a splint and carry the victim to medical attention. Do not use tourniquets or try to suck the venom out. Antivenom is available for most species.

Women's Health

Pregnant women should receive specialised advice before travelling. The ideal time to travel is between 16 and 28 weeks, when the risk of pregnancy-related problems is at its lowest and pregnant women generally feel their best. During the first trimester there is a risk of miscarriage and in the third trimester complications – such as premature labour and high blood pressure – are possible. It's wise to travel with a companion. Always carry a list of quality medical facilities available at your destination and ensure that you continue your standard antenatal care at these facilities. Avoid rural travel in areas with poor transportation and medical facilities. Most of all, ensure that your travel insurance covers all pregnancy-related possibilities, including premature labour.

Malaria is a high-risk disease in pregnancy. WHO recommends that pregnant women do *not* travel to areas with Chloroquine-resistant malaria. None of the more effective antimalarial drugs are completely safe in pregnancy.

Traveller's diarrhoea can quickly lead to dehydration and result in inadequate blood flow to the placenta. Many of the drugs used to treat various diarrhoea bugs are not recommended in pregnancy. Azithromycin is considered safe.

Birth-control options may be limited, so bring adequate supplies of your own form of contraception. Heat, humidity and antibiotics can all contribute to thrush. Treatment is with antifungal creams and pessaries such as Clotrimazole. A practical alternative is a single tablet of Fluconazole (Diflucan). Urinary tract infections can be precipitated by dehydration or long bus journeys without toilet stops; bring suitable antibiotics.

Traditional Medicine

Throughout Myanmar traditional medical systems are widely practised. Folk remedies should be avoided, as they often involve rather dubious procedures with potential complications. In comparison, traditional healing systems such as Chinese medicine are well respected, and aspects of them are being increasingly used by Western medical practitioners.

All traditional Asian medical systems identify a vital life force, and see blockage or imbalance as causing disease. Techniques such as herbal medicines, massage and acupuncture are used to bring this vital force back into balance or to maintain balance. These therapies are best used for treating chronic fatigue, arthritis, irritable bowel syndrome, skin conditions and other chronic ailments. Don't use traditional medicines to treat serious acute infections, such as malaria.

Be aware that 'natural' doesn't always mean 'safe', and there can be drug interactions between herbal medicines and Western medicines. If you are using both systems ensure that you inform both practitioners what the other has prescribed.

Language

Burmese is part of the Tibeto-Burman language family. As the national language of Myanmar (Burma), it has more than 40 million speakers, of whom more than 30 million use it as their first language. The variety of Burmese of Mandalay and Yangon, spoken throughout the central area of Myanmar, is considered the standard language. Many other languages are spoken in Myanmar, but with Burmese you'll be understood in the whole country.

There are two varieties of Burmese – one used in writing and formal situations, the other in speaking and informal context. The main differences are in vocabulary, especially the most common words (eg 'this' is di in spoken Burmese, but i in the written language). The phrases in this chapter are in the informal spoken variety, which is appropriate for all situations you're likely to encounter. Note that many Burmese nouns are borrowed from English, though the meaning and sound may be somewhat different.

In Burmese, there's a difference between aspirated consonants (pronounced with a puff of air after the sound) and unaspirated ones – you'll get the idea if you hold your hand in front of your mouth to feel your breath, and say 'pit' (where the 'p' is aspirated) and 'spit' (where it's unaspirated). These aspirated consonants in our pronunciation guides are said with a puff of air after the sound: ch (as in 'church'), k (as in 'kite'), ş (as in 'sick'), t (as in 'talk'); the following ones are pronounced with a puff of air before the

sound: hl (as in 'life'), hm (as in 'me'), hn (as in 'not'), hng (as in 'sing'), hny (as in 'canyon'). Note also that the apostrophe (') represents the sound heard between 'uh-oh', th is pronounced as in 'thin' and ţh as in 'their'.

There are three distinct tones in Burmese (the raising and lowering of pitch on certain syllables). They are indicated in our pronunciation guides by the accent mark above the vowel: high creaky tone, as in 'heart' (á), plain high tone, as in 'car' (à), and the low tone (a – no accent). Note also that ai is pronounced as in 'aisle', aw as in 'law', and au as in 'brown'.

BASICS

Burmese equivalents of the personal pronouns 'I' and 'you' have masculine and feminine forms, depending on the gender of the person indicated by the pronoun. These forms are marked as 'm/f' in phrases throughout this chapter. Depending on the pronoun (ie 'I' or 'you'), these abbreviations refer to the speaker or the person addressed.

Hello.	မင်္ဂလာပါ။	ming·guh·la·ba
Goodbye.	သွားမယ်နော်။	thwà·me·naw
Yes.	ဟုတ်ကဲ့။	hoh'·gé
No.	ဟင့်အင်း။	híng·ìn
Excuse me.	ဆောရီးနော်။	sàw·rì·naw
Sorry.	ဆောရီးနော်။	sàw·rì·naw
Please.	တဆိတ်လောက်။	duh·şay'·lau'
Thank you.	ကျေးဇူး တင်ပါတယ်။	jày·zù ding·ba·de
You're welcome.	ရပါတယ်။	yá·ba·de
How are you?	နေကောင်းလား။	nay·gàung·là
Fine. And you?	ကောင်းပါတယ်။ ခင်ဗျား/ရှင်ရော။	gàung·ba·de king·myà/ shing·yàw (m/f)

WANT MORE?

For in-depth language information and handy phrases, check out Lonely Planet's *Burmese Phrasebook*. You'll find it at **shop.lonelyplanet.com**, or you can buy Lonely Planet's iPhone phrasebooks at the Apple App Store.

What's your name?

နာမည် ဘယ်လိုလို့   nang·me be·loh
ခေါ်သလဲ။   kaw·ţhuh·lè

My name is ...

ကျနော့်/ကျမ   juh·náw/juh·má
နာမည်က- - - ပါ။   nang·me·gá ... ba (m/f)

Do you speak English?

အင်္ဂလိပ်လို့   ìng·guh·lay'·loh
ပြောတတ်သလား။   byàw·da'·thuh·là

I don't understand.

နားမလည်ဘူး။   nà·muh·le·bòo

ACCOMMODATION

Where's a ...?   - - - ဘယ်မှာလဲ။   ... be·hma·lè

   bungalow   ဘန်ဂလို   buhng·guh·loh
   guesthouse   တည်းခိုခန်း   dè·koh·gàn
   hotel   ဟိုတယ်   hoh·te

Do you have   - - - ရှိသလား။   ... shí·ţhuh·là
a ... room?

   single   တစ်ယောက်ခန်း   duh·yau'·kàng
   double   နှစ်ယောက်ခန်း   hnuh·yau'·kàng
   twin   ခုတင်နှစ်လုံး   guh·ding·
     ပါတဲ့အခန်း   hnuh·lòhng·
      ba·dé·uh·kàng

How much is it per night/person?

တစ်ည/တစ်ယောက်   duh·nyá/duh·yau'
ဘယ်လောက်လဲ။   be·lau'·lè

Is there a campsite nearby?

ဒီနားမှာ   di·nà·hma
စခန်းချဝရာနေရာ   suh·kàng·chá·zuh·ya·nay·ya
ရှိသလား။   shí·ţhuh·là

DIRECTIONS

Where is ...?
- - - ဘယ်မှာလဲ။   ... be·hma·lè

What's the address?
လိပ်စာက ဘာလဲ။   lay'·sa·gá ba·lè

Could you please write it down?
-ရေးမှတ်ထားပါ။   yày·hmuh'·tà ba

Can you show me (on the map)?
(မြေပုံပေါ်မှာ)   (myay·bohng·baw·hma)
ညွှန်ပြပေးပါ။   hnyoong·byá·bày·ba

Turn ...   - - - ကွေ့ပါ။   ... gwáy·ba

   at the corner   လမ်းထောင့်မှာ   làng·dáung·hma
   at the traffic   မီးပွိုင့်မှာ   mì·pwáing·hma
   lights

It's ...

   behind ...   - - - အနောက်မှာ။   ... uh·nau'·hma
   far away   အရမ်းဝေးတယ်။   uh·yàng wày·de
   in front of ...   - - - ရှေ့မှာ။   ... sháy·hma
   left   ဘယ်ဘက်မှာ။   be·be'·hma
   near ...   - - - နားမှာ။   ... nà·hma
   next to ...   - - - ဘေးမှာ။   ... bày·hma
   right   ညာဘက်မှာ။   nya·be'·hma
   straight   ရှေ့တည့်တည့်မှာ။   sháy·dé·dé·hma
   ahead

EATING & DRINKING

Can you   - - - တစ်ခု   ... duh·kú
recommend   အကြံပေးနိုင်မလား။   uh·jang·bày·
a ...?   naing·muh·là

   bar   အရက်ဆိုင်   uh·ye'·şaing
   cafe   ကော်ဖီဆိုင်   gaw·pi·şaing
   restaurant   စားသောက်ဆိုင်   sà·thau'·şaing

I'd like a/the   - - - လိုချင်ပါတယ်။   ... loh·jing·ba·de
..., please.

   table for   (၄)ယောက်စာ   (lày)·yau'·sa
   (four)   စားပွဲ   zuh·bwè
   nonsmoking   ဆေးလိပ်   şày·lay'
   section   မသောက်ရတဲ့နေရာ   muh·thau'·yá·
      dé·nay·ya

I'd like (the)   - - - ပေးပါ။   ... bày·ba
..., please.

   bill   ဘောက်ချာ   bau'·cha
   menu   မီနူး   mì·nù
   that dish   အဲဒီဟင်းခွက်   è·di hìng·gwe'
   wine list   ဝိုင်စာရင်း   waing·suh·yìng

Could you   - - - မပါဘဲ   ... muh·ba·bè
prepare a meal   ပြင်ပေးနိုင်မလား။   bying·bày·
without ...?   naing·muh·là

   butter   ထောပတ်   tàw·ba'
   eggs   ကြက်ဥ   je'·ú
   fish sauce   ငံပြာရည်   ngang·bya·yay
   meat   အသား   uh·thà
   meat stock   အသားပြုတ်ရည်   uh·thà·
      byoh'·yay

Do you have vegetarian food?
သက်သတ်လွတ် စားဖွရာ   the'·tha'·lu· sà·zuh·ya
ရှိသလား။   shí·ţhuh·là

What would you recommend?
ဘာအကြံပေးမလဲ။   ba uh·jang·pày·muh·lè

What's the local speciality?
ဒီမြို့ကစပယ်ရှယ် · di·myóh·gá suh·be·she
အစားအစာက ဘာလဲ။ · uh·sà·uh·sa·gá ba·lè

Cheers!
ချီးယား။ · chì·yà

Key Words

breakfast	မနက်စာ	muh·ne'·sa
lunch	နေ့လည်စာ	náy·le·za
dinner	ညစာ	nyá·za
snack	အဆာပြေ	uh·ṣa·byay
	စားစရာ	sà·zuh·ya
fruit	အသီးအနှံ	uh·thì·uh·hnang
meat	အသား	uh·thà
vegetable	ဟင်းသီးဟင်းရွက်	hìng·thì·hìng·ywe'
bottle	တစ်ပုလင်း	duh·buh·ling
bowl	ပန်းကန်လုံး	buh·gang·lòhng
chopsticks	တူ	doo
cup	ခွက်	kwe'
fork	ခက်ရင်း	kuh·yìng
glass	ဖန်ခွက်	pang·gwe'
knife	ဓား	dà
napkin	လက်သုတ်ပုဝါ	le'·thoh'·buh·wa
plate	ပန်းကန်	buh·gang
spoon	ဇွန်း	zòong
teaspoon	လက်ဖက်ရည်ဇွန်း	luh·pe'·yay·zòong

Drinks

(cup of) coffee ...	ကော်ဖီ (၁)ခွက် - - -	gaw·pi (duh·)kwe' ...
(cup of) tea ...	လက်ဖက်ရည် (၁)ခွက် - - -	luh·pe'·yay (duh·)kwe' ...
with milk	နို့နဲ့	nóh·né
without	သကြား	ṭhuh·jà
sugar	မပါဘဲ	muh·ba·bè
wine	ဝိုင်	waing
red	အနီ	uh·ni
white	အဖြူ	uh·pyu
beer	ဘီယာ	bi·ya
drinking water	သောက်ရေ	thau'·yay
hot water	ရေနွေး	yay·nwày

milk	နို့	nóh
mineral water	ရေသန့်ဘူး	yay·ṭháng·bòo
orange juice	လိမ္မော်ရည်	layng·maw·yay
soft drink	ဖျော်ရည်	pyaw·yay
sugarcane juice	ကြံရည်	jang·yay

Signs

အဝင်	Entrance
အထွက်	Exit
ဖွင့်	Open
ပိတ်ထားသည်	Closed
အခန်းအားရှိသည်	Vacancies
အခန်းအားမရှိပါ	No Vacancies
စုံစမ်းရန်	Information
ရဲစခန်း	Police Station
တားမြစ်နယ်မြေ	Prohibited
အိမ်သာ	Toilets
ကျား	Men
မ	Women
ပူ	Hot
အေး	Cold

EMERGENCIES

Help!	ကယ်ပါ။	ge·ba
Go away!	သွား။	thwà
Call ...	- - - ခေါ်ပေးပါ။	... kaw·bày·ba
a doctor	ဆရာဝန်	ṣuh·ya·wung
the police	ရဲ	yèh

I'm lost.
လမ်းပျောက်နေတယ်။ · làng·byau'·nay·de

Where are the toilets?
အိမ်သာ ဘယ်မှာလဲ။ · ayng·ṭha be·hma·lè

I'm sick.
နေမကောင်းဘူး။ · nay·muh·gàung·bòo

It hurts here.
ဒီမှာနာတယ်။ · di·hma na·de

I'm allergic to (antibiotics).
(အင်တီဘားရောဂတ်) · (ing·di·bà·yàw·di')
နဲ့မတဲ့ဘူး။ · né muh·dé·bòo

SHOPPING & SERVICES

Where can I buy (a padlock)?
(သော့လောက်) ဘယ်မှာ · (tháw·guh·lau') be·hma
ဝယ်လို့ရမလဲ။ · we·lóh·yá·muh·lè

Numbers

1	တစ်	di'
2	နှစ်	hni'
3	သုံး	thòhng
4	လေး	lày
5	ငါး	ngà
6	ခြောက်	chau'
7	ခုနစ်	kung·ni'
8	ရှစ်	shi'
9	ကိုး	gòh
10	တစ်ဆယ်	duh·şe
20	နှစ်ဆယ်	hnuh·şe
30	သုံးဆယ်	thòhng·ze
40	လေးဆယ်	lày·ze
50	ငါးဆယ်	ngà·ze
60	ခြောက်ဆယ်	chau'·şe
70	ခုနစ်ဆယ်	kung·nuh·şe
80	ရှစ်ဆယ်	shi'·şe
90	ကိုးဆယ်	gòh·ze
100	တစ်ရာ	duh·ya
1000	တစ်ထောင်	duh·towng

Can I look at it?
ကြည့်လို့ရမလား။ jí·lóh yá·muh·là

Do you have any other?
တခြားရှိသေးလား။ duh·chà shí·ţhày·là

How much is it?
ဒါဘယ်လောက်လဲ။ da be·lau'·lè

Can you write down the price?
ဈေးရေးပေးပါ။ zày yày·bày·ba

That's too expensive.
ဈေးကြီးလွန်းတယ်။ zày·ji·lùng·de

What's your lowest price?
အနည်းဆုံးဈေးက ဘယ်လောက်လဲ။ uh·nè·zòhng·zày·gá be·lau'·lè

There's a mistake in the bill.
ဒီပြေစာမှာ အမှား ပါနေတယ်။ di·byay·za·hma uh·hmà ba·nay·de

Where's a ...?	- - - ဘယ်မှာလဲ။	... be·hma·lè
bank	ဘဏ်တိုက်	bang·dai'
internet cafe	အင်တာနက် ကဖေး	ing·ta·ne' gá·pay
market	ဈေး	zày
post office	စာတိုက်	sa·dai'
tourist office	တိုးရစ်ရုံး	dòh·yi'·yòhng

TIME & DATES

What time is it?
အခု ဘယ်အချိန်လဲ။ uh·gòo be·uh·chayng·lè

It's (two) o'clock.
နှစ်နာရီ(ရှိပြီ) (hnuh·na·yi) shí·bi

Half past (one).
(တစ်နာရီ) ခွဲ။ (duh·na·yi) gwè

morning	မနက် - - - နာရီ	muh·ne' ... na·yi
afternoon	နေ့လည် - - - နာရီ	náy·le ... na·yi
evening	ညနေ - - - နာရီ	nyá·nay ...na·yi
yesterday	မနေ့က	muh·náy·gá
tomorrow	မနက်ဖြန်	muh·ne'·puhng

Monday	တနင်္လာနေ့	duh·nìng·la·náy
Tuesday	အင်္ဂါနေ့	ing·ga·náy
Wednesday	ဗုဒ္ဓဟူးနေ့	boh'·duh·hòo·náy
Thursday	ကြာသပတေးနေ့	jà·thuh·buh·dày·náy
Friday	သောကြာနေ့	thau'·ja·náy
Saturday	စနေနေ့	suh·nay·náy
Sunday	တနင်္ဂနွေနေ့	duh·nìng·guh·nway·náy

January	ဇန်နဝါရီလ	zuhn·nuh·wa·yi·lá
February	ဖေဖော်ဝါရီလ	pay·paw·wa·yi·lá
March	မတ်လ	ma'·lá
April	ဧပြီလ	ay·byi·lá
May	မေလ	may·lá
June	ဇွန်လ	joong·lá
July	ဇူလိုင်လ	joo·laing·lá
August	ဩဂုတ်လ	àw·goh'·lá
September	စက်တင်ဘာလ	se'·ding·ba·lá
October	အောက်တိုဘာလ	ow'·toh·ba·lá
November	နိုဝင်ဘာလ	noh·wing·ba·lá
December	ဒီဇင်ဘာလ	di·zing·ba·lá

TRANSPORT

Public Transport

Is this the ... to (Moulmein)?	ဒါ (မော်လမြိုင်) သွားတဲ့ - - - လား။	da (maw·luh·myaing) thwà·dé ... là
boat	သင်္ဘော	thìng·bàw
bus	ဘတ်စကား	ba'·suh·gà
plane	လေယာဉ်	lay·ying
train	ရထား	yuh·tà

At what time's the ... bus?	- - - ဘတ်စကား ဘယ်အချိန် ထွက်မလဲ။	... ba'·suh·gà be·uh·chayng twe'·muh·lè
first	ပထမ	buh·tuh·má
last	နောက်ဆုံး	nau'·sòhng
next	နောက်	nau'

One ... ticket to (Taunggyi), please.	(တောင်ကြီး) - - - လက်မှတ် တစ်စောင် ပေးပါ။	(daung·jì) ... le'·hma' duh·zaung bàmy·ba
one-way	အသွား	uh·thwà
return	အသွား အပြန်	uh·thwà uh·byang

At what time does it leave?

ဘယ်အချိန် ထွက်သလဲ။ — be·uh·chayng twe'·thuh·lè

How long does the trip take?

ဒီခရီးက ဘယ်လောက် ကြာမလဲ။ — di·kuh·yì·gá be·lau'·ja·muh·lè

Does it stop at (Bago)?

(ပဲခူး)မှာ ရပ်သလား။ — (buh·gòh)·hma ya'·thuh·là

What's the next station?

နောက်ဘူတာက ဘာဘူတာလဲ။ — nau'·boo·da·gá ba·boo·da·lè

Please tell me when we get to (Myitkyina).

(မြစ်ကြီးနား) ရောက်ရင် ပြောပါ။ — (myi'·jì·nà) yau'·ying byàw·ba

Is this ... available?	ဒီ - - - အားသလား။	di ... à·ṭhuh·là
motorcycle-taxi	အငှား မော်တော်ဆိုင်ကယ်	uh·hngà maw·daw·şaing·ke
rickshaw	ဆိုက်ကား	şai'·kà
taxi	တက္ကစီ	de'·guh·si

Sightseeing

monument	အထိမ်းအမှတ် ကျောက်တိုင်	uh·tàyng·uh·hma' jau'·taing
museum	ပြတိုက်	pyá·dai'
old city	မြို့ဟောင်း	myóh·hàung
palace	နန်းတော်	nàng·daw
ruins	အပျက်အစီး	uh·pye'·uh·sì
statues	ရုပ်ထု	yoh'·tú
temple	စေတီ	zay·di

Please take me to (this address).

(ဒီလိပ်စာ)ကို ပို့ပေးပါ။ — (di·lay'·sa)·goh bóh·bàmy·ba

Please stop here.

ဒီမှာရပ်ပါ။ — di·hma ya'·ba

Driving & Cycling

I'd like to hire a ...	- - - ငှားချင်ပါတယ်။	... hngà·jing·ba·de
bicycle	စက်ဘီး	se'·bàyng
car	ကား	gà
motorbike	မော်တော်ဆိုင်ကယ်	maw·taw·şaing·ge

Is this the road to (Moulmein)?

ဒါ (မော်လမြိုင်) သွားတဲ့လမ်းလား။ — da (maw·luh·myaing) thwà·dé·làng·là

I need a mechanic.

မက္ကင်းနစ်လိုချင်ပါတယ်။ — muh·gìng·ni' loh·jing·ba·de

I've run out of petrol.

ဓါတ်ဆီကုန်သွားပြီ။ — da'·şi gohng·thwà·bi

I have a flat tyre.

ဘီးပေါက်နေတယ်။ — bàyng·pau'·nay·de

GLOSSARY

See p361 for some useful words and phrases dealing with food and dining.

Bamar – Burman ethnic group

betel – the nut of the areca palm, which is chewed as a mild intoxicant throughout Asia

Bodhi tree – the sacred banyan tree under which the Buddha gained enlightenment; also 'bo tree'

chaung – (gyaung) stream or canal; often only seasonal

chinlon – extremely popular Myanmar sport in which a circle of up to six players attempts to keep a rattan ball in the air with any part of the body except the arms and hands

chinthe – half-lion, half-dragon guardian deity

deva – Pali-Sanskrit word for celestial beings

dhamma – Pali word for the Buddhist teachings; called dharma in Sanskrit

furlong – obsolete British unit of distance still used in Myanmar; one-eighth of a mile

gaung baung – formal, turban-like hat for men; made of silk over a wicker framework

gu – cave temple

haw – Shan word for 'palace', a reference to the large mansions used by the hereditary Shan sao pha

hintha – mythical, swanlike bird; hamsa in Pali-Sanskrit

hneh – a wind instrument like an oboe; part of the Myanmar orchestra

hpongyi – Buddhist monk

hpongyi-kyaung – monastery; see also kyaung

hsaing – traditional musical ensemble

hsaing waing – circle of drums used in a Myanmar orchestra

hti – umbrella-like decorated pinnacle of a stupa

in – lake; eg Inle means little lake

IWT – Inland Water Transport

Jataka – stories of the Buddha's past lives; a common theme for temple paintings and reliefs

ka – city bus

kalaga – embroidered tapestries

kamma – Pali word for the law of cause and effect; called karma in Sanskrit

kammahtan – meditation; a kammahtan kyaung is a meditation monastery

kammawa – lacquered scriptures

kan – (gan) beach; can also mean a tank or reservoir

karaweik – a mythical bird with a beautiful song; also the royal barge on Inle Lake; karavika in Pali

KNLA – Karen National Liberation Army

kutho – merit, what you acquire through doing good; from the Pali kusala

kyaik – Mon word for paya

kyauk – rock

kyaung – (gyaung) Myanmar Buddhist monastery; pronounced 'chown'

kyi – (gyi) big; eg Taunggyi means big mountain

kyun – (gyun) island

lain ka – 'line car' or pick-up truck

lei bein – 'four wheels' or blue taxi

Lokanat – Avalokitesvara, a Mahayana Bodhisattva (buddha-to-be) and guardian spirit of the world

longyi – the Myanmar unisex sarong-style lower garment; sensible wear in a tropical climate; unlike men in most other Southeast Asian countries, few Myanmar men have taken to Western trousers

MA – Myanma Airways

Mahayana – literally 'Great Vehicle'; the school of Buddhism that thrived in north Asian countries

like Japan and China, and also enjoyed popularity for a time in ancient Southeast Asian countries; also called the Northern School of Buddhism

MTT – Myanmar Travels & Tours

mudra – hand position; used to describe the various hand positions used by buddha images, eg abhaya mudra (the gesture of fearlessness)

myint hlei – horse cart

myit – river

myo – town; hence Maymyo (after Colonel May), Allanmyo (Major Allan) or even Bernardmyo

myothit – 'new town', usually a planned new suburb built since the 1960s

naga – multiheaded dragon-serpent from mythology, often seen sheltering or protecting the Buddha; also the name of a collection of tribes in northwest Myanmar

nat – spirit being with the power to either protect or harm humans

nat-gadaw – spirit medium (literally 'spirit bride'); embraces a wide variety of nat

nat pwe – dance performance designed to entice a nat to possess a nat-gadaw

NDF – National Democratic Force

ngwe – silver

nibbana – nirvana or enlightenment, the cessation of suffering, the end of rebirth; the ultimate goal of Buddhist practice

NLD – National League for Democracy

pagoda – generic English term for zedi or stupa as well as temple; see also paya

pahto – Burmese word for temple, shrine or other religious structure with a hollow interior

Pali – language in which original Buddhist texts were recorded; the 'Latin' of Theravada Buddhism

parabaik – folding Buddhist palm-leaf manuscripts

paya – a generic Burmese term meaning holy one; applied to buddha figures, *zedi* and other religious monuments

pwe – generic Burmese word for festival, feast, celebration or ceremony; also refers to public performances of song and dance in Myanmar, often all-night (and all-day) affairs

pyatthat – wooden, multiroofed pavilion, usually turretlike on palace walls, as at Mandalay Palace

sai-ka – bicycle rickshaw or tri-shaw

Sanskrit – ancient Indian language and source of many words in the Burmese vocabulary, particularly those having to do with religion, art and government

sao pha – 'sky lord', the hereditary chieftains of the Shan people

sawbwa – Burmese corruption of the Shan word *sao pha*

saya – a teacher or shaman

sayadaw – 'master teacher', usually the chief abbot of a Buddhist monastery

shinpyu – ceremonies conducted when young boys from seven to 20 years old enter a monastery for a short period of time, required of every young Buddhist male; girls have their ears pierced in a similar ceremony

shwe – golden

sikhara – Indian-style, corncob-like temple finial, found on many temples in the Bagan area

sima – *see thein*

Slorc – State Law & Order Restoration Council

SPDC – State Peace & Development Council

stupa – *see zedi*

Tatmadaw – Myanmar's armed forces

taung – (daung) mountain, eg Taunggyi means 'big mountain'; it can also mean a half-yard (measurement)

taw – (daw) a common suffix, meaning sacred, holy or royal; it can also mean forest or plantation

tazaung – shrine building, usually found around *zedi*

thanakha – yellow sandalwood-like paste, worn by many Myanmar women on their faces as a combination of skin conditioner, sunblock and make-up

thein – ordination hall; called *sima* in Pali

Theravada – literally 'Word of the Elders'; the school of Buddhism that has thrived in Sri Lanka and Southeast Asian countries such as Myanmar and Thailand; also called Southern Buddhism and Hinayana

Thirty, the – the '30 comrades' of Bogyoke Aung San who joined the Japanese during WWII and eventually led Burma (Myanmar) to independence

thoun bein – motorised three-wheeled passenger vehicles

Tripitaka – the 'three baskets'; the classic Buddhist scriptures consisting of the Vinaya (monastic discipline), the Sutta (discourses of the Buddha) and Abhidhamma (Buddhist philosophy)

USDP – Union Solidarity & Development Party

UWSA – United Wa State Army

vihara – Pali-Sanskrit word for sanctuary or chapel for buddha images

viss – Myanmar unit of weight, equal to 3.5lb

wa – mouth or river or lake; Inwa means 'mouth of the lake'

ye – water, liquid

yoma – mountain range

ywa – village; a common suffix in place names such as Monywa

zat pwe – Classical dance drama based on Jataka stories

zawgyi – an alchemist who has successfully achieved immortality through the ingestion of special compounds made from base metals

zayat – an open-sided shelter or resthouse associated with a *zedi*

zedi – stupa, a traditional Buddhist religious monument consisting of a solid hemispherical or gently tapering cylindrical cone and topped with a variety of metal and jewel finials; *zedi* are often said to contain Buddha relics

zei – (zay or zè) market

zeigyo – central market

Behind the Scenes

SEND US YOUR FEEDBACK

We love to hear from travellers – your comments keep us on our toes and help make our books better. Our well-travelled team reads every word on what you loved or loathed about this book. Although we cannot reply individually to postal submissions, we always guarantee that your feedback goes straight to the appropriate authors, in time for the next edition. Each person who sends us information is thanked in the next edition – the most useful submissions are rewarded with a selection of digital PDF chapters.

Visit **lonelyplanet.com/contact** to submit your updates and suggestions or to ask for help. Our award-winning website also features inspirational travel stories, news and discussions.

Note: We may edit, reproduce and incorporate your comments in Lonely Planet products such as guidebooks, websites and digital products, so let us know if you don't want your comments reproduced or your name acknowledged. For a copy of our privacy policy visit lonelyplanet.com/privacy.

OUR READERS

Many thanks to the travellers who used the last edition and wrote to us with helpful hints, useful advice and interesting anecdotes:

A Alejandro Chehebar, Andrew Hart, Andrew Selth, Ann Tennant, Anna Kurihara, Anna Reilly, Anthoula Madden, Åsta Skjervøy, Axel Bruns **B** Birney Mae Smith **C** Cameron Potts, Charlotte McWilliam, Chris Howard, Chris Thomas, Christian Stegen, Clifford Roberts, Colin Merrilees, Connie Van den Bergh **D** Dace Berg, Daniel Atzbach, Danielle Van Melle, Daniëlle Wolbers, David Brown, David Holdorf, Dona Chilcoat **E** Eddie Joseph, Elise Silber, Elizabeth Goofers, Eric Neemann, Erik & Davina, Erin McNeaney, Evert van Leerdam **F** Francis Geldart, Francis Lu, Frederik J Jurriaanse **G** Gerri Lee George, Giorgia Paoloni, Gretchen Powers **H** Haim Borovski, Hanne van Lier, Helen Bonser, Helen Jackson, Henk Hollaar, Henning Siegert **I** Ian Brown **J** Jakob Heinemann, Jan Kline, Janet Clements, Jean Roberts, Jeannie Browne, Jelmar ter Beek, Joanne Steele, Johan Dittrich Hallberg, Johan Kruseman, John Fleming, Joshua Saul, Juan Gallardo, Judah Labovitz, Juliet Purssell **K** Karen Butcher, Kath Gardiner, Katharine Gordon, Kerry O'Boyle **L** Laurence McAdam, Laurie McLean, Lieve Vanhoecke, Limmer Klaus **M** Marie Catignani, Mark Tewari, Mark Thomas, Marlies Reimering, Marvin Lee, Matthew Sample, Michael Haring, Michael Wynne, Monica Villarindo **N** Natascha Möller, Neal Irvine, Nicolai Reimann, Niels de Pous **O** Orly Flax **P** Patrick Wheeler, Paul Rank, Peggy Lange, Peter Kabell Nissen, Peter Smith, Phil Sutcliffe, Philadelphia Stockwell, Pia Pedersen, Priya Koel **Q** Qian Xiaoyan **R** Richard Cohan, Robert Dewar, Robert Martyniecki **S** Sabine Gerull, Safia Weeks, Sandra Rosenhouse, Sarah Robinson, Stephen Barker, Steven Lin, Susan Johnson, Suzanne Jacob **T** Thierry Boitier, Tim Blight, Timothy Pink, Tino Onandia, Tobias Feld, Tracy Hammerstrom **U** Ur Omry **Y** Yannicke Gerretsen, Yin Naing **Z** Zsombor Barta

AUTHOR THANKS

Simon Richmond

Many thanks to my fellow authors and the following: William Myatwunna, Thant Myint-U, Edwin Briels, Jessica Mudditt, Greg Klemm, Vicky Bowman, Marcus Allender, Tun Lin Htaik (Tom Tom), Andrea Martini Rossi, Amelie Chan, Aung Soe Min, Wanna Aung, Allison Morris, Pete Silverster, New Ni Thien (Nina), Soe Moe Aung, Nay Aung, Patrick Kyaw Khin, Patrick Winn and Sean Turnell.

Austin Bush

I'd like to thank LPers for Life Ilaria Walker and Bruce Evans, and the very accommodating carto Diana Von Holdt. In Myanmar, I owe a lot to, in no special order, Ko Htay Aung and Ko Win Naing; Thu Thu; Ni Ni Htun and family; U Myint Thoung; William and Ohn Mar; Sai Leng, Song and family; Naing Naing; the kind guys of the Regional Guides Society – Mrauk U; Phu Phu, Pauksa and U Aung Soe; Mr Antony; MiMi Aye; and Aung Kyaw Kyaw, Captain Herbert and Janis Vougioukas.

David Eimer

Much gratitude to Htwe Htwe in Hsipaw for tips and transport and to Moe In Bhamo for his guidance. Thanks to Simon Richmond for his patience, and to Ilaria Walker and Diana Von Holdt at Lonely Planet. As ever, thanks to everyone who passed on advice along the way, whether knowingly or unwittingly.

Mark Elliott

Thank you Bo Thin, Thuang Nai U, Yeh Tut, Aung Aung, Mei Kyo Win, Bhikku Tilawka, Mr Bamaw, Mr Mango, San San Ee, Nang at Mya Kyauk, Guneikssara at Masoe, Pyu Papa Myu, Thanthanini, Aung Aung, Myothu and the RQ gang, Ko Zaw, Carolyn, Jeremy, Zach, Thomas and Lisbeth, Tina Friedman, Dan, Iain and Cheryl. Special thanks to Harriet Einsiedel and to my unbeatable family.

Nick Ray

A big thanks to the people of Myanmar, whose warmth and humour, stoicism and spirit make it a happy yet humbling place to be. Thanks to fellow travellers and residents, friends and contacts in Myanmar who have helped shape my knowledge and experience in this country, particularly Win Zaw, May Thu and Philippe. Biggest thanks are reserved for my wife, Kulikar Sotho, and children, Julian and Belle, as without their support and encouragement the occasional adventure would not be possible.

ACKNOWLEDGMENTS

Climate map data adapted from Peel MC, Finlayson BL & McMahon TA (2007) 'Updated World Map of the Köppen-Geiger Climate Classification', Hydrology and Earth System Sciences, 11, 1633¬44.

Illustration pp48-9 by Michael Weldon Cover photograph: Bagan. Felix Hug/ Getty ©

THIS BOOK

This 12th edition of Lonely Planet's *Myanmar (Burma)* guidebook was researched and written by Simon Richmond, Austin Bush, David Eimer, Mark Elliott and Nick Ray.

This guidebook was commissioned in Lonely Planet's Melbourne office, and produced by the following:

Commissioning Editor
Ilaria Walker

Coordinating Editors
Andrea Dobbin, Amanda Williamson

Senior Cartographer
Diana Von Holdt

Book Designer Jessica Rose

Managing Editor
Sasha Baskett

Senior Editor
Catherine Naghten

Assisting Editors Katie Connolly, Bruce Evans, Carly Hall, Kate James, Jodie Martire

Assisting Cartographer
James Leversha

Cover Research
Naomi Parker

Language Content
Branislava Vladisavljevic

Thanks to Anita Banh, Brendan Dempsey, Samantha Forge, James Hardy, Anna Harris, Elizabeth Jones, Kate Mathews, Virginia Moreno, Stephen Nolan, Luna Soo, Angela Tinson

Index

NOTES